Venezuela

Krzysztof Dydyński

LONELY PLANET PUBLICATIONS
Melbourne • Oakland • London • Paris

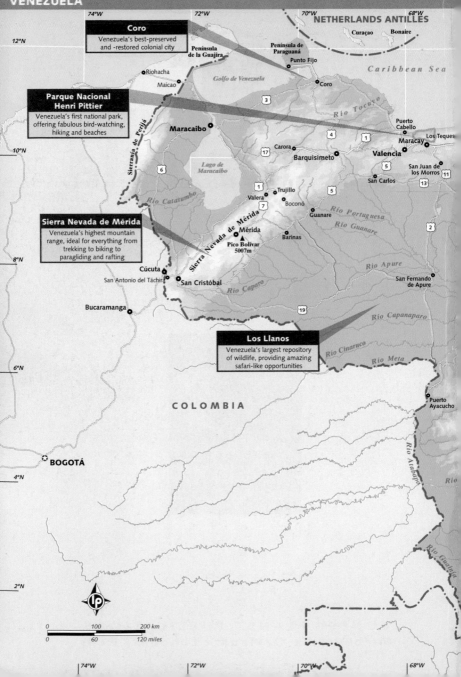

VENEZUELA

Coro
Venezuela's best-preserved and -restored colonial city

Parque Nacional Henri Pittier
Venezuela's first national park, offering fabulous bird-watching, hiking and beaches

Sierra Nevada de Mérida
Venezuela's highest mountain range, ideal for everything from trekking to biking to paragliding and rafting

Los Llanos
Venezuela's largest repository of wildlife, providing amazing safari-like opportunities

NETHERLANDS ANTILLES
Curaçao   Bonaire

Caribbean Sea

Península de la Guajira
Península de Paraguaná
Punto Fijo
Riohacha
Maicao
Coro
Golfo de Venezuela
Río Tocuyo
Puerto Cabello
Los Teques
Maracay
Valencia
San Juan de los Morros
Maracaibo
Carora
Barquisimeto
San Carlos
Lago de Maracaibo
Trujillo
Valera
Boconó
Guanare
Río Portuguesa
Río Guanare
Sierra de Perijá
Río Catatumbo
Sierra Nevada de Mérida
Mérida
Pico Bolívar 5007m
Barinas
Río Apure
San Fernando de Apure
Cúcuta
San Antonio del Táchira
San Cristóbal
Río Caparo
Bucaramanga
Río Capanaparo
Río Cinaruco
Río Meta
COLOMBIA
Puerto Ayacucho
BOGOTÁ
Río Atabapo
Río

3   1   4   1   17   5   13   11   2   6   1   7   5   19

0   100   200 km
0   60   120 miles

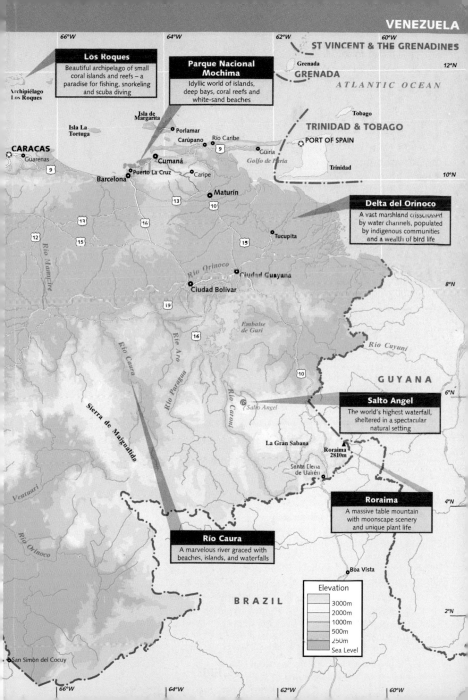

VENEXUELA

Los Roques
Beautiful archipelago of small coral islands and reefs – a paradise for fishing, snorkeling and scuba diving

Parque Nacional Mochima
Idyllic world of islands, deep bays, coral reefs and white-sand beaches

ST VINCENT & THE GRENADINES

Grenada

GRENADA

ATLANTIC OCEAN

Tobago

TRINIDAD & TOBAGO

PORT OF SPAIN

Archipiélago Los Roques

Isla La Tortuga

Isla de Margarita

Porlamar

Carúpano   Río Caribe

Güiria

Golfo de Paria

Trinidad

CARACAS

Guarenas

9

Cumaná

Puerto La Cruz

Barcelona

Caripe

Maturín

13

10

Delta del Orinoco
A vast marshland crisscrossed by water channels, populated by indigenous communities and a wealth of bird life

13

16

12

15

Río Manapire

Tucupita

15

Río Orinoco

Ciudad Guayana

Ciudad Bolívar

19

Río Aro

Río Caura

Río Paragua

Embalse de Guri

Río Cuyuní

GUYANA

10

Sierra de Maigualida

Río Caroní

Salto Angel

Salto Angel
The world's highest waterfall, sheltered in a spectacular natural setting

La Gran Sabana

Roraima 2810m

Santa Elena de Uairén

Roraima
A massive table mountain with moonscape scenery and unique plant life

Ventuari

Río Orinoco

Río Caura
A marvelous river graced with beaches, islands, and waterfalls

Boa Vista

BRAZIL

San Simón del Cocuy

Elevation
3000m
2000m
1000m
500m
250m
Sea Level

Venezuela 3
3rd edition – June 2001
First published – October 1994

Published by
Lonely Planet Publications Pty Ltd ABN 36 005 607 983
90 Maribyrnong St, Footscray, Victoria 3011, Australia

Lonely Planet Offices
Australia Locked Bag 1, Footscray, Victoria 3011
USA 150 Linden St, Oakland, CA 94607
UK 10a Spring Place, London NW5 3BH
France 1 rue du Dahomey, 75011 Paris

Photographs
Many of the images in this guide are available for licensing from
Lonely Planet Images.
email: lpi@lonelyplanet.com.au

Front cover photograph
Squirrel monkey (Edward Paine)

ISBN 1 86450 219 3

Printed by SNP SPrint (M) Sdn Bhd
Printed in Malaysia

Contents

2   Contents

GUAYANA
349

LANGUAGE
402

GLOSSARY
410

FOOD & DRINK GLOSSARY
415

ACKNOWLEDGMENTS
419

INDEX
425

MAP LEGEND
432

MAP INDEX

NETHERLANDS ANTILLES

ST VINCENT & THE GRENADINES

Caribbean Sea

GRENADA

The Central North page 158

The Northwest page 201

Caracas page 111

TRINIDAD & TOBAGO

The Northeast page 297

The Andes page 246

Los Llanos page 280

GUYANA

Guayana page 349

COLOMBIA

OTHER MAPS
Venezuela at front of book
Administrative Divisions page 22
National Parks page 31
Major Indian Groups Living Today page 33

BRAZIL

0   100   200 km
0   60   120 miles

The Author

Krzysztof Dydyński

Krzysztof was born and raised in Warsaw, Poland. Though he graduated in electronic engineering and became an assistant professor in the subject, he soon realized that there's more to life than microchips. In the mid-1970s he took off to Afghanistan and India and has been back to Asia several times since. In the 1980s, a newly discovered passion for Latin America took him to Colombia, where he lived for over four years, during which he traveled throughout the continent. In search of a new incarnation, he made Australia his home and worked for Lonely Planet as a designer. Apart from this guide, he is the author of Lonely Planet's guides to *Poland, Kraków* and *Colombia* and has contributed to other books.

FROM THE AUTHOR

Many friends, colleagues, travelers on the road and the staffs of various Venezuelan institutions and agencies have contributed to this book and deserve the highest praise.

Warmest thanks to Nico de Greiff, Hernando Arnal, Antonio Aranguren, César Luis Barrio, Dharío Borges, Gladis Dornheim, Billy Esser, Raquel & Tom Evenou, Jesús García, Henry González, Erick Migliore, Eugenio Molina, Eugenio Opltz, Emilio Pérez, Miro Popic, Román Rangel, Tulio Reyes, Guillermo Rodríguez, Kokyean Segnini, Christina Vareschi, Fridhelm Wegener and Luis Zavarce. My special appreciation goes to Angela Melendro.

This Book

FROM THE PUBLISHER

This edition of Venezuela was edited in Lonely Planet's Oakland office by Vivek Waglé. Maria Donohoe provided expert editorial guidance and supervision, while Wendy Taylor applied her eagle eye to proofreading the book. Thanks go to Brigitte Barta and Wade Fox for getting the project rolling.

A veritable army of cartographers did the maps, headed by field marshals Patrick Bock and Naoko Ogawa; its ranks comprised John Culp, Molly Green, Brad Lodge, Andrew Rebold, Stephanie Sims, Kat Smith and Herman So. Senior cartographers Kimra McAfee and Annette Olson oversaw the mapping. Monica Lepe assisted with the project's development.

Henia Miedzinski laid out the guide and designed the color pages, while Susan Rimerman designed the cover and provided layout guidance. Beca Lafore coordinated the illustrations, which were done by Mark Butler, Hugh D'Andrade, Justin Marler, Henia Miedzinski, Hannah Reineck, Jennifer Steffey, Alan Tarbell and Mick Weldon. Ken DellaPenta indexed the guide.

Special thanks to Krzysztof Dydyński for his support during the editing process.

Foreword

ABOUT LONELY PLANET GUIDEBOOKS

The story begins with a classic travel adventure: Tony and Maureen Wheeler's 1972 journey across Europe and Asia to Australia. Useful information about the overland trail did not exist at that time, so Tony and Maureen published the first Lonely Planet guidebook to meet a growing need.

From a kitchen table, then from a tiny office in Melbourne (Australia), Lonely Planet has become the largest independent travel publisher in the world, an international company with offices in Melbourne, Oakland (USA), London (UK) and Paris (France).

Today Lonely Planet guidebooks cover the globe. There is an ever-growing list of books, and there's information in a variety of forms and media. Some things haven't changed. The main aim is still to help make it possible for adventurous travelers to get out there – to explore and better understand the world.

At Lonely Planet we believe travelers can make a positive contribution to the countries they visit – if they respect their host communities and spend their money wisely. Since 1986 a percentage of the income from each book has been donated to aid projects and human-rights campaigns.

Updates Lonely Planet thoroughly updates each guidebook as often as possible. This usually means there are around two years between editions, although for more unusual or more stable destinations the gap can be longer. Check the imprint page (following the color map at the beginning of the book) for publication dates.

Between editions, up-to-date information is available in two free newsletters – the paper *Planet Talk* and email *Comet* (to subscribe, contact any Lonely Planet office) – and on our Web site at www.lonelyplanet.com. The *Upgrades* section of the Web site covers a number of important and volatile destinations and is regularly updated by Lonely Planet authors. *Scoop* covers news and current affairs relevant to travelers. And, lastly, the *Thorn Tree* bulletin board and *Postcards* section of the site carry unverified, but fascinating, reports from travelers.

Correspondence The process of creating new editions begins with the letters, postcards and emails received from travelers. This correspondence often includes suggestions, criticisms and comments about the current editions. Interesting excerpts are immediately passed on via newsletters and the Web site, and everything goes to our authors to be verified when they're researching on the road. We're keen to get more feedback from organizations or individuals who represent communities visited by travelers.

Lonely Planet gathers information for everyone who's curious about the planet – and especially for those who explore it firsthand. Through guidebooks, phrasebooks, activity guides, maps, literature, newsletters, image library, TV series and Web site, we act as an information exchange for a worldwide community of travelers.

Research Authors aim to gather sufficient practical information to enable travelers to make informed choices and to make the mechanics of a journey run smoothly. They also research historical and cultural background to help enrich the travel experience and allow travelers to understand and respond appropriately to cultural and environmental issues.

Authors don't stay in every hotel because that would mean spending a couple of months in each medium-size city and, no, they don't eat at every restaurant because that would mean stretching belts beyond capacity. They do visit hotels and restaurants to check standards and prices, but feedback based on readers' direct experiences can be very helpful.

Many of our authors work undercover; others aren't so secretive. None of them accept freebies in exchange for positive write-ups. And none of our guidebooks contain any advertising.

Production Authors submit their raw manuscripts and maps to offices in Australia, the USA, the UK or France. Editors and cartographers – all experienced travelers themselves – then begin the process of assembling the pieces. When the book finally hits the shops, some things are already out of date, we start getting feedback from readers and the process begins again....

WARNING & REQUEST

Things change – prices go up, schedules change, good places go bad and bad places go bankrupt – nothing stays the same. So, if you find things better or worse, recently opened or long since closed, please tell us and help make the next edition even more accurate and useful. We genuinely value all the feedback we receive. Julie Young coordinates a well-traveled team that reads and acknowledges every letter, postcard and email and ensures that every morsel of information finds its way to the appropriate authors, editors and cartographers for verification.

Everyone who writes to us will find their name in the next edition of the appropriate guidebook. They will also receive the latest issue of *Planet Talk*, our quarterly printed newsletter, or *Comet*, our monthly email newsletter. Subscriptions to both newsletters are free. The very best contributions will be rewarded with a free guidebook.

Excerpts from your correspondence may appear in new editions of Lonely Planet guidebooks, the Lonely Planet Web site, *Planet Talk* or *Comet*, so please let us know if you *don't* want your letter published or your name acknowledged.

Send all correspondence to the Lonely Planet office closest to you:

Australia: Locked Bag 1, Footscray, Victoria 3011
USA: 150 Linden St, Oakland, CA 94607
UK: 10A Spring Place, London NW5 3BH
France: 1 rue du Dahomey, 75011 Paris

Or email us at: talk2us@lonelyplanet.com.au

For news, views and updates, see our Web site: www.lonelyplanet.com

HOW TO USE A LONELY PLANET GUIDEBOOK

The best way to use a Lonely Planet guidebook is any way you choose. At Lonely Planet, we believe the most memorable travel experiences are often those that are unexpected, and the finest discoveries are those you make yourself. Guidebooks are not intended to be used as if they provided a detailed set of infallible instructions!

Contents All Lonely Planet guidebooks follow the same format. The Facts about the Country chapters or sections give background information ranging from history to weather. Facts for the Visitor gives practical information on issues like visas and health. Getting There & Away gives a brief starting point for researching travel to and from the destination. Getting Around gives an overview of the transport options available when you arrive.

The peculiar demands of each destination determine how subsequent chapters are broken up, but some things remain constant. We always start with background, then proceed to sights, places to stay, places to eat, entertainment, getting there and away, and getting around information – in that order.

Heading Hierarchy Lonely Planet headings are used in a strict hierarchical structure that can be visualized as a set of Russian dolls. Each heading (and its following text) is encompassed by any preceding heading that is higher on the hierarchical ladder.

Entry Points We do not assume guidebooks will be read from beginning to end, but that people will dip into them. The traditional entry points are the list of contents and the index. In addition, however, some books have a complete list of maps and an index map illustrating map coverage.

There may also be a color map that shows highlights. These highlights are dealt with in greater detail later in the book, along with planning questions. Each chapter covering a geographical region usually begins with a locator map and another list of highlights. Once you find something of interest in a list of highlights, turn to the index.

Maps Maps play a crucial role in Lonely Planet guidebooks and include a huge amount of information. A legend is printed on the back page. We seek to have complete consistency between maps and text, and to have every important place in the text captured on a map. Map key numbers usually start in the top left corner.

Although inclusion in a guidebook usually implies a recommendation, we cannot list every good place. Exclusion does not necessarily imply criticism. In fact, there are a number of reasons why we might exclude a place – sometimes it is simply inappropriate to encourage an influx of travelers.

Introduction

Emerging from a turbulent history of despots and disasters, tremendous wealth and desperate poverty, Venezuela today provides a nearly unimaginable array of opportunities for the traveler. The nation combines enchanting traditional cultures contained within a beautiful natural setting with decent, western-style tourist facilities – it does, after all, have a reputation as the most 'Yankeefied' country in South America.

Visitors can travel smoothly, enjoying familiar comfort, and at the same time experience a kaleidoscope of exotic landscapes, people and wildlife. It's the easy bit of South America, yet it has all you could wish for, from the Caribbean to the Andes to the Amazon. Indeed, it's the perfect introduction to the continent.

Modern Venezuela has been strongly influenced by oil – or, more precisely, oil

money – which has turned the country into one of South America's wealthiest nations. As a result, Venezuela has an extensive road network, spectacular new architecture and a developed tourism infrastructure. Yet deep in the countryside, people still live their lives in traditional ways, as if the 20th century got lost somewhere down the road. A number of Indian groups remain unconquered by encroaching civilization, including the mysterious Yanomami, whose Stone Age culture seems forgotten by time along the Venezuela-Brazil border.

The variety of Venezuela's landscapes is unlikely to disappoint visitors. The nation boasts the northern tip of the Andes, topped with snowcapped peaks, and the vast Delta del Orinoco, crisscrossed by a maze of natural channels. The country's southern portion is taken up by the legendary wilderness of the Amazon, while the north is bordered by 2800km of Caribbean coastline and countless beaches.

Venezuela's most unusual natural formations are the *tepuis* – flat-topped mountains with vertical flanks that loom more than 1000m above rolling savannas. Their tops are noted for bizarre, moonlike landscapes and peculiar endemic flora. About 100 tepuis are scattered throughout the southeast of the country. From one of them spills Salto Angel (Angel Falls), the world's highest waterfall (979m) and Venezuela's most famous tourist sight.

In practical terms, Venezuela is a relatively safe and friendly country in which to travel, with a wide choice of lodging and eating facilities everywhere, as well as fast and efficient domestic transportation. Venezuela also sports South America's cheapest air links with both Europe and the USA, and is thus a convenient gateway to the continent. However, don't make the mistake of treating Venezuela as a mere bridge. Give yourself some time to discover this land – it's well worth it.

Facts about Venezuela

HISTORY
Pre-Columbian Times

Radiocarbon dating of archaeological samples has shown that people first arrived in what is now Venezuela somewhere around the 14th millennium BC. The oldest examples have been excavated at El Jobo, in the present-day state of Falcón, in the country's northwest.

Various primitive nomadic groups' cultures evolved from that time, using rough stone for tools and weapons for hunting. Around the fifth millennium BC, bone and marine shells also came into use. Pottery began to appear only in the first millennium BC. Around the same time, agriculture developed, and this phenomenon gradually led to the establishment of sedentary settlements. From this stage on, separate groups began to evolve into distinct cultures.

The more settled way of life resulted in an increase in population growth. It's estimated that by the time of the Spanish conquest, about half a million Indians inhabited the region that is now Venezuela. There were isolated communities of various ethnic backgrounds belonging to three main linguistic families: Carib, Arawak and Chibcha.

The warlike Carib tribes inhabited the central and eastern coast, living off fishing and shifting agriculture. Various Arawak groups were scattered over a large area of western Llanos and north up to the coast. They lived off hunting and gathering, and only occasionally practiced farming.

The Timote-Cuica, members of the Chibcha linguistic family (to which the Muisca and Tayrona of Colombia belonged as well) were the most advanced of Venezuela's pre-Hispanic societies. They chose the Andes as their home, where they founded settlements and linked them by a network of trails. They developed fairly advanced agricultural techniques, including irrigation and terracing where the topography required it.

Venezuela's pre-Hispanic cultures didn't reach the level of architectural or artistic development of the great civilizations such as the Maya or Inca. They did not leave behind many significant artifacts, save for some fine pottery pieces found during excavations. No important samples of their architectural legacy have survived.

Petroglyphs (drawings or carvings on rock), which have been discovered on numerous locations throughout the country, are some of the most remarkable testimonies to the culture of Venezuela's indigenous people. However, exactly when they were done and by whom remains a mystery.

The Spanish Conquest

Christopher Columbus was the first European to set foot on Venezuelan soil – indeed, it was the only South American mainland country Columbus landed on. In 1498, on his third trip to the New World, he anchored at the eastern tip of the Península de Paria, across from Trinidad. He at first thought he had discovered yet another island, but continuing along the coast, he

Columbus Discovers the New World (1493), by an anonymous artist

found the voluminous mouth of the Río Orinoco – sufficient proof that the place was much more. Astonished with his discovery, he wrote in his diary, 'Never have I read or heard of so much sweet water within a salt ocean,' and named the gulf El Mar Dulce (Sweet Sea). Today it is called the Golfo de Paria.

A year later, another explorer – Alonso de Ojeda – accompanied by Juan de la Cosa and the Italian Amerigo Vespucci, sailed up to the Península de la Guajira, at the western end of present-day Venezuela. On entering Lago de Maracaibo in August 1499, the Spaniards saw the local Indians living in *palafitos*, thatched huts on stilts above the water. Perhaps as a sarcastic sailor joke, they called the place 'Venezuela' (Little Venice), as the rustic reed dwellings they saw didn't exactly match the opulent palaces of the Italian city they knew. The name of Venezuela appeared for the first time on the map drawn by Juan de la Cosa in 1500 and has remained to this day.

The first Spanish settlement on Venezuelan soil, Nueva Cádiz, was established on the small island of Cubagua, just south of Isla de Margarita, in about 1500 (although it was not until 1519 that it was granted a formal act of foundation). The town swiftly developed into a busy port engaged in pearl harvesting, but was completely destroyed by an earthquake and tidal wave in 1541. The earliest Venezuelan town still in existence, Cumaná, on the northeast coast, dates from 1521.

Officially, most of what is now Venezuela was ruled by Spain from Santo Domingo (the present-day capital of the Dominican Republic), except for its western part, which was governed from Lima. Following the 1717 creation of the Virreynato de la Nueva Granada, with its capital in Bogotá, all of present-day Venezuela fell under the administration of the new viceroyalty. It remained so until independence.

In practice, however, the region was allowed a large degree of autonomy. It was, after all, such an unimportant and sparsely populated backwater, with an uninviting steamy climate, that the Spaniards gave it low priority, focusing instead on gold- and silver-rich Colombia, Peru and Bolivia. In many ways, Venezuela remained a backwater until the oil boom of the 1920s.

The colony's population, initially consisting of indigenous communities and the Spanish invaders, diversified with the arrival of slaves, brought from Africa to serve as the work force. Most of them were set to work on plantations, mainly along the Caribbean coast. During the 16th and 17th centuries, the Spaniards shipped in so many Africans that they eventually surpassed the indigenous population in number.

The demographic picture became still more complex when the three racial groups began to mix, producing various fusions, including *mestizos* (people of European-Indian blood), *mulatos* (of European-African ancestry) and *zambos* (African-Indian). Yet, throughout the whole of the colonial period, the power was almost exclusively in the hands of the Spaniards.

Independence Wars

Apart from three brief rebellions against colonial rule between 1749 and 1797, Venezuela had a relatively uneventful history for 300 years after the arrival of the Europeans. All this changed at the beginning of the 19th century, when Venezuela gave Latin America its greatest ever hero, Simón Bolívar. El Libertador, as he is commonly known, together with his most able lieutenant, Antonio José de Sucre, were largely responsible for ending colonial rule all the way to the borders of Argentina.

The revolutionary flame was lit by Francisco de Miranda in 1806, but his efforts to set up an independent administration at Caracas came to an end when he was handed over to the Spanish by his fellow conspirators. He was shipped to Spain and died a few years later in a Cádiz jail. Leadership of the revolution was taken over by Bolívar. After unsuccessful attempts to defeat the Spaniards at home, he withdrew to Colombia, then to Jamaica, until the opportune moment came in 1817.

At the time, events in Europe were in Bolívar's favor. The Napoleonic Wars had ended, and Bolívar's agent in London was able to raise money and arms and to recruit some 5000 British veterans of the Peninsular War who were being demobilized from the armies that had been raised to fight Napoleon. With this mercenary force and an army of horsemen from Los Llanos, Bolívar marched over the Andes and defeated the Spanish at the battle of Boyacá, thus bringing independence to Colombia in August 1819.

Four months later in Angostura (present-day Ciudad Bolívar), the Angostura Congress proclaimed Gran Colombia, a new state unifying Colombia, Venezuela and Ecuador (though the last two were still under Spanish rule). The liberation of Venezuela was completed with Bolívar's victory over the Spanish forces at Carabobo in June 1821, though the royalists continued to put up a desultory rearguard fight from Puerto Cabello for another two years. With these victories under their belts, Bolívar and Sucre went on to liberate Ecuador, Peru and Bolivia, which they accomplished by the end of 1824.

Although both economically and demographically the least important of Gran Colombia's three provinces, Venezuela bore the brunt of the fighting. Venezuelan patriots fought not only on their own territory, but also in the armies that Bolívar led into Colombia and down the Pacific coast. It is estimated that a quarter of the Venezuelan population died in these wars.

Gran Colombia managed to exist for only a decade before it split into Venezuela, Ecuador and Colombia. Bolívar's dream of a unified republic fell apart even before his death in 1830.

After Independence

Venezuela's postindependence period was marked by serious governmental problems that continued for over a century. For the most part, these were times of despotism and anarchy, with the country being ruled by a series of military dictators known as *caudillos*. It wasn't until 1947 that the first democratic government was elected.

The first of the caudillos, General José Antonio Páez, controlled the country for 18 years (1830–48), though not as president for

all that time. Despite his tough rule, he succeeded in establishing a certain political stability and put the weak economy on its feet. He is perhaps the most warmly remembered of the caudillos.

The period that followed was an almost uninterrupted chain of civil wars and political strife, stopped only by another long-lived dictator, General Antonio Guzmán Blanco. He came to power in 1870 and kept it, with few breaks, until 1888. A conservative with liberal leanings, he launched a broad program of reforms, including a new constitution, compulsory primary education, religious freedom and a package of regulations designed to improve the economy. No doubt he tackled some of the crucial domestic issues and assured temporary stability, yet his despotic rule triggered wide popular opposition, and when he stepped down, the country plunged again into civil war.

Things were not going much better on the international front. In the 1840s, Venezuela raised the question of its eastern border with British Guiana (present-day Guyana). Based on vague preindependence territorial divisions, the Venezuelan government laid claim to as much as two-thirds of Guiana, up to the Río Essequibo. The issue was a subject of lengthy diplomatic negotiations, severely straining international relations in the 1890s. It was eventually settled in 1899 by an arbitration tribunal, which gave rights over the questioned territory to Great Britain. Despite the ruling, Venezuela maintains its claim to this day. All maps produced in Venezuela have this chunk of Guyana within Venezuela's boundaries, labeled 'Zona en Reclamación.'

Another conflict that led to serious international tensions was Venezuela's failure to meet payments to Great Britain, Italy and Germany on loans accumulated during the irresponsible government of yet another caudillo, General Cipriano Castro (1899–1908). In response, the three European countries in 1902 sent their navies to blockade Venezuelan seaports.

It's worth noting that the independence movement and subsequent governments were almost entirely in the hands of Creoles

Simón Bolívar

'There have been three great fools in history: Jesus, Don Quixote and I.' This is how Simón Bolívar summed up his life shortly before he died. The man who brought independence from Spanish rule to the entire northwest of South America – today's Venezuela, Colombia, Panama, Ecuador, Peru and Bolivia – died abandoned, rejected and poor.

The Bolívar family came to the New World from Spain in 1557. They first settled in Santo Domingo, but in 1589, they moved to Venezuela, where they were granted a hacienda in San Mateo, near Caracas. Members of Venezuela's colonial elite, they were well off and steadily extended their possessions. One of their descendants, Juan Vicente Bolívar, acquired a town house in Caracas. He was 47 years old when, in 1773, he married 15-year-old María de la Concepción Palacios y Blanco. They had four children; the second, born on July 24, 1783, was named Simón.

Juan Vicente died in 1786 (Simón was then three years old) and María six years later. The boy was brought up by his uncle and given a tutor, Simón Rodríguez, an open-minded mentor who had a strong formative influence on his pupil.

In 1799 the young Bolívar was sent to Spain and France to continue his education. After mastering French, he turned his attention to that country's literature. Voltaire and Rousseau became his favorite authors. Their works introduced him to new, progressive ideas of liberalism and – as it turned out – were to determine the course of his career.

In 1802, Bolívar married his Spanish bride, María Teresa Rodríguez del Toro, and a short time later the young couple sailed to Caracas. Their married life lasted only eight months: María Teresa died of yellow fever. Bolívar never married again, although he had many lovers. The most devoted of these was Manuela Sáenz, whom he met in Quito in 1822 and who accompanied him almost until his final days.

The death of María Teresa marked a drastic shift in Bolívar's destiny. He returned to France, where he met with the leaders of the French Revolution, and then traveled to the USA to take a close look at the new order after the American Revolutionary War. By the time he returned to Caracas in 1807, he was full of revolutionary theories and experiences taken from these two successful examples. It didn't take him long to join clandestine, pro-independence circles.

At the time, disillusionment with Spanish rule was close to breaking out into open revolt. On April 19, 1810, the Junta Suprema was installed in Caracas, and on July 5, 1811, the congress declared independence. This turned out to be only the beginning; the declaration triggered a long, bitter war, most of which was to be orchestrated by Bolívar.

Bolívar's military career began under Francisco de Miranda, the first Venezuelan leader of the independence movement. After Miranda was captured by the Spaniards in 1812, Bolívar took over command. Over the following decade, he had hardly a moment's rest; battle followed battle with astonishing frequency until 1824. Of those battles personally directed by Bolívar, the forces of independence won 35. Of these, the key strategic achievements were the battle of Boyacá (August 7, 1819), which secured the independence of Colombia; the battle of Carabobo (June 24, 1821), which brought freedom to Venezuela; and the battle of Pichincha (May 24, 1822), which led to the liberation of Ecuador.

Bolívar's long-awaited dream materialized: Gran Colombia, the unified state comprising Venezuela, Colombia and Ecuador, became reality. However, the task of setting the newborn country on its feet proved to be even more difficult than that of winning battles. 'I fear peace more than war,' Bolívar wrote in one of his letters, aware of the difficulties ahead.

Simón Bolívar

The main problem was the question of Gran Colombia's political organization. Bolívar, then the president, favored strong central rule, but the central regime was increasingly incapable of governing an immense country with such great racial and regional divisions and differences. Gran Colombia began to collapse from the moment of its birth.

Bolívar insisted on holding the weak union together, but matters began to slip out of his hands. His impassioned and vehement speeches – for which he was widely known – no longer swayed the growing opposition. His glory and charisma faded.

As separatist tendencies escalated dangerously, Bolívar removed his vice president, Santander, from office by decree and, in August 1828, assumed dictatorship. This step brought more harm than good. His popularity waned further, as did the circle of his personal friends and supporters. A short time later, he miraculously escaped an assassination attempt in Bogotá. Disillusioned and in bad health, he resigned the presidency in early 1830 and decided to travel to Europe. The formal disintegration of Gran Colombia was just months away.

Following Venezuela's separation from Gran Colombia, the Venezuelan Congress approved a new constitution and – irony of ironies – banned Bolívar from his homeland. A month later, Antonio José de Sucre (remembered for inflicting final defeat on Spain in the battle of Ayacucho on December 9, 1824), the closest of Bolívar's friends, was assassinated in southern Colombia. These two pieces of news reached Bolívar shortly before he was to have boarded a ship bound for France. Depressed and ill, he accepted the invitation of a Spaniard, Joaquín de Mier, to stay at his house, Quinta de San Pedro Alejandrino, in Santa Marta, Colombia. A bitter remark written in Bolívar's diary at this time reads, 'America is ungovernable. Those who serve the revolution plow the sea.'

Bolívar died on December 17, 1830, of pulmonary tuberculosis. A priest, a doctor and a few officers were by his bed, but none of his close friends. Joaquín de Mier donated one of his shirts to dress the dead body, as there had been none among Bolívar's humble belongings. So died perhaps the most important figure in South America's history.

It took the Venezuelan nation 12 years to acknowledge its debt to the man who won its freedom. In 1842 Bolívar's remains were brought from Santa Marta to Venezuela and deposited in Caracas' cathedral. In 1876, they were solemnly transferred to the National Pantheon, where they now rest.

El Libertador – as he was named at the beginning of the liberation campaign and is still commonly called today – was without doubt a man of extraordinary gifts and talents. An idealist with a poetic mind and visionary ideas, Bolívar's goal was not only to topple Spanish rule but also to create a unified America. This, of course, was an impossible ideal, yet the military conquest of some 5 million square kilometers remains a phenomenal accomplishment. This inspired amateur without any formal training in war strategy won battles in a manner that still confounds experts today. The campaign over the Andean Cordillera in the rainy season was described 100 years later as 'the most magnificent episode in the history of war.'

Voices critical of Bolívar's faults and shortcomings are now almost never heard, yet he was frequently accused of despotism and dictatorship when he ruled Gran Colombia. It was Bolívar himself who once said, 'Our America can only be ruled through a well-managed, shrewd despotism.'

Today Bolívar's reputation is polished and inflated to almost superhuman dimensions. His cult is particularly strong in Venezuela, but he is also widely venerated in all the other nations he freed. His statue graces almost every central city square, and at least one street in every town bears his name. One of the final, prophetic remarks in Bolívar's diary reads, 'My name now belongs to history; it will do me justice.' And history has duly done so.

(persons of European descent). They paid little attention to Indians and blacks, and not much more to mestizos or mulatos, who continued to be exploited under conditions similar to or worse than those prevailing under Spanish rule. Although slavery was officially abolished in 1854, in many regions it continued well into the 20th century.

20th-Century Dictatorships

The first half of the 20th century was dominated by five successive military rulers from the Andean state of Táchira, the first of whom was the incompetent Cipriano Castro. The longest lasting and most despotic was General Juan Vicente Gómez, who seized power in 1908 and didn't relinquish it until his death in 1935. Gómez phased out the parliament, squelched the opposition and thus monopolized power, supported by a strong army, an extensive police force and a well-developed spy network.

Thanks to the discovery of oil in the 1910s, the Gómez regime was able to stabilize the country. By the late 1920s, Venezuela became the world's largest exporter of oil, which not only contributed notably to economic recovery but also enabled the government to pay off the country's entire foreign debt.

Little of the oil-related wealth filtered down to people on the street. The vast majority continued to live in poverty, with little or no educational or health facilities, let alone reasonable housing. Oil money also resulted in the neglect of agriculture. Food had to be imported in increasing amounts, and prices rose rapidly. When Gómez died in 1935, the people of Caracas went on a rampage, burning down the houses of his relatives and supporters and even threatening to set fire to the oil installations on Lago de Maracaibo.

Gómez was succeeded by his war minister, Eleázar López Contreras, and six years later by yet another Táchiran general, Isaías Medina Angarita. Meanwhile, popular tensions rose dangerously, exploding in 1945 when Rómulo Betancourt, the founder and leader of the left-wing Acción Democrática party (AD), took control of the government.

A new constitution was adopted in 1947, and noted novelist Rómulo Gallegos became president in the first democratic election in the country's history. On the wave of political freedom, the conservative Partido Social Cristiano (known as 'Copei') was founded by the young activist Rafael Caldera to counterbalance the leftist AD.

The pace of reforms was too fast, however, given the strength of the old military forces greedy for power. The inevitable coup took place only eight months after Gallegos' election, with Colonel Marcos Pérez Jiménez emerging as leader. Once in control, Pérez Jiménez began to ruthlessly crush the opposition, at the same time plowing the oil money back into public works, into industries that would help diversify the economy and, particularly, into the modernization of Caracas. However, spectacular buildings mushrooming in the capital were poor substitutes for a better standard of living and access to political power for the majority of the population, and opposition grew rapidly.

Democracy at Last

In 1958, Pérez Jiménez was overthrown by a coalition of civilians and navy and air force officers. The country returned to democratic rule, and an election elevated AD founder Betancourt to the presidency. He put an end to the former dictator's solicitous policy toward foreign big business, but was careful this time not to act impetuously.

Betancourt enjoyed widespread popular support and succeeded in completing the constitutional five-year term in office – the first democratically elected Venezuelan president to do so. He voluntarily stepped down in 1963. Since then, all changes of president have been by constitutional means, with the two traditional parties, AD and Copei, being the major forces on the political scene until the mid-1990s.

Presidents Raúl Leoni of AD (1964–69) and Rafael Caldera of Copei (1969–74) had relatively quiet terms, since the steady stream of oil money that flowed into the country's coffers kept the economy buoyant. President Carlos Andrés Pérez of AD

(1974–79) witnessed the oil bonanza. Not only did production of oil rise but, more importantly, the price quadrupled following the Arab-Israeli war in 1973. Pérez nationalized the iron-ore and oil industries and went on a spending spree. Imported luxury goods crammed the shops, and the nation got the impression that El Dorado had finally materialized. Not for long, though.

Back to Instability

In the late 1970s, the growing international recession and oil glut began to shake Venezuela's economic stability. Oil revenues declined, pushing up unemployment, inflation and foreign debt. Presidents Luis Herrera Campins of Copei (1979–84) and Jaime Lusinchi of AD (1984–89) witnessed a slowing of the economy as well as increasing popular discontent.

The 1988 drop in world oil prices cut the country's revenue in half, threatening Venezuela's ability to pay off its foreign debt. Austerity measures introduced in February 1989 by the government of President Pérez (elected for the second time) triggered a wave of protests in Caracas, culminating in three days of bloody riots, known as the 'Caracazo,' and the loss of more than 300 lives. All further measures (basically, price increases) spurred protests, mostly beginning in universities, that often escalated into riots. Strikes and street demonstrations came to be part of everyday life, as they continue to be today.

To make matters worse, there were two attempted coups d'état in 1992. The first, launched in February by a faction of mid-rank military officers led by Colonel Hugo Chávez, was a shock to most Venezuelans. The president escaped from the presidential Palacio de Miraflores minutes before rebel tanks broke in. There was shooting throughout Caracas, claiming over 20 lives, but the government regained control. Chávez was sentenced to a long term in prison.

Another attempt, in November, was led by junior air-force officers. The air battle over Caracas, with warplanes flying between the skyscrapers, gave the coup a cinematographic, if not apocalyptic, dimension. The Palacio de Miraflores was bombed and partially destroyed. The army was again called to defend the president, which it dutifully did. This time, more than 100 people lost their lives.

Things became even more complicated when President Pérez was charged with embezzlement and misuse of public funds. He was automatically suspended from his duties and tried in court. On a continent where the trial of a president is a rare occurrence, it's remarkable that Pérez was eventually sentenced. He was released in 1996 after spending 28 months under house arrest.

Caldera's Difficult Second Term

The December 1993 elections brought Rafael Caldera back to the presidency. He no longer represented Copei, the party he founded, but ran as an independent backed by a coalition of 16 small parties, known as the Convergencia Nacional. He narrowly defeated Andrés Velásquez of the Causa Radical (Causa R), the relatively new, progressive left-wing party founded by unionists. The candidates of the two traditional parties, Copei and AD, were beaten into third and fourth place, respectively.

The election result reflected the social climate of the day. Amid general political instability, and with both traditional parties embroiled in corruption scandals, voters opted for their charismatic former president, probably hoping he would repeat his success of the previous term. However, 25 years on, the economic situation was quite different, as was the man himself, 77 years old by the time of the election.

Caldera's problems began even before he officially took office. In February 1994, Venezuela's second-largest bank, Banco Latino, collapsed and had to be rescued by a government takeover costing US$2 billion. The domino-like failure of a dozen other banks throughout 1994 cost the government another US$8 billion to pay off depositors. Several more banks failed in 1995. In all, the disaster cost state coffers the equivalent of 20% of the gross domestic product, making it one of the largest financial collapses in recent history.

Unlike previous free-market-oriented governments, Caldera's opted for a state-controlled economy and fixed the exchange rate of the local currency. In 1995, the government was forced to devalue the currency by more than 70%, yet Venezuela's economic situation continued to worsen. Facing an economic mess, in 1996 the government introduced a package of drastic rescue measures, including an increase of gas prices by about 500% and the abolition of exchange controls.

Throughout Caldera's presidency, Venezuela was plagued by strikes for higher wages by workers of most major job groups, including teachers, civil servants and doctors. By 1998, more than three-quarters of the country's 23 million inhabitants found themselves below the poverty line, and unemployment hit a new record of 15%. Crime and drug trafficking have increased, and there has been a dramatic expansion of Colombian guerrillas into Venezuela's frontier areas over recent years.

Venezuela Today

As the country reached perhaps its deepest economic crisis in living memory, challengers for the December 1998 presidential election jockeyed for position. This time there were no candidates from the traditional AD and Copei among the front-runners. Instead, the campaign was between two unusual independents – ex–Miss Universe Irene Sáez and the leader of the 1992 failed coup, Hugo Chávez – poignantly reflecting the frustration and the discontent of the electorate. Yale-educated businessman Henrique Salas Römer joined the race later, but Chávez eventually won with 56% of the vote.

Chávez, pardoned by Caldera in 1994, became a radical leftist politician, campaigning with a blend of nationalism, populist rhetoric and anticorruption overtones that made him popular with Venezuela's poor majority. As a platform for his campaign, he founded the Movimiento Bolivariano Revolucionario party, which in 1997 was transformed into the Movimiento Quinta República (MVR).

During the campaign, Chávez replaced his army uniform with business suits and modeled himself on the UK's Tony Blair, pledging to seek 'a third way between brutal neoliberalism and hard-line socialism.' It was not quite clear what he had in mind, but he showed little enthusiasm for privatization and a free-market economy, voting instead to declare a moratorium on repaying the country's US$22 billion foreign debt.

Shortly after taking office, Chávez set about putting into action his great 'peaceful and democratic social revolution' that he had pledged in his presidential campaign. In order to do this, however, he insisted that he first needed to rewrite the existing constitution, which he described as 'moribund.' A 131-member Constituent Assembly was formed and put together the wholly new document in 100 days. The constitution was approved in a referendum held nationwide on December 15, 1999.

Precisely on the same day, violent mudslides were cascading down the Litoral Central on the coast of Vargas state, just north of Caracas, burying everything in their paths. The result of torrential rains soaking the region since late November, the sea of mud devastated a 100km stretch of the coast populated by nearly half a million people. In what is considered South America's worst natural disaster in the 20th century, some 30,000 to 50,000 people lost their lives, and another 150,000 lost their homes. The disaster caused an estimated US$15 to US$20 billion in damage.

With the nation still deeply traumatized by the disaster, the new constitution came into force on December 30, 1999, symbolically giving the country a new legal platform for the new millennium. Described by political analysts as a 'blank check for the presidency,' the constitution gave the chief executive sweeping powers. It also introduced extensive changes – so extensive, in fact, that they necessitated a new round of general elections, which were held in late July 2000.

Still experiencing widespread popular support, Chávez easily won again, this time

Who is Hugo Chávez?

Born in 1954 in the town of Sabaneta, in Barinas state, this former paratrooper and now president of Venezuela is not exactly your average politician. To start with, not everybody chooses a coup d'état as a form to express their political standpoint, as did Chávez in February 1992. The coup was a failure and Chávez ended up in a jail, but the event put him firmly on the political scene. The seeds had been sown.

Pardoned by President Caldera in 1994, Chávez embarked on an aggressive populist campaign, with nationalist Bolivarian rhetoric targeting the poor – roughly 80% of Venezuelans. Four years later, he was head of state, this time legally.

Once in office, he swiftly embarked on changing the constitution, which he achieved within a year. The new constitution gives him extraordinary powers and extends presidential terms to six years with the possibility of immediate reelection. This means Chávez can potentially stay in office until 2012. Critics haven't missed the opportunity to comment that the era of the caudillos is back.

On the international front, Chávez has caused a lot of talk. His friendly links with Colombian guerrillas, Cuba and China have been carefully watched by Uncle Sam, who sees him as a destabilizing force in the region. His April 2000 visit to Havana for the Group of 77 summit of Third World nations (he was the only attending Latin American head of state, apart from Fidel Castro) was also met with regional criticism.

Chávez has remained defiant. In August 2000 he toured all the OPEC countries and became the first foreign head of state to visit Baghdad and meet Saddam Hussein since the Gulf War of 1991. As if this were not enough, he then paid a visit to former Libyan head of state Ghaddafi, attracting a red-carpet reception and further infuriating the USA.

A strong opponent of globalization, Chávez has been credited with the revitalization of OPEC and the campaign to keep oil prices high by carefully controlling supply. He also tries to portray OPEC as a consumer-friendly advocacy organization and blames high fuel prices on the heavy taxes charged by western governments.

Chávez burst upon the scene in 1992.

beating Francisco Arias Cárdenas, another 1992 coup leader and onetime friend and ally of Chávez. In the provincial elections, held together with the presidential ones, Chávez' MVR party garnered the position of governor in 13 of 23 states.

The results of the elections, combined with the presidential powers provided by the new constitution, gave Chávez a monopoly on authority, allowing him to govern virtually without opposition. How he will use these powers to produce his 'social revolution' is yet to be seen.

GOVERNMENT

Venezuela is a federal republic. The fully new 1999 constitution – the 26th in the country's history – replaced the document that was in force since 1961. The new act introduced a number of significant changes, including nothing less than the change of country's name (it's now República Bolivariana de Venezuela). The previously bicameral Congress has been replaced by a unicameral National Assembly, the members of which are elected by popular vote. In addition, the constitution provided for an

ADMINISTRATIVE DIVISIONS

executive post – vice president – that had previously been absent from the government.

The new constitution has given the presidency far-reaching powers. The president is now elected by direct vote for a six-year term (before, it was five years) and can be reelected for one consecutive term (previously the president had to stay two terms out of office before running for reelection). The president is both the chief of state and head of government. She or he appoints the cabinet, the commander in chief of the armed forces, and members of the Supreme Court (thus raising the prospect of political interference in the judiciary). The president can also dissolve the National Assembly.

There are a number of political parties, of which the Acción Democrática (AD) and Partido Social Cristiano (Copei), both founded in the 1940s, were the major traditional forces until the early 1990s. For more than 30 years, up to the 1993 elections, Venezuelan presidents were always members of one of these parties.

The picture diversified in the 1990s, with other parties, including the Causa Radical (Causa R) and Movimiento al Socialismo (MAS), gaining political weight. Recent years have seen dramatic changes, with Movimiento Quinta República (MVR) becoming a significant political power.

Administratively, the country is divided into 23 *estados* (states) and the federal district of Caracas. The youngest state, Estado Vargas (the one devastated by mudslides in December 1999), was created only in July 1998. The islands of Margarita, Coche and Cubagua collectively form a state on their own, Nueva Esparta; the remaining 72 islands are all federal dependencies. The states are further divided into *municipios* (municipalities) and are ruled by *gobernadores* (governors) elected by direct vote at provincial elections.

Venezuela is a member of the United Nations (UN), Organization of American States (OAS), Latin American Integration Association, Organization of Petroleum Exporting Countries (OPEC), the Andean Pact (trade pact between Bolivia, Colombia, Ecuador, Peru and Venezuela) and the Grupo de los Tres (Group of Three, a trade block of Colombia, Mexico and Venezuela).

The Venezuelan flag, adopted in 1811, has three horizontal belts of equal width: from top to bottom, the belts are yellow, blue and red. There's an arc of seven white stars on the blue portion, representing the seven original provinces of Venezuela in 1811.

GEOGRAPHY

With an area of 916,445 sq km, Venezuela is South America's sixth-largest country. It's bigger than the UK and France combined, or twice the size of California. About eight Venezuelas would fit on the Australian continent. Stretching some 1500km east to west and 1300km north to south, it occupies the northern part of South America, neighboring Colombia (which lies to the west), Brazil (south) and Guyana (east).

In the north, Venezuela is bordered by 2813km of coastline, dotted with countless beaches. Just south of the coast looms a chain of mountain ranges, the Cordillera de la Costa, with a number of peaks exceeding 2000m. This is a structural continuation of the Andes, even though it's separated from the main Andean massif by lowlands. The

coastal mountain chain rolls southward into a vast area of plains known as 'Los Llanos,' which stretches as far as the Ríos Orinoco and Meta. Los Llanos occupies a third of the national territory.

The land south of the Orinoco, constituting half the country's area, is called 'Guayana'; it can be broadly divided into three different geographical regions. To the southwest is a chunk of the Amazon – thick tropical forest, partly inaccessible. To the northeast lies the Delta del Orinoco, a vast swamp crisscrossed by a labyrinth of water channels. Finally, the central and largest part of Guayana is taken over by extensive highlands, with the plateau of open savanna known as 'La Gran Sabana' being its most visited part. It's here that the majority of *tepuis* (table mountains) are located. These gigantic mesas, with vertical walls and flat tops, are all that's left of the upper layer of a plateau that gradually eroded over millions of years. They rise up to 1000m above the surrounding countryside but reach nearly 3000m above sea level.

The northwestern part of Venezuela is another area of geographical contrasts. Here lies the Sierra Nevada de Mérida, the northern end of the Andean chain. The Sierra constitutes Venezuela's highest mountain range, topped by the snowcapped Pico Bolívar (5007m). Just north of the Andes is the marshy lowland basin around the shallow and brackish Lago de Maracaibo. At 13,500 sq km (200km long and 120km wide), it's South America's largest lake and is linked to the Caribbean Sea by a narrow strait. The basin is the country's main oil-producing area. Northeast of the lake, near the town of Coro, is Venezuela's sole desert, the Médanos de Coro.

The 2150km-long Río Orinoco is by far the longest river in the country. The second longest is the Río Caroní (640km), a tributary of the Orinoco.

Venezuela possesses 72 islands scattered around the Caribbean Sea off the country's northern coast. The largest of these is Isla de Margarita. Other islands and archipelagos of importance include Las Aves, Los Roques, La Orchila, La Tortuga and La Blanquilla.

CLIMATE

Venezuela is close to the equator, so average temperatures vary little throughout the year. They do, however, change with altitude, dropping about 6°C with every 1000m increase. Since over 90% of Venezuela lies below 1000m, you'll experience temperatures between 22°C and 30°C in most places. The Andean and coastal mountain ranges have more moderate temperatures.

Venezuela experiences dry and wet seasons. Broadly speaking, the dry season (known as *verano* – 'summer') goes from December to April, while the wet season (*invierno* – 'winter') lasts the remaining part of the year. There are many regional variations in the amount of rain and the length of the seasons. For example, the upper reaches of the mountains receive more rainfall than

the coast and can be relatively wet for most of the year, while you can visit the Coro desert almost any day of the year and not need to worry about rain. The Amazon has no distinct dry season, with annual rainfall exceeding 2000mm, distributed roughly evenly throughout the year.

Recent climatic anomalies throughout the world, including El Niño and La Niña, have affected Venezuela with abnormal periods of rain and drought. As a result, the previously clearly defined dry and rainy seasons have become difficult to determine. These anomalies contributed to the mudslide disaster on the Vargas coast in December 1999.

ECOLOGY & ENVIRONMENT

A short walk along a city street or a bus ride in the countryside will give you insight into

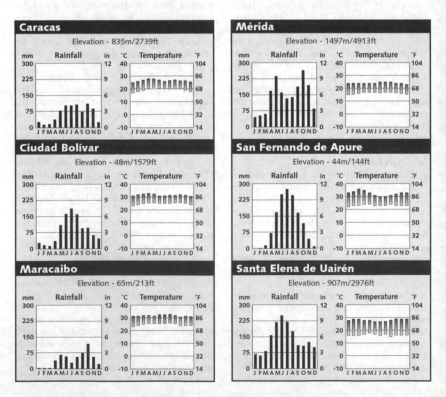

Venezuelans' attitude toward the environment. Unfortunately, it won't be a pleasant experience. Many locals throw away everything they don't need wherever they may happen to be. Without ecological education, the indifference to such behavior is passed on through generations. Some cities and many smaller towns don't have sufficient designated waste heaps or landfill areas, so garbage is simply trucked to the nearest out-of-sight place and dumped. Disturbing as it may be for a visitor, it's only the tip of the iceberg of Venezuela's environmental problems.

A more serious issue is indiscriminate deforestation and the subsequent erosion it promotes. Every year large areas of forest are cleared for agricultural use, pastureland, construction and industrial projects, and timber. The shrinking forest area affects local wildlife, and consequently an increasing number appear on the endangered-species list.

Industry poses a serious threat to the environment. Plants and installations have been built at economically prime locations, with little or no attention paid to the preservation of the ecosystem, and these intruders have introduced several long-term sources of contamination.

Lago de Maracaibo has been so heavily contaminated by decades of oil drilling and untreated sewage from the city of Maracaibo that cleaning it would cost at least US$1 billion. The discovery of oil deposits in the Delta del Orinoco, as well as the recent commencement of its exploitation, has put at risk the ecological balance of one of the best-preserved regions, including the pristine Parque Nacional Mariusa. Right on the edge of the fragile Parque Nacional Mochima, a gigantic cement plant has been built and recently extended considerably. The alleged leak of a chemical from one of the northwestern Venezuelan oil refineries in 1996 is thought to be responsible for the partial death of the coral in Parque Nacional Morrocoy. And mercury is widely used in gold and diamond mining in Guayana, polluting rivers and causing health hazards for local inhabitants and wildlife.

But wildlife is threatened not only by industry. Given the amazing variety of exotic species, it's no surprise that legions of poachers comb remote forests in search of rare animals, mostly birds. Today Venezuela is one of South America's major exporters of wildlife, which is smuggled across the border by air and sea.

The lack of conservation of both wildlife and ecosystems is alarming, despite the existence of environmental institutions and legislation. Ironically enough, Venezuela was at the forefront of Latin America's green movement. The Sociedad Conservacionista Audubon de Venezuela was founded as early as 1970. It is now the leading non-governmental environment promoter, yet it lacks sufficient funds to develop a thorough program.

On the government side, an environmental protection law was enacted in 1975; three years later the Ministerio del Ambiente (Ministry of the Environment) was created, becoming the very first governmental department of its kind on the continent. In 1992, Venezuela passed a comprehensive environmental law specifying dozens of punishable crimes, including the pollution of soil, water and air; damaging the ozone layer; and setting forest fires. This comes complete with a package of detailed technical standards defining protected areas, limits on pollution levels etc.

All this looks highly impressive on paper, yet compliance has been minimal at most. The lack of personnel to enforce the law, a weak judicial system, widespread bureaucracy and notorious corruption are all obstacles to the successful prosecution of violators. And the government's current predisposition toward rescuing the crumbling economy at any cost doesn't make things easier.

If there's any redeeming feature of the situation, it is that most of Venezuela lacks the population pressures of, say, Brazil, so environmental problems have not yet reached apocalyptic proportions. Nonetheless, if decisive measures aren't implemented promptly, the country's forests and wildlife resources face bleak prospects.

Río Orinoco

The 2150km Río Orinoco is South America's third-longest river (after the Amazon and La Plata) and drains an area of roughly 1 million square kilometers in Venezuela and Colombia. Its entire course, from source to mouth, lies in Venezuela. Its major left-bank tributaries are the Ríos Apure, Arauca, Meta and Vichada, while the main right-bank tributaries include the Ríos Caroní and Caura.

The Orinoco is also the third most voluminous river on the continent. Its flow and discharge depend largely on the season. The difference between the low and high water levels (in March and August, respectively) can exceed 15m.

The river carries about 50 billion metric tons of sediment annually and, as a consequence, its delta spreads out into the Atlantic. The delta consists of a maze of natural channels that cut a swath through predominantly marshy land. The Delta del Orinoco covers an area of about 25,000 sq km, which is not much less than the total size of Belgium. There are more than 40 major mouths, which are distributed along 360km of the Atlantic coast.

One of these mouths, the outlet of Caño Manamo, was discovered by Christopher Columbus in 1498, shortly after he landed at the tip of the Paria Peninsula, opposite Trinidad. The Orinoco was thus the first major river discovered in the New World by a European. From that moment on, the river began to draw in adventurers and explorers, mostly because they supposed it to be the gateway to the legendary El Dorado. In one of the earliest big expeditions, in 1531, Diego de Ordaz sailed upstream as far as the Raudales de Atures (near present-day Puerto Ayacucho), but the rapids effectively defended the river's upper course from penetration.

International Environmental Organizations

Many organizations promote the preservation of rain forests and other endangered environments. For more details contact any of the following groups:

Australia
Friends of the Earth (☎ 03-9419 8700) 312 Smith St, Collingwood, Vic 3066
Web site: www.foe.org.au
Greenpeace Australia Ltd (☎ 03-9670 1633) 24/26 Johnston St, Fitzroy, Vic 3065

UK
Friends of the Earth (☎ 020-7490 1555) 26/28 Underwood St, London N17JQ Survival International (☎ 020-7492 1441) 11-15 Emerald Rd, London WC1N 3QL
World Wildlife Fund (☎ 01483 426 444) Panda House, Weyside Park, Godalming, Surrey GU7 1BP
Web site: www.wwf.org

USA
Conservation International (☎ 202-429 5660) 2501 M St NW, Suite 200, Washington, DC 20037
Web site: www.conservation.org

Friends of the Earth (☎ 202-783 7400) 1025 Vermont Ave NW, Washington, DC 20005
Web site: www.foe.org
Rainforest Action Network (RAN; ☎ 415-398 4404) 221 Pine St, Suite 500, San Francisco, CA 94104
Web site: www.ran.org
The Nature Conservancy (☎ 703-841 5300) 4245 N Fairfax Drive, Suite 100, Arlington, VA 22203
Web site: www.tnc.org

FLORA & FAUNA

As a tropical country with a diverse geography, Venezuela boasts varied and abundant flora and fauna. Over millions of years, distinctive biohabitats evolved in different regions, each with its own peculiar wildlife. These species developed relatively uninterrupted, unlike their counterparts in North America and Western Eurasia, which were affected by the ice ages. In effect, Venezuela is among the world's top 10 most biodiverse countries.

German naturalist Alexander von Humboldt and French botanist Aimé Bonpland were both among the first serious explorers

Río Orinoco

Alexander von Humboldt managed to explore some of the upper reaches of the Orinoco in 1800. His major goal was the intriguing Brazo Casiquiare, discovered earlier by missionaries. The Casiquiare is a 220km-long natural channel linking the Orinoco with the Río Negro. It spans the two vast fluvial systems of the Orinoco and the Amazon, being one of the very few phenomena of its kind in the world.

The uppermost reaches of the Orinoco were rarely seen by explorers. This has always been an inaccessible land and home to the mysterious Yanomami tribe, who have not been particularly open to outsiders. Actually, it wasn't until 1951 that the exact source of the Orinoco was determined, when a joint French-Venezuelan expedition found the 70m-high cliff of the Cerro Delgado Chalbaud (at an altitude of 1047m), close to the Brazilian border, where the river originates.

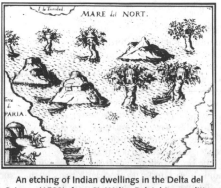

An etching of Indian dwellings in the Delta del Orinoco (1599), from Sir Walter Raleigh's expedition

dedicated to studying and recording local species, and their work was continued by subsequent expeditions. Despite a number of scientific explorations over recent decades, the picture is still very incomplete.

Flora

Generally speaking, Venezuela's plant life is stratified by thermal zones, which means that some species are confined to particular altitudes with optimal growing conditions. Since the country's topography goes from sea level up to 5000m, there's quite a diversity, from rain forest at the bottom end up to *páramos* – boggy highland meadows just below the highest peaks.

Bosque húmedo (rain forest) – which still covers nearly a quarter of the country's area – is quite different from the temperate woodlands to which Europeans and North Americans are accustomed. It is home to a diversity and abundance of plants. Even more diversified is *bosque nublado* (cloud forest), which is confined to mountain slopes between 1000 and 3000m. It is common to

the Andes and upper reaches of the Cordillera de la Costa.

Higher up in the Andes, from about 3300 to 4400m, are the páramos, which are found only in limited mountainous areas of Venezuela and Ecuador, as well as in Colombia, where they are more numerous and diversified. A typical feature of the páramo is the *frailejón*, or espeletia, a plant with long, down-covered, pastel green leaves arranged in a rosette pattern. The flower generally blooms from September to December. There are many species of espeletia, the tallest of which reaches up to 10m (in Colombia). The tallest found in Venezuela are about 3m high.

The flora on top of the tepuis is most unusual. Isolated from the savanna below and from other tepuis for millions of years, the plant life on top of each of these plateaus developed independently. In effect, these biological islands have totally distinctive flora, half of which is considered endemic and typical to only one or a group of tepuis.

The *flor de mayo*, one of several thousand species of *orquídea* (orchid), is Venezuela's national flower. The *araguaney* (trumpet tree) is the national tree and is particularly spectacular at the end of the dry season, when it is covered with bright yellow blossoms.

Birds

There are some 1360 bird species in Venezuela (more than in Europe and North America combined). There are a number of excellent bird-watching areas, of which the largest and one of the best is Los Llanos. Parts of the coast, especially those with a developed mangrove ecosystem (Parque Nacional Morrocoy), and cloud forest (Parque Nacional Henri Pittier) are also excellent territories for bird-watchers.

The bird world ranges from species commonly associated with tropical forests, such as the macaw *(guacamaya)*, parrot *(loro)* and toucan *(tucán)*, to a variety of waterbirds, including ibis *(ibis)*, heron *(garza)*, pelican *(pelícano)* and flamingo *(flamenco)*. (Names given in italics in this section are common local names.)

The hummingbird *(colibrí)* is one of the most unusual birds. This colorful little 'helicopter' beats its wings up to 80 times a second as it hovers, producing its characteristic hum. Various species of hummingbird inhabit different climatic zones, including one living high in the páramo above 4000m.

Commonly associated with

Andean countries, the famous condor *(cóndor)* was wiped out in Venezuela decades ago (apart from those in zoos), but 10 specimens were introduced in the early 1990s from abroad and set free in the Mérida region. Sadly, only a few birds can still be seen; others have allegedly been shot down.

The oilbird *(guácharo)*, a nocturnal fruit eater, inhabits dozens of Venezuelan caves. See the Cueva del Guácharo section, in the Northwest chapter, for details. The *turpial*, noted for its magnificent yellow, white and black plumage, is the national bird.

Mammals

South America is not famous for large mammals, but nonetheless has a great diversity and number of smaller species. About 340 mammal species have been recorded in Venezuela alone.

The largest terrestrial local species include the tapir *(danta)*, found in the rain forests throughout the country, and the spectacled bear *(oso frontino)*, which lives in the Andean cloud forest.

The jaguar *(tigre* or *jaguar)* is the largest cat in the New World. It had a significant mythological importance in various pre-Columbian civilizations. Today its existence is threatened by illegal hunting and the shrinking of its natural habitat. Other feline mammals typical of Venezuela include the puma *(puma)* and

The mysterious jaguar holds a lofty place in indigenous lore.

ocelot *(ocelote)*, both of which inhabit the local forests and are endangered species.

What does abound is the capybara *(chigüire)*, the world's largest rodent, weighing up to 60kg. It's typical of Los Llanos, and you can even find it on the local menu. Its smaller cousin, the agouti *(lapa)*, is also numerous, but it's probably at greater risk of overhunting because of its excellent meat.

Venezuela boasts a variety of monkeys, including the red howler monkey *(mono araguato)*, capuchin monkey *(mono capuchino)* and spider monkey *(mono araña)*. You are likely to see some of these when traveling deeper into the forest. Easier to see, even in city parks, are sloths *(perezas)*, invariably hanging motionless from tree limbs.

Other terrestrial mammals found in Venezuela include the armadillo *(armadillo)*, the anteater *(oso hormiguero)*, the peccary *(báquiro)*, the deer *(venado)*, the coati *(guache)* and the opossum *(rabipelado)*.

Local rivers and lakes are home to a variety of aquatic mammals, the most characteristic of which are the pink dolphin *(tonina)*, the giant otter *(perro de agua* or *nutria gigante)* and the manatee *(manatí)*, which is facing serious risk of extinction.

Finally, Venezuela features a number of bat species (which are mammals), the most mysterious of which is perhaps the vampire bat *(vampiro)*, found throughout the country. It does feed on blood, but contrary to popular belief, it's not dangerous to humans.

Reptiles

Venezuela is home to about 300 species of reptiles, including crocodiles, snakes, lizards and turtles. Among the most characteristic local reptiles are the caimans, or American crocodiles. There are five species of caiman, ranging from the most common, the spectacled caiman *(baba or caimán de anteojos)*, to the huge Orinoco caiman *(caimán del Orinoco)*. The latter inhabits the rivers of the Orinoco basin and can sometimes exceed 5m in length. Its favorite diet is fish, but birds, other reptiles and mammals are a frequent diversion. It has been extensively hunted since the 1920s for its skin, which is highly valued as leather on local and international markets. This has put its existence in jeopardy. At present, its population is estimated at between 500 and 1000.

Another giant, the *caimán de la costa*, lives, as its name suggests, along the coast, principally in the lower reaches of rivers emptying into the Caribbean Sea and Lago de Maracaibo. It can reach 6m from head to tail and has a rare ability to live in both salt water and freshwater. It's also very rare today.

Nonvenomous snakes include the legendary anaconda *(anaconda)*, the world's greatest snake, reaching up to 8m in length, which lives in Los Llanos and the Amazon. There are several species of the equally famous boa, including the red-tailed boa *(boa constrictor)*, common tree boa *(boa arborícola)*, emerald tree boa *(boa esmeralda)* and rainbow boa *(boa arco iris)*.

There exist four groups of venomous ophidians, including two species of rattlesnake *(cascabel)*, typical of the arid areas, and nine species of the pit viper *(mapanare)*, common in most regions. Also very characteristic of Venezuela are 12 species of coral snake *(coral)*, which live throughout the country. Though not aggressive, they're highly venomous. They are recognizable by brightly colored bands that differ depending on the particular species (red, white, yellow etc). Finally, there's the rare venomous bushmaster *(cuaima piña)*, which lives deep in the rain forest of Guayana, and you're unlikely to have many close encounters with it. It's much easier to see the iguana *(iguana)*, which despite its alarming size is only a large herbivorous lizard.

Among the turtles, you may have a chance to see the matamata turtle *(mata mata)*, but it's harder to spot an arrau sideneck turtle *(tortuga arrau)*, the shell of which can be up to 80cm in diameter; it's now a seriously endangered species.

Insects

This is certainly the most populous wildlife group. Of some 30,000 species so far recorded, butterflies *(mariposas)* are arguably the favorite of most travelers. There's a great variety of them, including spectacular morphos, which have intensely blue wings spanning up to 15cm.

The insect family comprises less pleasant creatures, such as two that are commonly known as the *jején* and *puri puri*. These are small gnats that infest the Gran Sabana and, to a lesser extent, some other regions. Their bites are desperately itchy for days. Also, beware of a large ant, colloquially referred to as the *hormiga veinticuatro* (ant 24). The mysterious number is reputedly due to the fact that the inch-long ant's bite results in a high fever for a full day; it can be fatal.

Marine Life

With some 2800km of coastline and a maze of islands, islets, cays and coral reefs, it's no wonder that submarine flora and fauna are enormously abundant. All the multicolored fish, starfish, sea urchins, sea anemones and coral that you've seen in TV documentaries are here and thriving. There are many good areas for snorkelers and scuba divers – see the Activities section in the Facts for the Visitor chapter.

NATIONAL PARKS

The first nature reserve, Parque Nacional Henri Pittier, was established in 1937. It took another 15 years for the next park to be established, but today Venezuela boasts 43 national parks. Between 1987 and 2000, 17 new parks appeared on the map, and new ones may be declared in the near future.

Apart from national parks, Venezuela has an array of 21 nature reserves called *monumentos naturales*. These are usually smaller than the parks and are intended to protect a particular natural feature, such as a lake, a mountain peak or a cave. The whole system of parks and other reserves covers about 15% of the country's territory.

The Instituto Nacional de Parques, commonly referred to as 'Inparques,' is the governmental body created to run and take care of national parks and other nature reserves. Unfortunately, its control seems only nominal. Deforestation, contamination, hunting and fishing haven't been eliminated by simply declaring an area a national park,

and funds and personnel are insufficient to enforce protection.

Only a small handful of the parks have any Inparques-built tourist facilities. Most others either are wilderness or have been swiftly taken over by local private operators, who have built their own tourist facilities and provide transportation.

No permits are needed to enter national parks, but some parks charge admission fees. Los Roques charges US$15, the western part of Canaima charges US$12, and half a dozen others have smaller fees, none of which exceeds US$1.

In theory, you have to pay a fee (usually no more than US$2) for camping in the parks – you do this in regional Inparques offices. However, except for a few parks, you'll probably never be asked to pay.

ECONOMY

Oil is Venezuela's major natural resource and the heart of its economy. The main deposits are in the Maracaibo basin, but other important reserves have been discovered and exploited on the eastern outskirts of Los Llanos (in Anzoátegui and Monagas states) and in the Delta del Orinoco.

Since its discovery in 1914, oil turned Venezuela – at that stage a poor debtor nation – into one of the richest countries in South America. Until 1970 Venezuela was the world's largest exporter of oil, and though it was later overtaken by some Middle Eastern countries, its oil production expanded year after year.

As cofounder of OPEC, Venezuela was influential in the fourfold rise in oil prices introduced in 1973 and '74, which quadrupled the country's revenue overnight. Oil revenues peaked in 1981 with export earnings of US$19.3 billion, representing over 95% of the country's exports. On the strength of this wealth, Venezuela borrowed heavily from foreign banks to import almost everything other than petroleum. As of 1999, Venezuela was OPEC's third-largest oil producer, after Saudi Arabia and Iran.

Oil has overshadowed other sectors of the economy. Agriculture, which had never been strong, has been largely neglected, and

NATIONAL PARKS

1 Perijá	
2 Ciénagas del Catatumbo	
3 Páramos Batallón y La Negra	23 San Esteban
4 Chorro El Indio	24 Henri Pittier
5 El Tamá	25 Macarao
6 Río Viejo	26 El Ávila
7 Tapo-Caparo	27 Guatopo
8 Sierra Nevada	28 Laguna de Tacarigua
9 Sierra La Culata	29 Mochima
10 Guaramacal	30 Laguna de La Restinga
11 Dinira	31 Cerro El Copey
12 El Guache	32 El Guácharo
13 Yacambú	33 Turuépano
14 Terepaima	34 Península de Paria
15 Cerro Saroche	35 Mariusa
16 Sierra de San Luis	36 Aguaro-Guariquito
17 Médanos de Coro	37 Cinaruco-Capanaparo
18 Cueva de la Quebrada El Toro	38 Canaima
19 Yurubí	39 Jaua Sarisariñama
20 Tirgua	40 Yapacana
21 Morrocoy	41 Duida Marahuaca
22 Archipiélago Los Roques	42 Parima-Tapirapecó
	43 Serranía La Neblina

only 4% of the country's territory is under cultivation. The major crops include bananas, sugarcane, maize, coffee, cacao, cotton and tobacco. Despite its long coastline, Venezuela hasn't realized the potential of the fishing industry, which accounts for only 4% of the total catch of South America and comprises principally shrimp, sardine and tuna.

But even apart from oil, Venezuela is rich in natural resources. Iron ore, with huge deposits found south of Ciudad Bolívar, is the most important mineral, followed by extensive reserves of bauxite (from which alu-

minum ore is extracted), also in Guayana. These minerals gave birth (in 1961) to Ciudad Guayana, the center of these industries, as the government attempted to diversify the economy. Other major subsoil riches include gold and diamonds, both in Guayana, and coal near the border with Colombia, north of Maracaibo.

The government also invested heavily in developing manufacturing, such as the motor-vehicle-assembly, chemical, textile, footwear, paper and food industries. Taking advantage of a considerable hydroelectric potential, the gigantic Guri Dam was built (at a cost of US$5 billion) south of Ciudad Guayana. This is the second-largest hydroelectric plant in the world, with a potential power of 10 million kilowatts. More than half of Venezuela's electricity needs are supplied by hydroelectric power.

In spite of the development of non-oil sectors, petroleum has remained Venezuela's bread-and-butter industry, generating around 80% of export earnings. In the early 1980s, when global recession struck, oil prices declined. Venezuela's export earnings from oil fell drastically to a low of US$7.2 billion in 1986. This left the country with an unsustainable foreign debt and forced a 1987 agreement with creditors to 'reschedule' some US$20 billion in repayments. Political uncertainty, the collapse of the major banks and the government's economic mismanagement contributed to what is now Venezuela's worst economic crisis.

In 1999 Venezuela's gross domestic product shrank by 7.2% – the worst economic performance for any country on the continent for that year and Venezuela's worst figure on record for over a decade. Unemployment in 1999 hit a high of 18% according to the official statistics. Inflation ended up at around 20%, down from 29% in the previous year and from the record high of 103% in 1996. However, most analysts consider the apparently low inflation to be mostly due to the 12% consumption drop over that year. In fact, 1999 consumption (expenditure on goods and services for personal use) fell to the levels of 1967.

As of 2000, minimum monthly wages were about US$200. Chronic inflation has caused the middle class to shrink, while the share of the population living in poverty has increased dramatically. By 1999, 83% of the population lived below the poverty level, according to official statistics.

POPULATION & PEOPLE

Venezuela traditionally conducted the national census every 10 years, in the years ending in zero, but the 2000 census was postponed owing to a lack of funds. Consequently, population figures are estimates

calculated on the basis of the previous census and projection.

As of 2000, Venezuela's total population was estimated at 23.5 million, of which over one-fifth lived in Caracas. The rate of population growth stands at around 1.6%, one of the highest in Latin America. Venezuela is a young nation, with over half of its inhabitants under 18 years of age. Yet, at about 73 years, average life expectancy is remarkably high.

The mean population density, at about 26 people per square kilometer, is low, although it varies a great deal. The central coastal region, including the cities of Valencia, Maracay and Caracas, is the most densely inhabited, while Los Llanos and Guayana are very sparsely populated. More than 75% of Venezuelans live in towns and cities.

Venezuela is a country of mixed races. About 70% of the population is a blend of European, Indian and African ancestry, or any two of the three. The rest are whites (about 21%), blacks (8%) and Indians (1%). Indians don't belong to a single ethnic or linguistic family, but form different independent groups scattered throughout the country.

There are about two dozen indigenous groups comprising some 200,000 to 250,000 people. The main Indian communities include the Guajiro, north of Maracaibo; the Piaroa, Guajibo, Yekuana and Yanomami, in the Amazon; the Warao, in the Delta del Orinoco; and the Pemón, in southeastern Guayana.

Venezuela was the destination for significant post–World War II immigration from Europe (estimated at about a million), mostly from Spain, Italy and Portugal, but it nearly stopped in the 1960s, and many migrants returned home. From the 1950s on, there has been a stream of immigrants from other South American countries, particularly Colombia. Venezuela also has some Middle Eastern communities, most notably from Lebanon, which live principally in Caracas and Isla de Margarita. According to official statistics, about 600,000 foreigners live in the country today, but unofficial estimates put the number of Colombians alone

Let sleeping jaguars lie.

The unique flora of Roraima

"You lookin' at me?"

Vegetation atop the tepuis

Just another lazy day in the stream

A spectacular example of the Orinoco caiman

The delights of road travel in Venezuela

Warao beauties, Delta del Orinoco

Prepping for the beauty contest

MAJOR INDIAN GROUPS LIVING TODAY

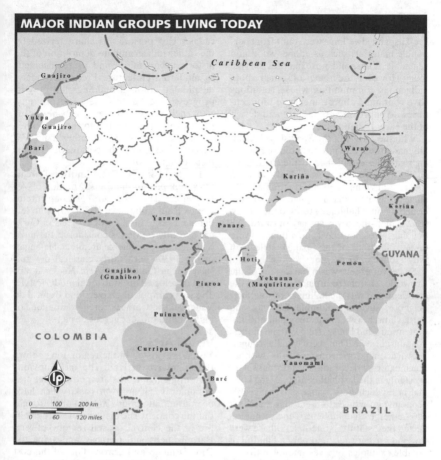

at more than a million. Caracas is the country's most cosmopolitan city.

EDUCATION

The education system has been expanded and modernized over the past few decades to meet the needs of the country's developing economy. However, it has recently suffered budgetary and administrative problems and has been plagued by strikes by both students and staff.

There's compulsory six-year primary education for children over seven years old.

Then there is also an optional four-year secondary-school education, followed by a one-year preparatory course for university. There are 31 universities in the country, of which the Universidad Central de Venezuela, in Caracas, is the largest and oldest (70,000 students, founded in 1725), followed by the Universidad de los Andes, in Mérida (35,000 students, founded in 1785). Primary education is state-run and free, as are some of the secondary schools and government-sponsored universities. The literacy of the population over 15 years old is about 91%.

ARTS
Architecture

Pre-Hispanic dwellings were built from perishable materials such as adobe, wood and vegetable fibers, and no examples survive today. However, the homes of some remote indigenous communities, whose traditions have continued almost unchanged for centuries, do approximate the form and design of the early Indian homes.

With the arrival of the Spanish, brick and tile made their way into the colony. Following rigid rules established by the Crown, the newly founded towns were laid out on a square grid with streets intersecting at right angles. The main plaza, cathedral and government house habitually formed the center, from which the town spread outward. All buildings – religious, civil and military – were direct reflections of the Spanish style, with only a touch of local color showing through.

Since Venezuela was a backwater of the Crown, local architecture never reached the grandeur that was the hallmark of wealthier neighbors such as Colombia, Ecuador and Peru. Churches were mostly small and unpretentious, and houses followed the modest Andalusian style. They were usually straightforward one-story constructions, without much external decoration or internal splendor. Only in the last half-century of the colonial era, which bore witness to noticeable economic growth, did a wealthier merchant class emerge that built residences that reflected their stature. Nonetheless, these were few and far between, and only a handful of notable examples survives, mainly in Coro.

The first 50 years of independence had little impact on Venezuelan architecture, but things began to change in the second half of the 19th century. In the 1870s a thorough modernization program for Caracas was launched by Guzmán Blanco, resulting in a number of monumental public buildings in a hodgepodge of styles, from neo-Gothic to neoclassical, depending on the whim of the architect in charge. You can admire the results of this modernization while strolling about Caracas' center.

The second rush toward modernity came with oil money and culminated in the 1960s and '70s. (The pace of urban change has slowed considerably over the last two decades.) This period was characterized by the rather indiscriminate demolition of the historic urban fabric and its replacement by modern architecture. Predictably, many dilapidated colonial buildings fell prey to progressive urban planners. Accordingly, Venezuela's colonial legacy can be disappointing when compared to those of other Andean countries. On the other hand, Venezuela has some of the best modern architecture on the continent.

Plenty of international and local architects took part in the transformation of Venezuelan urban centers. Among them, Carlos Raúl Villanueva (1900–75), who left behind a large number of projects in Caracas and other cities, is considered the most outstanding Venezuelan architect. He began in the 1930s with fairly classical designs, such as the Galería de Arte Nacional, but soon developed his individual modern style. The vast campus of Universidad Central de Venezuela, in Caracas, is regarded as one of his best and most coherent designs.

Visual Arts

Visual art existed in the region long before the Spaniards arrived. The most obvious surviving early works are petroglyphs, predominantly carvings on rock, which have been found at about 200 locations throughout the country. The majority of petroglyphs are in the central coastal region between Barquisimeto and Caracas, and along the Ríos Orinoco and Caroní. One of the best examples is on Cerro Pintado, a 50m-high cliff near Puerto Ayacucho. A number of cave paintings have also been discovered, almost all of them in Bolívar and Amazonas states. The most common colors used by these unknown artists from pre-Columbian tribes were black, white and various tones of ocher.

The painting and sculpture of the colonial period had an almost exclusively religious character. Although mostly executed by local artists and artisans, the style was largely influenced by the Spanish art of the day. Some of that work, consisting mainly of paintings of saints, carved wooden statues and retables (ornamental altar screens), can be seen in old churches and museums.

With independence, painting departed from strictly religious themes and began to immortalize important historical events. The first artist to do so was Juan Lovera (1778–1841), whose two most famous paintings, *April 19, 1810* and *July 5, 1811,* can be seen in the Capilla de Santa Rosa de Lima, in Caracas.

The most outstanding historical painting figure was Martín Tovar y Tovar (1827–1902), particularly remembered for his monumental works in Caracas' National Capitol. Other artists who contributed to 19th-century Venezuelan painting include Cristóbal Rojas (1860–90) and Arturo Michelena (1863–98). The latter received wide international recognition despite his short life and artistic career. He lived in Paris, and thus his works were exhibited at important salons in what was then the world's art capital. Another Venezuelan living in France, Emilio Boggio (1857–1920) also acquired an international reputation. Influenced by his French colleagues, and by Van Gogh in particular, he became Venezuela's first impressionist.

The epic historical tradition of Tovar y Tovar was continued by Tito Salas (1888–1974), who dedicated himself to commemorating Bolívar's life and achievements, producing a number of paintings on the subject. His best-known works are the wall paintings in the National Pantheon in Caracas.

Modern painting began with Armando Reverón (1889–1954), who made his home in Macuto (near Caracas), where he executed most of his expressionist works. Another painter who made his mark in the transition from traditional to modern painting was Carlos Otero (1886–1977). Other artists working in the same period include Rafael Monasterios (1884–1961), Federico Brandt (1879–1932), Marcos Castillo (1897–1966) and Manuel Cabré (1890–1984).

Francisco Narváez (1905–82) is commonly acclaimed as Venezuela's first modern sculptor. The art museum in Porlamar, on Isla de Margarita, where he was born, has the largest single collection of his works, but there are also a number of his sculptures distributed throughout Caracas.

The recent period in Venezuelan art has been characterized by a proliferation of artists representing a wide range of schools, trends and techniques. One of the most remarkable is the painter Héctor Poleo (1918–1989), who expressed himself in a variety of styles, easily switching from realism to surrealism, with some metaphysical exploration in between. Equally captivating is the expressionist painting of Jacobo Borges (born 1931), who by deforming human figures turns them into caricatures.

Other leading contemporary figures in painting and sculpture include Oswaldo Vigas (born 1926), Alejandro Otero (1921–90), Carlos Cruz Díez (born 1923), Mateo Manaure (born 1926), Alirio Palacios (born 1938) and Marisol Escobar (born 1930).

There's a lot of activity among the younger generation. Watch out, for example, for works of Carlos Zerpa (painting), José Antonio Hernández Díez (photo, video, installations), Miguel von Dangel (painting) and Abigail Varela (sculpture).

Jesús Soto is Venezuela's number one internationally renowned contemporary artist. This leading representative of kinetic art (ie, art, particularly sculpture, that contains moving parts) was born in Ciudad Bolívar in 1923. His easily recognizable, often fairly large works have adorned many public buildings and plazas in Venezuela and beyond (including Paris, Toronto and New York). The largest collection of his work is in the museum dedicated to him, which opened in 1971 in his natal city (see Ciudad Bolívar, in the Guayana chapter).

Literature

There was no written language on the continent before the Spanish conquest apart from a variety of petroglyphs, which remain undeciphered. Accordingly, there wasn't, in the strict sense of the word, a pre-Hispanic Indian literature. Yet there must have been a rich world of tales, legends and stories created, conserved and passed orally from generation to generation. This 'literature' provided invaluable information on the pre-Columbian culture for the first Spanish chroniclers.

The first chronicles narrating the early history of Venezuela include *Brevísima Relación de la Destrucción de las Indias Occidentales,* by Fray Bartolomé de las Casas; *Noticias Historiales* (1627), by Fray Pedro Simón; and *Elegías de Varones Ilustres de Indias* (1589), by Juan de Castellanos. Much more analytical and comprehensive is one of the later and perhaps best chronicles, *Historia de la Conquista y Población de la Provincia de Venezuela* (1723), by José de Oviedo y Baños.

Almost all literature during the colonial period was written by the Spanish, who imposed not only their language but also the cultural and religious perspective of the mother country. A more independent approach emerged with the dawn of the 19th century, with the birth and crystallization of revolutionary trends. The first 30 years of that century were more or less dominated by political literature.

Among the works of significant historical value was the autobiography of Francisco de Miranda (1750–1816). Simón Bolívar (1783–1830) has left an extensive literary heritage, including letters, proclamations, discourses and dissertations, and also literary achievements such as *Delirio sobre El Chimborazo.* As literature, it has strong merits, notably for its expression of ideals and ambitions for the nation fighting for independence, as well as for its prophetic visions.

Bolívar was influenced by his close friend Andrés Bello (1781–1865), the first important Venezuelan poet. Bello was also a noted philologist, essayist, historian, journalist, literary critic, jurist and translator.

With independence achieved, political writing gave way to other literary manifestations. However, it wasn't until the early 20th century that more mature literature began to emerge. In the 1920s, Andrés Eloy Blanco (1896–1955) appeared on the scene to become one of the best poets Venezuela has ever produced. This Cumaná-born writer went into exile in Mexico, escaping the persecution of the dictator Pérez Jiménez, and tragically died in a car accident. *Angelitos Negros* is probably the most popular of his numerous poems.

At the same time, several notable novelists emerged, among whom Rómulo Gallegos (1884–1969) was the most outstanding and remains, perhaps, the internationally best-known writer in the country's literary history. *Doña Bárbara,* his most popular novel, was first published in Spain in 1929 and has since then been translated into a dozen languages. Other important novels by this writer, who was also Venezuela's first democratically elected president (in 1947), include *Canaima* and *Cantaclaro.*

Mariano Picón Salas (1901–65) worked in a variety of literary forms, of which essays were possibly his favorite. A professor, minister and ambassador, he frequently touched on historical and political issues. His extensive literary output includes *El Último Inca* and *Preguntas a Europa.* Miguel Otero Silva (1908–85) was another remarkable novelist of the period. He's best remembered for *Casas Muertas,* a bestseller published in 1957.

Andrés Bello, poet friend of Bolívar's

Arturo Uslar Pietri (born 1906) stands out as an authority in the field of literature. A novelist, essayist, historian, literary critic and journalist, he also has been a prominent figure in politics, having been a minister on various occasions and even a presidential candidate. He's not only the most versatile writer in the country, but also the man with the longest involvement in literature. Since writing his first important novel, *Lanzas Coloradas,* published in the 1930s, he has written a great deal and is still active on the literary scene.

Other veteran Venezuelan writers of note include Denzil Romero (novels), Salvador Garmendia (short forms), Aquiles Nazoa (humor, poetry), Rafael Cadenas (poetry) and Francisco Herrera Luque (historical novels). The books of Herrera Luque (born 1928) may be particularly interesting for foreigners, as they give profound insight into Venezuela's history and are at the same time beautifully readable. His novels include *Los Viajadores de la India* (about the Spanish conquest), *Los Amos del Valle* (colonization from 1567 to 1783) and *En la Casa del Pez que Esculpe el Agua.*

There's quite a number of younger yet already well established novelists, essayists and poets. Try, for example, the novels of Luis Brito García, Carlos Noguera, Orlando Chirinos and Ednodio Quintero, who are among the most interesting authors on the local literary scene today.

Music

Almost nothing is known about the early forms, functions and instruments utilized by pre-Hispanic musicians. The Spanish, and with them the Africans, introduced new rhythms and instruments, bringing diversity to the colony's musical world. European and African traditions gradually merged with one another and with indigenous music, eventually producing what is now Venezuela's folk music. It's not uniform, as different forms have evolved in different regions of the country.

Venezuela's most popular folk rhythm is the *joropo,* also called *música llanera,* which developed in Los Llanos and gradually con-

quered the country (see the boxed text 'The Music of Los Llanos' in the Los Llanos chapter). The joropo is usually sung and accompanied by harp, *cuatro* (small, four-stringed guitar) and maracas. The joropo song 'Alma Llanera' has become a sort of unofficial national anthem.

Joropo apart, there are plenty of traditional beats still largely confined to their regions. In the eastern part of the country you'll hear, depending on the particular region, the *estribillo, polo margariteño, malagueñas, fulías* and *jotas.* In the west, on the other hand, the *gaita* is typical of the Maracaibo region, while the *bambuco* is one of the popular rhythms of the Andes. The central coast echoes with African drumbeats, a mark of the sizable black population.

In addition to locally rooted musical forms, various foreign rhythms have made their way into the country. Of these, salsa and merengue from the Caribbean basin and *vallenato* from Colombia have been best absorbed. And, of course, western pop – everything from rock to rap – has become hugely popular among urban youth. All these musical imports fomented the creation of local composers and interpreters of these forms. Oscar D'León is Venezuela's leading *salsero.* Most discotheques now play a cocktail of salsa, merengue and western beats. In city streets you also hear quite a bit of vallenato and joropo. Jazz, except for Latin jazz, is not popular.

European classical music emerged in Venezuela only in the 19th century. The first composers of note include José Angel Lamas (1775–1814) and Cayetano Carreño Rodríguez (1774–1836), both of whom wrote religious music. The beginnings of concert music are accredited to Felipe Larrazábal (1818–73), a pianist, composer and founder of the Caracas Conservatory.

The most prominent figure in Venezuela's classical music of the 19th century (and of the country's entire history, for that matter) was Teresa Carreño (1853–1917), a pianist and composer. Born in Caracas, she was just seven years of age when she composed her first work, a polka that was performed by a military band in Caracas. She held her first concert at the Irving Hall in New York at the age of nine. She lived most of her life in Germany, visiting her native country only twice.

The first half of the 20th century saw no outstanding musical talents, except perhaps for pianist Reinaldo Hahn (1874–1947), who lived and composed in Paris, and Juan Bautista Plaza (1898–1965), another pianist and composer, whose career was tied to Rome.

During the last few decades, Venezuelan musical culture has developed more swiftly. This has been due to both the opening of musical schools and the building of new concert halls. In 1930 the Symphony Orchestra of Venezuela was founded in the capital and was followed by three other city orchestras.

Dance & Ballet

Integrally linked to music, dance was a part of the ritual celebrations and everyday life of the early civilizations. The region's dance forms diversified during colonial and postcolonial times. Dance traditions are possibly most alive among black communities on Venezuela's central coast, where locals rush to dance as soon as homegrown drummers take to their instruments – this happens spontaneously, mostly on weekend nights. Elsewhere, folk dance is not part of local lifestyle to that extent, though you can often see amateur dance ensembles in action during some annual feasts.

Folk dance has sown seeds for the creation of professional groups that now promote their musical folklore in a polished form to the public. The Danza Venezuela, directed by Yolanda Morreno, is the country's prime national folk-dance ensemble. It has traveled intensively and has delighted audiences on several continents. Some members of the company have formed their own folk groups.

Among the neoclassical dance and ballet groups, perhaps best known is the Ballet Nuevo Mundo de Caracas, led by Venezuela's most famous ballerina, Zhandra Rodríguez. The Ballet Teresa Carreño, under the artistic direction of Vicente Nebreda, and the Ballet de Cámara de Caracas, run by María Barrios, also perform in the neoclassical style.

Contemporary dance is probably best represented by Coreoarte, directed by Carlos Orta; the Danza Hoy, led by Adriana Urdaneta; the Dramo, run by Miguel Issa; and the Acción Colectiva, directed by Julie Bernsley. All of these companies are based in Caracas.

Theater

Venezuela's first theater, Teatro del Conde, was founded in Caracas in 1784, and since then a theater tradition has slowly developed. Several theaters opened at the end of the 19th century, in Caracas (Teatro Nacional and Teatro Municipal), Maracaibo (Teatro Baralt), Valencia (Teatro Municipal), Barquisimeto (Teatro Juares) and Barcelona (Teatro Cajigal). However, mostly European fare was presented; infrequent local productions mimicked the style and content of Old World works.

The national theater was born only a few decades ago, with its major center in Caracas. Today, there are a few dozen theatrical groups, most in Caracas. Rajatabla, tied to the Ateneo de Caracas, has been Venezuela's best-known theater on the international scene. However, since the death (in 1993) of its creator and director, Carlos Giménez, the company seems to have undergone rougher times. Other Caracas-based groups of note include La Compañía Nacional de Teatro and the Teatro Profesional de Venezuela. It's also worth watching out for the Teatro Negro de Barlovento, formed by the black community of the central coast and taking inspiration from African roots.

Cinema

The first films were publicly screened in Maracaibo in January 1897, only 13 months after the famous show by the Lumière brothers took place in Paris. Venezuela's first short film was shot in 1909; the first silent feature film, *La Dama de las Cayenas,* was made in 1913; and the first sound film,

La Venus de Nacar, was produced in 1932. Venezuelan film's first international success was *La Balandra Isabel Llegó Esta Tarde* (1950), by Carlos Hugo Christensen, a prizewinner at the 1951 Cannes festival.

It wasn't until the 1970s that local cinematography began to develop at a faster pace, producing several thought-provoking films. Román Chalbaud, who began his career in that period, is possibly the internationally best known Venezuelan film director. His film *El Pez que Fuma* (The Fish That Smokes), made in 1977, received some noteworthy critical acclaim abroad. Apart from various theatrical works, Chalbaud made 18 films. His best-known works include *La Quema de Judas* (1974), *La Oveja Negra* (1987) and *Pandemónium, La Capital del Infierno* (1997).

Serious film buffs interested in recent highlights of Venezuelan cinematography should check out some of the following films: *Macu, la Mujer del Policía* (1987), by Solveig Hoogesteijn; *Jericó* (1991), by Luis Alberto Lamata; *El Misterio de Los Ojos Escarlata* (1993), by Alfredo Anzola; *Sicario* (1995), by José Ramón Novoa; *Mecánicas Celestes* (1995), by Fina Torres; *Aire Libre* (1995), by Luis Armando Roche; *Cien Años de Perdón* (1999), by Alejandro Saderman; and *Amaneció de Golpe* (1999), by Carlos Azpúrua.

On the whole, however, Venezuelan cinema hasn't reached the artistic heights achieved by other Latin American nations such as Mexico or Argentina, and it hasn't gained much acclaim abroad. Local film production is sparse, and few domestically produced films reach the screens of commercial cinemas. Because public demand for Venezuelan films is low, profits are small. Hence, film distributors prefer foreign movies, which are more likely to realize a profit. Half of the Venezuelan film industry's profit is made in Caracas.

In contrast to cinema, TV production is booming. Venezuelans are great fans of *telenovelas,* or soap operas, and producers and directors do everything they can to meet demand. Over the last two decades Venezuela has become one of the major Latin American producers of such fare, catching up with the two traditional telenovela powers, Mexico and Brazil.

SOCIETY & CONDUCT

Western visitors will probably find Venezuela more accessible than most other Andean countries, such as Colombia, Ecuador, Peru and Bolivia. Although Venezuela is a palette of ethnic blends, and traditional culture is still very much alive in the countryside, the urban population went through an intensive 'course' of westernization when oil money hit the nation from the 1960s through to the 1980s. Local shops glittered with all the latest in styles and gadgets, US cars were imported in the thousands, and many middle-class Venezuelans traveled regularly to vacation or shop in the USA, principally to Miami. Many western-style facilities were built in Venezuela over that period.

However, although some manifestations of western culture are evident, you'll find many local habits, manners and attitudes quite different from those at home. Some may be strange or even irritating if you haven't been to this country before.

On the whole, Venezuelans are courteous, polite and hospitable to guests. They are open, willing to talk and not shy about striking up a conversation with a stranger. This may vary from a city to the countryside and from region to region, but wherever you are, you are unlikely to be alone or feel isolated, especially if you can speak a little Spanish.

You will probably meet many friendly people promising you the earth, but keep in mind that such effusiveness often has a short life. Their statements may well gloss over reality, promises can be just wishful thinking, and appointments are often not kept. Few locals will return your phone call after you've left a message, and the passionate friend of one day might hardly recognize you the next. This attitude (common in most of the continent) is largely rooted in the Latin American concept of life *aquí y ahora* (here and now), with little importance given to the future. Don't worry; there will be plenty of new faces and new promises coming your way.

Everyday life is remarkably open and public. One reason might be the restricted space of the humble Venezuelan homes, in which a vast majority of the population live. The climate, too, invites the outdoor life. Consequently, much of family life takes place outside the home: in front of the house, in the street, in a bar or at the market. And many Venezuelans seem indiscreet about their behavior in public places. A party in a bar may discuss personal problems at a volume that allows all the patrons to follow the conversation. A female employee in a bank or travel agency may talk by phone for quite a while about private matters (including love affairs) and not seem embarrassed or ashamed that you're waiting right there to be served. The driver may urinate on the tire of his bus after he has stopped for a break on the road and disembarked along with most passengers. People waiting to use public phones will be squashed up against the person calling. And couples hug and kiss passionately in parks and in the street.

Noise is a constant companion in Venezuela, and locals seem to be undisturbed by volume levels many decibels above what most Europeans or North Americans are used to. Music blares in restaurants, is pumped into buses, and climaxes at night in discos, taverns and private parties. Powerful portable tape players are an important part of equipment for beachgoers and holidaymakers. Televisions are at full volume, especially during telenovelas and sports transmissions. Some vehicles are as noisy as tanks, and horns are used constantly, even in traffic jams. Street vendors screech at potential customers, and people converse at a volume that to outsiders might suggest a heated argument.

Like noise, litter is an integral part of Venezuelan life, so be prepared to get used to it. Venezuelans are accustomed to throwing things away wherever they happen to be – streets, restaurants, hotel rooms, buses, cinemas, beaches and the countryside. Garbage cans are virtually nonexistent, except for a smattering in central streets of the major cities. In budget hotels and restaurants you will rarely find an ashtray, and asking for one may embarrass the management because they often simply don't have them. It's normal to throw cigarette butts on the floor; nobody pays the slightest attention. In buses, all disposables, including empty glass bottles, are thrown out the windows.

Venezuelans (like most other Latin Americans) seem to have their own notion of time. Time-related terminology does exist, but its interpretation is not necessarily what visitors might expect. For example, *mañana* (literally 'tomorrow') can mean anytime in the indefinite future. Similarly, the word *ahora* (literally 'now,' or 'in a moment'), often used in its more charming, diminutive forms such as *ahorita* or *ahoritica,* also has a flexible meaning.

If, for example, you're waiting for a bus and ask bystanders when the bus should arrive, their *ahorita viene* ('it's coming') may mean anytime from a minute to a few hours. By the same token, when the driver of the bus waiting at the terminal assures you that *ya nos vamos* ('we are leaving right now'), take it easy – it may still take an hour before the bus departs.

Venezuelans invited to lunch or a party might arrive a few hours late and regard it as normal. The same applies to meetings in the street, cafés, pubs etc. Arriving half an hour later than arranged may still give you time to read a newspaper before your friends arrive (if they arrive at all). Many offices and institutions have a similarly flexible grasp of their official working hours. Don't expect to arrange anything in an office if you arrive less than half an hour before either its statutory lunch break or the end of work in the afternoon.

Some Venezuelans, particularly rural dwellers, also have a different notion of space. If they say that something you're looking for is *allí mismito* (just around here) or *cerquitica* (very close), it may still be an hour's walk to get there.

If you ask for information or directions, don't always expect a correct answer, especially in the countryside. The campesinos (country folk), even if they have no idea, may often tell you anything just to appear helpful and knowledgeable. Ask several people the same question; if one answer seems to pop up more frequently than others it may be the correct one. Avoid questions that can be answered by just 'yes' or 'no'; instead of 'Is this the way to ...?' ask 'Which is the way to ...?'

Never show any disrespect for Bolívar – he is a saint to Venezuelans. For instance, sitting on a bench in Plaza Bolívar with your feet on the bench, crossing the plaza wearing shorts, or carrying bulky parcels (or even a backpack) may be considered disrespectful, and police may hassle you.

RELIGION

About 95% of Venezuelans are Roman Catholics. Many Indian groups were converted to Catholicism, and only a few, primarily those living in isolation, still practice their ancient beliefs. There are Protestant churches in Venezuela, and lately they have been gaining in importance, taking some adherents away from the Roman Catholic Church. There are small populations of practicing Jews and Muslims. One religious curiosity is the cult of María Lionza, today widespread throughout the country (see Cerro de María Lionza, in the Northwest chapter, for details).

LANGUAGE

Spanish is Venezuela's official language, and except for some remote Indian groups, all of the population speaks it. There are over 25 Indian languages spoken in the country as well.

English-speakers can be found in large urban centers, but it's certainly not a commonly understood or spoken language, even though it's taught as a mandatory second language in the public school system. However, it is easier to find somebody speaking English in Venezuela than in, say, Colombia, Ecuador, Peru or Bolivia.

Most of the time you'll be in an exclusively Spanish-speaking environment. You'll probably manage to travel without knowing a word of Spanish, but you will miss out on a good part of the pleasure of meeting people. Your experience of the country will be limited as a result.

Spanish is quite an easy language to learn, and it's useful in most other Latin American countries as well. It's well worth making some effort to learn at least the essentials before setting off. Lonely Planet's *Latin American Spanish phrasebook* is a worthwhile addition to your backpack.

See the Language chapter, near the end of the book, for a practical guide to pronunciation and for some vocabulary and grammar essentials.

Facts for the Visitor

HIGHLIGHTS

Salto Angel (Angel Falls) is Venezuela's promotional landmark, and few tourists want to miss a view of this 1km-high waterfall. For more adventurous travelers, a trek to the top of Roraima is without doubt a fascinating and unforgettable experience. Other natural highlights include Andean peaks around Mérida, the *tepuis* (table mountains) and waterfalls of La Gran Sabana, the wildlife of Los Llanos, the Delta del Orinoco and the Río Caura.

Beachgoers will find it difficult to decide which patch of sand to choose from several hundred fine beaches along the country's Caribbean coast. Some of the most beautiful are in the Mochima, Henri Pittier and Morrocoy national parks, east of Río Caribe and on the Isla de Margarita.

SUGGESTED ITINERARIES

Your itinerary will largely depend on your particular interests, your budget, your customary pace of traveling (mad dash versus staying longer in fewer places), the season (dry or wet), your companions etc. Some travelers will rush through half of the country in a week, while others will prefer to spend the same time on one beach. One person may be crazy about colonial architecture; another, about bird-watching. Some visitors would like to see briefly most major attractions regardless of how distant they are from each other, whereas others are more interested in visiting some regions in depth, bypassing the rest of the country.

Organized tours are an important variable in your itinerary. Some of the country's major attractions can be reached only by taking a tour (Salto Angel, Delta del Orinoco and Los Llanos, among others). If you can't afford tours, you unfortunately have to delete these places from your program. On the other hand, if money is no problem, reputable tour operators will whisk you comfortably around important sights of their or your choice.

Since Venezuela is the cheapest entry point to the continent from both the USA and Europe, many travelers treat the country as just a stopover on their South American trip before heading to Colombia or Brazil. Depending on the route, many will be inclined to concentrate on Venezuela's west or southeast, respectively.

Finally, for almost all visitors arriving in Venezuela by air, Caracas will be the entrance gate. Some travelers will want to visit the capital before setting off around the country, while others will skip over Caracas as quickly as possible because of its crime, pollution, higher costs or simply a dislike of large cities.

To sum up, it's difficult to recommend any specific itineraries for a visitor. The following suggestions have been made assuming that you arrive at Caracas and plan on visiting just Venezuela, but please consider them as rough guidelines only. For more suggestions, see the Highlights at the beginning of each regional chapter.

One week
Spend one to three days exploring Caracas and its environs, possibly including a trip to the Archipiélago Los Roques; go to Choroní and/or Rancho Grande in Parque Nacional Henri Pittier, and also take a tour to Canaima and/or Salto Angel.

Two weeks
To the above, add one of the three following options: Mérida and the surrounding mountains, Ciudad Bolívar and La Gran Sabana, or a trip to the top of Roraima.

One month
You'll be able to do all the options listed above, possibly even including a tour to Los Llanos from Mérida.

Two months
To the above, add Coro with its environs and Parque Nacional Morrocoy in the west, and Parque Nacional Mochima, Cueva del Guácharo and Península de Paria in the east; if time allows and your wallet is still thick enough, you may consider adding a tour to the Delta del Orinoco and/or Río Caura.

PLANNING

While planning your trip to Venezuela, or to South America in general, it may be worth checking Lonely Planet's *Read This First: Central & South America* guide.

When to Go

The tourist season in Venezuela runs year-round, so theoretically, any time you visit is OK. There are two factors, however, that you might want to consider before you finalize travel plans.

The first is climate. Venezuela has one dry season (roughly November or December to April or May) and one wet season (the rest of the year). The dry season is certainly more pleasant for traveling – particularly if you plan on hiking or indulging in some other outdoor activities. In the wet season, paths are muddy and views obscured, and it's not much fun trudging in the rain all day anyway. If you plan on mountaineering high in the Andes, the rainy (or, more correctly, snowy) season not only is unpleasant but can be dangerous. Conventional sightseeing in the cities or towns won't be greatly disturbed by rain.

It may be better to visit some regions in the rainy period. For example, Salto Angel, a must for many tourists, is certainly more impressive in the wet season. Furthermore, boat trips to the waterfall (which arguably are a more attractive option than flights) may go only in the rainy season, when the river level is sufficiently high.

Keep in mind, too, that the weather pattern is not uniform throughout the country. Some regions (eg, parts of Lara, Falcón, Anzoátegui and Sucre states, as well as Isla de Margarita) are relatively dry for most of the year, so the season doesn't really matter much. On the other hand, parts of Amazonas are wet more or less year-round.

The second consideration when planning your trip is the periods when Venezuelans take their holidays. They are crazy about visiting friends and family over Christmas, Carnaval and Holy Week (Easter).

During these three periods, air and bus transportation get pretty busy and hotels fill up quickly, so you'll have to plan ahead and do more legwork to find a place to stay. On the other hand, these periods are colorful and alive, with a host of festivities. Schools break for annual vacations in August, but this doesn't significantly affect public transportation or accommodations.

Maps

You'll probably find it difficult to buy anything other than general maps of Venezuela outside the country itself. Check with good travel bookshops and map shops to see what is available. In the USA, Maplink (☎ 805-965 4402), 25 E Mason St, Dept G, Santa Barbara, CA 93101, has an excellent supply of maps. A similarly extensive selection of maps is available in the UK from Stanfords (☎ 020 7836 1321), 12-14 Long Acre, London WC2E 9LP.

Both these distributors, as well as many other map retailers in North America, Europe and Australia, should have the folded map of Venezuela (scale 1:1,750,000) published by International Travel Maps (ITM; ☎ 604-687 3320, fax 687 5925), 736A Granville St, Vancouver, BC, Canada V6Z 1G3. This is the best general map of the country published so far. It has excellent topographical detail and heaps of information, and it's better than any general country map produced in Venezuela. The map may be available from some bookshops and travel agencies in Venezuela, mostly in Caracas, but it's difficult to find, and it won't be any cheaper than you'd pay at home.

ITM has also published three sectional maps of South America (North West, North East and South), plus individual maps to several Latin American countries. All are excellent.

Within Venezuela, folded road maps of the country are produced by Lagoven and Corpoven oil companies (available at their gasoline stations, but currently out of print) and several other publishers (distributed through bookshops).

For large-scale regional maps, try the Caracas-based state map publisher, Servicio Autónomo de Geografía y Cartografía

Nacional (☎ 02-408 11 15, 408 12 19), Calle Este 6, Colón a Dr Díaz (Ⓜ La Hoyada). The office sells 1:100,000 and 1:25,000 maps, but so far only the northern part of the country is well covered; there is only a small handful of maps of Amazonas and Guayana. Unfortunately, virtually all these maps are long out of date, often more than 20 or 30 years old.

If the office runs out of color originals (which is usually the case), it will make a black-and-white copy for you on the spot. Maps cost somewhere between US$3 and US$5 per sheet, depending on size.

What to Bring

The first and most important rule of travel is to bring with you the minimum possible – a large, heavy backpack soon becomes a nightmare. Almost everything you need can easily be bought in Venezuela. Clothes, footwear, toiletries, stationery etc are readily available in shops, supermarkets and markets, and they are usually cheaper than their equivalents in western countries. There's absolutely no need to bring large stocks of envelopes, spare batteries, or a bottle of shampoo big enough to last the whole trip. Instead, pay attention to the most important items, such as a good backpack, comfortable shoes, a basic set of clothes and photographic gear.

The overwhelming majority of the country is lowlands, so you don't need much in the way of warm clothing. If you stick to hotels, you don't need bedsheets or blankets, as even the most basic *residencias* provide them.

Some essentials that might be worth packing include: a travel alarm clock (for those early-morning buses), a small flashlight, sunglasses, a hat, a Spanish/English dictionary, flip-flops or thong sandals (to protect feet against fungal infections in shabby hotel bathrooms), and a good-quality pocketknife.

Make sure to bring any prescription medications you would normally take and a spare pair of glasses or contact lenses if applicable. A small medical kit is recommended if you plan on leaving the beaten

track – refer to the Health section, later in this chapter, for specifics.

Rain gear will come in handy if you're visiting the country during the wet season. A swimming suit is essential if you're heading to one or more of the hundreds of beaches on the coast. Bring a mask and snorkel (to save on rental fees). Plastic bags will protect your gear from rain and dust. Consider a set of nice clothes for dining out in fancy restaurants and special occasions. Bookworms might want to bring along some paperbacks, as the choice offered by local bookshops may not be extensive.

Think about bringing some small gifts to give people for hospitality or help. Foreign coins, stamps, postcards and small handicrafts from your country are just a few obvious suggestions.

If you plan on overnight hiking in the mountains, ideally you should include in your luggage the necessary equipment, such as a tent, sleeping bag, warm clothes, cooking stove etc. Camping Gaz Bluet is the most common brand of cooking gear. You can stock up on gas canisters in Caracas, Mérida and some other large cities.

Camping equipment is available in Venezuela, but it can be quite expensive, and the choice is limited. It also can be rented in some cities (mostly in Caracas and Mérida), but if you need it for a longer period, it may be better to bring your own. The weeklong Roraima trip alone probably justifies bringing your camping gear with you (see the Guayana chapter). You will also save quite a bit of money by camping at Canaima and the Archipiélago Los Roques, and you'll enjoy more flexibility in your itinerary while traveling around the country.

RESPONSIBLE TOURISM

A responsible tourist is, perhaps, one who treats the visited place as if it were home. Would you wander into your hometown church during a service and start taking flash photos? Would you bluntly point your camera at your neighbors while they go on about their daily business?

Respect rituals and ceremonies, traditions and beliefs. Also be aware that some customs can challenge your own belief system, and avoid trying to impose on the locals your own view of the world.

Encourage ecotourism projects that aim to preserve or restore local environments and that do not exploit indigenous people as circus oddities. Support native communities by buying their products, but avoid those made from corals, turtles or fossils.

Littering in Venezuela is widespread, but you don't have to follow suit. Make a little extra effort and carry your own rubbish until you find an appropriate disposal bin. Be particularly careful when visiting areas with delicate ecological balances, such as coral reefs, the tepuis and rain forests.

Carry your own trash out of all national parks. Remember that the plastic bag, can, silver foil, tampons or condoms you leave behind can endanger wildlife. Burying your rubbish won't solve the problem – it disturbs soil and ground cover and encourages erosion. It can also be dug up by animals, who may be injured or poisoned by it.

TOURIST OFFICES
Local Tourist Offices
Corporación de Turismo, or Corpoturismo, is the government agency promoting tourism and providing tourist information. Its head office is in Caracas (see that chapter for details). It publishes material on the country's attractions, but these publications are not always available.

Outside Caracas, the provision of tourist information has been taken over by regional tourist bodies with offices in state capitals and some other cities. Some are better than others, but on the whole they lack city maps and brochures. The staff members may be friendly but don't often speak English. The practical information they provide sometimes leaves something to be desired, especially if you are a budget traveler. For example, they seldom know which banks currently change money and which is the cheapest hotel in town. We don't comment in this book how useful particular offices are, because this changes constantly and largely depends on the person who attends to you.

Tourist Offices Abroad
Outside Venezuela there aren't many tourist-information agencies that focus specifically on Venezuela. One of the few is the Venezuelan Tourism Association (VTA; ☎ 415-331 0100, vtajb@hotmail.com), PO Box 3010, Sausalito, CA 94966, USA, which provides general information and maps. Their Web site is www.venezuelatuya.com. Some of the Venezuelan consulates and embassies can provide limited tourist information; see Embassies & Consulates, later in this chapter.

Other Sources of Information Abroad
One of the most useful resources for visitors to South America is the South American Explorers (☎ 607-277 0488, fax 277 6122, explorer@samexplo.org), 126 Indian Creek Rd, Ithaca, NY 14850, USA. The club provides services, information and support to travelers, researchers, mountaineers and explorers. It sells a range of books, guides and maps of South America, and publishes a quarterly journal and a mail-order catalog. It maintains clubhouses in Quito (Ecuador) and Lima (Peru). Membership is US$40 a year per individual, US$70 per couple. Check the club's Web site (www.samexplo.org) for more information.

The counterpart in Germany is the Lateinamerikanischer Freundeskreis eV (☎ 0421-239 245, fax 234 267), Schwachhauser Heerstrasse 222, D-28213, Bremen.

A useful contact in the UK is the Latin American Bureau (☎ 020-7278 2829, fax 7278 0165), 1 Amwell St, London EC1R 1UL, which keeps up-to-date with all Latin American happenings and publishes a list of titles dealing with politics, culture and travel throughout the region.

The Latin American Travel Consultants (fax 02-562 566, rku@pi.pro.ec), PO Box 17-17-908, Quito, Ecuador, publishes a quarterly news bulletin, *The Latin American Travel Advisor,* which features news on travel, public safety, health, climate, costs and so on for travelers in the region. Books, maps and videos are available from them by mail order.

VISAS & DOCUMENTS
Passports

A valid passport is your essential document, and it must be stamped with a visa if you need one. If your passport is due to expire within a year, get a new one before you leave on a South American circuit. Many countries won't issue a visa or admit you at the border if your passport has less than six months or even one year of validity remaining. Even if expiry isn't a problem, make sure that your passport has a few blank pages left for visas and stamps for entry and exit.

Once in Venezuela, you must carry your passport with you at all times. Identity checks are not uncommon on country roads and city streets. Your passport is the first document the police will ask for. Some police officers may be satisfied with a certified photocopy of your passport, but most won't accept it as valid.

Visas & Tourist Cards

Since 1992, nationals of the USA, Canada, Australia, New Zealand, South Africa, Japan, the UK and most western and Scandinavian European countries don't need visas if they fly into Venezuela. A Tourist Card (Tarjeta de Ingreso, officially denominated DEX-2) is given to these visitors free of charge from the airline they fly with. The tourist card is valid for 90 days and can be extended (see Visas & Tourist Card Extensions, later in this section).

Until not long ago, all foreigners who entered Venezuela by land from Colombia or Brazil needed a visa, but this strict rule has been liberalized in the mid-1990s. Overland visitors bearing passports of the countries listed above are now allowed to enter Venezuela with the tourist card. It can be obtained, in theory at least, from Venezuelan consulates and at border crossings, and it's free. In practice, though, border posts are a sort of lottery. You're strongly advised to get a tourist card from a consulate beforehand; though, yet again, not all consulates provide tourist cards. Some may still insist that you need a tourist visa, which they can issue for US$30 to US$40; others

can only give you a 72-hour transit visa (these visas cannot be extended in Venezuela, whatever the consulate tells you!). Still others may offer you nothing at all. Plan ahead, inquire at the consulates you pass on your route, and get the tourist card from the first consulate willing to give one to you. According to recent reports, Venezuelan consulates in Cartagena and Cúcuta (Colombia) and Manaus and Boa Vista (Brazil) were issuing tourist cards.

The tourist card is a small form with a yellow carbon copy. You must fill it in and present it, together with your passport, to immigration officials at the border. They will put an entry stamp in your passport and on the yellow copy, which will be given back to you (make sure that both documents are stamped). You then have to keep the yellow copy at all times while traveling in Venezuela (you may be asked for it by the police or Guardia Nacional during passport controls), and return it to immigration officials when leaving the country (although not all are interested in collecting the cards).

Matters related to foreigners and immigration (border passport control, visas, visa extensions, work permits etc) are handled by a department of the Ministry of Interior Affairs commonly known as DIEX (Dirección de Identificación y Extranjería) or DEX (Dirección de Extranjería). It has offices in Caracas, in state capitals and also at border crossings.

Visa & Tourist Card Extensions Extensions are handled by the DIEX office in Caracas only. The office is on Avenida Baralt, facing Plaza Miranda (Ⓜ Capitolio), and it's a classic example of Venezuelan bureaucracy and chaos: It's crowded and confusing, and officials may not be particularly friendly or helpful.

Visas and tourist cards can be extended for a maximum of up to three months, and the cost is US$70 regardless of whether you need three days or three months. Your passport, two photos and a letter explaining the purpose of the extension are required, plus the form they'll give you to fill in. The processing takes three working days.

Onward Tickets

Officially, every tourist entering Venezuela should have an onward ticket. You may occasionally be asked by immigration officials to present it, though that happens very rarely these days.

Travel Insurance

Ideally, all travelers should have a travel insurance policy, which will provide some sense of security in case of a medical emergency or the loss or theft of money or belongings. Even if you never use it, it will probably help you sleep more peacefully during the trip. It may seem an expensive luxury, but if you can't afford a travel health insurance policy, you probably can't afford medical emergency charges abroad either if something goes wrong. See the Health section, later in this chapter, for details.

If you do need to make a claim on your travel insurance, you must produce a police report detailing the loss or theft (refer to the Dangers & Annoyances section, later in this chapter). You also need proof of the value of any items lost or stolen. Receipts are the best bet, so if you buy a new camera for your trip, for example, hang onto the receipt.

Driver's Licenses

If you plan on driving in Venezuela, make sure you bring your driver's license. According to Venezuelan law, driver's licenses valid in other countries are also valid in Venezuela for a period of one year from the date of arrival, provided the license is not used to drive vehicles for profit. Despite this, some police and rental company staff may be unfamiliar with foreign driving licenses, so it's best to bring along an International Driving Permit as well. The minimum driving age in Venezuela is 18 years, but in order to rent a car you must be at least 21 and have a credit card. For more information on automobile travel in Venezuela, see the Car & Motorcycle section, in the Getting Around chapter.

Hostel & Student Cards

An International Youth Hostel card is useless in Venezuela, as the country lacks youth hostels. A student card is of rather limited use. Some airlines give a 15% discount on domestic flights to full-time local students, but they may be reluctant to sell discounted tickets to foreign students identifying themselves with an International Student Identity Card (ISIC). There are no student discounts on other means of transportation such as buses or ferries. A student card will save a few bolívares at museums, but most have free admission to all visitors anyway. See IVI Idiomas Vivos, under Travel Agencies in the Caracas chapter, for other possible student discounts.

Vaccination Certificates

The International Health Card is not required for entry into Venezuela unless you're arriving from an area infected with yellow fever or cholera, but even in this case you'll rarely be asked for the card. However, it's a good idea to get inoculated against some diseases before you set off for the trip. See the Health section, later in this chapter, for details.

Copies

Make photocopies of important documents such as your passport (data pages plus visas), credit cards, airline tickets, travel insurance policy and traveler's check receipt slips. Take notes of the serial numbers of your cameras, lenses, camcorders, laptop computer and any other pieces of high-tech stuff you'll be taking on the trip. Make a list of phone numbers for emergency assistance services (credit cards, insurance, your bank etc). Keep that material separate from your passport, money and other valuables. It's a good idea to keep one copy with you and one copy inside your luggage, and (if applicable) deposit another with a traveling companion. Also leave a copy of all these things with someone at home. Slip US$50 or US$100 into an unlikely place to use as an emergency stash.

It's also a good idea to store details of your vital travel documents in Lonely Planet's free online Travel Vault in case you lose the photocopies or can't be bothered with them. Your password-protected Travel

Vault is accessible online anywhere in the world – create it at www.ekno.lonelyplanet.com.

EMBASSIES & CONSULATES
Venezuelan Embassies & Consulates

Venezuelan embassies abroad include the following:

Australia
(☎ 02-6290 2967, fax 6290 2911)
5 Culgoa Circuit, O'Malley, Isaacs, ACT 2606

Belgium
(☎ 2-287 284, fax 292 370)
10 Avenue Franklin Roosevelt, 1050 Brussels

Canada
(☎ 613-235 5151, 235 5697, fax 235 3205)
32 Range Rd, Ottawa, Ontario K1N 8J4

France
(☎ 1-45 53 29 98, fax 47 55 64 56)
11 Rue Copernic, 75116 Paris

Germany
(☎ 0228-400 920, 466 057, fax 400 922)
Im Rheingarten 7, D-53225 Bonn 3

Italy
(☎ 06-807 9797, 807 9464, fax 808 4410)
Via Nicolo Tartaglia 11, 00197 Rome

Japan
(☎ 3-3409 1501, fax 3409 1505)
38 Kowa Building, Room 703, 12-24 Nishi Azabu, 4 Chrome, Minato Ku, Tokyo 106

Netherlands
(☎ 70-352 3851, 352 4351, fax 365 6954)
Nassaulaan 2, 2514 JS The Hague

Spain
(☎ 1-555 8452, 555 8455, fax 597 1583)
Calle Capitan Haya No 1, Edificio Eurocentro, Planta 13, Madrid

Sweden
(☎ 8-411 0996, fax 213 100)
Engelbrektsgatan 35-B, 11432 Stockholm

Switzerland
(☎ 31-371 3282, fax 371 0424)
Morillonstrasse 9, 3007 Bern

UK
(☎ 020-7581 2776, 7584 4206, fax 7589 8887)
1 Cromwell Rd, London SW7 2HW

USA
(☎ 202-342 2214, fax 387 2489)
1099 30th St NW, Washington DC 20007

In the USA, Venezuela has consulates in Baltimore, Boston, Chicago, Houston, Miami, New Orleans, New York, Philadelphia, San Francisco, San Juan and Washington. In Canada, there are consulates in Montreal and Toronto. There's no Venezuelan embassy in New Zealand; that country is under the jurisdiction of the embassy in Australia.

In Colombia, there's a Venezuelan embassy and consulate in Bogotá, and consulates in Arauca, Barranquilla, Bucaramanga, Cartagena, Cúcuta, Medellín, Puerto Carreño, Puerto Inírida and Riohacha. In Brazil, Venezuela has its embassy and consulate in Brasilia, and consulates in Belém, Boa Vista, Manaus, Rio de Janeiro and São Paulo.

Other Venezuelan representatives in the region include embassies and consulates in Argentina (Buenos Aires), Barbados (Bridgetown), Bolivia (La Paz), Chile (Santiago), Costa Rica (San José), Cuba (Havana), Dominican Republic (Santo Domingo), Ecuador (Quito), El Salvador (San Salvador), Grenada (St Georges), Guatemala (Guatemala City), Guyana (Georgetown), Haiti (Port-au-Prince), Jamaica (Kingston), Mexico (Mexico City), Nicaragua (Managua), Panama (Panama City), Paraguay (Asunción), Peru (Lima), St Lucia (Castries), St Vincent (Kingstown), Suriname (Paramaribo), Trinidad & Tobago (Port of Spain), Uruguay (Montevideo) and the Netherlands Antilles (Aruba, Bonaire and Curaçao).

Embassies & Consulates in Venezuela

All countries that maintain diplomatic relations with Venezuela have embassies in Caracas. Some are listed in this section. If you can't find your home embassy, check the Caracas phone directory, which includes a full list. Consulates are at the same address as the embassies unless indicated otherwise. There are also some consulates in other large cities and border towns; these have been listed in the relevant sections throughout the book.

Australia
(☎ 263 40 33, 261 46 32) Quinta Yolanda,
Avenida Luis Roche entre 6a y 7a Transversal,
Altamira

Austria
(☎ 991 38 63, 992 29 56)
Torre Las Mercedes, Piso 4, Oficina 408,
Avenida La Estancia, Chuao

Barbados
(☎ 991 67 21)
Edificio Los Frailes, Piso 5, Oficina 501, Calle
La Guairita con Avenida Principal de Chuao

Belgium
(☎ 262 14 45, 262 04 21)
Quinta La Azulita, 11a Avenida entre 6a y 7a
Transversal, Altamira

Bolivia
(☎ 261 45 63, 263 30 15)
Quinta Embajada de Bolivia, Avenida Luis
Roche con 6a Transversal, Altamira

Brazil
(☎ 261 44 81, 261 55 05)
Centro Gerencial Mohedano, Piso 6, Calle Los
Chaguaramos con Avenida Mohedano, La
Castellana

Canada
(☎ 951 61 66, 951 61 71)
Torre Europa, Piso 7, Avenida Francisco de
Miranda, Campo Alegre

Colombia
Embassy: (☎ 261 55 84, 261 83 58) Torre Credi-
val, Piso 11, 2a Avenida de Campo Alegre con
Avenida Francisco de Miranda, Campo Alegre
Consulate: (☎ 951 36 31, 951 66 92) Edificio
Consulado de Colombia, Calle Guaicaipuro, El
Rosal

Costa Rica
(☎ 265 78 89, 267 11 04) Edificio For You, Pent
House, Avenida San Juan Bosco entre 1a y 2a
Transversal, Altamira

Denmark
(☎ 951 46 18, 956 06 18) Torre Centuria, Piso 7,
Avenida Venezuela con Calle Mohedano, El
Rosal

Ecuador
(☎ 781 13 48, 781 32 77) Centro Empresarial
Andrés Bello, Torre Oeste, Piso 13, Avenida
Andrés Bello, Maripérez

France
(☎ 993 66 66, 993 85 92) Edificio Embajada de
Francia, Calle Madrid con Avenida La Trinidad,
Las Mercedes

Germany
(☎ 261 01 81, 261 32 53) Edificio Panaven, Piso
12, Avenida San Juan Bosco con 3a Transversal,
Altamira

Guyana
(☎ 977 11 58, 978 27 81) Quinta Roraima,
Avenida El Paseo, Prados del Este

Israel
(☎ 239 45 11, 239 49 21) Centro Empresarial
Miranda, Piso 4, Oficina 4-D, Avenida Francisco
de Miranda con Avenida Principal de Los
Ruices, Los Ruices

Italy
Embassy: (☎ 952 73 11, 952 89 39) Edificio
Atrium, Pent House, Calle Sorocaima entre
Avenidas Tamanaco y Venezuela, El Rosal
Consulate: (☎ 261 07 55, 261 28 03)
6a Avenida entre 3a y 5a Transversales, Altamira

Japan
(☎ 261 83 33) Edificio Bancaracas, Piso 12,
Plaza La Castellana

Your Own Embassy

It's important to realize what your own
embassy – the embassy of the country of
which you are a citizen – can and can't do to
help you if you get into trouble. Generally
speaking, it won't be much help in emergencies if the trouble you're in is remotely your
own fault. Remember that you are bound by
the laws of the country you are in. Your
embassy will not be sympathetic if you end
up in jail after committing a crime locally,
even if such actions are legal in your own
country.

In genuine emergencies you might get
some assistance, but only if other channels
have been exhausted. For example, if you
need to get home urgently, a free ticket is ex-
ceedingly unlikely – the embassy would
expect you to have insurance. If you have all
your money and documents stolen, it might
assist with getting a new passport, but a loan
for onward travel is out of the question.

Some embassies used to keep letters for
travelers or have a small reading room with
home newspapers, but these days the mail-
holding service has usually been stopped,
and even newspapers tend to be out of date.

Mexico
(☎ 952 44 57, 952 57 77) Edificio Forum, Piso 5, Calle Guaicaipuro con Avenida Principal de Las Mercedes, El Rosal

Netherlands
(☎ 263 30 76, 263 36 22) Edificio San Juan, Piso 9, 2a Transversal con Avenida San Juan Bosco, Altamira

Norway
(☎ 253 06 71, 253 19 73) Centro Lido, Torre A, Piso 9, Avenida Francisco de Miranda, El Rosal

Peru
Embassy: (☎ 264 14 20, 264 14 83) Edificio San Juan, Piso 5, 2a Transversal con Avenida San Juan Bosco, Altamira
Consulate: (☎ 261 93 89, 266 49 36) Quinta Uno, 4a Avenida entre 3a y 4a Transversal, Altamira

Spain
Embassy: (☎ 263 28 55, 263 38 76) Quinta Marmolejo, Avenida Mohedano entre 1a y 2a Transversal, La Castellana
Consulate: (☎ 266 02 22) Edificio Bancaracas, Piso 7, Plaza La Castellana

Suriname
(☎ 261 27 24, 263 15 54) Quinta Los Milagros, 4a Avenida entre 7a y 8a Transversal, Altamira

Sweden
(☎ 952 20 58, 952 20 70, 952 21 11) Torre Europa, Piso 8, Avenida Francisco de Miranda, Campo Alegre

Switzerland
(☎ 951 40 64, 951 41 66, 951 46 06) Torre Europa, Piso 6, Avenida Francisco de Miranda, Campo Alegre

Trinidad & Tobago
(☎ 261 37 48, 261 57 96) Quinta Serrana, 4a Avenida entre 7a y 8a Transversal, Altamira

UK
(☎ 993 41 11, 993 42 24) Torre Las Mercedes, Piso 3, Avenida La Estancia, Chuao

USA
(☎ 977 20 11, 977 41 11, 977 02 21) Calle F con Calle Suapure, Colinas del Valle Arriba

CUSTOMS

Customs regulations don't differ much from those in other South American countries. You are allowed to bring in personal belongings and presents you intend to give to Venezuelan residents. The quantity, kind and value of these items shouldn't arouse any suspicion that they may have been imported for commercial purposes. You can bring cameras (still, video and movie), a cassette recorder, a radio set, camping equipment, sports accessories, a laptop computer and the like without any problems.

The entry of products derived from milk or pork is prohibited. It's also forbidden to introduce seeds, flowers, fruit or plants of any kind. According to Venezuelan law, the possession, trafficking or consumption of drugs is a serious offense and subject to heavy penalties. You would be crazy to try smuggling them across the border.

When leaving the country, you can take souvenirs and handicrafts with you, but not in quantities that could be suspected of being commercial.

Customs formalities are usually not much more than that – formalities. However, you may encounter a thorough check. If you're coming overland from Colombia, your baggage is likely to be searched at the border and/or at *alcabalas* (police road checkpoints). This is because of the considerable drug traffic that passes this way.

MONEY
Currency

The unit of Venezuelan currency is – yes, you guessed it – the bolívar. In written listings, it's abbreviated to Bs, which is usually written before the figure it refers to.

ULRICIE WELSCH

Notes come in denominations of 5, 10, 20, 50, 100, 500, 1000, 2000, 5000, 10,000 and 20,000 bolívares. There are also the new coins of 10, 20, 50, 100 and 500 bolívares, intended to replace their paper counterparts, but it will take a while. You may also occasionally come across the old 1-, 2- and 5-bolívar coins, though they have virtually disappeared from the market. They are almost worthless and are collector's items rather than money.

Exchange Rates

Following are approximate exchange rates at the time of going to press.

country	unit		Bs
Australia	A$1	=	Bs 381
Canada	C$1	=	Bs 464
Euro	€1	=	Bs 643
France	1FF	=	Bs 98
Germany	DM1	=	Bs 329
Japan	¥100	=	Bs 599
New Zealand	NZ$1	=	Bs 304
UK	UK£1	=	Bs 1020
USA	US$1	=	Bs 699

Exchanging Money

An essential question for many travelers is what to bring: cash, traveler's checks or credit cards. All three are OK in Venezuela, but the easiest and fastest way of getting local currency is a credit card, and it is strongly recommended that you bring one with you. You may also bring some traveler's checks, though there are fewer places to cash them and it takes more time to do it. Then there's cash, the riskiest form of carrying money, but useful on various occasions, including in case of emergency.

Cash By far the most popular foreign currency in Venezuela is the US dollar, so stick strictly to the greenback. Bring a balanced variety of denominations, large and small, to be able to pay airport departure tax, for example, if you have run out of bolívares. Other internationally known currencies, such as the pound sterling or Deutschmark, can occasionally be exchanged, but places

that accept them are few and far between, and the rate will usually be poor. Don't bring anything too exotic for Venezuelans, such as Australian dollars or Japanese yen.

The usual place to change cash is a *casa de cambio*, an authorized money-exchange office. There are a number of them in Caracas, Puerto La Cruz and Porlamar, but in other large cities there may be just one or two. In smaller cities and towns they are virtually nonexistent, except for border towns.

Casas de cambio change cash at a slightly lower rate than you would get for traveler's checks in the banks, but you save a lot of time, as the whole operation takes under a minute. Casas de cambio also sell foreign currency, mostly US dollars.

Banks, which previously happily changed foreign currencies at good rates, are now very reluctant to do so. Other places that may change US dollars include top end hotels and some travel agencies, but the rate they give will usually be poorer than in casas de cambio.

US dollars are accepted by many tour operators as payment and are also useful for buying currencies of neighboring countries from money changers at the borders.

There is no black market for currency.

Traveler's Checks The only really useful brand of traveler's checks in Venezuela is American Express. It is accepted by most outlets of Corp Banca, which has a wide array of branches around the country. The bank changes checks at a good rate and normally doesn't charge commission. Some other major banks may also exchange Amex checks, but there are not many of them and they will usually charge commission. Some banks may occasionally change other brands of checks and (as mentioned above) cash, but you'll be lucky to find them.

Bank hours are the same throughout the country: weekdays 8:30 am to 3:30 pm. Banks are closed on Saturday, Sunday and public holidays. In addition, banks are always closed on the first Monday after January 6 (Epiphany), March 19 (St Joseph's Day), Ascension Day (May), June 29 (St Peter's &

St Paul's Day), August 15 (Assumption), November 1 (All Soul's Day) and December 8 (Immaculate Conception).

However, banks usually handle foreign-exchange operations within limited hours, which sometimes can mean during morning hours only. Each branch of every bank seems to have its own schedule, which moreover can change from day to day. Some banks set limits on the number of foreign-exchange transactions they do per day (or the total amount of money they can change daily), so if you arrive too late they may refuse to change your money. The best time to try is between 9 and 10 am.

Major branches in big cities are usually more reliable (and handle foreign exchange for longer times) than minor outlets in smaller provincial localities. It's always wise to change enough money to last you through to the next large city.

Another frustrating feature of Venezuelan banks is that they are almost always crowded, inefficient and painfully slow. It can easily take an hour to change traveler's checks. Local branches have to call the main bank to ask for the day's exchange rates, and sometimes they can't get through for an hour or two, or not at all, in which case they don't change money.

If you are in a provincial bank, ask more than one teller whether the bank changes money. Not all tellers are sure of what the bank can do, so they usually take the safest (and easiest) line and say that no exchange is possible.

Your passport is required in any bank transaction. When it comes to changing checks, some banks may also require you to produce your purchase receipt (the form titled 'purchase record customer's copy,' which you get when buying the checks). Make sure to carry this copy with you.

Some casas de cambio exchange traveler's checks; others don't. Some tour operators will accept traveler's checks as a means of payment for their services.

The place to report the loss or theft of Amex checks and apply for a replacement or refund is the Turisol in Caracas (see that chapter for contact details). Keep in mind

that you may be asked for details of where and when you bought the checks.

Credit Cards & ATMs Although the use of credit cards in Venezuela is still not as common as in western countries, they have become extremely popular over the past

ATM Warning

Withdrawing money from an ATM in Venezuela is easy, fast and convenient, but it has some small if potentially serious risks. To start with, the machine can swallow your card, as some travelers have reported. It's still OK if it happens during the bank's business hours, because someone from the bank is likely to help you to retrieve your card. It will be less fun, however, when the bank is closed: no money, no card, and nothing much to do.

A more concerning case may be when you do get your card back, but no money. One traveler reported that he tried once but the money didn't come out. Believing that there might have been some temporary problem with the machine, he repeated the operation, with the same negative result. A couple of months later at home, he wasn't particularly happy with his bank statement, which featured records of the two withdrawals.

The variant where you get your card back and also the requested money may not always have a happy ending either. The problem is that some of the ATMs are targeted by robbers. They simply watch discreetly and then decide whom to approach. By doing this, they kill two birds with one shot: They get a credit card and cash, and may even extract the PIN number from the victim. So far, we've heard of gangs targeting ATM users only in Caracas, but diseases like these may spread quickly.

The risk that something like this will happen to you is slim, but if you want to minimize it anyway, it's probably better to get a cash advance on your card inside the bank from a cashier, even if this can take half an hour or more.

decade. They can be used for cash advances from banks and ATMs, and for purchases of goods and services in a wide variety of establishments.

The most useful card for cash advances is Visa, as it's accepted by the largest number of banks, including Banco Unión, Banco de Venezuela, Banco Mercantil and Banco Provincial. The second best is MasterCard, which is also honored by a number of banks. It's much easier to find a bank that will service your Visa or MasterCard than it is to find a bank that will exchange US dollars or traveler's checks. Moreover, advance payments on cards take less time than changing checks or cash. All in all, bringing a credit card will save you a lot of time and hassle.

Many of the major banks, including those listed above, have adjacent ATMs, and they usually work fine with cards issued outside Venezuela. Some ATMs even offer a choice of instructions displayed in Spanish or English. However, there are some risks in using ATMs – read the boxed warning.

Visa, MasterCard and the American Express charge card, are most useful as a means of payment. They are accepted in most upmarket hotels and restaurants, airline offices and many stores. If you plan on renting a car, they are essential. Curiously, many regional tour operators may refuse payment by credit card or charge 10% to 15% more. To avoid this surcharge, get a cash advance and pay in bolívares.

Make sure you know the number to call if you lose your credit card, and be quick to cancel it if it's lost or stolen.

International Transfers If you need money sent to you quickly, it's probably best to use Western Union, which has over 80,000 agencies worldwide. Your sender pays the money at their nearest Western Union branch, along with a fee, and gives the details on who is to receive it and where. You can have the money within 15 minutes. When you pick it up, take along photo identification.

Western Union is represented in Venezuela by the Grupo Zoom, which has offices in most cities around the country. There are about 25 offices in Caracas alone. In Venezuela, call toll-free ☎ 800 227 82 for information. In the USA, call toll-free ☎ 800-325 6000. Or simply check their Web site: www.westernunion.com.

Security

Although Venezuela is not a particularly dangerous country to travel in, you should always keep money and documents as secure as possible. The most common protection used by travelers is money belts. They come in a variety of types and styles, of which the most popular are those that can be worn around the waist. Those made of leather or cotton are more comfortable than the synthetic variety. Money belts are useful only if worn under clothing – pouches worn outside clothes attract thieves' attention and are easy prey. In order to stash emergency cash, some travelers sew cloth pouches into their trousers or other items of clothing.

While most of your money should be well hidden, give yourself easy access to enough cash to cover your expected daily expenditure. You can then pay expenses without extracting money from your belt or pouch and attracting attention. This money is also useful in case you are assailed – muggers can become annoyed if you don't have anything for them, and they may react unpredictably. Leave your wallet at home, as it's an easy mark for pickpockets. Don't carry money or documents in back pockets.

Costs

Venezuela is no longer one of the cheapest Latin American destinations, as it was in the mid-1990s. Over the past several years, the prices of goods and services roughly doubled (in US$ terms), with the result that Venezuela is now one of the more expensive countries on the continent. By and large, it's pricier than most Andean countries, including Ecuador, Peru and Bolivia, and roughly comparable to Chile.

How much you spend in Venezuela largely depends on what degree of comfort you require, what kind of food you eat, where you go, how fast you travel and the means of transportation you use. If, for instance, you are used to rental cars and plush hotels, you will probably spend just as much as in North America or Europe. If you're a budget traveler, though, and are prepared for basic conditions and willing to endure some discomfort on the road, you should find that you get by on US$25 to US$30 per day. This would cover accommodations in budget hotels, food in low- to middle-range restaurants and bus transportation at a reasonable pace, and probably still leave a small margin for some beers, movies and taxis. These averages obviously don't include rental cars, tours and flights.

If you economize, it's possible to cut the average daily cost down to US$20, but this may limit your experience of the country and can turn your trip into more of an endurance test than a holiday. After all, you don't set off on a trip to put yourself through hell.

Accommodations, food and transportation are the three major expenses. If you are prepared for basic conditions, you shouldn't have to spend more than US$8 to US$10 a night (on average) for a budget hotel. The cost will be lower (or the standard better) if you travel with someone else, best if you're sharing a bed.

If budget dining is what you're used to, you shouldn't have to spend more than US$10 to US$15 a day on food. Since Venezuela's average temperatures are fairly high, you'll drink a lot, but soft drinks and mineral water are inexpensive.

Buses are the main means of transportation, and they're still reasonably priced. City buses cost next to nothing. Taxis aren't expensive either, particularly when you're in a group and split the cost. They are well worth considering for trips to or from the airport or bus terminal, when you're carrying all your gear.

Most museums don't charge an admission fee – a welcome custom – and those that do usually keep the fee low. In this book, we usually list admission fees only when they were higher than about US$1. Cultural events (cinema, theater, music etc)

are all fairly inexpensive. On the other hand, drinking sessions in nightclubs can deplete your funds quickly, especially if you drink at the same rate as Venezuelans.

What can really eat into your budget, however, are organized tours. They cost roughly between US$40 and US$120 per day and rarely are just day trips. A tour to Salto Angel is a considerable expense.

On the whole, travel in the countryside is cheaper than in the cities. Caracas is the most expensive Venezuelan city. There will be a hell of a difference in cost between camping on the beach for a week and exploring Caracas nightspots for the same length of time.

Prices in this book were correct as we went to press, but keep in mind that economic instability may affect them considerably, even though we list them in US dollars.

Tipping

In virtually every dining or drinking establishment with table service, a 10% service charge will automatically be added to the bill, so further tipping is theoretically unnecessary. In practice, few people leave any tip in budget eateries, but in upmarket restaurants a small tip is customary. One way to avoid a service charge is to eat and drink *en la barra* (at the bar), if the place provides such a facility. The barra is common in *tascas* (Spanish-style bar-restaurants), taverns, pubs, and some other types of eating outlets.

Tipping in hotels is essentially restricted to four- and five-star establishments, which usually have decent room service and porters, all of whom expect to be tipped. Going down the star ladder, the service thins out, so tipping is uncommon, unless you want to reward someone for his or her particularly outstanding effort, help or dedication.

Taxi drivers are seldom tipped. Since taxis don't have meters and the fare is just a verbal agreement between the driver and passenger, the tip is simply not expected.

Bargaining

As in most Latin American countries, bargaining in Venezuela is a part of everyday life. Obviously, not everything is a matter of negotiation: Prices of things such as airfares, goods in supermarkets, food in restaurants and rates of finer hotels are fixed, and no one will try to bargain over them. However, since a good part of the economy is informal, quasi-legal or uncontrolled, prices for some goods and services, including products purchased at the market, taxi fares, and even rates at less reputable hotels, are to some extent negotiable.

No matter how adept your bargaining skills, you probably won't get things as cheaply as the locals can, particularly if your Spanish is limited. Nonetheless, you should not be intimidated about haggling over prices. You can save some bolívares while buying handicrafts at the markets or negotiating a taxi fare, and perhaps have occasional success in beating down a hotel price. You also can try negotiating tour fares offered by regional operators and independent guides, particularly if you are traveling in a large party.

Whenever and wherever you bargain, do it in a friendly and easygoing manner, with a smile and in a jocular fashion. Don't lose your temper or express anger, even if you know that you've been given a 'gringo' price.

Taxes

Many goods and services in Venezuela (including luxury products, hotels, restaurants, car rentals and tours) are officially subject to a 15.5% sales tax levy, called IVA (impuesto de valor agregado), or value-added tax (VAT). Like many financial aspects of the local economy, however, IVA seems to be a flexible concept, and it's not exactly clear if and when you'll pay it. For example, many upmarket hotels charge the tax, but budget residencias and posadas usually don't. Some retailers will sell you products at a tax-free price, but if you ask for a factura (receipt), they will add the tax.

Businesses that charge IVA usually state the total price to the customer, but some list net prices. In some finer hotels or restaurants, for instance, you may find a displayed price list with a discreet comment in small print below that says no incluye IVA (doesn't include VAT).

POST & COMMUNICATIONS
Post

The postal service is run by Ipostel, which has post offices throughout the country. There are a score of Ipostel offices in Caracas and a few in each of the other big cities, but only one post office in the smaller cities and towns. The Ipostel offices in the major cities are usually open during normal office hours (8 am to noon and 2 to 6 pm weekdays), but elsewhere they tend to open later and close earlier.

Postal Rates Airmailing a letter of up to 20g costs US$0.80 to anywhere in the Americas, US$1 to Europe or Africa and US$1.40 elsewhere. Mailing letters between 20g and 50g costs US$1.60/2/2.80, respectively.

A 1kg airmail parcel costs US$16 to the Americas, US$20 to Europe or Africa and US$28 elsewhere. A 10kg parcel will cost US$100/120/160. Ipostel staff will assure you it takes only eight days for a parcel to reach its destination, but you shouldn't take this claim too seriously.

It is cheaper to send parcels by surface mail. A 1kg parcel costs US$12/15/18 and a 10kg parcel costs US$52/58/75. You will be told that it will take up to a month for delivery, but this is Ipostel's rather wishful thinking.

Sending Mail Ipostel service is slow, inefficient and unreliable. Airmail to the USA or Europe can take up to a month to arrive, if it arrives at all. Aerograms are more likely to arrive safely, although perhaps no more quickly than stamped letters. Internal mail is also painfully slow.

A more secure way of sending letters is by correo certificado (certified mail), although its delivery rate is not perfect either. Bear this in mind before sending an important letter or a valuable parcel through Ipostel. Avoid problems by using telephones, faxes, email or courier services. If you are on your way to Colombia or Brazil, wait and mail items from there, as both these countries have more reliable postal services.

As might be expected, Ipostel's inefficiency has spawned a rash of courier services, both national and international. DHL and other big companies are well established in Caracas and other large cities, and offer fast and secure service at their usual rates.

Receiving Mail Expect similar problems: Letters and parcels sent to Venezuela from abroad take a long time to be delivered and sometimes simply never make it. The confusing and imprecise local system of addresses only exacerbates the problems. Mail sent to an *apartado* (PO box) has a better chance of arriving safely than mail posted to a home or office address.

Poste restante (general-delivery mail) is handled by Ipostel offices, but if you decide to use its services, stick to the main offices in a few major cities. If you can use somebody's PO box address, it will probably be more reliable than Ipostel's poste restante service. In any case, if there's anything to be sent to you that you can't risk losing, ask your senders to use courier services.

Telephone

Venezuela's telephone network is operated by CANTV (Compañía Anónima Nacional de Teléfonos de Venezuela). This once fully state-owned company was partially privatized in 1991, and the sale of the remaining 60% of shares should be finalized by the time you read this.

In addition to CANTV, there are two cellular providers, Movilnet and Telcel. Since its introduction in 1991, cellular telephony expanded so dramatically that today Venezuela has the highest cellular-phone-per-capita ratio in Latin America. In absolute terms, it comes in third after Brazil and Mexico, both of which have far larger populations. Cellular phones have become both a status symbol and a more reliable alternative to CANTV's jammed lines and often inoperable public phones.

The telephone system is largely automated for both domestic and international connections. Public telephones exist in cities and large towns, but many are out of order. Those that do work often have lines of people waiting to place calls. Street phones are usually the most besieged, so look for public phones in more secluded locations, such as hotel lobbies and shopping malls. As a rule, CANTV offices have some operable phones. Also keep in mind that every metro station in Caracas has public phones.

Almost all public telephones operate only on phone cards known as *tarjetas CANTV*. It's worth buying a card as soon as you arrive, unless you don't plan on calling from public phones at all. Phone cards come in denominations of 3000 and 5000 bolívares, and they are useful for local, long-distance and international calls. The cards can be bought from CANTV offices, various establishments such as stationers and pharmacies, and countless street vendors.

Most of the newly installed card phones are incorporated into the long-distance direct-dialing system, both domestic and international, so you can call anywhere without having to place your call through an operator. You will probably be obliged to call direct anyway, as most CANTV offices eliminated the service of connecting long-distance calls through the operator from their offices (though they do this for customers using private phones).

International Collect Calls

Following are international access numbers for collect and international calls:

Australia	☎ 800-11-61-0
Canada	☎ 800-11-10-0
France	☎ 800-11-33-0
Germany	☎ 800-11-49-0
Italy	☎ 800-11-39-0
Japan	☎ 800-11-81-0
Netherlands	☎ 800-11-31-0
UK	☎ 800-11-44-0
USA	(AT&T) ☎ 800-11-1-21
	(IDB) ☎ 800-11-1-51
	(MCI) ☎ 800-11-1-41
	(Sprint) ☎ 800-11-1-11

Don't dial '00' (Venezuela's international access code) before the numbers listed.

Domestic Calls You can call direct to virtually every city and town in Venezuela. A three-minute local call within a city costs about US$0.10. The normal cost of long-distance calls is US$0.25 per minute, and it doesn't depend on the distance, so calling the neighboring city costs the same as calling right across the country. A *tarifa reducida* (reduced rate) of US$0.20 is applied from 7 to 11 pm, and there's an even cheaper *tarifa económica* of US$0.15, which is available from 11 pm to 7 am.

Area codes are listed just under the headings of the relevant destinations. Drop the initial 0 if you are calling from abroad.

Cellular phone numbers begin with the 014 (Telcel) or 016 (Movilnet) prefix, followed by the proper seven-digit number. You don't dial any area codes beforehand. Note that calling cellular numbers eats quickly into your phone card, even if your recipient is just a block away, so try to use the regular phone system as long as you can before appealing to the cellular network.

International Calls International connections are possible to just about any corner of the world, but not all countries can be called collect (reverse charge). In most cases, you'll be calling from a public phone using the phone card. You may have an opportunity to call from a private telephone to which you have access. Alternatively, you may prefer to call collect through the operator in the country you are calling.

When you're dialing direct, either from a public phone booth or from a private telephone, the call will be charged according to the length of time you talk. Sample per-minute rates are US$0.80 to the USA; US$1 to the UK, France, Italy, Germany and Canada; and US$2 to Australia and New Zealand. The rates are the same any time of the day or night. Collect calls *(llamadas de cobro revertido)* are possible to a number of countries and are easy to place (see the boxed text 'International Collect Calls').

The country code for Venezuela is 58. To call a number in Venezuela from abroad, dial the international access code of the country you're calling from, the country

Telephone Code Changes

In 2001, Venezuela began to change its telephone codes according to a rolling schedule. Most new codes were created by adding 2 to the existing code (eg, the Coro code will change from 068 to 0268). Exceptions are Greater Caracas (02 will become 0212), Tucacas and Chichiriviche (042 will become 0259) and Santa Elena de Uairén (088 will become 0289). Additionally, the Movilnet cell-phone code will change from 014 to 0414, and the Telcel code from 016 to 0416. For updates, visit www.cantv.com.ve.

This guide includes old and new codes at the beginning of regional sections along with the planned date of transition (except in Anzoátegui and Cojedes states, which changed in January 2001).

code (58), the area code (they are given in the relevant sections, but drop the initial 0) and the local phone number.

To call abroad from Venezuela, first dial 00, which is Venezuela's international access code. A click should follow the first 0 before the next one is dialed. Then dial the country code, area code and local number.

Fax
Faxes can be sent from major branches of CANTV offices. There's also a growing number of private companies in large cities offering fax services. The best hotels, too, will send and receive faxes for you, but they will charge heavily for this already expensive service. Finally, faxes can be sent from most cybercafés.

Email & Internet Access
Though it's way behind the west, the popularity of the Internet has become huge in Venezuela over recent years, and there are today a number of service providers on the market. Cybercafés that offer public access to the Internet began to open around 1998, but it wasn't until 2000 that they were popping up like mushrooms. By late 2000, most large cities had cybercafés, and they also began appearing in smaller localities.

Many cybercafés are not exactly 'cafés,' but rather officelike establishments tightly crammed with computer workstations. They don't necessarily serve coffee and sometimes serve nothing at all, yet they provide what they should, and by and large do a good job. Since most of these places are pretty new, they usually have good modern equipment, providing fast connections, large screens and often a range of related facilities, such as printing, scanning and faxing.

An hour of surfing the Web or emailing will cost anywhere between US$1 and US$10, depending on the region, city and particular place. Mérida has the cheapest facilities, while Caracas is around the most expensive. Incidentally, Mérida and Caracas are the two cities with the largest number of cybercafés. Most places have fixed one-hour, half-hour and 15-minute rates, with the latter being usually a minimum period. Only a few cybercafés charge by the minute. Many places are open Monday to Saturday, though some are also open on Sunday.

We have included a number of cybercafés in the relevant sections in this book, complete with some guidelines about their rates and opening hours, but note that this is one of the fastest-developing facilities, so there are likely to be many more (and perhaps better) places by the time you come.

INTERNET RESOURCES

The World Wide Web is a rich resource for travelers. You can research your trip, hunt down bargain airfares, book hotels, check on weather conditions or chat with locals and other travelers about the best places to visit (or avoid!).

There's no better place to start your Net explorations than the Lonely Planet Web site (www.lonelyplanet.com). Here you'll find succinct summaries on traveling to most places on earth, postcards from other travelers and the Thorn Tree bulletin board, where you can ask questions before you go or dispense advice when you get back. You can also find travel news and updates for many of our most popular guidebooks, and the subWWWay section links you to the most useful travel resources elsewhere on the Web.

Venezuela Web Sites

There are quite a few Web sites concerning Venezuela, and the number is growing. Useful sources of general and tourist information about the country include the following sites:

www.venezuelavirtual.com
www.think-venezuela.net
www.latinworld.com/sur/venezuela
www.venezuelavoyage.com
www.auyantepuy.com
www.gosouthamerica.about.com

If you want to keep track of the country's current political and economic affairs, read Venezuela's two leading papers at www.el-universal.com and www.el-nacional.com.

BOOKS

You will get far more out of your visit if you read about the country before you go. There are plenty of books in English that cover various aspects of Venezuela, some of which are recommended below. If you want to study a particular aspect of the country in detail, have a look at *Venezuela: World Bibliographic Series,* by DAG Waddell, which lists over 800 books concerning Venezuela.

If you read Spanish, you'll find invaluable sources of information in Venezuela itself. The country churns out many books and other publications, few of which have been translated into foreign languages.

Several books are published in different editions by different publishers in various countries. As a result, a book might be a hardcover rarity in one country while it's readily available in paperback in another. Fortunately, bookshops and libraries search by title or author, so your local bookshop or library is probably the best place to advise you on the availability of the following recommendations.

Lonely Planet

If you're planning a wider journey than just Venezuela, consider taking LP's *South*

America on a shoestring, which covers the whole continent. *Read This First: Central & South America* may be a useful predeparture reading. You may also want to consult *Healthy Travel: Central & South America.* Also note that Lonely Planet has individual guidebooks to most Latin American countries, including Venezuela's neighbors, Brazil and Colombia. Finally, the *Latin American Spanish phrasebook* can prove a worthwhile addition to your backpack.

Guidebooks

There are some English-language guides published in Venezuela. They are almost inaccessible outside the country, but you can buy them in some local bookshops.

Ecotourism Guide to Venezuela (Miro Popic, Caracas) is a bilingual Spanish/English guidebook focusing on ecological tourism. Updated annually, the guide features brief descriptions of all the national parks and nature reserves, plus information on over 500 lodging options located mostly in the countryside, including protected areas.

Even more detailed is the *Guide to Camps, Posadas and Cabins in Venezuela,* by Elizabeth Kline. Also a bilingual edition, the guide details 1200 mostly rural accommodation options. Both of these publications can be particularly useful for visitors planning outdoor activities.

Gourmets may be interested in the *Caracas Gastronomic Guide,* another bilingual Spanish/English publication by Miro Popic, also updated annually. The guide provides excellent insight into the local eating scene, covering more than 650 restaurants, plus dozens of cafés, delicatessens, bars, pubs and discotheques.

History & Politics

A good overview of the period of Spanish colonization is provided by John Hemming's *The Search for El Dorado.* The book provides fascinating insight into the conquest of Venezuela and Colombia. Equally captivating is *The Explorers of South America,* by Edward J Goodman, which brings to life some of the more incredible explorations of the continent, from Columbus to Humboldt. You'll read more about explorers and their studies in the following Geography & Wildlife section.

In Focus: Venezuela – A Guide to the People, Politics and Culture, by James Ferguson, is a good introduction to the country, as well as its history and contemporary issues. *Venezuela: the Search for Order, the Dream of Progress,* by John V Lombardi, provides general reading on history, politics, geography and people.

For a comprehensive 20th-century history, try *Venezuela, a Century of Change,* by Judith Ewell, or *Venezuela,* by David Eugene Blank. *Paper Tigers and Minotaurs,* by Moisés Naim, gives a good insight into economic policies of recent decades.

Geography & Wildlife

Venezuela's unique geological phenomenon, the tepui, has captivated explorers, scientists and writers for ages. One of the first authors attracted by the tepuis was Sir Arthur Conan Doyle, who – although he had never been to Venezuela – was inspired by fabulous stories of Colonel Fawcett's explorations of the plateaus. Conan Doyle gave play to his imagination in *The Lost World* (originally published 1912), a rollicking science-fiction tale set in a prehistoric world.

For something less fanciful, read 'Venezuela's Islands in Time,' an article by Uwe George published in *National Geographic* (May 1989). It has good general information about the tepuis and how they emerged, and it is illustrated with spectacular photos of these unique formations.

The Lost World of Venezuela and its Vegetation, by Charles Brewer-Carías (Caracas, 1987), looks at the mysterious and endemic plant life of the tepuis. The study contains a photographic record of the plants and describes the research carried out by the author on the top of several tepuis. The book also has a Spanish edition, but neither is easy to find in local bookshops, let alone outside Venezuela.

Another explorer's account of the tepuis is *Churún Merú, the Tallest Angel,* by Ruth Robertson, which is the report of the expedition to Auyantepui. It was on this expedition that the height of Salto Angel was measured for the first time, confirming its status as the world's highest waterfall.

The famous German geographer and botanist Alexander von Humboldt didn't make it to the tepuis, but he explored and studied other regions of Venezuela (as well as parts of Colombia, Ecuador and Peru). He describes it all in amazing detail in his three-volume *Personal Narrative of Travels to the Equinoctial Regions of America, 1799–1801*. Volume No 2 covers the Venezuelan section of his journey.

Travelers with a serious interest in South American wildlife have quite a choice when it comes to background reading and practical guides. *A Neotropical Companion: An Introduction to the Animals, Plants, and Ecosystems of the New World Tropics*, by John C Kricher, is an excellent source of information and fascinating reading. *World of Wildlife – Animals of South America*, by FR de la Fuente, is a good basic reference work. *Neotropical Rainforest Mammals – A Field Guide*, by Louise H Emmons, is a practical guide containing descriptions and illustrations of several hundred species, many of which can be found in Venezuela.

If birds are what interest you, you could start with *A Guide to the Birds of South America*, published by the Academy of Natural Science, Philadelphia. Alternatively, try the valuable reference work *The Birds of South America*, by RS Ridgley & G Tudor. It comes in several volumes, and amateurs may find it extremely detailed and technical. There's also the helpful *Where to Watch Birds in South America*, by Nigel Wheatley.

For the trip itself, get a copy of *A Guide to the Birds of Venezuela*, by Rodolphe Meyer de Schauensee & William H Phelps, which is a good, illustrated field guide. *South American Birds – A Photographic Aid to Identification*, by John S Dunning, might be another good companion on your trip. A number of the bird species featured in the book are found in Venezuela. You can also consider getting the useful *Birding in Vene-*zuela, by Mary Lou Goodwin (Sociedad Conservacionista Audubon de Venezuela, Caracas, 1994), which advises the best areas for birding and lists the bird species that can be found there. The guide is available in Venezuela.

A recommended rain forest guide is *Rainforests – A Guide to Research and Tourist Facilities at Selected Tropical Forest Sites in Central and South America*, by James L Castner. This book has useful background information and has descriptions of 40 rain forests in half a dozen countries.

Society & Culture

What is probably most intriguing for foreign travelers to Venezuela is the native Indian population. By far the most complete work on the subject is the three-volume *Los Aborígenes de Venezuela* (Fundación La Salle, Caracas). Volume No 1 (1980) refers to the Indian groups of the past, whereas volume Nos 2 and 3 (1983 and 1988, respectively) feature all the major communities (15 groups) currently living in Venezuela. The work was researched and written by an international group of anthropologists and ethnologists, and gives insight into the social organization, religion and culture of each group. It is well illustrated with maps and photos. There is only a Spanish edition and it's hard to get ahold of outside Venezuela; for those who read Spanish it's a treasure trove of information.

Internationally, the most widely publicized Indian group is the Yanomami. The tribe was considered to have an essentially Stone Age culture when it was first discovered in modern times. Perhaps the best authority on the matter is Jacques Lizot, who published a score of research studies on the group, including *Le Cercle des Feux: Faits et Dits des Indiens Yanomami* (Recherches Anthropologiques, Editions du Seuil, Paris, 1976). The work has been translated into English.

Another noted investigator of Yanomami culture is Napoleon Chagnon, whose doctoral dissertation emphasized the Indians' warrior culture. Read *Yanomamo, the True*

People, his article in *National Geographic* (August 1976). Also, have a look into *Aborigines of the Amazon Rain Forest: The Yanomami,* by Robin Hanbury-Tenison (Time Life Books, 1982).

NEWSPAPERS & MAGAZINES

All the main cities have their own daily newspapers. The two leading Caracas papers, *El Universal* and *El Nacional,* have countrywide distribution. Both have good coverage of national and international affairs, sports, economics and culture. Both cost US$0.60 except on Sunday, when they cost US$0.80. Caracas has several other newspapers and periodicals, including *Economía Hoy, El Mundo* and *El Globo.*

The major newspaper in Maracaibo is *Panorama,* in Valencia it's *El Carabobeño,* and in Barquisimeto they have *El Informador* and *El Impulso.*

The Daily Journal is Venezuela's main English-language newspaper. This general-interest daily published in Caracas will keep you up-to-date on local and international news, culture, sport and entertainment. It's available at major newsstands and at select bookshops in Caracas. Elsewhere, it can be difficult to come by.

Major international dailies and periodicals, such as *The New York Times, The International Herald Tribune, Der Spiegel, Le Monde, Time, Newsweek* and *The Economist,* can be bought in Caracas and some large cities from select newsstands and bookshops. The best place to look for them is at the newsstands in five-star hotels.

RADIO & TV

There are over a hundred radio stations in Venezuela, broadcasting on either AM or FM. Every fair-sized town has its own local radio station. In Caracas, there are at least 15 stations broadcasting on FM stereo alone.

Most of the programming is dominated by imported pop, rock, disco and the like. Jazz and classical music are less popular, but some stations do grant them airtime. Of these, Radio Nacional, which broadcasts on 630 kHz (AM), is a good example. In Caracas, La Emisora Cultural broadcasts a balanced menu of classical music, jazz and talk programs on 91.1 and 97.7 MHz (FM).

Almost all radio programs are transmitted in Spanish. If you need English-language news, tune in to the BBC World Service, which can be picked up on various shortwave AM frequencies.

Three private and two government TV stations broadcast on VHF out of Caracas and reach most of the country. The three commercial networks, Radio Caracas Televisión (Channel 2), Venevisión (Channel 4) and Televén (Channels 10), have the usual mix of news, music, feature films, sports and cultural programs. Prime time is dominated by *telenovelas* (soap operas), Venezuelans' favorite TV entertainment. The government-owned Venezolana de Televisión (Channel 8) also has general-interest fare, similar to the commercial stations. The second government broadcaster, Vale TV (Channel 5), focuses more on educational and cultural programs, news and some of the more mentally stimulating films.

Apart from the aforementioned stations, there are two UHF broadcasters, Globovisión (Channel 31), which features news and opinion, and Meridiano Televisión (Channel 37), which covers sports. Almost all programming is in Spanish, including dubbed foreign films.

There are several pay-TV providers, including Omnivisión, Cablevisión, Supercable and DirecTV, which offer mixed Spanish/English packages of feature films, sports, music, soap operas and news.

Satellite TV has boomed in Caracas and, to a lesser extent, in the other major cities. The *parabólica* (satellite dish) has become the ultimate status symbol and a feature of the Caracas skyline. They are conspicuous in the wealthier suburbs and are spreading like wildfire in other districts.

Major national and regional papers list the programs of TV channels (including some satellite stations) that can be picked locally.

VIDEO SYSTEMS

If you want to record or buy videotapes to play back home, you won't get a picture if the image registration system is different. Venezuela uses the NTSC system, the same as in North America and Japan, but incompatible with both the French SECAM system and PAL, which is used in most of Europe and Australia.

PHOTOGRAPHY & VIDEO

Given the country's spectacular and varied geography, wildlife, architecture and ethnic mosaic, there's plenty to capture on film or video. How you go about it is up to you. Some travelers are happy with a small automatic camera, while others travel with backpacks almost brimful with photographic gear.

Film & Equipment

Bring all necessary equipment from home. Cameras and accessories can be bought in Venezuela, but the choice is limited and unpredictable, and prices are hardly welcoming. It's difficult to get cameras repaired in Venezuela, so make sure your gear is reliable.

Film is easier to come by, and there's quite a choice in Caracas and some other big cities. Elsewhere, particularly in the outback, it may be difficult to get the film type and speed you require. Film is not cheap in Venezuela, so it may be advisable to bring some stock with you, particularly if you are coming from the cheap-film countries, such as the USA.

Kodak, Fuji and, to a lesser extent, Agfa are the most popular brands in Venezuela. Negative film is found almost everywhere. Slide film, especially the high-speed and professional type, is harder to find. Prints can be processed in any number of laboratories, often within an hour or two, and the quality is usually acceptable, but E6 slide processing is not common and the quality is not always good.

Don't be caught without a healthy supply of film. And also remember to bring a variety of film – rain forests are surprisingly dark and may require fast film (eg, 400 ASA), whereas the snowy peaks of the Andes and the sunny white beaches along the coast usually don't need anything faster than 50 ASA.

Technical Tips

One of the first things to consider before you leave home is what camera and accessories you will need while traveling. An automatic 35mm reflex with a zoom lens is universally considered appropriate for general purposes, including landscapes, portraits and architecture. The choice between a zoom and a set of straight lenses is a matter of individual preference.

Serious wildlife photography requires a long telephoto lens. A reasonable length would be somewhere between 200mm and 300mm. A wide-angle lens can be useful, sometimes indispensable, for photographing architecture or tight interiors. The macro, which comes as a standard feature in most zooms, is handy for taking photos of small insects, tiny flowers and the like. A UV filter is important when photographing at high altitudes.

A tripod is an important but heavy and bulky piece of equipment. Other useful accessories include a flash, a spare set of batteries for your camera, a lens-cleaning kit and plenty of silica-gel packs and plastic bags to protect your gear from humidity, dust, sand and water.

Whatever combination of lenses and accessories you decide to bring, make sure they are carried in a sturdy bag that will protect them from the elements and the hard knocks they're sure to receive. It's much better if the bag looks scruffy, because it will be less likely to attract the attention of thieves. And make sure your equipment is insured.

Heat and humidity can ruin film, so remember to keep it in the coolest, driest place available, both before and after exposure. Film should be processed soon after exposure, but don't panic about it; you might get a better result by waiting for two months to have it developed in a professional laboratory at home rather than processing it immediately in an unknown local venue.

Restrictions

Except for usual restrictions on photographing military installations and other strategic facilities (eg, oil refineries), you can take pictures almost anywhere and of just about anything. Taking photos is permitted in virtually every church and in some museums (although few allow flash).

Photographing People

Be sensitive about photographing people; if in doubt, ask for permission, and don't insist or take a picture if permission is denied. Indigenous people in particular may be reluctant to be photographed. It's not a good idea to photograph soldiers, police, Guardia Nacional etc.

Airport Security

To avoid possible damage to your high-speed film by airport X-ray machines, have it hand-inspected. Normal-speed film should not be affected, though some professionals might still want to have it hand-inspected, especially to avoid a cumulative effect if they pass through a number of airports on their route.

TIME

All of Venezuela lies within the same time zone, four hours behind Greenwich Mean Time. There's no daylight saving time (see the boxed text).

ELECTRICITY

Electricity is 110 volts, 60 cycles AC throughout the country. US-type flat two-pin plugs are used.

WEIGHTS & MEASURES

Venezuela uses the metric system. There's a conversion chart on the inside back cover of this book.

LAUNDRY

The dry cleaners in large cities usually take a couple of days to get your clothes cleaned. Top-class hotels offer laundry facilities for guests, but prices for this service are rather high. In budget hotels, you can usually make arrangements with the hotel staff, or their

When it's Noon in Caracas

Keep in mind that Venezuela does not observe daylight saving time.

city	time
Auckland	4 am (next day)
Berlin	5 pm
Bogotá 1	1 am
Buenos Aires	1 pm
Frankfurt	5 pm
Hong Kong	midnight
Lima	11 am
London	4 pm
Los Angeles	8 am
Melbourne	2 am (next day)
Mexico	10 am
Montreal	11 am
New York	11 am
Paris	5 pm
Quito	11 am
Rio de Janeiro	1 pm
San Francisco	8 am
Sydney	2 am (next day)
Tokyo	1 am (next day)
Toronto	11 am
Vancouver	8 am

relatives, to have clothes washed (usually by hand) at fair rates.

Self-service launderettes are scarce, but several establishments offer full-service washes. They exist in the cities and many larger towns, and are particularly numerous in major tourist destinations, such as Mérida and Porlamar. They may be a bit hard to find without help, but ask the locals for the *lavandería automática*. The machines may not be of the most modern technology, but they do the job reasonably well. Most laundries offer full service, including washing, drying and ironing, if requested. It usually takes a few hours to wash and dry, and will cost US$2.50 to US$5 for a 5kg load, detergent included.

TOILETS

There are virtually no self contained public toilets in Venezuela. If you are unexpectedly caught in need, use a toilet in a restaurant.

Choose better-looking establishments, because basic eateries either have no toilets or, if they do, you're better off not witnessing them. If you feel uncomfortable about sneaking in just to use the toilet, order a soft drink, a coffee or whatever. Museums and large shopping malls usually have toilets, as do bus and airport terminals. Toilets are usually the sit-down style, but they often lack boards, so they effectively become the squat variety.

You will rarely find toilet paper in toilets, so make sure you carry some at all times. Some toilets charge fees (normally not exceeding US$0.25), but in return you can generally receive a short piece of single-ply toilet paper. If it seems to be too small for your needs, do not hesitate to ask for more.

Except for toilets in some upmarket establishments, the plumbing might not be of a standard you are accustomed to. The tubes are narrow and water pressure is weak, so toilets can't cope with toilet paper. A wastebasket is normally provided.

The most common word for toilet is *baño*. Men's toilets will usually bear a label reading *señores, hombres* or *caballeros,* while women's toilets will be marked *señoras, mujeres* or *damas.*

HEALTH

Venezuela's health service has deteriorated over the past decade, and it's better not to get into its clutches. There are, to be just, an array of pharmacies, private clinics and hospitals, but the economic decline is putting their standards at risk. Be sure to have a good health-insurance policy to cover an emergency flight home or to the USA if something goes terribly wrong. If you need hospital treatment in Venezuela, by far the best facilities are in Caracas.

Your health while traveling depends on your predeparture preparations, your day-to-day health care, and how you handle medical problems or emergencies that develop. The list of potential dangers included in this section may seem frightening, but don't panic: With some basic precautions, few travelers experience anything more than minor stomach upsets.

This section includes preventative measures, descriptions of symptoms and suggestions about what to do if there is a problem. It isn't meant to replace professional diagnosis or prescriptions, and visitors to South America should discuss with their physician the most up-to-date methods used to prevent and treat the health threats that may be encountered.

If a serious medical problem arises during the trip, seek qualified help wherever possible, as self-diagnosis and treatment can be risky. Your embassy or consulate can usually recommend a good place to go for medical help. So can five-star hotels, although they often recommend doctors with five-star prices – this is when medical insurance really comes in useful.

Predeparture Preparations

Health Insurance Purchasing a travel-insurance policy to cover medical problems is highly recommended. However fit and healthy you are, do take out medical insurance. Even if you don't get sick, you might be involved in an accident.

There are a wide variety of policies, and your travel agent can make recommendations. The international student travel policies handled by STA and other student travel organizations are usually particularily good values.

When buying a policy, it's important to check the small print. Some policies specifically exclude coverage for dangerous activities, which can include scuba diving, motorcycling or even trekking. If these activities are on your agenda, such a policy would be of limited value.

You may prefer a policy that pays doctors or hospitals directly rather than having you pay them on the spot and claim later. If you have to claim later, make sure you keep all documentation. Some policies ask you to call back (reverse charges) to a center in your home country where an immediate assessment of your problem is made.

Check if the policy covers ambulances or an emergency flight home – someone has to pay if you have to stretch out across a few airline seats.

Five million people and an oil economy make for a hell of a rush hour in Caracas.

Simón Bolívar gazes over his plaza in Caracas.

The National Congress, Caracas

From point A to point B underneath the capital

A touch of the modern, Caracas

The beautiful Santa Capilla in the old center, Caracas

The towering affluence of Parque Central, Caracas

A monument to the bad boys of Caracas

The Museo Militar in San Mateo

Medical Information Services Useful health information is available from several public information services. In the USA, the Center for Disease Control & Prevention (CDC) has an international travelers' hot line (toll-free ☎ 877-394 8747). In Canada, there's Health Canada (☎ 613-957 8739). In the UK, you can obtain a printed health brief for any country by calling Medical Advisory Services for Travelers Abroad (MASTA; ☎ 0906-8-224 100). In Australia, call the Australian Government Health Service or consult the Travelers Medical & Vaccination Center (TMVC; ☎ 1300 658 844), which has 19 clinics in Australia and New Zealand.

There are a number of excellent travel health sites on the Internet. From the Lonely Planet Web site, there are links to the CDC, MASTA and TMVC (which offers online personal travel-health reports).

Travel Health Guides If you plan to travel in remote areas for a long period of time, you might consider taking a more detailed health guide. Here are some suggestions:

Healthy Travel Central & South America, by Isabelle Young, includes guidelines on treating travel illnesses in the region.

Travelers' Health, by Richard Dawood, is comprehensive, easy to read, authoritative and highly recommended, although it's rather large to lug around.

Travel with Children, by Maureen Wheeler, includes advice on travel health for children.

Immunizations No immunizations are necessary for Venezuela, unless you are coming from an area infected with cholera or yellow fever. However, the farther off the beaten track you go, the more necessary it is to take precautions. All vaccinations should be recorded on an International Health Certificate, which is available from your physician or government health department.

Plan your vaccinations ahead of time; some of them require an initial shot followed by a booster, and some vaccinations should not be administered at the same time. Most travelers from western countries will have been immunized against various diseases during childhood, but your doctor may still recommend booster shots. The period of protection offered by vaccinations differs widely. Note that some are not advisable for pregnant women.

The list of possible vaccinations includes the following:

Cholera Venezuelan authorities may still occasionally require that you have a cholera vaccination if you are coming from an infected area, particularly from Colombia, where there were outbreaks in recent years. In Venezuela itself there was a recent outbreak. However, the World Health Organization no longer recommends cholera vaccinations, as the vaccine offers incomplete and unreliable protection.

Diphtheria & Tetanus Diphtheria can be a fatal throat infection and tetanus can be a fatal wound infection. Vaccinations for these two diseases are usually combined and are recommended for everyone. Most people in developed countries have been vaccinated against them at school age. Boosters are necessary every 10 years and are recommended as a matter of course.

Hepatitis A This is the most common travel-acquired illness after diarrhea, and it can put you out of action for weeks. A vaccine such as Havrix 1440, Avaxim or VAQTA provides long-term immunity (possibly more than 10 years) after an initial injection and a booster at six to 12 months. Gamma globulin is not a vaccination, but rather a ready-made antibody collected from blood donations. It should be given close to departure because, depending on the dose, it protects for only two to six months.

Hepatitis B Vaccination involves three injections, the quickest course being over three weeks with a booster at 12 months. A combined Hepatitis A and Hepatitis B vaccine called Twinrix is also available. It's recommended for people wanting protection against both types of viral hepatitis. Three injections over a six-month period are required for this treatment.

Malaria There are malaria-carrying mosquitoes in Venezuela. So far, there is no effective vaccine against malaria, only antimalarial drugs. They don't prevent infection, but they kill the malaria parasites during a stage of their development and reduce the risk of serious illness or death. Expert advice on medication should be sought, as there are many factors to consider, including the area to be visited, the risk of exposure to malaria-carrying mosquitoes, the side effects of medication, your medical history etc.

Polio This has been wiped out in Venezuela but is endemic in Brazil, where outbreaks have been reported in the southern states. Westerners will usually have had an oral polio vaccine while in school, but you should undertake a booster course if more than 10 years have elapsed since your last vaccination.

Rabies Vaccination should be considered by those who will spend a longer period in Venezuela (or South America in general), especially if they will be handling animals or traveling to remote areas. Pre-travel rabies vaccination requires three injections over 21 to 28 days. If someone who has been vaccinated is bitten or scratched by an animal, they will require two booster injections of the vaccine; those not vaccinated require more shots.

Typhoid This is an important vaccination to have in areas where hygiene is a problem and is recommended to anybody traveling for longer periods in rural tropical areas. It is available either as an injection or as oral capsules.

Yellow Fever This vaccination is a legal requirement for entry into many countries when a visitor comes from an infected area. Protection lasts 10 years and is recommended for travel in most lowland tropical areas of South America (which includes Venezuela), where the disease is endemic. You usually have to go to a special yellow-fever vaccination center. Vaccination isn't recommended during pregnancy, but if you must travel to a high-risk area, it is probably better to take the vaccine.

Medical Kit Give some thought to a medical kit for your trip. The size and contents of your first-aid kit will depend on your knowledge of first-aid procedures, where and how far off the beaten track you are going, how long you will need the kit for, and how many people will be sharing it. See the boxed text for what a possible kit might include.

It's not necessary to take every remedy for every illness you might contract during your trip. Venezuelan pharmacies stock all kinds of drugs, and medication can be cheaper than in western countries. There are few restricted drugs; almost everything is sold over the counter. Many drugs are manufactured locally under foreign license. Be sure to check expiration dates.

Travelers should be aware of any drug allergies they may have, and avoid using such drugs or their derivatives. Since common names of prescription medicines in South America may be different from the ones you're used to, ask a pharmacist before taking anything you're not sure about.

Ideally, antibiotics should be administered only under medical supervision and should never be taken indiscriminately. Overuse of antibiotics can weaken your body's ability to deal with infections naturally and can reduce the drug's efficacy in future. Take only the recommended dose at the prescribed intervals, and continue using the antibiotic for the prescribed period, even if the illness seems to have been cured.

Remember that antibiotics are quite specific to the infections they treat, so if there are any serious unexpected reactions, discontinue use immediately. If you are not sure whether you have the correct antibiotic, don't use it at all.

Other Preparations Make sure you're healthy before you start traveling. Have your teeth checked and make sure they are OK. If you wear glasses or contact lenses, bring a spare pair and your optical prescription. Losing your glasses can be a real problem, although in many Venezuelan cities you can get new ones made up quickly, cheaply and competently.

At least one pair of good-quality sunglasses is essential because of the strong glare, as well as the dust and sand that can get into the corners of your eyes. A hat, sunscreen lotion and lip protection are also very important.

If you require a particular medication, take an adequate supply with you, as it may not be available locally. Take the original prescription specifying the generic rather than the brand name; it will make getting replacements easier. It's also wise to have the prescription with you to prove that you're using the medication legally.

Basic Rules
Paying attention to what you eat and drink is the most important health rule. Stomach

upsets are the most common travel health problem, but most of these will be relatively minor. Don't be paranoid about trying local food – it's part of the travel experience, and you wouldn't want to miss it.

Water & Drinks The tap water in Caracas and several other large cities is considered safe to drink, but it's better to avoid it. Fortunately, that's pretty easy: Bottled water and soft drinks are readily available in shops, supermarkets, restaurants, bakeries etc. Outside the big cities, tap water should never be drunk. Generally speaking, if you don't know for certain whether or not the water is safe, don't drink it. This goes for ice as well.

In rural areas, take care with fruit juice, particularly if water may have been added. Milk should be treated with suspicion because it is often unpasteurized. Boiled milk is fine if it is kept hygienically, and yogurt is always good. Hot tea or coffee should also be OK, since the water will probably have been boiled. Even in the most remote villages, bottled drinks are almost always available.

Problems begin when you venture into wilderness areas, where there are no Coca Cola stands. One solution is to bring drinkable water with you; the other is to purify local water. The simplest way of purifying water is to boil it thoroughly; technically this means boiling it for 10 minutes. Remember that at higher altitudes, water boils at lower temperatures, so germs are less likely to be killed.

Simple filtering will not remove all dangerous organisms, so if you cannot boil suspect water, it should be treated chemically. Chlorine tablets (Puritabs, Steritabs or other brand names) will kill many but not all pathogens. Iodine is an effective water purifier and is available in tablet form (such as Potable Aqua), but follow the directions carefully and remember that too much iodine is harmful. If you can't find tablets, tincture of iodine (2%) or iodine crystals can be used.

Food Salads and fruit should, theoretically at least, be washed with purified water, or

Medical Kit Checklist

Following is a list of items you should consider including in your medical kit – consult your pharmacist for brands available in your country.

❑ **Aspirin or paracetamol** (acetaminophen in the USA) – for pain or fever

❑ **Antihistamine** – for allergies, eg, hay fever; to ease the itch from insect bites or stings; and to prevent motion sickness

❑ **Cold and flu tablets, throat lozenges and nasal decongestant**

❑ **Multivitamins** – for long trips, when dietary vitamin intake may be inadequate

❑ **Antibiotics** – consider including these if you're traveling well off the beaten track; see your doctor, as they must be prescribed, and carry the prescription with you

❑ **Loperamide or diphenoxylate** – 'blockers' for diarrhea

❑ **Prochlorperazine or metaclopramide** – for nausea and vomiting

❑ **Rehydration mixture** – to prevent dehydration, which may occur, for example, during bouts of diarrhea; particularly important when traveling with children

❑ **Insect repellent, sunscreen, lip balm and eye drops**

❑ **Calamine lotion, sting relief spray or aloe vera** – to ease irritation from sunburn and insect bites or stings

❑ **Antifungal cream or powder** – for fungal skin infections and thrush

❑ **Antiseptic (such as povidone-iodine)** – for cuts and grazes

❑ **Bandages, Band-Aids (plasters) and other wound dressings**

❑ **Water purification tablets or iodine**

❑ **Scissors, tweezers and a thermometer** – note that mercury thermometers are prohibited by airlines

❑ **Sterile kit** – in case you need injections in a country with medical hygiene problems; ask your doctor for a note explaining why you have them

peeled whenever possible. Ice cream is usually OK, but beware of street vendors selling ice cream that has melted and been refrozen. Thoroughly cooked food is safe – but not if it has been left to cool or if it has been reheated. Take great care with shellfish or fish, and avoid undercooked meat. If a place looks clean and well run and if the vendor also looks clean and healthy, then the food is probably all right. In general, places that are packed with locals will be fine, while empty restaurants are questionable.

Nutrition If your diet is poor or you're traveling hard and fast and missing meals, you can soon start to lose weight and place your health at risk.

It's important to make sure that your diet is well balanced. Eggs, beans, lentils and nuts are all safe sources of protein. Fruit you can peel (bananas, oranges or mandarins, for example) is always safe and is a good source of vitamins. Eat sufficient rice and bread. Remember that although food is generally safer if it is cooked well, overcooked food loses much of its nutritional value. If your diet isn't well balanced or if your food intake is insufficient, it's a good idea to take vitamin and iron pills.

Most of Venezuela is hot lowland terrain, so make sure you drink enough – don't rely on thirst alone to tell you when to drink. Not needing to urinate and dark yellow urine are signs of dehydration. Always carry a water bottle with you on trips off the beaten path. On the other hand, excessive drinking can cause excessive sweating. This can lead to a loss of salt, resulting in muscle cramps. If you find that your sweat is not salty, add more salt than usual to your food.

Environmental Hazards

Altitude Sickness Popularly referred to as *soroche,* altitude sickness, along with the more serious acute mountain sickness (AMS), occurs at high altitudes and in extreme cases can be fatal. Both are caused by ascending to high altitudes so quickly that the body does not have time to adapt to the lower oxygen concentration in the atmosphere. Light symptoms can appear at

---

Everyday Health

Normal body temperature is 37°C (98.6°F); more than 2°C (4°F) higher is a high fever. A normal adult pulse rate is 60 to 80 beats per minute (children 80 to 100, babies 100 to 140). You should know how to take a temperature and a pulse rate. As a general rule, the pulse increases about 20 beats per minute for each 1°C (2°F) rise in fever.

Respiration rate can also be an indicator of health or illness. Count the number of breaths per minute: Between 12 and 20 is normal for adults and older children (up to 30 for younger children, 40 for babies). People who have a high fever or serious respiratory illness (like pneumonia) breathe more quickly than normal. More than 40 shallow breaths a minute usually means pneumonia.

Many health problems can be avoided by taking care of yourself. Wash your hands frequently – it's quite easy to contaminate your own food. Clean your teeth with purified water rather than water straight from the river. Avoid extremes of temperature – keep out of the sun when it's hot, dress warmly when it's cold.

Some diseases can be avoided by dressing sensibly. Worm infections can be caught by walking barefoot, and dangerous cuts are likely if you walk over dead coral without shoes. (*Never* walk on live coral.) Avoid insect bites by covering bare skin and using insect repellents or a mosquito net at night. Seek local advice – if you're told water is unsafe owing to crocodiles or piranhas, don't go in.

---

altitudes as low as 2500m, and they become increasingly severe the higher you go. Most people are affected to some extent at altitudes between 3500 and 4500m. You may reach these altitudes if trekking in the Andes around Mérida.

The best way to minimize the risk of altitude sickness is to ascend slowly, to increase liquid intake and to eat meals containing energy-rich carbohydrates. Even with acclimatization, however, you may still have trouble if you visit high-altitude areas.

Headaches, nausea, dizziness, a dry cough, breathlessness and loss of appetite are the most frequent symptoms. As long as they remain mild, there's no reason to panic, but the ascent should be halted and the sufferer watched closely and given plenty of fluids and rest. If the symptoms become more pronounced or there is no significant sign of improvement after a few hours, descend to a lower altitude.

Often a descent of a few hundred meters is enough to provide considerable relief. Descend farther and rest for a day or two. Don't take risks with altitude sickness; many people have died because they have ignored the early symptoms and pressed on to higher altitudes.

Altitude sickness is completely unpredictable – youth, fitness and experience at high altitudes are no protection. Even people who have had no problems at high altitudes before may suddenly suffer soroche at relatively low altitudes.

Heat Exhaustion Serious dehydration or salt deficiency can lead to heat exhaustion. Salt deficiency, which can be brought on by diarrhea or vomiting, is characterized by fatigue, lethargy, headaches, giddiness and muscle cramps. Salt tablets may help. The best way to avoid heat exhaustion is by drinking lots of liquids and eating salty foods.

Heatstroke This serious, occasionally fatal, condition can occur if the body's heat-regulating mechanism breaks down and the body temperature rises to dangerous levels. Long, continuous periods of exposure to high temperatures can leave you vulnerable to heatstroke. Alcohol intake and strenuous activity can increase chances of heatstroke, especially among new arrivals to a hot climate.

Symptoms include minimal sweating, a high body temperature (39°C to 41°C or 102°F to 106°F) and a general feeling of being unwell. The skin may become flushed and red. Severe throbbing headaches, decreased coordination, and aggressive or confused behavior may be signs of heat-stroke. Eventually, the victim may become delirious and go into convulsions. Get the victim out of the sun, if possible, remove clothing, cover with a wet towel and fan continuously. Seek medical help as soon as possible.

Hypothermia Too much cold is just as dangerous as too much heat and may lead to hypothermia. There are not many really cold areas in Venezuela, but nonetheless hypothermia can be a threat in the highest reaches of the Andes and, occasionally, on the top of Roraima.

Hypothermia occurs when the body loses heat faster than it can produce it. It is caused by exhaustion and exposure to cold, wet or windy weather. It is surprisingly easy to progress from being very cold to dangerously cold owing to a combination of wind, wet clothing, fatigue and hunger, even if the air temperature is well above freezing.

It is best to dress in layers; silk, wool and some of the new artificial fibers are all good insulating materials. A hat is important because a lot of heat is lost through the head. A strong, waterproof outer layer is essential, and keeping dry is vital. Carry food containing simple sugars to generate heat quickly, and lots of fluid to drink.

Symptoms of hypothermia include exhaustion, numb skin (particularly toes and fingers), shivering, slurred speech, irrational or violent behavior, lethargy, stumbling, dizzy spells, muscle cramps and violent bursts of energy.

To treat hypothermia, get sufferers out of the wind or rain, remove wet clothing and replace it with dry, warm garments. Give them hot liquids – not alcohol – and easily digestible food. This should be enough for the early stages of hypothermia, but if it has gone further, it may be necessary to place sufferers in a sleeping bag and get in with them in order to provide as much warmth as possible.

If no improvement is noticed within a few minutes, seek help, but don't leave the victim alone while doing so. The body heat of another person is more important in the short term than medical attention.

Jet Lag Jet lag is experienced when a person travels by air across more than three time zones (each time zone usually represents a one-hour time difference). It occurs because many of the functions of the human body (such as temperature, pulse rate and emptying of the bladder and bowels) are regulated by internal 24-hour cycles. When you travel long distances rapidly, your body takes time to adjust to the 'new time' of your destination, and you may experience fatigue, disorientation, insomnia, anxiety, impaired concentration and loss of appetite. These effects will usually be gone within three days of arrival, but take the following steps to minimize the impact of jet lag:

• Rest for a couple of days prior to departure.

• Try to select flight schedules that minimize sleep deprivation; arriving late in the day means you can go to sleep soon after you arrive.

• Avoid excessive eating (which bloats the stomach) and alcohol (which causes dehydration) during the flight. Instead, drink plenty of noncarbonated, nonalcoholic drinks, such as fruit juice or water.

• Avoid smoking.

• Make yourself comfortable by wearing loose-fitting clothes and perhaps bringing an eye mask and earplugs to help you sleep.

• Try to sleep at the appropriate time for the time zone of your destination.

Motion Sickness If you are prone to motion sickness, try to choose a place that minimizes disturbance – near the wing on an aircraft, midship on a boat, or between the front and the middle of a bus. Eating lightly before and during a trip will reduce the chances of motion sickness. Fresh air almost always helps, while reading or cigarette smoking makes matters worse.

Commercial motion-sickness preparations, which can cause drowsiness, have to be taken before the trip; if you're already feeling sick, it's too late. Dramamine tablets, one of the most popular medications, should be taken three hours before departure. Ginger can be used as a natural preventative and is available in capsule form.

Prickly Heat This is an itchy rash caused by excessive perspiration trapped under the skin. It usually strikes people who have just arrived in a hot climate and whose pores have not yet opened sufficiently to cope with increased sweating. Frequent baths and the application of talcum powder will help relieve the itchiness.

Sunburn The sun's rays in tropical zones are more direct and concentrated than in temperate zones. In highland areas, such as the Andean region, you will be additionally exposed to hazardous UV rays and can become sunburned surprisingly quickly, even through clouds. Use sunscreen and take extra care to cover areas that are not normally exposed to sunlight – for example, your feet. A hat provides added protection, and sunglasses will prevent eye irritation (especially if you wear contact lenses).

Infectious Diseases

Diarrhea Simple things like a change of water, food or climate can all cause a mild bout of diarrhea, but a few rushed toilet trips with no other symptoms is not indicative of a major problem.

Dehydration is the main danger with any diarrhea – particularly in children or the elderly, as dehydration can occur quite quickly. Under all circumstances, fluid replacement (at least equal to the volume being lost) is the most important thing to remember. Lightly sugared weak black tea, soda water, or soft drinks allowed to go flat and diluted 50% with clean water are all good. With severe diarrhea, a rehydrating solution is preferable to replace minerals and salts lost. Commercially available oral rehydration salts (ORS) are useful; add them to boiled or bottled water. In an emergency you can make up a solution of six teaspoons of sugar and a half teaspoon of salt to a liter of boiled or bottled water. You need to drink at least the same volume of fluid that you are losing in bowel movements and vomiting. Urine is the best guide to the adequacy of replacement – if you have small amounts of concentrated urine, you need to drink more. Keep drinking small amounts often. Stick to a bland diet as you recover.

Lomotil or Imodium can be used to bring relief from the symptoms, although they do not actually cure the problem. Only use these drugs if you do not have access to toilets – for example, if you must travel. For children under 12 years old, Lomotil and Imodium are not recommended. Do not use these drugs if the person has a high fever or is severely dehydrated.

In certain situations, antibiotics may be required: diarrhea with blood or mucus (dysentery), any fever, watery diarrhea with fever and lethargy, persistent diarrhea not improving after 48 hours and severe diarrhea. In these situations, gut-paralyzing drugs like Imodium or Lomotil should be avoided.

A stool test is necessary to diagnose which kind of dysentery you have, so you should seek medical help urgently. Where this is not possible, the recommended drugs for dysentery are 400mg norfloxacin twice daily for three days or 500mg ciprofloxacin twice daily for five days. These are not recommended for children or pregnant women. The drug of choice for children would be co-trimoxazole (Bactrim, Septrin, Resprim), with dosage dependent on weight. A five-day course is given. Ampicillin or amoxycillin may be given in pregnancy, but medical care is necessary.

Amoebic dysentery is more gradual in the onset of symptoms, with cramping abdominal pain and vomiting less likely; fever may not be present. It will persist until treated and can recur and cause other health problems.

Giardiasis is another type of diarrhea. The parasite causing this intestinal disorder is present in contaminated water. The symptoms are stomach cramps, nausea, a bloated stomach, watery foul-smelling diarrhea and frequent gas. Giardiasis can appear several weeks after you have been exposed to the parasite. The symptoms may disappear for a few days and then return; this can go on for several weeks. Tinidazole, known as Fasigyn,

or metronidazole (Flagyl) are the recommended drugs. Treatment is a 2g single dose of Fasigyn or 250mg of Flagyl three times daily for five to 10 days.

Cholera This disease is transmitted orally by the ingestion of contaminated food or water. The symptoms, which appear one to three days after infection, consist of a sudden onset of acute diarrhea with rice-water stools, vomiting, muscular cramps and extreme weakness. You need medical attention, but your first concern should be rehydration. Drink as much water as you can – if it refuses to stay down, keep drinking anyway. If there is likely to be a considerable delay in getting medical treatment, begin a course of Tetracycline, but that should not be administered to children or pregnant women.

Fungal Infections These infections occur more commonly in hot weather and are most likely to be found between the toes or fingers or around the groin. They are spread by infected animals or humans; you may contract them by walking barefoot in damp areas, for example. Moisture encourages fungal infections.

To prevent these infections, wear loose, comfortable clothes, avoid artificial fibers, wash frequently and dry thoroughly. Use thong sandals (flip-flops) while taking a shower in the bathrooms of cheap hotels.

If you become infected, wash the infected area daily with a disinfectant or medicated soap, and rinse and dry well. Apply an antifungal cream or powder like tolnifate (Tinaderm). Try to expose the infected area to air or sunlight as much as possible, change all towels and underwear often, wash them in hot water and let them dry in the sun.

Hepatitis A general term for inflammation of the liver, hepatitis is a common disease worldwide. The symptoms are fever, chills, headache, fatigue, feelings of weakness and aches and pains, followed by loss of appetite, nausea, vomiting, abdominal pain, dark urine, light-colored feces and jaundiced (yellow) skin. The whites of the eyes may turn yellow.

The most common strain is Hepatitis A, which is transmitted by contaminated food and drinking water. If you contract it, you should seek medical advice, but there is not much you can do apart from resting, drinking lots of fluids, eating lightly and avoiding fatty foods. People who have had hepatitis should avoid alcohol for some time after the illness, as the liver needs time to recover. Hepatitis E is transmitted in the same way as Hepatitis A and can be particularly serious in pregnant women.

The next most common strain worldwide, Hepatitis B, is spread through contact with infected blood, blood products or body fluids – for example, through sexual contact, unsterilized needles and blood transfusions, or contact with blood via small breaks in the skin. Other risk situations include being shaved, getting a tattoo or having your body pierced with contaminated equipment. The symptoms of Hepatitis B may be more severe than type A, and the disease can lead to long-term problems, such as chronic liver damage or liver cancer. Hepatitis C and D are spread in the same way as type B and can also lead to long-term complications.

There are vaccines against Hepatitis A and B, but there are currently no vaccines against other types.

HIV & AIDS As almost everywhere else, these diseases have become a concern in Venezuela. Although there are no credible statistics, it's estimated that at least 100,000 Venezuelans are HIV-positive. HIV (Human Immunodeficiency Virus) is likely to develop into AIDS (Acquired Immune Deficiency Syndrome).

Any exposure to blood, blood products or body fluids may put the individual at risk. The disease is often transmitted through sexual contact, and in South America it's transmitted primarily through contact between heterosexuals.

HIV and AIDS can also be contracted through infected blood transfusions, and you should be aware that not all the hospitals screen blood supplies. The virus may also be picked up through injection with an unsterilized needle. Acupuncture, tattooing and body piercing are other potential dangers. There is currently no cure for AIDS.

Intestinal Worms These parasites are common in most humid, tropical areas. They can be present on unwashed vegetables or in undercooked meat, or you can pick them up through your skin by walking barefoot. Infestations may not show up for some time, and although they are generally not serious, they can cause further health problems if left untreated. A stool test upon your return home is not a bad idea if you think you may have contracted them. Once the test pinpoints the problem, medication is usually available over the counter, and treatment is easy and short.

The most common form you're likely to contract are hookworms. They are usually caught by walking barefoot on infected soil. The worms bore through the skin, attach themselves to the inner wall of the intestine and proceed to suck your blood, resulting in abdominal pain and sometimes anemia.

Rabies Rabies, caused by a bite or scratch from an infected animal, is present in most of South America. Bats and dogs are the most notorious carriers. Any bite, scratch or lick from a mammal should be cleaned immediately and thoroughly. Scrub the area with soap and running water, and then clean it with an alcohol solution. If there is any possibility that the animal is infected, seek medical help. Even if the animal is not rabid, all bites should be treated carefully, because they can become infected or result in tetanus. Avoid any animal that appears to be foaming at the mouth or acting strangely. If bitten, try to capture the offending animal for testing. If that's impossible, you must assume the animal is rabid. Rabies is fatal if untreated, so don't take the risk. Medical attention should not be delayed.

A rabies vaccination is now available and should be considered if you intend to spend a lot of time around animals.

Health Glossary

This basic glossary of illnesses and other health-related terms may be useful. See the Language chapter, near the end of the book, for emergency terms and phrases.

abortion – *aborto*
AIDS – *SIDA (síndrome de inmunideficiencia adquirida)*
allergy – *alergia*
altitude sickness – *soroche*
antibiotic – *antibiótico*
bite – *picadura* (insect, snake), *mordedura* (dog)
blood – *sangre*
blood test – *examen de sangre*
cholera – *cólera*
cold or flu – *gripe*
condom – *condón*
contraceptive pills – *pastillas anticonceptivas*
cough – *tos*
cramp (menstrual) – *cólico*
cramp (muscular) – *calambre*
cut – *cortadura, cortada*
diarrhea – *diarrea*
disease – *enfermedad*
dizziness – *mareo*
dysentery – *disentería*
earache – *otitis, dolor de oído*
fatigue – *fatiga, cansancio*
fever – *fiebre*
headache – *dolor de cabeza*
health – *salud*
heart attack – *ataque cardíaco, infarto*
heatstroke – *insolación*
hepatitis – *hepatitis*
HIV – *VIH (virus de inmunodeficiencia humana)*

infection – *infección*
injection – *inyección*
insurance – *seguro*
itching – *ardor*
malaria – *malaria*
medication – *droga, medicamento, remedio*
miscarriage – *aborto*
nausea – *náusea*
pain – *dolor*
penicillin – *penicilina*
pneumonia – *neumonía*
polio – *polio*
pregnancy – *embarazo*
prescription – *receta, fórmula*
rabies – *rabia*
rash – *escozor, rasquiña*
sore throat – *dolor de garganta*
stomach – *estómago*
sunburn – *quemadura de sol*
symptom – *síntoma*
syringe – *jeringa*
tablets – *pastillas*
tetanus – *tétano*
toothache – *dolor de muelas*
typhoid – *fiebre tifoidea*
vaccination – *vacuna*
vomiting – *vómito*
weakness – *debilidad*
wound – *herida*
yellow fever – *fiebre amarilla*

Schistosomiasis Also known as bilharzia, this disease is carried in water by minute worms. It is found in rivers and streams in northern central Venezuela. The worm enters through the skin and attaches itself to your intestines or bladder.

The first symptom may be tingling and sometimes a light rash around the area where it entered. Weeks later, a high fever may develop. A general feeling of being unwell may be the first symptom, or there may be no symptoms. Once the disease is established, abdominal pain and blood in the urine are other signs. The infection often causes no symptoms until the disease is well established (several months to years after exposure) and damage to internal organs is irreversible.

The main method of preventing the disease is to avoid swimming or bathing in fresh water where bilharzia is present. Even deep water can be infected. If you do get wet, dry off quickly and dry your clothes as well.

A blood test is the most reliable procedure to determine infection, but it will not show positive until a number of weeks after exposure.

Sexually Transmitted Diseases Sexual contact with an infected partner can result in your contracting a number of diseases. While abstinence is the only 100% effective prevention, the use of condoms lessens the risk of infection considerably.

The most common sexually transmitted diseases are gonorrhea and syphilis, which in men first appear as sores, blisters or rashes around the genitals and a discharge or pain when urinating. Symptoms may be less marked or not present at all in women. Syphilis' symptoms eventually disappear, but the disease continues and may cause severe problems in later years. Gonorrhea and syphilis are treatable with antibiotics.

Tetanus This potentially fatal disease is difficult to treat but is easily prevented by immunization. Tetanus occurs when a wound becomes infected by a germ that lives in soil and in the feces of horses and other animals. It enters the body via breaks in the skin, so the best prevention is to clean all wounds promptly and thoroughly with an antiseptic. Use antibiotics if the wound becomes hot or throbs, or if pus is seen. The first symptom may be discomfort in swallowing, or stiffening of the jaw and neck; this can be followed by painful convulsions of the jaw and whole body.

Typhoid This is a gut infection that travels via contaminated water and food. Vaccination against typhoid is not 100% effective, and since it is one of the most dangerous infections, medical attention is necessary if you are infected. Early symptoms are similar to those of many other travelers' illnesses – you may feel as though you have a bad cold or the flu combined with a headache, a sore throat and a fever. The fever rises a little each day until it exceeds 40°C (104°F), while the pulse rate slows – unlike a normal fever, when the pulse increases. These symptoms may be accompanied by vomiting, diarrhea or constipation.

In the second week, the high fever and slow pulse continue, and a few pink spots may appear on the body. Trembling, delirium, weakness, weight loss and dehydration set in. If there are no further complications, the fever and other symptoms will slowly fade during the third week. Medical attention is essential, however, since typhoid is extremely infectious, and possible complications include pneumonia or peritonitis (burst appendix).

When feverish, the patient should be kept cool and watch for dehydration. The recommended antibiotic is Chloramphenicol.

Insect-Borne Diseases

Malaria This serious and potentially fatal disease is spread by anopheles mosquito bites. If you are traveling in endemic areas, it is important to avoid mosquito bites and to take antimalarial tablets. Symptoms range from fever, chills and sweating, headache, diarrhea and abdominal pains to a vague feeling of ill health. Seek medical help immediately if malaria is suspected. Again, without treatment, malaria can rapidly become more serious and can be fatal.

If medical care is not available, malaria tablets can be used for treatment. You need to use a medication different from the one you were taking when you contracted malaria. The treatment dosages are mefloquine (two 250mg tablets and another two six hours later) or fansidar (single dose of three tablets). If you were previously taking mefloquine, then alternatives are halofantrine (three doses of two 250mg tablets every six hours) or quinine sulfate (600mg taken every six hours). There's a greater risk of side effects with these dosages than in normal use, so medical advice is preferable.

Antimalarial tablets are not 100% effective, so the primary prevention should always be to avoid mosquito bites. The mosquitoes that transmit malaria bite from dusk to dawn, but it's best to take precautions at all times. These include:

- Wear light-colored clothing.
- Wear long trousers and long-sleeved shirts.
- Use mosquito repellents containing the compound DEET on exposed areas (but remember that it may decrease the efficacy of sunblock).
- Avoid highly scented perfumes or aftershaves.
- Use a mosquito net – it may be worth bringing your own – and consider spraying it with some insecticide.

Mosquitoes are prevalent throughout Venezuela and can live at altitudes of up to about 3000m. However, the Anopheles mosquito is mostly confined to lowland areas. The risk of infection is higher during the wet season. The areas of greatest risk include Amazonas, Los Llanos and the Delta del Orinoco.

The symptoms of malaria appear only several weeks after contraction, which may lead to confusion in diagnosis. By the time symptoms appear, you may be home and local doctors will not be looking for such an exotic disease. Make sure you give your doctor details of your trip. Malaria can be diagnosed by a simple blood test.

Dengue Fever This serious disease is a rapidly growing problem in tropical South America. The *Aedes aegypti* mosquito, which transmits the dengue virus, is most active during the day and is found mainly in urban areas, in and around human dwellings.

Signs and symptoms of dengue fever include a sudden onset of high fever, headache, joint and muscle pains, nausea and vomiting, and sometimes a rash of small red spots appearing three to four days after the onset of fever.

In the early phase, dengue may be mistaken for other diseases, including malaria and influenza. Later it can progress to the potentially fatal dengue hemorrhagic fever (DHF), a severe illness characterized by heavy bleeding. Full recovery even from simple dengue fever may be prolonged, with fatigue lasting for several weeks.

If you think you may be infected, seek medical attention quickly. A blood test can exclude malaria and indicate the possibility of dengue fever, for which there is no spe-

cific treatment. Aspirin should be avoided, as it increases the risk of hemorrhaging.

There is no vaccine against dengue fever. The best prevention is to avoid mosquito bites at all times, as for malaria.

Yellow Fever This viral disease is found in most of South America, except for the Andean highlands and the southern part of the continent. Yellow fever, which is transmitted by mosquitoes, first manifests itself as fever, headaches, abdominal pain and vomiting. There may appear to be a brief recovery before it progresses into its more severe stages, including possible liver failure. There is no treatment apart from keeping the fever as low as possible and avoiding dehydration. The yellow-fever vaccination gives good protection for 10 years and is highly recommended for every person traveling on the continent.

Typhus This illness is spread by ticks, mites and lice. It begins as a severe cold followed by a fever, chills, headaches, muscle pains and a body rash. There is often a large and painful sore at the site of the bite, and nearby lymph nodes will become painfully swollen.

Trekkers may be at risk from wild-game or cattle ticks. Seek local advice about whether or not ticks are present in the area and check yourself carefully after walking in suspect areas. A strong insect repellent can help.

Cuts, Bites & Stings
Cuts & Scratches In warm, moist, tropical lowlands, skin punctures can easily become infected and may have difficulty healing. Even a small cut or scratch can become infected, which can lead to serious problems.

The best treatment for cuts is to cleanse the affected area frequently with soap and water and to apply an antiseptic cream. Whenever possible, avoid using bandages, which keep wounds moist and encourage the growth of bacteria. If the wound becomes tender and inflamed, use a mild, broad spectrum antibiotic. Remember that bacterial immunity to certain antibiotics may build up, so it's not wise to take these medicines indiscriminately or as a preventative measure.

Coral cuts are notoriously slow to heal because coral injects a weak venom into the wound. Avoid coral cuts by never walking on reefs.

Bites & Stings The plethora of ants, gnats, mosquitoes, bees, spiders, flies and other exotic creatures living in Venezuela means that you may experience a variety of bites and stings. Some are more dangerous or annoying than others, but it's best to protect yourself from bites altogether. Cover your skin, especially from dusk to dawn, when many insects, such as malaria-transmitting mosquitoes, feed. The problem is more serious in rural areas than in cities, and dense rain forests are probably the worst.

Wear long-sleeved shirts and long pants (trousers) instead of T-shirts and shorts, and wear shoes instead of sandals. Use insect repellent on exposed skin and, if necessary, spray it over your clothes. Sleep under a mosquito net if you are outdoors or if your hotel room does not have a sufficiently strong fan. Burning incense also lowers the risk. Good repellents, mosquito nets and incense are available in Venezuela.

If you are bitten, avoid scratching, as this easily opens bites and may cause them to become infected. Use creams and lotions that alleviate itching and deal with infection; they are sold in local pharmacies.

Bee and wasp stings are usually more painful than dangerous. Calamine lotion will give some relief, and ice packs will reduce the pain and swelling.

Body lice and scabies mites are common, but shampoos and creams are available to eliminate them. In addition to hair and skin, clothing and bedding should be washed thoroughly to prevent further infestation.

Bedbugs love to live in the dirty mattresses and bedding of seedy hotels. If you see spots of blood on bedclothes, look for another hotel. Bedbugs leave itchy bites; calamine lotion may help alleviate them.

Leeches may be present in damp rain forests. They attach themselves to your skin and suck your blood. Trekkers may get them on their legs or in their boots. Salt or a lighted cigarette end will make them fall off. Do not pull them off, because the bite is more likely to become infected and the head of the leech can remain in your body. An insect repellent may keep them away.

Vaseline, alcohol or oil will persuade a tick to let go. You should always check your body if you have been walking through a tick-infested area, because ticks can spread typhus. They like the warmest parts of the body and often go to the genital area or the armpits, so be sure to inspect all of these areas.

It's rather unlikely that you'll get stung by a scorpion or a spider, but if you do, it may be severely painful (though rarely more than that). They tend to shelter in shoes and clothing, so check them before putting them on. Also, check your bedding or sleeping bag before going to sleep.

Snakebite There's only a small chance of being bitten by a snake in Venezuela, but you should take precautions. To minimize the chances of being bitten, wear boots, socks and long pants (trousers) when walking through undergrowth. A good pair of canvas gaiters will further protect your legs. Don't put your hands into holes and crevices, and be careful when collecting firewood. Check shoes, clothing and sleeping bags before use.

Snakebites do not cause instantaneous death, and antivenins are available. If someone is bitten, it's vital that you identify the snake immediately, or at the very least, are able to describe it. Keep the victim calm and still, wrap the bitten limb tightly, as you would a sprain, then attach a splint to immobilize it. Seek medical help immediately and, if possible, bring the dead snake along for identification.

Don't attempt to catch the snake if there is a chance of being bitten again. Tourniquets and sucking out the poison are now comprehensively discredited.

For those who plan on a serious expedition into the wilderness, antivenins for some local snakes (but not all) can be bought at Universidad Central de Venezuela (UCV) in Caracas. Antivenins must be kept at a low temperature; otherwise their efficiency quickly decreases. It's a good idea to carry a field guide with photographs and detailed descriptions of snakes.

Women's Health
Antibiotic use, synthetic underwear, sweating and contraceptive pills can lead to fungal vaginal infections when travelling in hot climates. Maintaining good personal hygiene and wearing loose-fitting clothes and cotton underwear will help prevent these infections.

Fungal infections, characterized by a rash, itch and discharge, can be treated with a vinegar or lemon-juice douche, or with yogurt. Nystatin, miconazole or clotrimazole pessaries or vaginal cream are the usual treatment.

Sexually transmitted diseases are a major cause of vaginal problems. Symptoms include a pungent discharge, painful intercourse and sometimes a burning sensation when urinating. Male sexual partners must also be treated. Medical attention should be sought. Remember that in addition to these diseases, HIV or hepatitis B may also be acquired from sexual contact. Besides abstinence, the best thing is to practice safe sex using condoms.

Women who are pregnant need to take especial care while on the road. Most miscarriages occur during the first three months of pregnancy, so this is the most risky time to travel. The last three months should also be spent within reasonable reach of good medical care, because serious problems can develop at this stage. Pregnant women should avoid all unnecessary medication, but vaccinations and malarial prophylactics should still be taken when possible. Additional care should be taken to prevent illness, and particular attention should be paid to diet and nutrition.

It is also worth noting that the use of antibiotics significantly affects the effectiveness of birth-control pills.

Back Home
Be aware of illnesses after you return home; take note of odd or persistent symptoms of any kind, get a check-up and remember to give your physician a complete travel history. Most doctors in temperate climates will not be looking for unusual tropical diseases. If you have been traveling in malarial areas, have yourself tested for the disease.

WOMEN TRAVELERS
Like most of Latin America, Venezuela is very much a man's country. Machismo and sexism are palpable throughout society, so it's not difficult to imagine how a gringa traveling by herself is regarded.

Women travelers will attract more curiosity, attention and advances from local men than they would from men in the west. Many Venezuelan men will stare at women, use endearing terms, make comments on their physical appearance and, in some cases, try to make physical contact. It is just the Latin American way of life, and local males would not understand if someone told them that their behavior constituted sexual harassment. On the contrary, they would argue that they are just paying the woman a flattering compliment.

Gringas are often seen as exotic and challenging conquests. Local males will quickly pick them out in a crowd and use a combination of body language and flirtatiousness to capture their attention. These advances may often be lighthearted but can sometimes be more direct and rude.

Men in large cities, especially when they are in male-only groups, and particularly when they are drunk, will generally display more bravado and be more insistent than those in small villages. Male travelers also have reported that they have felt hassled by Venezuelan women, who are seen as being rather sexually aggressive.

The best way to deal with unwanted attention is usually to ignore it. Maintain your self-confidence and assertiveness and don't let macho behavior disrupt your holiday. Dressing modestly may lessen the chances of you being the object of macho interest, or at least make you less conspicuous to the local peacocks. Wearing a wedding band and carrying a photo of a make-believe spouse may minimize harassment.

Don't follow local fashions in dressing. Most Venezuelan women are dressed up and beautifully turned out – whether it is on the beach or the bus. You can guarantee they will wear lots of makeup, high heels and plenty of gold, silver and bright colors on usually skintight clothes.

Harassment aside, women traveling alone face more risks than men. Rape is a potential danger. Women are often targets for bag-snatchers and assault, but female travelers need not walk around Venezuela in a constant state of fear. Just be conscious of your surroundings and aware of situations that could be dangerous. Shabby barrios, solitary streets and beaches, and all places considered male territory, such as bars, sports events, mines and construction sites, should be considered risky. Do not hitchhike alone.

There isn't much in the way of women's support services in Venezuela, let alone resources specifically for women travelers. Books that might be worth looking at before the trip include the *Handbook for Women Travelers,* by Maggie & Jemma Moss, and *Women Travel – Adventures, Advice & Experience,* by Natania Jansz & Miranda Davies.

GAY & LESBIAN TRAVELERS

Homosexuality isn't illegal in Venezuela, but the overwhelmingly Catholic society tends to both deny and suppress it. The gay and lesbian movement is still very underdeveloped. Caracas has the largest gay and lesbian community and the most open gay life, and is therefore the best place to make contacts and get to know what's going on. Get as much information there as you can, because elsewhere in Venezuela, it can be difficult to contact the community.

Caracas' contact links include the Movimiento Ambiente de Venezuela (☎ 02-321 94 70) and the *En Ambiente* gay 'what's on' guide (☎ 014-219 18 37, enambiente@ latinmail.com). You may also check local

gay Web sites, including www.gayvenezuela .com and www.republicagay.com (these Web sites are in Spanish).

Gay bars, discos and other venues are limited to the larger cities, but because of social pressures they come and go frequently. Again, Caracas offers the largest choice. See that chapter for some gay hangouts.

DISABLED TRAVELERS

Venezuela offers very little to people with disabilities. Wheelchair ramps are available only at a few upmarket hotels and restaurants, and public transportation will be a challenge for any person with mobility problems. Hardly any office, museum or bank provides special facilities for disabled travelers, and wheelchair-accessible toilets are virtually nonexistent.

Much to blame for the lack of any infrastructure is the general perception of disabled people. The relatively enlightened attitudes toward disability that prevail in many western countries haven't yet taken hold in Venezuela. Here, as in much of the developing world, people with visible disabilities are expected to beg, sell lottery tickets on the street, or stay at home. They are generally not perceived as capable of living a normal active life, let alone handling the rigors of traveling.

Organizations

Disabled travelers in the USA might wish to contact the Society for the Advancement of Travel for the Handicapped (☎ 212-447 7284; fax 725 8253), 347 Fifth Ave, Suite 610, New York, NY 10016. In the UK, a useful contact is the Royal Association for Disability & Rehabilitation (☎ 020-7242 3882), 25 Mortimer St, London W1N 8AB. You may also be interested in picking up *Nothing Ventured: Disabled People Travel the World,* which provides helpful general advice.

SENIOR TRAVELERS

By and large, senior travelers may often expect more respect and help from locals than young visitors. This attitude doesn't necessarily prevail with some attendants in shops, bank tellers and employees of public institutions. The difference in attitudes toward the youth and elderly is likely to be more pronounced among rural communities.

As far as discounts go, senior travelers get reductions on airfares with some airlines, but that's about it. So far, there are no discounts for senior citizens on bus fares, accommodation rates, cinema and theater tickets etc.

TRAVEL WITH CHILDREN

As do most Latin Americans, Venezuelans adore children. Owing to a high rate of population growth, children are a significant proportion of the population, and they are omnipresent. Few foreigners travel with children in Venezuela, but if you do plan on taking along your offspring, he or she will easily find plenty of local companions.

Children enjoy numerous privileges on local transportation and in accommodations and entertainment. Age limits for particular freebies or discounts vary from place to place but are rarely rigidly enforced. Free rides on buses and the Caracas metro formally mean that the child doesn't occupy a separate seat, but this is not always the case.

Basic supplies are usually no problem in the cities. There are quite a few shops devoted to kids' clothes, shoes and toys, and you can buy disposable diapers (nappies) and baby food in supermarkets and pharmacies. Health is a bit more of a problem, given numerous potential hazards (see Health, earlier in this chapter). For general suggestions on how to make a trip with kids easier, pick up the current edition of Lonely Planet's *Travel with Children,* by Maureen Wheeler.

DANGERS & ANNOYANCES

Venezuela is a relatively safe country to travel in, though robbery is becoming more common every day, and violent crime is on the increase in large cities. Caracas is by far the most dangerous place in the country, and you should take serious care while strolling about the streets, particularly at night. Elsewhere, you can travel more peacefully, but you should nonetheless always observe basic precautions and use common sense.

This section covers a variety of potential dangers and may look alarming, but don't panic; the intention is not to frighten you, but to demonstrate how many things you can do to prevent mishap.

Predeparture Precautions

When choosing things for your trip, try to take only those items that you are prepared to lose, such as used clothes, a cheap watch or an ordinary raincoat. Take as little as possible, because the less you carry with you, the less you have to lose. Don't bring jewelry, chains or anything flashy – this will only increase the chances of robbery. Don't bring anything of such sentimental value that its loss would cause significant grief. If you have to take an expensive item (such as a camera), try to make sure it's a standard model that is easy to replace.

The only guarantee of replacement is to have travel insurance. A good policy is essential for two reasons – it gives you peace of mind while traveling, and it gives you the actual security of replacement if something is lost (touch wood). Loss through violence or petty theft is always a stressful experience, but an insurance policy can relieve some of the pain.

If you are careful about choosing what you take, you'll find there is only a handful of items that you really wouldn't like to lose, including money, documents, your passport and air tickets. Keep these items as secure as possible (see Security in the Money section, earlier in this chapter). Make photocopies of your documents (see Copies in the Visas & Documents section, also in this chapter).

It's best if your backpack is fitted with double zippers, which can be secured with small combination locks. Padlocks are also good, but are easier to pick. A thick backpack cover or modified canvas sack improves protection against pilfering, the planting of drugs, and general wear and tear. A spare combination lock or padlock is useful for replacing the padlocks on your hotel door.

A swanky camera bag is not a good idea; take something less conspicuous. Many travelers carry their photographic equipment in daypacks. If you have a choice, bring a plain daypack rather than one that is a fluorescent orange or purple. If you wear glasses, secure them with an elastic strap to prevent them from falling off and breaking, and to deter petty theft.

Traveling with a friend or two is theoretically always safer than traveling on one's own. An extra pair of eyes makes a lot of difference.

Precautions While Traveling

First, don't put all your eggs in one basket; distribute your valuables about your person and luggage to avoid the risk of losing everything in one fell swoop. It's a good idea to carry a small emergency packet containing important records of your passport, checks, credit cards, tickets etc plus a few US$20 bills. While keeping the packet separately in a safe place – for example, sewn inside your trousers – always keep in mind that good-looking, expensive clothes are also appreciated by robbers.

Try not to attract the attention of thieves and robbers. Your dress is an important piece of information for them. One rule that works quite well in risky areas is the shabbier you look, the better, but use common sense and wear more decent clothes in less dangerous places. Your dress should be casual and inexpensive.

If you carry a daypack, it's safer to wear it strapped to your front rather than your back, so you can keep a constant eye on it. Many local youths now carry their packs that way, particularly in Caracas, so you won't stand out in a crowd. If you carry a handbag, keep it in the hand away from the street – there have been some reports about purse-snatchers in Caracas operating from motorcycles.

If you're in a bus terminal, restaurant, shop or any other public place and have to put your daypack down, put your foot through the strap. If you have a camera, don't wander around with it dangling over your shoulder or around your neck – keep it out of sight as much as possible. In genuinely risky areas, you shouldn't carry your camera at all. If you absolutely have to, camouflage it the best you can – an ordinary plastic bag from a local supermarket is one possible disguise.

Behave confidently when you're on the street; don't look lost or stand with a blank expression in the middle of the road or in front of the bus terminal. Helpless-looking tourists are favorite targets of thieves and robbers.

Before arriving in a new place, make sure you have a map or at least a rough idea about orientation. Try to plan your schedule so you don't arrive at night, and use a taxi if this seems the appropriate way to avoid walking through risky areas. Be vigilant and learn to move like a street-smart local.

Keep your eyes open while you're leaving the hotel, bank, casa de cambio, ATM etc. (We've had some reports about muggers targeting ATM users in Caracas.) Look around to see whether there is anyone watching you, and if you notice you're being followed or closely observed, let them understand that you are aware and alert.

If you happen to be in a crowded place (urban bus, market, bus terminal, busy street etc) keep a close eye on your pockets and daypack. Even if you have a cheap watch, it's better to keep it in your pocket rather than on your wrist – it attracts unwanted attention.

On intercity bus journeys, put your backpack in the luggage compartment, where it will be relatively safe. Don't put your daypack or handbag on the floor or on the luggage rack – keep it under your arm next to you or, if you are with a companion, wedge it between the two of you. On long nighttime bus rides, it is better if one of your party is awake.

Theft & Scams

Theft is the most common travelers' danger. Generally speaking, the problem is more serious in the largest cities, with Caracas being the worst. The more rural the area, the quieter and safer it is. Favorite settings for thieves are crowded places such as markets, festivals and fiestas, bus terminals and buses (both long-distance and urban).

The most common methods of theft are snatching your daypack, camera or watch; pocket picking; or taking advantage of a moment's inattention to pick up your gear and run away. Distraction is often part of the thieves' strategy.

Thieves often work in pairs or groups; one or more will distract you while an accomplice does the deed. There are hundreds, if not thousands, of possible ways to distract you, and new scams are dreamt up every day. Here are some common ones: Someone 'accidentally' bumps into you (sometimes throwing you off balance); a group of strangers appear in front of you and greet you jovially as if you were lifelong friends; a woman drops her shopping bag right at your feet; a character spills something on your clothes or your daypack; several kids start a fight around you. Try not to get distracted – of course, it's easier said than done.

Some thieves are even more innovative and will set up an opportune situation to separate you from your belongings. They may begin by making friends with you, or by pretending to be the police and demanding to check your belongings. Their imagination is infinite in this respect, so keep your wits about you. Stay aware of changes and innovations by talking to other travelers on the road.

Mugging

Mugging is far more dangerous than theft. Armed holdups can happen anywhere in Venezuela, on the beach or in a town, but they are most frequent in Caracas. Sadly, they have become more and more common over the last several years. The favorite places for robbery are slum areas, but some Caracas gangs now comfortably work in the central districts during daylight hours. The usual weapon is a knife, but guns are not unheard of.

The assault usually goes something like this: You are stopped on the street by a man or, more often, a group of men; they show you a knife or gun and either ask for your money and valuables or set about searching for themselves. Even if they don't show you their arms, you can take it for granted that they have them. They will usually be satisfied with your daypack, watch and a bundle of currency notes you keep in your pocket for daily expenditure, but some more determined criminals may keep searching, trying to get to your money belt. If this is the case, it's best to give them whatever they are after. Don't try to escape or struggle – your chances are slim. Don't count on any help from passersby.

Police

Cases of police corruption, abuse of power and use of undue authority have been documented, so it's probably best to stay a safe distance from them if you don't need them, just in case. This, of course, doesn't mean that they will stay away from you.

In the cities, ID checks by the police are not common, but they do occur, so always have your passport with you. If you don't, you may end up at the police station. By law, you must carry your passport with you at all times. A certified photocopy of the passport is not a legal identity document, although some police officers may be satisfied with it.

While traveling in the countryside, you'll experience plenty of stops at *alcabalas* (road checkpoints operated by the police or, more often, by the Guardia Nacional). They stop and control traffic, including cars, trucks and public buses. They then check the identity documents of the driver and passengers and, sometimes, search their luggage.

If your passport, valuables or other belongings are stolen, go to the nearest PTJ (Policía Técnica Judicial) office to make a *denuncia* (report). The officer on duty will write a statement according to what you tell them. It should include the description of the events and the list of stolen articles. Pay attention to the wording you use, make sure you include every stolen item and document, and carefully check the statement before signing it to ensure it contains exactly what you've said. They will give you a copy of the statement, which serves as a temporary identity document, and you will need to present it to your insurer in order to make a claim. Don't expect your things to be found, as the police are unlikely to even try to do anything about it. Stolen cars and motorcycles should also be reported at the PTJ.

If you happen to get involved with the police, keep calm and be polite, but not overly friendly. Don't get angry or hostile – it only works against you.

Be wary of criminals masquerading as plainclothes police. They may stop you on the street, identify themselves with a fake ID, then request to inspect your passport and money. If you follow suit, forget about your stuff. If you hesitate, the 'officers' may try to persuade you to go with them to the 'police station' in their car or in a taxi (which are, of course, as genuine as the officers themselves), and probably will clean you out in the vehicle. Under no circumstances should you agree to a search or a ride. Call a uniformed police officer, if there happens to be one around, or decent-looking passersby to witness the incident, and insist on phoning a bona fide police station. By that time, the 'officers' will probably walk discreetly away.

This scam is still rare in Venezuela, but it's well known in other South American countries, including Colombia, and, unfortunately, this sort of disease spreads quickly over the borders.

Drugs

The presence of Colombian cocaine in Venezuela is on the rise. Drugs pass through Venezuela en route to US and European destinations. The number of locals involved in drug trafficking is increasing, and so is corruption and other crimes that accompany this illicit business. Fortunately, planting drugs on tourists in order to extort bribes hasn't, as yet, been reported.

Keep well away from drugs, don't carry even the smallest quantity, and watch carefully while police officers search your luggage. Always refuse if a stranger at an airport asks you to take their luggage on board as part of your luggage allowance. Needless to say, smuggling dope across borders is a crazy idea. Have you ever seen the inside of a Venezuelan prison?

Some isolated cases of drugging tourists with *burundanga* have recently been reported. Burundanga – which also comes from Colombia, where it is widespread – is a drug used by thieves to eliminate the victim's ability to respond, thus enabling them to clean them out without resistance. The drug can be added to almost any substance – sweets, cigarettes, chewing gum, spirits, beer – and it has no noticeable taste or smell. It therefore can be easily applied to the potential victim. If circumstances appear suspicious, think twice before accepting a cigarette from a stranger or a drink from a new friend.

Kidnapping

Recent years have seen a spate of 'express kidnappings' in Caracas. In an attempt to quickly garner some money, armed groups kidnap individuals or groups and hold them hostage until the victims or their friends provide a specific amount of money. Usually the victims are released upon delivery of the cash. While foreigners aren't especially targeted for express kidnappings, bear in mind that foreign travelers may be viewed as wealthy and thus a tempting source of income.

Guerrillas

Venezuela doesn't have its own guerrillas, but two major Colombian guerrilla fronts, the FARC and the ELN, have shown an increasing presence in Venezuela's remote border areas of Zulia, Táchira, Apure and Amazonas states. Consequently, travel in these areas may be risky owing to potential dangers of violence, skirmishes or even kidnapping.

LEGAL MATTERS

Foreigners here, as elsewhere, are subject to the laws of the host country. Penalties for trafficking, possessing and using illegal drugs are stiff in Venezuela, and perpetrators usually end up with long jail terms.

While your embassy or consulate is the best stop in any emergency, bear in mind that there are some things it cannot do for you. These include getting local laws or

Emergency Numbers

The nationwide toll-free 24-hour emergency phone numbers include the following:

Police	☎ 169
Traffic Police	☎ 167
Fire	☎ 166
Emergency Center (Police, Fire, Ambulance)	☎ 171
Phone Directory Assistance	☎ 113

Don't expect the attendants of any of these services to speak English. If your Spanish is not up to scratch, try to get a local to call on your behalf.

regulations waived because you're a foreigner, investigating a crime, providing legal advice or representation in civil or criminal cases, getting you out of jail, and lending you money. A consul can, however, issue emergency passports, contact relatives and friends, advise on how to transfer funds, provide lists of reliable local doctors, lawyers and interpreters, and visit you if you've been arrested or jailed.

BUSINESS HOURS

The office working day is, theoretically at least, eight hours long, usually from 8 am to noon and 2 to 6 pm Monday to Friday. In practice, offices tend to open later and close earlier, and the opening hours for the public may be only until 4 pm. Many offices in Caracas are adopting the so-called *horario corrido*, a working day without a lunch break that finishes two hours earlier. However, it's nearly impossible to arrange anything between noon and 2 pm, as most of the staff are off for their lunch anyway.

All banks in Venezuela have the same business hours – weekdays from 8:30 am to 3:30 – and keep pretty close to them. Most tourist offices are closed on Saturday and Sunday, and travel agencies usually only work on Saturday until noon.

As a rough guide only, the usual shopping hours are from 9 am to 6 or 7 pm Monday to Saturday. Many shops close for lunch, but some work without a lunch break. Large

stores and supermarkets in the cities usually stay open until 8, 9 or sometimes even 10 pm, and some are also open on Sunday. Shopping hours vary considerably from shop to shop and from city to countryside. In remote places, business hours are shorter and are often taken less seriously.

Pharmacies employ a rotation system for Sunday and all-night hours. Check local newspapers for the list of pharmacies on 24-hour duty. You can recognize them by a board or a neon sign saying 'Turno' ('On Duty').

Most of the better restaurants in the larger cities, particularly in Caracas, tend to stay open until 11 pm or midnight (some even longer), whereas restaurants in smaller towns often close by 9 pm or earlier. Many restaurants don't open at all on Sunday.

The opening hours of museums and other tourist sites vary greatly. Most museums are closed on Monday but are open on Sunday. The opening hours of churches are even more difficult to pin down. Some are open all day, others only for certain hours, while the rest remain locked except during mass, which in some villages may be only on Sunday morning.

PUBLIC HOLIDAYS

Official public holidays include January 1 (New Year's Day), the Monday and Tuesday before Ash Wednesday (Carnaval), Maundy Thursday and Good Friday (before Easter Sunday), April 19 (Declaration of Independence), May 1 (Labor Day), June 24 (Battle of Carabobo), July 5 (Independence Day), July 24 (Bolívar's birthday), October 12 (Discovery of America) and December 25 (Christmas).

SPECIAL EVENTS

Given the strong Catholic character of Venezuela, many feasts and celebrations follow the Church calendar. Accordingly, Christmas, Easter, Corpus Christi and the like are celebrated all over the country. The religious calendar is dotted with saints' days, and every village and town has its own patron saint – you can take it for granted the locals will be holding a celebratory feast on that day. In many cases, solemn church ceremonies are accompanied by popular feasts that may include beauty pageants and bullfights. Some events are celebrated throughout the country, but most are local, confined to a particular region or town.

One of the biggest nationwide events is Carnaval, which takes place on the Monday and Tuesday prior to Ash Wednesday. Feasting usually breaks out by the end of the preceding week. The festival is characterized by plenty of music and dancing, parades and masquerades, bullfighting and *toros coleados* (a local sort of rodeo), lots of food and, particularly, beer and spirits. Carnaval varies from region to region in terms of its length, intensity and character. In Santa Elena de Uairén, for example, it has a distinct Brazilian feel, a reflection of the town's proximity to that border. Carúpano is known nationwide for its elaborate Carnaval, as is, to a lesser extent, El Callao.

One of the most colorful regional events is the Diablos Danzantes, or the Dancing Devils. It's held on Corpus Christi in San Francisco de Yare and several other villages in Venezuela's central north. The ceremony consists of a parade and the ritual dance of devils, performed by dancers disguised in elaborate, if grotesque, masks and costumes.

Cultural events such as festivals of theater, film or classical music are almost exclusively confined to Caracas.

Venezuela's main religious and cultural events include:

Paradura del Niño – Mérida state; January

La Divina Pastora – Barquisimeto; January 14

Feria de San Sebastián – San Cristóbal; second half of January

Carnaval – throughout the country; February or March

Semana Santa – many towns; processions on Maundy Thursday and Good Friday (March or April)

Festival Internacional de Teatro – Caracas; March/April of even years

Velorio de la Cruz de Mayo – throughout the country; May

Diablos Danzantes – San Francisco de Yare, Chuao, Naiguatá and some other villages in the region; Corpus Christi (May or June)

Fiesta de San Juan – Curiepe, Higuerote, Chuao, Cuyagua and many other towns of the central coastal region; dances to drum music, with an African flavor (the region is the center of black culture); June 23 & 24, but usually extending till June 28

Fiesta de la Virgen María – La Asunción (Isla de Margarita); August 15

Fiesta de la Virgen de Coromoto – Guanare; September 8

Fiesta de la Virgen del Valle – Valle del Espíritu Santo (Isla de Margarita); September 8

Feria de la Chinita – Maracaibo; November 18

ACTIVITIES

Venezuela has much to offer those who love the great outdoors. Its 40-odd national parks provide a good choice of walks ranging from easy, well-signposted trails to jungle paths where a machete might be a useful tool. If you arrive in Venezuela at Caracas, try Parque Nacional El Ávila first before heading for less developed trails in Guatopo, Henri Pittier, San Esteban and Canaima national parks.

Sierra Nevada de Mérida is Venezuela's best region for high-mountain trekking, and, if you're up for it, you can try mountaineering and rock climbing there; guides and equipment are available in Mérida. Incidentally, Mérida state is also the best area for mountain biking, which has become quite popular; bikes and guides can be hired in the city of Mérida.

Mérida is also the best place to go paragliding. It's a relatively new activity but is becoming widespread in Caracas and Mérida. Double gliders are available, so even greenhorns can try this breathtaking experience.

Rafting is also gaining in popularity. Rafting trips are run on some Andean rivers (arranged in, again, Mérida), in the Mochima national park (organized from Mochima), and over Orinoco rapids (arranged in Puerto Ayacucho). The newest craze, canyoning, took off recently in, again, the Mérida region.

Some national parks, including Henri Pittier and Yacambú, are good for wildlife watchers, particularly for bird-watchers. You can go on your own, combining hiking and

Considerations for Responsible Diving

The popularity of diving is placing immense pressure on many sites. Please consider the following tips when diving, and help preserve the ecology and beauty of reefs:

- Do not use anchors on the reef, and take care not to ground boats on coral. Encourage dive operators and regulatory bodies to establish permanent moorings at popular dive sites.

- Avoid touching living marine organisms with your body or dragging equipment across the reef. Polyps can be damaged by even the gentlest contact. Never stand on corals, even if they look solid and robust. If you must hold on to the reef, touch only exposed rock or dead coral.

- Be conscious of your fins. Even without contact, the surge from heavy fin strokes near the reef can damage delicate organisms. When treading water in shallow reef areas, take care not to kick up clouds of sand. Settling sand can easily smother the delicate organisms of the reef.

- Practice and maintain proper buoyancy control. Major damage can be done by divers descending too fast and colliding with the reef. Make sure that you are correctly weighted and that your weight belt is positioned so that you stay horizontal. If you have not dived for a while, do a practice dive in a pool before heading to the reef. Be aware that buoyancy can change over the period of an extended trip: Initially, you may breathe harder and need more weight; a few days later, you may breathe more easily and need less weight.

- Take great care in underwater caves. Spend as little time within them as possible, as your air bubbles may be caught within the roof and thereby leave previously submerged organisms high and dry. Taking turns to inspect the interior of a small cave reduces the chances of damaging contact.

- Resist the temptation to collect or buy corals or shells. Aside from the ecological damage, taking home marine souvenirs depletes the beauty of a site and spoils others' enjoyment. The same goes for marine archaeological sites (mainly shipwrecks). Respect their integrity; some sites are even protected from looting by law.

- Ensure that you take home all your rubbish and any litter you may find as well. Plastics in particular are a serious threat to marine life. Turtles can mistake plastic for jellyfish and eat it.

- Resist the temptation to feed fish. You may disturb their normal eating habits, encourage aggressive behavior or feed them food that is detrimental to their health.

- Minimize your disturbance of marine animals. In particular, do not ride on the backs of turtles, as this causes them great anxiety.

bird-watching. Alternatively, if you'd prefer a more comfortable way to observe wildlife, go to one of the *hatos* (ecological ranches) in Los Llanos, where a boat or a jeep will take you on a guided safari through the animal world. Wildlife safaris in Los Llanos are also organized from Mérida, and these are much cheaper.

With 2800km of coastline, beach enthusiasts can sunbathe to their hearts' content. For good beaches, try Morrocoy, Mochima or Henri Pittier national parks, the environs of Río Caribe, or Isla de Margarita.

Venezuela is also excellent for snorkeling and scuba diving, which is probably best around the offshore archipelagos such as Los Roques. There is also some good snorkeling around the islands closer to the mainland, including in Mochima and Morrocoy national parks. In all these places, local operators offer courses and diving trips, and rent relevant equipment.

Fishing enthusiasts can try their luck on Los Roques, or they can go fishing in rivers; the Orinoco and some of its tributaries are good places for this, as are mountain lakes around Mérida.

Spelunkers can explore some of Venezuela's several hundred caves. The most famous and among the most spectacular is the Cueva del Guácharo. There are about 20 other, less known caves in the same area.

LANGUAGE COURSES

Spanish-language courses are available in some cities, of which Caracas and Mérida offer the widest choice. Isla de Margarita also has some facilities. See the relevant sections for details.

WORK

Travelers looking for paid work on the spot in Venezuela will probably be disappointed. First of all, to work legally, you need a work visa, and getting one is a journey through hell. It's a complex and lengthy paperwork procedure, and it's practically impossible to start the process unless you already have a job lined up. Secondly, wages are low in Venezuela, unless you are a highly qualified specialist. Lastly, forget about unskilled casual jobs (such as picking grapes or playing waiter, which you might remember fondly from trips to more developed countries), as there will always be plenty of competing Venezuelans eager to work for much less than you would ever expect to be paid.

Qualified English teachers have perhaps the best chance of getting a job, but it's not that easy. Try English-teaching institutions such as the Centro Venezolano Americano, the British Council, linguistic departments at universities and private language schools. If you don't have bona fide teaching credentials, you may still try to organize some informal arrangements, eg, giving private language lessons.

If you are interested in voluntary work with an emphasis on environmental protection, contact environmental organizations (see the Ecology & Environment section, in the Facts about Venezuela chapter), which may sponsor some projects in Venezuela. Inquire well in advance of your trip.

ACCOMMODATIONS

Establishments listed in Places to Stay sections of this book are ordered according to price, from the bottom to the top. Where sections are broken down into price categories, the budget accommodations include anything costing less than about US$25 double, the mid-range bracket covers hotels rated from approximately US$25 to US$50 double, and the top end is anything over US$50 double. Caracas has slightly higher price brackets – see that chapter for details.

Venezuela doesn't belong to Hostelling International and has no youth hostels. In some resorts, mostly on the coast, locals rent out rooms in their homes in order to provide additional accommodations for beachgoers, who arrive en masse on weekends and holidays.

Camping

Purpose-built campgrounds – fenced-off compounds for camping equipped with electricity, running water, showers, a cooking area and on-site trailers – are virtually nonexistent in Venezuela. What you can find here are bivouac sites, or just open grounds for camping with scarce or – more often – no facilities, but even these places are few and far between.

Locals who vacation with camping in mind pitch their tents wherever they feel like doing so, practically anywhere outside urban centers. Accordingly, if you plan on camping, follow the local style. Camping on the beach is particularly popular (that's where most local holidaymakers go), but be careful and don't leave your tent unattended.

If you camp in wilderness or other fragile areas, try to minimize your impact on the environment. Ideally, all food residue, cigarette butts and other rubbish should be removed. If there are no toilet facilities, select a site at least 50m from water sources, and bury waste. Use biodegradable soap products. Wash dishes and brush your teeth well away from watercourses. Make sure you have a sufficient stock of sturdy bags to take your garbage out of the area.

Hotels

There are heaps of hotels for every budget, and it's usually easy enough to find a room, except perhaps on major feast days. The cheapies tend to be grouped together in certain areas, such as around the market, bus terminal and in the backstreets of the city center.

Top-class hotels, on the other hand, are usually scattered around the wealthier districts, which aren't necessarily close to the center. You can expect to find at least one mid-priced hotel on the Plaza Bolívar or in its immediate vicinity.

Hotels charge a 15.5% VAT tax on top of the room price, though few budget places do it. The prices listed in this book have included this tax already. Most top-end hotels will accept payment by credit card.

Budget Hotels Budget places to stay appear under a variety of names, such as *hotel, residencia, hospedaje, posada* and *pensión*. The last two are meant to be small, family-run guesthouses. Posadas, which have mushroomed recently in both the cities and countryside, often have more character and offer more personalized attention than the rest, but not always. Don't jump to conclusions by just seeing the label on the door; check inside.

Most of the cheapies have a private bathroom (in this book, simply called 'bath'), which includes a toilet and shower. The bath is sometimes separated from the room by only a partial partition (eg, a section of wall that doesn't even reach the ceiling), and there is hardly ever a door between the two areas. Note that cheap hotel plumbing can't cope with toilet paper, so throw it in the wastebasket that is normally provided.

As most of the country lies in the lowland tropics, a fan or air-conditioning is a staple in cheap hotel rooms, but hot water in the shower is rare. Air-conditioning may not always be advantageous. The equipment often dates from oil-rich years and, after a decade or more of use, it may be in a desperate state of disrepair and as noisy as a tank. There's usually only the on/off option, and it's not always clear which is better. Sometimes they're *very* efficient and turn the room into a freezer; other times they don't cool the room at all.

Always have a look at the room before booking in and paying. When inspecting the room, make sure the toilet flushes and the water runs in the shower. Check that the fan (or air-conditioning) works and that the lock on the door is sufficiently secure. If you're not satisfied with the room you're shown, ask to see another. After checking in, you'll usually get a towel, a small piece of soap and a roll of toilet paper.

Venezuclans enjoy TV, so many budget hotels provide TV sets in rooms. Since the insulation between the rooms is often flimsy, TV noise can be a nightmare. If there are no TV sets in rooms, you can be sure that there's one around the reception area, and it's usually kept at top volume until late at night. Look around to see where this noisemaking box stands and try to take a room as far from it as possible. Check also that there isn't a bar or *taberna* downstairs or next door, especially on a Friday or Saturday night.

The price of budget hotels varies throughout the country. It's much higher in Caracas or Puerto La Cruz than in Mérida. Count on roughly US$8 to US$12 for a single room *(habitación sencilla)* and US$10 to US$18 for a double *(habitación doble)*. In this book, a double denotes a room with two beds. Many hotels don't have singles, and the cheapest is the so-called *habitación matrimonial*. This is a room with one wide double bed intended for couples. It often costs the same for one as for two, so traveling as a couple considerably reduces the cost of accommodations. Payment is almost exclusively up front and in cash.

By and large, hotels are reasonably safe places, but precautions and common sense are always advisable. Most budget places lock their doors at night, and some even keep them locked during the day, opening them only for guests. The biggest danger of being ripped off is most likely to come from other guests (and occasionally from the staff). The thieves' task is made easier by only partial hardboard partitions between rooms, and flimsy catches and easily picked padlocks on doors. Hotels provide padlocks, but it's recommended that you use your own combination lock (or padlock) instead. As a rule, bigger hotels are less safe than smaller ones, because the atmosphere is more impersonal and a thief won't stand out in a crowd.

Some budget hotels offer a deposit facility, which in practice means that the management will guard your gear in their own room, as there are no other safe places. This reduces the risk but doesn't eliminate it completely. In most cheapies, the staff won't want to give you any receipt for receiving your valuables, and if you insist on one, they may simply refuse to guard them. Decide for yourself if it's safe.

Mid-Range & Top End Although often lacking in character, mid-range hotels provide more facilities than budget establishments. They will almost always have private baths, but air-conditioning may be as noisy as in the cheapies. Some of these hotels are reasonably priced for what they offer, while others are outrageously overpriced. It's a good idea to inspect the room in these hotels before you commit yourself.

In top-end hotels, you can be more sure about standards, including silent central airconditioning and a reception desk open around the clock with proper facilities to safeguard guests' valuables. However, prices vary greatly and don't always reflect quality. Except for Caracas, where prices seem to be inflated, you can normally grab a quite good double with facilities for somewhere between US$60 and US$100.

Only Caracas and Isla de Margarita, and to a lesser extent Puerto La Cruz and Maracaibo, have a reasonable choice of five-star hotels. Be prepared to pay about US$100 and up for a single and US$120 and up for a double.

Love Hotels Informally known as *tiraderos,* these places – which rent rooms by the hour – are common in Venezuela. Many budget (and some mid-range) hotels double as love hotels, and it's often impossible to recognize them and to avoid staying in one from time to time. They are probably as safe as other places (the guests have more interesting things on their minds than stealing your belongings), and the staff normally keep the sex section separate from other hotel rooms. There are also upmarket love hotels, but these are well outside the downtown areas, usually tucked away on the city outskirts.

Campamentos

The *campamento* (literally 'camp') is a place to stay in the countryside that often also provides food and sometimes tours (which can be optional or compulsory). The campamento can be anything from a rustic shelter with a few hammocks to a posh country lodge with a swimming pool and its own airstrip. Most commonly, however, it will be a collection of *cabañas* (cabins) plus a restaurant. Quite scarce until recently, today campamentos spring up like mushrooms in the most remote areas.

A campamento is rarely a place for just an overnight stop on the road, but rather a destination in itself and a base for tours organized from there. Most camps are off the beaten track anyway, and some are sheltered deep in the wilderness and accessible by a jeep track or sometimes only by air.

Some more upmarket camps require you to buy an all-inclusive package that covers lodging, full board and tours. This usually has to be done in advance at a designated travel agency or from the camp's representative. The cost of such packages can easily reach hundreds of dollars. Tours offered in the package depend on the region's characteristics and may include anything from walks in the environs to wildlife safaris by jeep or boat, bird-watching, fishing or even helicopter flights.

FOOD

Venezuelans like to eat well, and restaurants are abundant. On the whole, food is good, though it's no longer a great bargain. Apart from a variety of typical local dishes, there are plenty of western cuisines available. Gourmets will enjoy their stay in Caracas, which offers the widest range of eating establishments and international cuisines.

Since Venezuela is one of the most Americanized countries on the continent, there's a dense array of gringo fast-food outlets, including McDonald's, KFC, Burger King and Pizza Hut. Spanish and Italian restaurants are well represented thanks to the sizeable migration from these two countries. There are also some good Chinese and Middle Eastern restaurants, mostly in the main cities. For self-caterers, there's a satisfactory choice of supermarkets and shops.

Budget travelers should look for restaurants that serve the so-called *menú del día* or *menu ejecutivo*, a set lunch consisting of soup and a main course, which is cheaper than any à la carte dish. Depending on the establishment, the set lunch will cost between US$3 and US$6.

A cheap alternative might be spit-roasted chicken, served at a variety of restaurants, including specialist chicken eateries called *pollo en brasas*. Half a chicken with potatoes, yucca or another side dish shouldn't cost more than US$6. Another option is the *arepa*, a wonderful Venezuelan snack (see the Food & Drink Glossary at the back of the book) for about US$2 to US$3, served in places called *areperas*, which are everywhere.

For breakfast, go to any of the ubiquitous *panaderías* (bakeries), which serve sandwiches, pastries and a variety of typical snacks, plus usually delicious espresso. The market is, as in most of South America, a good cheap option, offering food that is usually tasty and fresh.

Etiquette and table manners are more or less the same as in the west, and there are no particular oddities to observe. When beginning a meal, it's good manners to wish your fellow diners *buen provecho* ('bon appetit'). When drinking a toast, the Spanish equivalent of 'cheers' is *salud*.

Venezuelan cuisine is varied and regional. The most typical snacks and dishes, collectively referred to as *comida criolla*, include arepa, *cachapa, hallaca, hervido, lechón, mondongo, muchacho, pabellón criollo* and *sancocho*. See the Food & Drink Glossary at the back of the book for details.

DRINK

Nonalcoholic Drinks Espresso coffee is strong and excellent in Venezuela. It's served in panaderías and a variety of other establishments. Ask for *café negro* if you want it black; for *café marrón* if you prefer half coffee, half milk; or *café con leche* if you like very milky coffee.

Fruit juices are popular and readily available in restaurants, *fuentes de soda, fruterías, refresquerías* and other eating outlets. Given the variety of fruit in the country, you have quite a choice. Juices come either pure or watered-down *(batidos),* or as milk shakes *(merengadas).*

Bottled and canned soft drinks *(refrescos)* can be bought everywhere (accordingly, you can find empty bottles and cans everywhere).

Alcoholic Drinks The favorite alcoholic drink is beer, particularly Polar beer, which is the dominant brand. It is sold everywhere in either cans (0.3L) or bottles (0.22L) and costs about US$0.35 in shops and US$0.50 in the cheapest bars and eateries. The Brazilian Brahma beer is now making inroads into the local market.

The local production of wine is small and the quality poor, except for the acceptable Altagracia wines. There are plenty of imported wines available from other South American countries, Europe and the USA. Chilean and Argentine wines are fine and come at affordable prices, but European wines are expensive, especially so in restaurants.

Among spirits, *ron* (rum) heads the list and comes in numerous varieties and different qualities. The Ron Añejo Aniversario Pampero is one of the best dark rums Venezuela produces. The 0.75L bottle, elegantly packed in a leather pouch, will cost about US$10 in a liquor store. If you want to take one home, buy it in the city; it's rarely available in the airport duty-free shops.

ENTERTAINMENT

Cinemas

Movies are popular and there are cinemas in almost every town. In Caracas alone, there are more than 40 cinemas. Most movies are the regular US commercial fare. If you need something more mentally stimulating, try the *cinematecas* (art cinemas) in Caracas.

Most movies are screened in their original language with Spanish subtitles. A cinema ticket costs between US$3 and US$5. Cinemas in the lowlands are air-conditioned and may sometimes be cool; come prepared. In some towns, men in T-shirts or shorts will not be let in.

Theater & Classical Music

Most theater activity is confined to Caracas, where there are a dozen theaters. In other large cities, the choice of theaters, and usually the quality of productions, doesn't match that of Caracas. Much the same can be said about other areas of artistic expression such as ballet, opera and classical music. Refer to Entertainment in the Caracas chapter for further information.

Discos

Venezuelans love to dance and are good dancers. By far the largest choice of discos is in Caracas, followed by Porlamar. The usual fare is a mix of western rock, reggae, salsa and merengue, but some discos focus mainly on Cuban/Caribbean rhythms. There may be live music on weekends in some places.

Some discos operate nightly (sometimes except Sunday and Monday, which are the slowest days), but many open from Thursday to Saturday only. Discos open their doors around 9 pm, but the action doesn't usually begin before 11 pm, when most of the patrons turn up. There may be an entry fee on weekends, but rarely on other days of the week.

Discos don't usually serve food but offer plenty of drinks, which can be cheap or expensive, depending on the particular establishment. Most Caracas discos won't let you enter in a T-shirt and sneakers, but provincial venues tend to be more tolerant. Some discos are of suspicious reputation, stocked with prostitutes and with drugs sold openly – be careful.

Bars & Pubs

Don't worry – there are plenty of watering holes open late into the night, although they don't necessarily remind you of classic English or Irish pubs. Bottles are emptied quickly, so if you keep up with your Venezuelan friends, you may have some problems returning safely to your hotel.

SPECTATOR SPORTS

Baseball (*béisbol*) is the most popular sport, attracting large crowds. The professional league is composed of eight teams (based in Caracas, La Guaira, Maracaibo, Valencia, Barquisimeto, Maracay, Puerto La Cruz and Cabimas), which often feature US players. The season goes from October to February.

One Venezuelan baseball player, Luis Sojo, has gone on to fame and fortune in US Major League Baseball. On October 26, 2000, crowds gathered in front of an enormous screen in Caracas to watch his dramatic ninth-inning hit that scored the winning runs in the World Series, defeating the New York Mets and preserving the New York Yankees' title.

The second-most popular sport is probably basketball (*baloncesto*), with a professional league also comprising eight teams and the season running from March to July.

Horse races have been run in Los Llanos for centuries, but they are now run on racetracks built according to international rules, betting included. La Rinconada in Caracas is the best racetrack in the country, but other large cities, such as Maracaibo and Valencia, have their own tracks.

Unlike in most other South American countries, soccer (*fútbol*) has found few fans in Venezuela, though it does exist and there's even a professional league that plays from August till May.

The *corrida* (bullfight) was imported from Spain and found fertile soil in Venezuela, and now most major cities have their own *plaza de toros* (bullring). The bullring in

Valencia, capable of seating 27,000 people, is the largest in the country, followed by the one in San Cristóbal, with 22,000 seats. The Plaza de Toros Maestranza, in Maracay, is among the country's most stylish bullrings. The bullfighting season peaks during Carnaval, when top-ranking matadors are invited from Spain and Latin America (especially Mexico and Colombia).

Another cruel and breathtaking spectator sport is cockfighting. As in most countries on the continent, it's popular in Venezuela, and *galleras* (cockfight rings) can be found in most cities.

Also thrilling – but bloodless – is the *coleo* or *toros coleados,* a sort of rodeo popular in Los Llanos, in which four riders compete to bring down a bull. The aim is to ground the bull after grabbing it by the tail from a galloping horse.

Another popular game, and an easier one to participate in, is *bolas criollas,* the Venezuelan variety of lawn bowling. Two teams, each consisting of two players, throw eight wooden balls, aiming to place them as close as possible to the smaller ball, known as the *mingo*.

Chess and dominoes have plenty of addicts throughout the country, and these games are played as much in the villages as they are in Caracas.

SHOPPING

Given the number of Indian communities living in the country, there is a variety of crafts to buy. Some of the most interesting are the crafts of the Guajiro, Warao and the groups of Amazonas. For example, a *chinchorro* (hammock) of the Warao, a *manta* (colorful, long loose-flowing dress) of the Guajiro, or some fine baskets of the Yanomami make excellent collector's items and are as decorative as they are useful.

Although there are handicraft shops in Caracas and most major cities, you should always try to buy crafts in their region of origin, ideally from the artisans themselves; not only are the crafts more authentic, but they are also much cheaper (and the money goes directly to the artisan). If you can't get to the Indian communities, shop in the markets in nearby towns.

If you are interested in local music, comb Caracas' music shops, which have the best selection. Most of the music is now recorded on CDs. The price of a CD ranges from about US$10 to US$20.

Venezuela is noted for gold and diamonds, but don't expect to find great bargains everywhere. Possibly the best place to buy gold jewelry is El Callao. Leather footwear is a good buy in Venezuela, and shops selling shoes are plentiful.

Getting There & Away

AIR
Sitting at the northern edge of South America, Venezuela has the cheapest air links with both Europe and North America and is therefore the most convenient northern gateway to the continent.

Airports & Airlines
Caracas is by far Venezuela's major international air hub, and most visitors arrive at Caracas' airport in Maiquetía. Other cities servicing international flights include Valencia and Maracaibo. Charter flights bringing international package tourists also fly into Porlamar, on Isla de Margarita.

The country is serviced by a number of major intercontinental airlines, including British Airways, Air France, KLM, American Airlines and United Airlines.

As for the Venezuelan carriers, Viasa was once the country's flagship, with flights to Europe and much of the Americas, but it was grounded and liquidated in 1997. In its absence, Avensa/Servivensa temporarily became Venezuela's main international carrier, but it went almost bankrupt by mid-2000. It still has some international flights, including Miami and Mexico City, but its situation is precarious. The reborn Aeropostal is now better established and operates more international routes, including Lima, Havana, Port of Spain and Miami. Other Venezuelan carriers servicing international flights include Santa Bárbara (Aruba, Barranquilla) and Aserca (Aruba, Santo Domingo).

Buying Tickets
Your plane ticket will probably be the single most expensive item in your budget, but you can reduce the cost by finding discounted fares. Stiff competition has resulted in widespread discounting, and these days there are plenty of discount tickets valid for 12 months, allowing multiple stopovers with open dates.

Air tickets bought from travel agents are generally cheaper than those bought directly from an airline, even if they cover the same route and have similar conditions or restrictions. How much you save largely depends on where you buy. In some countries or cities there is a big trade in budget tickets; in others, the discount-ticket market is limited, and the prices are not very attractive.

> ### Warning
>
> The information in this chapter is particularly vulnerable to change: Prices for international travel are volatile, routes are introduced and canceled, schedules change, special deals come and go, and rules and visa requirements are amended. Airlines and governments seem to take a perverse pleasure in making price structures and regulations as complicated as possible. You should check directly with the airline or a travel agent to make sure you understand how a fare (and any ticket you may buy) works. In addition, the travel industry is highly competitive, and there are many lurks and perks.
>
> The upshot of this is that you should get opinions, quotes and advice from as many airlines and travel agents as possible before you part with your hard-earned cash. The details given in this chapter should be regarded as pointers and are not a substitute for your own careful, up-to-date research.

It is always worth putting aside a few hours to research the current state of the market. Start early, as some of the cheapest tickets have to be bought well in advance and as some popular flights sell out quickly. Look at ads in newspapers and magazines (including the Latin American press published in your country), surf the Internet and keep an eye out for special offers. Read the Air Travel Glossary, later in this chapter, to get familiar with basic terms. Then phone travel agents for bargains.

If you are traveling from the UK or the USA, you will most likely find that the cheapest flights are advertised by obscure bucket shops (known as 'consolidators' in the USA) whose names haven't yet reached the telephone directory. The days when some travel agents would routinely fleece travelers by running off with their money are, happily, almost over. Paying by credit card generally offers protection, as most card issuers provided refunds if you can prove you didn't get what you paid for. Agents who accept only cash should hand over the tickets straight away and not tell you to 'come back tomorrow.' If you feel suspicious about a firm, go somewhere else.

You may decide to pay a bit more than the rock-bottom fare by opting for the safety of a better-known travel agent. Firms such as STA Travel, which has offices worldwide, Council Travel in the USA or Travel CUTS in Canada offer good prices to most destinations and are not going to disappear overnight.

Use fares quoted in this book as a guide only. They are approximate and based on rates advertised by travel agents as we went to press. Remember that quoted airfares do not necessarily constitute a recommendation for that carrier.

Onward Ticket Requirements

Venezuela requires, technically at least, that visitors have an onward ticket before they're allowed into the country. This is quite strictly enforced by airlines and travel agents, and probably none of them will sell you a one-way ticket unless you already have an onward ticket.

Upon arrival in Venezuela, however, hardly any immigration official will ask you to present your onward ticket. However, the ticket may be necessary if you want to extend your visa.

If you come without a return ticket and want to go home, you may be disappointed: Venezuela is not a good place to buy international air tickets. Airfares to Europe and Australia are high, and there are virtually no discounted tickets available. Only flights to Florida are reasonably cheap, simply because it's close and the route is serviced by local airlines that may offer discount fares. It's always better to have the whole route covered by a ticket bought at home.

Travelers with Special Needs

If you have special needs of any sort – you've broken a leg, you're vegetarian, traveling in a wheelchair, taking a baby or just terrified of flying – you should let the airline know as soon as possible so that it can make appropriate arrangements.

You should remind the staff of your needs when you reconfirm your booking and again when you check in at the airport. It may be worth calling various airlines before you make your booking in order to find out how they can handle your particular requirements.

Airports and airlines can be surprisingly helpful, but they do need advance warning. Most international airports will provide escorts from the check-in desk to the plane when needed, and there should be ramps, elevators, and accessible toilets and phones. Aircraft toilets, on the other hand, are likely to present a problem; travelers should discuss this with the airline at an early stage and, if necessary, with their doctor.

Guide dogs for the disabled will often have to travel separately from their owners in a specially pressurized baggage compartment with other animals, though smaller guide dogs may be admitted to the cabin.

All guide dogs are subject to the same quarantine laws (six months in isolation etc) as other domestic animals when entering or returning to countries currently free of rabies, such as the UK or Australia. Deaf

Air Travel Glossary

Bucket Shops These are unbonded travel agencies specializing in discount airline tickets.

Cancellation Penalties If you have to cancel or change a discounted ticket, heavy penalties are often involved; insurance can sometimes be taken out against these penalties. Some airlines impose penalties on regular tickets as well, particularly against 'no-show' passengers.

Courier Fares Businesses often need to send urgent documents or freight securely and quickly. Courier companies hire people to accompany the package through customs and, in return, offer a discount ticket that is sometimes a phenomenal bargain. However, you may have to surrender all your baggage allowance and take only carry-on luggage.

Full Fares Airlines traditionally offer 1st-class (coded F), business-class (coded J) and economy-class (coded Y) tickets. These days, so many promotional and discounted fares are available that few passengers pay full economy fare.

Lost Tickets If you lose your airline ticket, an airline will usually treat it as a traveler's check and, after inquiries, issue you another one. Legally, however, an airline is entitled to treat it like cash: If you lose it, it's gone forever. Take good care of your tickets.

Onward Tickets An entry requirement for many countries is a ticket out of the country. If you're unsure of your next move, the easiest solution is to buy the cheapest onward ticket to a neighboring country or a ticket from a reliable airline that can later be refunded if you do not use it.

Open-Jaw Tickets These are roundtrip tickets that permit you to fly into one place but return from another. If available, these tickets can save you backtracking to your arrival point.

Overbooking Because almost every flight has some passengers who fail to show up, airlines often book more passengers than they have seats. Usually excess passengers make up for the no-shows, but occasionally somebody gets 'bumped' onto the next available flight. Guess who it is most likely to be? The passengers who check in late.

Promotional Fares These are officially discounted fares, available from travel agencies or direct from the airline.

Reconfirmation If you don't reconfirm your flight at least 72 hours prior to departure, the airline may delete your name from the passenger list. Call to find out if your airline requires reconfirmation.

Restrictions Discounted tickets often have various restrictions – for example, they may need to be paid for in advance, or altering them may incur a penalty. Other restrictions include minimum and maximum periods you must be away.

Round-the-World Tickets RTW tickets give you a limited period (usually a year) in which to circumnavigate the globe. You can go anywhere the carrying airlines go as long as you don't backtrack. The number of stopovers or total number of separate flights is decided before you set off, and these tickets usually cost a bit more than a basic roundtrip flight.

Transferred Tickets Airline tickets cannot be transferred from one person to another. Travelers sometimes try to sell the return half of a ticket, but officials can ask you to prove that you are the person named on the ticket. On an international flight, tickets are compared with passports.

Travel Periods Ticket prices vary with the time of year. There is a low (off-peak) season and a high (peak) season, and often a low-shoulder season and a high-shoulder season as well. Usually the fare depends on your outward flight – if you depart in the high season and return in the low season, you pay the high-season fare.

travelers can ask for airport and in-flight announcements to be written down for them.

Children under two years of age travel for 10% of the standard fare (or free on some airlines), as long as they don't occupy a seat. They don't get a baggage allowance either. Skycots should be provided by the airline if requested in advance; these are capable of carrying a child weighing up to about 10kg.

Children between two and 12 years of age can usually occupy a seat for half to two-thirds of the full fare, and they do get a baggage allowance. Strollers can often be taken aboard as hand luggage.

Departure Tax

On leaving Venezuela by air, all passengers pay the airport tax (tasa aeroportuaria) of US$21. This apart, there's the departure tax (impuesto de salida) of US$18 for all visitors who have stayed in Venezuela for more than one month (which together makes for a hefty US$39 expense). The taxes are payable in either US dollars or bolívares at the current exchange rate, but not by credit card.

The USA

Two of the most reputable discount travel agencies in the USA are STA Travel and Council Travel Services. Although they both specialize in student travel, they may offer discount tickets to nonstudents of all ages. Their national head offices are the following:

Council Travel
(☎ 800-226 8624, 212-822 2700, fax 212-822 2719)
205 East 42nd St, New York, NY 10017
Web site: www.counciltravel.com

STA Travel
(☎ 800-777 0112, 213-937 8722, fax 213-937 2739)
5900 Wilshire Blvd, Suite 2110, Los Angeles, CA 90036
Web site: www.sta-travel.com

Both Council Travel and STA Travel have offices in Boston, Chicago, Los Angeles, Miami, Philadelphia, New York, San Diego, San Francisco, Washington and other major cities. Check their Web sites for addresses.

For more discount travel agencies, check the Sunday travel sections in major newspapers such as the *Los Angeles Times,* the *San Francisco Examiner* and the *Chronicle* on the west coast and the *New York Times* on the east coast.

The major US gateway for Venezuela is Miami, from where several carriers, such as American Airlines, United Airlines, Lan-Chile, Aeropostal and Avensa/Servivensa, fly to Caracas. A 30-day APEX roundtrip ticket normally costs about US$400 to US$500, depending on the season, but Aeropostal and/or Avensa may offer cut-down airfares, occasionally as cheap as US$150 or even less one-way. Contact the Miami outlets of both airlines: Aeropostal (☎ 305-371 6717 or toll-free ☎ 888-912 8466) and Avensa (☎ 305-381 8541, 871 0071 or toll-free ☎ 800-381 8001). Aeropostal also has direct flights from Miami to Maracaibo and Valencia.

Another important gateway to Venezuela is New York, from where American Airlines and Continental Airlines have flights to Caracas. A 60-day APEX round-trip ticket is likely to be around US$600 to US$750, depending on the season. Avensa/Servivensa offered attractive budget fares when it serviced this route, but it had no flights when we were going to press. Call its New York airport office anyway, to check the current state of affairs, at ☎ 718-244 6857 or toll-free ☎ 800-428 3672.

On the west coast, the major departure point is Los Angeles, but flights to Caracas are expensive. The cheapest 60-day roundtrip fares will be probably somewhere between US$900 and US$1000. Contact American Airlines (☎ 800-433 7300) and United Airlines (☎ 800-538 2929). It may work out cheaper to go on a low-cost domestic flight to Miami and fly to Caracas from there, but check beforehand to see what discount fares are available from Miami.

Canada

American Airlines and United Airlines have connections from Calgary, Montreal, Toronto and Vancouver to Miami, and on to Caracas. Prices vary according to the length of stay. For example, a roundtrip ticket from Toronto costs about C$1200 for less than 60 days and C$1500 for longer.

To start with, check the fares offered by Travel CUTS, Canada's national student travel agency (you don't have to be a student to use its services). Their head office is in Toronto (toll-free ☎ 800-667 2887), and branch offices are in Edmonton, Halifax, Montreal, Ottawa, Saskatoon, Vancouver and Victoria. Check their Web site (www .travelcuts.com) for further information and a full list of their offices.

It's also worth contacting Andes Travel, one of the travel agents specializing in flights to South America. Call its office in Toronto at ☎ 416-537 3447, or the one in Montreal at ☎ 514-274 5565. Adventure Centre, which has offices in Calgary, Edmonton, Toronto and Vancouver, can also be useful. You'll find advertisements for other travel agencies in the travel sections of weekend editions of newspapers such as the *Toronto Star,* the *Montreal Gazette,* the *Vancouver Sun* and the *Globe & Mail.*

Europe

A number of airlines, including British Airways, Air France, KLM, Lufthansa, Alitalia, Iberia and Air Portugal, link Caracas with European cities. Venezuela is usually the cheapest South American destination to reach from Europe, and most travel agents will offer flights to Caracas.

London, where bucket shops abound by the dozen, usually has the cheapest fares to Caracas. Other cities with long-standing traditions in ticket discounting include Amsterdam, Brussels, Frankfurt and Paris. Elsewhere, special deals come and go, but there is usually less to choose from and airfares are generally higher. This is particularly true in Scandinavia, where budget tickets are difficult to find.

It may be worthwhile checking the London market before buying an expensive ticket from a local agent in, say, Oslo or Helsinki. Some London travel agents will make arrangements by phone, email or fax, so you don't actually have to go to London to shop around. However, you may be obliged to go to London to pick up your ticket in person, as not many British agencies will want to send the ticket outside the UK.

The UK London is Britain's major hub for discounted tickets. You'll find plenty of deals listed in the travel sections of weekend editions of London newspapers. Advertisements for many travel agents appear in the travel pages of the weekend broadsheets, such as the *Independent* on Saturday and the *Sunday Times*. Look out for the free magazines, such as *TNT,* which are widely available in London – start by looking outside the main railway and underground stations.

A word of warning, however – don't take advertised fares as gospel. To comply with advertising laws in the UK, companies must be able to offer some tickets at their cheapest quoted price, but they may have only one or two of them per week. If you're not one of the lucky ones, you'll be looking at higher-priced tickets. It's best to begin looking for deals well in advance of your intended departure so that you can get a fair idea of what's available.

Following is a list of recommended agencies selling discounted tickets:

Flynow.com
(☎ 020-7835 2000) 125A Gloucester Rd, London SW7 4SF
Web site: www.gofly.com

Journey Latin America (JLA)
(☎ 020-8747 3108, fax 8742 1312) 12–13 Heathfield Terrace, Chiswick, London W4 4JE
Web site: www.journeylatinamerica.co.uk

Scott Dunn Latin America
(☎ 020-8767 8989, fax 8767 2026) Fovant Mews, 12 Noya Rd, London SW17 7PH

South American Experience
(☎ 020-7976 5511, fax 7976 6908) 47 Causton St, Pimlico, London SW1P 4AT

STA Travel
Telesales Europe (☎ 020-7361 6161)
Telesales Worldwide (☎ 0207-7361 6262)
Head Office (☎ 0207-7361 6100)
Web site: www.statravel.co.uk

Trailfinders
(☎ 020-7938 3366) 42–48 Earls Court Rd, London W8 6FT
(☎ 020-7938 3939) 194 Kensington High St, London W8 7RG

usit Campus
(☎ 020-7730 3402) 52 Grosvenor Gardens, London SW1W 0AG
Web site: www.usitcampus.com

STA Travel and usit Campus sell tickets to all travelers but cater especially to young people and students.

Apart from selling tickets, some of these travel agencies offer a variety of other services. JLA, consistently recommended by travelers, will arrange itineraries for both independent and escorted travel. It will make arrangements for you over the phone or by fax. Ask for its helpful free magazine, *Papagaio*. The equally reputable Trailfinders publishes a free quarterly magazine, *Trail finder*, packed with useful information on tickets, vaccinations, visas etc. The company has regional branches in Bristol, Glasgow and Manchester. STA Travel has regional offices in Bristol, Cambridge, Leeds, Oxford and Manchester.

Direct flights between London and Caracas are operated twice weekly by British Airways, but agents often use services of other carriers flying indirect routes via one of the mainland European cities, and they can work out to be cheaper.

Prices for discounted flights from London to Caracas start at around UK£250 one-way and UK£400 roundtrip. Bargain hunters should have little trouble finding even lower prices, but make sure you use a travel agent affiliated with ABTA (Association of British Travel Agents). If you have purchased your ticket from an ABTA-registered agent who then goes out of business, ABTA will guarantee a refund or an alternative. Unregistered bucket shops are sometimes cheaper but can be riskier.

France The Paris-Caracas route is serviced directly four times a week by Air France, but – as in London – travel agents may offer you cheaper indirect routes on board other carriers, eg, via Lisbon with TAP Air Portugal, which is one of the cheapest airlines. Following is a list of selected travel agencies selling discounted tickets in Paris. Many have branch offices in other major French cities.

Forum Voyages
(☎ 01-47 27 89 89) 49 Ave Raymond Poincaré, 75016 Paris
(☎ 01-55 26 71 60, fax 55 26 71 74) 114 Rue de Flandres, 75019 Paris

Fuaj (Fédération Unie des Auberges de Jeunesse)
(☎ 01-48 04 70 30, fax 44 89 87 10) 9 Rue Brantôme, 75003 Paris
Web site: www.fuaj.org

OTU (Organisation du Tourisme Universitaire)
(☎ 01-40 29 12 12) 39 Ave Georges Bernanos, 75005 Paris
Web site: www.otu.fr

usit Connect Voyages
(☎ 01-42 44 14 00, fax 42 44 14 01) 14 Rue Vivienne, 75002 Paris
Web site: www.usitconnect.fr

Voyageurs en Amérique du Sud
(☎ 01-42 86 17 70, fax 42 86 17 92) 55 Rue Sainte-Anne, 75002 Paris
Web site: www.vdm.com

The cheapest Paris-Caracas roundtrip tickets can be bought for about 3500FF in the low season and around 5000FF in the high season. Some agencies offer cheaper fares for students. Most discounted roundtrip tickets have a maximum stay period of two or three months, but sometimes they may allow for a stay of up to six months.

Australia & New Zealand

To start with, travel between Australasia and Venezuela is arduously long – at least 20 hours in the air alone. Add to it several stopovers, as there are no direct flights. Secondly, there are a number of routes, none of which is clearly better or cheaper than the others. Lastly, fares are high, and there is not much in the way of budget tickets to be found in Australia or New Zealand.

In theory, there are four air routes to Venezuela. Many travelers first think about the route through Los Angeles as the seemingly best option, but note that getting from there to Venezuela is expensive (see The USA, earlier in this section). Moreover, even a couple of days in the USA would eat up all the savings in airfares, so it's only a good value if you want to visit the USA anyway or if you go through without stopping. Arrange the ticket for the whole route at home. A roundtrip ticket is likely to cost somewhere between A$2400 and A$3000, depending on the season, length of stay etc.

The route through Europe is the longest, but not as absurd as it may sound. Given the discounted airfares to various European cities, including London and Paris, and interesting fares on to Caracas, the total fare may be comparable to or even lower than traveling via Los Angeles.

The shortest route between Australasia and South America goes over the South Pole. Aerolíneas Argentinas flies three times a week between Auckland and Buenos Aires, and has arrangements with other carriers that cover the Auckland-Australia leg. It may be an interesting proposition if you plan on beginning your overland trip from Argentina, but note that Venezuela is at the opposite end of the continent. Aerolíneas Argentinas can fly you to Caracas, but the total fare will be pretty high; expect to pay between A$2400 and A$3000 for the Sydney-Caracas roundtrip flight, depending on the length of stay and the season. The Auckland-Caracas fare will be only marginally lower.

Finally, you can fly right across the South Pacific to Santiago de Chile. LanChile flies from Papeete (Tahiti) via Easter Island to Santiago and also has flights on to Caracas. Associated carriers take passengers from Australia and New Zealand to Papeete. The LanChile Sydney-Caracas roundtrip fares cost much the same as those of Aerolíneas Argentinas.

Unless you are particularly interested in any of the four aforementioned routes, it's worth thinking about a RTW (Round-the-World) ticket. RTW tickets with various stopovers can still be found for as little as A$2200, but these tend to include only Northern Hemisphere stopovers; RTWs that include Latin America or the South Pacific will automatically cost at least A$1000 more.

Of these, one of the more interesting options may be a one-year RTW ticket with Aerolíneas Argentinas and KLM on their Sydney-Auckland-Buenos Aires-Caracas-Amsterdam-Singapore-Sydney route. It's possible to include a couple of other South American destinations, such as Santiago, Lima or Rio de Janeiro.

Alternatively, look for a cheap Northern Hemisphere RTW that includes Miami, from where you can make a side trip to Venezuela (see The USA, earlier in this section).

The Saturday editions of major newspapers such as the *Sydney Morning Herald* and the *Age* carry travel sections that have discount airfare ads, but very few of them include South American destinations. It may be worth getting a copy of some of the Spanish-language newspapers published in Australia, such as *El Español* or *Extra Informativo*, that list travel agents specializing in South America.

STA Travel has Australian offices in Adelaide, Brisbane, Cairns, Canberra, Darwin, Melbourne, Perth, Sydney and Townsville. Call ☎ 131 776 Australia-wide for the location of your nearest branch, or visit the Web site at www.statravel.com.au. In New Zealand, STA Travel (☎ 09-309 0458) has its main office at 10 High St, Auckland, and branches in Auckland, Christchurch, Dunedin, Hamilton, Palmerston North and Wellington.

Flight Centre (☎ 131 600 Australia-wide) has its central office at 82 Elizabeth St, Sydney, and dozens of offices throughout Australia. Its Web site is www.flightcentre.com.au. In New Zealand, Flight Centre (☎ 09-309 6171) has its central office in Auckland at National Bank Towers (corner of Queen and Darby Sts) and many branches throughout the country.

Central America

Lacsa (a Costa Rican carrier) can take you to Caracas from most Central American capitals, including San José (US$395 for a 30-day roundtrip), Guatemala (US$435) and Tegucigalpa (US$500). From Panama, you can fly direct to Caracas with Mexicana or Copa (both US$435).

You can also go from Central America to Venezuela via Colombia, using San Andrés Island (a Colombian sovereignty) as a bridge. The cheapest options are to fly to San Andrés from either Guatemala City, Guatemala (US$125), or Tegucigalpa, Honduras (US$120), and continue on to Cartagena, on the Colombian mainland, on a domestic flight (US$130).

South America & the Caribbean

Colombia Avianca and Servivensa operate flights between Bogotá and Caracas (US$218 one-way, US$251 for a 30-day roundtrip, US$281 for a 60-day roundtrip). Santa Bárbara flies daily between Barranquilla and Maracaibo (US$135 one-way, US$190 for a 30-day roundtrip). There are no longer Servivensa flights between Bogotá and San Antonio del Táchira, nor between Medellín and San Antonio del Táchira.

Note that all international tickets bought in Colombia are subject to a 16% tax (8% on roundtrip flights) on top of the listed fares.

Brazil Flying between Brazil and Venezuela is painfully expensive. The flight from São Paulo or Rio de Janeiro to Caracas will cost around US$840 one-way, or US$905 for a 60-day roundtrip. There are no direct flights between Manaus and Caracas, nor between Boa Vista and Santa Elena de Uairén.

Trinidad Aeropostal has five flights a week from Port of Spain to Caracas (US$120 one-way), two of which stop en route at Porlamar (US$120). BWIA flies four times a week direct from Port of Spain to Caracas (US$120). Rutaca operates three flights a week between Port of Spain and Maturín (US$90, US$120 for a 30-day roundtrip).

Guyana There are no direct flights between Venezuela and Guyana. You have to fly via Port of Spain, Trinidad, with BWIA (US$222/327 for a 30-day roundtrip in low/high season).

Netherlands Antilles ALM flies between Caracas and Aruba, Curaçao and Bonaire, but is expensive (about US$200 one-way for any of the three routes). Aeropostal services Aruba and Curaçao from Caracas and is much cheaper (about US$115 either route). Aserca flies between Caracas and Aruba, and between Maracaibo and Aruba (US$115 either route). Discount fares are available on seven- and 14-day roundtrip flights with all three carriers.

There are charter flights on light planes from Aruba and Curaçao to Coro (see Coro, in the Northwest chapter, for details).

LAND
Border Crossings

Venezuela has road connections with Colombia and Brazil only. There is no road link with Guyana; you must go via Brazil.

Colombia You can enter Venezuela from Colombia at four border crossings. Going from north to south, there's a coastal smuggling route between Maicao and Maracaibo (see Maracaibo, in the Northwest chapter, for details). Farther south is the most popular border crossing, between Cúcuta and San Antonio del Táchira (see San Antonio del Táchira, in the Andes chapter). Next comes an unpopular, dangerous (because of Colombian guerrilla activity) and inconvenient crossing from Arauca to El Amparo de Apure. Finally, there's an unusual but interesting outback route from Puerto Carreño, in Colombia, to either Puerto Páez or Puerto Ayacucho, in Venezuela (see Puerto Ayacucho, in the Guayana chapter).

Brazil There's only one road connecting Brazil and Venezuela. It leads from Manaus to Boa Vista (Brazil) to Santa Elena de Uairén (Venezuela) and then continues on to Ciudad Guayana. See Santa Elena de Uairén, in the Guayana chapter, for details.

You may also enter Venezuela via the Amazon at San Simón de Cocuy. This is an adventurous river/road route seldom used by travelers. See the Puerto Ayacucho section, in the Guayana chapter, for additional information on this route.

SEA
Lesser Antilles

There was a ferry service between the Lesser Antilles (St Lucia, Barbados, St Vincent and Trinidad) and Pampatar (Isla de Margarita) and Güiria in Venezuela, but it was suspended in the early 2000. See Güiria, in the Northeast chapter, for details.

Netherlands Antilles

Ferry services between Curaçao and La Vela de Coro (the port of Coro) and between Aruba and Punto Fijo, on the Paraguaná Peninsula, were closed in 1992. They may reopen one good day, but this opening has been in the works since soon after they closed, so have a bit of patience.

ORGANIZED TOURS

Tours to South America have become popular, and there are hundreds of tour companies in the USA, the UK and elsewhere providing organized trips. They range from easy hotel-based sightseeing excursions, designed mainly for first-time tourists, to expeditions tailored to the particular interests of experienced independent travelers. The latter tours feature activities rather than sightseeing and may include anything from trekking and bird-watching to mountain biking and rock climbing. An increasing number of tours are designed with some sort of ecotourism angle in mind. You'll find ads for these tours in hiking, mountaineering and wildlife magazines.

If you plan on taking an organized tour, start shopping early enough to make sure you get what you want. Some operators may offer slow-selling tours at considerably lower prices close to their scheduled departure. However, on the whole, tours to South America bought outside the continent tend to be an expensive way to travel.

Many overseas companies contract the services of local operators, obviously charging you more than you'd pay directly to that operator. Accordingly, you can save quite a bit by setting off on your own and arranging the tour in the country you go to. Fortunately, Venezuela has quite a developed tour business, with lots of tour operators (see the Organized Tours sections in the Getting Around and Caracas chapters). Naturally, flexibility is essential, as tours may take a while to be put together, unless you arrange one in advance from home.

The USA Given the proximity to South America and numerous flight connections, the USA has probably more tour companies specializing in the neighboring continent than the rest of the world combined. They are advertised in travel and outdoor magazines such as *Outside, Escape* and *Ecotraveler,* as well as magazines of a more general nature, including *Natural History* and *Audubon*. Here is a list of some reputable operators:

Eco Voyager
(☎ 617-769 0676 or toll-free ☎ 800-326 7088, fax 617-769 0667, info@ecovoyager.com) 79 Parkingway, Suite 10, Quincy, MA 02169
Web site: www.ecovoyager.com

International Expeditions
(☎ 205-428 1700 or toll-free ☎ 800-633 4734, fax 205-428 1714, ietravel@aol.com) One Environs Park, Helena, AL 35080
Web site: www.ietravel.com

Lost World Adventures
(☎ 404-373 5820 or toll-free ☎ 800-999 0558, fax 404-377 1902, info@lostworldadventures.com) 112 Church St, Decatur, GA 30030
Web site: www.lostworldadventures.com

Mountain Travel Sobek
(☎ 510-527 8100 or toll-free ☎ 888-687 6235, fax 510-525 7710, info@mtsobek.com) 6420 Fairmount Ave, El Cerrito, CA 94530
Web site: www.mtsobek.com

Southwind Adventures
(☎ 303-972 0701 or toll-free ☎ 800-377 9463, fax 303-972 0708, info@ southwindadventures.com) PO Box 621057, Littleton, CO 80162
Web site: www.southwindadventures.com

Venezuela Ventures
(☎ 914-273 6333 or toll-free ☎ 800-810 5021, fax 914-273 6370, info@venez.com) 156 Bedford Rd, Armonk, NY 10504
Web site: www.venez.com

Wilderness Travel
(☎ 510-558 2488 or toll-free ☎ 800-368 2794 fax 510-558 2489, info@wildernesstravel.com) 1102 Ninth St, Berkeley, CA 94710
Web site: www.wildernesstravel.com

Wildland Adventures
(☎ 206-365 0686 or toll-free ☎ 800-345 4453, fax 206-363 6615, info@wildland.com) 3516 NE 155th, Seattle, WA 98155
Web site: www.wildland.com

All the listed companies place emphasis on responsible tourism. Further information about responsible traveling can be obtained from the following organizations: Center for Responsible Tourism (☎ 415-843 5506), 2 Kensington Rd, San Anselmo, CA 94960; The Ecotourism Society (☎ 802 447 2121, fax 447 2122, ecotsocy@igc.apc.org), PO Box 755, North Bennington, VT 05257; and The Earth Preservation Fund, c/o Wildland Adventures (see the previous list).

Earthwatch organizes trips for volunteers to work overseas on scientific and cultural projects with an emphasis on the protection and preservation of ecology and environment. Other organizations that handle voluntary work include Conservation International and The Nature Conservancy. For the addresses of these and other environmental organizations, see the Ecology & Environment section, in the Facts about Venezuela chapter.

The UK Following is a list of some overland operators offering tours in South America:

Dragoman
(☎ 01728-861 133, fax 861 127, info@dragoman.co.uk) Camp Green, Kenton Rd, Debenham, Suffolk IP14 6LA
Web site: www.dragoman.co.uk

Encounter Overland
(☎ 020-7370 6845, fax 7244 9737, adventure@encounter.co.uk) 267 Old Brompton Rd, London SW5 9JA
Web site: www.encounter.co.uk

Exodus Travels
(☎ 020 8673 0859, fax 8673 0779, info@exodus.co.uk) 9 Weir Rd, London SW12 0LT
Web site: www.exodus.co.uk

Geodyssey
(☎ 020 7281 7788, fax 7281 7878, enquiries@geodyssey.co.uk) 116 Tollington Park, London N4 3RB
Web site: www.geodyssey.co.uk

Guerba Expeditions
(☎ 01373-826 611, fax 858 351) Wessex House, 40 Station Rd, Westbury, Wiltshire BA13 3JN
Web site: www.guerba.co.uk

Last Frontiers
(☎ 01296-658 650, fax 658 651, info@lastfrontiers.co.uk) Fleet Marston Farm, Aylesbury, Buckinghamshire HP18 0QT
Web site: www.lastfrontiers.co.uk

Top Deck
(☎ 020-7244 8641, fax 7373 6201) Top Deck House, 131/135 Earls Court Rd, London SW5 9RH
Web site: www.topdecktravel.co.uk

Geodyssey specializes in Venezuela and offers a variety of tours to almost every corner of the country. Also see the travel agencies listed in the Air section, earlier in this chapter; some of these, including JLA, South American Experience and Scott Dunn Latin America, offer tours to South America and may have Venezuela in their programs.

As with US operators, many UK tour companies are environmentally aware. Should you need more information on responsible traveling, contact the Centre for the Advancement of Responsible Travel (☎ 01732-352 757) and Tourism Concern (☎ 020-7753 3330).

Australia Few tour companies in Australia specialize in South America, and even fewer operators have Venezuela on their list. What is easiest to find in Australia are general tours covering several South American countries, mostly Argentina, Chile, Peru and Bolivia. Venezuela appears on some of these routes, and occasionally it is a destination in its own right.

Following is a list of Australian travel agencies offering tours to South American countries including Venezuela. Some may offer programs tailor-made for you.

Contours Travel
(☎ 03-9670 6900, contourstravel@bigpond.com) 84 Williams St, Melbourne, VIC 3000

Destination Holidays
(☎ 03-9725 4655, fax 9729 9211, desthols@ acepia.net.au) Suite 3, 36 Main St, Croydon, VIC 3136
Web site: www.south-america.com.au

Inca Tours
(☎ 02-4351 2133 or toll-free ☎ 1800 024 955, fax 02-4351 2526, inca@southamerica.com.au) 3 Margaret St, Wyong, NSW 2259

Peregrine Travel Centre
Represents UK's Exodus Travels (☎ 02-9290 2770, fax 9290 2155, enq@peregrine.net.au) 38 York St, Sydney, NSW 2000 (☎ 03-9662 2700, fax 9662 2422, travelcentre@peregrine.net.au) 258 Lonsdale St, Melbourne, VIC 3000
Web site: www.peregrine.net.au

South America Travel Centre
(☎ 03-9642 5353 or toll-free ☎ 1800 655 051, fax 03-9642 5454, satc@satc.com.au) 104 Hardware St, Melbourne, VIC 3000

Sundowners
Represents UK's Encounter Overland (☎ 03-9670 1123 or toll-free ☎ 1800 654 152, fax 03-9642 5838, adventure@sundowners.com.au) 600 Lonsdale St, Melbourne, VIC 3000
Web site: www.sundowners-travel.com.au

Getting Around

AIR

Venezuela has a number of airlines and an extensive network of national air routes. Caracas (or more precisely, Maiquetía, where Caracas' airport is located) is the country's major aviation hub for domestic flights, much the same way as it is for international air traffic. It handles departures to most major cities around the country and flights to minor destinations. Cities most frequently serviced from Caracas include Porlamar, Maracaibo and Puerto Ordaz (Ciudad Guayana).

Domestic Air Services

Avensa and Servivensa have long been Venezuela's main domestic airlines, controlling up to half of the national market. It's actually one company, although the planes are labeled with their own distinct logos. Servivensa was created by Avensa in 1978 as its subsidiary. Avensa itself has flown Venezuelan skies since 1943. The company had the widest network of internal routes over recent years, but unexpectedly, it ran into serious problems in 1999 and was almost grounded by mid-2000. It was apparently slowly recovering by the time were we going to press, but it may take a while until it regains its previous position, if ever.

Aeropostal is another Venezuelan carrier with a long tradition and a checkered history. Founded in 1929, it had up to 40% of the domestic market in its heyday, but ceased operations after a strike in 1994. Following the government's unsuccessful attempts to sell it, Aeropostal eventually found a private buyer and returned to the air in early 1997. It was quite successful and speedy in its recovery, with the result that it's now Venezuela's major carrier, servicing a dozen national destinations plus another dozen international airports.

Meanwhile, Venezuelan skies have become pretty crowded. In recent years, several new airlines, including Aserca, Laser, Air Venezuela, Avior, Lai and Santa Bárbara, have appeared on the market. They have successfully made their way into some of the most popular and lucrative routes, in addition to opening others not previously serviced by air.

To complete the picture, there are perhaps a dozen minor provincial carriers that cover regional and remote routes on a regular or charter basis. They fly light planes, so they can reach even the most obscure destinations.

Airfares

Domestic air travel in Venezuela is still relatively cheap when compared to neighboring Colombia or Brazil, but it's no longer the bargain it used to be a decade ago. Air fares have doubled or even tripled over the past several years. Fortunately, they recently seem to have grown at a slower pace, mostly because of fierce competition between airlines. Approximate fares are given in the relevant sections in the book, but treat them as guidelines only.

Fares vary between carriers, so if the route you're flying is serviced by several airlines, check their fares before buying your ticket. Travel agencies, where you are most likely to buy your tickets, will know who is flying which route and how much it costs. Since the air war is full-blown, there may be various promotional and discounted fares, particularly on the more popular routes serviced by various carriers.

Avensa/Servivensa, Aeropostal, Aserca and Laser use mainly jets and have higher fares than other airlines that predominantly fly propeller planes. The latter are mostly small planes, which sometimes don't even have a toilet, and the in-flight service is minimal, but you can save a lot over the jet fare.

Some airlines offer discount fares for students and/or senior citizens, but these change frequently and may apply only to Venezuelans. Check with the airlines or agencies for news.

Make sure to reconfirm your flight at least 72 hours before departure (preferably in person rather than by phone). Remember, not all flights depart on time, so be patient and have a flexible itinerary, particularly if you have flight connections.

Air Passes

Avensa Air Pass In its good days, Avensa offered an air pass that operated on a coupon system, allowing travelers to fly relatively cheaply within its network over a period of 45 days. You could buy the air pass both outside and inside Venezuela, but it was not sold to residents of any Latin American country. The pass may be reintroduced in the near future; check for news with Avensa offices in the USA (phone numbers are included in the USA section of the Getting There & Away chapter) or in Venezuela. Avensa's Web site is at www.avensa.com.ve.

Avianca Air Pass If you plan on traveling on to Colombia, you may be interested in the Colombian domestic air pass offered by Avianca. It can be bought only outside Colombia – so Venezuela will actually be your last place to decide – and you have to fly into Colombia with Avianca. The pass allows for five stopovers of your choice serviced by Avianca and SAM (two major Colombian carriers) and is valid for 30 days from the date of the first flight.

The pass costs US$260 (including San Andrés and Leticia as two of the five stopovers) or US$180 (excluding these two destinations). It's US$290 or US$200, respectively, in the high season (June to August and December). Up to three additional stopovers can be purchased at US$40 each. The pass is an excellent value when compared with regular airfares. For further information, contact Avianca offices in the USA, Europe or Latin America. In Venezuela, there's an Avianca office in Caracas. Avianca's Web site is at www.avianca.com.

Domestic Departure Tax

There's an airport tax of around US$0.80 on all domestic flights.

BUS

As there's no passenger train service in Venezuela, most traveling is done by bus. Buses are generally OK, especially on main roads, which are all paved and run regularly day and night between major population centers. Bus transportation is still reasonably cheap in Venezuela; you probably won't go wrong if you allow US$2 for one hour of a bus ride, or roughly 60km.

There are dozens of bus companies, each owning a plethora of buses ranging from archaic pieces of junk to the most recent models. The antiques usually ply the regional secondary roads, while the modern technology is put to service on major long-distance routes. If various companies operate the same route, fares are much the same with them all. The standard of service, though, may differ from one company to another, and you'll soon become familiar with the better ones.

No matter how low or high the standard, however, you can be pretty sure of having a lot of music on the bus ride – anything from *joropo* (see the boxed text 'The Music of Los Llanos,' in the Los Llanos chapter) to salsa – according to the driver's taste. The volume is also at the whim of the driver, and you may experience a whole night of blasting merengue or rap – not necessarily great fun. Another feature of local buses is the shading of windows with a dirty-purple tinted sticker. It's meant to be protection against strong sun, but it ruins the view, unless you get access to an open window.

Most major companies have introduced the so-called *servicio ejecutivo* in modern air-conditioned buses, which provide better standards and shorter traveling time, and cost about 20% to 30% more than the ordinary service *(servicio normal)*. These buses have their windows shut, tinted and usually curtained, and the air-conditioning can be *very* efficient, so have plenty of warm clothing at hand to avoid being frozen solid. They usually feature video entertainment, yet bloody US action movies played most of the night and often at full volume – not to mention the usually disastrous technical quality of the image and sound – can be real torture.

All intercity buses depart from and arrive at a *terminal de pasajeros*. Every city has such a terminal, usually outside the city center but always linked to it by local transportation. Caracas, with its two terminals, is the most important transportation hub, handling buses to just about every corner of the country. Many terminals charge a *tasa de salida* (departure tax), usually not higher than US$0.20.

In general, there's no need to buy tickets in advance for major routes. You usually just go to the terminal, find which company has the next bus due to depart, buy your ticket and board the bus. On some minor routes, where there are only a few departures a day, it's worth considering buying your ticket several hours before the scheduled departure. The only times you really need to book well in advance are during and around Christmas, Carnaval and Easter, when Venezuelans rush to travel.

Many short-distance regional routes are serviced by the so-called *por puesto* (literally 'by the seat'). It's a cross between a bus and a taxi – a similar kind of service as a *colectivo* in Colombia or Peru.

Por puestos are usually US-made large cars of the '60s and '70s vintages (less often, vans or minibuses) that ply fixed routes and depart when all seats are filled. They cost somewhere between 50% and 100% more than ordinary buses but are faster and may be more comfortable. On some routes, they are the dominant or even the exclusive means of transportation. Depending on the region and kind of vehicle, por puestos may also be called *carros* or *carritos*.

TRAIN
Venezuela had a railway network, but when the oil boom hit the nation, it was largely discarded in favor of road transportation. The last railway that carried passengers, the 173km Barquisimeto–Puerto Cabello line, ceased this service in the mid-1990s and now only carries freight. There are plans to reintroduce the passenger service.

CAR & MOTORCYCLE
Traveling by an independent means of transportation – be it a car or motorcycle, owned or rented – is a comfortable and attractive way of getting around the country. Some advantages are schedule flexibility, access to remote areas, and the ability to seize fleeting photographic opportunities.

Venezuela is relatively safe, the road network is extensive and usually in acceptable repair, gas stations are everywhere, and fuel costs next to nothing – US$0.10 to US$0.20 per liter, depending on the octane level. It's among the cheapest gasoline in the world, despite the fact that prices jumped by 500% in 1996.

This rosy picture appears to be slightly obscured by Venezuelan traffic and local driving manners. Traffic in Venezuela, especially in Caracas, is not exactly what you may be used to at home. It's wild, chaotic, noisy, polluting and anarchic.

You may still find some similarities if you're coming from, say, Italy or Spain, but if you're a novice traveler from Australia, Germany or Canada, you're in for a shock. It's not that road rules don't exist; it's just that nobody respects them and they're not enforced.

Road Rules
Watching crazy traffic, reminiscent of Formula 1 racing, you'd never suspect that there are speed limits, but they do legally exist. Unless traffic signs say otherwise, the maximum speed limit in urban areas is 40km per hour, and outside built-up areas it's 80km per hour.

Officially, traffic coming from the right has priority, unless indicated otherwise by signs. In practice, however, it seems that right-of-way depends on the size of vehicle rather than the regulations. Accordingly, trucks generally take priority over cars, cars over motorcycles, and motorcycles over pedestrians.

Cars must be equipped with seat belts for front seats (which always have to be used), and they must have a spare tire, wheel block, jack and a special reflector triangle, which in case of accident or breakdown has to be placed 50m behind the car. Motorcyclists have to wear a crash helmet, and motorcycles cannot be ridden at night. However, once again, all this is theoretical.

The minimum driving age in Venezuela is 18. Although there are limits on your blood alcohol level, driving drunk is not unusual, and rules relating to this are seldom enforced. See the Facts for the Visitor chapter for information about driver's licenses.

Rental

There are several international car rental companies, including Hertz, Avis and Budget, and a number of local operators. They have offices at most major airports and in city centers, usually in top-end hotels. Any top-class hotel, tourist office or travel agency will provide you with detailed information about where to look for them. Many travel agents are only too willing to arrange car rental for you.

Car rental is not cheap in Venezuela – prices are higher than in the USA – and there are seldom any discounts. Local companies may be cheaper than international operators, but their cars and rental conditions can leave something to be desired.

When you get rental quotes, make sure they include insurance. Otherwise, you'll have to pay for it on top of the quoted price, as it's compulsory. Some companies allow a set number of free kilometers per day or week, but others will apply a per-kilometer rate from the moment you take the car.

As a rough guide only, a small car will cost around US$50 to US$60 per day (including insurance), while the discount rate for a full week will be about US$300 to US$350. A 4WD vehicle is usually considerably more expensive and harder to obtain.

Rental agencies will require you to produce your driver's license and a credit card (Visa, MasterCard and American Express are the most common). You need to be at least 21 years of age to rent a car, although renting some cars (particularly luxury models and 4WDs) may require you to be at least 23 or 25. Some companies also have an age ceiling, usually 65.

Read the rental contract carefully before signing (most contracts are in Spanish only). Pay close attention to any theft clause, as it will probably load any loss onto the renter. Look at the car carefully, and insist on listing any defects (including scratches) on the rental form. Check the spare tire, and take note of whether there is a jack.

Bringing Your Own Vehicle

Bringing a car into South America is expensive. Since there is no road through the Darien Gap (an area of undeveloped rain forest between Panama and Colombia), it's impossible to drive all the way from North to South America. You can continue by road as far as Panama, from where the only way to move your vehicle farther south is by sea or air.

The cheapest way will probably be by boat from Colón (Panama) to Barranquilla or Cartagena (Colombia). Prices are extremely variable and negotiable; you may end up paying anything between US$300 and US$800 for shipping your car, and US$100 to US$300 for a motorcycle. Prices apart, the procedure is time-consuming, as there's a lot of paperwork involved at both ends. The security of shipping is minimal, so take every possible precaution and the best insurance you can. Some smaller vessels are sometimes contraband boats, and their service may be risky.

Motorcyclists may consider the airplane option, which is safer, easier and faster than boat, but more expensive. Start by asking the cargo departments of the airlines that fly to Colombia, or at the cargo terminal at Tocumen international airport in Panama City. Travel agents can sometimes help.

Another possibility is to ship your vehicle directly from the USA to Venezuela, in which case you are most likely to arrive in La Guaira, Puerto Cabello or Maracaibo. The cheapest point of departure from the USA will probably be Miami; look in the yellow pages under automobile transporters for toll-free 800 and 888 numbers. You usually need to give the shipping company one or two weeks' notice; expect it to take a month or more from the date of sailing.

Prices are variable, so call several companies before committing yourself; the cost of shipping a car can be anywhere between US$500 and US$1500.

Drivers and motorcyclists will need their vehicle's registration papers, liability insurance and a Carnet de Passage en Douane, known in Spanish as a Libreta de Pasos por Aduana (Customs Passage Document). Contact your local automobile association and Venezuelan consulate for details about all documentation. Touring y Automóvil Club de Venezuela (see Automobile Clubs, later in this section) can be useful, and the South American Explorers in the USA (see the Tourist Offices section in the Facts for the Visitor chapter) may also have some helpful advice.

If planning to take your own vehicle with you, check in advance to see what spares are likely to be available. Fuel is usually no problem and a bargain. You can readily get diesel and leaded gasoline in three octane grades (87, 91 and 95 octanes). Unleaded gasoline was introduced only in 1999, but it's now available at most gas stations.

Venezuela has quite a developed automobile industry. Various foreign brands, including Chrysler, Fiat, Ford, General Motors, Mitsubishi, Renault and Toyota, are assembled locally, and most spare parts for these cars are easily available. Popular imported brands include Honda, Mazda, BMW, Hyundai, Peugeot and Volkswagen, so you can also expect a reasonable supply of their spare parts. However, spare parts for unpopular cars can be hard to get, so bring along a good supply if you bring your Jaguar.

See also Driver's License, in the Visas & Documents section of the Facts for the Visitor chapter.

Driving in Venezuela

Whether you bring your own vehicle or rent one, drive carefully and defensively. Don't expect local drivers to obey the rules. Never assume, for example, that a vehicle will stop at a red light or stop sign. Using signals (indicators) before making a turn is rare, while driving the wrong way on one-way streets is not unusual. Pedestrians leap into traffic and often walk across highways and sometimes freeways.

Although many roads look to be in good shape, you should always be prepared for unexpected potholes and occasional missing manhole covers. Some roads, including the notorious Caracas–La Guaira highway, have poor-quality surfacing material and can be slippery, particularly when wet.

Road signposting is poor, and it's often difficult to find the right way without stopping and asking locals for directions. Signs are frequently vandalized or destroyed, and nobody seems to care much about replacing them.

When you drive in Caracas and other big cities, it's best to have the doors locked and windows rolled up (or almost rolled up), to prevent unexpected theft at red lights or in traffic jams. If you can't stand the windows closed, don't have handbags and packets lying around on the seats, and wear your watch on the hand away from the window.

Just don't look out the window.

When driving on country highways, you'll be frequently stopped at the *alcabalas* (road checkposts operated by the Guardia Nacional), where the guards will examine your passport, and often your car papers and driver's license as well. Sometimes they will even search the vehicle and your luggage.

Car security is a problem, so never leave valuables in the vehicle, and lock it securely. If possible, always leave the vehicle in a guarded parking lot *(estacionamiento vigilado)*. If your car is stolen, report the theft immediately to the police, where a written report (known as a *denuncia)* will be produced. It is absolutely essential for making an insurance claim, or if the car is rented, you must submit a copy to the car rental company.

If you are involved in a road accident, don't move your car – regardless of how badly traffic is blocked – until the transit police arrive. They should be called as soon as possible at ☎ 167. If you move your vehicle before the transit police make a report, you can't claim insurance. If you have an accident resulting in injuries or death, you'll be detained and your vehicle impounded temporarily, even if you're not at fault.

Automobile Clubs

Touring y Automóvil Club de Venezuela (☎ 02-781 97 43, 782 15 77), Torre Phelps (the board on the top of the building says 'Philips'), Piso 15, Plaza Venezuela, Caracas, can be useful for travelers with their own vehicles. The club provides general driving information and publishes a manual of traffic laws and regulations. It also offers a range of services, such as towing, car maintenance, documentation and legal assistance in accident cases; these are usually discounted for members. The club can provide information and aid on importing and exporting vehicles into and out of Venezuela.

BICYCLE

Cycling is a cheap, convenient, healthy, environmentally sound and above all fun way of traveling. All this sounds terrific, but Venezuela is not the best place for cyclists.

There are almost no bike tracks, bike rentals or any other facilities. Drivers don't show much courtesy to cyclists either. Cycling is not popular among locals, and foreign travelers with their own bikes are a rarity. Mérida is one of the few places so far where mountain biking has started to become popular and bikes can be hired.

This doesn't mean that cycling is impossible or not worth the bother. Roads are usually in good shape and most of the country is flat. Except for cities (particularly Caracas), where cycling can be annoying and dangerous, there are no major problems for independent cyclists. Cycling will let you cover a fair amount of ground without going too fast to enjoy the scenery. Locals will certainly be curious if you are traveling by bike, and it's a good way to get talking.

Before you leave home, go over your bike with a fine-tooth comb and fill your repair kit with every imaginable spare. As with cars and motorcycles, you won't necessarily be able to buy that crucial gizmo for your machine when it breaks down somewhere in the back of beyond just as the sun sets. Bring along a solid lock to protect your bike.

Bicycles can be taken with you on the plane. You can dismantle them and put them in a bike bag or box, but it's much easier to simply wheel your bike up to the check-in desk, where it should be treated as a piece of baggage. You may have to remove pedals and handlebars so that it takes up less space in the aircraft's hold; check all this with the airline well in advance, preferably before you pay for your ticket.

HITCHHIKING

Hitchhiking is never entirely safe in any country in the world, and we don't recommend it. Travelers who decide to hitchhike should understand that they are taking a small but potentially serious risk. People who do choose to hitchhike will be safer if they travel in pairs and let someone know where they are planning to go.

Safety apart, Venezuela is not that good for hitchhiking. Although many people have cars, they are reluctant to stop to pick up strangers. If you decide to hitch, be prepared for long waits, and even then don't count on reaching your destination. As bus transportation is fast, efficient and relatively cheap, it's probably not worth wasting time hitchhiking. Women traveling on their own shouldn't hitchhike at all.

BOAT
Venezuela has a number of islands off its Caribbean coast, the main one being Isla de Margarita. See the sections on Puerto La Cruz, Cumaná and Isla de Margarita for details about boats and ferries going to and from the island. There are no regular boat services to Venezuela's other islands.

The Río Orinoco is the country's major waterway, and it is navigable from its mouth up to Puerto Ayacucho. However, there's no passenger service operating along the river.

LOCAL TRANSPORTATION
Bus
All cities and many major towns have their own urban transportation, which in most places is serviced by a small bus or minibus. It is called, depending on the region, a *buseta, carro, carrito, micro, camioneta* or *camionetica*. The standard, speed and efficiency vary from place to place, but on the whole, city buses are often crowded.

Local buses cost next to nothing; the fare doesn't normally exceed US$0.25 and in most cities is a flat rate, so you pay the same to go one block as to go right across the city. Luggage is free, and drivers usually don't hassle passengers getting on with large backpacks, even into a crowded bus.

You get on and off by the front door and pay the driver or assistant directly when entering or, more often, when you get off. You never get a ticket. To let the driver know that you intend to get off, simply shout *parada* (bus stop) or clap your hands twice, and he will stop at the nearest bus stop.

In many larger cities, buses are supplemented by por puestos, which are faster and more comfortable. The fare is somewhere between 20% and 100% higher than buses still a bargain. An urban por puesto has no designated stops; you just wave it down anywhere you happen to be on its route, and it

will stop if it has a free seat. A por puesto also comes under a variety of names, of which 'carro' or 'carrito' are the most popular.

Metro
Caracas is the only Venezuelan city that has an underground railway system. See the Caracas chapter for details.

Taxi
Especially if you're traveling with companions, taxis are a fairly inexpensive and convenient means of getting around. The fare will usually be the same regardless of the number of passengers, though some drivers may demand more if you have a lot of luggage.

Taxis are particularly useful when you arrive in an unfamiliar city and want to get from the bus terminal or the airport to the city center to look for a hotel. A taxi may also be chartered for longer distances. This is convenient if you want to visit places near major cities that are serviced by local transportation infrequently or not at all.

Taxis are identifiable by a sign reading 'Taxi' or 'Libre.' Curiously enough, taxis in Venezuela don't have meters, so fares are a matter of agreement between the driver and the passenger. On the more popular routes, there are commonly accepted fares, known to the locals. Taxi drivers in touristy areas often try to charge foreign visitors a gringo fare, obviously much higher than they would charge locals. It's advisable to find out the correct fare beforehand from an independent source, eg, from terminal officials or a hotel reception desk. Always fix the fare with the driver *before* boarding the cab. If you can't agree on a price with the first driver, try another taxi.

ORGANIZED TOURS
Tours are a popular way to visit some parts of Venezuela, largely because vast areas of the country are virtually inaccessible by public transportation (eg, the Delta del Orinoco or Amazonas) or because a visit on one's own to scattered sights over a large territory (as in La Gran Sabana) may be considerably more time-consuming and, eventually, more expensive than a tour.

Many companies in Caracas can send you on a tour to just about every corner of the country – see the Caracas chapter for details about the local tour operators and their offers. However, it will be cheaper, and may even be better, to arrange the tour from the regional center closest to the area you are going to visit. Accordingly, for hikes in the Andes, the place to look for a guide or a tour is Mérida; for excursions around La Gran Sabana and treks to the top of Roraima, the cheapest organized trips are found in Santa Elena de Uairén; for Amazonas, the obvious point for talking to agents is Puerto Ayacucho; for the Delta del Orinoco, Tucupita is the right address; and for tours to Salto Angel, Ciudad Bolívar is the place to shop around. Refer to the relevant sections of this book for information.

Many Venezuelan tour companies receive mixed reports, sometimes totally contradictory. As a matter of fact, tours are probably some of the most difficult aspects of travel to be judged objectively. What some travelers consider great others can hardly stand. Furthermore, many variables, such as the particular guide you go with, weather or even the company of other travelers in your tour, may affect your general impression. It also seems that once a company is mentioned in a guidebook, it may get lazy and deliver a poor product or an overly expensive one. To sum up, you shouldn't always jump to the first operator listed in this book, but shop around and check various options, getting a rundown on a variety of companies, prices, records, references etc.

We try to provide as detailed contact information about the tour companies as possible, to give you all the available tools for information and booking. It may be advisable to contact the companies in advance from home, particularly if your trip to Venezuela is going to be on a tight schedule, but always leave a few extra days for unexpected developments, which are likely to happen.

Caracas

☎ 02 (☎ 0212 from Feb 24, 2001)

With 440 years of history under its belt, Caracas today is a sprawling metropolis of almost five million inhabitants. Like most of the large cities on the continent, it's a striking mixture of all things Latin American, with its own distinctive traits. Perhaps most characteristic of the city are its spectacular setting, pleasant climate and modern architecture. 'Yankeefied' and almost denuded of its colonial charm, Caracas is a vibrant, fast-paced, progressive and cosmopolitan city – attractive and captivating in some aspects, depressing and disappointing in others. It's a huge Latin American city with every modern convenience and every third-world problem.

It cannot be denied that Caracas today has some impressive modern architecture, and numerous sculptures, bas-reliefs, mosaics and murals grace streets, metro stations and the foyers of public buildings. However, unbalanced city growth has produced vast expanses of shantytowns that creep up hillsides all around the central districts. Caracas' setting in a valley amid rolling hills only highlights the contrast between wealth and poverty.

Caracas also has a web of motorways not often seen in other South American capitals, but the vast amount of motor vehicles in the city causes a kind of traffic frenzy, not to mention serious environmental problems. Traffic jams are a way of life, probably more so than in most other large cities on the continent.

Its size and status as the capital city make Caracas the unquestioned center of Venezuela's political, scientific, cultural, intellectual and educational life. Whether you're interested in good food, plush hotels, theater, museums, nightlife or shopping, nowhere else in the country will you find as much to choose from.

Set at an altitude of about 900m, Caracas enjoys an agreeable, relatively dry and sunny climate with a mean temperature of about 22°C. The rainy season lasts from June to October.

On a less enticing note, Caracas is the least secure of all Venezuelan cities. Petty crime in general, and robbery and armed assaults in particular, are on the rise.

Highlights

- Visit the Museum of Contemporary Art.
- Hike In rugged Parque Nacional El Ávila.
- Explore the nightspots of Las Mercedes.
- Tour the Museum of Colonial Art.
- Take a weekend trip to El Hatillo.

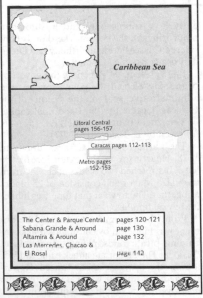

Caribbean Sea

Litoral Central
pages 156–157

Caracas pages 112–113

Metro pages
152–153

HISTORY

Caracas had a precarious beginning in 1560. It was then that Francisco Fajardo of Isla de Margarita discovered the verdant valley (today entirely taken up by the city) inhabited

CARACAS

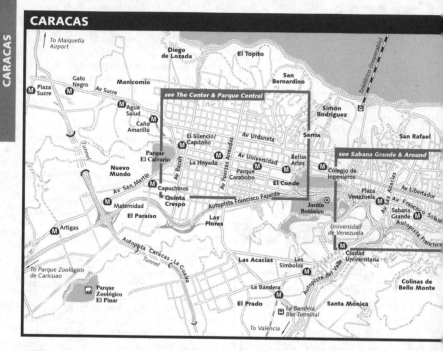

To Maiquetía
Airport

Diego
de Lozada

El Topito

San
Bernardino

Teleférico (inoperable)

Gato
Negro

Manicomio

Plaza
Sucre

Av Sucre

Simón
Rodríguez

Agua
Salud

see The Center & Parque Central

Caño
Amarillo

San Rafael

El Silencio/
Capitolio

Av Urdaneta

Sarria

Parque
El Calvario

Av Bolívar

Av Universidad

Bellas
Artes

see Sabana Grande & Around

Nuevo
Mundo

Av San Martín

La Hoyada

Av Fuerzas Armadas

Parque
Carabobo

El Conde

Colegio de
Ingenieros

Plaza
Venezuela

Av Acacias

Av Libertador

Capuchinos

Quinta
Crespo

Autopista Francisco Fajardo

Jardín
Botánico

Av Francisco Solar

Sabana
Grande

Autopista Francisco

Maternidad

Las
Flores

El Paraíso

Universidad
de Venezuela

Artigas

Autopista Caracas - La Guaira

Tunnel

Las Acacias

Los
Símbolos

Ciudad
Universitaria

To Parque Zoológico
de Caricuao

La Bandera

Autopista del Valle

Colinas de
Bello Monte

Parque
Zoológico
El Pinar

El Prado

La Bandera
Bus Terminal

Santa Mónica

To Valencia

by Toromaima Indians. He founded a settlement named San Francisco, but was soon driven out by the natives. A year later, Juan Rodríguez Suárez, the founder of Mérida, arrived and resurrected San Francisco, which by then had been razed by the Indians. Years of struggle followed as the village tried to survive repeated Indian attacks, in which many members of the small population were killed, including Rodríguez.

In 1567, a complete conquest of the valley was ordered by the governor of the province, Pedro Ponce de León. An expedition of 136 men under the command of Captain Diego de Losada was sent from El Tocuyo. They overcame a brave Indian resistance before reestablishing the settlement yet again on July 25, 1567. The new township was named Santiago de León de Caracas: 'Santiago' after the patron saint of Spain, 'León' after the governor, and 'Caracas' after the Indian group that inhabited the coastal cordillera and was apparently less troublesome and hostile than other tribes in the region. The date is considered Caracas' formal birthday and Diego de Losada its official founder.

In 1577, Juan de Pimentel, the governor of the day, elected the young town as the administrative seat of the colony. Thus Caracas became the third and final capital of Venezuela (Coro was the first, 1527–46, followed by El Tocuyo, 1547–77).

The earliest map of Caracas, drawn in 1578, clearly shows the extension of the 'city.' It stretched two blocks each way from the Plaza Mayor and consisted of 25 blocks altogether. The town at that time was inhabited by 60 families.

From the beginning, Caracas' development was hindered by constant setbacks, including pirate raids, plagues and natural disasters. The first pirate attack came in 1595, leaving the town sacked and razed. Reconstructed and revived, Caracas went on to be destroyed by a violent earthquake in 1641,

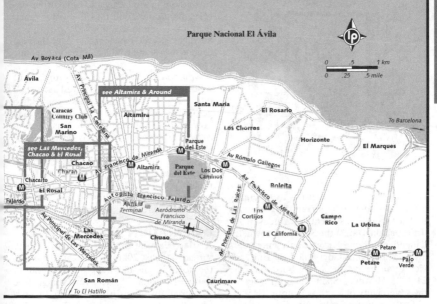

CARACAS

Parque Nacional El Ávila

see Altamira & Around

see Las Mercedes, Chacao & El Rosal

To Barcelona

only four years after the bishops had moved the archdiocese here from Coro. Some 500 inhabitants died in the ruins.

The 18th century proved to be more fortunate. In 1725, the Universidad Real y Pontificia de Caracas (the present-day Universidad Central de Venezuela) became the province's first university. Three years later, the Real Compañía Guipuzcoana was created. This trading company, comprised of 700 captains and merchants from Spain's Basque region, was given a monopoly over trade between the mother country and the colony. In Venezuela, the company had its headquarters in the port of La Guaira and a branch in Puerto Cabello.

Although Guipuzcoana traders initially contributed greatly to Caracas' progress, later on their aggressive practices and corruption aroused widespread discontent among the colonists. In 1749, Juan Francisco de León marched on Caracas with 800 men to protest against the company's oppressive tactics. In the opinion of many historians, this riot was the first open protest of importance, sowing the seeds of what became the independence movement. The company was eventually dissolved in 1785.

On March 28, 1750, Caracas became the birthplace of Francisco Miranda, and on July 24, 1783, that of Simón Bolívar. The former was to pave the way to independence, the latter was to realize that aim.

On April 19, 1810, a group of councilors, supported by some notable *caraqueños* (as inhabitants of Caracas are known), denounced the authority of the Spanish governor and formed a Supreme Junta to replace the government. The political struggle continued for over a year, until July 5, 1811, when the congress convened in Caracas and solemnly declared the independence of Venezuela. The document was signed by all but one delegate.

On Maundy Thursday of 1812, an earthquake wrecked the town and killed some

The Caracas coat of arms

10,000 people. The conservative clergy swiftly seized the opportunity to declare that it was a punishment from heaven for the rebellion against the Spanish Crown. Independence, however, was only nine years away, to be eventually sealed by Bolívar's victory at the battle of Carabobo on June 24, 1821. However, Spain did not recognize the sovereignty of Venezuela until 1845.

Despite its political merits, Caracas continued to grow at a very modest pace. It wasn't until the 1870s that an extensive modernization program was launched by General Guzmán Blanco, the ruler at the time, known as 'El Modernizador.' A number of monumental buildings, among them the National Capitol, were erected over the following decades, considerably changing the face of the city center. Unfortunately, in 1900, yet another serious earthquake ruined much of the urban fabric, and reconstruction had to begin all over again.

Then came the oil boom, and things began to change at breakneck speed. Oil money was pumped into modernization, successfully transforming the somewhat bucolic colonial town into a vast concrete sprawl. In the name of progress, most colonial buildings were demolished and their place taken by spanking commercial centers and steel-and-glass towers. Some ambitious projects – including the freeways to Maiquetía and Valencia, the UCV university

campus, La Rinconada horse-racing track and the cable car up to Pico El Ávila – were carried out in the 1950s, and rapid urban development continued into the 1980s, when the metro system was opened. Growth has, however, slowed considerably over the past decade as a result of the country's economic crisis.

Spurred on by the illusory dream of wealth, thousands of rural dwellers rushed into Caracas, but most never managed to get their share of the city's prosperity; they now lead a hand-to-mouth existence in *ranchos* (ramshackle huts) covering the hills around the central districts. Over the last 50 years, the city's population has expanded from around 400,000 to about five million, though some unofficial estimates place the current population within the metropolitan boundaries as high as six million.

ORIENTATION

Nestled in a long and narrow valley, the city spreads at least 20km from west to east. To the north looms the steep, verdant wall of Parque Nacional El Ávila, refreshingly free of human dwellings. To the south, by contrast, the city is expanding up the hillsides, with modern *urbanizaciones* (suburbs) and derelict *barrios* (shantytowns) invading and occupying every acceptably flat piece of land.

The valley itself is a dense urban fabric, with forests of skyscrapers sticking out of a mass of low-rise buildings. The area from El Silencio to Chacao can be considered the greater downtown area, packed with commercial centers, banks, offices, shops, hotels, eating establishments and public buildings. The metro's main line (No 1) goes right along this axis.

The historic quarter (called 'the center' in this chapter) is at the west end of the greater downtown area and is clearly recognizable on the map by the original chessboard layout of the streets. About 1.5km to the east is the Parque Central area, noted for good museums, theaters and cinemas. Another 2km east is Sabana Grande, centered on an attractive pedestrian mall that's lined with shops and restaurants. Continuing east, you come to Chacao, a commercial district of rather low priority for tourists, and then to the trendy Altamira, which boasts a good number of upmarket restaurants and nightspots. El Rosal and Las Mercedes, to the south of Chacao, are two other districts catering to gourmets and night trippers.

Although Caracas' attractions are scattered throughout the city, many of them are easily accessible by metro. In the addresses listed in this chapter, the nearest metro station is usually included if the place is within walking distance of the station.

A curiosity of Caracas is the center's street address system, which might be difficult for newcomers to follow. It's actually not the streets that bear names but rather the *esquinas*, or street corners. A place is identified by the street corners on either side, and its address is given 'corner to corner.' If, for instance, the address is 'Piñango a Conde,' you know that the place is between these two street corners. If the place were right on the corner, its address would be 'Esquina Conde.' Authorities have given numbers and cardinal-point designations to the streets (Este, Oeste, Norte and Sur), but locals continue to stick with the esquinas.

Outside the colonial center, a conventional system is used wherein the streets, and not the corners, indicate where the place is located. Major streets are commonly named 'Avenidas.' Street numbers are seldom used, and you'll rarely find one on facades or entrance doors.

The Venezuelan system of designating floors is the same as that used in the UK. The ground floor is the *piso bajo* or *planta baja*, the 1st floor is the *primer piso*, then comes the *segundo piso* (2nd floor) etc. In addresses, floors are usually written in the form 'Piso 1,' 'Piso 2' etc. In elevators, abbreviations used on the buttons include PB (ground floor), M (mezzanine), S (basement level) and PH (penthouse).

Maps
Some of the better bookshops sell folded Caracas city maps that have a map of Venezuela on the reverse. Perhaps the best Caracas/country map was published by the Lagoven oil company, but it's virtually out of print.

If you can't get any of these, look for the reasonable Caracas city map at the back of the local phone directory. It's also worth remembering that most metro stations have a Caracas map posted somewhere near the ticket booth and usually another copy on the train platform.

For information on where to buy maps for the rest of Venezuela, see Maps in the Facts for the Visitor chapter.

INFORMATION
Tourist Offices
The Corpoturismo tourist office (☎ 574 87 12, 574 95 56, fax 573 89 83, corpoturismo@platino.gov.ve) is on the 35th floor of the Torre Oeste (West Tower), Parque Central (Ⓜ Bellas Artes). When you enter the tower, take the elevator from Nivel Lecuna (elevators from other levels don't go to this floor). The office is open 8:30 am to 12:30 pm and 2 to 5 pm weekdays.

Corpoturismo has two outlets at the Maiquetía airport: in the international terminal (☎ 355 25 98), open daily 7 am to midnight; and in the national terminal (☎ 355 11 91), open daily 7 am to 8 pm.

Hotel Hilton Caracas (☎ 503 50 00) has a tourist information desk (open daily 7 am to 10 pm) in the main lobby. It's officially a service for hotel guests only, but the friendly and knowledgeable English-speaking staff is likely to attend to you if they are not too busy.

Park Information
Venezuela's Instituto Nacional de Parques Nacionales, commonly known as 'Inparques' (☎ 285 41 06, 285 48 59, fax 285 30 70), has its main seat just east of the Parque del Este metro station. The office doesn't provide maps or brochures about the parks, but it has a specialized library, open to the public 9 am to noon Monday; 9 am to noon and 2 to 4 pm Tuesday, Thursday and Friday; and 2 to 4 pm Wednesday. You don't have to go to Inparques for permits to the parks, as they are no longer necessary.

Money

There's a constellation of banks in Caracas, but probably none of them will exchange your US cash dollars unless you have an account with them. The usual places to change foreign cash are *casas de cambio,* and there are quite a number of them. One with a good reputation is Italcambio, which has offices on Avenida Urdaneta in the old center, Avenida Casanova in Sabana Grande, Calle California in Las Mercedes and Avenida Ávila in Altamira, plus outlets in several shopping centers, including Sambil and El Recreo (see the maps for locations). They are all open 8:30 am to 5 pm weekdays and 9 am to 1 pm Saturday. There are also Italcambio exchange desks at the international terminal of Maiquetía airport (see Getting There & Away, later in this chapter, for more information on changing money at the airport).

All Italcambio offices also sell foreign currency and change traveler's checks as well. However, American Express checks can be exchanged at a better rate at Corp Banca (though the transaction will take longer), which has plenty of branches around the city.

The refund assistance point for holders of American Express traveler's checks is Turisol (☎ 959 60 91, 959 94 17), in Centro Ciudad Comercial Tamanaco (CCCT), Nivel PB (see Metro, under Getting Around, later in this chapter, for information on getting to CCCT).

Cash advances on Visa and MasterCard can be easily obtained at Banco de Venezuela, Banco Unión, Banco Mercantil, Banco Provincial and some other banks. Many of them have ATMs.

If you need money sent to you quickly, it's probably best to use Western Union. It's represented by the Grupo Zoom, which has about 25 offices scattered around the city. Call toll-free ☎ 800 227 82 for information.

Post

The main Ipostel post office, Avenida Urdaneta, Esquina Carmelitas, close to Plaza Bolívar, has a poste restante service. Letters sent to you should be addressed as follows:

your last name capitalized and underlined, your first name, Lista de Correos, IPOSTEL, Carmelitas, Caracas 1010.

Another central post office is on Plaza La Candelaria, next to the church. Other convenient post offices around the city include one in Sabana Grande (in the Centro Comercial Arta on Plaza Chacaíto), in Chacao (Avenida Blandín) and in Altamira (Avenida Francisco de Miranda).

There are a number of international and local courier companies, including FedEx (☎ 205 33 33), DHL (☎ 800 345 74), UPS (☎ 204 14 41) and TNT (☎ 205 05 81). Shop around, as rates vary considerably.

Telephone & Fax

Almost all of Caracas telephone numbers have seven digits, but there are still some old six-digit numbers, which are gradually being changed. The 02 telephone area code for Caracas applies for both six- and seven-digit numbers. As elsewhere in Venezuela, toll-free 800 numbers are followed by five digits.

You can call virtually anywhere in Venezuela from public phones. They are everywhere, though many are out of order and those that work may be besieged by people. Most public phones have access to an international network, so you can call abroad using a phone card or by making a collect (reverse-charge) call.

CANTV has been recently opening its own telecommunication offices (called 'Centros de Comunicaciones CANTV'), which offer domestic and international calls from their cabins; calls are charged by the minute, without the three-minute minimum charge. So far there are half a dozen outlets in Caracas, including the ones at Esquina El Conde and El Chorro a Dr Díaz in the center, one in the Parque Central, and another one in Centro Plaza on Avenida Francisco de Miranda in Los Palos Grandes (Ⓜ Altamira). Many top-end hotels will place your call through the CANTV operator but will add a hefty charge on top of this service. All the CANTV offices listed above also provide fax service.

Email & Internet Access

Caracas already has a number of places offering Internet services, and new ones are popping up every month. The facilities include:

Business Center
(☎ 503 50 00) in Hotel Hilton Caracas
(Ⓜ Bellas Artes)

CANTV Net
(☎ 901 35 00) Centro Lido, Avenida Francisco de Miranda, El Rosal (Ⓜ Chacaíto)
(☎ 263 08 81) Centro Sambil, Nivel Acuario, Chacao (Ⓜ Chacao)

CompuMall
(☎ 993 01 11) Edificio CompuMall, Piso 1, Avenida Orinoco, Las Mercedes

Cyber Café M@dness
(☎ 267 83 26) Centro Sambil, Nivel Acuario, Chacao (Ⓜ Chacao)

Cyber Office 2020
(☎ 762 94 07) Edificio San Germán, Calle Pascual Navarro at Avenida Francisco Solano (Ⓜ Plaza Venezuela)

Digital Planet
(☎ 261 05 09) Yamin Family Center, Piso 1, Avenida San Juan Bosco, Altamira (Ⓜ Altamira)

Internet Para Todos
(☎ 992 41 55) Centro Comercial Paseo Las Mercedes, Nivel Mercado, Local 143, Las Mercedes

Internet Solution Center
(☎ 793 51 22) Torre Capriles, Planta Baja, Plaza Venezuela (Ⓜ Plaza Venezuela)

Naveg@ Center
(☎ 564 93 96) Edificio Iberia, Piso Bajo, Avenida Urdaneta, Esquina Animas, La Candelaria (Ⓜ Parque Carabobo)

Postnet
(☎ 952 20 05) Mezzanina, Local C3 (Ⓜ Chacaito)

SCAI (Servicio de Cabinas de Acceso a Internet) Biblioteca Metropolitana Simón Rodríguez, Calle Norte 4, Esquina El Conde; and Avenida Universidad, La Bolsa a San Francisco; both in the center (Ⓜ Capitolio)

The places listed above conveniently cover just about all the areas of tourist interest, from Plaza Bolívar to Altamira. Most outlets are open Monday to Saturday, but some, including CompuMall, Cyber Café M@dness, Cyber Office 2020 and Digital Planet, also open on Sunday. Caracas' cybercafés are not that cheap – expect to pay about US$4 to US$7 per hour of surfing the Web or emailing. Of the places listed, Cyber Office 2020 and Postnet are among the cheapest.

Travel Agencies

IVI Idiomas Vivos (☎ 993 39 58, 993 71 74, 992 37 39, fax 992 96 26, info@ividiomas.com), Residencia La Hacienda, Piso Bajo, Local 1-4-T, Final Avenida Principal de las Mercedes, offers attractive airfares to Europe and elsewhere for foreign students, teachers and people under 26 years of age. It issues ISIC and ITIC cards for full-time students or teachers. IVI has agreements with various businesses around the country that give cardholders discounts (about 10% to 30%) on their goods or services (hotels, restaurants, shops, medical services etc) – check IVI's Web site (www.ividiomas.com) for details on the providers and their discounts.

Bookstores

The best bookshops specializing in English-language publications include The American Book Shop (☎ 263 54 55, 267 41 34), Edificio Belveder, Avenida San Juan Bosco, near the corner of 1a Transversal (Ⓜ Altamira) and The English Book Shop (☎ 979 13 08, 979 40 98), Centro Comercial Concresa, Prados del Este. The former has a fair selection of Lonely Planet guidebooks and also offers secondhand books in English. Another bookstore that carries a range of Lonely Planet titles is Read Books Import (☎ 991 55 62), Plaza Urape, in Urbanización San Román.

The Librería La France (☎ 952 08 18), in the Centro Comercial Chacaíto (basement level), Plaza Brión (commonly called Plaza Chacaíto), has the best selection of books in French, while the Librería Alemana Oscar Todtmann (☎ 762 52 44), in the Centro Comercial El Bosque, Avenida Libertador (Ⓜ Chacaíto), offers the most extensive choice of German-language publications.

For books in Italian, try El Libro Italiano (☎ 763 19 64), Avenida Francisco Solano, Sabana Grande; or the Librería Rizzoli (☎ 286 24 42), Centro Plaza, 1a Transversal between 1a Avenida and Avenida Andrés Bello, Los Palos Grandes (❿ Altamira).

The Tecni-Ciencia Libros is one of Venezuela's best bookshops. It has half a dozen branches around the city, including the two largest in the Centro Ciudad Comercial Tamanaco (☎ 959 55 47, 959 50 35), Nivel C-2, Chuao; and the Centro Sambil (☎ 264 17 65, 267 15 78), Nivel Acuario, Chacao. Both have heaps of publications, including dictionaries, specialist fare and coffee-table books. Their well-stocked travel sections (arguably the best in town) feature plenty of Lonely Planet titles.

Nature lovers may enjoy the small bookshop of the Sociedad Conservacionista Audubon de Venezuela (☎ 993 25 25), in the Centro Comercial Paseo Las Mercedes (next to the public toilets on the ground floor).

Specialist bookshops apart, Caracas has plenty of general-interest bookshops, which mostly deal in locally published Spanish-language books. If you've already mastered the language, you'll find a wide choice of tomes on Venezuelan history, politics, ethnology, ethnography, nature and the like, not to mention Latin American literature. You'll also find a large variety of lavishly illustrated coffee-table books on Venezuela's art, architecture and nature – a tempting buy to take back home. They also often stock dictionaries, maps and some locally produced guidebooks.

Books are not cheap in Venezuela. If you want to save some bolívares, first check the secondhand bookshops and markets. The cheapest place to buy books is the street market on Avenida Fuerzas Armadas, Romualda a Plaza España (❿ La Hoyada). The bookstalls there have a haphazard range of new and secondhand books, including some rare old editions that are virtually unobtainable elsewhere. A similar street market, but smaller and not so cheap, is on Paseo Anauco just off Avenida México (❿ Bellas Artes). There are also a dozen or so bookstalls in the grounds of Universidad Central de Venezuela. They sell new books below normal bookshop prices. All these markets deal almost exclusively in Spanish-

language books. For secondhand books in English, check The American Book Shop, listed earlier in this section.

Libraries

Caracas has a number of libraries, the largest one being the Biblioteca Nacional (☎ 505 90 05, 564 30 43), next to the Panteón Nacional. Another major facility is the Biblioteca Metropolitana Simón Rodríguez, on Calle Norte 4, Esquina El Conde.

For those interested in English-language publications, the widest selection is in the library of the British Council (☎ 952 97 57), Torre Credicard, Piso 3, Avenida Principal El Bosque (❿ Chacaíto). Alternatively, try the library of the Centro Venezolano Americano (CVA; ☎ 993 79 11), Edificio CVA, Avenida Principal de las Mercedes.

The Asociación Cultural Humboldt (☎ 552 64 45, 552 76 34), Avenida Jorge Washington at Avenida Juan Germán Roscio, San Bernardino, has a library featuring German-language books, papers and periodicals. The library of the Alianza Francesa (☎ 762 74 55), Edificio Centro Solano, Piso 1, Avenida Francisco Solano (❿ Chacaíto), has publications in French.

Laundry

Many hotels offer laundry facilities; alternatively, you can use *lavanderías*. There are few self-service laundries – almost all provide service washes. They include Lavandería El Metro (the cheapest of all listed here), Lavandería El Rey, Lavandería Chapultepex (the only self-service laundry included here) and Lavandería De-Blan-Ro, all four in the Sabana Grande area, and the Lavandería Autolanka in the Centro Comercial Doral Centro in La Candelaria (see the maps for locations). Bring your dirty clothes in the morning and pick them up all clean and dry in the afternoon. A 5kg load will cost US$2.50 to US$4.

Medical Services

Many minor health problems, such as mild diarrhea, colds, coughs, pains, and small cuts or wounds, can be solved by just applying a proper remedy, which you can buy in a *farmacia* (pharmacy). Caracas has a wide array of pharmacies, and there's always one in every suburb of the city that takes its turn and stays open the whole night. They are listed in the local press, and you'll recognize them by a lit board or neon sign reading 'Turno.' Some drugs that can be bought only with a prescription in western countries (eg, antibiotics) are readily available over the counter in local pharmacies. Always make sure you buy the proper drug (it may appear under a different name in other countries) and check the expiration date.

If you happen to get really sick, seek qualified medical help promptly. Your embassy or consulate may recommend doctors or clinics, but if you can't get that advice, act on your own without delay. Fortunately, Caracas has a number of public hospitals, private clinics, specialist medical centers and dentist offices.

If you're insured, it's preferable to use private clinics rather than government-owned institutions, which are cheaper but may not be as well equipped. Most private clinics offer inpatient and outpatient services, carry out laboratory tests and have specialist doctors, some of whom speak English. Some reputable medical facilities include:

Clínica El Ávila
(☎ 276 11 11) Avenida San Juan Bosco at 6a Transversal, Altamira

Clínica Instituto Médico La Floresta
(☎ 285 21 11, 285 32 22) Avenida Principal de la Floresta at Calle Santa Ana

Policlínica Metropolitana
(☎ 908 01 00, 908 01 40) Calle A at Avenida Principal de Caurimare

Centro Médico de Caracas
(☎ 552 22 22, 555 91 11) Plaza El Estanque, Final de Avenida Eraso, San Bernardino

Most private clinics also offer vaccinations, but you can get them at no cost in public health centers called *unidades sanitarias*, which are in most suburbs. They can inoculate you against yellow fever and will also administer a series of injections against rabies if you've been bitten by a suspect animal.

The Escuela de Farmacia (☎ 605 26 86) at the Universidad Central de Venezuela has antivenins for some snake species.

Caracas tap water is heavily chlorinated and is said to be safe to drink, but it's better to avoid it. Bottled water is readily available from most food shops, supermarkets, cafés, restaurants etc.

Emergency
All the services listed below operate 24 hours a day. Don't expect the attendants to speak English. If your Spanish is not up to scratch, try to get a local to call on your behalf.

Police	☎ 169
Traffic Police	☎ 167
Fire	☎ 166
Emergency Center (Police, Fire, Ambulance)	☎ 171

Dangers & Annoyances
Since the late 1980s, Caracas has become increasingly unsafe, more so than any other city in the country. One obvious reason for this is the city's large and rapidly growing population, many of whom live in ranchos far below the poverty level. Another cause is a declining standard of living – the result of a precarious economy and political instability. Predictably, poor barrios are where the majority of violent crimes are reported, but criminals of the slums are venturing into more affluent districts.

So be on your guard. Refer to Dangers & Annoyances in the Facts for the Visitor chapter for general tips. Don't venture into shantytowns at any time of the day, let alone at night. Central districts are OK during the day, though armed robberies occasionally occur. Holdups have been reported around the airport area (see To/From the Airport in the Getting Around section, later in this chapter). Expensive jewelry, watches and cameras will definitely multiply your chances of being mugged.

The historic center is reasonably safe for daytime strolls but may be risky after dark. The Sabana Grande is heading the same way, though so far it's quite secure until around 8 or 9 pm, when crowds rapidly

THE CENTER & PARQUE CENTRAL

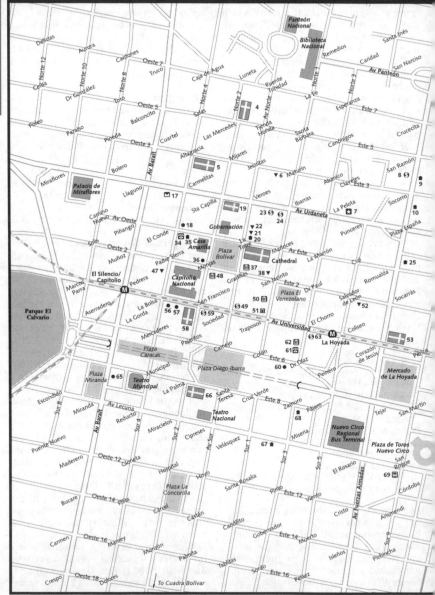

THE CENTER & PARQUE CENTRAL

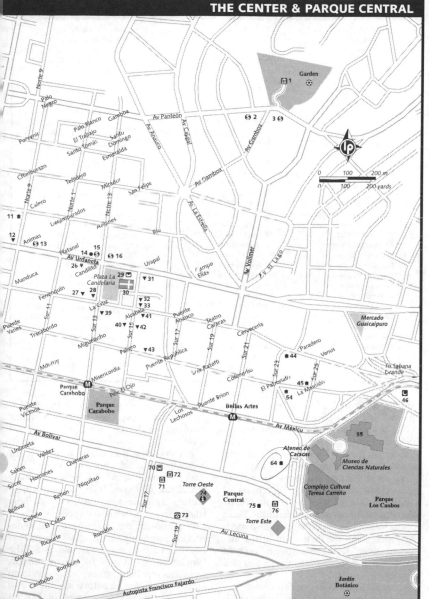

Garden

🏛1

😊 2   3 😊

Av Panteón

Av Chuao

Av Gamboa

Av Panteón

Av Gamboa

Norte 9

Palo Negro

Palo Blanco

Gamboa

Porvenir

El Trabajo

Santo Domingo

Santo Tomás

Esmeralda

Chimborazo

Tejedero

Mirador

San Felipe

Av Gamboa

Norte 9

Norte 1

Norte 13

Calero

Av La Estrella

Av Vollmer

11 🏛

Desamparados

Riu

12 ▼

Animas

😊 13

Pajaritos

Platanal   15

14 ●😊   😊 16

Av Urdaneta

26 ▼

Candilito

Urapal

Campo Elías

Av El Lago

Manduca

Plaza La
Candelaria

29 ✉

▼31

Av Vollmer

Ferrenquín

27 ▼   28
       ▼

30

▼32
▼33

Mercado
Guaicaipuro

Puente
Yanes

La Cruz

Sur 11

▼39

Alcabala

▼41

Sur 13

Puente
Anauco

Teatro
Caracas

Cervecería

Tracabordo

Miguelacho

40▼   ▼42

Paligro

Sur 15

Paradero

Venus

Móran

▼43

Puente República

Viale Racotti

Columerio

Sur 21

▪44

To Sabana
Grande

Misericordia

Perez El Ojo

El Patronato

45 ▪   La Marción

54

🅱
46

Parque
Carabobo   Ⓜ

Puente
Victoria

Los
Lechosos

Puente Brion

Bellas Artes

Ⓜ

Av México

Av Bolívar

Urdaneta

Valdez

Queseras

Salom

Horcones

Sucre   Niquitao

Bolívar

Retón

El Callao

Cedeño

Ricaurte

Rondón

Parque
Carabobo

Sur 17

Ateneo de
Caracas

64 ▪

Museo de
Ciencias Naturales

55

Complejo Cultural
Teresa Carreño

70 🖼

🏛72

71

Torre Oeste

74 🔷

Parque
Central

75 🏛

🏛76

Parque
Los Caobos

📷73

Torre Este

Av Lecuna

Gardot

Carabobo

Bombona

Carabobo

Autopista Francisco Fajardo

Jardín
Botánico
✿

0   100   200 m
0   100   200 yards

THE CENTER & PARQUE CENTRAL MAP KEY

PLACES TO STAY
9 Hotel Terepaima
10 Hotel Metropol
11 Hotel Inter
20 Plaza Catedral Hotel;
   Restaurant Les Grisons
25 Hotel Hollywood
35 Hotel El Conde
44 Hotel New Jersey
45 Hotel Ribot
54 Hotel Renovación
64 Hotel Hilton Caracas
67 Hotel Center Park
68 Hotel Guarapiche
75 Hilton Caracas
   Residencias Anauco

PLACES TO EAT
6 Restaurant Dama Antañona
12 La Barra Vegetariana;
   Naveg@ Center
21 Restaurant La Torre
22 Restaurant Las Vegas
26 Restaurant El Coyuco
27 Tasca de Manolo
28 Tasca La Mansión de
   Altamira
31 Tasca La Carabela
32 Tasca La Tertulia
33 Tasca La Cita
38 Restaurant Kafta
39 Lunchería Doña Agapita
40 Tasca Guernica
41 Tasca Mallorca

42 Bar Basque
43 Casa Farruco
47 Restaurant Padre Sierra
52 Restaurant Beirut

OTHER
1 Museo de Arte Colonial
2 Banco Unión
3 Corp Banca
4 Iglesia Las Mercedes
5 Iglesia Altagracia
7 PTJ Police
8 Banco Unión
13 Italcambio
14 Lavandería Autolanka
15 Banco de Venezuela
16 Banco Unión
17 Ipostel Main Post Office
18 Biblioteca Metropolitana
   Simón Rodríguez
19 Iglesia Santa Capilla
23 Italcambio
24 Corp Banca
29 Ipostel Post Office
30 Iglesia de la Candelaria
34 Centro de Comunicaciones
   CANTV
36 Edificio La Francia
37 Museo Sacro de Caracas;
   Café del Sacro
46 Mosque
48 Concejo Municipal; Capilla de
   Santa Rosa de Lima; Museo
   Caracas

49 Banco de Venezuela
50 Museo Bolivariano
51 Casa Natal de Bolívar
53 Iglesia Sagrado Corazón
   de Jesús
55 Galería de Arte Nacional;
   Museo de Bellas Artes;
   Cinemateca Nacional
56 Former Supreme Court
57 Palacio de las Academias;
   Biblioteca Metropolitana
58 Iglesia de San Francisco
59 Banco Mercantil
60 Cartografía Nacional
61 Centro de Comunicaciones
   CANTV
62 Museo Fundación John
   Boulton
63 Banco Unión
65 DIEX Office
66 Basílica de Santa Teresa
69 Carritos to El Junquito
70 Buses to Maiquetía Airport
71 Museo del Teclado
72 Museo de los Niños
73 Centro de Comunicaciones
   CANTV
74 Corpoturismo;
   Mirador de la Torre Oeste
76 Museo de Arte
   Contemporáneo

dwindle. Altamira, La Castellana, Los Palos Grandes and Las Mercedes have a reputation of being relatively safe at night. Travelers have repeatedly been robbed at knife or gunpoint in the hillside Parque El Calvario by what seem to be professional gangs.

Be careful when withdrawing money from ATMs – there have been reports of gangs targeting ATM users (see the 'ATM Warning' in the Money section of the Facts for the Visitor chapter). There are also security problems in the metro and at the airport terminal – see the Metro and To/From the Airport sections toward the end of this chapter for details.

Caracas' traffic is heavy, fast and wild – be careful! Drivers don't obey traffic rules, and they may run red lights or crawl against

the flow up a one-way street if that's what they feel like doing. Crossing the street may involve some risk; take it for granted that no driver will stop to give you the right-of-way.

Air pollution is largely a by-product of heavy traffic and the poor mechanical condition of many vehicles, which often spew out clouds of fumes. Pollution may appall visitors from cleaner countries, especially when there is no wind to disperse it.

Nonsmokers may have a hard time. Venezuela is a smoking nation, and it's permitted nearly everywhere: in just about all the restaurants, in offices, at the bus and airport terminals etc. Public transportation is technically no-smoking territory, and the metro is probably the ultimate example of that, but in taxis much depends on the driver's habits.

THE CENTER & AROUND

The historic sector, where the city was born, has lost much of its original identity. In a rush toward modernization, many colonial houses were replaced with modern buildings, which range from nondescript plain edifices to futuristic tinted-glass towers. Architectural ragbag that it is, the center is colorful and alive and boasts some important sights, many of which are related to Bolívar. All are within easy walking distance of each other.

Plaza Bolívar

This is the nucleus of the old town, with the inevitable monument to Bolívar in the middle. The equestrian statue was cast in Europe, shipped in pieces, assembled and unveiled in 1874 – later than planned, because the ship carrying it had foundered on the Archipiélago de Los Roques. The plaza is a favorite playground for all sorts of political visionaries and religious messiahs, who deliver their passionate speeches to a casual audience, mostly at lunchtime. The leafy square is lined on all sides by a collection of buildings from different epochs, some of which are detailed in the following sections.

Catedral

Set on the eastern side of Plaza Bolívar, the cathedral was built from 1665 to 1713 after the 1641 earthquake had destroyed the previous church. A wide five-nave interior supported on 32 columns was largely remodeled in the late 19th century. The Bolívar family chapel is in the middle of the right-hand aisle and can be easily recognized by a modern sculpture of El Libertador mourning his parents and wife. Note the fine colonial altarpiece at the back of the chapel.

Museo Sacro de Caracas

Accommodated in a meticulously restored colonial building next to the cathedral, the museum displays a modest but carefully selected collection of religious art. It also has an interesting cultural program featuring theater, poetry, musical recitals and concerts, which are staged on the premises, plus a pleasant café (see Places to Eat). The

museum is open 10 am to 5 pm daily except Monday.

Concejo Municipal

Occupying half of Plaza Bolívar's southern side, this building was erected by the Caracas bishops from 1641 to 1696 to house the Colegio Seminario de Santa Rosa de Lima. In 1725, the Real y Pontificia Universidad de Caracas, the province's first university, was established here. Bolívar renamed it the Universidad Central de Venezuela, the moniker it continues to keep to this day, though it moved away and now occupies a vast campus outside the historic center. Today the building is the seat of the Municipal Council, but part of it is open to the public (9 to noon and 2 to 4:30 pm Tuesday to Friday, 10 am to 4:30 pm weekends).

The **Museo Caracas**, on the ground floor, features exhibits related to the town's history, including historic paintings and elaborate models of central Caracas as it looked in the 1810s and 1930s. Also on display is a collection of dioramas depicting the life of turn-of-the-19th-century Caracas, all created by a local artist, Raúl Santana.

On the 1st floor is a collection of 80 paintings by Emilio Boggio (1857–1920), a Venezuelan artist who lived in Paris. It's normally closed to the public, but the attendants by the main entrance might show you around.

The western side of the building houses the **Capilla de Santa Rosa de Lima**, where on July 5, 1811, the congress declared Venezuela's independence (though it was another 10 years before this became a reality). The chapel has been restored with the decoration and furniture of the time.

While strolling around the spacious courtyard with a fountain in the middle, look for the famous Caracas map of 1578; its enlarged reproduction is displayed in the courtyard's cloister.

Casa Amarilla

The 17th-century balconied mansion called the 'Yellow House,' on the western side of Plaza Bolívar, was originally the infamous royal prison. Wholly revamped and painted yellow (hence its name) after independence, the building was converted into a presidential residence. Today it's the seat of the Ministry of Foreign Affairs and can't be visited, but have a look at the well-preserved colonial appearance of its exterior.

Iglesia Santa Capilla

The Holy Chapel, one block north of Plaza Bolívar, is a neo-Gothic church that was modeled on the Sainte Chapelle of Paris and looks a bit like a wedding cake. It was ordered by Guzmán Blanco in 1883 and built on the site of the rustic San Mauricio chapel, where the first mass was allegedly celebrated after the foundation of the town.

Illuminated by the warm light passing through colorful stained-glass windows, the decorative interior boasts an elaborate stone high altar and an unusual openwork vault. One of the treasured possessions of the church is the sizable painting *Multiplication of the Bread,* by Arturo Michelena, hanging in the right-hand aisle.

Capitolio Nacional

The neoclassical National Capitol, the seat of the congress, occupies the entire block just southwest of Plaza Bolívar. It's a two-building complex, commissioned in the 1870s by Guzmán Blanco and erected on the site of a convent, whose occupants had been expelled by the dictator (who proceeded to raze the old building).

In the central part of the northern building is the famous **Salón Elíptico**, the oval hall with a large mural on its domed ceiling. The painting, depicting the battle of Carabobo, was done in 1888 by perhaps the most notable Venezuelan artist of the day, Martín Tovar y Tovar. The southern wall of the hall is crammed with portraits of distinguished leaders of the independence wars. In front of this wall is Bolívar's bust on top of a marble pedestal; the original Act of Independence of 1811 is kept in the chest inside the pedestal. It's put on public view on July 5, which is Independence Day.

Tovar y Tovar left behind more military works of art in two adjoining halls: The Salón Amarillo has on its ceiling a depiction

of the battle of Junín, while the Salón Rojo has been embellished with a scene from the battle of Boyacá. The Capitolio is open for visits daily 9 am to noon pm and 2 to 5 pm.

Iglesia de San Francisco

Just south of the Capitolio Nacional, the San Francisco church was built in the 1570s but was remodeled on several occasions during the 17th and 18th centuries. Guzmán Blanco, unable to resist his passion for modernizing, placed a new neoclassical facade on the church to match the just-completed capitol building. Fortunately, the interior of the church didn't undergo such an extensive alteration, so its colonial character and much of its old decoration has been preserved. Have a look at the richly gilded baroque altarpieces distributed along both side walls, and stop at the statue of San Onofre, in the right-hand aisle. He is the most venerated saint in the church due to his miraculous powers of bringing health, happiness and a good job.

It was in this church in 1813 that Bolívar was proclaimed 'El Libertador,' and also here that his much-celebrated funeral was held in 1842, after his remains had been brought from Santa Marta in Colombia, 12 years after his death.

Casa Natal de Bolívar

Bolívar's funeral took place just two blocks from the house where, on July 24, 1783, he was born. The house's reconstructed interior (which lost almost all of its colonial features in the process) has been decorated with a score of large paintings by Tito Salas depicting Bolívar's heroic battles and scenes from his life. The house is open 9 am to noon and 2 to 5 pm Tuesday to Friday, 10 am to 1 pm and 2 to 5 pm weekends.

Museo Bolivariano

This museum, a few paces north from the Casa Natal, is also in a colonial house (which has preserved a bit more of its original style). It displays a variety of independence memorabilia, documents, period weapons and banners, plus a number of Bolívar's portraits. Among the exhibits is the coffin in which the remains of Bolívar were brought from Santa Marta. The ashes were then kept in the cathedral, from where they were moved in 1876 in the *arca cineraria* (a funeral ark, also exhibited in the museum) to their eventual resting place, the National Pantheon. The opening hours are the same as for Casa Natal.

Museo Fundación John Boulton

This museum features a collection of historic and artistic objects that have been accumulated over generations by the family of British merchant John Boulton (1805–75). Among the exhibits are paintings by Arturo Michelena, colonial furniture, Bolívar memorabilia and an extensive collection of ceramics from all over the world. The museum is in the Torre El Chorro, Piso 11, Esquina El Chorro, and is open 8 to 11 am and 2 to 5 pm weekdays.

Cuadra Bolívar

Located in the far southern section of the historic center, this is the Bolívar family's summer house, where Simón spent much of his youth. Restored to its original appearance and stuffed with period furniture, the house is today a museum dedicated to El Libertador. It's open 9 am to noon and 2 to 5 pm Tuesday to Friday, 10 am to 1 pm and 2 to 4 pm weekends.

Panteón Nacional

The National Pantheon is at the opposite, northern edge of the old town, five blocks due north of Plaza Bolívar. There was once a church on the site, but it was destroyed in the 1812 earthquake. After being reconstructed, it continued as a place of worship until 1874, when by decree Guzmán Blanco turned it into the pantheon. Since then it has been the last resting place for eminent Venezuelans.

The entire central nave is dedicated to Bolívar – his bronze sarcophagus is placed in the chancel instead of the high altar – while 140 tombs of other revered personages, including only three women (War of Independence heroine Luisa Cáceres de Arismendi, pianist Teresa Carreño, and writer Teresa de la Parra) have been pushed out to the aisles.

One tomb is empty and open, awaiting the remains of Francisco de Miranda, who died in a Spanish jail in 1816 and was buried in a mass grave. There are two more empty tombs, but they are sealed. One is dedicated to Antonio José de Sucre, who was assassinated in Colombia and whose remains are in the Quito Cathedral, as he is considered by Ecuadorians as the liberator of their country. The other tomb commemorates Andrés Bello, a Caracas-born poet, writer and friend of Bolívar's who later went to live in Chile. He died and was buried in Santiago.

The vault of the pantheon is covered by paintings depicting scenes from Bolívar's life, all done by Tito Salas in the 1930s. Note the huge crystal chandelier, made and hung in 1883 on the centennial of Bolívar's birth. It consists of 4000 pieces and 230 lights. The pantheon is open 9 am to noon and 2 to 5 pm Tuesday to Friday, 10 am to noon and 2 to 4:30 pm weekends. Be sure to wait for the ceremonial changing of the guard, which is held several times a day during the opening hours.

Guzmán Blanco, 'El Modernizador'

José Gregorio Hernández

Ask Venezuelans who their most important saint is and most will give you the same answer – 'José Gregorio,' as people familiarly refer to Hernández. Indeed, his image is omnipresent in private homes and in stalls that carry religious paraphernalia, where you can buy a range of pictures or plaster statues of him. At first sight, you might be confused by his appearance – he is always portrayed in a well-tailored suit with a white shirt and tie, usually with a black felt hat on his head, which you'd hardly associate with a saint – but don't worry, it's him. A more serious

Candle wrapper bearing José Gregorio's image

problem is his fragile holy credentials; in fact, Hernández doesn't appear on the Vatican's list of saints. So far, the church has elevated him to venerable status (in 1985), but further steps along the way to sainthood – beatification and canonization – seem to be still a ways off.

Hernández was born in 1864 in the obscure Andean village of Isnotú, near Valera, in Trujillo state. He was the eldest of seven kids of a humble campesino family that fled up the mountains seeking refuge from the federation wars that plagued their native Los Llanos. His mother died when he was nine, and young José Gregorio helped his father take care of the youngsters before going to Caracas to study.

Iglesia de la Candelaria

This church, seven blocks east of Plaza Bolívar, stands amid an area tingling with a Spanish flavor, thanks to Iberian migrants who settled here and opened up *tascas* (Spanish-style bar-restaurants). The church itself is noted for the richly gilded monumental retables that cover the chancel's walls. The central retable dates from about 1760, while the lateral ones are modern replicas.

For the majority of the faithful, however, the holiest place in the church is the tomb of José Gregorio Hernández, in the first chapel off the right-hand aisle. Though not canonized, José Gregorio is considered the most important saint by many Venezuelans, more so than many official saints, whose images adorn the altars of this and other churches (see the boxed text).

Museo de Arte Colonial

This museum is housed in a beautiful colonial country mansion known as Quinta de

Anauco, laid out around a charming patio and surrounded by gardens. When built in 1797, the quinta was well outside the historic town; today it's just a green oasis in the inner suburb of San Bernardino, a 10-minute walk northeast of La Candelaria.

If you make the effort to go there, you'll be rewarded with a guided tour around meticulously restored interiors filled with carefully selected works of art, furniture and household implements. The museum is open 9 to 11:30 am and 2 to 4:30 pm Tuesday to Friday, 10 am to 5 pm weekends. Entry costs US$1.25 and covers the guide service. Tours depart roughly every half-hour and last around 45 minutes. Chamber-music concerts are held in the adjacent former stables, usually on Saturday at 5 pm and Sunday at 11 am.

PARQUE CENTRAL & AROUND

Parque Central is a good place to go for a taste of modern Caracas. It's an easy 1.5km

José Gregorio Hernández

Reputedly extraordinarily gifted and a hardworking student, Hernández graduated in medical sciences from the Universidad Central de Venezuela (UCV) in 1888. The following year, he went to Paris to specialize in histology, physiology and bacteriology in some of the best laboratories, led by world-class medical eminences. Back home in 1891, he was appointed to the UCV to research, teach and oversee studies of the newly created subjects he had mastered in Europe.

Hernández has commonly been considered the founder of experimental medicine in Venezuela. He was also a creator of the so-called Commission of Public Health, the embryo of the present-day Ministry of Health. He began his brilliant career as a university professor at the age of 27 and was the personal doctor of the president. He also left behind some literary work (including a philosophical treatise) and was allegedly a skilled pianist.

José Gregorio also was a devotedly religious person, following God's gospel to the word. He distinguished himself by treating the poor without charging a fee, and even bought medicine for his patients. He intended to dedicate himself completely to a monastic life on various occasions. In his most decisive attempt, in 1913, he went to Rome to study theology and Latin, but his developing tuberculosis forced him to resign and search for more favorable climatic conditions. He returned to Caracas and gave his energy and time to treating the poor.

Hernández died in a car accident in Caracas in 1919. Soon after his tragic death, a cult emerged around him and has spread throughout the country and beyond. Countless miracles are attributed to him, including numerous healings. Interestingly, Hernández was adopted as one of the principal deities of the mysterious María Lionza cult. Some consider him to be the second-holiest figure in the cult's pantheon, after María Lionza herself.

southeast of Plaza Bolívar, but if it's too far for you to walk, take the metro to the Bellas Artes station.

The park is not, as you might expect, a green area, but rather a concrete complex consisting of five high-rise residential slabs of somewhat apocalyptic appearance, crowned by two 53-story octagonal towers, the tallest in the country. You may not be much impressed by the architecture, but don't retreat, for there are some important sights around, especially if you are after cultural fare.

Actually, the Parque Central area is Caracas' art and culture hub, boasting half a dozen museums, the major performing-arts center, two art cinemas and arguably the best theater in town. Additionally, you can go to the top of one of the towers for an impressive 360-degree bird's-eye view of the city.

Mirador de la Torre Oeste

This open-air viewpoint on the 52nd floor of the Torre Oeste (the same tower that houses the Corpoturismo tourist office) provides some of the best views of the city. It's not a typical tourist sight, but rather a courtesy of the tower's security department, which manages the *mirador* (lookout) and lets tourists go there free of charge, 9 to 11 am and 2 to 4 pm Tuesday to Friday.

You first need to go to the department's office, CSB División y Departamento de Seguridad, on the tower's basement level, called 'Nivel Sótano Uno.' Upon exiting the elevator, you'll see the office right in front of you. The staff will probably ask you for your passport to write down your name before somebody accompanies you up to the lookout.

Museo de Arte Contemporáneo

Occupying the eastern end of the Parque Central complex, this is by far the best contemporary art museum in the country, if not the entire continent. In 16 halls on five levels, you'll find works by many prominent

Venezuelan artists, including Jesús Soto, noted for his kinetic pieces.

There are also some remarkable paintings by international giants such as Picasso, Chagall, Matisse, Monet, Leger and Miró, and – the pride of the museum – a collection of a hundred or so engravings by Picasso, created by the artist from 1931 to 1934. Part of the exhibition space is given to changing displays; since its opening in 1974, the museum has presented over 400 temporary exhibitions dedicated to both locally and internationally renowned artists. The museum is open 10 am to 6 pm Tuesday to Sunday.

Museo de los Niños

The Children's Museum is at the opposite, western end of the complex and is open 9 am to noon and 2 to 5 pm Wednesday to Sunday. Admission is US$6 (US$4 for children 14 years of age and under).

The office stops selling tickets one hour before closing, but it's best to allow at least two hours anyway. It's an excellent hands-on museum where adults have as much (or perhaps more) fun as the kids. Avoid weekends, when the museum is besieged by families.

Museo del Teclado

This small museum of musical instruments has a collection of two dozen historic keyboard instruments. It's in Parque Central, next to the Museo de los Niños, and is open 9 to noon and 2 to 4 pm weekdays. Concerts and recitals are usually held here on Saturday at 4 pm and Sunday at 11 am.

Complejo Cultural Teresa Carreño

Looking like a gigantic concrete sculpture or bunker, just to the east and across the street from Parque Central (and linked to it by a footbridge), the Complejo Cultural is a modern performing-arts center. Opened in 1983, it has a spacious main auditorium capable of seating 2400 patrons, as well as a 400-seat side hall. The center hosts concerts, ballets, plays, recitals etc by both local and visiting performers.

Hourlong guided tours around the complex are conducted several times a day from 10 am to 5 pm Tuesday to Friday and cost US$1. Call ☎ 800 673 72 a day or two before you go if you need an English-speaking guide. At the back of the building is a small museum dedicated to Teresa Carreño (1853–1917), the best pianist Venezuela has ever produced (see Music, under Arts, in the Facts about Venezuela chapter).

Ateneo de Caracas

Next to the Complejo Cultural, the Ateneo is another cultural center, complete with a concert hall, theater, cinema, art gallery, bookshop and café. The Ateneo is home to the Rajatabla, probably the best-known (both in and outside the country) local theater company. For more information on the Rajatabla, see Theater in the Entertainment section, later in this chapter.

Museo de Ciencias Naturales

The Natural Sciences Museum, behind the Ateneo, tracks the history of evolution, displaying minerals, fossils, stuffed animals and artifacts of pre-Hispanic communities from Venezuela and beyond. It also stages temporary exhibitions. The museum is open 9 am to 5 pm Tuesday to Friday, 10:30 am to 5 pm weekends. Admission is US$2.

Galería de Arte Nacional

Opposite the Museo de Ciencias Naturales, the National Art Gallery has a vast collection of artwork embracing five centuries of Venezuela's artistic expression, plus some pre-Hispanic art, but only a small part is in exhibition on diverse temporary shows. The building, which owes much to the neo-classical style, was designed in 1935 by a renowned Venezuelan architect, Carlos Raúl Villanueva. Note the three bas-reliefs by Francisco Narváez, Venezuela's first modern sculptor, placed over the doors at the entrance to the building. The gallery is open 9 am to 5 pm Tuesday to Friday, 10 am to 5 pm weekends. The gallery houses Caracas' leading art cinema.

Museo de Bellas Artes

Adjoining the gallery, the Museum of Fine Arts, in the modern six-story building also designed by Villanueva, features mostly temporary exhibitions. Go to the rooftop terrace for views over the city and of the spankingly modern US$33-million modern mosque (the largest in South America) just to the north. The museum, open the same hours as the gallery, has a shop that sells contemporary art.

SABANA GRANDE & AROUND

Sabana Grande, 2km east of Parque Central, is a thrilling district packed with hotels, restaurants and shops. There are no particular tourist sights here, but the place is enjoyable and popular with both locals and visitors, who come en masse and stroll along its trendy, vibrant mall, the **Boulevard de Sabana Grande**, which stretches between the metro stations of Plaza Venezuela and Chacaíto. It is pretty wide at its western end, with room for several open-air street cafés – a good place to sit over a cup of espresso and watch the world go by.

Jardín Botánico

If Sabana Grande is too busy or crowded for you, relax in the botanical gardens, a 10-minute walk from the western end of the mall. The gardens, open 8 am to 5 pm daily, are extensive, but only part of them are open to the public. They are well maintained and feature a good variety of local flora, yet their northern fringe, along the Autopista Francisco Fajardo, suffers badly from traffic noise. Occasional exhibitions are held in the Instituto Botánico building on the grounds. The only entrance to the gardens is from Avenida Interna UCV, a short walk south of Plaza Venezuela (there's no access from Parque Central or Parque Los Caobos).

Universidad Central de Venezuela

With its 70,000 students, this is Caracas' (and Venezuela's, for that matter) largest university and is a hotbed of frequent student protests. The vast campus was designed by Carlos Raúl Villanueva and is considered to be one of the milestones of his career. It was built from scratch in one go in the early 1950s.

Although its architecture may look pretty dull today, the campus is still a pleasant place to stroll around, thanks to a number of abstract sculptures and murals adorning its grounds and buildings. There's an excellent concert hall, Aula Magna, on the grounds, with a fairly regular and interesting schedule (see Entertainment, later in this chapter, for more details). The Aula Magna is capable of seating 2700 patrons and is thought to have the best acoustics in the country. A US sculptor, Alexander Calder, largely contributed to this by hanging a set of *platillos volantes* (flying saucers) from the ceiling.

At the eastern side of the campus is a sports complex, which includes soccer and baseball stadiums. The campus is just south of the botanical gardens and can be easily reached on foot from Sabana Grande; alternatively, you can get there by metro (Ciudad Universitaria station).

ALTAMIRA & EASTERN SUBURBS

East of Sabana Grande lie some of Caracas' most fashionable suburbs, possibly reaching their peak at Altamira and its environs. Proceeding farther east, you gradually descend the social ladder, reaching a low point at Petare. Eastward from here are vast expanses of appalling shantytowns.

Parque del Este

Directly south of the metro station of the same name, the Parque del Este is the largest city park. It's a good place for leisurely walks, and you can visit the snake house, aviary and cactus garden, and (only on Saturday and Sunday afternoons) enjoy a show in the Planetario Humboldt. The park is open 5 am to 5 pm daily except Monday.

Museo del Transporte

The Museum of Transportation is just to the east of the Parque del Este and can be reached directly from the park by a pedestrian bridge (if it's closed, go through the nearby parking-lot gate). The museum features some old steam locomotives, vehicles and planes scattered over the grounds, but

SABANA GRANDE & AROUND

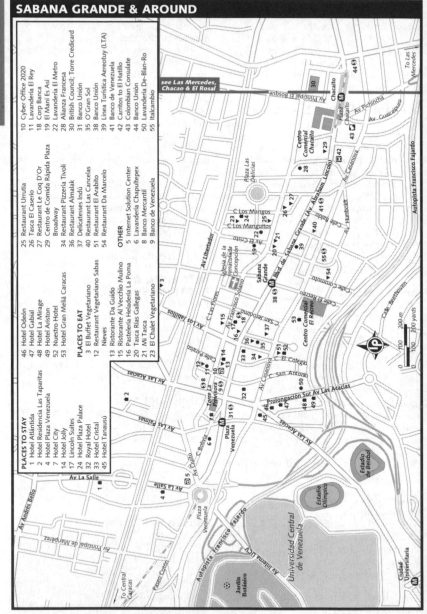

10	Cyber Office 2020
11	Lavandería El Rey
18	Corp Banca
19	El Maní Es Así
22	Lavandería El Metro
28	Alianza Francesa
30	British Council; Torre Credicard
31	Banco Unión
35	O'Gran Sol
38	Banco Unión
39	Línea Turística Aereotuy (LTA)
41	Banco de Venezuela
42	Carritos to El Hatillo
43	Colombian Consulate
44	Banco Unión
50	Lavandería De-Blar-Ro
55	Italcambio

PLACES TO STAY
1 Hotel Atlántida
2 Hotel Residencia Las Tapatías
4 Hotel Plaza Venezuela
14 Hotel City
17 Hotel Jolly
24 Lincoln Suites
32 Hotel Plaza Palace
33 Royal Hotel
45 Hotel Cristal
46 Hotel Odeón
47 Hotel Gabial
48 Hotel La Mirage
49 Hotel Ariston
52 Nuestro Hotel
53 Hotel Gran Meliá Caracas
Hotel Tanausú

PLACES TO EAT
3 El Buffet Vegetariano
12 Restaurant Vegetariano Sabas Nieves
13 Ristorante Da Guido
15 Ristorante Al Vecchio Mulino
16 Pastelería Heladería La Poma
20 Tasca Rías Gallegas
21 Mi Tasca
23 El Chalet Vegetariano
25 Restaurant Urrutia
26 Tasca El Caserío
27 Restaurant Le Coq D'Or
29 Centro de Comida Rápida Plaza Broadway
34 Restaurant Pizzería Tívoli
36 Restaurant Almalak
37 Delicatesses Indú
40 Restaurant Las Cancelas
51 Restaurant El Arabito
54 Restaurant Da Marcelo

OTHER
5 Internet Solution Center
6 Lavandería Chapultepec
8 Banco Mercantil
9 Banco de Venezuela

see Las Mercedes, Chacao & El Rosal

most exhibits are kept indoors. The highlights are extensive collections of old horse-drawn carts and carriages, as well as vintage cars, many of which are linked with eminent personages of Venezuelan social and political life, including former presidents and military rulers. The museum is open 8 am to 2 pm Wednesday and 9 am to 5 pm Sunday. Admission is US$1.

La Casona

A short walk south of the museum is La Casona, the home of Venezuela's presidents. Established at the beginning of the 18th century as a cacao hacienda, it was decreed the presidential residence by Rómulo Gallegos. After remodeling was completed in 1966, Raúl Leoni moved in and became its first resident.

The complex consists of several buildings – some dating from the colonial period, others from the late 19th century – and seven internal patios and gardens. The interiors are fitted with Spanish-Creole furnishings and graced with paintings by prominent Venezuelan artists. A part of the hacienda (not the area where the president lives, of course) was opened to the public, but the visits were very recently suspended. It is unclear if or when tours will recommence. Call ☎ 286 80 30 or 286 80 70 for news.

Petare

Today, Petare is an outer suburb of Caracas, easily accessible by metro, but it was once a town in its own right. It was founded in 1621 and developed independently side by side with Caracas. Although it has been swallowed up by the metropolis, it has preserved much of its historic character.

The town is centered on the restored Plaza Sucre, with an equestrian statue of the Gran Mariscal himself in the middle. The eastern side of the square is occupied by the large mid-18th-century **Iglesia del Dulce Nombre de Jesús**, which still boasts some of the original retables dating from the time of the church's construction.

Two blocks south of the plaza, on the corner of Calles Guanche and Lino de Clemente, is the **Museo de Arte Popular de Petare**, in a beautiful colonial house. The museum features temporary exhibitions of naive art, open for visitors 10 am to 5 pm daily except Mondays.

Stroll around the town's central streets and have a look at the old houses, some of which have been adorned with paintings by local artists. Take precautions, though: The suburb doesn't seem to be absolutely secure.

SOUTHERN SUBURBS

The southern part of Caracas, set on the rolling hills, is the most heterogeneous. Here are some of Caracas' wealthiest suburbs and also numerous pockets of ramshackle barrios, sometimes neighboring each other.

Parque Zoológico de Caricuao

This is Caracas' main zoo, located in the far southwestern suburb of Caricuao, about 10km from the center, but easily accessible by metro. Get off at Zoológico station (terminus of the line), from where it's a seven-minute walk to the zoo's entrance.

The zoo has a selection of native birds, reptiles and mammals, plus some imported big cats and elephants. Most animals seem to enjoy a fair degree of freedom in their enclosures, and some, including monkeys, peacocks, ibis, flamingos and macaws, are virtually free. The zoo is open 9 am to 4 pm Tuesday to Sunday.

There's also the small Parque Zoológico El Pinar, 4km southwest of the center, but it's poorer and not as convenient to get to.

Fundación de Etnomusicología y Folklore

Commonly referred to as FUNDEF, this foundation aims at preserving traditional popular Latin American culture, carrying out research programs and collecting artifacts. The museum on the premises features changing exhibitions of popular arts and crafts, including pottery, basketry, wood carving and textiles. It's open 8:30 am to noon and 2 to 4:30 pm weekdays, 10 am to 3 pm weekends. The foundation (☎ 693 95 08, 693 98 45) is in a fine old house known as 'Mansión Zuloaga' and is in Quinta Micomicona, Avenida Zuloaga, Los Rosales.

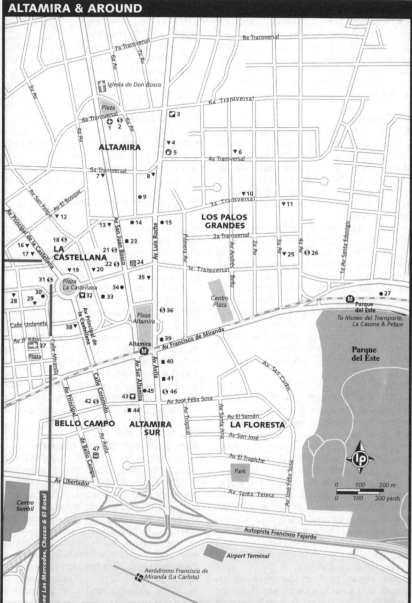

ALTAMIRA & AROUND

Iglesia de Don Bosco

7a Transversal
7a Av
6a Av
8a Transversal

3a Av

Plaza
6a Transversal
1 2
6a Av

ALTAMIRA

6a Transversal

3

4a Av

▼ 4
5

▼ 6

4a Transversal

Av San Felipe
Av El Bosque
5a Transversal
7 ▼
8 ▼

▼ 12

● 9

Av Principal de la Castellana
13 ▼
● 14
● 15
3a Transversal
▼ 10
▼ 11

LOS PALOS GRANDES

Av San Juan Bosco
Av Luis Roche

18
LA CASTELLANA
16 ▼
17 ▼
21
23
2a Transversal
Primera Av
Av Andrés Bello
2a Av
3a Av
4a Av
▼ 25
26
1a Av Santa Edurvigis

19 ▼
22
▼ 20
24
1a Transversal

31
Plaza La Castellana
34 ●
35 ▼

● 27

28 ▼
29 ▼
30 ●
32
33
Centro Plaza

M Parque del Este
To Museo del Transporte, La Casona & Petare

Av Principal de la Castellana
36
Plaza Altamira

Parque del Este

Calle Urdaneta
38 ▼

Av JF Ribas
37
Plaza

● 39
Altamira **M**
Av Francisco de Miranda

Calle Coromoto
Av Sur Altamira
Av Ávila
● 40

● 41
Av San Carlos

42
43
45
46
Av José Félix Sosa

44

Calle Miranda
Av Principal de Bello Campo

BELLO CAMPO
ALTAMIRA SUR
Av Tropical
Av Santa Ana
Av El Samán
LA FLORESTA
Av San José

47
Av Ávila
Av El Trapiche
Park

Av José Félix Sosa

Av Libertador

Centro Sambil

see Las Mercedes, Chacao & El Rosal

Av Santa Teresa

0   100   200 m
0   100   200 yards

Autopista Francisco Fajardo

Airport Terminal

Aeródromo Francisco de Miranda (La Carlota)

ALTAMIRA & AROUND MAP KEY

PLACES TO STAY
23 Hotel Continental Altamira
33 Hotel Residencial El Cid
39 Four Seasons Hotel
40 Hotel Residencia Montserrat
41 Hotel La Floresta
44 Hotel Altamira

PLACES TO EAT
4 El Alazán de Altamira
6 Art Café
7 Restaurant Japonés
   Hatsuhana
8 Restaurant El Barquero
10 Ri-K-Chapa
11 Pollo en Brasas El Coyuco
12 Steak House de Lee Hamilton
13 Fritz & Franz
16 Restaurant El Gran Charolais

17 Spizzico
19 Restaurant Chez Wong
20 Le Petit Bistrot de Jacques
25 Restaurant El Presidente
28 El Mundo del Pollo
29 Pizzería La Romanina
35 Café L'Attico
38 Restaurant La Estancia

OTHER
1 Clínica El Ávila
2 Banco Unión
3 Bolivian Embassy & Consulate
5 Gas Station
9 Little Rock Café
14 Marmmen Store
15 Casa de Rómulo Gallegos
18 Corp Banca
21 Banco Provincial

22 Banco de Venezuela
24 Digital Planet
26 Corp Banca
27 Inparques
30 El Solar del Vino
31 Corp Banca; Centro Cultural
   Corp Group
32 Gran Pizzería El León
34 The American Book Shop
36 Banco Unión
37 Iglesia San José de Chacao
42 Corp Banca
43 Greenwich Pub
45 Tiffany's
46 Italcambio
47 Aeroexpresos Ejecutivos Bus
   Terminal

It's two blocks east from La Bandera metro station.

El Hatillo

A small old town 15km southeast of the city center, El Hatillo is today a distant suburb of Caracas. Like Petare, it lived its own life for centuries until becoming a part of Caracas' metropolitan area. Centered on Plaza Bolívar, the town still retains some of its colonial architecture. The parish church on the plaza has preserved its exterior pretty well, but its interior was radically (and rather controversially) modernized. Many central houses have been restored and painted in bright colors, which gives the town an attractive and lively look.

El Hatillo has become a trendy weekend getaway for caraqueños and is packed with cars and people on Saturday and Sunday. Every house is a restaurant, café, boutique, art gallery or handicraft shop. The biggest craft shop, the Hannsi, is half a block north of the church. The recent explosion of eating outlets has been extraordinary, and today you can find most major foreign cuisines, from French and Italian to Japanese and Thai.

Frequent *carritos* (small buses) run to El Hatillo from Avenida Humboldt, just off Boulevard de Sabana Grande, near the Chacaíto metro station.

ACTIVITIES

The best place for **hiking** near Caracas is Parque Nacional El Ávila – see the Around Caracas section, later in this chapter. If you're looking for organized hiking trips, contact one of the *centros excursionistas* – see Excursion Centers in the Organized Tours section, later.

The favorite **rock-climbing** spot within the city is the Parque de Recreación Cuevas del Indio, Avenida Principal de la Guairita (southern continuation of Avenida Principal del Cafetal). Local climbers flock here on weekends.

There are a few public **tennis** courts in the city, but some private clubs hire out their courts to nonmembers. Contact the Federación Venezolana de Tenis (☎ 979 74 62, 979 70 95).

Public **golf** courses are nonexistent in Caracas, but some private golf clubs are willing to offer their facilities to the general public – for a fee, of course. If you absolutely must play, you can obtain information from the Federación Venezolana de Golf (☎ 730 46 80, 730 47 03).

LANGUAGE COURSES

Caracas has quite a choice of institutions offering Spanish-language courses, and most can also provide teachers for individual classes. The places to check include the following:

Centro de Idiomas Berlitz
(☎ 993 55 74, 993 68 51) Quinta Manuela, Calle Madrid, Las Mercedes
Web site: www.berlitz.com

Centro Venezolano Americano (CVA)
(☎ 993 84 22, 993 79 11, fax 993 68 12) Avenida Principal de las Mercedes
Web site: www.cva.org.ve

Centro Venezolano de Español
(☎ 793 92 65, 793 24 34, fax 793 40 45) Torre Phelps, Piso 19, Plaza Venezuela
Web site: www.ceves.org.ve

ORGANIZED TOURS

Caracas tour companies can send you almost anywhere in Venezuela, but the trips won't be cheap. It's cheaper to reach the region on your own and contact a local operator (see Organized Tours in the Getting Around chapter). But remember that some tours organized from Caracas may be unavailable in the region, and Caracas companies may conveniently link various regional tours into one chain to reduce transfer time. If you plan on taking tours, carefully read the information on regional operators in this book before leaving Caracas.

Tour Companies

There are over 600 travel agencies in Caracas, and most offer tours. Some of them (the so-called *mayoristas,* or wholesalers) simply sell tours organized by other companies. Many agencies use some of the services of selected regional operators, adding their own guides and transfers, and sometimes altering routes and upgrading lodging facilities. Some Caracas operators, though, organize the entire trip themselves, using their own camps and means of transportation. Some companies can prepare tailor-made trips, which will usually take a while and cost considerably more than standard tours.

Following are some reputable tour companies. Listed prices are approximate and per person; they don't include transportation to/from the tour's area, and they may vary significantly depending on the number of people in the tour.

All the listed companies focus on responsible tourism and have English-speaking guides (some also have guides that speak German and/or French). For more information on responsible traveling, contact the Sociedad Conservacionista Audubon de Venezuela (☎ 992 28 12, 992 32 68, fax 991 07 16), Edificio Matisco, Piso 1, Oficina 5, Calle Veracruz, Las Mercedes. This leading environmental society can provide information on ecological issues and recommend tour companies; it organizes bird-watching tours itself. Check out their Web site at www.audubonvenezuela.org for details.

Akanan Travel & Tours
(☎ 234 21 03, 234 23 23, fax 237 38 79, akanan@sa.omnes.net) Edificio Claret, Mezzanina, Avenida Sanz at Calle La Laguna, El Marqués. This company specializes in adventure trips not often offered by mainstream operators, including treks to the top of Auyantepui (eight days, US$780) and Roraima (eight days, US$650), as well as bicycle trips from La Paragua to Canaima (six days, US$450). Web site: www.akanan.com

Alpi Tour
(☎ 283 14 33, 283 66 77, fax 285 60 67, alpitour@viptel.com) Torre Centro, Piso 1, Oficina 11, Centro Parque Boyacá, Avenida Sucre, Los Dos Caminos. One of the more expensive operators, this company specializes in fishing trips, but also offers a range of mainstream packages and some adventurous tours in the Amazonas. Web site: www.alpi-group.com

Cacao Expediciones
(☎ 977 12 34, 977 27 98, fax 977 01 10, cacaotravel@cantv.net) Quinta Orquidea, Calle Andrómeda, Urbanización El Peñón, Vía Baruta. This agency has expertise in Caura River tours (five days, US$400), where it has its own lodge. It also has a lodge in the Amazonas, serving as a base for boat trips in the region. Web site: www.cacaotravel.com

Cóndor Verde
(☎ 975 43 06, 975 36 60, fax 975 23 85, condor@etheron.net) Torre Humboldt, Mezzanina 03, Avenida Caura, Prados del Este. This German-run agency offers one of the widest spectrums of tours, ranging from leisurely beach holidays on Isla de Margaritato adventurous boat trips in the Amazonas, plus special-interest packages such as fishing, diving and golf. Tours include Delta del Orinoco (three days, US$380), Gran Sabana (four days, US$300), Roraima (seven days, US$500) and Caura River (five days,

US$350). It also has a special no-frills offer for budget travelers.

Orinoco Tours
(☎ 761 77 12, 761 40 30, fax 761 68 01, info@ orinocotours.com) Edificio Galerías Bolívar, Piso 7, Oficina 75-A, Boulevard de Sabana Grande (Ⓜ Plaza Venezuela). This German-run agency offers various levels of adventure tours. Programs include Gran Sabana, Roraima and Los Llanos. Web site: www.orinocotours.com

Trotamundos Internacional
(☎ 576 07 36, 576 00 78, fax 576 60 83, trotamundos@ cantv.net) Hotel Hilton Caracas, Torre Sur, Piso 3, Oficina 313 (Ⓜ Bellas Artes). This is one of Caracas' well-established wholesalers, with wide if not budget offerings of mainstream and mild-adventure tours to most regions. Web site: www.trotamundos.com

Tucaya
(☎ 234 94 01, 237 78 15, fax 232 53 90, tucaya@ cantv.net) Quinta Santa Marta, 1a Avenida Urbanización Campo Claro, Los Dos Caminos. This small, French-run agency caters principally to the French-speaking clientele, but it also organizes tours guided in English. The tours feature some major tourist destinations, including Gran Sabana (four days, US$420), Roraima (nine days, US$900), Los Llanos (four days, US$415) and Delta del Orinoco (three days, US$230). Web site: www.tucaya.com

Salto Angel Tour Operators Hoturvensa, an offspring of Avensa airlines and owner of the Canaima camp, offers two packages (two days for US$295/485 single/double room, and three days for US$570/675), which include room and board at the Canaima camp plus the flight over the falls (the Caracas-Canaima flight costs extra). This is probably the most expensive offer you can find on the market. You can buy these packages at any Avensa office and at most travel agencies throughout the country.

Since Salto Angel is one of Venezuela's top tourist attractions, many Caracas tour companies (including most listed above) have the falls in their programs, and they are likely to have more innovative and cheaper tours than Hoturvensa.

However, possibly the cheapest tours will be offered by the small Canaima-based tour operators. Fortunately, the most major of these, Tiuna Tours, has a desk at the domes-

tic terminal of Maiquetía airport (☎ 014-287 16 25), and still more conveniently, an office in Caracas (☎ 235 87 40, 235 48 32), Edificio Centro Gerencial Los Andes, Piso 3, Oficina 3-G, Avenida Rómulo Gallegos, Boleíta Norte. The staff can sell you the boat tour from Canaima to the falls for the same price you'd pay in Canaima, and they can inform you about ways of getting to Canaima. See Salto Angel in the Guayana chapter for further information, and Ciudad Bolívar in the same chapter for more tour options.

Los Roques Tour Operators Archipiélago Los Roques is serviced from Maiquetía airport by a number of small airlines. They all offer a flight-only option, and some also offer tours.

There are more than half a dozen of these airlines at the airport terminal (either domestic or auxiliary), including Sol de América (☎ 355 17 97, 355 17 26), Rutaca (☎ 355 16 43, 355 18 38), AeroEjecutivos (☎ 014-939 78 51), Chapi Air (☎ 355 27 86, 355 19 65), Island Air (formerly Viprovías; ☎ 355 11 57), Transavén (☎ 355 11 79) and Línea Turística Aereotuy (LTA; ☎ 355 20 60). LTA is the largest operator and has its main office in Caracas (☎ 761 80 43, 761 62 31), Edificio Gran Sabana, Piso 5, Boulevard de Sabana Grande (Ⓜ Sabana Grande). See Archipiélago Los Roques in the Central North chapter for further information.

Los Llanos Representatives If you plan on taking tours to the *hatos* (ranches) in Los Llanos (see the Hatos section in the Los Llanos chapter for full details), note that some hatos may require you to book and pay beforehand through a Caracas agent. They include:

Hato El Cedral
(☎ 781 89 95, ☎/fax 793 60 82, hatocedral@ cantv.net) Edificio Pancho, Piso 5, Oficina 33, Avenida La Salle, Los Caobos

Hato Piñero
(☎ 991 11 35, 992 44 13, fax 991 66 68, hatopinerovzla@telcel.net.ve) Biotur Hato Piñero, Edificio General de Seguros, Piso 6, Oficina 6-B, Avenida La Estancia, Chuao
Web site: www.branger.com/pinero.html

Excursion Centers

Not precisely tour companies, the centros excursionistas are associations of outdoor-minded people who organize excursions for themselves. These are essentially one- or two-day weekend trips around Caracas and the central states, but longer journeys to other regions are often scheduled for long weekends and holiday periods. The trips include walking in the countryside, and though the focus is usually on nature, cultural sights are often part of the program. Each trip is prepared by a member of the group, who then serves as a guide. The excursionists use public transportation and take their own food and camping gear if necessary. Foreign travelers are welcome to take part, and you can usually find a companion for conversation in English, German etc.

Founded in 1929, the Centro Excursionista Caracas (CEC) is the oldest and best-known club of this kind. Its members include people of all ages, and it has regular weekend trips, which are detailed in a CEC monthly bulletin. Club meetings are on Saturday (if there is no excursion that day) between 2:30 and 5 pm, in the Polideportivo in Urbanización Santa Sofía.

It's best to call a club member beforehand to ask about forthcoming trips and to check the meeting's details. Contacts include Samuel Bendayán (speaks English; ☎ 731 64 78), Fritz Werner (German; ☎ 945 09 46) and Andrea Würz (English and German; ☎ 235 30 53 or 267 14 11).

Younger travelers may be interested in the Centro Excursionista Universitario (CEU), which bands together mostly university students. They walk faster and may have some more adventurous trips. They meet on Tuesdays between 6 and 8 pm in the basement (sótano) under the swimming pool (piscina) of the sports compound at the Universidad Central de Venezuela (Ⓜ Ciudad Universitaria).

The CEU contacts include Henry Guerra (☎ 562 42 49), Raniero de Lima (☎ 662 87 27) and Ubaldo Oloyola (☎ 979 89 06).

The most recent addition is the Centro Excursionista Los Montañeros, which still hasn't found a permanent seat for their meetings. Contact persons include Lucy Alió (English, German and French; ☎ 782 41 82), Faustino Valdés (☎ 561 48 62) and Jesús González (some degree of English; ☎ 014-320 44 98).

Guides

The Asociación Venezolana de Instructores y Guías de Montaña is an association of over 30 guides, some of whom are very experienced. They can provide mountain-guide services (mountaineering, rock climbing, mountain trekking etc) and may find guides for other activities, such as caving, kayaking, paragliding or bird-watching. They have their office (☎ 751 23 19, ☎/fax 751 22 19, loby@telcel.net.ve) in Quinta Nenena, Piso Bajo, Local 6, Calle Caurimare, Colinas de Bello Monte.

Henry González (hegori65@hotmail.com) can organize and personally guide expeditions to the top of Auyantepui in Canaima national park. These are 12- to 15-day strenuous treks from the base of the tepui to the point from which Salto Angel spills down. The return can be on foot the same way or by helicopter. The cost of an all-inclusive trip will run around US$1800 to US$2200 per person, depending on the particular version, with a minimum of eight participants.

SPECIAL EVENTS

Caracas is not particularly renowned for its religious or popular festivities, though Christmas, Carnaval and Easter are celebrated with due fervor. During these times, all offices close, as do most shops, and inter-city bus transportation is frantic. Flights are fully booked for a week or two beforehand.

Possibly the biggest religious feast in Caracas is the Easter celebration in Chacao, which begins with the Bajada de Palmeras, on the Friday before Palm Sunday, and goes on for over a week, culminating with solemn processions on Maundy Thursday and Good Friday. It concludes with the Quema de Judas (Burning of Judas) on Easter Sunday.

Traditional suburbs are likely to celebrate holy days with more vigor than central districts. El Hatillo boasts local feasts on several occasions during the year (including May 3, July 16 and September 4), as does Petare (January 30 and 31 and the last Sunday of September).

More characteristic of Caracas are cultural events, of which the Festival Internacional de Teatro is the city's highlight. Initiated in 1976, it has been held in March/April of every even-numbered year.

El Hatillo is home to the still very young and small Festival de Música El Hatillo, which covers everything from jazz to ethnic to classical to contemporary music and takes place somewhere between September and November. A similarly wide range of musical genres characterizes the new Festival El Piano de Bach a Chick Corea, which is held in the Complejo Cultural Teresa Carreño in June/July. Another new event, the Temporada de Danza, goes for several weeks in July and August, bringing together some of the leading national dance groups, plus occasional international guests.

The week around July 25 usually witnesses an increase in cultural activities such as concerts, exhibitions and theater performances, organized to celebrate the anniversary of Caracas' foundation on that date in 1567.

PLACES TO STAY

There are loads of hotels scattered throughout the city, but most are located in the central districts, particularly in the center and Sabana Grande. Note that staying in a distant district of the city is not a problem, as long as you are close to the metro.

Accommodations in Caracas are more expensive than elsewhere in the country. A simple budget hotel that costs, say, US$15 double in a provincial city won't go for less than US$20 in Caracas. Therefore, the price brackets in the following sections have been pushed a bit upward compared to those in the rest of the book. The budget section has been extended to cover anything up to about US$30 double, and the mid-range bracket up to roughly US$60 double.

All hotels listed in the following sections have rooms with private baths and either fan or air-conditioning (as indicated), and

almost all have TV sets. Many budget establishments, as well as almost all mid-range and top-end places, offer parking-lot facilities. In high-rise hotels, it may be worth asking for a room on one of the upper floors, for better views and less noise. Always try to see the room before booking in and paying.

Places to Stay – Budget

On the whole, Caracas' budget accommodations are poor and styleless, and they are usually located in unimpressive, sometimes unsafe areas. Many budget hotels double as love hotels, and some as brothels; business is particularly brisk on Friday and Saturday. Consequently, some hotels may turn you down on weekends. If your itinerary is flexible, try to avoid arriving in Caracas on these days, or at least come reasonably early so as to allow some time for possible hotel hunting.

The Center This area roughly corresponds with what is covered by the left page of the Central Caracas map. The cheapest accommodations in this sector are found south of Avenida Bolívar. There are at least 50 basic hotels there, most of which are concentrated in two areas: between Teatro Nacional and Cuadra Bolívar, and south of Plaza de Toros Nuevo Circo. However, this entire area is unattractive and is unsafe at night; even during the daytime you should be on your guard. Furthermore, most of the hotels are scruffy shelters, many renting rooms by the hour.

One of the few acceptable places in the area is *Hotel Center Park* (☎ 541 86 19), Avenida Lecuna, Velásquez a Miseria. It's clean and well kept and is sometimes used by travelers. It offers small *matrimoniales* (beds for two people) with fan for US$15 (US$20 with air-con), which is about the minimum you need to pay for the cheapest acceptable room in town. Alternatively, try the nearby family-run *Hotel Guarapiche* (☎ 542 30 73), Calle Este 8, Esquina Zamuro, which has spacious if dim air-conditioned matrimoniales/doubles/triples for US$20/24/30.

It's more convenient for sightseeing, and perhaps safer, to stay north of Avenida Universidad. One of the cheapest options in the area is *Hotel Hollywood* (☎ 561 49 89), Avenida Fuerzas Armadas, Esquina Romualda, which costs US$18/22 matrimonial/double with fan.

Two blocks north along the same road is *Hotel Metropol* (☎ 562 86 66), Plaza España a Socorro, and *Hotel Terepaima* (☎ 562 51 84), Socorro a San Ramón. Both have air-conditioned rooms and are OK, if a bit noisy due to heavy traffic. Each costs US$20/24/28 matrimonial/double/triple.

One block east, on Esquina Calero, is *Hotel Inter* (☎ 564 02 51, 564 70 31). It costs much the same as the Metropol and Terepaima, but is quieter and better kept. It's popular with businesspeople and is often full. It's no wonder, as this is one of the best options in the center in this price bracket.

Parque Central The area just north of Parque Central has a few budget hotels, which may be alternative options to those in the center. They are merely a couple of blocks from the Bellas Artes metro station and are conveniently close to several museums.

The cheapest place here is *Hotel Ribot* (☎ 571 32 44), Esquina La Mansión, with its striking ancient Egyptian facade. Don't expect too much inside – it's truly basic at US$16/20 matrimonial/double with fan.

The nine-story *Hotel New Jersey* (☎ 571 46 24), Esquina Paradero, is better and has air-con rooms for US$22/28. Ask for a room on one of the top floors. The best budget option in the area, *Hotel Renovación* (☎ 571 01 33, 571 07 44), El Patronato a La Mansión, costs US$24/30; here, too, the rooms on the upper floors are more attractive.

Sabana Grande This area is a popular place to stay among travelers. It has plenty of hotels and feels a little bit safer than the center, and it sits on the metro line, so you can easily get around to other districts.

Many of the budget hotels are concentrated in the western end of the district, on

Prolongación Sur Avenida Las Acacias and neighboring streets. There are perhaps more than 30 hotels here, packed in a small area just a few minutes' walk south of the Plaza Venezuela metro station. Note that many of these hotels cater not only to tourists but also to couples just wanting to have sex.

One of the cheapest is *Hotel Tanausú* (☎ 793 19 22, 793 76 91), charging US$18/24 double/triple; it's basic and rents out rooms by the hour. Just across the street is the better *Hotel Odeón* (☎ 793 13 45, 793 13 22), which has air-conditioned matrimoniales/doubles/triples for US$20/25/30. There are over a dozen budget hotels farther south on Prolongación Sur Avenida Las Acacias, including *Hotel La Mirage* (☎ 793 27 33) and *Hotel Ariston* (☎ 782 77 23), both costing much the same as the Odeón.

More cheapies lie on Calles San Antonio and El Colegio, two parallel streets to the east. One of the cheapest here is *Nuestro Hotel* (☎ 761 54 31), Calle El Colegio, costing US$20 for a simple matrimonial with fan, but it too doubles as a love hotel.

If you need somewhere more central, try *Hotel Cristal* (☎ 761 91 31), perfectly located on Boulevard de Sabana Grande, at Pasaje Asunción. It's not the classiest place around, but it has reasonable matrimoniales/doubles with air-conditioning for US$30/32. Ask for a room with a balcony overlooking the mall. Slightly cheaper is the nearby *Hotel Jolly* (☎ 761 48 87, 763 18 92), Avenida Francisco Solano, which is priced at US$28/30, though the rooms facing the street can be noisy.

Places to Stay – Mid-Range

This section includes hotels that charge around US$30 to US$60 double. These hotels have private baths with hot water and air-conditioning as standard facilities, but otherwise they may be quite nondescript and styleless. They sometimes don't offer much more than some of the budget places, though fewer of them double as love hotels. Mid-range hotels are in good supply in the Sabana Grande area, but elsewhere there aren't many of them.

The Center The center is certainly not an upmarket district, and there are few mid-range hotels in the area. Few travelers would want to spend much money on staying in a central hotel. One that you might consider is *Plaza Catedral Hotel* (☎ 564 21 11, 563 33 94, fax 564 17 97), at Plaza Bolívar. It is the best-located mid-range hotel in the area, and though increasingly unkempt, it's perhaps still worth US$42/48/56 single/double/triple, especially if you get the room overlooking the plaza. It's not for light sleepers, though, as the cathedral's bells ring every 15 minutes. A bonus is the hotel's own restaurant on the top floor – a handy facility if you don't feel like strolling the streets after dark.

Sabana Grande This district has a choice of hotels in the mid-range bracket, though few of them are really good values. One that is certainly worth checking is *Hotel Plaza Palace* (☎ 762 48 21, fax 762 63 75), in a quiet area on Calle Los Mangos, yet close to Boulevard de Sabana Grande. It has good matrimoniales for US$55; add a mere US$5 and you can stay in an excellent, spacious double suite.

Even closer to the boulevard is the small *Royal Hotel* (☎ 762 54 94, 762 29 43, fax 762 64 59), Calle San Antonio, which offers singles/doubles for US$54/58. A bit farther south in the same area, the eight-story *Hotel Gabial* (☎ 793 11 56, 793 09 56, fax 781 14 53), Prolongación Sur Avenida Las Acacias, is not as well located as the Royal, but is cheaper and a better value at US$45 matrimonial or double. Another reasonable option is *Hotel City* (☎ 793 57 85, 793 17 35, fax 782 63 54), Avenida Bolivia, just next to the Plaza Venezuela metro station. It costs much the same as the Gabial.

There are more places farther away from the boulevard. *Hotel Plaza Venezuela* (☎ 781 78 11, 781 73 44, fax 781 95 42), on Avenida La Salle, provides decent standards and good service for US$45 double, but it's worth paying just US$8 more for a large suite. A few minutes' walk uphill on the same street is the *Hotel Atlántida*

(☎ 793 32 11, fax 781 36 96), which doesn't offer many luxuries but is nonetheless quiet and clean and costs US$52/60 double/triple.

Still more tranquil is *Hotel Residencia Las Taparitas* (☎ 782 65 33, fax 793 04 94), well located on a small side street, Calle San Camilo, just off Avenida Las Palmas. It has cozy studio apartments complete with kitchenette and fridge, for US$50 per two persons.

Altamira Although Altamira is essentially an upmarket suburb, it has some affordable, if not budget, accommodations. It's worth considering, for it's a pleasant and fairly safe area dotted with a number of good restaurants and nightspots, and it lies just a 15-minute trip by metro from the center (or seven minutes from Sabana Grande).

Hotel Residencia Montserrat (☎ 263 35 33, fax 261 13 94), Avenida Ávila, Plaza Altamira Sur, just a few steps from the Altamira metro station, is still a reasonable value for money, though it has passed its best days and some refurbishing wouldn't be a bad idea. It costs US$45/55/65 for a spacious double/triple/quad.

If you are unsuccessful there, try *Hotel La Floresta* (☎ 263 19 55, fax 262 12 43), next door. At US$45/50/60 single/double/triple, it's not as good a deal and the rooms are much smaller, but it is more likely to have a vacancy. However, before booking in you may want to check the nearby *Hotel Altamira* (☎ 267 42 55, 267 42 84, fax 267 19 26), Avenida José Félix Sosa, which is cheaper but not worse (US$44 matrimonial or double). Generally speaking, it's easier to get a room in these hotels on weekends.

Places to Stay – Top End
The city has quite a number of four- and five-star hotels, though their standards don't always match their hefty rates. It's often better to stay in a decent three-star establishment for a fraction of the price, spending the saved money on dining, tours, shopping etc. Possibly the biggest single advantage of upmarket hotels is noiseless central air conditioning, instead of noisy

room conditioners commonly used in budget and most mid-range hotels. Some top-end hotels will offer lower rates on weekends.

The Center The top end in the center is represented by three-star *Hotel El Conde* (☎ *864 12 79, 860 12 71, fax 862 09 28)*, Esquina El Conde, one block west of Plaza Bolívar. It's not one of the city's best hotels, but it's not particularly expensive either at US$60/70/80 single/double/triple.

Parque Central The five-star *Hotel Hilton Caracas* (☎ *503 50 00, fax 503 50 03)*, facing Parque Central, is one of the well-established upmarket hotels in town. Its trump cards are a convenient location, good views from the top floors, a helpful tourist information desk, a swimming pool, tennis courts and a gym. However, the hotel is not that cheap at US$280 double, though US$170 weekend rates may be more tempting.

Cheaper is the four-star *Hilton Caracas Residencias Anauco* (☎/fax 573 41 11)*, in one of the apartment buildings within the Parque Central complex. Suites range from studios to three bedrooms, kitchen included, and may be particularly suitable for larger parties. Reservations for both Hilton hotels can be made through any Hilton worldwide.

Sabana Grande The 11-story, 125-room *Lincoln Suites* (☎ *761 27 27, 762 85 75, fax 762 55 03)*, on Avenida Francisco Solano between Avenida Los Jabillos and Calle San Jerónimo (also accessible directly from Boulevard de Sabana Grande), has comfortable, spacious suites with full amenities for around US$120 for up to three people, as well as a reasonably priced restaurant.

The 660-room five-star *Hotel Gran Meliá Caracas* (☎ *762 81 11, fax 762 37 37, caracas@gran-melia.com.ve)*, on Avenida Casanova, has finally opened, following a decade-long snail's-pace construction, to become the largest, poshest and most expensive hotel in town. It has just about all the facilities you could wish for, including a gym, a swimming pool, four restaurants,

four bars and a conference center for 1250 people. A double room will cost about US$320 (US$180 on weekends), but be prepared to pay at least twice that for a junior suite.

Las Mercedes Should you want to stay close to Caracas' major nightlife hub, the four-star *Hotel Paseo Las Mercedes* (☎ *991 00 33, fax 993 03 41)*, in the shopping mall of the same name, on Avenida Principal de Las Mercedes, is handy. It offers decent standards and services, and costs US$150 double (US$100 on weekends). Across the road is the more costly five-star *Hotel Tamanaco Inter-Continental* (☎ *909 71 11, fax 909 89 50)*. The nearby *Hotel Eurobuilding Caracas* (☎ *902 11 11, 959 11 33, fax 907 21 89)* is another five-star option.

Altamira The alternative center of nighttime entertainment, Altamira can accommodate you in its modern, three-star *Hotel Continental Altamira* (☎ *261 06 44, fax 262 02 43)*, Avenida San Juan Bosco. Its ample double rooms cost US$130 (US$100 on weekends).

Cheaper than the above is the well-kept *Hotel Residencial El Cid* (☎ *263 26 11, 263 17 15, fax 263 55 78)*, Avenida San Felipe, which offers spacious suites with kitchenette for US$70 double – a good value.

By the time you read this, the huge *Four Seasons Hotel*, on the corner of Avenidas Francisco de Miranda and Luis Roche, should be open, providing some of the ultimate luxuries Altamira has to offer – at a price, of course.

PLACES TO EAT

Caracas has an enormous choice of places to eat, and you could easily stay in town a full year and eat out three times a day without visiting the same restaurant twice. This unfortunately makes any objective and comprehensive selection difficult. However, the food is generally good, even in budget eateries, so you can safely explore the culinary market by yourself. Many restaurants place their menus outside, so you can get an idea of what's offered and how much it costs. The *Caracas Gastronomic Guide* (listed under Guidebooks in the Books section of the Facts for the Visitor chapter) is a great help in discovering the local cooking scene.

There's a range of budget eateries that have a *menú del día* or *menú ejecutivo* for about US$3 to US$5. An alternative can be chicken, and the places that serve it, usually called *pollos en brasas,* are also in good supply. Don't forget *arepas* (small, stuffed maize pancakes) – a perfect snack or even a meal – sold in numerous *areperas.*

For breakfast, go to any of the ubiquitous *panaderías,* which will invariably have a choice of croissants, *pasteles* (pastries), *cachitos* (filled croissants) and fresh bread. Sandwiches are rarely precooked and on display, but they can be prepared in a minute on request. Wash it all down with a *batido* or coffee. In the evening, countless Spanish *tascas* (bar restaurants) dot many streets of inner suburbs, particularly in La Candelaria and Sabana Grande. If you can't live without your burgers and pizzas, numerous outlets of McDonald's, Burger King, Pizza Hut, KFC and other big chains will keep you alive.

Going more upmarket, suburbs such as Las Mercedes, Altamira and La Castellana boast dozens of well-appointed restaurants that will serve you a worldwide range of delicacies, though these may eat a little bit into your pocket. With a massive rise in prices over recent years, fine eating is no longer a bargain by western standards. A great dinner in Caracas can be nearly as expensive as in Paris or New York.

The menus of upscale establishments are in English (sometimes also in German and/or French) in addition to Spanish, but be warned: A notorious practice of Caracas restaurants is that they usually don't include the 15.5% IVA tax, and never the 10% service, so your dinner will effectively cost you over 25% more than the price listed in the menu (or, more precisely, at least 35%, because they obviously expect their customary 10% tip on top of the bill).

Many restaurants, particularly cheaper ones, aren't open on Sunday, but fast-food outlets operate seven days a week. Some areperas keep going 24 hours a day. Most upmarket restaurants are open until 10 pm or later.

A phone number after the restaurant's name in the following text suggests that it's an upper-middle to top-end establishment, and that you might want to book a table, especially on weekends.

The Center & Parque Central

While it doesn't abound in chic restaurants, the center does have a great variety of low- to middle-priced eateries, many of which serve local fare known as *comida criolla.* Reasonable central options of that kind include *Restaurant La Torre* and *Restaurant Las Vegas*, next to each other just off Plaza Bolívar, and *Restaurant Padre Sierra*, La Bolsa a Padre Sierra. You will find more places like these around the central streets. They get particularly busy at lunchtime, when crowds of office workers rush to have their lunch. The number of patrons inside the establishment is usually a good indicator of how good or bad the place is.

One of the finest central places for local cuisine is the *Restaurant Dama Antañona*, Jesuitas a Maturín. It offers traditional cooking at affordable if not budget prices in appropriately craft-decorated surroundings.

Café del Sacro, in the Museo Sacro de Caracas, at Plaza Bolívar, is an ideal place to escape from the city rush and enjoy some delicious (if not cheap) fresh salads and sandwiches, plus great espresso. It's open noon to 4 pm Tuesday to Saturday. Another pleasant place on the plaza, though of a completely different character, is the top-floor *Restaurant Les Grisons*, in the Plaza Catedral Hotel. It does local and international dishes, including some Swiss specialties, and you have the whole plaza at your feet.

For an inexpensive vegetarian lunch, go to *La Barra Vegetariana*, Edificio Iberia, Avenida Urdaneta, Esquina Animas. For falafel and other popular Middle Eastern food, try *Restaurant Kafta*, Esquina San Jacinto, or the slightly better *Restaurant Beirut*, Salvador de León a Socarrás (both closed on Sunday).

CARACAS

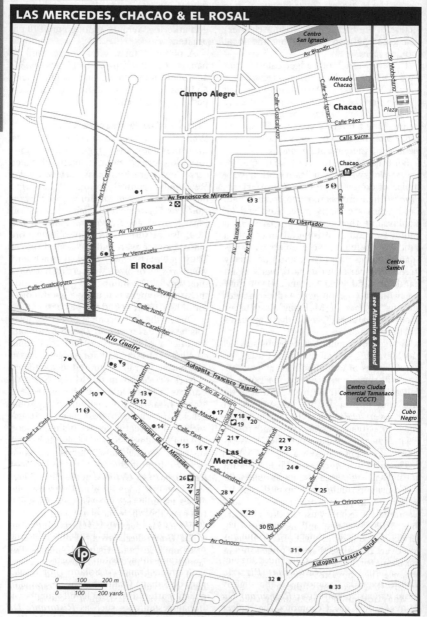

LAS MERCEDES, CHACAO & EL ROSAL

LAS MERCEDES, CHACAO & EL ROSAL MAP KEY

PLACES TO STAY
32 Hotel Paseo Las Mercedes
33 Hotel Tamanaco Inter-
Continental; Le Gourmet

PLACES TO EAT
9 Restaurant Real Past
10 Restaurant Doña Caraotica
13 Restaurant Aranjuez
15 Avanti
16 Restaurant La Castañuela
18 Restaurant Taiko
20 Maute Grill
21 Jardín des Crêpes

22 El Granjero del Este
23 Hereford Grill
25 Pollo en Brasas Los Riviera
27 Restaurant Kuates
28 La Romanissima
29 Las Tapas de Madrid

OTHER
1 Avianca
2 Centro Lido
3 Corp Banca
4 Banco de Venezuela
5 Banco Unión
6 Juan Sebastián Bar

7 Centro Venezolano
Americano
8 Berlitz
11 Italcambio
12 Banco Unión
14 Da Dío
17 Ozono
19 French Embassy
24 Fire
26 Birras Pub & Café
30 CompuMall
31 IVI Idiomas Vivos

The area east of Avenida Fuerzas Armadas, known as La Candelaria, is swamped with tascas, where you can try some traditional Spanish cooking, including a variety of tapas, or dedicate yourself to drinks, of which there's always a good choice. Many tascas are near the Plaza de la Candelaria, including *Tasca La Carabela*, *Tasca de Manolo*, *Tasca Mallorca*, *Bar Basque* and *Casa Farruco*. You'll find the location of these and other good tascas on the Central Caracas map.

La Candelaria also has some good eateries serving local food. The *Restaurant El Coyuco*, Avenida Urdaneta, Platanal a Candilito, is one of the better budget places for chicken and *parrillas* (mixed grills). It's popular with locals and often crowded at mealtimes, despite its enormous size. Some of the best and cheapest *cachapas* (corncakes) with ham and/or cheese can be had at the tiny *Lunchería Doña Agapita*, off Plaza La Candelaria. Don't miss trying one.

Sabana Grande

The Sabana Grande area boasts enough restaurants, cafés and snack bars to suit any budget and taste. For somewhere on the lower end of the price scale, check the unpretentious, cheap *Restaurant Pizzería Tivoli*, Avenida Casanova, or the slightly more expensive but better *Restaurant Da Marcelo*, on Calle Coromoto. The budget *Centro de Comida Rápida Plaza Broadway*, Boulevard de Sabana Grande, features

a collection of fast-food outlets serving anything from pizza and chicken to falafel and Chinese fried rice. A larger but more expensive fast-food center is on the top floor of the *Centro Comercial El Recreo*, on Avenida Casanova.

Vegetarians can get set lunches (US$4 to US$5) at *Restaurant Vegetariano Sabas Nieves*, Calle Pascual Navarro; *El Chalet Vegetariano*, Calle Los Manguitos (both open for lunch only, Monday to Saturday); or *El Buffet Vegetariano*, Avenida Los Jardines, La Florida, one block north of Avenida Libertador (open lunchtime on weekends only). You can get appetizing Indian veggie dishes (including a set lunch for US$4) until 8:30 pm at *Delicatesses Indú*, Calle Villaflor (closed Sunday)

For reasonable Middle Eastern fast food, including tabbouleh, falafel and the like, go to *Restaurant Almalak*, Calle Villaflor, or, better, to *Restaurant El Arabito*, half a block away on Avenida Casanova. *Restaurant Las Cancelas* has some of the better paellas in town (US$20 for two people). *Restaurant Le Coq D'Or*, on Calle Los Mangos, offers classic French cooking at prices lower than those of trendy French restaurants in the eastern suburbs.

Avenida Francisco Solano (not Boulevard de Sabana Grande) is the area's major culinary artery. Here you'll find a number of Italian restaurants, such as *Ristorante Da Guido* and *Ristorante Al Vecchio Mulino*, and several Spanish tascas, including *Tasca*

Rías Gallegas, *Mi Tasca* and *Tasca El Caserío*. Here also is the upmarket *Restaurant Urrutia* (☎ 763 04 48), considered one of the best (though not the cheapest) Basque restaurants in town.

The western end of the Boulevard de Sabana Grande is filled with a number of open-air cafés, which are popular with both locals and visitors. *Pastelería Heladería La Poma*, a short walk eastward, has some of the best ice cream and also offers a large selection of creative high-calorie cakes and pastries.

Las Mercedes

With a long-standing reputation as a fashionable dining district, Las Mercedes features perhaps a hundred restaurants, bars, cafés etc, all of which become particularly lively in the evening. It's a pleasant area to stroll around and explore gastronomic diversity, and you'll discover many more attractive eating venues than just those included in this text.

Most restaurants cater to a more affluent clientele, but some do serve cheap food. A good example is *Restaurant Real Past*, Avenida Río de Janeiro, which is the cheapest pasta house in the area. None of its appetizing plates costs more than US$2.50. *Pollo en Brasas Los Riviera*, Calle París, is another inexpensive place, specializing in spit-roasted chicken and parrillas. Slightly more expensive is the popular *El Granjero del Este*, Avenida Rio de Janeiro, which is open round the clock. This full-service arepera offers hearty comida criolla, including a variety of arepas, cachapas, soups, chicken and parrillas, in informal, cheerful surroundings. Similar in menu and price is *Restaurant Doña Caraotica*, another 24-hour arepera, on Avenida Principal de Las Mercedes.

There's a choice of restaurants offering international cuisine at affordable (though not budget) prices. *Jardín des Crêpes*, Calle Madrid, is an enjoyable place that does a variety of French-inspired crêpes (both sweet and savory versions) as well as some fish and meat dishes. *La Romanissima*, Calle New York, cooks good home-style pastas. The new, two-story *Avanti*, Avenida

Principal de Las Mercedes, has reasonable Italian fare. *Restaurant Kuates*, Calle California, does some appetizing Mexican standards, including tacos.

Las Mercedes is particularly known for its upmarket establishments, which abound by the dozen and offer a variety of delicacies from most of the world. *Restaurant La Castañuela* (☎ 993 22 05), Calle París, is one of the finer Spanish restaurants in the area, and there's probably nothing better for Japanese specialties than *Restaurant Taiko* (☎ 993 56 47), Avenida La Trinidad. *Le Gourmet* (☎ 909 72 20), in Hotel Tamanaco (see Places to Stay – Top End), provides some of the best French cooking in town. *Las Tapas de Madrid* (☎ 991 78 94), Avenida Principal de Las Mercedes, is a popular tasca that offers a large variety of typical Spanish tapas, *tapitas* and more elaborate dishes. For grilled beef, there's *Hereford Grill* (☎ 993 96 10), Calle Madrid; *Maute Grill* (☎ 993 38 46), Avenida Rio de Janeiro; and *Restaurant Aranjuez* (☎ 993 13 26), Calle Madrid.

Altamira & Around

Along with its neighboring suburbs of La Castellana and Los Palos Grandes, Altamira is another trendy area dotted with posh restaurants, spiffy cafés, discos and bars. Like Las Mercedes, it's essentially an upmarket zone, catering to Caracas' young and wealthy, yet budget travelers will find something too.

Pollo en Brasas El Coyuco, 3a Transversal at 4a Avenida, Los Palos Grandes, offers chicken and parrillas and will fill you up nicely for US$6 to US$8. One block west, the tiny *Ri-K-Chapa* serves cachapas. South of El Coyuco, the simple, plain *Restaurant El Presidente* provides home-style meals at lunchtime. La Castellana also has some down-to-earth options, including the good chicken outfit *El Mundo del Pollo* and *Pizzería La Romanina*.

A step up the price ladder, *Café L'Attico* (☎ 261 28 19), Avenida Luis Roche, is an attractive, charmingly informal bar-restaurant and one of the trendiest places in town. It serves good food (including some North

American offerings) at affordable prices, a lively bar, videos, music and a usually great atmosphere. It's hard to get a table on weekday evenings, let alone on weekends, when it's completely packed with joyful folks. The open-air *Art Café*, Avenida Andrés Bello at 4a Transversal, serves exquisite sandwiches with chips and salad – a filling meal in itself for US$8. *Fritz & Franz*, Avenida San Juan Bosco at 3a Transversal, offers reasonably priced German fare, including grilled sausages, potato salads, sauerkraut and apple strudel.

Turning to the upper price bracket, *Le Petit Bistrot de Jacques* (☎ 263 86 95), Avenida San Felipe, has a reputation as one of the most authentic French bistros outside France. *Restaurant La Estancia* (☎ 261 18 74), Avenida Principal de La Castellana, is well known for its grilled meats of every cut and style, as is *Restaurant El Gran Charolais* (☎ 263 55 02), farther north on the same street. *Spizzico* (☎ 267 88 20), Avenida Principal de La Castellana, is a beautiful Mediterranean-style place with a predominantly Italian menu. *Restaurant Chez Wong* (☎ 266 50 15), Plaza La Castellana, is one of the best Chinese restaurants in town.

Other commendable upmarket restaurants in the area include *Restaurant El Barquero* (☎ 261 46 45), on Avenida Luis Roche (Spanish cuisine with an emphasis on seafood); *Restaurant Japonés Hatsuhana* (☎ 264 18 19), Avenida San Juan Bosco (Japanese fare); *El Alazán de Altamira* (☎ 285 02 08), Avenida Luis Roche (steaks); and *Steak House de Lee Hamilton* (☎ 263 84 29), Avenida San Felipe.

ENTERTAINMENT

The Thursday edition of *El Universal* carries a 'what's on' section called the *Guía de la Ciudad*. It gives brief descriptions of selected coming events, including music, theater, cinema and exhibitions, along with short reviews of some restaurants, nightspots etc.

Cinema

Caracas has about 40 cinemas screening the usual commercial fare, peppered with big-budget US blockbusters, which come here soon after their release at home. For something more intellectually demanding, check the program of the *Cinemateca Nacional* (☎ 576 71 18), the leading art cinema, in the Galería de Arte Nacional. *Cine La Previsora* (☎ 709 18 41), in the Torre La Previsora, also focuses on quality art-house films, as does the cinema in the *Ateneo de Caracas* (☎ 577 69 65) and the cinema of the *Fundación Celarg* (☎ 285 29 90), in the Casa de Rómulo Gallegos, on Avenida Luis Roche in Altamira.

There are usually three afternoon shows. Films are shown with the original soundtrack and Spanish subtitles. A movie ticket costs US$3 to US$5. Programs of both commercial and art cinemas are listed in the local daily press (including *The Daily Journal*).

Theater

There are a dozen regular theaters in the city. They are usually open from Wednesday to Sunday, but some have performances only on weekends. Tickets cost between US$3 and US$8, and there are student discounts in some theaters. Midweek sessions (usually on Wednesday) may be cheaper than weekend performances. The Ateneo de Caracas (see Cinema, earlier) often has something interesting in its theater, and you can see here the productions of Rajatabla, Venezuela's best-known theater company. It may be also worth checking the programs of La Compañía Nacional de Teatro, presenting their plays in the *Teatro Nacional* (☎ 484 59 56), and the Teatro Profesional de Venezuela, based at the *Teatro El Paraíso* (☎ 462 44 61, 462 67 44).

If you are lucky enough to arrive during Caracas' Festival Internacional de Teatro, in March and/or April of even-numbered years, you'll have a chance to see some of the best theater productions from Latin America and beyond. Festival performances are staged at theaters around the city.

European Classical Music & Ballet

The city's major stage for concerts and ballet, by both local and invited foreign performers, is **Complejo Cultural Teresa Carreño** (☎ 800 673 72). Also check the program of the **Aula Magna** (☎ 605 45 16), in the Universidad Central de Venezuela, which hosts performances by the symphony orchestra, usually on Sunday morning, among other spectacles. Tickets for Sunday concerts (US$1, half price for students) can be bought from the Aula's ticket office directly before the concerts.

Other places that stage concerts include the Ateneo de Caracas (see Cinema, earlier), Museo Sacro de Caracas (see the Center & Around section, earlier), Museo del Teclado (see the Parque Central & Around section, earlier), **Quinta Anauco**, **Centro Cultural Corp Group**, Centro Venezolano Americano and Asociación Cultural Humboldt (see Libraries under Information, earlier).

Nightlife

The nighttime entertainment scene is centered on Las Mercedes, El Rosal, Altamira and La Castellana, where most discos, bars and other nightspots are located. Incidentally, these are relatively safe areas for night strolls. The picture changes frequently, with the nighttime hot spots (especially discotheques) opening and closing and changing owners, names, locations etc.

Bar & Pubs The **Gran Pizzería El León**, on Plaza La Castellana (Ⓜ Altamira), is possibly the largest nighttime drinking hole, with dozens of tables placed outdoors on a vast terrace in front of the pizzeria. If you turn up on a weekend night, you'll find a large college crowd jovially debating over rows of beer bottles that completely cover the tables. And yes, you can also get pizza, though this is not what attracts people to the premises.

Completely different is **Greenwich Pub**, Avenida Sur Altamira (Ⓜ Altamira), an intimate indoor place with taped (or, at times, live) music, often at high volume, and a variety of beer and *pasapalos* (finger food). The place is trendy but so small that getting a table at night is a challenge.

There are plenty of watering holes in Las Mercedes, of which the informal **Birras Pub**

& Café, in Edificio Itaca on Avenida Principal de las Mercedes, is one of the cheapest.

Don't forget Café L'Attico (listed under Altamira & Around in the Places to Eat section), which is as much a place to drink as to eat.

Discos Caracas has quite a few discos scattered throughout the city, with Las Mercedes heading the league. Most are open nightly except Monday and sometimes also Sunday, which are the slowest days, but some are open only Thursday to Saturday. The music is usually a ragbag of western and Caribbean rhythms, though some discos focus on specific genres, such as salsa or rock & roll oldies, which may be their general musical theme or the theme of a particular day of the week.

Thursday, Friday and Saturday, especially after midnight, are when things are hottest. On these days there may be live music in some places. There's usually no entrance fee on weekdays, but there may be on the weekend. This may include a voucher that covers the cost of a few beers. Discos don't usually serve snacks or meals (so come after dinner) but do have plenty of drinks. Most Caracas discos won't let you in if you wear sneakers or a T-shirt, and some don't even accept jeans. Don't take handbags or cameras, as you will have to keep a constant eye on them; these places are often crowded, and thieves never sleep.

Da Dío (formerly Boomker), Avenida Principal de Las Mercedes, is one of the largest discos, with different levels, a well-stocked bar, pool tables and lots of bells and whistles. **Fire** (formerly the Magic Discotheque), Calle Madrid, is quieter and more formal, though not more expensive, and its musical program includes pop classics and oldies. It attracts a more mature clientele than most other discos. Other discos in Las Mercedes include **Ozono** and **Moebius**, both on Calle Madrid, and **El Sitio**, on Calle París.

In other suburbs, try **El Sarao**, in the Centro Comercial Bello Campo (which has mostly salsa, sometimes performed live), **Exit**, on Calle La Guairita in Chuao (which also focuses on Caribbean rhythms), *So Club*, in CCCT in Chuao (various rhythms), and *Masai*, in the Centro San Ignacio in La Castellana (also a bit of everything).

Live Music The *Juan Sebastián Bar*, on Avenida Venezuela in El Rosal (Ⓜ Chacaíto), is both a bar-restaurant and one of the few real jazz spots in the city. Live jazz performed by various groups goes from the afternoon until 2 am. There's no cover charge.

El Maní es Así, Calle El Cristo, Sabana Grande, has a long-standing reputation as a hot live salsa spot. Another place in Sabana Grande that hosts salsa bands (Tuesday to Saturday) is *O'Gran Sol*, a two-level restaurant on Calle Villaflor. The music is staged on the upper floor.

In La Castellana, *El Solar del Vino* is similar to O'Gran Sol; it's a Spanish restaurant that features live music (usually salsa, *antillana* and other Caribbean rhythms) on Wednesday to Saturday nights.

The castle-style *Little Rock Café*, 6a Avenida between 3a and 5a Transversal in Altamira, features rock bands on weekends.

Gay & Lesbian Venues Gathering places in Sabana Grande include *Tasca Pullman*, on Avenida Francisco Solano, *Tasca Don Sol*, on Pasaje Asunción, and *Sublime Café*, on the terrace of the Torre La Previsora. There are also several haunts on Calle San Antonio opposite the Royal Hotel, including *Tasca de La Tortilla*, *Petro's Bar* and *Vía Libre*. In Altamira, try *Tiffany's*, in Edificio Teatro Altamira on Avenida San Juan Bosco.

SPECTATOR SPORTS
Professional-league baseball games are played from October to February at the baseball stadium on the grounds of the Universidad Central de Venezuela (Ⓜ Ciudad Universitaria). Tickets should be bought early in the morning, particularly for games featuring the local Leones de Caracas (Caracas Lions).

The neighboring soccer stadium hosts major soccer matches, though Venezuelans don't seem to be as crazy about this sport as the Brazilians and Colombians are. Most matches take place between December and March, with the major events usually scheduled on Saturday evening.

Caracas' excellent horse-racing track, the Hipódromo La Rinconada, features racing on Saturday and Sunday afternoons starting at 1 pm. The track is 6km southwest of the center, off the Caracas-Valencia freeway.

SHOPPING
Caraqueños love shopping, and some don't stop until they drop or completely run out of money. There are plenty of shopping areas, including the historic center, La Candelaria, Sabana Grande, Chacaíto and Chacao, all of which are tightly packed with stores, shopping malls, street stalls and ambulant vendors. With the huge price increases over recent years, there has been an explosion of informal outdoor trading on the streets and markets, which offer most everyday products at prices lower than in shops.

Shopping Malls
Caracas has plenty of shopping malls, and despite the precarious economic situation of recent years, new ones keep appearing. Traditionally, one of the largest and most popular malls has been the Centro Ciudad Comercial Tamanaco, commonly known as CCCT, in Chuao. With a multiplex cinema, banks, hotel, fast-food complex and plenty of shops, it's still popular and busy, but is feeling increasing competition from the more modern developments.

Of the more recent projects, the biggest success story has been the Centro Sambil, opened in 1998 on Avenida Libertador in Chacao, and since then packed with shoppers and casual visitors seven days a week. Said to be South America's largest shopping mall, this vast five-level establishment comes complete with an aquarium, cybercafés, money-changing facilities, two multiplex cinemas, pool tables, video games, an amphitheater, a food court and a waterfall that is incorporated into the front wall of the building.

Another recent mall, the Centro San Ignacio, was opened on Avenida Blandín, in La Castellana, though this one doesn't seem to have had an easy start and has yet to attract big crowds. The one that does draw crowds is the large Centro Comercial El Recreo, on Avenida Casanova in Sabana Grande.

Other popular shopping malls include the Centro Comercial Chacaíto, on Plaza Chacaíto; the Centro Comercial Paseo Las Mercedes, in Las Mercedes; the Centro Lido, on Avenida Francisco de Miranda, in El Rosal; and the Centro Comercial Concresa, in Prados del Este.

Markets

Caracas has a number of markets, but don't expect the color and atmosphere normally associated with postcard South American bazaars full of traditionally dressed Indians along with their children and animals. Markets in the city are largely plain and nondescript. They mostly sell ordinary-quality, everyday products such as clothing, shoes, toiletries, electrical home appliances, watches and stationery. Some deal in food, including fruits and vegetables. Few feature any craft or art stalls or high-quality items.

One of the most central markets is the shabby Mercado de La Hoyada, near the metro station of the same name. After various attempts, Caracas' mayor eventually succeeded in closing it down altogether in 1998, giving room to a planned recreational area, but then came President Chávez' populist rule. The governor overturned the mayor's decision, and the market is back in place. A few blocks to the west is another outdoor market, which has actually invaded – and now occupies – the Plaza Diego Ibarra. Outside the center are the Mercado Guaicaipuro, on Avenida Andrés Bello (Ⓜ Bellas Artes), and the Mercado Chacao, three blocks north of the Chacao metro station.

Clothing & Footwear

The city center is one of the cheapest areas to hunt for clothes and shoes. If you just need ordinary jeans or sneakers, central markets (including the two listed above) may be the cheapest options, but there are also plenty of cheap shops around the central streets. The area just east of Plaza Bolívar boasts a bewildering wealth of shoe shops – actually, every third shop is a *zapatería* – creating the suspicion that Venezuelans are shoe-crazy.

Another good budget shopping area for clothes and shoes is Sabana Grande and, particularly, its central boulevard, which is lined with stores and shopping malls. If you're after upmarket, trendy stuff, it's probably best to start off combing some of the large shopping malls, particularly Centro Sambil or CCCT (see Shopping Malls, earlier), which have a variety of European and American fashion stores.

Crafts

Caracas doesn't have many craft shops to speak of. In the center, the best place to try is the Maquita, Tracabordo a Miguelancho in La Candelaria, which has particularly good wood carvings. Possibly the largest craft shop of all is the Hannsi, in El Hatillo (see Southern Suburbs, earlier), and it's best to check it first if you plan on any substantial craft buys.

On Sunday, artisans and artists set up small tables at the plaza in front of the Galería de Arte Nacional and sell their wares.

Jewelry

Venezuela is a major gold producer, so it's no wonder that gold jewelry is common and reasonably cheap. The artistic quality is rarely anything extraordinary, but most locals are more interested in how much gold rather than how much creativity is involved in the product.

The nucleus of Caracas' gold market is the legendary Edificio La Francia, on the southwestern corner of Plaza Bolívar, which boasts 10 stories of jewelry shops – about a hundred in all. It's always packed with shoppers, and you too are welcome to join the crowds, if only to observe Venezuelans' gold craze. If you can't find what you want here, try the Minicentro París, just a few steps away, with 20-something more jewelers; the Multicentro Capitolio, a further few steps on, with another 30 shops; or plenty of other businesses around.

Camping & Outdoor Equipment

Imported camping and trekking gear is increasingly available but expensive. Locally produced gear is cheaper and often of satisfactory quality. Gas canisters for common camping stoves (such as Gas Bluet) can be bought without major problems.

Corporación Verotex (☎ 951 36 70, 977 45 03), Centro Comercial Arta, Piso 2, Oficina 2-6, Plaza Chacaíto, has a reasonable choice of camping, trekking and mountaineering equipment and is one of the cheapest retailers around.

Possibly even cheaper is Loby (☎ 751 23 19, 751 22 19), Quinta Nenena, Piso Bajo, Local 6, Calle Caurimare, Colinas de Bello Monte. It makes backpacks, sleeping bags and high-mountain clothing, and imports other camping and mountaineering items.

A bit more upmarket is the well-stocked Marumen Store (☎ 261 81 34, 262 06 61), 3a Transversal, between Avenidas Luis Roche and San Juan Bosco, Altamira, which also has some fishing gear, maps and various guidebooks.

GETTING THERE & AWAY
Air

Simón Bolívar airport is in Maiquetía, near the port of La Guaira on the Caribbean coast, 26km from central Caracas. It's linked to the city by a freeway (built from 1950 to 1953) that cuts through the coastal mountain range with three tunnels, the main one being 2km long.

The airport has two terminals, one for international and the other for domestic flights, separated by 400m. There's free shuttle service between the terminals.

The international terminal has a range of facilities, including a tourist office, car rental desks, three or four casas de cambio, a bank, three ATMs, post and telephone offices, a restaurant, several cafés, snack bars and a bunch of travel agencies. It even has a chapel, but lacks a left-luggage office.

Note that arriving passengers are not allowed to take luggage trolleys beyond the customs area.

The domestic terminal doesn't have money-changing facilities, but does have a tourist office and a dozen desks of car rental companies, domestic airlines and tour operators, plus a collection of fast-food outlets.

If you fly into Venezuela via Maiquetía airport, you can change your money upon arrival. There are several casas de cambio in the main hall on the ground floor, including Italcambio, which changes cash and traveler's checks and usually offers the best rates. It's open daily until the last flight. There are also two casas de cambio before customs, and it may be worth changing money here if you don't want to line up at the casas de cambio in the concourse. Advances on Visa and MasterCard can be obtained in the Banco de Venezuela, on the upper level, during its opening hours (8:30 am to 3:30 pm weekdays). Otherwise you can get local currency from one of the three ATMs (all on the upper level).

For a budget breakfast, lunch or dinner, possibly the best place is the little-known 24-hour Cafetería Mocol, well hidden on the basement level – look out for the stairs leading down behind the men's bathroom opposite the post office, roughly in the middle of the main hall.

Ignore any individuals who approach you claiming that they are from the tourist office (they're not) and offering help and information; they'll demand a hefty fee for anything they do. The genuine Corpoturismo office (open 7 am to midnight daily) is on the ground floor and may have some brochures on Caracas. If you plan on phoning from the terminal, buy a phone card in CANTV or at the newsstand (both on the upper level). Since 1998, Maiquetía has had the same area code as Caracas, so when calling Caracas, you just dial the local Caracas number, without the 02 area code.

There are plenty of international and domestic flights. For international connections, see the Getting There & Away chapter. As for domestic air traffic, the airport offers direct flights to most major cities around

CARACAS

the country – see the table. The figures given are minimum and maximum airfares. They vary considerably over a given route, depending on the particular airline, and tend to change frequently.

Destination	Airfare (min-max in US$)
Barcelona	65–98
Barinas	58–67
Barquisimeto	48–92
Carúpano	58–65
Ciudad Bolívar	82–88
Coro	66–74
Cumaná	66–74
Las Piedras (Punto Fijo)	66–74
Maracaibo	68–87
Maturín	72–97
Mérida	58–70
Porlamar	46–74
Puerto Ayacucho	60–65
Puerto Ordaz (Ciudad Guayana)	52–88
San Antonio del Táchira	105–127
Valera	62–68

Airline Offices There's no need to go to a particular airline office to buy tickets for its flights. Just about every travel agency – and there are about 600 of them in the city – will sell you tickets for flights by most airlines and, consequently, will know which is the cheapest carrier on a particular route and which are the best connections. This essentially refers to domestic routes and popular international flights, such as Caracas to Miami. When it comes to more complex intercontinental connections, not all agencies are experts, so shop around.

For those looking for a flight to Europe, some of the cheapest airfares are offered by TAP Air Portugal (☎ 951 05 11, 951 55 08, 951 64 03), Edificio Canaima, Avenida Francisco de Miranda (Ⓜ Chacaíto). However, it may be cheaper to fly with Avensa to Miami and take one of the relatively cheap transatlantic flights (eg, with United Airlines). Some Caracas travel agencies will sell combined tickets for the whole route. Students and teachers will find the best deals at IVI (see Travel Agencies, earlier in this chapter).

If you plan on traveling to Colombia and flying within the country, inquire about the domestic air pass offered by Avianca (☎ 953 57 32), Edificio Roraima, Avenida Francisco de Miranda, Chacao (Ⓜ Chacaíto). See Air Passes under Air in the Getting Around chapter.

Bus

The central Nuevo Circo long-distance bus terminal was closed in 1998 (although the terminal for shorter routes remains open), and Caracas now has two new intercity bus terminals. The Terminal La Bandera, 3km south of the center (and accessible by metro), handles long-distance buses to anywhere in the country's west and southwest. The terminal is just 300m from La Bandera metro station, and you can easily and safely walk the distance during the day, but take precautions when arriving or departing late at night, because the terminal's surroundings may be unsafe. The terminal itself has several modern facilities, including computerized ticket booths, a telephone office, a left-luggage office, an information desk and a collection of food outlets.

The city's other bus terminal, the Terminal de Oriente, is on the eastern outskirts of Caracas, on the highway to Barcelona, 5km beyond the suburb of Petare (about 18km from the center). It's accessible by local buses from both the city center and Petare. The modern and functional terminal features computerized ticket booths. It handles all traffic to the east and southeast of the country.

Approximate fares and traveling times from Caracas to major destinations around the country are listed in the boxed text. Also see the chapters covering your destinations, which contain more specific information and comments.

The upscale Aeroexpresos Ejecutivos bus company (☎ 266 23 21) services several major cities – including Valencia, Barquisimeto, Maracaibo, Maturín and Puerto La Cruz – in modern, comfortable air-conditioned buses with a TV and toilet. It's more expensive than other companies, but some travelers have reported that it's worth

Fares & Traveling Times from Caracas to Major Destinations

Destination	Distance (km)	Ordinary Fare (US$)	Deluxe Fare (US$)	Time (hrs)
Barcelona	310	9	12	5
Barinas	515	11	15	8½
Barquisimeto	341	8	10	5½
Carúpano	521	14	18	8½
Ciudad Bolívar	591	15	19	9
Ciudad Guayana	698	17	21	10½
Coro	453	10	13	7
Cumaná	402	11	15	6½
Guanare	427	9	12	7
Güiria	663	–	22	12
Maracaibo	706	–	20	10½
Maracay	109	2.50	3	1½
Maturín	518	14	17	8½
Mérida	682	17	23	12
Puerto Ayacucho	841	–	25	16
Puerto La Cruz	320	9	12	5
San Antonio del Táchira	877	–	25	14
San Cristóbal	841	–	24	13
San Fernando de Apure	404	10	14	8
Tucupita	730	–	20	11
Valencia	158	3	4	2½
Valera	602	11	14	9½

it. Acroexpresos Ejecutivos has its own private bus terminal on Avenida Bello Campo (Ⓜ Altamira).

Short-distance buses servicing regional destinations (La Guaira, Los Teques, Santa Teresa, Ocumare del Tuy etc) still depart from the chaotic and dirty old central Nuevo Circo terminal, and when and where new facilities will be built remains unknown.

Car & Motorcycle

Driving into/out of Caracas is pretty straightforward. The major western access route is the Valencia-Caracas freeway, which enters the city from the south and joins Autopista Francisco Fajardo, the main east-west city artery, next to the Universidad Central de Venezuela. From anywhere in the east, access is by the Barcelona-Caracas freeway, which will take you directly to Avenida Francisco Fajardo.

If you need a car in Venezuela, try to make arrangements at home with one of the international car rental companies such as Avis, Hertz, Budget or Dollar (all of which operate here). That way you can have a car waiting for you upon arrival.

If you fly into Caracas without any previous arrangements, contact car rental companies at the Maiquetía airport. There are half a dozen operators in the international terminal, including Avis, Hertz and Dollar, but they can't always provide a car on demand. You'll find desks of another dozen or so (mostly local) companies in the domestic terminal, and these may have something on the spot. Major rental companies also have offices in Caracas and desks in the lobbies of top-end hotels, including the Hilton, Tamanaco Inter-Continental and Eurobuilding Caracas. Cars can also be rented through travel agencies. For more information about rental conditions, prices and driving, see Car & Motorcycle in the Getting Around chapter.

Boat

La Guaira, the port of Caracas, was affected by the disaster of December 1999 (see Litoral Central, in the Around Caracas section, later in this chapter), but is already operating normally again. However, there's no passenger service to any of Venezuela's offshore possessions, only freight boats to Los Roques.

GETTING AROUND
To/From the Airport

There's bus service between the Maiquetía airport and Caracas daily from 5:30 am until the evening. Buses are supposed to depart every half-hour, but, as is common everywhere in Venezuela, they usually don't leave until they're full. In the city, the buses depart until about 7 pm from Calle Sur 17, directly underneath Avenida Bolívar, next to Parque Central. Stairs connect the two levels next to the Museo de los Niños; you can also get down to the buses by Calle Sur 17 from Avenida México (or Avenida Lecuna). At the airport, buses leave from in front of both the domestic and international terminals. The last bus is supposed to depart from the international terminal around 8 pm and from the domestic terminal around 9 pm.

The bus trip either way costs US$2 to US$3 and normally takes about 40 minutes, but traffic jams, particularly on weekends and holidays, can double that time. If you are going from the airport to the city during rush hour, it's faster to get off at the Gato Negro metro station and continue by metro to your final destination.

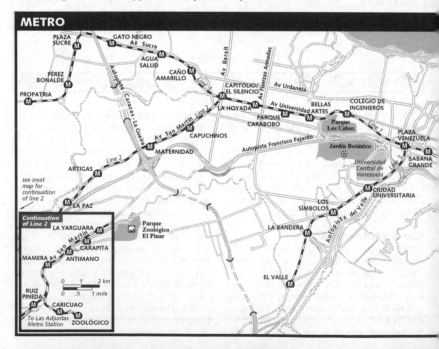

The taxi fare from the airport to Caracas depends on which suburb you go to. Sample daytime (6 am to 6 pm) rates are: the center US$22, Sabana Grande US$26, and Altamira US$30. Nighttime tariffs are about 10% higher. The fares from the city back to the airport are about 10% lower. Air-conditioned taxis may charge more. A taxi takes up to four passengers and shouldn't charge extra for luggage.

Before boarding a taxi, check the correct fare (eg, with the tourist office) in order to avoid the usual overcharging. Nonetheless, drivers may overcharge you in the evening, after all the buses are gone, because they know you don't have other options. Travelers have told of drivers asking exorbitant, nonnegotiable prices. Therefore, when you book your air ticket before your trip, make sure that you arrive at Maiquetía reasonably early during the day.

You may be approached by 'taxi drivers' inside the international terminal who will offer you a ride to Caracas for less than the official fare, but this should be viewed with suspicion. Their taxis are usually not in the regular taxi line, but are parked elsewhere. Some of these drivers are honest, but there may be some who mug you in the middle of nowhere.

If you have just an overnight stop in Maiquetía, there's probably no point in going to Caracas. Instead, you may prefer to stay the night on the coast, although accommodation options became drastically reduced after the December 1999 disaster (see Litoral Central in the Around Caracas section, later in this chapter).

If you're arriving late at night in Maiquetía, don't venture outside the terminal farther than the bus stop and taxi stand (both of which are just at the building's doors). Holdups at gunpoint have been reported by travelers, and you probably wouldn't want to lose all your bags right after arrival in Venezuela.

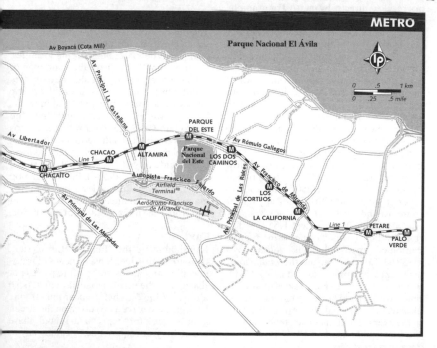

Metro

This is the major means of getting around Caracas. It's fast, well organized, easy to use, clean and cheap, and it provides access to most major city attractions and tourist facilities.

The French-made metro system has three lines, with a total length of 44km and 39 stations. The longest line, No 1, goes east-west all the way along the city axis, and you will use it most frequently. Line No 2 leads from the center southwest to the distant suburb of Caricuao and the zoo. The newest and shortest line, No 3, runs from Plaza Venezuela southwest to El Valle. More lines are planned, but it will take a while before they open.

The system also includes a number of bus routes, called 'Metrobús,' which link some of the suburbs to metro stations. You can thus easily reach San Bernardino, El Cafetal, Prados del Este, La Trinidad and other suburbs (plus intermediate points) that are not reached directly by metro. For example, the Centro Ciudad Comercial Tamanaco (CCCT) is accessible by Metrobús No 211 (La Trinidad) from the Chacao station and No 201 (El Cafetal) from the Altamira station (ask the driver to indicate where to get off – it's not immediately obvious). All of the metro lines and Metrobús routes are marked on the Caracas maps posted in every metro station.

The metro operates daily from 5:30 am to 11 pm. The air-conditioned trains run every few minutes, but less frequently early in the morning and late in the evening. Yellow single-ride tickets cost US$0.45 for a ride of up to three stations, US$0.50 for four to seven stations, and US$0.55 for any longer route. Roundtrip tickets (boletos de ida y vuelta) of any distance cost US$0.95. The transfer ticket (boleto integrado) for the combined metro-plus-bus route costs US$0.60. Consider buying the multiabono, an orange multiple ticket costing US$4, which is valid for 10 metro rides of any distance. Not only do you save money, but you also avoid the seemingly interminable waits in the ever-present lines each time you're at the ticket counters.

To get to the train platform, put your ticket into the slot on the turnstile, which opens and flips it back out to you. Keep it, because you have to use it again to open a similar turnstile at your destination. This time your ticket won't be flipped back, unless it's a multiabono. Bulky packages that might obstruct other passengers – as the regulations say – are not allowed in the metro. Backpacks are usually no problem, but use common sense and don't carry large bags during rush hours, when trains are really crowded.

The metro is generally safe, though there have been some comments about pickpockets that operate in groups on the escalators of the busy stations, eg, La Hoyada, Bellas Artes and Plaza Venezuela. An example scenario might run as follows: The man in front of you drops something and bends down to retrieve it. His accomplices at the back push you, while the one directly behind you tries to pick your pockets.

Bus

The bus network is extensive and covers all suburbs within the metropolitan area, as well as all the major neighboring localities. Carritos (small buses) are the main type of vehicle operating city routes. They run frequently but move only as fast as the traffic allows, sometimes getting trapped in traffic jams. However, they cost only half the metro fare (US$0.25). You will use carritos when going to destinations that are inaccessible by metro. It's probably worth taking a carrito ride anyway, just to get a taste of local culture; the radio will be blasting pop and the driver undertaking breathtaking maneuvers – definitely a different kind of trip from the smooth and silent metro ride.

Taxi

Identifiable by the 'Taxi' or 'Libre' sign, taxis are a fairly inexpensive means of transportation and are useful to get to places not reached by the metro. None have meters, so always fix the fare before boarding. It may be difficult to wave a taxi down on the street, so either look for them at a taxi stand (there are plenty), or request one by calling any of the numerous companies that provide a radio service. Several companies, such as Teletaxi (☎ 752 91 22, 752 41 55) and Móvil-Enlace (☎ 577 09 22, 577 33 44), service the entire Caracas area 24 hours a day.

Around Caracas

This section includes only places in the immediate vicinity of the capital – basically, what lies between the city and the coast. You will find other one-day destinations out of Caracas in the Central North chapter.

PARQUE NACIONAL EL ÁVILA

El Ávila national park consists of a steep, verdant mountain that looms just to the north of Caracas. The park encompasses about 90km of the range, running east-west along the coast and separating the city from the sea. The highest peak is Pico Naiguatá (2765m).

The southern slope, overlooking Caracas, is virtually uninhabited but is crisscrossed with dozens of walking trails. The northern face, running down to the sea, is dotted with hamlets and haciendas, yet few tourist trails are on this side. The park is crossed north to south by a few 4WD tracks and the inoperable *teleférico* (cable car).

Teleférico

The cable car was built by a German company from 1956 to 1957, during the dictatorship of Marcos Pérez Jiménez. It consists of two lines: the one-stage, 4km run from Caracas up to Pico El Ávila; and the three-stage, 7.5km run from El Ávila down to Macuto on the coast. Both lines have been closed since 1988. (Pérez Jiménez also commissioned the teleférico in Mérida, which is operating and is a great attraction – see that section, in the Andes chapter.)

The teleférico used to go from the Maripérez station (980m), located next to Avenida Boyacá in Caracas, up to El Ávila station (2150m). The terminus is close to Pico El Ávila (2175m), which is crowned by the sparkling, circular 14-story Hotel Humboldt, built in 1956. The hotel was closed soon after the cable car stopped running.

Today it's just a fantastic landmark overlooking Caracas, visible from almost every point in the city. The area around the upper station and the hotel offers breathtaking views of Caracas and the Valle del Tuy beyond, and toward the north is a beautiful panorama of the coast with the Caribbean Sea stretching to the horizon.

The cable car was privatized in 1998, and the new owner expects to open up the Maripérez–El Ávila run by 2001. Hopefully, it will be operating by the time you read this. Otherwise, you'll still need to walk to enjoy these fabulous views.

Hiking

Of all Venezuela's national parks, El Ávila provides the best infrastructure for walkers. There are about 200km of walking trails, most of them well signposted. Half a dozen camping grounds distributed around the park are equipped with sanitary facilities, and there are many more places designated for camping (though they're without facilities).

A dozen entrances lead into the park from Caracas; all originate from Avenida Boyacá, commonly known as 'Cota Mil' because it runs at an altitude of 1000m. Whichever route you choose, you'll have a short ascent before you get to a guard post, where you pay a nominal park entrance fee. The *guardaparques* (park rangers) may provide information about routes and suggest one if you haven't yet decided. Before you come, however, buy the useful *Mapa para el Excursionista – Parque Nacional El Ávila* (scale 1:40,000), which has marked trails and camping facilities.

You have plenty of options for a half- or full-day hike. You can, for example, go up to Pico El Ávila; at least four routes lead there. Start early, as it can get extremely hot by midmorning. For those who are prepared to camp, probably the most scenic route is the two-day hike to Pico Naiguatá. Take rain gear and warm clothes. Water is scarce, so bring some along. Don't forget plastic bags to bring all your rubbish back down. The dry season is from December to April, but even then it may rain in the upper reaches.

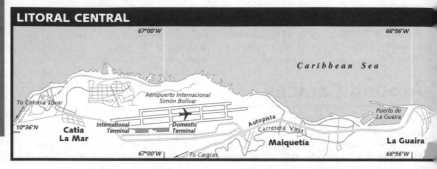

LITORAL CENTRAL

LITORAL CENTRAL

The northern face of El Ávila park slopes steeply down almost right into the sea, leaving only a narrow, flat strip of land between the foothills and the shore, referred to as the 'Litoral Central.' Still, the area developed into a chain of coastal towns, including, from west to east, Catia La Mar, Maiquetía, La Guaira, Macuto, Caraballeda and Naiguatá. Sadly, most of the area was devastated by mudslides caused by torrential rains in December 1999.

The whole area from La Guaira to Naiguatá has become a sea of ruins, and up to 50,000 people were buried under the mud. Macuto, Caraballeda and Naiguatá, once thrilling seaside resorts for caraqueños, were turned into ruined ghost towns, and they remained much the same half a year after the disaster. One can only guess how many people have remained in the area, which had a population of nearly half a million before the disaster. It will take long years before life returns to anything resembling normal, and perhaps two decades before the urban tissue is fully rebuilt, if ever.

Understandably, the region is not a tourist destination at the moment and won't be so for a while. Entire beaches are gone, complete with their infrastructure and facilities, and the colonial town of La Guaira – the major cultural sight – is, for the most part, destroyed. Almost all hotels and restaurants have been closed, but even if some open by the time you read this, there's not much to see or do here anyway.

Places to Stay & Eat

Catia La Mar was the least affected by the disaster, and is for the time being the only town in the region that offers a reasonable choice of places to stay and eat. Conveniently, it's close to the airport, but otherwise it's not attractive. It is just a large and uninspiring town, except, perhaps, for the northern seaside suburb, where a collection of modern residential towers has sprung up. Furthermore, most hotels are overpriced for what they offer, perhaps taking advantage of the scarcity of lodging options elsewhere in the region.

One of the cheapest places to stay is the basic *Hotel de París* (☎ 351 12 48), on Avenida Atlántida, which will set you back US$18/24 matrimonial/double. A little bit better, though equally lacking in style, is *Hotel Luna Mar* (☎ 351 13 14), Avenida Club Náutico, for US$28/34. Just a stone's throw from that is the slightly more agreeable *Hotel Skorpio* (☎ 351 91 95, 351 95 12), costing US$30/32/38 matrimonial/double/triple, as well as the more respectable seven-story *Hotel Aeropuerto* (☎ 351 12 59, 351 11 45), at US$38/ 46/54. Right next door to the Skorpio is *Restaurant Crisol*, the best place to eat in the area.

All the places listed above have rooms with air-conditioning and private baths. They are close to each other in the seaside suburb of Atlántida, in the northwestern part of town, and there are more hotels in the area. Half a kilometer east from the Skorpio is the upmarket *Hotel Puerto Viejo* (☎ 351 14 01, 352 40 44).

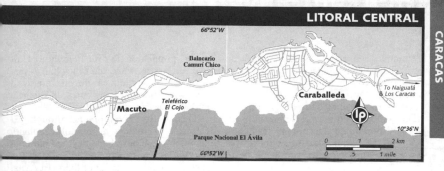

Getting There & Away

Carritos leave regularly from Nuevo Circo regional bus terminal in Caracas for Catia La Mar, passing next to the airport, where you can catch them. To do this, leave the terminal through the passageway leading from the building's upper level to the parking lot, get to the main road and wave down the carrito. Don't do it after dark. For the hotels listed in this section, get off at the road fork next to the McDonald's and walk along Avenida Atlántida. It's a 10-minute walk to the Hotel de París, and another five minutes to most of the others.

The Central North

Commonly referred to as 'El Centro,' the central north encompasses the states of Carabobo, Aragua, Miranda and Vargas, as well as the Distrito Federal. This is Venezuela's most developed region, both industrially and agriculturally. It is also the most densely populated: Occupying less than 2.5% of the national territory, these five states are home to around 45% of Venezuela's population (ie, over 10 million). Half live in Caracas, while the other half is distributed throughout a dozen fair-sized towns and the two large cities of Valencia and Maracay.

Despite its development, though, El Centro boasts extensive areas of woodland, some of which have been decreed national parks. There are six mainland parks in the region (the most popular of them, El Ávila, has been included in the Around Caracas section of the previous chapter) plus the marine park of Los Roques off the coast. The central north also has a number of other attractions, including the mountain town of Colonia Tovar and Venezuela's best hot-spring complex, at Las Trincheras.

Some of the places included in this chapter, such as Colonia Tovar, San Francisco de Yare and Parque Nacional Guatopo, can be visited as one-day trips out of Caracas. Caracas is also the departure point for the Archipiélago Los Roques.

Highlights

- Enjoy bird-watching in Parque Nacional Henri Pittier.
- See the Dancing Devils of San Francisco de Yare on Corpus Christi.
- Go snorkeling in Los Roques archipelago.
- Dance to nighttime drumbeats in Puerto Colombia.
- Visit the German town of Colonia Tovar.

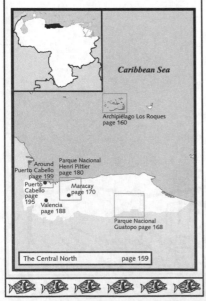

Caribbean Sea

Archipiélago Los Roques page 160

Parque Nacional Henri Pittier page 180

Around Puerto Cabello page 199

Puerto Cabello page 195

Maracay page 170

Valencia page 188

Parque Nacional Guatopo page 168

The Central North page 159

Archipiélago Los Roques

☎ 02 (☎ 0212 from Feb 24, 2001)

Los Roques is a beautiful archipelago of small coral islands lying about 160km due north off the central coast. Stretching 36km east to west and 25km north to south, it consists of about 40 islands big enough to deserve names, and perhaps 250 other unnamed islets, sandbars and cays. Gran Roque is the only mountainous island and is the focal point of the archipelago, being home to virtually all of its population (about 1200) and transportation facilities. All of the other islands are flat sandy cays, and shelter any human dwellings.

The archipelagos has swiftly become a popular tourist destination. What draws people here are soft, white sandy beaches and extensive coral reefs – a paradise for

THE CENTRAL NORTH

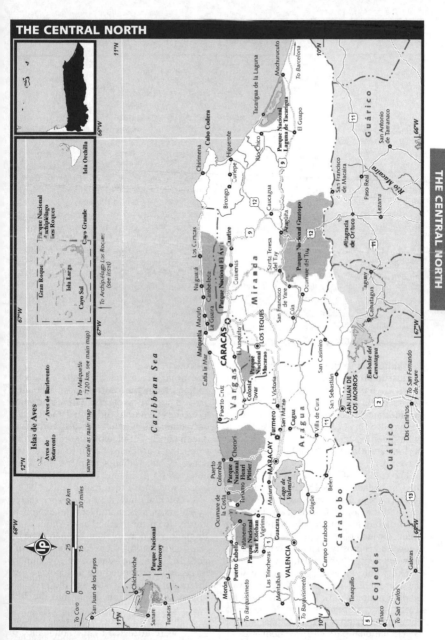

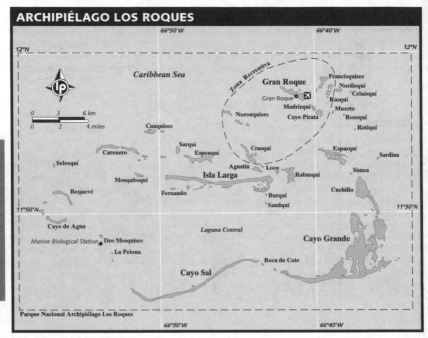

ARCHIPIÉLAGO LOS ROQUES

Caribbean Sea

Zona Recreativa

Gran Roque

Gran Roque

Francisquies
Nordisquí
Celuisquí
Rasquí
Madrizquí
Muerto
Noronquises
Cayo Pirata
Botoquí
Ratiquí

Canquises

Sarquí
Espenquí
Crasquí
Esparquí
Sardina

Carenero

Selesquí

Agustín   Loco
Simea

Mosquitoquí
Isla Larga
Rabusquí

Bequevé
Fernando
Burquí
Cuchillo
Sandquí

Cayo de Agua

Marine Biological Station   Dos Mosquises
Laguna Central
Cayo Grande

La Pelona

Boca de Cote

Cayo Sal

Parque Nacional Archipiélago Los Roques

snorkeling and scuba diving. The tourist infrastructure has expanded over recent years, as have flight services, providing access to the archipelago. Tourist peaks include late December and early January, Carnaval, Semana Santa (Holy Week, culminating in Easter) and August. The slowest periods are May to July and September to November.

The climate of Los Roques is typical of the Caribbean islands. The average temperature is about 28°C, with highs of 33°C in July and lows of 24°C in January. The days are hot but are pleasantly refreshed by breezes, which blow frequently. The rainfall is low and is mostly confined to the period between September and January.

The whole archipelago, complete with the surrounding waters (2211 sq km), was made a national park in 1972. Administratively, it's a dependency of the Distrito Federal. All visitors to Los Roques pay the US$15 national-park entry fee upon arrival.

History

The archipelago was originally settled by Indians from the central coast, who first arrived possibly as early as a thousand years ago. They generally inhabited the islands only temporarily – to catch fish, turtle and queen conch – until about the 16th century, when the Europeans began to arrive. Evidence of the Indian settlements has been detected on 21 islands, of which Dos Mosquises was one of their major seats.

In colonial times, the islands were visited by sailors, pirates, marauders and explorers, mostly from the Netherlands Antilles and England, but none of them seemed to be interested in settling there for good. It wasn't until 1871 that the Venezuelan government formally incorporated the archipelago into the national territory, though the presence of the Dutch continued well into the 20th century.

In the 1920s, fishermen from Isla de Margarita were attracted by the abundance of

Festival de Los Diablos Danzantes painting, San Francisco de Yare

A dancing devil in the flesh

A colonial church in Choroní

Typical transportation in the Archipiélago de Los Roques

Playa Grande's version of spring break

Frolicking at the beach on the Península de Paraguaná

Traditional Zulia *palafitos*, whose Venice-like appearance gave the country its name

Rows of happily restored houses, Maracaibo

fish and gradually settled the archipelago's main island, Gran Roque, completely pushing out the Dutch by the 1950s. Known as *roqueños,* their descendants now make up the majority of the local population.

Flora & Fauna

The islands' vegetation consists mainly of grasses, cacti, low bushes and mangroves. Local fauna is best represented by birds – 92 species have been recorded on the archipelago, including 50 that migrate down from North America. There's just one native mammal on the islands – the fishing bat – and some reptiles, including four species of turtle and some small lizards, salamanders and iguanas.

In contrast to the relatively limited variety of flora and fauna above sea level, the marine ecosystem is extremely varied and rich in species. The waters teem with fish, rays, barracudas, sea stars, mollusks, crabs, octopuses, sea urchins and lobsters, to name just a few. The latter have been overfished during the past decade, yet Los Roques still accounts for about 90% of national production. There's now a ban on fishing lobster from May to October, so don't expect it on the local tables during these months.

GRAN ROQUE

Lying on the northern edge of the archipelago, Gran Roque is the main island. On its southern side is a fishing village of the same name, with a population of 1200. It has a Plaza Bolívar, an Inparques office, a Guardia Nacional post, 60-odd posadas, five grocery shops and several public phones. There are no banks, casas de cambio or ATMs, so bring enough local currency, though some establishments may accept cash dollars.

The sandy streets are lined with brightly painted houses, and there are no traffic problems, as the only vehicles are garbage and water trucks and five small electric trolleys. The village has desalinization and electricity plants, both of which have recently been upgraded and are pretty reliable.

Gran Roque is the transportation hub of the archipelago. It has an airstrip, just to the

east of the village, which handles all flights. The village's waterfront is packed with fishing boats, tour operators' vessels, visiting yachts and pelicans.

Unlike all the other islands, which are sandy and completely flat, Gran Roque has several massive rocky humps along its northwestern coast – the tallest is 110m – and cliffs that drop almost vertically into the sea. Climb the hump crowned with an old lighthouse, known as the *faro holandés,* for sweeping views over the village, the neighboring islands, their coral reefs and the surrounding crystal-clear turquoise sea. The lighthouse itself was built in the 1870s and used until the early 1950s (it's now been replaced by an iron beacon on the highest hump, farther to the west).

Other Islands

The nearest island to Gran Roque is **Madrizquí**, about 1km to the southeast. It was the favorite island among affluent *caraqueños* (people from Caracas) who discovered Los Roques several decades ago and built their summer beach houses here before the archipelago was made a national park. Other nearby islands with dwellings are **Cayo Pirata** and **Crasquí**, which have fishing shelters known as *rancherías,* and **Rasquí**, which has a posada.

On the island of **Dos Mosquises Sur**, at the far southwestern edge of the archipelago, is the Marine Biological Station, run by the Fundación Científica Los Roques. The station, which can be visited, has breeding tanks, where turtles and other endangered species are raised before being released around the archipelago; more than 5000 turtles have already been reared.

In order to preserve the habitat, protective zones have been created in parts of the archipelago where tourists are not allowed or where access is limited to daytime visits. The only area with unrestricted access and the possibility of camping is the so-called Zona Recreativa, which comprises Gran Roque and the nearby islands (see the map).

You may wonder about the islands' strange names. Many were first named by English explorers. Local fishermen preserved most of the original names but wrote them down phonetically. Then apparently along came the linguistically correct cartographers, who changed the spelling according to standard Spanish orthography. This is how the original Northeast Cay in English was recorded as 'Nordisky,' to eventually become 'Nordisquí.' Similarly, the Sails Cay went through 'Selesky' to 'Selesquí,' and St Luis Cay has become 'Celuisquí.' You may find various spellings on different maps.

Activities

Many visitors, mostly Venezuelans, come to Los Roques to **sunbathe** on the beaches (it's not exactly clear if this is an 'activity'), which are numerous, clean, tranquil and unspoiled. The longest uninterrupted strip of sand is on the island of Crasquí, but there are plenty of other beaches to choose from. Note that the beaches on Los Roques are shadeless, and the incidence of solar rays is extremely high, mostly due to the reflection from the immaculately white sand, so be sure to bring along sufficient sun protection, such as sunblock, a hat and sunglasses.

The archipelago is one of Venezuela's best areas for **snorkeling**. Among the most amazing places are the Boca de Cote and Noronquises, but there are other fine sites closer to Gran Roque, including the so-called *piscina* next to Francisquí de Arriba, which is the most popular snorkeling spot on Los Roques. You actually don't even need to leave Gran Roque – there's a reasonable place for snorkeling beyond the airstrip in the southeastern part of the island. You can rent snorkeling equipment in Gran Roque for about US$8 a day. It may be a good idea to bring your own gear from the mainland.

Scuba diving is also fabulous, and there are plenty of good places for divers. Diving is operated by the Gran Roque–based Sesto Continente dive company (☎ 014-924 18 53, divelosroques@scdr.com), which offers diving trips, PADI courses and equipment. The company can be contacted in Caracas at ☎ 730 38 73 or ☎/fax 730 90 80. Check out www.scdr.com for information and prices.

Los Roques is renowned as one of the world's finest areas for **game fishing**, particularly for bonefish. These trips are pretty expensive, and it's best to arrange one in advance through a specialized company (eg, Alpi Tour in Caracas). In Gran Roque, Posada Mediterráneo (☎ 014-929 06 21) and Posada La Lagunita (☎ 014-290 40 11) organize game-fishing stays.

Another attractive activity you may try in Los Roques is **windsurfing**. It's organized by Vela Windsurf Center, based on the island of Francisquí de Abajo, which rents equipment (US$20/50 per hour/day) and can provide lessons for beginners (US$40 for two hours including equipment). For more information, inquire at Posada El Canto de la Ballena in Gran Roque.

You can also go **sailing** on Los Roques, in one of several sailing yachts that anchor off Gran Roque and wait for tourists. They have cabins equipped with berths and provide meals on board, and can take you for several days around the islands. Prices range from about US$120 to US$150 a person per day, all-inclusive.

Finally, you can have a fantastic bird's-eye **view** of the islands from the ultralight plane parked at the airport (US$40/60 for a 15-/25-minute flight).

Organized Tours

The easiest and most popular way of visiting the archipelago is on a one- or two-day tour. Tours are run by most of the small airlines with flights to Los Roques, and they all have their desks at the domestic or auxiliary terminals of the Maiquetía airport (see Organized Tours in the Caracas chapter for airlines and their phone numbers). The prices and services may vary between operators. Línea Turística Aereotuy (LTA) is the major operator.

The all-inclusive one-day tour from Maiquetía airport normally costs about US$140 to US$150 and includes the roundtrip flight, a boat excursion from Gran Roque to one or two of the nearby islands, lunch, soft drinks, one hour of snorkeling (equipment provided) and free time on the beach. The tour program is pretty similar among all the operators, though they go to different islands and have their own preferred snorkeling areas. LTA is the only company that runs trips in large catamarans (others have single-hull boats only).

The two-day tour includes accommodations in Gran Roque and all meals, and it costs around US$250 to US$350, depending on the season, lodging standards and the number of people per room. An additional day will cost another US$100 to US$150. Note that tour prices don't include the US$15 entry fee to the archipelago.

Some operators, including LTA, also run tours from Isla de Margarita (US$200 for a one-day tour, US$300 to US$450 for a two-day tour). LTA also offers fishing and scuba-diving packages.

A day tour is an enjoyable escape from Caracas, but it gives just a brief taste of what the archipelago has to offer. If this is all you want, the package is a good value, as it's not much more expensive than the airfare. Two-day tours give better insight but are far more expensive, largely because the tour companies use upmarket accommodations. Some travelers consider them a poor value.

If you plan on staying two or more days, it's worth considering going on your own, which is pretty straightforward and far cheaper than taking a tour. You just buy a roundtrip ticket from one of the airlines and arrange all the rest in Gran Roque. Avoid tourist peaks, when flights and accommodations are in short supply and prices can be stiff. In the slow season, you may be able to negotiate the price of the bed and sometimes even of the flight back to Maiquetía (in which case you may consider buying only a one-way ticket to Los Roques). See Getting There & Away, later in this section.

Upon arrival at Gran Roque, go to the Angel & Oscar Shop (☎ 014-370 37 13), by the airport. It's a combination of shop, tour agency, boat operator and tourist office, all run by the knowledgeable Oscar. He provides boat transportation to the islands, organizes full-day boat tours, and rents outs snorkeling equipment and beach chairs. He

can provide information on the activities listed above and will have current prices for the posadas, including the cheapest ones. Oscar's longest and most expensive excursion includes the magnificent Cayo de Agua and Dos Mosquises, and costs US$25 per person, with a minimum of six passengers.

Places to Stay & Eat

Responding to tourism, locals have moved swiftly to transform their homes into hotels, and the result is truly impressive. There are now 64 posadas in the tiny village of Gran Roque, providing some 500 beds in about 230 rooms (by comparison, in 1995 there were just seven posadas). Most of them are small and simple places that offer both lodging and dining. Food is expensive and limited, because everything except fish has to be shipped in from the mainland.

The minimum you'll pay in the low season is about US$30 (occasionally US$25 after bargaining) per person for a bed, breakfast and supper. Prices vary from weekdays to weekends and depend also on demand. The cheapest places are **Posada El Botuto** (☎ 014-369 46 14), **Posada Paraíso Azul** (☎ 014-213 16 90) and **Posada Roquelusa**, all three close to the Inparques office near the far end of the village. Slightly more expensive are some no-frills places around Plaza Bolívar, including **Posada Mi Recuerdo** (☎ 014-936 47 09), **Posada Coralky** (☎ 014-369 46 29), **Posada Doña Carmen** and **Posada Doña Magalys**.

There are plenty of more stylish places, some with a fine Mediterranean touch. **Posada Acuarela** (☎ 014-932 35 02), designed and managed by architect and painter Angelo, is one of the most amazing places. Bed and breakfast here will cost around US$70 per person.

Many upmarket posadas offer packages that include bed, all meals and boat trips to other islands, for US$80 to US$120 or even more. Be warned that these packages are not often a good value, as trips include only the closest islands, usually Madrizquí or Francisquises (these boat trips on their own will cost just US$5 or US$6 per person with any boat operator). It may be better to stay in a budget posada and take boat trips separately, with Oscar or other boat operator. You can thus go on an attractive full-day excursion to the outer islands, and it all may still be cheaper than a package sold by an overpriced posada.

Since almost all posadas serve meals for their guests, there are few self-contained eating places in Gran Roque. They include the budget *Aquarena CaféTours Shop*, which serves pizzas, hamburgers and sandwiches, and the upmarket *Restaurant El Canto de la Ballena*.

The cheapest option for staying on Los Roques is to camp. Camping is allowed on all the islands within the recreation zone, including Gran Roque, and is free. After arrival, go to the Inparques office (☎ 014-373 10 04) at the far end of the village (open daily 8 am to noon and 2 to 6 pm) for a free camping permit. The staff will tell you which islands are good for camping and snorkeling, and can give you other practical tips as well.

On Gran Roque, the camping site is next to the Inparques office, but it has no toilets or showers. The only public toilet (no shower) is at the airport on the opposite end of the village. Try to arrange access to the bath at a nearby posada for a price. You can buy bottled water in shops.

If you prefer staying outside Gran Roque, Oscar or other boat operators will take you to the island of your choice and pick you up at a prearranged time in the afternoon of the same day or on a later date. Roundtrip fares per person are: Madrizquí, US$5; Francisquises, US$6; and Crasquí or Noronquises, US$10. Use the following figures as a rough guide only – they may vary depending on your party's size and other conditions. You pay after they bring you back to Gran Roque.

If you plan on camping on any island other than Gran Roque, then you should be self-sufficient with camping gear, food and water. The only eating options outside Gran Roque are *Restaurant Casamarina*, on Francisquí de Arriba, and the meals prepared by fishers on Crasquí – ask for Juanita. Don't forget to bring along snorkeling gear and good sun protection.

Getting There & Away

Air The fares of the airlines that fly to Los Roques may differ, so shop around if you want to save. The Maiquetía–Los Roques one-way fare is about US$50 to US$75, and the roundtrip fare is US$90 to US$110. The flight takes about 40 minutes.

LTA offers budget one-way fares of US$35 on their afternoon flights to Los Roques and morning flights back to Maiquetía. In effect, you can have a roundtrip for US$70. This may be a great saving if you plan on camping but less so if you'll stay in a posada. LTA also flies to Los Roques from Isla de Margarita, offering a similar budget option (US$90 regular one-way, US$65 discounted one-way, US$135 regular roundtrip).

Normally, only 10kg of free luggage is permitted on flights to Los Roques, and you pay US$0.50 for every additional kilogram. Some airlines may be more tolerant about excess luggage.

Boat There are no passenger boats to Los Roques, only cargo boats, which depart two or three times a week (usually in the evening) from Muelle 7 in La Guaira port. They often take passengers for a small fee or sometimes even free of charge. The problem is that these boats have no schedule, and it's virtually impossible to find out in advance the departure day and time. You have to personally go to the port and look for the captain. The trip itself normally takes about 12 hours and can be rough.

Miranda State

SAN FRANCISCO DE YARE
☎ 039 (☎ 0239 from July 14, 2001)
A small, quiet town, San Francisco de Yare (population 18,000) lies about 70km by road southeast of Caracas. The town was founded in 1718 and boasts a fine mid-18th-century church, the Iglesia de San Francisco, and some well-preserved colonial architecture.

However, what has really made the place famous are the colorful celebrations of Diablos Danzantes (see the boxed text, later in this section), when up to 1000 devils take to the streets, performing their ritual dance to the rhythm of drums and maracas. The feast has been celebrated here annually on Corpus Christi since 1742.

Corpus Christi is one of the major holy days in the Roman Catholic tradition, falling on the 60th day after Easter Day. It's a movable feast, coming in May or June, always on a Thursday. It's not an official public holiday in Venezuela, but it's definitely very much so in San Francisco de Yare.

Festival de los Diablos Danzantes

The celebrations begin at noon on the Wednesday one day prior to Corpus Christi, when crowds of devil dancers wearing their colorful masks and red costumes depart from the Casa de los Diablos Danzantes and take up the central streets for the whole afternoon. In the evening, they go to El Calvario for the lengthy Velorio (Vigil), which lasts until dawn.

In the morning of Corpus Christi, the devils gather at the Casa de los Diablos Danzantes for a short dancing session before heading for the local cemetery to pay respects to their predecessors. They then go to the parish church (but don't enter it) and continue in a joyful pageant to the Plaza de los Diablos Danzantes, four blocks from the church, where they again take to dancing.

The dancing stops when the procession from the church arrives, bringing the top of the ecclesiastical hierarchy of Miranda state, including the bishop from Los Teques. A lengthy, solemn mass is celebrated on the square, with all the devils taking part in it. Once the mass is over, the ceremony of the Juramentación is held, in which young apprentices to devil dancers take a symbolic oath. The bishop gives God's blessing to the devils, and they all set off for the procession back to the church, carrying the image of the Holy Sacrament.

The devils continue their dancing throughout the afternoon, wandering around the streets, stopping at the makeshift street altars and visiting homes of their relatives before returning to the church at about 6 pm for another procession, after which they head to El Calvario, where the celebrations conclude. The script of the festivities may differ slightly from year to year, but nonetheless, there will always be a lot of fascinating devil dancing all over the town. This is easily one of Venezuela's most authentic and colorful festivals.

Other Attractions

Obviously, Corpus Christi is the best day to visit the town, but it may still be worth coming at other times. The ambience of the Diablos Danzantes is omnipresent any time, particularly in the weeks prior to the festival.

The Casa de los Diablos Danzantes (where the Corpus Christi celebrations begin), on Calle Rivas next door to the police station, shelters a museum that has a collection of devil masks and photos from previous festivals. It's open 7 to 11 am and 2 to 4 pm Tuesday to Friday, 7 to 11 am Sunday. The family living in the house next door to the museum has the keys and may open it for you at other times.

There are several workshops manufacturing devil masks, where you can see the production process and buy masks (at more reasonable prices than anywhere else). One of the best is Artesanía El Mocho, led by Manuel Sanoja. It's on Calle Rivas, opposite the Monumento de los Diablos Danzantes, above the Bodega San Antonio – inquire in this shop. Artesanía Morgado, one block away on the same street, is run by another noted local artisan, Juan Morgado.

Places to Stay & Eat

There are no regular hotels in San Francisco de Yare – the nearest reliable accommodation options are in Santa Teresa del Tuy and Ocumare del Tuy. There are several basic places to eat in town, including *Bar Restaurant El Deporte*, on Plaza Bolívar, and

Diablos Danzantes

The Dancing Devils is one of Venezuela's most colorful events. Its central feature is the devils themselves, portrayed by dancers wearing monstrous masks. The dance can be anything from ceremonial marchlike movements in double file to spasmodic squirms accompanied by the beat of drums. Strangely enough, the devil dancers take to the streets on Corpus Christi, one of the holiest days on the Roman Catholic calendar, held in honor of the Eucharist.

KRZYSZTOF DYDYŃSKI

The Dancing Devils – a hell of a good time

The ceremony is thought to manifest the struggle between Evil and Good, and the eventual triumph of the latter. Effectively, no matter how profane the devil dances may look, the devils come at some stage to the steps of the church to submit themselves to the Eucharist. In turn, they get the priest's blessing and can then return to their whirling dances.

The event has a magical-religious appearance and meaning. Locals believe that the dance ritual will ensure abundant crops, welfare, prosperity and protection against misfortune and natural disasters. For the devils, the dance is their religion.

Broadly speaking, Diablos Danzantes is the product of the blend of Spanish and African traditions. The event has its roots in Spain, where the devils' images and masks were featured in Corpus Christi feasts in medieval Andalusia. When the festival was brought to the New World by the Spanish missionaries in colonial times, it found a fertile soil among the black slaves, who reinterpreted the Catholic devotion in their own way. They happily put on traditional masks from their homeland and danced to the rhythm of familiar drumbeats. Some academics consider this an act of protest by the black community against the white god, a symbol of Spanish oppression and cruelty. Whatever the reason, the profane and the divine gradually merged, producing a striking cross-cultural ritual.

The ceremony's African origins are palpable, even though the dances today are not performed exclusively by blacks. Devil dances have been preserved only in areas that have traditionally had a significant black population. Some of the modern masks are similar to those of West African countries such as Congo, Benin and Nigeria. The usual accompanying instruments are the drum and maracas, though the *cuatro* (a small, four-stringed guitar) is also used in some areas.

The towns and villages that boast devil dances today include Naiguatá (Vargas); Cata, Chuao, Cuyagua, Ocumare de la Costa and Turiamo (Aragua); Canoabo, Guacara, Los Caneyes, Patanemo and Tocuyito (Carabobo); Tinaquillo (Cojedes); and San Francisco de Yare (Miranda). All these localities are in the area that witnessed the heaviest import of African slaves. The celebrations in Chuao and San Francisco de Yare are best known throughout the country, as are their masks.

Dances, costumes and masks of each community have developed their own forms and features. Although masks today are commonly made of papier-mâché, they differ notably from town to town. Those from San Francisco de Yare, for example, are large, elaborate and brightly painted in just about every color of the rainbow. They depict horned demons, monsters, fantastic animals and the like. The masks from Chuao are smaller and more modest. They are painted essentially with three colors – white, black and red – and clearly share characteristics with those from Congo.

Lunchería La Flor de Yare, which is just off the plaza.

Getting There & Away

There's no direct transportation from Caracas to San Francisco de Yare, but you can get there easily with one connection. Take one of the frequent buses to Ocumare del Tuy (US$0.80, 1½ hours) or Santa Teresa del Tuy (US$0.80, 1½ hours) from the Nuevo Circo regional bus terminal, and change at your destination. Buses shuttle between Ocumare and Santa Teresa every 15 minutes or so, and pass through San Francisco de Yare, providing convenient access.

PARQUE NACIONAL GUATOPO

Established in 1958, Guatopo is Venezuela's third-oldest national park. About 100km by road (60km as the crow flies) southeast of Caracas, it encompasses 1225 sq km of the rugged Serranía del Interior, a mountain range that splits off the Cordillera de la Costa and winds inland. The altitude in the park ranges between 200m and 1430m above sea level.

Most of the park is covered by lush rain forest, which makes it an important biological enclave in the otherwise heavily developed and populated hinterland of Caracas. Guatopo is also a major water supplier for the region, since several dams have been built in or just off the park, creating water reservoirs *(embalses)*.

The climate here is wet and warm. The average annual rainfall ranges from about 1500mm in low-lying areas to nearly 3000mm in the upper reaches. The rainiest months are October to December, while the driest ones are March and April, but even then rains are not uncommon. Reliable rain gear is recommended for travel here any time of the year. The temperatures in the lower parts of the park range between 25°C and 30°C, dropping to about 15°C on the highest tops.

Thanks to the wide range of elevations and copious rainfall, the park's vegetation is varied and exuberant, with numerous species of trees (some up to 40m high), palms, ferns and orchids. The rich mammal world includes the jaguar, puma, tapir, peccary, armadillo, margay and sloth, to name just a few. Guatopo is also good for bird-watching. Macaws, parakeets, woodpeckers, hummingbirds, honeycreepers, tanagers, trogons, grosbeaks and dozens of other bird species can be observed quite easily. There are also some poisonous snakes, including the coral snake, tigra mariposa, rattlesnake and (the most common and dangerous) macagua *(Bothrops colombiensis)* – so keep an eye out when you walk. Insects are plentiful, so it's worth bringing along an effective insect repellent.

Orientation

The paved road between Santa Teresa del Tuy and Altagracia de Orituco runs through the middle of the park, providing both access to all recreational areas and starting points for walks. It was affected at several points by landslides caused by the December 1999 torrential rains, but has since been mostly repaired and is navigable by any car. Public transportation from Caracas travels along this road, but it's infrequent and dies in the afternoon. Given this, a one-day trip to the park from Caracas gives you a pretty limited time in the park. If you decide to do this, make an early start and go to Agua Blanca (see that section, later), which is a good starting point for walking. If you have your own transportation, you can easily visit several areas in the park and still have reasonable time for walking.

The park offers some basic lodging and camping facilities, which allows for longer stays in the heart of the rain forest. The following sections detail the major stopovers on the route, from north to south (the exception being Hacienda La Elvira, which is accessible only from Altagracia de Orituco), along with their tourist facilities.

Los Alpes del Tuy

About 30km from Santa Teresa, Los Alpes is just a roadside cafetería, *Parador Turístico Los Alpes*, sitting on a Y-junction and serving hot snacks and drinks. The road branching to the south will take you to a viewpoint (3.5km from Los Alpes), then to

PARQUE NACIONAL GUATOPO

another viewpoint (1km beyond). Five kilometers farther on, you reach La Macanilla.

La Macanilla

The Inparques visitors center here has a very small exhibition on the park's flora, fauna and geology. The *guardaparque* (park ranger) can give you information about the park. La Macanilla was the starting point for a beautiful 9km trail that winds through thick forest up to the mountain ridge, continues along the ridge, and comes back down to the road 4km from La Macanilla. However, the trail hasn't been maintained and became overgrown several years ago. It was impassable at the time of writing. There are no accommodations or food in La Macanilla, and camping is not allowed.

Agua Blanca

Thirteen kilometers by road from La Macanilla, Agua Blanca is the park's major

recreational area. It can be swamped with day-trippers on weekends, but is usually quiet on weekdays. You can visit a reconstructed *trapiche* (traditional sugarcane mill) and have a bath in the *pozo* (pond) on the opposite side of the road, though the water is not particularly clean.

From the pond, a 3km walking trail goes to Santa Crucita. This trail is steep in parts and often muddy; allow up to 1½ hours to walk it at a leisurely pace. There's another, shorter trail between Agua Blanca and Santa Crucita (1650m, 45 minutes), running on the opposite, eastern side of the road, which allows for a roundtrip without returning the same way. See the following Santa Crucita section for more walks.

Agua Blanca has a picnic area, toilets, a parking lot (guarded on weekends), a snack kiosk (open on weekends) and some accommodation options. *Campamento Los Monos* is a 26-bed dormitory that is rented as a whole (US$20) through Caracas' Inparques office. Bring your own sheets and blankets. There are also five **cabañas**, rustic timber structures on stilts, scattered around the forest. You actually get just a bare wooden floor under the roof, but it's a pleasant shelter and doesn't cost much: US$4 for the whole cabaña (four people will fit). Bring your mats, sheets, blankets or a sleeping bag. There's also a **camping ground**. Bring your food if you come on weekdays.

Santa Crucita
The next stop down, Santa Crucita is 1.5km by road from Agua Blanca. There is a small lagoon here, and you can pitch your tent on the grassy **camping ground**. Apart from the two trails coming here from Agua Blanca (see that section, earlier), there are two short local walking loops, one skirting around the lagoon (700m) and another one going through the nearby forest (800m).

El Lucero & Quebrada de Guatopo
The park's administrative center is El Lucero, 5.5km down the road from Santa Crucita. There's a **camping ground** here, but no food is available.

Quebrada de Guatopo, 2km beyond El Lucero, has a picnic area, a creek and yet another **camping ground**. Again, bring your own food.

Altagracia de Orituco
Lying beyond the national park's boundaries, Altagracia de Orituco is 24km south of Quebrada de Guatopo. It's quite an ordinary town, but it's big enough to be a terminus for buses from Caracas and to have a collection of hotels and restaurants.

Buses to Caracas depart from the junction where the gas stations are located, 1km from Plaza Bolívar. Here you'll also find several hotels, including the inexpensive **Hotel La Avenida** and the more decent **Hotel Amazon**, which has a good restaurant. Halfway between the Plaza Bolívar and the bus terminus is the budget **Pensión Los Angeles**.

Hacienda La Elvira
This old coffee hacienda is 26km northeast of Altagracia. The central feature is the 19th-century country mansion, which is open to visitors. There are no accommodations, but camping is permitted.

To get there from Altagracia, you have to drive 8km east on the road to Paso Real and take the left turnoff north to San Francisco de Macaira. Follow this paved but pothole-riddled road for 14km, and take the jeep track branching off to the northwest and leading to La Elvira (4km). Getting anywhere nearby by public transportation is difficult.

Getting There & Away
The usual starting point for Parque Nacional Guatopo is Caracas. There are hourly buses from the Nuevo Circo regional terminal to Altagracia de Orituco (US$3.50, four hours), but they go by the road via Cúa and San Casimiro and don't pass through the park. There are also minibuses operating as por puestos to Altagracia. They run from about 5 am to 2 pm, depart when full and are faster than buses. They go via Santa Teresa and the park, and can let you off at any point on the road, eg, Agua Blanca (US$4, two hours).

Aragua State

MARACAY
☎ 043 (☎ 0243 from Apr 21, 2001)
The capital of Aragua state, Maracay (population 540,000) is the center of an important agricultural area. It's also quite developed industrially, though most factories are outside the city limits. There's almost nothing left of the colonial legacy in this 300-year-old city, and modern architecture is not Maracay's strong point either. What the city does possess are plenty of parks and leafy plazas, including the largest Plaza Bolívar in the country. Justifiably, Maracay is called the 'Ciudad Jardín' (Garden City).

At an altitude of about 450m, Maracay has a relatively hot yet tolerable climate

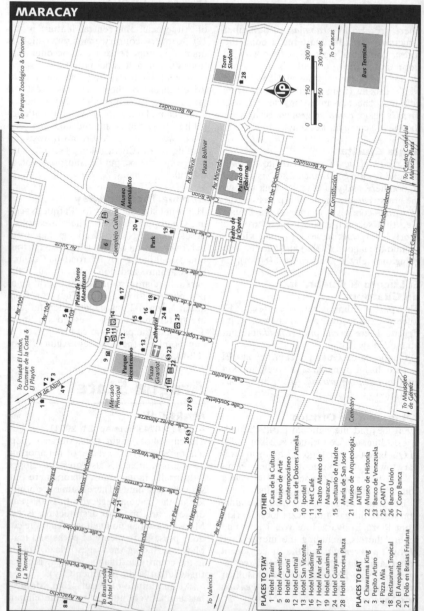

MARACAY

To Parque Zoológico & Choroni

To Caracas

Torre Sindoni

● 28

To Centro Comercial Maracay Plaza

Bus Terminal

Av Bermúdez

Plaza Bolívar

Av Bolívar

Palacio de Gobierno

Av 10 de Diciembre

Av Bermúdez

Av Constitución

Calle Brión

Av Miranda

Teatro de la Ópera

Av Independencia

Av Los Cedros

Museo Aeronáutico

Complejo Cultural

7 🏛
6 ■

Av Sucre

20 ▼

Park

19 ■

Calle Junín

Calle Sucre

To Posada El Limón, Ocumare de la Costa & El Playón

Av 105

Av 104
Av 103

5 ■

Plaza de Toros Maestranza

■ 17

18 ▼
16 ■

15 ■

Calle 5 de Julio

Calle López Aveledo

9 🏛

10 ▼
🏛 11

■ 12

■ 13

Cathedral

24 ■
🛇 25

Calle Mariño

To Posada El Limón

Av 19 de Abril

1 ■ ▼ 2
▼ 3

4 ▼

Mercado Principal

Parque Bicentenario

Plaza Girardot

21 🏛
🛇 23
22

To Mausoleo de Gómez

Cemetery

Calle Soublette

27 🛇

Calle Pérez Almarza

26 🛇

Calle Vargas

Av Boyacá

Av Santos Michelena

Calle Sánchez Carrero

Av Bolívar

Calle Libertad

Av Páez

Av Negro Primero

Av Ricaurte

To Restaurant La Tenería

Av Pichincha

To Brasilandia & Hotel Cristi

Calle Carabobo

Av Miranda

Av Ayacucho

8 ■

To Valencia

300 m
300 yards
0   150
0   150

PLACES TO STAY
1 Hotel Traini
5 Hotel Aventino
8 Hotel Caroni
12 Hotel Central
13 Hotel San Vicente
16 Hotel Wladimir
17 Hotel Mar del Plata
19 Hotel Canaima
24 Hotel Guayana
28 Hotel Princesa Plaza

PLACES TO EAT
2 Chawarma King
3 Pepito Arturo
4 Pizza Mia
18 Restaurant Tropical
20 El Arepanito
21 Pollo en Brasas Friulana

OTHER
6 Casa de la Cultura
7 Museo de Arte Contemporáneo
9 Casa de Dolores Amelia
10 Ipostel
11 Net Café
14 Teatro Ateneo de Maracay
15 Santuario de Madre María de San José
21 Museo de Arqueología; IATUR
22 Museo de Historia
23 Banco de Venezuela
25 CANTV
26 Banco Unión
27 Corp Banca

(warmer than Caracas, but more pleasant than Maracaibo), with an average temperature of 25°C and most of the rain falling between April and October.

History

At the time of the Spanish conquest, the valley in which Maracay is set was inhabited by the Aragua Indian group, led by Cacique Maracay; this is where the name of the city and the state comes from.

A Spanish settlement was established somewhere around the mid-16th century, but it was not until 1701 that a formal act of foundation was signed. Ever since, this signing has been considered the official birth of Maracay. At that time, the town numbered about 750 inhabitants. Thanks to the valley's fertile soil, agriculture became the basis of the region's development – cacao, indigo, coffee, sugarcane, cotton and tobacco were the major crops – yet the town's growth was pretty slow; by 1900 the population had reached a mere 7000.

Maracay would have probably continued at this unhurried rate if it hadn't been for Juan Vicente Gómez, the most enduring and probably the most ruthless of Venezuela's *caudillos* (see History in the Facts about Venezuela chapter). He first came here in 1899 and fell in love with the town. After seizing power in 1908, he settled for good in Maracay in 1912 and five years later moved the Aragua state capital from La Victoria to Maracay, which became not only the state capital but also virtually the national capital. From here Gómez ruled the country until his death in 1935.

During the Gómez days, Maracay saw a rash of new construction, including the government house, a bullring, an opera house, a zoo, the most splendid hotel in the country and a military aviation school. This school, founded in 1920, was the cradle of Venezuelan aviation, both civil and military.

Gómez was well aware of threats to his life (a consequence of his iron rule). It is said that he slept in the same bed two nights in a row and that he built a system of escape tunnels from his office. He constructed a road from Maracay over the mountains to the coast, in case he was forced to flee the country, and he surrounded himself with a strong military force, for which vast barracks were built. Lastly, he didn't forget to erect a mausoleum for himself.

The city's second wave of development came with post–World War II industrialization. The freeway linking Caracas with Valencia via Maracay, built in the 1950s by another ruthless dictator, Marcos Pérez Jiménez, also contributed to the city's growth. During his rule, Venezuela had the most powerful air force in Latin America, much of it based in Maracay. The 1950 population of 65,000 doubled over the next decade, and doubled again during the 1960s. Maracay continues to grow quickly and is an important base for military operations. The unsuccessful military takeover in November 1992 began in Maracay, and the rebels' planes flew to Caracas from here.

Information

Tourist Offices The IATUR (Instituto Autónomo de Turismo del Estado Aragua) tourist office (☎ 86 56 19) is in the Museo de Arqueología, on Plaza Girardot. It's open 8 am to 3:30 pm weekdays.

Money Some of the banks useful for cash advances, such as Banco Unión and Banco de Venezuela, are indicated on the map. Corp Banca changes American Express traveler's checks. Foreign cash can be exchanged at Italcambio (☎ 35 69 45, 35 85 42) in Centro Comercial Maracay Plaza, Piso 1, Local 110-K, on the corner of Avenidas Aragua and Bermúdez, 1.5km south of Plaza Bolívar.

Email & Internet Access The Biblioteca Virtual, next to the Casa de la Cultura, Avenida Sucre, is somewhat slow but cheap at US$1.50 an hour. Faster is Net Café, in the Centro Comercial La Capilla, Piso 1, Local 24, Avenida Santos Michelana. It provides good service and costs US$2.50 an hour. There are also three Internet facilities – Comunicaciones MP, Mundo Internet and Cyber Show – in the Centro Comercial Paseo Las Delicias, and the fast Net Show

Cyber Café, located on the ground floor of the Torre Sindoni.

Plaza Girardot

This is the historic heart of Maracay (not Plaza Bolívar, as is the rule almost anywhere throughout the country). The monument in the middle of the square, an obelisk topped with a bronze eagle, was erected in 1897. It commemorates the North American volunteers who joined the antiroyalist forces led by Francisco Miranda, but who were captured and hanged in 1806 by the Spaniards. The adjacent Parque Bicentenario was added in 1983, forming a spacious two-block open-air public ground. There are no colonial buildings left around either square, except for the cathedral.

Catedral

This fair-sized, handsome church, on the eastern side of Plaza Girardot, was completed in 1743 (as the inscription over the side door reads), and not much has changed since. Whitewashed all over, the exterior is attractive, especially with late-afternoon sunlight striking the facade.

Museo de Historia & Museo de Arqueología

On the south side of Plaza Girardot is an arcaded building erected by Gómez as the seat of government. Today, there are two museums inside. The Museo de Historia has one room dedicated to Bolívar and one to Gómez, plus a handful of exhibits loosely related to Venezuelan history. It was closed for refurbishing as of late 2000.

The Museo de Arqueología features pre-Hispanic pottery from the region. In the basement of this museum is the Sala de Etnología (the ethnological section), displaying crafts of some Indian groups living today, including the Maquiritare, Warao, Piaroa, Sanema, Guajibo and Guajiro. The museum is open 8 am to 3:30 pm Tuesday to Friday, 9 am to 12:30 pm weekends.

Casa de Dolores Amelia

Set on the northern side of Parque Bicentenario, this fine mansion was built from 1927 to 1929 by Gómez for his favorite mistress, Dolores Amelia Núñez de Cáceres. Designed by Frenchman André Potel in the neo-Sevillan style, the building has been meticulously restored and is now occupied by an insurance company. It is not a tourist sight, but if you turn up during office hours, someone may let you in and show you around the patio and adjoining parts of the building, which are clad with *azulejos* (ornamental tiles) and reminiscent of the Alhambra in Granada. It's said that the house was linked by a tunnel with Gómez' office in Plaza Girardot.

Santuario de Madre María de San José

The sanctuary, one block east of Plaza Girardot, is probably the most revered and visited city site. Choroní-born Madre María (1875–1967) was venerated in 1992 by a papal decree and solemnly beatified in 1995. Her remains were exhumed and, to everybody's surprise, the corpse was allegedly intact. You can see it in a crystal sarcophagus in the Santuario (though the face and hands are covered with masks). The Santuario is open 8:30 to 11:30 am and 2:30 to 5 pm Tuesday to Sunday. Also see Colonial Towns, under Parque Nacional Henri Pittier, later in this chapter, for more information on Madre María.

Plaza de Toros Maestranza

This large Spanish-Moorish bullring was designed by Carlos Raúl Villanueva, modeled on the one in Seville and built in 1933; it's possibly the most stylish and beautiful in the country. It was originally called 'Calicanto,' but was then renamed in memory of César Girón, Venezuela's most famous matador, who died in a traffic accident in 1971. The monument to him, which shows him fighting a bull, stands in front of the bullring. If you want to see the bullring from the inside, try getting in through the back door on the eastern side.

Museo Aeronáutico

This is the only aeronautical museum in the country. There are about 40 aircraft on display, including four helicopters. Many are warplanes from the 1920s to the 1950s that once served in the Venezuelan air force. The majority of the planes are displayed outdoors, but some valuable exhibits are kept indoors. Of these, the collection's gem is a beautifully restored French plane from the 1910s, which is reputedly in perfect working order. The museum also has a replica of the famous Jimmie Angel plane, but this one is yet to be restored.

In the middle of the exhibition grounds is the statue of Juan Vicente Gómez. This is the first and so far only monument to the caudillo, unveiled amid great controversy in November 1995.

The museum is open only on Saturday and Sunday 10 am to 6 pm. If you happen to come to Maracay on a weekday, inquire at the side gate at the end of Avenida Santos Michelena (best between 8 and 11 am or between 2 and 3 pm) and somebody may show you around. The soldiers at the gate may be unaware of this and may tell you it's impossible to visit, in which case politely ask them to call the supervisor.

Museo de Arte Contemporáneo

The entire block opposite the aeronautical museum is occupied by the Complejo Cultural (opened in 1983), which contains several cultural institutions, including the Casa de la Cultura, a library, a music school and the contemporary art museum. The museum (open daily except Monday from 9 am to 5 pm) stages temporary exhibitions of modern art.

Plaza Bolívar

A shady three blocks long, this is the largest Plaza Bolívar in the country and, some claim, Latin America. It was laid out by Carlos Raúl Villanueva and opened in 1930. The monument to Bolívar is a replica of the Caracas statue.

Palacio de Gobierno

This large edifice, on the southern side of Plaza Bolívar, was once the splendid Hotel Jardín. Designed by Villanueva and inaugurated in 1930 by Gómez, the hotel over-shadowed all other Venezuelan hotels of the day and became a playground for the rich and beautiful. The place witnessed many important episodes of the country's political, social and cultural life, and Carlos Gardel even sang his nostalgic tangos here.

The hotel closed down in 1959 and was largely remodeled for its new function, yet you can still feel some of the charm of the cloisters and interior gardens. It's now the government house, not a tourist sight, but the police security guards may let you in. If they refuse you entry at the front, try the back (south) gate, from Avenida Páez.

Teatro de la Opera

Commissioned by Gómez in 1934, this theater was intended to be the best in the country, to match the capital status of the city. It was designed by Luis Malaussena, and a huge budget of 2 million bolívares was allotted for the structure alone. Planned to be opened in 1936, the theater was constructed swiftly, and by December 1935 (the month Gómez died) it was almost ready; only the ceiling, imported from the USA, had to be fixed and the interior furnished. Nonetheless, the work was stopped by the new government, and part of the imported decoration was moved to Caracas for use in theaters there. It wasn't until 1973 that the theater finally opened. It can seat 860 and stages a variety of productions, including opera, ballet, theater, folkloric dance (performed mostly by visiting groups).

Mausoleo de Gómez

Also referred to as the 'Panteón de Gómez,' the mausoleum is south of the city center, just behind the cemetery. Interestingly, this was one of Gómez' earliest projects, built in 1919. A rather pretentious structure topped with a white Moorish dome, the pantheon houses the tomb of the general and members of his family. There are plenty of thanksgiving plaques placed on the interior walls. All have an almost identical inscription that reads 'Thanks for the favors,' but none is signed with a full name, only with initials.

Fresh flowers and lit candles are frequently left at the tomb, evidence that

Gómez is not forgotten. On the contrary, respect for Gómez seems to have been revived in Maracay over the past several years, partly as a result of the recent economic and political crisis. The mausoleum is open 6 am to 3 pm Tuesday to Sunday.

Parque Zoológico

At the northern city limits, the zoo is yet another of Gómez' achievements, established on one of his own estates. It is well laid out with reasonable cage space for most of the animals, many of which are typical of Venezuela. It's open 9 am to 5 pm Tuesday to Sunday. To get there from the city center, take the Castaño/Zoológico buseta, which goes all the way along Avenida Las Delicias and will deposit you right at the entrance to the zoo.

Special Events

The Fiesta de San José, Maracay's most important annual event, takes place over several days around March 19, the city patron saint's day. The major *corrida* (bullfight) is celebrated during the feast, but other corridas are held on some Sundays during the year, mostly between Christmas and Easter.

Maracay's Teatro de la Opera invites some groups taking part in Caracas' International Theater Festival to perform here (see the Caracas chapter for further information on the festival).

Places to Stay

Maracay has a fair choice of accommodations, by and large reasonably priced and conveniently located. All the hotels listed in this section have rooms with private bath and either fan or air-conditioning.

Budget There are several cheap but basic hotels right in the city center. *Hotel San Vicente* (☎ 47 03 21), just across Avenida Bolívar from the cathedral, is one of the cheapest options, at US$10 for a matrimonial with fan (US$14 for air-con). One block east along Avenida Bolívar is the similarly rudimentary *Hotel Guayana* (☎ 46 28 49),

which offers matrimoniales/doubles with fan for US$10/14.

The quieter (but not better) *Hotel Central* (☎ 45 28 34), Avenida Santos Michelena, has rooms with fans and costs much the same as the Guayana. It also has triples for US$16. *Hotel Canaima* (☎ 33 82 78), on Avenida Bolívar one block west of Plaza Bolívar, is another uninspiring budget option. Air-conditioned matrimoniales/doubles go for US$12/15. All these hotels have the odd loving couple passing through.

Appreciably better than anything listed above is the peaceful *Hotel Mar del Plata* (☎ 46 43 13, 47 21 01), Avenida Santos Michelena, which features neat and air-conditioned matrimoniales/doubles/triples for US$18/22/24 – a good value.

If you don't mind staying out of the city center, *Hotel Cristal* (☎ 54 06 68, 54 02 46), Avenida Bolívar, provides reasonable value. Its spacious and air-conditioned rooms cost much the same as those in the Hotel Mar del Plata. Hotel Cristal is four blocks west of Avenida Ayacucho, easily accessible by countless buses running along Avenida Bolívar. Alternatively, try *Hotel Caroní* (☎ 54 44 65, 54 78 55), Avenida Ayacucho, which has seen better days but is still probably worth US$16/25/30 for air-conditioned singles/doubles/triples with hot water.

Mid-Range Reasonable central options in this price bracket include *Hotel Traini* (☎ 45 55 02, 45 03 35), Avenida 19 de Abril, and *Hotel Wladimir* (☎ 46 11 15, 46 25 66), Avenida Bolívar. The Traini has air-conditioned singles/doubles/triples for US$24/28/34. The Wladimir costs about US$2 more per person. You may also try the newer *Hotel Aventino* (☎ 45 70 87, 45 78 96), Calle López Aveledo, which has ample matrimoniales/doubles for US$28/30.

Posada El Limón (☎/fax 83 49 25, caribean@telcel.net.ve, Calle El Piñal 64) is a world apart from anything else listed here. Run by two Dutch guys, Bernardus and Frank, it's a charming, stylish place that provides beds and hammocks, meals, Internet access, laundry, swimming pool, tours and transfers (for example, you can be picked up from Maiquetía airport and brought directly to the posada, for US$70 for up to three people). Comfortable double rooms with fan and air-conditioning cost US$45, and there are some cheaper beds and hammocks on a spacious balcony. Advance booking is recommended. The posada is in a leafy residential suburb of El Limón, about 8km from the city center. There's no public transportation all the way to the gate; you can either take the El Limón buseta and then walk or go by taxi – it shouldn't cost more than US$5 from the center.

Top End The *Hotel Princesa Plaza (☎ 32 01 77, 33 10 06, fax 33 79 72)* is on Avenida Miranda, next to the spanking 30 story brick-and-glass Torre Sindoni, the highest and most modern addition to the cityscape. Both convenient and decent, the hotel costs US$55 double.

Other top-end hotels are outside the center, mostly along Avenida Las Delicias in the northern residential districts. They include the modern high-rise *Hotel Byblos (☎ 42 03 11, fax 42 26 79)* and *Hotel Italo (☎ 32 05 22, fax 32 04 43)*, closer to the city center. Both are three-star establishments. The four-star *Hotel Pipo Internacional (☎ 41 31 11, fax 41 62 98)* is on Avenida Principal El Castaño (the road to Choroní), at the city limits.

Places to Eat
There are plenty of reasonably priced places to eat scattered throughout the city center. Some of the cheapest typical meals are to be found in the *Mercado Principal* (built by Gómez in 1921), which has half a dozen food stands.

Restaurant Tropical has tasty comida criolla, including arepas. *El Arepanito* is also good for local food and is open until late. *Pizza Mía* has some acceptable budget pizzas. *Pepito Arturo*, across the road, specializes in parrillas and batidos. Next door, *Chawarma King* serves falafel, kibbe and the like. *Pollo en Brasas Friulana* is the place for chicken. All these places are marked on the city map.

Brasilandia, on Avenida Bolívar close to the Hotel Cristal, is deservedly popular among locals for its hearty parrilla and chicken at good prices. Equally respectable is the *Restaurant La Ternera*, on Avenida Ayacucho next to the Mercado Libre Municipal (four blocks north of the Hotel Caroní), which has local-style cooked beef.

There are plenty of upmarket restaurants along Avenida Las Delicias north of the city center; *Restaurant El Riacho* and *Restaurant El Bodegón de Sevilla* are reputedly among the best. Not so chic but cheaper is *La Terraza del Vroster*, also on Avenida Las Delicias, which serves a good range of pasta and pizza, as well as Venezuelan cuisine.

Getting There & Away
Air Maracay's civil airport is in the air force base. Avior has direct flights to Porlamar (US$84) and Mérida (US$84).

Bus The bus terminal is on the southeastern outskirts of the city center. It's within walking distance of Plaza Bolívar, but it's quicker to take any of the frequent city buses.

The bus terminal is vast and busy, with frequent transportation to most major cities. Ordinary buses to Caracas depart every 15 minutes or so (US$2.50, 1½ hours), as do buses to Valencia (US$1, one hour).

There are at least a dozen departures a day to Barquisimeto (US$7, four hours), Maracaibo (US$17, nine hours) and San Cristóbal (US$21, 11½ hours). Half a dozen buses run to San Antonio del Táchira (US$23, 12½ hours), Coro (US$11, 6½ hours) and Mérida (US$21, 11 hours). There are direct buses to Puerto La Cruz (US$14, seven hours) and Ciudad Bolívar (US$18, nine hours); these buses bypass Caracas, saving time and money. The prices listed are for air-conditioned services, but there are also the 25% cheaper ordinary buses on some routes. Several ordinary buses per day go to San Fernando de Apure (US$7, seven hours).

For transportation to El Playón and Puerto Colombia, see the Parque Nacional Henri Pittier section, later in this chapter.

SAN MATEO
☎ 044 (☎ 0244 from Apr 21, 2001)

The town of San Mateo (population 24,000), 20km east of Maracay, is noted for a hacienda that once belonged to the Bolívar family. It was granted to them in 1593, after they came to settle in Venezuela from their native Spain. At the beginning of the 18th century, the Bolívars built a sugarcane mill on their land and used African slaves to work the crops, a common practice throughout the region.

In 1814, Simón Bolívar set up a military camp on the hacienda, which predictably became the target of fierce attacks by the royalist troops. The camp was saved thanks to a heroic act of defense by Antonio Ricaurte, one of Bolívar's lieutenants. Later on, Bolívar passed through San Mateo on various occasions, including a rest stop after the battle of Carabobo in 1821, when he freed the local slaves.

During the 19th century, the hacienda passed through the hands of various owners until it was bought by the government of Juan Vicente Gómez in 1924 and turned into barracks. It was later transformed into a museum.

Things to See
Restored in the 1980s to its original state, the hacienda now houses two museums, both open 10 am to 4 pm Tuesday to Sunday. The **Museo de la Caña de Azúcar** is centered on the original sugarcane mill. Exhibits include the mill itself and a variety of tools, implements and objects related to sugar production.

On the opposite side of the road is the **Museo Histórico Militar**. This finely restored historic house, on the top of a hill, features a collection of period armor, plus the usual Bolivariana, including documents and a number of Bolívar's portraits. The outbuildings, which served as the armory during Bolívar's days, were intentionally left in a state of ruin, as they have been since March 25, 1814. It was here that Antonio Ricaurte, a Colombian patriot in the service of Bolívar, sacrificed himself to save the battle that was almost lost to the Spaniards. Closely encircled by royalists, he led them into the armory, then set fire to the gunpowder kegs, blowing up both the enemies and himself.

Getting There & Away
The Bolívar hacienda is located on the old Maracay–La Victoria road (not the freeway), a couple of kilometers east of San Mateo town. The road is serviced by frequent buses and por puestos, which will let you off at the entrance to the museums. Ask the driver to drop you off at El Ingenio de Bolívar, as the place is commonly known.

If you plan to visit San Mateo from Caracas, take a bus to La Victoria (from La Bandera terminal) and from there catch a bus to San Mateo. There may also be some por puestos all the way to San Mateo through La Victoria.

LA VICTORIA
☎ 044 (☎ 0244 from Apr 21, 2001)

Founded in 1593, Nuestra Señora de Guadalupe de La Victoria was an important commercial center and the capital of Aragua state until 1917, when Juan Vicente Gómez moved the capital to Maracay, 30km to the west.

Today it's a busy city of 110,000 people, surrounded with factories, but its historic center, particularly the area around Plaza Ribas, retains some of its old architecture and flavor. Stroll around the central streets, between Plaza Ribas and Plaza Bolívar, five blocks apart. Both plazas boast a church – the large 18th-century neoclassical Iglesia de Nuestra Señora de la Victoria at Plaza Ribas, and the small Iglesia de Nuestra Señora de la Candelaria at Plaza Bolívar.

Places to Stay & Eat
It's not very likely that you'll hang around in town for long, but if you do, the most pleasant place to stay overnight is *Hotel El Recreo* (☎ 21 04 11, 21 02 44), in a converted sugar hacienda from 1724 on the road to San Mateo, a short walk west from Plaza Ribas. It has a large swimming pool, a fine restaurant arranged in a colonial mansion, and comfortable rooms for US$50/58/66 double/triple/quad.

Getting There & Away

A new bus terminal was opened in 1998 on the outskirts of the town, 4km east of the historic center. Local por puestos shuttle between the terminal and center.

There are frequent buses to Caracas, all running via freeway (US$2, 1¼ hours). Buses to Maracay go either via freeway (US$1, 30 minutes) or via the old road; the latter will drop you off at San Mateo (US$0.30, 15 minutes). Por puestos to Colonia Tovar depart regularly and wind up along a spectacular 36km mountain road offering dramatic views (US$2, 1½ hours). Sit on the right for better vistas.

COLONIA TOVAR

☎ 044 (☎ 0244 from Apr 21, 2001)

This unusual mountain town sits at an altitude of about 1800m amid the rolling forests of the Cordillera de la Costa, about 60km west of Caracas. It was founded in 1843 by a group of 376 German settlers from the Schwarzwald (Black Forest), recruited by Italian cartographer Agustín Codazzi (see the boxed text). The town was named after Martín Tovar y Ponte, who donated these lands.

Effectively isolated from the outer world by the lack of roads and by internal rules prohibiting marriage outside the colony, the village followed the mother culture, language and architecture for a century. It wasn't until the 1940s that Spanish was introduced as the official language and the ban on marrying outside the community abandoned. Furthermore, it was not until 1963 that a paved road reached Colonia Tovar from Caracas, marking a turning point in the history of the town, which by then had a mere 1300 inhabitants.

Today, Colonia Tovar has five times as many inhabitants (about 6500) and is a classic example of a tourist town, drawing in hordes of caraqueños on weekends, curious to see a bit of old Germany lost in Venezuelan cloud forest. They come to glimpse the traditional architecture, enjoy a German lunch or dinner, and buy bread or sausage made according to traditional recipes, as well as delicious strawberries, apples, peaches and blackberries, cultivated locally thanks to the temperate climate. Other town assets are beautiful, lush surroundings and the cordiality and hospitality of the inhabitants, some of whom are descendants of the original settlers.

Colonia Tovar has a distinct dual personality. On weekends it may be virtually swamped with visitors and their cars (which effectively block the access roads), while on weekdays it is almost dead and many restaurants are closed. Whichever time you come, though, take some warm clothing – it's hard to imagine how much the temperature drops as you climb into these upper reaches of the cordillera. Colonia Tovar's average temperature is 16°C, but it's much lower at night.

Things to See

Stroll about the steep, winding streets to see some fine examples of traditional German architecture. Call at the **Museo Histórico** (open 9 am to 6 pm weekends and holidays only) for a taste of the town's history. Visit the **Museo Arqueológico** (open weekends and holidays from 9 am to 5 pm) to learn a bit about the prehistory of the region.

Do not miss the local **church**, a curious L-shaped building with two perpendicular naves (originally, one for women, the other for men) and the high altar placed in the angle where the naves join. From there, the patron saint of the town, San Martín de Tours, overlooks both naves.

Hiking

There are various walking options around the town, including a hike up to **Pico Codazzi**, the highest peak in the area, at 2425m. To go there, you need to get first to the pass on the road to La Victoria, 5km out of Colonia Tovar (walk, hitch or take a por puesto to La Victoria), from where a path branches off to the right and leads up to the top (a half-hour walk).

Places to Stay & Eat

For most travelers, Colonia Tovar is a day trip from Caracas, but there are no problems if you want to stay longer. The town

Agustín Codazzi

Adventurer, sailor, explorer, corsair, soldier and merchant – but primarily remembered as a cartographer – Agustín Codazzi was born in 1793 in Lugo, a town in northern Italy. At the age of 17 he enrolled in the Napoleonic army and was trained in mathematics, geometry, topography and the like to become a professional artillery officer (which, as it turned out, gave him a solid basis for cartography). Later, he took part in various battles under Napoleon, but then came Waterloo. After that, there was not much of an army left and still less for Codazzi to do.

He turned his hand to commerce, but his boat sank in the Mediterranean with all his merchandise on board. Though he miraculously survived, Codazzi was financially ruined. His next endeavor was managing a casino in Constantinople (present-day Istanbul), but soon his passion for exploring overcame him and he took off to wander Europe and, in 1817, the USA.

When Codazzi heard that Bolívar was recruiting foreigners for a new Venezuelan army, he was the first to enroll. However, on his way south he met the French corsair Louis Aury, and together they landed on Old Providence (today Providencia, a Colombian island). From this island, the two adventurers regularly ransacked Spanish galleons, an activity that not only was profitable, but also contributed to the defeat of the Spaniards. Based on the island for three years, Codazzi didn't miss the chance to explore large parts of Nueva Granada (now Colombia), and it was on Providence that he drew his first maps.

Once the Spanish were defeated by Bolívar's troops, there was not much left to ransack. Codazzi returned to his native Lugo to dedicate himself to agriculture, yet before long his adventurous spirit took him back to the New World. Arriving in Cartagena in 1826, he made his way to Bogotá, where he met Bolívar. The Independence hero appreciated his military abilities more than his cartographic skills and sent him to Maracaibo to head the local military post in case the Spanish returned.

Four years later, Gran Colombia split into three separate countries. General José Antonio Páez, the first ruler of independent Venezuela, commissioned Codazzi to draft maps of the country's various regions. The job took him 10 years. Once he completed the work, Codazzi went to Paris,

has more than a dozen hotels and cabañas, and most of them have their own restaurants. Private bath and hot water are the norm in most places, and some also have heated rooms. Some hotels offer full board, which may be convenient but means that you are stuck with the same kitchen for the duration of your stay.

By and large, the accommodations in Colonia Tovar are good and stylish, but it's not cheap by Venezuelan standards. The room rates start at about US$30 double and more often than not are much higher than that.

Hotel Selva Negra (☎ 55 14 15, 55 17 15), near the church, is the oldest and the best-known lodge in town. Opened in 1936, it now has about 40 cabañas of different sizes,

sleeping from two to six guests and costing US$60 for two plus US$12 for each additional person. The old-style restaurant is in the original house.

Cheaper comfortable options include *Hotel Edelweiss* (☎ 55 12 60), *Hotel Kaiserstuhl* (☎ 55 18 10), *Hotel Drei-Tannen* (☎ 55 12 46) and *Hotel Bergland* (☎ 55 12 29). Any of these will cost about US$50 double. For somewhere still cheaper, take a look at *Cabañas Breidenbach* (☎ 55 12 11), *Residencias Baden* (☎ 55 11 51) or *Cabañas Silberbrunnen* (☎ 55 14 90).

Getting There & Away

The usual departure point for Colonia Tovar is Caracas, and the trip requires a change at El Junquito. All carritos to El

Agustín Codazzi

where in 1841 he published the *Atlas Físico y Político de la República de Venezuela* and the corresponding *Resumen de la Geografía de Venezuela*. His work received wide recognition among French scientific circles, and Codazzi was appointed an honorary member of the Académie Royale des Sciences in Paris.

About this time, the Venezuelan government began to look for European migrants eager to settle and work in Venezuela to help revive an economy devastated by the War of Independence. To facilitate the migration, the government proposed that Codazzi devise a colonization plan. First traveling to Venezuela to select a place with acceptable climatic conditions, Codazzi then returned to Europe and collected a group of several hundred German peasants (the nationality he thought was the most adaptable to foreign life), bringing them to Venezuela. After an arduous hike from the coast up the cordillera, they founded Colonia Tovar, in 1843. By then the Venezuelan authorities had lost all enthusiasm for continuing the colonization program, and Codazzi again dedicated himself to mapping.

The coup d'état of 1848, launched by Tadeo Monagas, brought Venezuela to the brink of civil war, and Codazzi fled to Colombia. After arriving in Bogotá in 1849, he was appointed head of the Comisión Corográfica. Over the next 10 years, until his death, he drafted detailed maps, region by region, of six of the eight existing departments of Colombia.

At the beginning, when he had the sponsorship of the government, his work advanced smoothly. Later on, however, internal political strife pushed cartographic concerns aside, and funds were cut off. Personal dedication and enthusiasm alone motivated Codazzi to set off north in order to completely map the two missing coastal provinces. Disillusioned and abandoned, he died of malaria in 1859 in the obscure village of Espíritu Santo (present-day Agustín Codazzi) in northern Colombia. His name and work sank into obscurity for a century.

The man who created Venezuelan and Colombian cartography was forgotten by the two countries. Only over the last few decades has Codazzi finally achieved the recognition he deserves, and his excellent maps have become the pride of national archives in both Colombia and Venezuela.

Junquito (US$1) depart from Esquina San Roque, the corner just south of the Plaza de Toros Nuevo Circo. There are also large buses to El Junquito (US$0.60); they don't have a terminal, but you can catch them on Avenida Lecuna or Avenida Universidad. From El Junquito, por puesto vans take you the remainder of the journey (US$1.20). The whole trip takes about two hours.

If you don't want to go back the same way to Caracas (or want to continue to Maracay or farther west), you can take an exciting ride south down to La Victoria. Over a distance of only 30km, the road descends about 1300m. Por puestos depart regularly from Colonia Tovar (US$2, 1½ hours); grab a seat on the left side for better views.

PARQUE NACIONAL HENRI PITTIER
☎ 043 (☎ 0243 from Apr 21, 2001)

This is Venezuela's oldest national park, created in 1937. It occupies most of the north of Aragua state, stretching from the Caribbean coast in the north almost as far south as the Valencia-Caracas freeway and the city of Maracay. The park was originally named 'Rancho Grande' but was later renamed in honor of the founder of Venezuela's national-park system, Henri Pittier (see the boxed text).

The national park covers 1078 sq km of the Cordillera de la Costa, the coastal mountain range (considered the northern continuation of the great Andean system), which exceeds 2000m in altitude in some of the park's areas. The park's highest point is Pico El Cenizo (2436m). From its east-west ridge, the cordillera rolls dramatically down to the coast to the north, and south to Maracay.

Given the wide range in elevation, the park has a staircase of thermal zones and corresponding strata of vegetation. Going from Maracay northward (ie, upward), you pass through semi-dry deciduous woods to ascend to evergreen rain forest and, farther up, to dense cloud forest. All this is found over a remarkably short distance – it takes just an hour to cover it in a bus or car. Over the crest and descending northward to the

sea, you get the same sequence in reverse, with the difference being that as you approach the coast, you also encounter arid coastal scrub before finally reaching the beaches, mangroves and coconut groves. The descent also takes only an hour or so.

The animal world here is also rich and diverse, including tapirs, deer, pumas, agoutis, peccaries, ocelots, opossums, armadillos, monkeys, snakes, frogs and bats. However, the park is most famous for its birds. About 580 species of birds have been identified in the park, which represents 43% of the bird species found in Venezuela and

PARQUE NACIONAL HENRI PITTIER

7% of all the birds known in the world. Given the small area of the park, it's not a bad total, and hardly any other park of that size in the world can match it.

This diversity is the combined result of the variety of habitats and their unspoiled condition. Additionally, Paso Portachuelo, the lowest pass in the mountain ridge, is on a natural migratory route for birds and insects flying inland from the sea (and back) from such distant places as Argentina and Canada.

Orientation

Two roads, both paved, cross the park from north to south. Both originate in Maracay and go as far as the coast. The western road, the one built by Gómez as an escape route, leads from Maracay to Ocumare de la Costa, and on to El Playón on the beach, and then continues on to Cata; it ascends to 1128m at Paso Portachuelo.

The eastern road heads from Maracay due north to Choroní and reaches the coast 2km farther on, at Puerto Colombia. It's narrower, poorer and more twisting, but it climbs up to 1830m and is more spectacular. Both roads are about 55km long and may occasionally be blocked by landslides, particularly in the rainy season. There's no road connection between the coastal ends of these roads; a boat is the only way to get from one end to the other.

The coast has rocky cliffs in some parts, interspersed with bays filled with coconut groves and bordered by beaches. Some beaches are developed, while others are virtually virgin. The town of Puerto Colombia, at the end of the eastern road, is the major tourist destination on the coast. It offers the widest choice of hotels, restaurants and boat-rental facilities. El Playón, on the western road, is also developing into a popular tourist hangout.

The park has something for nearly everyone, including beachgoers, bird-watchers, hikers, architecture buffs and fiesta lovers. It's good for day trips and longer stays. Unless you are particularly interested in bird-watching in Rancho Grande, it's better to take the eastern road, which provides access to more attractions and leads along a more spectacular route.

Colonial Towns

The coast has been inhabited for centuries, and some colonial towns have survived in the park (correctly speaking, these urban areas have been excluded from the park and are just outside its boundaries). It's interesting to note that all these old towns are set well back from the waterfront; Ocumare de la Costa, Cuyagua, Cata, Choroní and Chuao were all founded several kilometers inland, back from the sea. This was to provide the towns with some protection against the pirates who roamed the coast.

The tiny 385-year-old **Choroní** is the most charming of these towns. It's just a few narrow streets in all, but they are lined with fine pastel houses. Madre María de San José was born in one in 1875 and dedicated her life to the service for the poor. The house where she lived and worked is on the tree-shaded Plaza Bolívar. She later continued her work with the poor in Maracay, where she founded a religious congregation. She died at the respectable age of 92 and was beatified in 1995. See the Maracay section, earlier in this chapter, for a description of her miraculous exhumation.

On Choroní's plaza is a lovely parish church, Iglesia de Santa Clara, with a finely decorated ceiling. The wall over the high altar has been painted to look like a carved retable. The feast of Santa Clara, the patron saint of the town, is celebrated in August.

Puerto Colombia, on the coast just 2km north of Choroní, was that town's port. Over the recent decades, it has developed into the major travelers' haunt in the region. Unlike the sleepy and nostalgic Choroní, Puerto Colombia is full of young crowds, posadas and restaurants. It's an enjoyable enough place to hang around for a while, and a convenient base for excursions, eg, to Chuao.

Chuao, about 8km east of Choroní as the crow flies, is a small old village, well known as a center of cacao plantations. Featuring a very simple colonial church, the village is widely known for its Diablos Danzantes

Henri Pittier

Henri François Pittier Dormond was born in Bex, Switzerland, in 1857. Although he graduated in Sciences and Civil Engineering, it was botany that eventually became his real passion. Attracted by tropical nature, he went to Costa Rica in 1887, where he collected local plants, studied climates and drew maps. His 16-year Costa Rican adventure resulted in the 16,000-sample Herbario Nacional (National Herbarium), representative of about 5000 local plant species.

In 1904 Pittier was contracted by the US government as a botanist for the Agriculture Department. The job featured various research trips to the tropical and subtropical countries of the region, including Mexico, Guatemala, Honduras, Panama and Colombia. Then, in 1917, General Juan Vicente Gómez invited Pittier to Venezuela to organize an experimental station. The visit marked the beginning of Pittier's intense and fruitful career in Venezuela, which encompassed 33 years of his life and ended only with his death in 1950.

Pittier's extensive travels throughout the country resulted in the collection and classification of more than 30,000 specimens of local plants, the basis for the creation of the national herbarium. He was the author of about 160 studies on forests, herbs, fruit and other aspects of botany. Although he was essentially a botanist, his interest and work embraced many other fields, including agriculture, cartography, entomology and, finally, conservation.

Having judged the destruction of the soil and forests in Venezuela to be worse than in any other country he had visited, Pittier was well aware of the necessity for the protection of Venezuela's ecosystems, and he proposed the creation of the national-park system to the government. The struggle took several years, until, in 1937, President Eleázar López Contreras decreed the Parque Nacional Rancho Grande as Venezuela's first national park.

It took another 15 years, until 1952, before the government declared a second protected area, Parque Nacional Sierra Nevada. In 1953, three years after Pittier's death, Rancho Grande was renamed to commemorate the founder of Venezuela's national-park system.

(Dancing Devils) celebrations. (See the boxed text 'Diablos Danzantes' in the San Francisco de Yare section for more information on that festival.) Villagers live in almost complete isolation: The only road is a rough 4km trail between the village and the sea. Access to Chuao is by boat from Puerto Colombia, followed by a walk along the trail.

Other old towns noted for their Diablos Danzantes traditions are **Ocumare de la Costa**, **Cata** and **Cuyagua**, though the celebrations here are not as famous as those in Chuao. All these towns are located in the western, coastal section of the park, and are connected to one another and to Maracay by road.

There was a significant black population in all these towns, and some of their traditions have been preserved to this day. Drums

have been an integral part of life, and they can still be heard all year round on weekend nights and during holidays – particularly during the Fiesta de San Juan on June 23 and 24. The pulsating beat immediately sparks dancing, and the atmosphere is great.

Beaches

For most tourists (particularly Venezuelans), beaches are the principal attraction of the park, and indeed, some of them are really beautiful. Since the coastal bays are relatively small, the beaches are not long, but they are often pretty wide and shaded by coconut palms.

Some beaches are accessible by road, but those are the most popular and crowded, and they are left covered with rubbish on weekends. Other beaches can be reached only by boat; they are usually solitary. Boat business is well developed, and boats can take you to any isolated beach you wish. The charge is by boat, not by passenger, so the fare largely depends on how many people go with you on the trip (the boat's usual capacity is up to 10 passengers). Because the competition between boat operators is fierce, prices are negotiable: Always try to bargain. Puerto Colombia is the busiest tourist-boat hub.

Before you go, decide which road to take, as you have to choose between the beaches of either the Cata or Puerto Colombia areas. Boats can transfer you from Cata to Puerto Colombia or vice versa, but this trip will cost around US$100 per boat.

In the Puerto Colombia area, the most popular beach is **Playa Grande**, a five-minute walk by road east of town. It's about half a kilometer long and is shaded by coconut palms but is littered on weekends. There are several rustic shack restaurants at the entrance to the beach, serving good fried fish. You can camp on the beach or sling your hammock between the palms, but don't leave your stuff unattended.

If Playa Grande is too crowded or littered, go to the undeveloped **Playa El Diario**, on the opposite (western) side of the town. To get there, take the side road, Calle El Cementerio, which branches off midway along the Choroní–Puerto Colombia road, next to a small bridge. The road passes a few hotels before it reaches the cemetery (500m from the turnoff), where the asphalt becomes concrete. Follow the road uphill for 200m and take a path branching off to the left. It climbs a bit, then goes down to the small and shadeless El Diario beach (a 25-minute walk from the cemetery). If you take the concrete road to its end on the mountaintop (crowned with a CANTV communication mast), a 10-minute walk from the cemetery, you'll get sweeping panoramic views.

Other beaches in the area are normally visited by boat, though some of them can also be reached on foot after a long and hot walk. Boats crowd at the river mouth in Puerto Colombia, taking tourists to isolated beaches farther down the coat, including **Playa Aroa** (US$30 roundtrip per boat, 15 minutes one-way), **Playa Valle Seco** (US$30, 20 minutes), **Playa Chuao** (US$35, 30 minutes) and **Playa Cepe** (US$45, 45 minutes). The boat can pick you up at any time. The trip may be quite rough if the waves are high; be prepared to get wet.

In the Cata area, the first beach you can get to by road is **El Playón**, skirting the northern edge of the town of the same name. There are actually several small beaches here, the best of which is probably **Playa Malibú**, close to the Malecón.

Five kilometers eastward is the area's most famous beach, **Playa Cata**, a postcard crescent of sand bordering Bahía de Cata. Unfortunately, two bizarre, ugly apartment towers have been built just next to the beach. There are plenty of rustic restaurants along the beach but no accommodations.

Boats from Playa Cata take tourists to the smaller and quieter **Playa Catita**, on the eastern side of the same bay. It takes 10 minutes to get there, and the ride costs US$1.50 per person. You can also walk there – it takes longer but is worth it for the interesting xerophytic vegetation (ie, plants adapted to thrive in minimal-water conditions) on the way.

Farther east is the unspoiled and usually deserted **Playa Cuyagua**, which is good for surfers. You can get there by a 2.5km sand trail from the town of Cuyagua. Alternatively, boats from Playa Cata can take you to the beach for about US$30 roundtrip.

Estación Biológica Rancho Grande

Far away from the coastal towns and beaches, this biological station is on the Maracay-Cata road, a few hundred meters before the Paso Portachuelo. Surrounded by cloud forest, this station sits at an altitude of 1100m just off the road; a sign directs you to it. It's open for visitors daily from about 7 am to 6 pm, and admission is US$0.50.

The station is accommodated in an intriguing question-mark-shaped building. It was originally destined to be a posh country hotel, commissioned by Juan Vicente Gómez as one of his many grand projects. The building was only half completed by the time Gómez died and it was left by the workers when they heard news of the dictator's death. Two years later, after the national park was founded, Henri Pittier proposed to establish the research station here; his proposal became a reality in the mid-1940s. The station is run by the Faculty of Agriculture of the Universidad Central de Venezuela, based at El Limón, the northwestern outer suburb of Maracay.

An ecological path known as the Sendero Andrew Field has been traced through the forest behind the station, and it's open to the public. The path is named in memory of a young British botanist who lived and studied plants in the park for three years and tragically died here. The loop, which is easily walked in an hour, provides an opportunity to watch the local flora and fauna, particularly birds.

Serious bird-watchers may want to know that it's feasible to see up to 400 species of birds on a weeklong visit to the station. The best times for birds are early in the morning and late in the afternoon. October to November are the best months for viewing migratory birds. You may also see monkeys, agoutis, peccaries, snakes and butterflies.

More adventurous travelers may want to hike to the top of Pico Guacamaya (see Hiking). The station offers simple accommodations, but no food (see Places to Stay & Eat). Remember that it rains quite a lot in the area, so bring along reliable rain gear.

Hiking

There are no trails prepared specifically for tourists, but there are various rough paths, linking villages scattered throughout the area, that are used by locals. Some paths were originally traced centuries ago, but many were abandoned and eventually disappeared when the roads were built.

The area along the coast, where most of the villages are located, offers the best options for walkers and is relatively dry. It is possible, for example, to walk from Puerto Colombia west to Aroa (via Playa El Diario) and east to Chuao.

Various routes lead from the Choroní area to Chuao. One of the trails begins 6km south on the road from Choroní, at the place known as 'El Mamón'; the walk from here to Chuao will take five to seven hours. The route is confusing in parts because of various side paths, so you may want to look for a local guide – see Organized Tours, later.

Farther up the mountains, where virtually no people live, the trails are few and far between. The terrain is covered by thick forest, and rainfall is high. The cordillera's northern slopes receive more rain than the southern ones, and the upper parts are pretty wet most of the year. The driest months are January to March.

The trail going from Turmero, 14km east of Maracay, to Chuao is one of the few trails that traverse the cordillera. It has recently been signposted and is now reasonably easy to follow, though its upper reaches can be very wet and muddy in the rainy season. This hike can be done in two days, but it may run to three.

Beginning from Turmero, take a taxi over the paved road to the ranger's post in Pedregal (US$4). From here, a jeep trail goes northward to another ranger's post, Simón Machado (a five-hour walk), but this one is attended only in the tourist peak season. There's a water tank here and you are allowed to camp, but it's probably safer not to drink the water, and the scenery isn't particularly splendid. The walking trail goes from here up to about 1950m on the crest (a three- to four-hour walk) and descends gradually over the northern slope to the hamlet of El Paraíso (a six-hour walk), where you are likely to see a human being again. The trail continues downhill to Chuao (a 1½-hour walk), from where a 4km dust road (serviced by a few vehicles) goes down to the beach. The trip can also be done in reverse, from Chuao to Turmero.

Another challenging cross-cordillera trail links the Rancho Grande biological station with Cuyagua, but it has become overgrown over the years and is impassable. From the station, you can probably hike only as far as Pico Guacamaya (1828m). The path is faint and easy to lose; it will take you three to four hours uphill. Ask at the station for information and news on the condition of the trail.

Technically speaking, hikers who intend to camp overnight in the park should have an Inparques permit, obtainable at their office in the Maracay zoo (☎ 41 39 33).

Organized Tours

For hikes in the Choroní area (eg, Choroní to Chuao), look for guides in Puerto Colombia, Choroní or one of the small villages up the road. One of the good local guides for walks and bird-watching is the English-speaking Virgilio Espinal, who commonly goes by 'Vivi.' (Contact him at ☎ 91 11 06, 014-463 19 95, vivichoroni@latinmail.com, or just ask locals in Choroní or Puerto Colombia.) Knowledgeable about the park, he operates a mountain refuge known as 'El Cocuy,' near the village of Uraca, that serves as a base for tours ranging from two hours to several days and of any level of difficulty.

Another experienced tour guide, Tulio Reyes, is particularly recommended for the Turmero-Chuao hike. He charges US$110 per person for a three-day all-inclusive trip, providing food and camping equipment plus transfers from Maracay to Pedregal by car and from Chuao to Puerto Colombia by boat. He lives in Cagua, where you can contact him at ☎ 044-95 31 57 or liotu@yahoo.com.

Places to Stay & Eat

Accommodations and food are in good supply in Puerto Colombia and El Playón; both are also available in other localities. The telephone code for the following listings is ☎ 043, the same as Maracay. You can camp at no cost on the beaches, but never leave your tent unattended.

Puerto Colombia This tiny town already has more than two dozen places to stay – everything from rock bottom to luxury – and the number is growing swiftly. Locals also rent out rooms if there's demand. Prices usually rise on weekends and during major holiday periods (Christmas to early January, Carnaval, Holy Week, August). The rates listed in this section are for off-peak times. Restaurants, too, are numerous, so starving is improbable; fried fish is the local staple.

One of the cheapest places to stay is the German-run **Hostal Colonial** (☎ 91 10 87), on Calle Morillo (the main access road) opposite the bus terminus. It has a variety of rooms, some better than others (so check beforehand), but generally they are a reasonable value at US$12 for a matrimonial or double with fan (US$15 with bath as well). Similarly rated is another acceptable German-run place, the **Posada Alfonso** (☎ 91 10 37), about 200m up the same road.

Despite its name, the **Posada Alemania** (☎ 91 10 36), diagonally opposite the Alfonso, is no longer a German affair. It is, however, inexpensive at US$15/24 matrimonial/quad with bath, fan and access to the kitchen. Another budget place, the simple **Posada Los Guanches** (☎ 91 12 09), on Calle Trino Rangel close to the bus terminus, is not a bad value either at US$15/18 matrimonial/triple.

Those prepared to pay a bit more can choose from plenty of places, including some pretty stylish ones. A good example is the cozy and quiet **Posada La Parchita** (☎ 91 12 59), Calle Trino Rangel, which has just five rooms set around a lovely patio and costs US$20 per person, breakfast included. The cheaper **Posada Casablanca** (☎ 91 11 44), on Plaza Bolívar, also has much old colonial charm for US$20/34 matrimonial/double.

Another colonial-style place, **Posada La Montañita** (☎ 91 11 32), on Calle Morillo just off the waterfront, has doubles for US$35 with breakfast. Farther inland on the same street is the marginally cheaper **Posada Don Miguel** (☎ 91 10 81).

Going up the price scale, you can stay in the charming **La Casa de Las García** (☎ 91 10 56), on Calle El Cementerio outside town, for around US$60 double with breakfast. A hundred meters up the road is the beautiful **Hacienda El Portete** (☎ 91 12 55, fax 91 12 73). Established in the meticulously refurbished old colonial mansion, the hotel has its own restaurant and swimming pool. Air-conditioned doubles cost US$50 per person, including breakfast. Another pleasant place with a good swimming pool, **Hostal Piapoco** (☎ 91 12 53), on the main road at the entrance to the town, costs about US$75 double with breakfast.

If you need somewhere upmarket in the town's center, check out *Mesón Xuchitlán* (☎ 91 12 34) and the *Hostal Casagrande* (☎ 91 12 51), both on Calle Morillo near Plaza Bolívar. Both have air-conditioned rooms for about US$90 double with breakfast. Or try the posh, though unmarked, *Posada Humboldt* (☎ 91 10 50; in Caracas ☎ 02-976 22 22), farther inland on the same street. Set in a colonial-style building laid out around a flower-filled courtyard, it is a wonderful place to stay and eat (the food is excellent). Reservations are mandatory.

Budget eating is provided by a cluster of simple restaurants (including *Restaurant Araguaney* and *Tasca Bahía*) near the pedestrian bridge leading to Playa Grande. On Playa Grande itself, there's a colony of rustic restaurants that cook inexpensive meals, mostly fried fish, for US$5 to US$7 per plate.

Choroní An oasis of peace, Choroní is the place to escape the crowds of Puerto Colombia. The town has few tourist facilities apart from two pleasant colonial hotels located on the main street: *Hostería Río Mar* (☎ 91 10 38), which costs US$30 double and has a restaurant (the only reliable place to eat in town); and *Posada Colonial Choroní*, operated by Cacao Expediciones from Caracas (☎ 02-977 12 34), which has just four rooms and costs US$40 per person, breakfast included.

You can also stay in the charming *Hacienda La Aljorra* (☎ 91 12 12), 2km inland from Choroní, on the road to Maracay. It costs much the same as Posada Colonial and has a restaurant.

Chuao The new, simple but neat *Posada Tamaira*, Calle Real, has rooms with bunks and fans (but without private bath) and costs US$6 per person. Meals are available on request.

El Playón The counterpart of the eastern road's Puerto Colombia, El Playón is the major lodging center on the western road, sporting more than a dozen places to stay. The town is much larger than Puerto Colombia, but less attractive. Many places to stay are within two blocks of the waterfront, where tourist life is concentrated.

The simple *Posada Loley* (☎ 93 12 52), on Calle Fuerzas Armadas one block back from the beach, is one of the cheapest options. Doubles/quads with fan and shared bath cost US$15/24, and meals are available for guests.

Set in a pleasant garden facing the beach, *De La Costa Eco-Lodge* (☎ 93 19 86, dlcecolodge@hotmail.com), Calle California, provides reasonable rooms with fan (US$25/30/35 double/triple/quad), cabañas (US$40 for up to eight people), restaurant service, Internet access, boat trips, bike rental, snorkeling and scuba diving.

Also facing the sea, the new *Posada Costa de Oro* (☎ 93 19 57) offers spacious doubles with fan for about US$40 (US$45 with air-con). Try for a room with a good view. Cheaper air-con doubles (US$30) are available at *Hotel Montemar* (☎ 93 11 73), Calle Vargas, but they are smaller and not as good. There are more hotels nearby, similarly priced.

Rancho Grande The biological station has simple dormitory-style lodging facilities, providing about 40 beds. Though intended for visiting researchers, they're hardly ever all taken. Tourists are welcome to stay for US$7 per head (US$4 for students with an ISIC card). No camping is allowed and no food provided, but you can use the kitchen facilities. Bring a sleeping bag, food and a flashlight.

As of late 2000, there were plans to open a large visitors center in the research station building. Critics have already expressed strong anxiety about the possible impact of mass tourism on the fragile ecosystem of the park and the collapse of the station's research functions.

Getting There & Away
The departure point for the park is the Maracay bus terminal. Buses to El Playón (marked 'Ocumare de la Costa') depart every hour from 7 am to 5 pm (US$2, two hours). They can let you off at Rancho

Grande but will charge the full El Playón fare. The last bus back to Maracay departs at 5:30 pm. There are also hourly minibuses from Maracay to El Playón, but they depart from El Limón, not the bus terminal. The advantage is that they run longer, until about 7:30 pm. From El Playón, you can catch a carrito to Playa Cata (US$0.80, 10 minutes).

To Puerto Colombia, buses leave every one or two hours (US$2.50, 2¼ hours). The last bus back to Maracay theoretically departs from Puerto Colombia at 5 pm (later on weekends), but this departure is not reliable.

Carabobo State

VALENCIA
☎ 041 (☎ 0241 from Mar 24, 2001)
Founded in 1555 and named after its mother town in Spain, Valencia is Venezuela's third-largest city (population 980,000), after Caracas and Maracaibo, and the capital of Carabobo state. It's a prosperous, bustling urban sprawl nestled in the north-south valley of the Río Cabriales and bordered by mountains on the north and west. Set at an altitude of 480m, it has an annual average temperature of about 25°C, with hot days ameliorated by the evening breeze that comes down from the mountains.

Much like its Spanish namesake, Valencia is famous nationwide for its oranges. It's also renowned all over Venezuela for its Plaza de Toros Monumental. Capable of seating 27,000 spectators, it's the second-largest bullring in the Americas after the one in Mexico City. Internationally, however, the city isn't at the top of the average traveler's list of not-to-be-missed destinations. However, you may want to stop if you are coming this way, just to have a look some big-city tourist attractions.

History
Valencia has had a tumultuous and checkered history. It had not yet reached its seventh anniversary when Lope de Aguirre, the infamous adventurer obsessed with finding El Dorado, sacked the town and burned it almost to the ground. Twenty years later, the not-yet-fully-recovered town was attacked by Carib Indians, who did much the same as Aguirre. A century later, in 1667, the town was seized and destroyed again, this time by French pirates.

The town's proximity to Lago de Valencia didn't help development either. The disease-breeding marshes brought about smallpox epidemics that decimated the population. Survivors were scared away, and new settlers were few and far between. By the year 1800, ie, after 250 years of existence, Valencia had barely 6000 inhabitants.

In 1812, a devastating earthquake shook the Andean shell all the way from Mérida to Caracas, leaving Valencia – as well as several other large cities, including Barquisimeto, Trujillo, San Felipe, Mérida and Caracas – in ruins yet again. Two years later, the town was besieged by royalist troops under the command of José Tomás Boves (known as 'the Butcher') and taken 17 days later. The ensuing slaughter left 500 people dead, including many innocent inhabitants. For the next seven years, no fewer than two dozen battles were fought around the town. The violence lasted until June 24, 1821, when Bolívar's decisive victory at the battle of Carabobo clinched Venezuela's independence.

The year 1826 saw Valencia becoming the first town to oppose Bolívar's sacred union, Gran Colombia. Its inhabitants called for Venezuela to be declared a sovereign state. Four years later, this demand became a reality, when the Congress convened in Valencia and decreed formal secession from Gran Colombia. At the same time, Congress made Valencia the newborn country's capital. A year later, however, the newly elected government opted to move to Caracas.

Valencia experienced particularly rapid growth after World War II. With the acceleration of industrial development, the town caught the new economic wind in its sails. The Caracas authorities, concerned about over-industrialization of the capital, pushed some industries out of their city, and Valencia,

THE CENTRAL NORTH

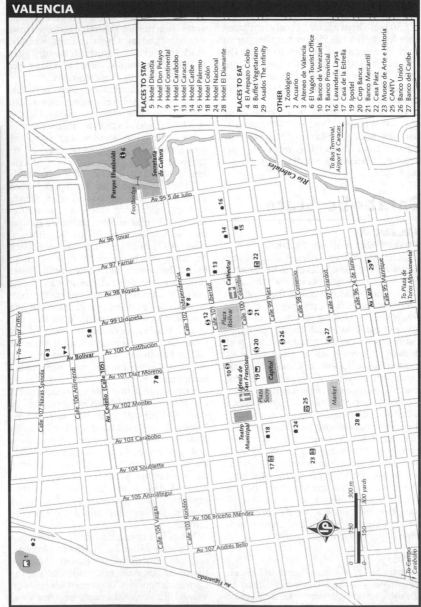

VALENCIA

PLACES TO STAY
5 Hotel Dinastía
7 Hotel Don Pelayo
9 Hotel Continental
11 Hotel Carabobo
13 Hotel Caracas
14 Hotel Caribe
15 Hotel Palermo
18 Hotel Colón
24 Hotel Nacional
28 Hotel El Diamante

PLACES TO EAT
4 El Arepazo Criollo
8 Buffet Vegetariano
29 Asados The Infinity

OTHER
1 Zoológico
2 Acuario
3 Ateneo de Valencia
6 El Vagón Tourist Office
10 Banco de Venezuela
12 Banco Provincial
16 Lavandería Laysa
17 Casa de la Estrella
19 Ipostel
20 Corp Banca
21 Banco Mercantil
22 Casa Páez
23 Museo de Arte e Historia
25 CANTV
26 Banco Unión
27 Banco del Caribe

which already had a good transportation infrastructure and other facilities, was one of the most blessed recipients.

Today, Valencia is Venezuela's most industrialized city (except for heavy industry, which is concentrated in Ciudad Guayana). Home to a thousand companies producing everything from pots to cars, the city generates nearly a quarter of the country's national manufacturing production and is justifiably called the 'Manufacturing Capital of Venezuela.' It is also the center of the most developed agricultural region, endowed with fertile soil and a favorable climate.

Information

Tourist Offices The main office, Dirección General de Turismo (☎ 25 70 64), is in Torre Venezuela, Piso 6, Avenida Bolívar Norte, about 3.5km north of Plaza Bolívar. The office is open 8 am to noon and 2 to 5 pm weekdays. There is an outlet, the Módulo de Información Turística El Vagón (same hours), in one of the old train carriages in Parque Humboldt (popularly known as Parque Los Enanitos), in the city center. The carriages and the former train station are relics of the railway built by the Germans in 1894 that provided service to Caracas until the 1960s. Dazzled by cars and freeways, Venezuelans have abandoned passenger-train transportation altogether.

Money Corp Banca exchanges American Express traveler's checks. Other banks on the map are useful for cash advances on Visa and MasterCard. For changing cash, Italcambio (☎ 21 81 73) is one of the very few casas de cambio; it's in Edificio Talía, Local 12, Avenida Bolívar Norte, Urbanización Los Sauces, about 2km north of Plaza Bolívar.

Laundry There are a few launderettes in the city center, including Lavandería Laysa, Calle Colombia No 95-48.

Plaza Bolívar

The heart of the historic town, the plaza boasts the inevitable monument to Bolívar in the middle. However, unlike the dozens of equestrian statues (often replicas of the Caracas monument) throughout the country, this one comes as a certain novelty. The bronze figure of Bolívar, pointing toward Campo Carabobo, stands on a 10m-high white Italian marble column cut from one block of stone. The monument was unveiled in 1889.

Catedral

The cathedral, on the eastern side of the plaza, is reputedly 420 years old, but it has experienced so many alterations in its history that today it's an eclectic hodgepodge of styles. In the most recent restoration, carried out in the early 1950s for the city's 400th anniversary, the ceiling was altered to resemble a wedding cake.

The cathedral's most revered treasure, the figure of Nuestra Señora del Socorro, is kept in the chapel in the left transept. Carved in the late 16th century, the sorrowful Virgin in black was the first statue in Venezuela to be crowned (in 1910) by Rome. The crown on her head is a replica – the original gold crown is encrusted with numerous precious stones and is stored in a safe. It is taken out of storage only for very special celebrations.

The two large paintings, *The Last Supper* and *The Entry into Jerusalem,* that hang opposite one another on the chapel's side walls are the work of Antonio Herrera Toro, a Valencia-born artist who left a number of murals and paintings in local churches and public buildings. Having studied in Rome, he was strongly influenced by the great masters of the Italian Renaissance.

Casa Páez

This large historic mansion, on the corner of Calle Páez and Avenida Boyacá, is the former home of Venezuela's first president, General José Antonio Páez. He distinguished himself by forging a formidable army of *llaneros* (plainsmen) who fought under Bolívar on numerous fronts, contributing greatly to the achievement of independence. In 1830, on the day Venezuela split from Gran Colombia, Páez took power as the first acting president of the newborn

General José Antonio Páez

sovereignty and established his residence in the new capital. A year later, Páez was elected president of the republic and moved with the government to Caracas.

Restored and furnished with period fittings, the house is today a museum, open 9 am to noon and 3 to 5:30 pm Tuesday to Friday, 9 am to 2 pm weekends. The walls of the cloister lining the lovely central patio are graced with murals depicting the nine battles the general fought. The work was done by Pedro Castillo and supposedly directed by Páez himself.

Capitol

Built in 1772 as a convent, this large building takes up half a block. It became the government house a century later, after Guzmán Blanco expelled the former occupants, as he did with many other religious institutions throughout the country. Part of it is open to visitors from 8 am to 4 pm on weekends; you'll be shown around some of the formal rooms, including the Salón Bolívar assembly hall, which boasts the famous portrait by Arturo Michelena of Bolívar mounted on his horse.

Teatro Municipal

Modeled on the Paris Opera House and inaugurated in 1894, the theater was thoroughly renovated in the 1970s. The ceiling of its 640-seat auditorium was painted by Antonio Herrera Toro in 1892 ; it depicts famous men of music and literature, including Rossini, Goethe, Shakespeare and Beethoven. If you want to see it during the day, enter through the back door (from Calle Libertad), which leads directly onto the stage; the guards should let you in.

Museo de Arte e Historia

The museum is accommodated in the Casa de los Celis, one of the most beautiful colonial mansions in the city, built in the 1760s and named after one of its owners, Colonel Pedro Celis. It closed for renovation in 1997 but should be open again by the time you read this. Planned sections include anthropology, colonial art and the city's founding, plus rooms dedicated to Antonio Herrera Toro (1857–1914) and Andrés Pérez Mujica (1873–1920), both artists born in Valencia.

Casa de la Estrella

In this building, the sovereign state of Venezuela was born on May 6, 1830, after Congress convened here and decreed secession from Gran Colombia. Erected as a hospital around 1710 (thus being the city's oldest existing house), the building underwent interior remodeling soon after independence to accommodate a college, which later became the Universidad de Valencia. Extensively restored over recent years, the Casa opened in 1999 as a museum (open 9 am to 5 pm weekdays, 10 am to 5 pm weekends). You'll de guided around the interior, though there's not much in the way of exhibits as yet, save for a brief history of Valencia's past posted on boards and a 15-minute video on the history of the house.

Museo de la Ciudad

Also opened in 1999, this museum is in the 19th-century palacelike Quinta La Isabela, better known as the Palacio de los Iturriza, on the corner of Calle Rojas Queipo and Avenida Paseo Cabriales, about 1.5km north of the center. The museum is dedicated to the city's history, but again, there's still not that much to see here, except for the fine historic interior of the palace. Its opening hours are the same as those of the Casa de la Estrella (see above).

Acuario & Zoológico

The aquarium and zoo are apparently the favorite attractions for local inhabitants. The stars of the aquarium are the *toninas*, or freshwater dolphins, kept in a large central pool. Feeding and shows are at 10 am and 2 and 4:30 pm Tuesday to Friday, and 11 am and 1, 3 and 5 pm weekends. Next to the pool is the aquarium-terrarium, which has a good collection of Venezuelan freshwater fish and snakes, including electric eels, piranhas and anacondas.

Beyond the aquarium is the small zoo, featuring some of Venezuela's typical animal species, including the jaguar, tapir, Orinoco caiman, turtles and a variety of birds.

Both the aquarium and zoo are open 9 am to 6 pm Tuesday to Sunday (they may also open Monday in August); the combined entry ticket costs US$1.50.

Special Events

The two major local events are Semana de Valencia, in late March, and the Fiestas Patronales de Nuestra Señora del Socorro, in mid-November. The former features cultural events, an agricultural fair, parades, bullfights etc. The latter is a religious feast in honor of the city's patron saint, in which the crowned Virgin is taken out of the church and paraded in a procession.

In October of every year, the prestigious Salón Arturo Michelena opens in the Ateneo de Valencia and goes on for three months until January. This is Venezuela's oldest visual-arts show, held every year since 1943. It presents a variety of styles and forms, including painting, sculpture, performance, video and installations.

Places to Stay

The cheapest accommodations are concentrated a few blocks east of Plaza Bolívar, but the hotels there are basic and do a lot of business renting rooms by the hour. The area itself is unpleasant and can be unsafe at night.

All the hotels included in this section feature private baths.

The conveniently located *Hotel Caracas* (☎ 57 18 49, Avenida Boyacá No 100-84), just behind the cathedral, is perhaps the best budget choice in this part of the center. It is reasonably clean and well kept and has spacious matrimoniales/doubles with fan for US$12/16. Other cheapies in the area include *Hotel Continental* (☎ 57 10 04, Avenida Boyacá No 101-70), *Hotel Caribe* (☎ 57 11 57, Calle Colombia No 96-68), and the cheapest, very basic *Hotel Palermo* (☎ 58 60 66, Calle Colombia No 96-39).

The area west of Plaza Bolívar seems to be marginally safer, but don't venture here at night either. There are some cheapies here as well, of which the *Hotel Nacional* (☎ 58 36 76, Calle Páez No 103-51) is a bit better than its neighbors. It costs US$12/18 matrimonial/double with fan, US$18/22 with air-conditioning. You may also check the nearby *Hotel Colón* (☎ 57 71 05, Calle Colombia No 103-37), though it doesn't look better despite its higher prices.

The ideally located *Hotel Carabobo* (☎ 58 88 60, 58 44 67, Calle Libertad No 100-37), just off Plaza Bolívar, passed its best days long ago and is in urgent need of renovation. However, it may still be worth US$30/34 for a large air-con double/triple. A better central option, though not as well positioned, is *Hotel El Diamante* (☎ 58 15 95, 58 83 64), on Avenida Carabobo, which is neat and well kept and costs US$32/40 matrimonial/double.

Top-end accommodations in the city center are represented by the modern highrise *Hotel Don Pelayo* (☎ 57 92 22, 57 93 52), on the corner of Avenida Díaz Moreno and Calle Rondón, and *Hotel Dinastía* (☎ 58 26 59, 58 18 78), on the corner of Avenidas Urdaneta and Cedeño. Either will charge about US$56/60/64 single/double/triple.

Other mid-range and top-end hotels are stranded away from the city center. Some of the cheapest, such as the *Hotel Le Paris* (☎ 21 67 51) or *Hotel Excelsior* (☎ 21 40 55), are on Avenida Bolívar Norte. They have air-conditioned rooms and don't cost much (roughly US$30/40 double/triple) but are otherwise nothing special.

Far better is ***Stauffer Hotel*** *(☎ 23 40 22, 23 66 63)*, on Avenida Bolívar Norte near the tourist office. Decent doubles with breakfast will cost around US$100.

The poshest place in town is the expensive five-star ***Hotel Inter-Continental Valencia*** *(☎ 24 70 70, 20 31 00)*, Calle Juan Uslar, Urbanización La Viña, about 4km north of the city center.

Places to Eat

The center is OK for cheap eating but not so good for quality dining. Plenty of budget eateries line the back streets, particularly in the area around basic hotels. These places serve set lunches for about US$3 to US$4. Restaurants tend to close by 8 pm, except for the *tascas* (restaurant-bars), which by that time turn into drinking venues.

Hotel Nacional and ***Hotel Colón*** both have reasonably priced restaurants; the former is cheaper and serves an inexpensive *menu del día* (daily menu) at lunchtime.

For vegetarians, the best budget option in the center is ***Buffet Vegetariano***, on the corner of Calle Independencia and Avenida Urdaneta. It offers hearty set meals for US$3 plus a variety of salads. It's open at lunchtime only, Monday to Saturday.

Asados The Infinity, Avenida Lara, is one of the central outlets for chicken, parrillas, churrasco etc. ***El Arepazo Criollo***, Avenida Bolívar, has a range of arepas and is open around the clock. ***Hotel Don Pelayo*** has a reasonably priced restaurant.

A better area for dining out is north of the center. There are plenty of restaurants on Avenida Bolívar Norte, including ***Marisquería El Marchica*** (seafood), ***La Trattoria Romana*** (Italian), ***La Villa de Madrid*** (Spanish) and ***El Regio*** (international). There's also a good choice of places to eat in El Viñedo, the area between Avenidas Sanda and Monseñor Adam to the west of Avenida Bolívar, about 2.5km north of the center. El Viñedo has become one of Valen-

cia's trendiest spots, packed with restaurants, cafés and bars that draw in some of the more affluent local folks, particularly on weekend evenings.

Getting There & Away

Air The airport is about 7km southeast of the city center; a taxi from the center costs around US$7. There are direct flights to Caracas (US$74), from where you can continue to anywhere around the country. Sample domestic destinations and fares from Valencia are: Barcelona, US$97; Maracaibo, US$118; and Porlamar, US$101.

Bus The bus terminal is about 4km northeast of the city center, in the Disneyland-style Big Low Center, and is easily accessible by frequent local buses; alternatively, take a taxi for US$4. The terminal is large and well organized and has a lot of facilities, including restaurants and snack bars.

Buses run regularly to most major cities. To Caracas, ordinary buses depart every 15 minutes or so (US$3, 1½ hours); there are also frequent services to Maracay (US$1, one hour). Half-hourly ordinary buses run to Puerto Cabello (US$1.25, 50 minutes), Tucacas (US$2.50, two hours) and Coro (US$8, five hours). Hourly ordinary buses run to Barquisimeto (US$4.50, three hours) and Chichiriviche (US$3.50, 2½ hours).

A number of buses depart (mostly in the evening) to more distant destinations, including Maracaibo (US$16, eight hours), San Cristóbal (US$20, 10½ hours), San Antonio del Táchira (US$22, 11½ hours) and Mérida (US$20, 10 hours). All these fares are for air-conditioned buses; the ordinary service, available on some routes, is about 25% cheaper.

There are half a dozen buses a day to San Fernando de Apure (US$7/10 ordinary/deluxe, eight hours), where you can change for the bus to Puerto Ayacucho.

CAMPO CARABOBO

The Carabobo Battlefield is the site of the great battle fought on June 24, 1821, in which Bolívar's troops defeated the Spanish

Pico Bolívar from a distance

The twisting streets of Jajó

Juan Félix Sánchez's chapel and grave, San Rafael

Mérida's thrilling *teleférico*

The cathedral in the clouds, Mérida

Santuario de La Virgen de Coromoto, inside…

…and out, near Guanare

royalist army. Bolívar's regiments were strengthened by the lancers of General Páez and the British legionnaires, and thanks to these two assisting forces, El Libertador was able to win the battle. A milestone in Latin American history, the victory effectively sealed Venezuela's independence. To commemorate the event, a complex of monuments has been erected on the site where the battle took place.

Things to See

The approach is by a wide entrance road, which turns into the **Paseo de los Héroes**, a formal promenade lined with bronze busts of the battle heroes. The promenade leads to the huge **Arco de Triunfo** (Triumphal Arch) and the **Tumba del Soldado Desconocido** (Tomb of the Unknown Soldier) beneath it. Two soldiers guard the tomb; their gala period uniforms seem more suitable for a Siberian winter than for the baking sun of Carabobo. Fortunately for them, the changing of the guard takes place every two hours.

A hundred meters beyond the arch is the **Altar de la Patria**, an impressive, massive monument, no doubt the largest in Venezuela. Designed by a Spanish sculptor, Antonio Rodríguez del Villar, and revealed in 1930, the monument depicts the main heroes and allegorical figures, all fashioned in stone and bronze. On the top is — you guessed it – an equestrian statue of Bolívar.

About 1km to the west is the **Mirador**, a viewpoint from which Bolívar commanded the battle. It houses a large model of the battlefield and provides a panoramic view over the whole site. The diorama cubicle, to the right of the access road, seems to have closed down.

Getting There & Away

The battleground is 32km southwest of Valencia, on the road to San Carlos. Frequent suburban buses (helpfully marked 'Campo Carabobo') go from Valencia to the battlefield. In Valencia, they go east along Calle Comercio and turn south onto Avenida Carabobo; catch them on either of these streets, eg, at the door of CANTV. They will leave you in Carabobo, at the end of the entrance road. The trip takes an hour and costs US$0.50 one-way.

PARQUE ARQUEOLÓGICO PIEDRA PINTADA

There are several petroglyphs in Carabobo state, the largest group of which is at the site known as Piedra Pintada, 22km northeast of Valencia, near the village of Tronconero. The place must have been an important ritual center for some pre-Hispanic communities, for they left behind a number of glyphs on the rocks, the age of which is still a matter of discussion.

Also referred to as the 'Cerro Pintado,' the place features dozens of weathered rocks and slabs scattered over a grassy slope. Many of the stones bear shallow engravings of mysterious designs and figures. Farther on, there's a group of upright megalithic stones.

The site, which was made an archeological park in 1996, is open to visitors 9 am to 5 pm weekdays, 10 am to 5 pm weekends. The 12-hectare park is well maintained and has a small museum.

Getting There & Away

To get to the park from Valencia, take the Maracay bus from the terminal and get off at Guacara, 13km east of Valencia (ask the driver to drop you off at the *puente de Guacara*). Go down the bridge and wave down the buseta that's marked 'Hospital-Tronconero,' which will bring you close to the Parque Arqueológico. Get off at the end of the line and walk for 10 minutes, following signs.

LAS TRINCHERAS
☎ 041 (☎ 0241 from Mar 24, 2001)

The village of Las Trincheras (population 3000), 18km north of Valencia, is noted for its hot springs. At about 92°C, the springs are reputedly the second-hottest in the world, and they are also widely acclaimed for their curative powers. A large bath complex, the Centro Termal Las Trincheras, has been built at the site; it includes a hotel, restaurant, baths, mud bath and sauna.

Known for centuries, the springs have attracted a number of explorers and naturalists, among them Alexander von Humboldt, who successfully used them to boil eggs in four minutes. In 1889, thermal baths were built that included a hotel and pools. The original hotel was reconstructed by General Gómez, who used to come here frequently. In 1980, the old hotel was restored, a new one constructed beside it, and the pools largely remodeled. There are now three pools with temperatures ranging from 36°C to 42°C, as well as a mud bath.

The springs are renowned for their therapeutic properties, recommended for the treatment of a variety of ailments, including rheumatic, digestive, respiratory and allergic problems. They are also useful for losing weight, making the skin feel fresh and smooth, and helping with general relaxation.

You can either come to the baths for the day (open daily 7 am to 10 pm, mud bath until 6 pm only, entrance fee US$5) or stay in the hotel, using the baths and other facilities at no extra cost. The hotel has its own pool for exclusive use by guests.

Places to Stay & Eat
Centro Termal Las Trincheras (☎ 91 00 03, 91 00 04) offers comfortable air-conditioned singles/doubles/triples for US$28/35/40 and suites for US$45 to US$75. The price includes use of the baths, sauna and other facilities. The restaurant offers breakfast, lunch and dinner for both hotel guests and day visitors.

It's usually easy to get a room during the week, but on weekends the hotel tends to fill up. Advance booking is available either directly or through the hotel's Caracas office (☎ 02-661 37 24, 661 27 03), Edificio Carini, Piso Bajo, Local A, Avenida Alma Mater, Los Chaguaramos.

Opposite the entrance to the baths complex is **Hotel Turístico El Bosque**, which has doubles/triples for US$18/24. It runs its own restaurant, which serves Venezuelan and European cuisine. The hotel price does not include entrance to the baths.

Getting There & Away
There are city buses from Valencia to Las Trincheras; catch them on Avenida Bolívar, north of Avenida Cedeño. They go by the old Valencia–Puerto Cabello road and deposit you at the entrance to the baths. The trip takes half an hour to one hour and costs US$0.50.

You can also get to the baths from the Valencia bus terminal by catching any of the frequent buses to Puerto Cabello. These buses go via the *autopista* (freeway) and charge the full fare to Puerto Cabello (US$1.25) but take only 20 minutes to get to Las Trincheras. They will put you down off the autopista, which is a 10-minute walk from the baths.

If you want to continue on from Las Trincheras north to Puerto Cabello, Tucacas or Chichiriviche, wave down the appropriate bus on the autopista.

PUERTO CABELLO
☎ 042 (☎ 0242 from Mar 24, 2001)
Somewhere around the mid-16th century, Puerto Cabello began life as a simple wharf built on the bank of an ample coastal lagoon. The site was a perfect natural anchorage: It provided protection from winds and waves and was connected with the open sea by a convenient strait. In fact, there was hardly a better place for a port on the Venezuelan coast.

During the 17th century, the port grew on a busy contraband trade – mostly dealing in cacao – with Curaçao. At that time, it was under Dutch control. It wasn't until 1730 that the Spanish took over the port, after the Real Compañía Guipuzcoana had moved in. The company built warehouses and wharves, plus an array of forts to protect the harbor. By the 1770s, Puerto Cabello came to be the most heavily fortified town on Venezuela's coast. Two forts remain from that period.

During the War of Independence, Puerto Cabello became an important royalist stronghold from which attacks were launched against Bolívar's troops. After losing the battle of Carabobo, the Spanish retreated to Puerto Cabello and kept it until

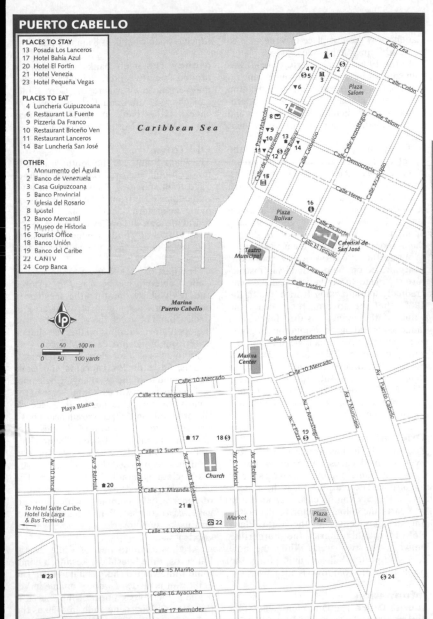

PUERTO CABELLO

PLACES TO STAY
13 Posada Los Lanceros
17 Hotel Bahía Azul
20 Hotel El Fortín
21 Hotel Venezia
23 Hotel Pequeña Vegas

PLACES TO EAT
4   Lunchería Guipuzcoana
6   Restaurant La Fuente
9   Pizzería Da Franco
10 Restaurant Briceño Ven
11 Restaurant Lanceros
14 Bar Lunchería San José

OTHER
1   Monumento del Águila
2   Banco de Venezuela
3   Casa Guipuzcoana
5   Banco Provincial
7   Iglesia del Rosario
8   Ipostel
12 Banco Mercantil
15 Museo de Historia
16 Tourist Office
18 Banco Unión
19 Banco del Caribe
22 CANTV
24 Corp Banca

Caribbean Sea

Calle Zea
Calle Colón
Plaza Salom
Calle Salom
Calle Anzoátegui
Calle Comercio
Calle Bolívar
Paseo Malecón
Calle de los Lanceros
Calle M Lindoño
Calle Democracia
Calle Heres
Plaza Bolívar
Calle R Caurín
Catedral de San José
Calle El Templo
Teatro Municipal
Calle Girardot
Calle Ustáriz

Marina Puerto Cabello

THE CENTRAL NORTH

0   50   100 m
0   50   100 yards

Calle 9 Independencia
Marina Center
Calle 10 Mercado
Calle 10 Mercado
Av J Puerto Cabello
Calle 11 Campo Elías
Av 2 Municipio
Playa Blanca
Av 3 Anzoátegui
Av 4 Páez
Av 5 Bolívar
Av 6 Valencia
Av 7 Santa Bárbara
Av 8 Carabobo
Av 9 Bahruñ
Av 10 Juncal
Calle 12 Sucre
Church
Calle 13 Miranda
To Hotel Suite Caribe,
Hotel Isla Larga
& Bus Terminal
Calle 14 Urdaneta
Market
Plaza Páez
Calle 15 Mariño
Calle 16 Ayacucho
Calle 17 Bermúdez

November 7, 1823, when they surrendered the town to General Páez. Thus, Puerto Cabello was the last place in Venezuela to be freed from Spanish rule.

In the 19th century, Puerto Cabello was Venezuela's busiest port, through which a good deal of cacao, coffee, indigo and cotton was shipped abroad. The port was modernized during the dictatorships of Gómez and Pérez Jiménez, and again over recent decades.

Today the port handles 65% of the country's import and export cargo (except oil) and boasts the best natural conditions and technical facilities of all Venezuelan ports. Occupying an area of 200 hectares, it features 150,000 inhabitants, 34 docks, a shipyard with a dry dock, large warehouses and extensive space for containers. Part of the harbor is occupied by the naval base.

While the attention of governors was concentrated on the port and its infrastructure, the old town was largely neglected and gradually fell into ruins. It wasn't until the 1980s that the government realized the value of the town's historic fabric and launched an extensive restoration program. Some streets have already been restored – with quite remarkable results – and work on others is in progress. Although there's still a long way to go, it's already worth seeing. You can also visit the attractive surrounding area, including beaches to the east and lush forests to the south.

Orientation

Puerto Cabello has grown considerably over recent decades, stretching westward for about 7km along the freeway, as far as the airport. The central area, at the eastern end of the city, can be clearly divided into two parts: the colonial sector, to the north, and the new center, to the south. Plaza Bolívar roughly marks the borderline between the two areas. While the new center is pretty dull and uninspiring, the partly renovated old town is attractive.

Information

Tourist Office The Dirección General de Turismo (☎ 61 39 21, 61 46 22, fax 61 32 55) is in the Edificio Gobierno de Carabobo, Calle Ricaurte, facing Plaza Bolívar. The office is open weekdays 8 am to 5 pm.

Money The main banks are scattered around the city center, including the colonial sector. As elsewhere, the Corp Banca can change American Express traveler's checks. Other banks marked on the map handle Visa and MasterCard cash advances.

Old Town

The **Plaza Bolívar**, at the southern edge of the colonial sector, boasts yet another equestrian statue of Bolívar. The massive, odd edifice built from coral rock and occupying the eastern side of the plaza is the **Catedral de San José**. It was begun in the mid-19th century and completed only some 100 years later, when the bell tower was added.

The part of the old town to the west of Calle Comercio has been largely restored and revived by painting the facades in bright colors. It's now a pleasant area to stroll around or watch the world go by from the open-air restaurants on the tree-shaded waterfront boulevard, **Paseo Malecón**.

Don't miss walking along the two historic streets, **Calle de los Lanceros** and **Calle Bolívar**, and note the overhanging balconies and massive doorways adorning some of the houses, including the fair-sized **Museo de Historia**. Built in 1790 as a residence, it has a graceful internal patio and facades over both streets; the blue balcony facing Calle Bolívar is particularly impressive. The museum has been closed since the early 1990s; it's unclear whether it will reopen. The building is now occupied by an association of local artists, complete with their art gallery. Do go inside to have a look around, and make sure to go up to the tower for good views.

At the northern end of Calle de los Lanceros is the **Iglesia del Rosario**, a handsome whitewashed church built in 1780. The bell tower is made of wood – unique in Venezuela. One block north of the church is the **Casa Guipuzcoana**, built in 1730 as the office for the Compañía Guipuzcoana.

Today it's a public library that you can enter and look around.

The library faces a triangular square with the **Monumento del Águila** (Eagle Monument) in the middle. The monument, a tall column topped by a condor rather than an eagle, was erected in 1896 to the memory of North Americans who gave their lives for Venezuelan independence. Recruited by Francisco de Miranda, in 1806 they sailed from New York to Ocumare de la Costa, north of Maracay. Upon dropping anchor, however, two boats with Americans aboard were surprised and captured by Spanish guard boats. Ten officers were hanged, and the remaining 50-odd recruits were sent to prison. Miranda arrived in Coro a few months later with new recruits, but this expedition proved a failure as well.

Spanish Forts

North of the old town, separated from it by the entrance channel to the harbor, is Fortín San Felipe, later renamed **Castillo Libertador** and commonly referred to as such. The fort was constructed in the 1730s by the Compañía Guipuzcoana to protect the port and warehouses. During the War of Independence, the fort was for a time in the patriots' hands, serving as the ammunition depot, but it was lost to the royalists in 1812. Francisco de Miranda was jailed here before the Spanish sent him to prison in Spain. The fort was recovered in 1823 after the eventual surrender of the royalists, and it subsequently served the Venezuelan army. General Gómez used the fort as a jail, mostly for political prisoners. Upon Gómez' death in 1935, the prison closed down and 14 tons of chains and leg irons were thrown into the sea.

The fort is within the naval base, which once operated a free boat across the channel, ferrying tourists there and back, but this service has been suspended (it may open in the future). Ask at the tourist office, which may help you arrange the visit.

On the 100m-high hill to the south of the city sits the **Fortín Solano** (another fort of the Guipuzcoana company), built in the 1760s to provide security for its commercial operations. Reputedly the last colonial fort built in Venezuela, it commands excellent views of the city and the harbor. The road to the fort branches off from the road to San Esteban on the outskirts of Puerto Cabello. Hence, you can easily combine a visit to the fort with the trip to San Esteban. Even if you want to visit only the fort, take a San Esteban carrito to the turnoff to avoid walking through a shabby barrio on the way.

Places to Stay

Budget accommodations in town are poor and overpriced. Most hotels double as basic love hotels, and there are a number of shady whorehouses (this is a port, after all). One of the cheapest acceptable places is the Italian-run **Hotel Venezia** (☎ 61 43 80), Avenida Santa Bárbara. It costs about US$10/12/16 for a small, simple single/double/triple with fan but no private bath, and US$18/24 for a larger matrimonial/double with bath and air-conditioning.

Better is the nearby **Hotel Bahía Azul** (☎ 61 40 34), Avenida Santa Bárbara, which has neat air-conditioned matrimoniales/doubles with bath for US$28/32. Cheaper but perhaps not as good is **Hotel El Fortín** (☎ 61 24 27), on Calle Miranda in the same area, which will set you back US$22/28/34 for a matrimonial/double/triple.

The **Hotel Pequeña Vegas** (☎ 61 23 80, 61 57 69), Calle Mariño, looks more attractive from the outside than it really is. Its dim rooms cost much the same as those in El Fortín. The best option in the area is probably **Hotel Isla Larga** (☎ 61 37 41, 61 32 90, fax 61 44 16), Calle Miranda, close to the bus terminal. It offers air-conditioned matrimoniales/doubles for US$45/50.

So far, the colonial sector has not a single hotel, but this may change. **Posada Los Lanceros** (☎ 62 08 92), in a colonial house on Calle Bolívar, was being furnished at the time of writing and may be open before you read this. It's supposed to be a budget place – check when you come.

If you need somewhere upmarket, try **Hotel Suite Caribe** (☎ 64 34 54, 64 26 21, fax 64 39 10), on the freeway, 5km west of the city center (2km east of the airport). It provides air-conditioned rooms with bath and TV (US$70 double), plus its own restaurant, a swimming pool, gym and sauna.

Places to Eat

There's a growing number of food outlets in the colonial sector, most of which are on or just off Paseo Malecón. The cheapest places in the area include the unpretentious *Lunchería Guipuzcoana*, opposite the Monumento del Águila, and *Bar Lunchería San José*, on Calle Bolívar. Both close early.

Pizzería Da Franco, on Paseo Malecón, serves more than just pizzas. Featuring outdoor tables, it's a pleasant and inexpensive place that stays open until 11 pm. Other good, slightly more expensive places on Paseo Malecón include *Restaurant Briceño Ven*, *Restaurant La Fuente* and *Restaurant Lanceros*.

Getting There & Away

Air The airport is 7km west of Puerto Cabello, next to the freeway, but it is of little interest, as there are no scheduled flights.

Bus The bus terminal is on Calle Urdaneta, about 800m west of Avenida Bolívar. Frequent carritos run between the terminal and the center, but you can walk the distance in 10 minutes. If you do decide to walk, never go via the Playa Blanca beach, even though it seems to be a considerable shortcut. It's notorious for the armed robbery of tourists, especially due north of the bus terminal.

Buses depart every 15 minutes to Valencia (US$1.25, 50 minutes), where you change for equally frequent buses to Caracas. There are also regular buses to Tucacas (US$1.25, 1¼ hours) and San Felipe (US$2, 1¾ hours), and less frequent departures to Chichiriviche (US$2, 1¾ hours) and Barquisimeto (US$3.50, three hours). For transportation to the nearby beaches and San Esteban, see the following Around Puerto Cabello section.

Train Puerto Cabello is the terminus of the railway line to Barquisimeto, but it now only handles freight transportation; the passenger service was suppressed in the mid-1990s, and it's unclear when, if ever, passenger service will resume.

AROUND PUERTO CABELLO
Beaches

Several beaches lie to the east of Puerto Cabello, off the road to Patanemo. First comes **Balneario Quizandal**, about 7km by road from the city. This beach is quite developed, with a parking lot, showers, restaurants and a drive-in cinema.

From the beach, boats can take you to **Isla Larga**, an island popular with beachgoers, swimmers and snorkelers. There are two wrecks near the island, a bonus attraction for snorkelers and scuba divers. Several food stalls will be more than happy to stuff you with fish (open weekends and sometimes weekdays as well). Take good sun protection, as there is no shade on the island. On weekends, which feature many holidaymakers, the two-way boat trip will cost US$4 per person, but during the week you'll probably have to pay the fare for the whole boat: US$25 roundtrip (negotiable).

The next exit off the Patanemo road, 1km beyond the one to Quizandal, leads to the small **Playa Huequito**. In the same place, another road branches off to the right and heads south to **Borburata**, the oldest town in Carabobo, founded in 1548. The town is widely known for its Fiestas de San Juan (June 23–24) and San Pedro (June 28). Borburata has some budget places to stay and eat, including *Posada de Mi Tío*.

Back on the main road and continuing eastward for about 1.5km from the junction, the Patanemo road brings you to the village known as **Rincón del Pirata**. This is the only place where the road runs close to the coast, but the area is unappealing and the beach poor.

From this point, the road winds up a hill, then descends to yet another turnoff (6km beyond Rincón), which leads 1.5km to **Playa Patanemo**. This is the best beach in the area, wide and shaded by coconut palms. It's full of holidaymakers on weekends but fairly solitary on weekdays. It's now lined with 33 food outlets, including some more-permanent *churuata*-style (thatched hut)

AROUND PUERTO CABELLO

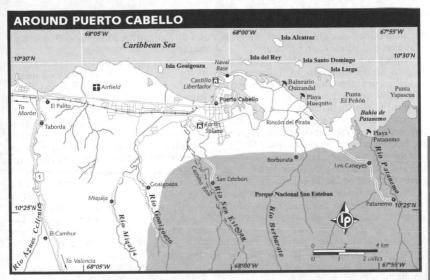

restaurants with their owners residing on site; these open daily. You can pitch your tent anywhere amid the palms, but it may be safer to camp next to one of the restaurants. There are mosquitoes at times – come prepared.

At the turnoff to the Patanemo beach is the pleasant *Campamento Turístico La Churuata* (014-949 92 09), which offers cabañas (US$24/30 matrimonial/triple with bath and fan, US$38/45 with air-con) and its own restaurant.

Shortly beyond the turnoff, the road enters the village of **Los Caneyes**, which hosts several places to stay. First comes the small and styleless *Posada Natal Mar* (☎ 014-943 23 50), just 300m past La Churuata, with a few air-con matrimoniales for US$24 each. About 400m down the road you'll find the charming if unkempt *La Fortaleza* (☎ 014-946 75 76), with two large basic cabañas (US$70/90 for up to six/eight persons) set in a vast garden. Another 200m farther down the road is *Casa de Playa El Eden* (☎ 016-442 49 55), which has rooms for up to four guests (US$40 double plus US$8 each additional person), some more

comfortable (and expensive) suites and a restaurant for guests.

The road continues 1.5km to the village of **Patanemo**, noted for the Diablos Danzantes celebrations on Corpus Christi (see San Francisco de Yare, earlier in this chapter) and for drumbeats on Fiesta de San Juan (June 23–24). At the entrance to Patanemo is the family-run *Posada La Chachita* (☎ 042-61 23 30), which offers simple matrimoniales for US$18 and can prepare meals for guests.

Carritos run regularly between the Puerto Cabello bus terminal and Patanemo, and will put you down at any turnoff of your choice, within reasonable walking distance of the beach. The ride to Patanemo village takes half an hour and costs US$0.60.

San Esteban

An enjoyable village 7km south of Puerto Cabello, San Esteban is surrounded by lush vegetation, has a more pleasant climate than the port and boasts a couple of attractions. It's also the starting point for the Camino Real, the old Spanish trail leading south to Valencia (see the following Parque Nacional San Esteban section). Carritos to

San Esteban depart regularly from the bus terminal in Puerto Cabello (US$0.30, 15 minutes). They reach as far as the bridge in San Esteban, where the road ends.

Walk south (600m from the bridge) along a path on the same side of the river and you'll get to a large rock known as the **Piedra del Indio**, covered with petroglyphs. The rock is just next to the path, on your left.

San Esteban was the birthplace of Bartolomé Salom, one of the heroes of the War of Independence, who accompanied Bolívar all the way to Ayacucho. The house where he was born is 800m back along the road from the point where the carritos terminate. Left half-ruined, it's open for visitors from 9 am to 4 pm. Inside the main room is a life-sized statue of the general sitting in a hammock – quite an unusual sight.

A bit up the main road from Salom's house lies the inexpensive *Posada Mi Jaragual*; there are also a few places to eat in the village.

Parque Nacional San Esteban

This national park, adjacent to the western part of Parque Nacional Henri Pittier, stretches from San Esteban southward almost to Naguanagua, on the northern outskirts of Valencia. Like its eastern neighbor, the park protects a part of the Cordillera de la Costa, noted for its rich and diverse flora and fauna.

There's a popular trail in the park known as the 'Camino Real.' In colonial times, it was the main route linking Puerto Cabello with Valencia, along which goods were transported. The trail leads from north to south, passing over the ridge at an altitude of about 1400m. You can still see traces of the cobbled Spanish road and will even encounter the original Spanish bridge, the 1808 Puente de los Españoles. The trail is relatively easy, though side paths joining it may be confusing. Although the walking time between San Esteban and Naguanagua is about eight hours, count on two days to take it at a leisurely pace. There have been problems reported at the southern end, as the northern suburb of Naguanagua, Bárbula, is noted for armed robbery.

Many walkers departing from the northern end (San Esteban) make it just a one-day roundtrip by only going as far as the Spanish bridge. It's about a three-hour walk up and a two-hour walk back down. The tourist office in Puerto Cabello can help you to find a guide, should you need one.

The Northwest

Venezuela's northwest is a land of contrasts, with such diverse natural features as coral islands and beaches, rain forests and waterfalls, caves and chasms, the country's only desert, and South America's largest lake – Lago de Maracaibo. The region combines the traditional with the contemporary, from living indigenous cultures (such as that of the Guajiros) and colonial heritage to the modern city of Maracaibo. Administratively, the northwest as described in this chapter covers the states of Falcón, Lara, Yaracuy and Zulia.

Highlights

- Meander around the colonial core of Coro.
- Discover the Sierra de San Luis.
- Enjoy the beaches and coral reefs of Parque Nacional Morrocoy.
- Marvel at the lightning phenomenon of Catatumbo.

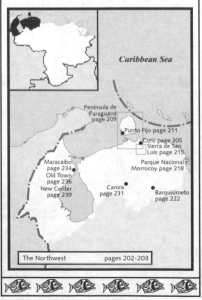

Caribbean Sea

Península de Paraguaná page 209

Punto Fijo page 211

Coro page 205
Sierra de San Luis page 215

Maracaibo page 234
Old Town page 236
New Center page 239

Parque Nacional Morrocoy page 218

Carora page 231

Barquisimeto page 222

The Northwest   pages 202-203

Falcón State

CORO
☎ 068 (☎ 0268 from Aug 18, 2001)

Set at the base of the curiously shaped Península de Paraguaná, the capital of Falcón state is a pleasant, peaceful city of 140,000 inhabitants. Thanks to a large university, it has a noticeably cultured air. More importantly, Coro features some of the best colonial architecture in all of Venezuela.

Founded by Juan de Ampiés in 1527, Coro was one of the earliest towns on the continent and the first capital of colonial Venezuela. In the same year, the city was leased, along with the entire province, to the Welsers of Germany to conquer, settle and exploit. The contract was made by King Carlos I of Spain, who was heavily in debt to German banking firms for loans he had used to buy the title of Holy Roman Emperor Karl V (Charles V) in 1519. The Germans were eager to share in the reputedly fabulous riches of the newly discovered continent. The Church was quick to follow, and in 1531 it established the Episcopal See in Coro, the first archdiocese founded in the New World.

Despite this promising start, Coro's development was bogged down right from the beginning. The town became little more than a jumping-off point for repeated expeditions in search of treasure, and El Dorado never materialized. In 1546 the contract with the Welsers was canceled and the administrative seat of the province moved to El Tocuyo, 200km to the south. The Church was more patient, but finally relocated the archdiocese to Caracas in 1637.

Having suffered from looting and burning by pirates on various occasions (in 1567, 1595 and 1659, among others), Coro struggled hard to survive and was revived only by contraband trade with Curaçao and Bonaire during the 18th century. Most of the historic buildings date from that time,

THE NORTHWEST

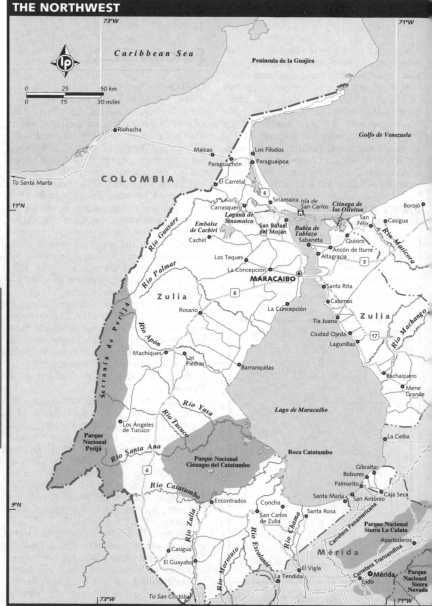

Caribbean Sea

Península de la Guajira

Golfo de Venezuela

Riohacha

Maicao

Los Filudos

Paraguaipoa

Paraguachón

El Carretal

To Santa Marta

COLOMBIA

11°N

Carrasquero

Sinamaica

Isla de
San Carlos

Ciénaga de
los Olivitos

Borojó

Casigua

San
Félix

Río Guasare

Embalse
de Cachirí

Laguna de
Sinamaica

San Rafael
del Moján

Bahía de
Tablazo

Quisiro

Río Matícora

Cachirí

Sabaneta

Ancón de Iturre

Río Palmar

Los Teques

La Concepción

Altagracia

3

MARACAIBO

Zulia

Santa Rita

Cabimas

Zulia

Rosario

La Concepción

6

Río Apón

Tía Juana

Río Machango

Ciudad Ojeda

17

Machiques

Las
Piedras

Lagunillas

Barranquitas

Bachaquero

Serranía de Perijá

Mene
Grande

Río Yasa

Lago de Maracaibo

Los Ángeles
de Tucuco

Río Tucuco

La Ceiba

Parque
Nacional
Perijá

Boca Catatumbo

Parque Nacional
Ciénagas del Catatumbo

Gibraltar

Río Santa Ana

Bobures

6

Palmarito

Río Catatumbo

Encontrados

Concha

Santa María

San Antonio

Caja Seca

9°N

Santa Rosa

San Carlos
de Zulia

Parque Nacional
Sierra La Culata

Río Zulia

Río Chama

Apartaderos

Casigua

Carretera Panamericana

Mérida

El Guayabo

Río Morotuto

Río Escalante

El Vigía

Carretera Transandina

Parque
Nacional
Sierra
Nevada

La Tendida

Mérida

To San Cristóbal

Ejido

73°W

71°W

0   25   50 km
0   15   30 miles

and it's no surprise that their architectural detail is influenced by the Dutch baroque.

Since Coro's historic center was declared a national monument in the 1950s, a number of the old houses have been restored. The cobblestone Calle Zamora, where most of the restoration work has been done, is the loveliest colonial-style street, and it's here that the majority of historic mansions are located. In 1993, Coro was made a World Heritage Site – Venezuela's only cultural site to appear on the official UNESCO list (along with Parque Nacional Canaima, the country's only natural site).

Information

Tourist Offices The Secretaría de Turismo (☎ 51 11 32, 51 27 32, fax 51 53 27) is on Paseo La Alameda, a pedestrian mall just north of Plaza Bolívar. It is open 8 am to noon and 1 to 4 pm weekdays.

Money Most of the major banks have their branches in the center. Corp Banca is on Calle Zamora, three blocks east of Avenida Manaure. Banco Mercantil is on Calle Falcón, two blocks east of Avenida Manaure. Banco Unión is on Avenida Manaure, eight blocks south of Calle Falcón. Cash can be exchanged at Casa de Cambio Falcón (☎ 52 98 63) in the airport terminal (open 8 am to noon and 1 to 4 pm weekdays).

Email & Internet Access Internet Coro (☎ 52 89 96), on the upper level of the Centro Comercial Punta del Sol, on the corner of Avenida Manaure and Calle Falcón, was the most reliable site at the time of writing. CANTV, on Calle Falcón, and La Colmena, on Calle Comercio, were also going to open their own facilities.

Colonial Churches

The massive fortresslike **cathedral** was begun in the 1580s and concluded half a century later, making it the oldest surviving church in Venezuela. There are no remainders of its early history inside, but the 1790 baroque main retable is a good example of late colonial art.

Two blocks north, the 18th-century **Iglesia de San Francisco** has been thoroughly restored, though the interior has not yet been fully furnished and decorated. The cupola of the Capilla del Santísimo Sacramento, at the top of the right aisle, was built in the 1760s and is a fine example of Mudejar art.

Just a stone's throw to the west of San Francisco is another 18th-century church, the **Iglesia de San Clemente**. It was laid out on a Latin cross plan and is one of the very few examples of its kind in the country. Note the anchor hanging from the middle of the ceiling, which commemorates St Clement's martyrdom.

In the barred pavilion on the plaza between the two churches is the **Cruz de San Clemente**. This is said to be the cross used in the first mass celebrated after the town's foundation. The cross is made from the wood of the *cují* tree, a xerophytic slow-growing species of acacia that grows in this arid region.

Historic Mansions & Museums

The city has a few good museums, all of which are in restored colonial buildings. The **Museo de Arte Coro**, established in a beautiful 18th-century mansion on Paseo Talavera, is a branch of the Caracas Museo de Arte Contemporáneo. All exhibits are temporary and are changed regularly. The museum is open 9 am to 12:30 pm and 3 to 7:30 pm Tuesday to Saturday, 9 am to 4 pm Sunday.

Diagonally opposite, in another great historic *casona* (large house), the **Museo de Arte Alberto Henríquez** features a small collection of modern paintings. At the back is the synagogue, founded in 1853. The present furnishings are all replicas, as almost nothing has survived of what was the first synagogue in Venezuela, and probably in all of Latin America. The museum is open 9 am to noon and 3 to 6 pm Tuesday to Saturday, 9 am to noon Sunday.

For insight into the colonial past, go two blocks north to the **Museo Diocesano Lucas Guillermo Castillo** (named after the 1923–48 bishop of Coro), in an old convent. An extensive collection of religious and secular art from the region and beyond, including

CORO

PLACES TO STAY
1 Hotel Miranda Cumberland
3 Posada Turística El Gallo
18 Hotel Intercaribe
30 Apart Hotel Sahara
31 Posada Turística Manena
33 Posada La Fonda Coriana

PLACES TO EAT
2 Pizzería La Barra del Jacal
12 Fonda Turística Sabor Latino
15 Restaurant El Tinajero
16 Comedor Popular
17 Centro Social Italo Venezolano
19 Panadería Costa Nova

OTHER
4 Casa del Tesoro
5 Casa de las Ventanas de Hierro
6 Casa de los Soto
7 Casa Nazaret

8 Casa del Sol
9 Casa de los Arcaya; Museo de Cerámica Histórica y Loza Popular
10 Iglesia de San Clemente
11 Cruz de San Clemente
13 Iglesia de San Francisco
14 Museo Diocesano Lucas Guillermo Castillo
20 Internet Coro
21 Iglesia de San Nicolás de Bari
22 Monument to Juan de Ampiés
23 Tourist Office
24 Banco de Venezuela
25 Museo de Arte Coro
26 Museo de Arte Alberto Henríquez
27 Ipostel
28 La Colmena
29 Public Telephones
32 Lavandería San Luis

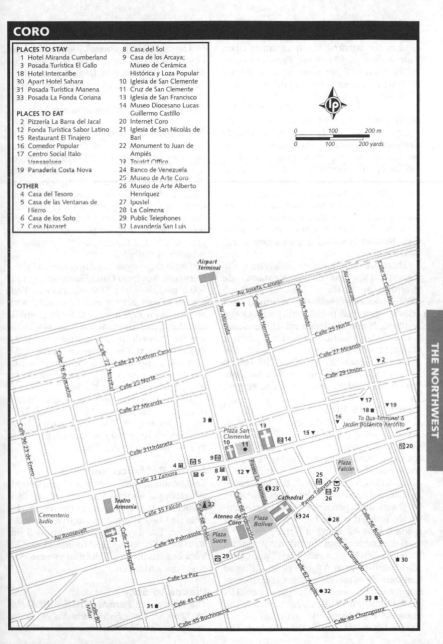

THE NORTHWEST

some extraordinary pieces, is displayed in 22 rooms. It's one of the best collections of its kind in the country. The museum is open 9 am to noon and 3 to 6 pm Tuesday to Saturday, 9 am to 2 pm Sunday; all visits are guided (in Spanish only), and the tour takes about 45 minutes. Admission is US$0.75.

A short walk west is the **Casa de los Arcaya**, noted for its long, tile-roofed balconies. The mansion houses the **Museo de Cerámica Histórica y Loza Popular**, a small but interesting museum of pottery and ceramics; opening hours are nearly the same as the Museo Diocesano, with the difference being that it closes at 1 pm Sunday.

Opposite Los Arcaya is the **Casa del Sol**, named for the decorative sun motif over its doorway. Next door is the more modest **Casa Nazaret**. Both buildings are now occupied by offices.

There are more great mansions on Calle Zamora. The **Casa de las Ventanas de Hierro** is noted for a splendid 8m-high plaster doorway and the wrought-iron grilles (imported from Spain) across the windows. It now shelters a private museum featuring a collection of historic objects (opening hours are the same as for the Museo de Cerámica). The **Casa del Tesoro** houses an art gallery. The **Casa de los Soto** is a private residence and cannot be visited.

Cementerio Judío
Established in the 1830s, this is the oldest Jewish cemetery still in use on the continent. Jews came to Coro from Curaçao in the early 19th century, a period of intensive trade with the Dutch islands. In the course of time, they formed a small but influential commercial community, despite persecution by the postindependence caudillo governments. Today there are perhaps at most half a dozen Jews still living in Coro.

The cemetery was founded by Joseph Curiel (1796–1886), a rich Jewish merchant who met Bolívar in Angostura and offered him the help of the Venezuelan Jewish community in the cause of independence. His tomb is one of the most elaborate, while the grave of his 10-year-old daughter, dated 1832, is the oldest tomb in the cemetery. The Curiel family name occurs more frequently than any other in the cemetery.

The cemetery is normally locked and the keys kept in La Colmena (☎ 51 14 46, 52 04 36), on Calle Comercio. Inquire there, and a guide will accompany you and show around the graveyard for about US$5 per group. Advance booking is recommended.

Médanos de Coro
A national park north of the city, Médanos de Coro was created in 1974 to protect the unusual environment of the isthmus of the Península de Paraguaná. The dominant feature of the isthmus' landscape is sand dunes, which rise up to 30m and give one the impression of being in the middle of a desert. The most spectacular desert area is just northeast of the city, easily accessible by urban transportation.

To get there from the city center, take the Carabobo bus from Calle Falcón and get off 300m past the large Monumento a la Federación. From here it is a 10-minute walk north along a wide avenue to another public sculpture, the Monumento a la Madre. A few paces north there is nothing but sand. Armed robberies were reported here in the past, but it appears that it's now reasonably safe to walk around since the Inparques employed more rangers in the area.

There's another point of access to the dunes from the highway to Punto Fijo. Take the urban bus to Plaza Concordia, from where it's a 10-minute walk north along the Punto Fijo road to the dunes.

Jardín Botánico Xerófito
This beautiful, well-kept xerophytic botanical garden is about 4.5km west of the Monumento a la Federación, on the road to La Vela de Coro. It's open 8 am to noon and 1 to 4 pm Tuesday to Friday, 9 am to 5 pm weekends. To get to the garden, take the La Vela bus from Calle Falcón anywhere east of Avenida Manaure.

Places to Stay
The eight-room *Posada Turística El Gallo* (☎ 52 94 81, Calle Federación No 26) is the cheapest place. Owned and managed by a

friendly Frenchman, Erick (who himself rebuilt the place from a colonial ruin), the posada is simple and lacks private baths, but otherwise is clean, pleasant and perfectly acceptable. The rooms (all with fan) are arranged around a leafy patio and cost US$6/10/18 single/double/quad. Erick provides good tourist information and organizes budget tours in his jeep to the Península de Paraguaná and Sierra de San Luis. This place is warmly recommended.

Posada Turística Manena (☎ 51 66 15, Calle Garcés No 119) is another small budget place, though it doesn't have colonial charm or a patio. On a positive note, its rooms (five in total) all have private bath, and some even have air-conditioning. They cost US$12/15/21 matrimonial/triple/quad with fan, US$18/28 matrimonial/triple with air-conditioning.

The new, seven-room *Posada La Fonda Coriana (☎ 52 62 45, Calle Comercio No 46)* offers good, comfortable matrimoniales/doubles/triples with bath and noiseless air-conditioning for US$22/25/28, which is an excellent value. The posada also has an inexpensive restaurant.

There are more budget hotels in the center, but nothing comparable to the three listed above. Actually, even mid-range hotels hardly match the style, charm or tranquility of the posadas.

The large *Hotel Intercaribe (☎ 51 18 11, 51 18 44)*, Avenida Manaure, offers perhaps more facilities, including TV, but has noisy air-conditioning and is nothing particularly special for US$30/36/42 single/double/triple. They require you to pay a security deposit equivalent to two nights, regardless of the duration of your stay.

Alternatively, you can try the 156-room *Apart Hotel Sahara (☎ 52 80 68, 52 68 64)*, Calle Bolívar, with an *ambiente familiar*, as they advertise this massive 12-story tower. The hotel is neither immaculately kept nor stylish, but it's in the highest building in town and provides good vistas from some of its upper-floor rooms, which all cost US$30/36/50 double/triple/suite.

Hotel Miranda Cumberland (☎ 52 33 44, 52 30 22, fax 51 30 96), on Avenida Josefa Camejo opposite the airport, is the best place to stay in town. Air-conditioned doubles/triples go for US$65/80. The hotel has its own restaurant, bar, swimming pool and sauna.

Places to Eat

Some of the cheapest meals can be had (at lunchtime only) in *Comedor Popular*, but don't expect much. On a similar basic side but open longer is *Fonda Turística Sabor Latino*, on Paseo La Alameda. Other unpretentious budget places in the same area include *Restaurant El Tinajero*, on Calle Zamora, and *Centro Social Italo Venezolano*, on Calle Urdaneta. The latter serves quite good pizzas.

The open-air *Pizzería La Barra del Jacal*, on Calle Unión, offers more than just pizzas. It's an enjoyable place with tasty food. Not only is it open until midnight, it's reasonably priced.

For breakfast, try the good *Panadería Costa Nova*, opposite the Hotel Intercaribe. Locals like it, and there are outside tables.

Getting There & Away

Air The sleepy airport is just a five-minute walk north of the city center. Avior, Santa Bárbara and Falcón Royal Air have daily flights to Caracas (US$67), where you need to change for other domestic destinations.

Aerocaribe Coro and Falcón Royal Air fly light planes to Aruba and Curaçao (about US$100 for a 14-day roundtrip to either), provided they collect a minimum of three passengers. You can charter their planes to take you on other routes as well.

Bus The bus terminal is on Avenida Los Médanos, about 2km east of the city center, and is easily accessible by frequent city transportation. Ordinary buses to Maracaibo (US$7, four hours), Punto Fijo (US$2, 1¼ hours) and Valencia (US$8, five hours) run every half-hour until 5 to 6 pm. Most of the direct buses to Caracas (US$10 ordinary, US$13 deluxe, seven hours) depart in the evening (and a few in the morning), but you can easily take one of the half-hourly buses to Valencia and change.

THE NORTHWEST

Several direct buses a day go to Mérida (US$20 deluxe, 13 hours) and to San Cristóbal (US$20 deluxe, 12 hours); all these buses depart in the evening and go via Maracaibo.

Within the region, there are buses to Adícora (US$1), on the eastern coast of Península de Paraguaná, as well as por puesto jeeps to Curimagua (US$2.50).

Boat Coro isn't on the coast; its port, La Vela de Coro, is 12km northeast of the city. Ferry services from La Vela to Curaçao (Netherlands Antilles) were closed down in the early 1990s, but there are plans to reintroduce them.

PENÍNSULA DE PARAGUANÁ
☎ 069 (☎ 0269 from Aug 18, 2001)
Shaped vaguely like a human head, the Península de Paraguaná is intriguing for more reasons than its topographical form. Its geography is quite different from the mainland's, as is its history, which was influenced by the Netherlands Antilles.

Stretching about 60km from north to south and 50km from east to west, Paraguaná is Venezuela's largest peninsula, covering an area of about 2500 sq km. It was once an island, but wind and waves gradually built up a sandbar, linking it to the continent. Paraguaná is flat except for an unusual mountain, the 830m Cerro Santa Ana, which juts out from the middle of the peninsula. The lowland vegetation is xerophytic, featuring a number of semidesert plant species, the most noticeable of which is the *cardón,* a columnar cactus tree. Only in the upper reaches of the mountain is the plant life lusher, including a variety of rain forest species.

The climate is dry, with a period of light rain extending from October to December. On average, there are only 40 rainy days per year. Owing to this relative lack of moisture, there are no permanent rivers on the peninsula.

The original inhabitants of Paraguaná were the Amuay, Guaranao and Caquetío Indians, all belonging to the Arawak linguistic family. Today these people are extinct.

Europeans first saw Paraguaná in 1499, when Alonso de Ojeda landed at Cabo de San Román, on the northern tip of the peninsula. Some 130 years later, the Dutch settled the nearby islands of Curaçao, Aruba and Bonaire, and since then there has been a steady mix of Spanish, Dutch and (at one point) indigenous cultural influences.

The region was never densely populated, as the lack of precious fresh water effectively hindered development. Today, freshwater is piped from the mainland to the whole of the peninsula.

The earliest colonial towns emerged not on the peninsular coast, but inland, close to Cerro Santa Ana, as it provided the only source of freshwater. They still preserve some of their old urban fabric, including their churches. The most remarkable colonial churches are in Moruy, Santa Ana and Jadacaquiva.

Another notable leftover from the colonial past is the number of large country mansions scattered around the region, outside the towns. These were once the farmhouses of the *hatos,* the country estates. Most of them were built in the late 18th century – a period of intensive trade with the Dutch Antilles – and they therefore reflect the Dutch-Caribbean architectural style. The **Casa de las Virtudes**, near Buena Vista, is one of the best examples of these mansions, but it can only be viewed from outside.

Things began to change with the oil boom. In the 1920s an oil terminal was built in Punto Fijo to ship oil overseas from Lago de Maracaibo. Refineries were constructed in the 1940s, and Punto Fijo embarked on a boom that continues today, rapidly becoming the largest urban center on the peninsula. The area around the city is dominated by the oil industry and crisscrossed by multilane highways. The rest of the peninsula, however, hasn't rushed into progress and modernity. It's still dotted with small old towns and their colonial churches.

Orientation
The peninsula offers a variety of attractions, including colonial towns, nature reserves, beaches, *salinas* (salt mines) and flamingos,

plus the general feeling of traveling through a remote semidesert outback.

There's an array of paved roads on the peninsula, except in the almost uninhabited northwest. Having an independent means of transportation is a great advantage here, but even if you don't, you'll manage to get around using local buses and por puestos. Public transportation is not frequent but does service most of the larger localities, including Punto Fijo, Santa Ana, Moruy, Pueblo Nuevo and Adícora.

The usual springboard for the peninsula is Coro, from where buses go to Adícora and Punto Fijo, the only places with a reasonable choice of accommodations and food.

Punto Fijo is much better serviced by public transportation, but otherwise it's an unremarkable place. It's better to go to the more pleasant Adícora and use it as a base for further excursions, such as viewing flamingos at Laguna de Tiraya or hiking up Cerro Santa Ana.

The owner of Posada Turística El Gallo (see the Coro section, earlier in this chapter) organizes day trips around the peninsula that are worth considering if you want just a quick taste of Paraguaná.

Punto Fijo

It was in 1925 that Punto Fijo first appeared on maps, following the construction of an oil terminal scrving Lago de Maracaibo. The building of two refineries, in Amuay and Punta Cardón, boosted the development of the young town. Today it's an industrial city of about 110,000 inhabitants, approaching the size of Coro. In some aspects, Punto Fijo has already outdistanced the state capital. Its airport, in Las Piedras, is busier than the one in Coro, as are trade and the general pace of life.

For tourists, Punto Fijo is of marginal interest, though you may need to stay overnight here if you are en route to or from the Netherlands Antilles. The only city on the peninsula, Punto Fijo has a range of hotels and restaurants – establishments that are scarce elsewhere on Paraguaná.

The city center is concentrated along two north-south streets, Avenida Bolívar and Avenida Colombia. It's in this area that most of the hotels, restaurants, banks and bus company offices are located. Plaza Bolívar is several blocks east of the center.

Places to Stay There are quite a number of reasonably priced hotels in the city center. The flip side of the coin is that these places are hardly memorable, as are their surroundings.

The basic *Hotel Euzcalduna* (☎ 45 15 34, *Avenida Ecuador No 18-160*) is one of the cheapest acceptable places. It has doubles/triples without bath for US$8/11 and matrimoniales with private bath for US$10. All rooms have fans.

Hotel Miami (☎ 45 85 32, *Calle Falcón No 21-96*), is the cheapest hotel with air-conditioned rooms, but it's also on the basic side. It costs US$15/17/20 matrimonial/double/triple with bath and TV. For much the same price you can stay in *Hotel Venicia* (☎ 45 57 43), on the corner of Calle Mariño and Avenida Bolívar, which offers better standards and quieter air-conditioning.

Slightly better is *Hotel El Cid* (☎ 45 52 45, 45 19 67), on the corner of Calle Comercio and Avenida Bolívar, which costs US$20/24/28 matrimonial/double/triple. Other similarly affordable central options include *Hotel Caribe* (☎ 45 04 21, 45 63 54, *Calle Comercio No 21-112*) and *Hotel Presidente* (☎ 45 89 64, 45 51 56), on the corner of Avenida Perú and Calle Cuba.

For somewhere upmarket, try the four-star *Hotel Península* (☎ 45 97 34, 45 97 76), at the entrance road to the city from Coro.

Getting There & Away Punto Fijo is the major transportation hub of the peninsula.

Air Punto Fijo's airport is about 10km northeast of the city and is labeled in all the air schedules as 'Las Piedras,' not 'Punto Fijo.' There are no public buses to the airport; a taxi from the city center will cost US$7. There are daily flights to Caracas (US$67) and Maracaibo (US$55).

Bus Punto Fijo has no central bus terminal; bus companies have their own offices

PUNTO FIJO

To Hotel Península & Coro

PLACES TO STAY
1 Hotel El Cid
4 Hotel Caribe
5 Hotel Presidente
8 Hotel Miami
10 Hotel Venicia
11 Hotel Euzcalduna

OTHER
2 Expresos Occidente
3 Banco de Venezuela
6 Banco Unión
7 Corp Banca
9 CANTV
12 Banco Mercantil
13 Regional Bus Terminal
14 Expresos San Cristóbal
15 Expresos Alianza

Market

To Puerto
del Guaranao

scattered throughout the city center. Expresos Occidente, Expresos Alianza and Expresos San Cristóbal service all the long-distance routes, including Caracas (US$15 deluxe, 8½ hours), Maracaibo (US$12 deluxe, 5½ hours) and Mérida (US$22 deluxe, 15 hours).

Regional buses depart from the market square. Buses to Coro (via an 82km freeway) run every half-hour until about 6 pm (US$2, 1¼ hours). There are also hourly buses to Pueblo Nuevo via the freeway and Santa Ana, and busetas to Pueblo Nuevo via Judibana and Moruy.

Boat Punto Fijo's port, Puerto del Guaranao, is about 2km south of the city center. The Punto Fijo–Aruba ferries were not operating at the time of writing, but service may recommence.

Santa Ana

Paraguaná's ancient capital and oldest town, Santa Ana is reputed to have existed since at least the 1540s, originally as a Caquetío Indian settlement. The church was built in the 16th century – thus being the first church on the peninsula – and was extended and remodeled at the end of the

17th century. The unusual bell tower was added around 1750. Since then the church has hardly changed and remains one of the prettiest country churches in Venezuela. It also has an amazing retable – a curious piece of popular art graced with naive elements, dating from the mid-18th century.

Except for the 9 am Sunday mass and the occasional cleaning, the church stays locked. The priest in the Casa Parroquial, on the northern side of Plaza Bolívar, may open it up for you.

Santa Ana has several basic places to eat, plus a few cheap rooms in a two-story house on the plaza's southern side. The Inparques office is one block north of the church. Buses between Pueblo Nuevo and Punto Fijo pass on the main road every hour or so.

Moruy

The small village of Moruy, 7km northwest of Santa Ana, sports another lovely colonial church. Built around 1760, the church is modest in internal furnishing and decoration. The village (along with the nearby hamlet of San Nicolás) is noted for the manufacture of *silletas paraguaneras,* chairs made from the cactus wood of the cardón.

Moruy is a popular starting point for hikes up Cerro Santa Ana (see the following section). There's nowhere to stay overnight in the village and not much to choose from as far as lunch or dinner goes. Busetas and buses run regularly to Punto Fijo, Pueblo Nuevo and Santa Ana.

Cerro Santa Ana

Rising 830m above the plains, this mountain is visible from almost any point on the peninsula. It actually has three peaks; the highest is the westernmost and looks dramatic from almost every angle. The mountain, along with the surrounding environs (19 sq km altogether), has been decreed a natural monument and is under the control of Inparques.

The mountain's vegetation is stratified according to altitude, going from xerophytic species at the base to a type of cloud forest above 500m. There are even some orchids and bromeliads in the upper reaches.

Two ways lead to the top. The main route begins at Moruy and heads eastward for 800m along an unpaved road to the Inparques post and a bivouac area. From there, a proper trail heads to the highest peak. It's about a three-hour walk up to the summit (two hours back down).

Another starting point is the town of Santa Ana, from where a rough road from the Inparques office heads north to another bivouac site (a 30-minute walk). The trail that begins there leads to the lowest, eastern peak, then continues up westward along the crest to the main peak.

Both Inparques posts allow tourists to start uphill until about 9 am. You should register before departure at the respective post, but there's no charge. Hikers need to return by 3 pm and mark their return on the list.

The peak is always windy and frequently shrouded in cloud. Occasionally it rains in the upper reaches, especially between September and January, the wet months. Take along a sweater, waterproof gear and proper shoes – the path near the top can be muddy.

Pueblo Nuevo

Home to about 8000 people, Pueblo Nuevo is the largest town in the inland portion of Paraguaná. It still contains some fine colonial houses and a church dating from 1758, although the latter was remodeled this century and modern fittings added.

Pueblo Nuevo has a small posada and several restaurants serving inexpensive meals. There are buses, busetas and por puestos to Punto Fijo (via Moruy) and Adícora, and there may be occasional direct busetas to Coro.

Reserva Biológica de Montecano

Montecano is a 16-sq-km biological reserve about 7km west of Pueblo Nuevo, created to protect the only remaining lowland forest on the peninsula. Surprisingly enough, this small wooded area features 62% of the plant species of Falcón state and attracts a great variety of birds. The reserve is run by Infalcosta, a Coro-based institute established in 1995 for the development and conservation of Falcón's arid coastal areas.

The reserve's visitors center is on a narrow road leading to the village of San José de Cocodite, which branches off from the Pueblo Nuevo–Buena Vista road 2km south of Pueblo Nuevo. There's no public transportation on this side road; you can hitch or walk 5km from the turnoff. From the visitors center (open daily 8 am to 5 pm), a guide will take you on a trip along a looped path that winds up and down through the reserve. It's an easy one-hour walk through an unusual habitat full of amazing plants and birds, and you'll even find a small lake on the way. The admission and guide service are so far free of charge.

Adícora

The small town of Adícora (population 4500), on Paraguaná's eastern coast, is one of the most popular tourist destinations on the peninsula. The town features several examples of old architecture, a beach, accommodations, food and a few local operators offering windsurfing and excursions around the peninsula.

Founded on a small headland jutting into the sea, Adícora was used in the 18th century by the Compañía Guipuzcoana as one of its trading bases, turning it into a prosperous town. Strolling around the streets, you'll still find brightly colored Dutch Caribbean houses characterized by barred windows with pedestals and decorated caps.

Windsurfing Over recent years, Adícora has gained international fame as a windsurfing center, with some of the best wave and wind conditions on Venezuela's coast. The winds are strongest and most consistent from January to June, and calmest from September to November. The surfing is safe because the breeze is always onshore, and the place is virtually untouched by big tourism, so it's beautifully unspoiled, informal and inexpensive.

There are a few windsurfing operators in town, including Carlos Wind Place (☎ 014-968 06 60, in Caracas ☎ 02-963 12 68, adicorart @yahoo.com), run by Carlos, as well as Windsurf Adícora (☎ 882 24, 014-693 87 31,

windsurf_adicora@yahoo.com), run by a German, Alex. Both offer windsurfing courses, equipment rental and simple accommodations, with Alex being a bit more expensive in all three categories. Alex also has bicycles and diving gear for rent, and he organizes excursions around the peninsula.

Places to Stay & Eat Adícora has a better choice of places to stay than any other town on the peninsula except for Punto Fijo. Accommodation prices tend to vary from weekdays to weekends and seem to be negotiable in some places on slow days, when there are few tourists around. In contrast, hotels can be packed with beachgoers on weekends and holidays.

Some locals rent out rooms in their homes, which can make for some of the cheapest and safest form of lodging – ask around. On the other hand, don't rent unattended cabañas or beach houses; these places are easy prey for robbers.

Posada La Carantoña, in a fine old house in the town's center, one block back from the beach, is a pleasant place to stay and one of the cheapest, starting at US$15 double with bath and fan. Another good choice is *Posada Montecano* (☎ 881 74), half a kilometer from the bus stop along the road to Pueblo Nuevo, run by a friendly Italian-Venezuelan couple. They were in the process of constructing a new posada-restaurant that should be ready by the time you arrive. They are also likely to serve hearty food in the new restaurant, as they did in the old one.

Places to eat closer to the beach include the budget *Restaurant El Guatacarazo* and the slightly more expensive *Restaurant Los Sartenes*, both near the lighthouse. There are more restaurants along the beach, though most of them are only open on weekends. There's also the good *Restaurant La Posada del Temporadista*, 1km beyond the Montecano toward Pueblo Nuevo.

Possibly the most spectacular place to stay in Adícora is the *Campamento Vacacional La Troja* (☎ 880 48), occupying an entire block in the middle of town. This walled complex, built in the traditional style and set in a lush garden (quite unusual on the peninsula), offers comfortable accommodations and food. A package including breakfast and dinner will cost around US$45 per person. It can be booked in Caracas at ☎ 02-952 83 52.

Outside Adícora, the small, tranquil *Hacienda La Pancha (☎ 014-969 26 49)* resides in a fine colonial country mansion on the road to Pueblo Nuevo, 2km beyond El Hato. Its four rooms overlook a leafy patio, and a side restaurant serves good food, including some Basque specialties. Bed, breakfast and dinner cost US$38 per person in a double or triple room decorated with folk paintings.

Getting There & Away Adícora is linked to Coro by several daily buses, the last departing at around 5 pm. There are also por puestos to Pueblo Nuevo and busetas to Punto Fijo.

Lagoons & Salt Mines
About 6km north of Adícora, **Laguna de Tiraya** is where flamingos feed. Though peak season is mostly from November to January, you can be pretty sure of finding some almost year-round. There is no public transportation to the lagoon, but you can walk or try to hitch (the traffic is mainly on weekends; at other times it's sporadic), or take a taxi from Adícora.

From Adícora, take the road to El Supí and turn left onto the recently paved road that branches off to the west 4km north of Adícora. This road leads to Santa Rita and skirts the lagoon. The flamingos may be either quite close to your shore or off in the distance, on the opposite, eastern side of the lagoon. As a (rough) rule, they often come to the near shore in the afternoon and prefer to do their fishing on the distant side in the morning.

Farther north, between Santa Rita and Las Cumaraguas, is the **Salina de Cumaraguas**, where salt is mined using rudimentary methods. Several kilometers northwest of Las Cumaraguas is the **Salina de Bajarigua**, which may also attract some flamingos, but fewer than Laguna Tiraya. There's

public transportation on a paved road from Las Cumaraguas to Pueblo Nuevo via El Vínculo.

Be prepared for the heat: Take sufficient water, sunscreen, sunglasses and a hat. If you have your own transportation, you can explore the region farther north as far as **Cabo de San Román**, which is the northernmost point in Venezuela.

Beaches
The beaches on Paraguaná don't match those of Morrocoy or Henri Pittier, and the dearth of coconut palms means that they usually lack shade. Like all other beaches in Venezuela, Paraguaná's beaches are quiet on weekdays and completely swamped on the weekends.

The beaches on the eastern coast stretch almost all the way from Adícora to Piedras Negras. **Adícora** is the most popular beach resort, though **El Supí** and **Buchuaco**, farther north, have arguably finer beaches. **Tiraya** is less popular with holidaymakers because it's harder to reach. On the western coast, the popular beaches include **Villa Marina** and **El Pico**, both serviced by local transportation from Punto Fijo.

SIERRA DE SAN LUIS
☎ 068 (☎ 0268 from Aug 18, 2001)
The Sierra de San Luis is the belt of verdant mountains stretching to the south of the arid coast of Coro. It is a vital source of water for the whole coastal area, including the Península de Paraguaná. About 200 sq km of the rugged terrain was made into a national park in 1987. Elevations within the park range from 200m up to 1501m on Cerro Galicia, the park's highest point. Average temperatures range between 25°C and 15°C, according to altitude. Annual rainfall is moderate, not exceeding 1500mm, and the wettest months are October to December.

The sierra boasts a few picturesque towns, several waterfalls, about 20 caves and a dozen *simas* (deep vertical holes in the earth). It offers a fresh, pleasant climate, exotic forests full of birds, an adequate array of hotels and restaurants, reasonable

SIERRA DE SAN LUIS

PLACES TO STAY
1 Posada El Conuquero
2 Casa de Campo
3 Finca El Monte
4 Posada La Soledad
5 Posada Monte Alto
6 Posada El Gigante del Sabor
7 Caravan
8 Hotel Apolo
9 Hotel Falconés
10 Posada El Trapichito
12 Posada El Duende
13 Club Campestre Camino Viejo
14 Hotel La Montaña

△ Cave

THE NORTHWEST

public transportation and a good choice of walking paths.

Orientation

San Luis, Cabure and Curimagua are the major towns of the sierra. All three are accessible by public transportation from Coro, each one by a different route. Curimagua is the closest to Coro (45km) and has the most frequent transportation. Curimagua and its environs also have the best choice of accommodations and provide the most popular and convenient base from which to explore the region.

Of the three towns, San Luis is possibly the most picturesque. Founded in 1590, it's the oldest Spanish settlement in the area and has preserved some of its colonial architecture, including a fine church. Of the waterfalls, the Cataratas de Hueque are the largest and perhaps the most spectacular. Among the caves, the Cueva de Zárraga and Cueva del Encanto are the most frequent tourist destinations. The Haitón de Guarataro is the most impressive local sima. It's 305m deep, but the mouth is only about 12m in diameter. Another highlight is the Camino de Los Españoles, an old Spanish trail between Cabure and La Negrita; its best-preserved part is near Acarite, where there is a brick bridge that dates from around 1790.

Places to Stay & Eat

With few exceptions, the places to stay in the region are clean, pleasant and friendly. They don't offer excessive luxuries but are adequate, comfortable and inexpensive. Most are family-run posada-style places operated directly by the owners. Many of the hotel owners/managers will offer visitors excursions around area sights, or at least provide them with information on how to get there.

Curimagua & Around There are at least four places to stay in the town alone. The Dutch-owned *Hotel Falconés* (☎ 51 82 71) has seven doubles with bath and hot water for US$30 each, plus a restaurant serving reasonable food, including set lunches priced at US$8.

The nearby *Hotel Apolo* (☎ 51 76 34) is bigger, provides comparable standards for much the same price, and has a slightly cheaper restaurant.

Posada El Gigante del Sabor, at the western end of the town, is one of the cheapest places around – costing US$12/18 matrimonial/triple – but is basic. It also serves some of the cheapest meals. Across the road, a Lithuanian family rents out a rundown *caravan* that can sleep up to four people for US$25.

About 2km west of Curimagua, on the road to La Tabla, the new *Posada Monte Alto* (☎ 014-682 10 89) offers good cabañas for US$30/35/45 double/triple/quad. About 3km farther, on the slope of Cerro Galicia, is *Posada La Soledad* (☎ 014-690 88 89). This is the most isolated and highest hotel in the sierra. Built with traditional techniques and materials, the colonial-style house with a central patio is one of the loveliest places in the region, and it is not that expensive, priced at US$28/32/36 double/triple/quad.

Two kilometers east of Curimagua, off the road to Coro, is *Posada El Trapichito*, which offers four simple matrimoniales at US$20 each and has a pleasant restaurant. Three kilometers farther along the road to Coro is *Finca El Monte*, a 9-hectare farm owned and run by a friendly Swiss couple, Ernesto and Ursula. They have four rooms at US$14/18 double/triple, which makes it about the cheapest place in the area and an excellent value. They prepare rich meals for guests, with just about everything homegrown and homemade, and organize hikes in the area. Their place is very warmly recommended.

San Luis Since the Posada Paraguariba closed down, there's nowhere to stay in town, but check for news when you come to the region.

Cabure The loveliest place to stay here is *Posada El Duende* (☎ 61 10 79), about 1.5km up a steep, rough road from the town. Built in a traditional rustic style, the posada has simple but comfortable doubles with bath for US$24 and a six-person dorm for US$34, plus an appealing restaurant.

Club Campestre Camino Viejo (☎ 61 10 16), next to the local cemetery, has four matrimoniales for US$28 each and two eight-bed cabañas for US$45, plus a restaurant and a swimming pool. The Spanish *camino de herradura* (bridle path, or old colonial trail) begins here. The least attractive place, *Hotel La Montaña* (☎ 61 11 77), has five matrimoniales for US$15 each.

Other Areas The *Casa de Campo* (☎ 729 17), halfway between Coro and Curimagua, provides the most upmarket accommodations in the region. This large hillside holiday complex offers a variety of rooms, suites and cabañas, plus a restaurant and bar service. Expect a double to cost US$45 to US$75. Information and reservation service are available through their Coro office (☎ 52 63 46).

Farther to the north, in the village of Santa María de la Chapa, is the pleasant and comfortable *Posada El Conuquero*, which costs US$20/28 matrimonial/double with bath and hot water and has its own restaurant.

Getting There & Away

The usual point of departure for the sierra is Coro's bus terminal. Por puesto jeeps to Curimagua (via La Chapa) depart from 5 am until midafternoon (US$2.50, 1½ hours). There are also infrequent carritos to San Luis (via El Tigre) and Cabure (via Pueblo Nuevo de La Sierra).

PARQUE NACIONAL MORROCOY

Established at the eastern edge of Falcón state, Morrocoy national park comprises a strip of coast and an offshore area dotted with islands, islets and cays. Many islands are skirted with white-sand beaches and surrounded by coral reefs. Owing to its geography, Morrocoy is one of the most spectacular littoral environments on Venezuela's coast.

The park is also well known for its variety of wading birds and waterbirds, including ibis, herons, cormorants, ducks, pelicans and flamingos. They permanently or seasonally inhabit some of the islands and coastal mangroves, especially the Golfete de Cuare, which is one of Venezuela's richest bird-breeding grounds and has been declared a wildlife refuge.

The park is a popular destination for Venezuelan beachgoers, who come en masse on holidays and weekends and leave the islands badly littered. The fragile island environment is unfortunately beginning to suffer from human interference, though you can still enjoy deserted and apparently virgin beaches on weekdays.

More significantly, some of the coral has died, purportedly the result of an early-1996 chemical leak from a nearby oil refinery. Official sources are silent on the issue, but independent biologists are monitoring the damage and claim that up to half of the coral is dead.

Orientation

The park lies between the towns of Tucacas and Chichiriviche (detailed in the following sections), which are its main gateways. Both have well-organized boat services to the islands, as well as an array of places to stay and eat. You can use them as a springboard for day trips to the islands or, if you have a tent or a hammock, you can stay on the islands themselves.

The most popular island is Cayo Sombrero, which has fine coral reefs and some of the best beaches. It's more exposed to the open sea than most other islands, and the breeze means that it has fewer insects. Other places good for snorkeling include Cayo Borracho, Cayo Peraza, Playa Mero and Playuela.

Places to Stay & Eat

Camping is officially permitted on four islands: Sal, Muerto, Sombrero, and Paiclás. If you plan on staying in a hammock, make absolutely sure you take along a good mosquito net. All four of the islands have beach restaurants and/or food kiosks, but some of them may be closed on weekdays in the slow season.

Before you go camping, you should contact the Inparques office in Tucacas and pay the camping fee of US$2 per person per night at the Banco Unión in Tucacas.

When camping on the islands, take food, sufficient water, snorkeling gear, good sun protection and a reliable insect repellent. The insects here – small biting gnats known locally as *puri-puri* – are most annoying in windless months, usually November and December. You can use gas camping stoves, but no open fire is permitted.

TUCACAS
☎ 042 (☎ 0259 from Mar 24, 2001)

This is a hot, ordinary town (population 17,000) on the Valencia-Coro road, with nothing to keep you for long. Yet, with the park just a stone's throw away, the town is quickly developing into a holiday center and has an array of hotels and other facilities. Plenty of new developments are springing up toward the south of town, between the Morón road and the beach.

The town's lifeline is Avenida Libertador (also known as 'Avenida Principal'), a 1km road stretching between the Morón-Coro highway in the west and the bridge to an island in the east. Many businesses are on or just off this street.

THE NORTHWEST

PARQUE NACIONAL MORROCOY

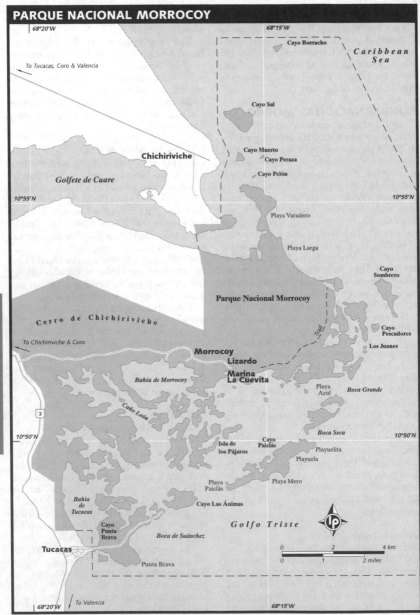

68°20'W

To Tucacas, Coro & Valencia

68°15'W

Cayo Borracho

Caribbean Sea

Cayo Sal

Cayo Muerto

Cayo Peraza

Cayo Pelón

Chichiriviche

Golfete de Cuare

10°55'N

10°55'N

Playa Varadero

Playa Larga

Cayo Sombrero

Parque Nacional Morrocoy

Cerro de Chichiriviche

To Chichiriviche & Coro

Cayo Pescadores

Los Juanes

Trail

Morrocoy
Lizardo
Marina
La Cuevita

Bahía de Morrocoy

Playa Azul

Boca Grande

Caño León

3

Boca Seca

10°50'N

10°50'N

Isla de los Pájaros

Cayo Paiclás

Playuelita

Playuela

Playa Paiclás

Playa Mero

Bahía de Tucacas

Cayo Las Ánimas

Cayo Punta Brava

Boca de Suánchez

Golfo Triste

Tucacas

0   2   4 km
0   1   2 miles

Punta Brava

68°20'W

To Valencia

68°15'W

The island across the bridge, Cayo Punta Brava, is part of the national park. A 15-minute walk along the paved road from the bridge will bring you to the beach, which is shaded with coconut palms; more beaches lie farther east on the same island, accessible by road. If you want to visit other islands of the park, go to the *embarcadero* (landing dock), in the town close to the bridge, from where boats can take you for a trip along the *caños* (channels) through mangroves or drop you off on one of the many islands.

Information

While there's no tourist office in Tucacas, you can get information from the managers of some budget hotels, including André, Norbert and Carlos (see Places to Stay & Eat), and from diving schools (see Diving & Snorkeling).

The area Inparques office (☎ 83 00 69, ☎/fax 83 00 53, toll-free ☎ 800 848 47) is at the eastern end of Avenida Libertador, close to the bridge.

The Banco Unión, on Avenida Libertador just off the Coro-Morón highway, gives cash advances on Visa and MasterCard, and it sometimes also changes cash and traveler's checks. Diving schools normally accept payments in cash dollars and traveler's checks. They may also change them, though the rates are often poor.

Diving & Snorkeling

There are two diving operators in town: Submatur (☎ 83 00 82, fax 83 10 51), Calle Ayacucho No 6 near Plaza Bolívar, owned by Mike Osborn, and Amigos del Mar Divers (☎ 83 17 54), Calle Democracia No 1 near the embarcadero, owned by André Nahon. Both offer diving courses and guided dives run by professional licensed instructors, and both have shops selling diving and snorkeling equipment, some of which can be rented. They can also organize boat trips around the islands of Morrocoy park and beyond. Amigos del Mar has received better reviews by travelers and is cheaper than Submatur.

Apart from these two diving schools, you can rent snorkeling gear from some of the boat operators and hotel managers (about US$8 per day).

Places to Stay & Eat

The 10-room *Posada Amigos del Mar* (☎ 83 39 62), run by André, the diving school manager mentioned above, is a good budget place and an excellent value. Overlooking a pleasant leafy garden, the posada has spacious doubles/triples/quads with bath and fan for US$12/15/18. On a less pleasant note, the place is beyond the Hospital Viejo, on the unsafe side of the road, and is unmarked. Don't try to look for it if you arrive after dark; call the owner from the bus stop and he will likely come and accompany you to his hotel.

Most of the budget hotels are close to each other on Avenida Libertador, halfway between the Morón-Coro road and the bridge. The cheapest is *Hotel La Esperanza* (☎ 83 09 50, 014-484 12 67), Avenida Libertador, managed by a German guy, Norbert (who also administers Hotel La Suerte; see that listing, later in this section). It costs US$10/12/14 matrimonial/double/quad with bath and fan, US$12/14/16 with bath and air-conditioning. Downstairs is the 24-hour *Arepera La Esperanza*, which serves good cheap arepas. Full meals are offered at the budget *Restaurant El Salmón*, 50m down the road.

Right across the road from La Esperanza is the small *Posada de Carlos* (☎ 83 14 93), named after the owner. The establishment's name isn't posted, but the place is recognizable by the *sí hay habitación* inscription on the door. The hotel has matrimoniales/doubles with bath and fan for US$15/18, and you can use the kitchen and fridge at no extra cost.

The 70-room *Hotel La Suerte* (☎ 83 13 32), next to Posada de Carlos, has cheaper rooms with fan (US$12/15 matrimonial/double) and also provides air-conditioned rooms for US$18/22. Behind La Suerte is *Posada Johnatan* (☎ 83 02 39), which offers much the same as La Suerte for marginally more.

The new *Posada Venemar* (☎ 83 26 69), on Avenida Libertador near the bridge, offers four good-quality suites, all with sea views, for US$40 per person. Downstairs is the upmarket *Restaurant Venemar*, perhaps the best place to eat in town.

The waterfront *Posada Balijú* (☎ *83 15 80)*, on Calle Libertad, is one of the most charming places around, providing tranquility, stylish surroundings and a family atmosphere. The package, which includes bed, breakfast, dinner and boat excursions, costs US$75 per person.

Getting There & Away
Tucacas sits on the main Valencia-Coro road, so there are frequent buses to both Valencia (US$2.50, two hours) and Coro (US$5.50, 3½ hours). Buses from Valencia pass through regularly on their way to Chichiriviche (US$1, 40 minutes).

Getting Around
Boats to the islands normally take up to seven or eight people and charge a flat rate per trip. Prices to all islands and beaches are posted next to the ticket office close to the dock. They are roundtrip fares per boat, not per person. The fare to the farthest islands, such as Cayos Sombrero or Pescadores, is around US$65. Closer destinations include Playa Paiclás (US$32), Playa Mero (US$36), Playuela (US$40) and Playa Azul (US$44). The boat will pick you up from the island in the afternoon or at a later date, depending on when you want to return. On weekdays during the off-season, you can usually bargain down the price.

Some hotels have their own boats (or have contracts with boat owners) and offer excursions. These are mostly full-day trips around the islands with stops for snorkeling and relaxing on beaches, usually including Cayo Sombrero. Such excursions can work out cheaper than those arranged at the boat wharf. For example, a full-day boat trip organized by André costs about US$12 per person.

CHICHIRIVICHE
☎ 042 (☎ 0259 from Mar 24, 2001)
Chichiriviche is the northern gateway to the park, providing access to half a dozen neighboring cays. The town (population 7000) is smaller than Tucacas, but it's equally undistinguished and unattractive. Accommodations, food and boats are in good supply here.

Access to the town is from the west, by the 12km road that runs along a causeway through mangrove swamps. The area lining this road is a favorite feeding ground for flamingos, which gather here mostly between August and January; however, a small community can remain up to March or even April, as long as there's sufficient water. November is usually the peak month, when up to 5000 birds are in the area.

Upon entering the town proper, the road divides. Its main branch, Avenida Zamora (also called Avenida Principal), continues straight ahead to the bus terminus and the town's center, ending at the waterfront next to the northern pier. The southern branch, Avenida Fábrica de Cemento, goes to the cement plant south of town, passing several hotels and providing access to the southern pier on the way.

Information
As in Tucacas, in the absence of a tourist office you can ask hotel managers and diving operators for local information. The Banco Industrial de Venezuela, Avenida Zamora, gives advances on Visa, but that's about all it can do for you; it doesn't change cash or traveler's checks and doesn't accept MasterCard. The Hotel Capri (see Places to Stay & Eat, later) may change your dollars, but don't expect good rates.

Diving
Run by a Swiss couple, Monika and Pierre, Agua-Fun Diving (☎/fax 862 65, aguafun@cantv.net), on Calle El Sol in the southern part of town, is a professional and well-equipped diving school. Visit their Web site, at www.venezuela-web.de/sport/sport_de/agua_fun_diving, for information.

Places to Stay & Eat
There are several pleasant budget places to stay in the town's center. Run by a friendly Spaniard, Aurelio, the stylish *Villa Gregoria* (☎ *863 59)*, on Calle Mariño one block

north of Avenida Zamora, has good singles/doubles/triples with bath and fan for US$7.50 per person. Choose a room on the 1st floor. The small **Residencias Delia** (☎ 860 89), a few paces west along the same street, costs much the same. It lacks character but has a very familiar atmosphere.

Another enjoyable option in the same area, the five-room **Posada Morena's Place** (☎ 85 09 36) is in a fine old house managed by Carlos. Most rooms have only a shared bath, but they are perfectly acceptable and cost US$7.50 per person. The posada offers laundry service and budget breakfasts.

Posada Milagro (☎ 85 08 64), on Avenida Zamora 60m from the waterfront, has seven matrimoniales with bath and sea views. Ask for a room in the Licorería Falcón, downstairs. About 30m from the Milagro on the same street, **Residenza Eva** (☎ 85 09 23) offers four air-conditioned studio apartments, all with kitchenette and fridge. At US$12 per person, it's a good value. Inquire downstairs at the Italian Paradise café.

Another 30m up the same street, **Hotel Capri** (☎ 860 26) provides a reasonable air-conditioned option. Matrimoniales/doubles/triples with bath and hot water are all US$22/26/30. The newer **Hotel Caribana** (☎ 868 37), a few hundred meters inland along the same road, offers similar standards for a bit more.

Several hotels lie farther away from the beach, including the German-run **Posada Alemania** (☎ 85 09 12), set in a pleasant coconut-palm garden on Avenida Fábrica de Cemento (US$30 double with bath and fan), and the upmarket **Hotel La Garza** (☎ 867 11, fax 863 47), on Avenida Zamora at Avenida Fábrica de Cemento (about US$60 double with air-con); the latter has a swimming pool.

For budget meals, try **Rancho Tropical**, on Avenida Zamora, or the pricier **Pizzería Casamare**, on the waterfront. Among the best places are **Restaurant Txalupa** and **La Brisa del Mar**, both on the waterfront.

Getting There & Away
Chichiriviche is about 22km off the main Morón-Coro highway and is serviced by hourly buses from Valencia (US$3.50, 2½ hours).

There are no direct buses to Chichiriviche from Caracas or Coro. To get there from Caracas, take any of the frequent buses to Valencia (US$3, 2½ hours) and change there. From Coro, take any bus to Valencia, get off in Sanare, the turnoff for Chichiriviche (US$5, 3¼ hours), and catch the Valencia-Chichiriviche bus.

Getting Around
The town has two piers: the Embarcadero Playa Norte, near the eastern end of Avenida Zamora; and the Embarcadero Playa Sur, about 1km southwest. Boat fares are the same at both piers. As in Tucacas, the boat takes a maximum of seven to eight passengers, and the fare given is per boat. Roundtrip fare to the closest cays, such as Cayos Muerto, Sal or Pelón, is about US$20, whereas the fare to the farthest cays, such as Cayos Borracho, Sombrero or Pescadores, is about US$50. The return time is up to you, and haggling over the price is also possible (bargaining is apparently easier at the southern pier). Some hotels and posadas (including Posada Tibisay and Posada Alemania) organize boat trips.

Lara & Yaracuy States

BARQUISIMETO
☎ 051 (☎ 0251 from July 14, 2001)

After Caracas, Maracaibo and Valencia, Barquisimeto is Venezuela's fourth-largest city (population 750,000). It's the capital of Lara state and an important commercial, industrial and transportation center. At 550m, the city has a warm, relatively dry climate with a mean temperature of 24°C.

Originally founded in 1552 on the Río Buría, Barquisimeto moved three times before eventually being established at its present-day location in 1563. Its growth was slow, as the indigenous tribes in the region were particularly fierce in defending their territory. Furthermore, the 1812 earthquake

THE NORTHWEST

★ Hotel Crepusculo

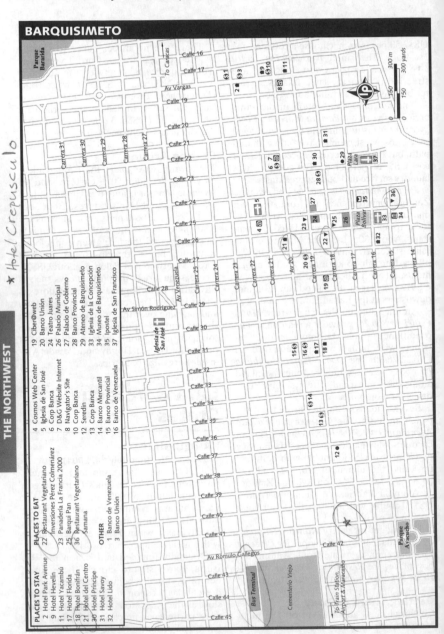

BARQUISIMETO

PLACES TO STAY
2 Hotel Park Avenue
9 Hotel Hevelin
11 Hotel Yacambú
17 Hotel Florida
18 Hotel Bonifrán
21 Hotel del Centro
30 Hotel Príncipe
31 Hotel Savoy
32 Hotel Lido

PLACES TO EAT
22 Restaurant Vegetariano
5 Inversiones Pérez Colmenárez
23 Panadería La Francia 2000
25 Barqui Pan
36 Restaurant Vegetariano Samana

OTHER
1 Banco de Venezuela
3 Banco Unión

4 Cosmos Web Center
5 Iglesia de San José
6 Corp Banca
7 D&G Website Internet
8 Navigator's Site
10 Corp Banca
13 Seredin
14 Banco Mercantil
15 Banco Provincial
16 Banco de Venezuela

19 Ciber@web
20 Banco Unión
24 Teatro Juares
26 Palacio Municipal
27 Palacio de Gobierno
28 Banco Provincial
29 Ateneo de Barquisimeto
33 Iglesia de la Concepción
34 Museo de Barquisimeto
35 Ipostel
37 Iglesia de San Francisco

destroyed much of the town and its colonial architecture.

As in almost every other large city in Venezuela, the rush to modernize in recent decades has been intensive and indiscriminate, and has been carried out at the expense of those few Spanish structures that had survived the earthquake. Today, Barquisimeto is a predominantly modern city dotted with a number of shady parks and plazas. It's not a major traveler destination, but it has some minor sights and a developed tourist infrastructure. There are also some interesting places around the town.

Information

Tourist Offices The Dirección de Turismo (☎ 53 75 44, 53 93 21) is in the Edificio Fundalara, on Avenida Libertador near the Complejo Ferial. It's over 2km northeast of the center, beyond Parque Bararida. It's open 8 am to 3:30 pm weekdays. There are also information desks in the bus terminal and at the airport.

Money Most of the major banks are on or just off Avenida 20 (the main commercial street in the city center). Italcambio is the only casa de cambio operating in the city. Its office (☎ 54 97 90) is in the Centro Empresarial Barquisimeto, Avenida Los Leones, and it has a desk (☎ 43 19 10) at the airport. Both outlets change cash and traveler's checks.

Email & Internet Access There has been a rash of cybercafé building since late 1999, most located in the new shopping malls. Local facilities are among the cheapest in the country at US$2 to US$2.50 an hour. Central places include:

Ciber@web
(☎ 32 56 04) Centro Comercial Country, Calle 28 between Carreras 18 and 19, Piso Bajo, Local 5

Cosmos Web Center
Centro Comercial Cosmos I, Nivel 2, Local 2A-21, Calle 25 between Carreras 21 and 22

D&G Website Internet
(☎ 32 28 26) Centro Comercial BarquiCenter, Nivel Sótano, Local 38-C-23, Avenida 20 between Calles 22 and 23

Navigator's Site
(☎ 32 76 96) Centro Comercial Capital Plaza, Piso 2, Local 96, corner of Avenida Vargas and Avenida 20

Seredin
Centro Comercial Cilara, corner of Carrera 19 and Calle 37 (on the floor above the Banco República; enter from the parking lot in the back)

Most places listed above are open 9 am to 8 pm Monday to Saturday; some, including Seredin and Ciber@web, are also open on Sunday.

Things to See

The **Plaza Bolívar** is the original center of the city, adorned with yet another replica of the Bolívar statue in Caracas. It's now lined with modern edifices, except for the **Iglesia de la Concepción**, on the square's southern side. This was Barquisimeto's first cathedral, but it was destroyed in the earthquake of 1812 and rebuilt 30 years later in a different style.

A few steps south of the church is the **Museo de Barquisimeto**, in a large building with a rectangular courtyard centered on a chapel. It was built in the 1910s as a hospital, and used from 1954 to 1977 for various purposes, until authorities decided to demolish it to make way for modern buildings. Thanks to public protests, it was restored and turned into a museum that now features temporary exhibits. It's open 9 am to 5 pm Tuesday to Sunday.

Plaza Lara, two blocks east of Plaza Bolívar, is the city's only area with colonial character, thanks to the restored historic buildings lining the square. The **Ateneo de Barquisimeto**, on the northern side of the plaza, stages changing exhibitions.

The **Iglesia de San Francisco**, on the southern side of Plaza Lara, was built in 1865 and carried the distinction of being Barquisimeto's second city cathedral. The modern **Catedral** was constructed in the 1960s on the corner of Avenidas Venezuela (Carrera 26) and Simón Rodríguez (Calle 29). Boasting an innovative design noted for the parabolic concrete roof, the cathedral is open only for mass (several times on

Sunday, at 6 pm on weekdays), so plan accordingly if you want to see its centrally located high altar.

Parque Bararida, on the northeastern outskirts of the center, features small botanical and zoological gardens.

Special Events

The city's biggest annual event is the Fiestas Patronales de la Divina Pastora. The patron saint's day is January 14, and its central feature is a solemn procession parading the image of the Virgin Mary from the shrine in Santa Rosa village into the city. The celebrations go for several days before and after the saint's day, and include agricultural fairs, concerts and sports events held in the Complejo Ferial (Fairgrounds).

Places to Stay

If you're just in transit, you can choose from half a dozen basic hotels on the northern side of the bus terminal. Check out a few before deciding – they differ significantly in standards and rates.

In the city center, one of the cheapest places is the basic **Hotel del Centro** (☎ 31 53 46), Avenida 20 near the corner of Calle 26. Doubles/triples with fan and bath cost US$11/13, while air-conditioned doubles/triples/quadruples go for US$14/15/16. Another basic shelter, the **Hotel Park Avenue** (☎ 31 13 67), Avenida Vargas at Carrera 22, costs US$12/16/18 matrimonial/double/triple with fan.

Hotel Lido (☎ 31 55 68), on Carrera 16 between Calles 26 and 27, one block west of Plaza Bolívar, is a small place with air-conditioning and TV, but otherwise it's nothing special. It is priced at US$18/22/25 matrimonial/double/triple. Similar in price and standards, and owned by the same people, is **Hotel Savoy** (☎ 31 51 34), on Carrera 18 between Calles 21 and 22. Marginally better is **Hotel Florida** (☎ 32 98 04), on Carrera 19 between Calles 31 and 32, which costs US$19/24/27.

Also available are two affordable options on Avenida Vargas: the **Hotel Hevelín** (☎ 52 24 87, 52 39 86), with doubles/triples for US$28/32, and **Hotel Yacambú** (☎ 52 30 78, 52 10 77), for US$35/40. None of the hotels listed above is a Hilton – their common problem is age (all are old and renovations have been minimal), and consequently their air-conditioning can be rather noisy.

Among the better hotels in the city center are the **Hotel Bonifrán** (☎ 32 03 02, 32 24 34), on the corner of Carrera 19 and Calle 31 (US$40/45 double/triple), and **Hotel Príncipe** (☎ 31 21 11, 31 25 44), on Calle 23 between Carreras 18 and 19 (US$45/50).

The best place is the five-star **Hotel Barquisimeto Hilton** (☎ 53 60 22, fax 54 43 65), in Urbanización Nueva Segovia, 2km southeast of the city center.

Places to Eat

A row of basic restaurants on Carrera 24 next to the bus terminal will keep you going if you're waiting for a bus or staying in one of the terminal area's budget hotels. There's no risk of starving in the city center either, as it's packed with eating outlets, particularly Avenida Vargas and its environs and, to a lesser extent, Avenida 20.

For an inexpensive vegetarian lunch, head for **Restaurant Vegetariano Samana**, Carrera 15 between Calles 24 and 25, or **Restaurant Vegetariano Inversiones Pérez Colmenárez**, on the corner of Carrera 18 and Calle 26. Both are open weekdays from about noon to 3 pm only.

Barqui Pan, on the corner of Calle 26 and Carrera 18, is one of the central panaderías that has tables outside – a good place for a breakfast or just a cup of coffee. Still better is the new, trendy **Panadería La Francia 2000**, on the corner of Carrera 19 and Calle 25, which has sandwiches, pizzas, pastries etc.

Getting There & Away

Air The airport is 4km southwest of the center. The Ruta 7 city bus runs between the bus terminal and airport; you can also take a taxi for about US$4. There are several departures a day to Caracas with Aeropostal, Aserca, Avior and Air Venezuela (US$48 to US$92). There are also direct flights to Coro

Hotel Crepusculo Calle 41 entre 18 y 19 ~$20⁰⁰
tel. (051) 46-34-11   Fax 46-39-25

(US$52), Mérida (US$45) and San Antonio del Táchira (US$85). All fares are one-way.

Bus Barquisimeto straddles an important crossroads, with roads (and, accordingly, buses) leading in all directions. The bus terminal is northwest of the center; and city buses frequently make the trip.

There are regular connections to Valencia (US$4 ordinary, three hours), Caracas (US$8 ordinary, US$10 deluxe, 5½ hours) and Maracaibo (US$7 ordinary, five hours). Half a dozen buses depart nightly to Mérida (US$10 ordinary, US$13 deluxe, seven hours) and San Cristóbal (US$14 deluxe, nine hours). Transporte Federación runs buses to Coro every two or three hours (US$8 ordinary, US$10 deluxe, seven hours). There are also ordinary buses to Valera (US$5), Guanare (US$4) and Barinas (US$5). Buses within the region (Quíbor, El Tocuyo, Sanare, Chivacoa etc) run frequently.

Train The train station is on the northwestern outskirts of Barquisimeto, but there are no longer passenger trains to Puerto Cabello.

CHIVACOA
☎ 051 (☎ 0251 from July 14, 2001)

Chivacoa (population 45,000), about 60km east of Barquisimeto on the road to Valencia, is the jumping-off point for Cerro de María Lionza, the holy mountain that is home to the cult of María Lionza (see the boxed text).

Chivacoa is a rather undistinguished town, except for an unusually large number of *perfumerías* selling everything imaginable related to the cult. It's an interesting experience to browse through these shops, to get a taste of the María Lionza phenomenon. Here you'll find an extensive collection of books and brochures dealing with magic, witchcraft, reading the future and the like; cigars; candles (indispensable ritual accessories); and an unbelievable range of essences, perfumes, lotions etc. You can also familiarize yourself with the cult's pantheon, as every perfumería has a complete stock of plaster figures of the deities in every size and color.

Places to Stay & Eat
Chivacoa has several budget places to stay within a few blocks of Plaza Bolívar. One of the cheapest options is *Hotel El Lusitano* (☎ 83 03 66), on the corner of Calle 10 and Avenida 12, which costs about US$10 for a matrimonial with bath and fan (US$14 with additional air-conditioning); it also has aircon doubles/triples for US$16/20. Similarly simple is *Hotel Abruzzese* (☎ 83 04 19), Avenida 9 between Calles 10 and 11, which costs marginally more. Possibly a bit better is *Hotel Venezia* (☎ 83 05 44), on the corner of Calle 12 and Avenida 9, which has all rooms with air-conditioning, priced at US$20/25 double/triple. All three hotels have their own restaurants, and there are more places to eat around the area.

Getting There & Away
Plenty of buses run between Barquisimeto and Valencia or San Felipe, all of which will let you off on the main road on Chivacoa's northern outskirts, a 10-minute walk to Plaza Bolívar.

There are also buses from Barquisimeto to Chivacoa (marked 'Chivacoa Directo') that will deposit you a couple of blocks south of Plaza Bolívar (US$1, one hour), as well as por puestos that go up to Plaza Bolívar and stop next to the church (US$1.50, 50 minutes).

CERRO DE MARÍA LIONZA
This mountain is the most sacred spot for followers of the María Lionza cult. The mountain outcrop stretches from east to west several kilometers south of Chivacoa and is part of a much larger mountain formation known as the 'Macizo de Nirgua.' Covered with thick rain forest, the range is rich in endemic species. It is the source of the state's largest river, the Río Yaracuy.

In 1960, Inparques declared the entire 117-sq-km area as the Monumento Natural María Lionza, in an attempt to protect the region from overuse by thousands of the

Cult of María Lionza

Venezuela's most curious quasi-religious phenomenon, the Cult of María Lionza is an amalgam of pre-Hispanic indigenous creeds, African voodoo and Christian practices. It involves magic, witchcraft, esoteric rites and trance rituals.

Few serious studies of the cult have been conducted, so many of its aspects, such as its origins or doctrines, are still obscure. What is clear, however, is that the cult attracts more and more followers every year, and spiritual centers proliferate in cities throughout the country. The 'guides,' or intermediaries, who run these centers claim to be able to communicate with deities and spirits, heal the sick, tell the future and the like.

In search of new inspiration – or in order to give more color and mystery to the cult – some guides adopt ideas and rites from other parts of the world, such as India, Japan and the Philippines. Consequently, the cult vocabulary is dotted with a plethora of exotic terms such as 'karma,' 'reincarnation,' 'yoga,' 'transmigration of souls' etc. This makes the María Lionza cult even more confusing, obscure and difficult to investigate.

The cult is pantheistic and involves a constellation of deities, spirits and other personalities with very diverse origins, the number of which is growing year by year. At the top of the hierarchy is María Lionza, a female deity usually portrayed as a beautiful woman riding a tapir. One story concerning her origin tells that centuries ago a woman from a dark-skinned tribe gave birth to a light-skinned, green-eyed girl of surpassing beauty. The girl grew up to be venerated by her tribe and, eventually, by the surrounding peoples. As the years passed, her life became the stuff of legends, and ever since she has been revered by her devoted followers.

La Reina (Queen) – as María Lionza is often referred to – is followed by countless divinities: historical or legendary personages, saints, powers of nature etc, usually grouped into *cortes* (courts). The list of the most popular deities includes Cacique Guaicaipuro, Negro Primero, the Virgen de Coromoto, Negro Felipe and Dr José Gregorio Hernández. For many followers, Hernández is second in importance after La Reina.

Although the María Lionza cult is practiced throughout Venezuela, its most sacred area and the focus for pilgrimages is the mountain range commonly referred to as the Cerro de María Lionza, south of the town of Chivacoa, in Yaracuy state. Devotees come here year-round, mostly on weekends, to practice their rites. The biggest celebrations, drawing in thousands, are held on October 12, El Día de la Raza (Discovery of America), and during Semana Santa (Holy Week, culminating in Easter).

cult's followers. However, the religious significance of the mountain overshadows its natural wealth.

Several sanctuaries have emerged along the northern foothill of the mountain, where pilgrims flock before heading up the slopes. The most important of these are Sorte and Quiballo (or Quibayo). Both have their own Altar Mayor, where the initial celebrations are performed before the group and its medium head off to the shrine of their choice, one of many that are

scattered all over the forest. It's at these shrines that the proper rites are performed; they may last the whole night or longer and usually include a trance seance.

Quiballo

Not really much of a town, Quiballo is just a collection of several dozen shabby shacks that are either perfumerías or basic places to eat. The Altar Mayor on the riverbank shelters a bizarre collection of images that you will have already seen in Chivacoa –

figures of Bolívar, various Indian caciques, and numerous statues of María Lionza herself. The faithful sit in front of the altar, smoke cigars and light candles. The Inparques office is 30m from the altar.

Quiballo is far larger than Sorte (so it has more frequent transportation) and seems to be more accustomed to casual visitors. However, it's not a tourist spot by any definition. Behave sensibly and modestly, and don't openly use your camera, which may easily arouse hostile reactions from cult believers.

Hiking the Mountain

From the Quiballo altar, a path goes over the bridge to the opposite bank of the river (in which the faithful perform ritual ablutions) and then splits into a maze of paths that wind up the mountain slope, some climbing to the very top. All along the paths are *portales* (literally, 'gates'), shrines dedicated to particular deities or spirits. On the top are Las Tres Casitas (Three Little Houses) of Cacique Guaicaipuro, Reina María Lionza and Negro Felipe. A sketch map of the route and portales is posted on the side of the Altar Mayor. Technically, the trip to the top takes three hours, but there are several dangers to watch out for along the way.

Followers of the cult point out that the trip to the top is full of drawbacks. At each portal you have to ask the respective spirit for permission to pass. This is done by smoking cigars, lighting candles and presenting offerings. Permission may or may not be granted. One of the devotees commented that he had tried on various occasions and hadn't succeeded. Those who continue on without permission may be punished by the spirits. Some, local stories claim, have never returned.

The Inparques staff have a far more rational standpoint. They don't recommend the trip to the summit because of muddy paths, snakes and the possibility of getting lost in the maze of paths.

An additional drawback is that, like any other place with crowds of people, the path attracts thieves: Robberies have been reported by travelers. Try not to venture too far on your own, and keep your wits about you. The question of to what degree you comply with the spirits' wishes is up to you.

Wandering around, especially on weekends, you may come across a group of faithful practicing their rituals. Keep away unless you're invited or unless you are with a guide who will introduce you.

Places to Stay & Eat

There are no hotels in either Sorte or Quiballo, but you can camp in a tent or sling a hammock as the pilgrims do. If this is the case, never leave your tent and belongings unattended. You won't starve at the shack restaurants, but their offerings are mostly basic and their prices inflated.

Getting There & Away

Jeeps to Quiballo depart when full from Chivacoa's Plaza Bolívar (US$0.80, 20 minutes). They run regularly on weekends, but there may be only a few departures on weekdays. Jeeps to Sorte (US$0.80, 15 minutes) are even less frequent. The jeeps travel 4km south on a good paved road to a large ceiba tree in the middle of the road, then turn right onto a rough road and continue through sugarcane plantations for another 4km to Quiballo. The road to Sorte branches off to the left 1km past the ceiba.

QUÍBOR

☎ 053 (☎ 0253 from July 14, 2001)

Quíbor, about 35km southwest by freeway from Barquisimeto, is a sizable (population 158,000) and swiftly growing satellite town of the state capital. It was founded in 1620, but little evidence of its colonial past remains. However, it may still be worth stopping if you're wandering around the region.

Things to See

One of the oldest colonial relics, dating from the town's foundation, is the **Ermita de Nuestra Señora de Altagracia**, a fortresslike church on Calle 13 between Avenidas 19 and 20, on the northern edge of the town. The large **Iglesia de Nuestra**

Señora de Altagracia, on Plaza Bolívar, is also named after the patron saint but was built only in 1808 and was reconstructed after the earthquake of 1881.

In the northwestern corner of Plaza Bolívar is the **Cementerio Indígena de Quíbor**, a pre-Hispanic cemetery excavated in the 1960s. Most of the finds from the cemetery are now on display in the **Museo Arqueológico**, on the corner of Calle 12 and Avenida 10, two blocks north of Plaza Bolívar. The museum, which opened in 1999 after an extensive, snail's-pace reconstruction, features a small but well-prepared and interesting collection that includes Indian tombs, funerary urns and other ceramic pieces. It can be visited 9 am to noon and 2 to 5 pm Tuesday to Friday, 10 am to 5 pm weekends.

Places to Stay
Quíbor has just a few hotels. For somewhere cheap, try *Hotel El Gran Duque* (☎ *41 01 49)*, next to La Ceiba gas station on Avenida Florencio Jiménez, at the entrance to the town from Barquisimeto. It costs US$10/12 matrimonial/double with fan, US$14/16 with air-conditioning.

The best place to stay in town is *Hostería Valle de Quíbor* (☎ *41 06 01)*, three blocks southeast of Plaza Bolívar on the corner of Avenida 5 and Calle 7. It offers rooms (US$33/38/42 for an air-con matrimonial/double/triple with bathroom and TV) and cabañas (US$26/28/30) and has its own restaurant, piano bar and swimming pool.

Getting There & Away
Buses between Barquisimeto and Quíbor run frequently from 6 am to 6 pm (US$0.75, 45 minutes). There are also por puestos (US$1, 30 minutes). In Barquisimeto, they depart from the bus terminal; in Quíbor, they line up at the corner of Avenida 6 and Calle 12, one long block south of Plaza Bolívar. Buses to El Tocuyo run along Avenida 7, lining Plaza Bolívar.

EL TOCUYO
☎ 053 (☎ 0253 from July 14, 2001)
The diminutive town of Nuestra Señora de la Pura y Limpia Concepción del Tocuyo

was founded in 1545 in a verdant valley of the Río Tocuyo. Two years later it became the capital of Venezuela, after the authorities moved the seat of government here from Coro following the revocation of the contract with the Welsers and the departure of the Germans (see the Coro section, earlier in this chapter). El Tocuyo remained the capital until 1577, when the capital was transferred to Caracas, and over that time, it evolved into a graceful colonial town. Despite its political downgrading, El Tocuyo continued to grow, taking advantage of its fertile soil, which is ideal for growing sugarcane and a variety of vegetables. Over the colonial period, seven churches and a number of splendid mansions were built.

Sadly, a serious earthquake in 1950 ruined a good number of the buildings. The job was completed by Colonel Marcos Pérez Jiménez, Venezuela's dictator at the time. On his orders, most of the damaged structures were demolished and a new town was built on the site. Hence, in effect El Tocuyo is now a modern town of 52,000, with just a handful of restored or reconstructed historic buildings.

Things to See
The most important monument related to colonial times is the **Iglesia de Nuestra Señora de la Concepción**, two blocks west of Plaza Bolívar. It shared the fate of most other buildings and was bulldozed (despite the fact that it could have been repaired) but was later reconstructed.

The church's whitewashed exterior is noted for its exceptional bell tower and fine façade. Inside, the splendid retable from the 1760s (which miraculously survived the earthquake) takes up the whole wall behind the high altar. Like almost all altarpieces of the period, it was carved entirely out of wood but, unusually, was not painted or gilded; it's the only one of its kind in the country. Look around the interior and you'll see other relics from the colonial past, among them the original pulpit. Unfortunately, the church is open only for religious services, normally held at 6 pm on weekdays, with more masses on Sunday.

None of the other colonial churches were restored or reconstructed, but two were left in ruins, untouched from the day of the earthquake: the **Iglesia de Santo Domingo**, on the corner of Carrera 10 and Calle 19, and the **Iglesia de Belén**, on Carrera 12 between Calles 15 and 17.

The town has two small museums. The **Museo Arqueológico JM Cruxent** (open 3 to 6 pm Wednesday to Friday, 9 am to 2 pm weekends), on the northern side of Plaza Bolívar, has some pre-Columbian ceramics found in the region. The **Museo Lisandro Alvarado** (named after the locally born politician, doctor and anthropologist), on Calle 17 near the corner of Carrera 11, features historic objects related to the town. It's open 9 am to noon and 2:30 to 5 pm Tuesday to Friday, 10 am to 4 pm weekends.

You can enter the **Casa de la Cultura**, a former convent on the Plaza Bolívar, to see its spacious courtyard and some photos depicting the damage by the 1950 earthquake that it somehow withstood.

Places to Stay
The most attractive place to stay is **Posada Colonial** (☎ 63 24 95), on Avenida Fraternidad between Calles 17 and 18, near Plaza Bolívar. It has a fine location, a restaurant and a swimming pool, and costs US$22/25/28 for an air-conditioned matrimonial/double/triple. Cheaper (but less stylish) lodging options include **Hotel Venezia** (☎ 63 12 67), on the corner of Calle Comercio and Carrera 9, and **Hotel Nazaret** (☎ 63 24 34), on Avenida Fraternidad between Calles 7 and 8.

Getting There & Away
Buses between Barquisimeto and El Tocuyo run at least every half-hour until about 6 pm (US$1.50, 1¼ hours). There are also por puestos (US$2, one hour).

SANARE
☎ 053 (☎ 0253 from July 14, 2001)
With its steep streets winding over hillsides, Sanare is pleasant town of 12,000 that radiates a distinctly mountain atmosphere. Founded in 1620, it features such historic relics as the three-nave Santa Ana church.

The town lies at about 1400m, making for a fresh climate with an average temperature of 20°C. In addition to these charms, Sanare is a gateway to the Parque Nacional Yacambú.

Places to Stay & Eat
The most charming place to stay is the well-kept **Posada Turística El Cerrito** (☎/fax 49 00 16), about half a kilometer south of Plaza Bolívar (take Calle 17 from the square). Built in a colonial style, the posada has doubles/triples/quads with bath and hot water for US$24/28/36.

Half a kilometer up the road, on the way to Yacambú national park, is **Posada Los Sauces** (☎ 49 08 53), which is slightly cheaper but isn't as good. Alternatively, you can stay in the very central **Hotel Taburiente** (☎ 49 01 48), on Avenida Miranda 40m from the church. Rooms cost US$15/18/22 matrimonial/double/triple.

Probably the most comfortable option, the new **Hotel La Fumarola** (☎ 49 07 53), 2km north of Sanare on the road to Quíbor, costs around US$35 triple and has a swimming pool.

All four hotels have their own restaurants, of which the ones in El Cerrito and La Fumarola are probably the best. There are more restaurants scattered throughout the town's center.

Getting There & Away
Por puesto minibuses run between Barquisimeto and Sanare until midafternoon (US$1.50, 1¼ hours).

PARQUE NACIONAL YACAMBÚ
This park was created in 1962 to protect a 145-sq-km chunk of the mountain range known as the 'Sierra de Portuguesa,' just southeast of Sanare. This is actually the northern part of the Andean massif, reaching elevations of up to 2200m within the park's boundaries. The park has Venezuela's only active volcano, locally called 'La Fumarola' after the cloud of smoke that floats over it.

Most of the park's area is covered with cloud forest featuring plant species typical of the Andes, many of which are endemic.

About 60 species of orchid have been recorded. There haven't been any detailed studies of the fauna, but it is remarkably rich and includes rare, endangered mammals such as the spectacled bear (*oso frontino*) and jaguar. The park is particularly good for bird-watchers.

Yacambú is an important water resource for the region, and there's a large reservoir, the Embalse Yacambú, formed by a dam built just south of the park. The rainy period is from April to November; the mean annual rainfall in some upper areas reaches up to 3000mm.

Orientation

Access to the park is from Sanare by the 30km road that goes to the dam. This road crosses the park and passes near the Inparques administrative center at El Blanquito, about 20km from Sanare. The rangers here can give you information about the walks and sights, including *miradores* (viewpoints), waterfalls and the Cañón de Angostura, the gorge formed by the Río Negro.

Places to Stay

The park provides accommodations in 12-bed cabins and dormitory modules (bring your sheets) in El Blanquito, but you need to pay for the whole cabin or module (US$30 each), not just the beds you're going to use. Camping is allowed for US$4 per tent. You should book cabins several days in advance at the Inparques office in Barquisimeto (☎ 051-54 81 18, ☎/fax 54 91 03), in the southeastern corner of the Parque del Este on Avenida Libertador. Payment for both cabins and camping has to be made at a bank before you go – Inparques will give you details.

Getting There & Away

There doesn't seem to be a regular form of public transportation to the park other than occasional por puestos from Sanare. Negotiate the ride with drivers in Sanare.

CARORA
☎ 052 (☎ 0252 from July 14, 2001)

Carora, about 100km west of Barquisimeto on the road to Maracaibo, is the second-largest town in the state of Lara (population 90,000), after Barquisimeto. Founded in 1569 on the bank of the Río Morere, the town has experienced several serious floods, the last in 1973. Despite considerable damage, Carora has preserved a good deal of its colonial architecture. The historic center has been extensively restored and is an attractive place to explore on foot.

The town's main thoroughfares are Avenida Francisco de Miranda and Avenida 14 de Febrero, and most of the shops, offices, hotels and restaurants lie here. The historic sector is about 1km to the northwest, close to the river. The town is small enough to get around on foot; alternatively, you can use *micros* (small buses), which link its old and new sectors.

Information

The Banco Unión is on the corner of Carrera Lara and Calle Rivas. The Corp Banca is on Avenida Francisco de Miranda, half a kilometer southeast of Avenida 14 de Febrero, and the Banco de Venezuela is one block farther.

Carora Viajes (☎ 21 59 81, ☎/fax 21 43 95), Calle San Juan, is a travel agency that can provide some tourist information and organize regional tours.

Old Town

The historic part of town, around Plaza Bolívar, is neat, well kept and colonial in style, even though not all the buildings date from that period. Some of the most interesting houses have been clearly labeled. They include the **Casa Amarilla**, the oldest surviving house in town (mid-17th century), now a public library, and **El Balcón de los Álvarez**, an 18th-century house where Bolívar stayed in 1821. The **Casa de Juan Jacinto Lara** was the birthplace of its eponymous hero of the War of Independence, who gave his name to the state.

The town has some fine colonial churches. The main one, **Iglesia de San Juan Bautista** (raised in 1992 to the rank of cathedral), on Plaza Bolívar, was built in the middle of the 17th century and has preserved its original external form intact. Its

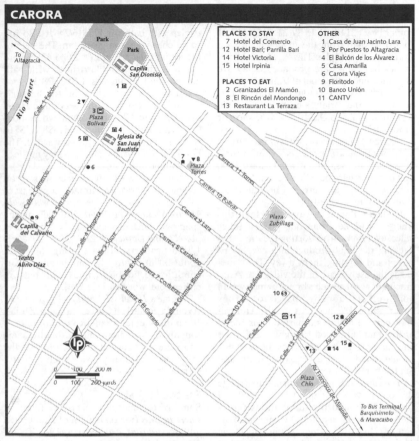

CARORA

PLACES TO STAY
7 Hotel del Comercio
12 Hotel Barí; Parrilla Barí
14 Hotel Victoria
15 Hotel Irpinia

PLACES TO EAT
2 Granizados El Mamón
8 El Rincón del Mondongo
13 Restaurant La Terraza

OTHER
1 Casa de Juan Jacinto Lara
3 Por Puestos to Altagracia
4 El Balcón de los Álvarez
5 Casa Amarilla
6 Carora Viajes
9 Floritodo
10 Banco Unión
11 CANTV

THE NORTHWEST

beautiful, richly gilded main retable dates from 1760. The church is open in the early morning and late afternoon.

The renovated **Capilla San Dionisio**, one block north of Plaza Bolívar, dates from 1743. It's used only for special ceremonies, including funerals, and is closed at other times. About 300m northeast of San Dionisio, in the middle of arid bushland, is the striking ruin of the **Iglesia de la Purísima Concepción**, commonly referred to as the 'Portal de la Pastora.' You'll get a good view of the ruin from the dike at the end of Calle Comercio.

On the opposite, southwestern end of Calle Comercio is the **Capilla del Calvario**. It has one of the most amazing church façades in Venezuela, an extraordinary example of local baroque. Its simple interior features an interesting main retable, plus two side retables on both walls. The chapel is often open in the morning, but if it's locked, the keys are kept in the Floritodo, a flower shop diagonally opposite the church.

The modern Teatro Alirio Díaz, next to the chapel, has a small archaeological collection displayed in its foyer. The guards will let you in during the day.

Bodegas Pomar

On Carora's southern outskirts, Bodegas Pomar (☎ 21 21 91, 21 18 89, 21 79 21, fax 21 70 14) lie 3km from the town's center on Carretera Lara-Zulia. This is where Venezuela's best wines are produced. They are marketed under the label of Viña Altagracia and distributed throughout the country. Depending on the variety, a bottle of wine will cost about US$5 to US$10 in a wine shop or supermarket.

Venezuela has almost no wine tradition. Viña Altagracia started its experimental phase only in 1985, and it wasn't until 1990 that commercial production began. A dozen varieties of wine are currently produced, including whites and reds.

Bodegas Pomar feature the facilities where the whole production process takes place: everything from sorting the grapes to packing the final product into cardboard boxes and sending them away. The vineyards themselves are in the village of Altagracia (hence the wine's brand name), 24km northwest of Carora by a paved road. They cover about 125 hectares in all. Altagracia's climate features a harmonious blend of low humidity, good sunlight, warm days and fresh nights year-round, so the crop can be harvested twice a year (in March and September).

You can visit Bodegas Pomar, but arrange this one or two days in advance. They will show you around the installations (commentary in Spanish only). They may also organize a visit to the vineyards in Altagracia in either their or (preferably) your means of transportation. If you want to go there on your own, contact them to arrange your visit to the vineyards. Por puestos to Altagracia depart infrequently from Plaza Bolívar.

Places to Stay

There are three hotels close to each other on Avenida 14 de Febrero, near Avenida Francisco de Miranda, in the town's new center. The cheapest is *Hotel Victoria*, on the corner of Carrera Carabobo. It's simple, but what would you expect for US$8 for a double room with bath and fan?

If you need air-conditioning, try *Hotel Barí* (☎ 21 67 45), which has matrimoniales/triples with bath for US$16/24. It also has some cheaper rooms with fan. The best of the lot is *Hotel Irpinia* (☎ 21 63 62), where spacious singles/doubles/triples with bath and air-conditioning cost US$22/28/34.

There are no hotels in the historic quarter. The closest is the very basic *Hotel del Comercio*, Carrera Bolívar, where doubles with bath and fan cost US$8 (US$10 with air-conditioning). But be warned: The hotel's *cervecería* (bar) likes to play music at full volume until late.

There are two better places to stay on Avenida Francisco de Miranda, southeast of the center. Closer to the center is *Posada Madre Vieja* (☎ 21 25 90, 21 37 87), in the spacious gardenlike grounds. The other place, *Hotel Catuca* (☎ 21 33 10, 21 33 02), is 1.5km farther southeast along the road, about 300m before the bus terminal. Air-conditioned doubles/triples with bath in either hotel will cost US$35/42.

The new *Hotel El Amparo* (☎ 21 01 11), Avenida Rotaria (Carretera Lara-Zulia), 100m off Avenida Francisco de Miranda, is roughly midway between the Madre Vieja and Catuca. It costs much the same as the other two, but does provide slightly better standards.

Places to Eat

Some of the cheapest meals are found at *Parrilla Barí* (the restaurant of Hotel Barí) and *Restaurant La Terraza*. The new *El Rincón del Mondongo*, on Plaza Torres, is also cheap. *Granizados El Mamón*, on Plaza Bolívar, has fruit juices, snacks and delicious *granizados* (a cross between ice cream and juice). *Posada Madre Vieja*, *Hotel Catuca* and *Hotel El Amparo* all have their own restaurants.

Getting There & Away

Carora lies about 3km north off the Barquisimeto-Maracaibo freeway. A new bus terminal opened on Avenida Francisco de Miranda, on the southeastern outskirts of town, about half a kilometer northwest off the freeway. The terminal is linked to the town's center by city minibuses.

Carora has half-hourly buseta connections with Barquisimeto (US$2.50, 1½ hours); there are also por puestos (US$3, 1¼ hours). It's an interesting trip on a good *autopista* (freeway) across arid, hilly countryside. Ordinary buses to Maracaibo (US$4.50, 3½ hours) come through from Barquisimeto every hour or so. To Caracas (US$12, seven hours), air-conditioned buses come through from Maracaibo; it may be faster to go to Barquisimeto and change there.

Zulia State

MARACAIBO
☎ 061 (☎ 0261 from May 19, 2001)

Although the region was explored as early as 1499, and Maracaibo was founded in 1574 (after several previous unsuccessful attempts), the town really began to grow only in the 18th century as the port that serviced trade between the Andean region and the Netherlands Antilles and beyond. The republicans' naval victory over the Spanish fleet, won on Lago de Maracaibo on July 24, 1823, brought political importance to the town. It was not, however, until 1914 that the first oil well, Zumaque No 1, was sunk in the area, precipitating the oil boom. The city developed into Venezuela's oil capital, with two-thirds of the nation's output coming from beneath the lake.

Maracaibo (population 1.3 million) is today the country's largest urban center after Caracas and a predominantly modern, prosperous city. It's the capital of Zulia, Venezuela's richest state, and is also an important port. The city's climate is hot, humid and often windless, with an average temperature of 30°C – among the highest on the continent. *Maracuchos,* as local inhabitants are called, have a more regional outlook than other Venezuelans, with some separatist tendencies apparent in local government circles and influential groups. Many feel that their state produces the money that the rest of the country spends. And it's not just oil

money: Zulia has large deposits of coal, and also shelters other mineral resources, including copper, clay and salt. The state produces 45% of Venezuela's poultry and 35% of its eggs, and provides important shares of other food products, such as milk, beef, fish, sugar and plantains.

The region around the city preserves some of its original culture and way of life. The Guajiros, to the north, and the Yukpa and Barí, to the west, are among the most traditional indigenous groups in the country. Maracaibo is probably the only city in Venezuela where you can still see Indians in their native dress, particularly the Guajiro women in their traditional *mantas* (colorful, long, loose dresses) and *alpargatas* (sandals with giant pompoms), and sometimes with their faces painted with a dark pigment.

Maracaibo has no absolute must-see attractions, and few tourists bother to come here. However, you may need to stop in the city on the way to or from the Colombian coast, or you may just want to catch a glimpse of what an oil capital is really like. As with any city of its size, Maracaibo offers developed tourist facilities, and you may even find it interesting and agreeable despite the nearly unbearable heat.

With more time, you can explore the surrounding region, which offers a range of attractions, from a community living in houses built on stilts on Laguna de Sinamaica to forests of oil derricks on Lago de Maracaibo. The Around Maracaibo section, later, details some of the regional sights.

Information
Tourist Offices The Corpozulia tourist office (☎ 92 18 11, 92 18 40) is on the 9th floor of the high-rise Edificio Corpozulia, on Avenida Bella Vista between Calles 83 and 84. It's about 2km north of the old town; the Bella Vista por puestos from Plaza Bolívar will take you there. The office is open 8 am to noon and 1 to 4 pm weekdays.

The Corzutur (Corporación Zuliana de Turismo) tourist office (☎ 83 49 28) is on the 4th floor of the Edificio Lieja, on the corner

THE NORTHWEST

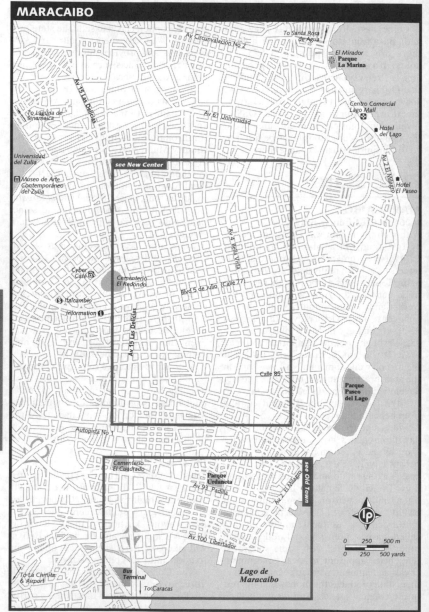

MARACAIBO

To Santa Rosa de Agua

Av Circunvalación No 2

El Mirador
Parque La Marina

To Laguna de Sinamaica

Av 67 Universidad

Centro Comercial Lago Mall

Hotel del Lago

Av 2 El Milagro

Universidad del Zulia

Museo de Arte Contemporáneo del Zulia

Hotel El Paseo

see New Center

Av 4 Bella Vista

Cyber Café

Cementerio El Redondo

Blvd 5 de Julio (Calle 77)

Italcambio

Information

Av 15 Las Delicias

Av 15 Las Delicias

Calle 85

Parque Paseo del Lago

Autopista No 1

Cementerio El Cuadrado

Parque Urdaneta

Av 93 Padilla

Av 2 El Milagro

see Old Town

Av 100 Libertador

To La Chinita & Airport

Bus Terminal

To Caracas

Lago de Maracaibo

0   250   500 m
0   250   500 yards

of Avenida 18 and Calle 78. It's open 8 am to noon and 1 to 5 pm weekdays.

Money Some of the major banks are marked on the maps. For changing cash, two casas de cambio are useful. Italcambio has offices in Centro Comercial Montielco (☎ 83 20 40), on Avenida 20 at Calle 72; in Centro Comercial Lago Mall (☎ 93 29 83), on Avenida El Milagro; and at the airport (☎ 36 25 13). Casa de Cambio Maracaibo has its offices on Avenida 9B between Calles 77 and 78 (☎ 97 25 76) and in Centro Comercial Lago Mall (☎ 92 21 74).

There are several casas de cambio in the bus terminal that change Venezuelan bolívares into Colombian pesos and vice versa.

Email & Internet Access La Casa de los Milagros (☎ 93 03 51), Calle 72 at Avenida 3F, is a charming café/art gallery and one of the few central places that provide budget email and Internet access; it's open late (8 am to midnight Monday to Saturday, 4 pm to midnight Sunday) and costs US$3 an hour. You can also try Cyber Café (☎ 59 24 55), Calle 72 between Avenidas 16 and 17, and Postnet (☎ 49 15 15, 49 05 97), on Avenida Las Delicias. Farther outside the center, you can find Internet facilities in Centro Comercial Lago Mall, Avenida El Milagro, and in Centro Comercial Galerías, Avenida La Limpia.

Old Town

Most of the tourist sights are in the oldest part of the city, only a short walk from each other. The axis of this sector is the **Paseo de las Ciencias**, a seven-block by one-block park created after the demolition of the colonial buildings that had previously stood on the site. This controversial plan was executed in 1973, effectively cutting the very heart out of the old town. The only structure not pulled down was the **Iglesia de Santa Bárbara** in the middle of the paseo. The park itself has been graced with fountains and works by contemporary artists, including one by Jesús Soto. Unfortunately, none of the fountains work anymore, and some of the sculptures have been vandalized.

At the western end of the paseo stands the **Basílica de Chiquinquirá**, with its opulent interior decoration. Its most venerated image is the Virgin of Chiquinquirá, affectionately referred to as 'La Chinita,' in the high altar. Legend has it that the image of the Virgin, painted on a small wooden board, was found in 1709 by a humble campesina on the shore of Lago de Maracaibo. Upon being brought to her home, the image began to glow. It was then taken to the church, and miracles started to happen. In 1942 the Virgin was crowned as the patron saint of Zulia state.

The image of the Virgin Mary, accompanied by San Andrés and San Antonio, is hardly recognizable from a distance. Special access is provided to allow you to get close to it. You can then also appreciate the large crown above the image, made of gold and encrusted with precious stones. Pilgrims gather here year-round, but the major celebrations – the Feria de la Chinita – are held in November, culminating with a procession on the 18th.

The eastern end of the Paseo de las Ciencias is bordered by the **Plaza Bolívar**, with the hero's statue in the middle, and the 19th-century **Catedral** on the eastern side. The most revered image in the cathedral is the Cristo Negro or Cristo de Gibraltar, so called as it was originally in the church of Gibraltar, a town on the southern shore of Lago de Maracaibo. The town was overrun and burned by Indians in 1600, but the crucifix miraculously survived, even though the cross to which the statue was nailed was incinerated. Blackened by smoke, Cristo Negro is also known, like La Chinita, for his miraculous powers, and he attracts pilgrims from the region and beyond. The image is in the chapel to the left of the high altar.

On the northern side of the plaza is the large, arcaded mid-19th-century **Palacio de Gobierno**, also called the Palacio de las Águilas (Palace of the Eagles) for the two condors placed on its roof. To the west is the **Casa de la Capitulación**, also known as 'Casa Morales,' built at the end of the 18th century as the residence of Maracaibo's governor. Today it is the only residential

OLD TOWN

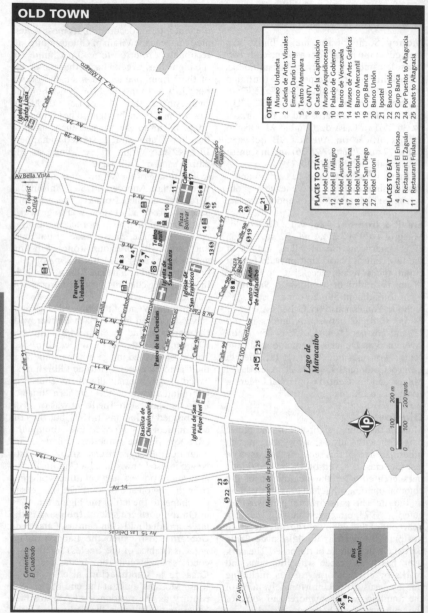

THE NORTHWEST

colonial building left in the city. It was here that on August 3, 1823, the act of capitulation was signed by the Spanish, after their defeat on Lago de Maracaibo. The house has been restored, fitted with period furniture and decorated with paintings of heroes of the War of Independence. It can be visited 9 am to 1 pm and 2 to 6 pm Tuesday to Saturday.

Just across the street from the casa is the monumental **Teatro Baralt**, inaugurated in 1883 and recently opened after extensive restoration. Half-hour guided tours around the site are run 9 am to noon and 2:30 to 6 pm weekdays, if there are no other activities in the theater. On the southern side of the plaza is the **Museo de Artes Gráficas**, which stages temporary exhibits. It's open 8 am to 4 pm weekdays.

One block north of Plaza Bolívar is the **Museo Arquidiocesano**, featuring religious artwork from the region. It was closed for restoration at the time of writing.

A short walk northwest will take you to the **Museo Urdaneta**. Born in Maracaibo in 1788, General Rafael Urdaneta is the city's greatest hero, distinguishing himself in numerous battles in the War of Independence. The museum, built on the site of Urdaneta's birth, features a collection of objects, documents, paintings and other memorabilia related to the general and the events of the period. It's open 9 am to noon and 2 to 5 pm Tuesday to Friday, 10 am to 1 pm weekends.

Calle 94, better known as **Calle Carabobo**, has been partially restored to its former appearance, characteristic for the brightly colored facades and grilled windows of the houses. The most spectacular part of the street is between Avenidas 6 and 8. Another area noted for fine old houses is around the Iglesia de Santa Lucía (see the Old Town map).

The sector south of the Paseo de las Ciencias is a wonder of heat, dirt and chaos. Countless street stalls give the area a market feel. The most striking sight here is the imposing old market building overlooking the docks. A curious metal structure with certain art nouveau features, it was built on the site of the previous market,

which was destroyed by fire in 1927. The building operated as the Mercado Principal from 1931 to 1973. It has been wholly remodeled and refurbished, and was turned into the **Centro de Arte de Maracaibo**, which opened in 1993. It now stages temporary exhibitions and has an arts-and-crafts gallery.

Other Attractions

Parque La Marina is on the lakeshore at the confluence of Avenidas El Milagro and Bella Vista, 5km north of the center. It features **El Mirador** (Lookout), on top of a high tower, which provides a good view over the city and the lake.

A few kilometers farther north is **Santa Rosa de Agua**, once a small lakeside village, today a suburb within the city boundaries. There are some *palafitos* (houses built on stilts) on the shore that might be worth a visit if you don't plan on a trip to Laguna de Sinamaica (see the Around Maracaibo section, later). Perhaps it was in Santa Rosa that the Spaniards in 1499 first saw these houses and gave Venezuela its name (see History, in the Facts about Venezuela chapter). There is a bust of Amerigo Vespucci, who took part in that Spanish expedition, on the plaza near the waterfront.

The new **Museo de Arte Contemporáneo del Zulia**, popularly known as MACZUL, has opened in the grounds of the Universidad del Zulia, on Avenida Universidad. It will still take a while to fill up the huge exhibition spaces, but it's easily one of the country's leading museums of its kind, probably the most important after the one in Caracas and undoubtedly far larger. It's open 9 am to 5 pm Tuesday to Sunday.

On the northern outskirts of Maracaibo, on the road to Sinamaica, is the **Planetario Simón Bolívar** (Simón Bolívar Planetarium), open 9 am to 3 pm Tuesday to Saturday, 9 am to 4 pm Sunday.

Special Events

Maracaibo's major annual event is the Feria de la Chinita, which springs to life around November 10 and continues until the coronation of the Virgin on November 18. Apart

The Music of Maracaibo

Gaita is the typical musical genre of Mara-caibo. This lively percussion-based music is performed by a band using a variety of typical instruments, such as the *cuatro* (a small, four-stringed guitarlike instrument) maracas, *furruco* (a percussion instrument) and *charrasca* (another percussion instru-ment). Lyrics are mostly either religious or political and are largely improvised. Ricardo Aguirre (1939–69), nicknamed 'El Monu-mental,' is considered one of the greatest gaita singers.

Gaita is particularly popular during the Christmas period, but the season usually extends from October to January. It can be heard less frequently in other months.

The genre came to Venezuela with the Spanish, but its origins are older, and some scholars claim that it has Persian roots. Gaita hasn't been overshadowed by the nation-wide *joropo*; on the contrary, it has made its way well outside Zulia to become the second most popular national beat.

from religious celebrations, the weeklong festival includes various cultural and pop-ular events such as bullfights, toros coleados, street parades and, obviously, music – above all the *gaita,* the typical local rhythm. The best time to listen to the gaita is on the eve of November 18, when musical groups ga-ther in front of the basilica to play the *Sere-nata para la Virgen* (Serenade for the Virgin).

Places to Stay

Maracaibo has notorious water-supply problems, which may affect you in hotels, particularly the budget ones. Inquire before checking in.

Budget If you're just trapped for the night in the city, head for one of several very basic hotels on the western side of the bus termi-nal. They are poor and overpriced, but you'll save on a trip to the center in search for a similarly primitive shelter. Try *Hotel San Diego* or *Hotel Caroní*, which are perhaps a bit more acceptable than the others around, but have a look at the room before checking in.

The historic center has very little to offer as far as accommodations go. The cheapest shelters, such as *Hotel Santa Ana* and *Hotel Aurora*, behind the cathedral, rent rooms by the hour and are really basic. Marginally better is *Hotel Caribe* (☎ 22 59 86), on Avenida 7 near Avenida Padilla, though it's not good either. Air-conditioned singles/doubles/triples with bath go for US$14/18/22. It's better to book into *Hotel El Milagro* (☎ 22 89 34), which costs a bit more but is cleaner and better kept.

The old-style *Hotel Victoria* (☎ 22 96 97, 22 94 66), overlooking Plaza Baralt and the old market building, must have once been a beautiful place. Increasingly unkempt and run-down, it's now a shade of its former glory, yet it's the only central hotel with character and is perhaps still worth consid-ering. It has spacious rooms with bath and air-conditioning for US$13/15/18 single/matrimonial/double. Make sure to choose a room with a balcony and a good view over the plaza.

If you plan on hanging around in town for a while, it's probably better and safer to stay farther north of the historic center, where there are a number of budget hotels with standards that are generally better than those of their old-town counterparts. From south to north, you have the older-style *Hotel Nuevo Montevideo* (☎ 22 27 62, Calle 86A No 4-96); the small *Nuevo Hotel Unión* (☎ 93 32 78, Calle 84 No 4-60); the family-run *Hotel Oasis Garden* (☎ 97 95 82, Calle 82B No 8-25); *Hotel San Martín* (☎ 91 50 95, Avenida 3Y No 80-11); and the simple *Hotel Astor* (☎ 91 45 10, 91 45 30), on Plaza República. All the listed hotels have air-conditioned rooms with private bath. The Astor is the cheapest of the lot, priced at US$13/15 matrimonial/double, while the Oasis Garden is the most expensive (US$23/27). The remaining three charge about US$15/18. All the hotels are easily ac-cessible by frequent por puestos running along Avenida Bella Vista.

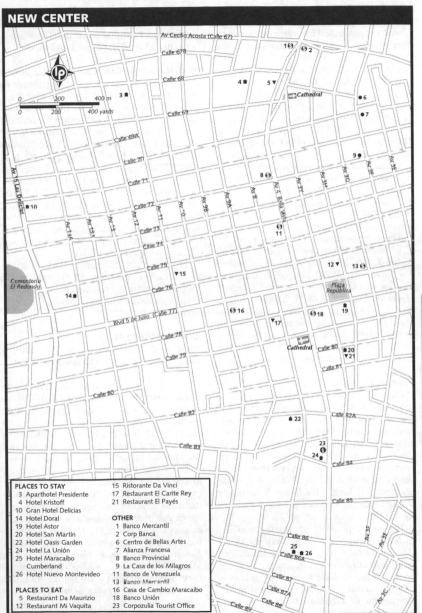

NEW CENTER

PLACES TO STAY
3 Aparthotel Presidente
4 Hotel Kristoff
10 Gran Hotel Delicias
14 Hotel Doral
19 Hotel Astor
20 Hotel San Martín
22 Hotel Oasis Garden
24 Hotel La Unión
25 Hotel Maracaibo
    Cumberland
26 Hotel Nuevo Montevideo

PLACES TO EAT
5 Restaurant Da Maurizio
12 Restaurant Mi Vaquita
15 Ristorante Da Vinci
17 Restaurant El Carite Rey
21 Restaurant El Payés

OTHER
1 Banco Mercantil
2 Corp Banca
6 Centro de Bellas Artes
7 Alianza Francesa
8 Banco Provincial
9 La Casa de los Milagros
11 Banco de Venezuela
13 Banco Mercantil
16 Casa de Cambio Maracaibo
18 Banco Unión
23 Corpozulia Tourist Office

Mid-Range & Top End There are no mid-priced and upmarket hotels in the old city center; they all opted for more elegant, new districts, mainly in the northern part of the city.

One of the cheapest in this price bracket is the small *Hotel Doral* (☎ 97 83 85), Avenida 14A at Calle 75, which has doubles for about US$30, though it isn't anything memorable. More expensive and better is the three-star *Gran Hotel Delicias* (☎ 97 61 11, fax 97 30 37), on Avenida Las Delicias in the same area, which costs US$55 double.

Other three-star establishments include *Aparthotel Presidente* (☎/fax 98 31 33, Avenida 11 No 68-50), for about US$60 double; and *Hotel Maracaibo Cumberland* (☎ 22 29 44, 22 23 35, Calle 86A No 4-150), for around US$70 double.

There are several classier hotels in the city, among them the four-star *Hotel Kristoff* (☎ 97 29 11, fax 98 07 96, Avenida 8 No 68-48), at US$80 double. Better, and also more expensive, is the large lakeside *Hotel del Lago* (☎ 92 40 22, fax 93 03 92), on Avenida El Milagro (about US$130 double). There's another waterfront option nearby: *Hotel El Paseo* (☎ 92 40 84, fax 91 94 53), which costs US$160 double, but offers half-price room rates on weekends.

Places to Eat

Budget There are a lot of cheap eateries in the old town that serve set lunches for about US$3, but the quality of the food often mirrors the price. After 6 pm or so it's difficult to find a budget place to eat. One of the few cheap central outlets that keeps going until about 8 pm is *Restaurant Friulana* (Calle 95 No 3-06). While the white tiles make it look a bit like a hospital or public toilet, the portions are large and the food is OK.

Far more pleasant is *Restaurant El Enlosao*, in the Casa de los Artesanos, on Calle 94, which serves unpretentious but tasty food at low prices. A few paces away, on the corner of Calle 94 and Avenida 6, is another attractive eating establishment: *Restaurant El Zaguán*. The place consists of a restaurant serving comida criolla at reasonable prices, a bar, and an open-air café shaded by a beautiful old ceiba. The place is open until 11 pm but closed on Monday.

Mid-Range & Top End Like the hotels, the cream of the restaurants has gathered in the northern sector of the city. Many are concentrated around Boulevard 5 de Julio and Avenida Bella Vista, Maracaibo's new center. To name a few: *Restaurant Mi Vaquita* (steaks), on Avenida 3H; *Restaurant El Payés* (French), on Avenida 3Y; *Restaurant El Carite Rey* (seafood), on Calle 78 at Avenida 8A; *Ristorante Da Vinci* (Italian), on Avenida 11; and *Restaurant Da Maurizio* (Italian), on Avenida Bella Vista at Calle 68. Prices in these restaurants aren't low, but it's easy to find somewhere cheap to eat in this area. Many of the city's restaurants don't open on Sunday.

For something different, go to the revolving rooftop *Restaurant El Girasol* in the Hotel El Paseo. It's not cheap, but the food (international cuisine) is good and the views are excellent.

Entertainment

Have a look in *Panorama,* Maracaibo's major daily paper, for what's going on in the city.

Check the program of the *Centro de Bellas Artes CBA; Avenida 3F No 67-217,* in the new city center. It has a multipurpose auditorium used for concerts, art film and theater performances. CBA is also home to the Orquesta Sinfónica de Maracaibo and the Danza Contemporánea de Maracaibo.

In the old town, the *Centro de Arte de Maracaibo* (CAM) hosts musical and stage events and art films. The *Teatro Baralt* is the main central venue for theater performances, but it also presents other events. Additionally, the restored Calle 94 is coming to life. Pop into the *Galería de Artes Visuales Emerio Darío Lunar* (also known as the Museo Udón Pérez), which stages temporary arts-and-crafts exhibitions. On the same street is the *Teatro Mampara*, which also has an exhibition space.

Spectator Sports

Baseball games are played at the stadium of the Complejo Polideportivo, southwest of the Universidad de Zulia. Basketball games are played in the nearby gym in the same sports complex.

The horse-racing track, the Hipódromo de Santa Rita, is on the eastern side of Lago de Maracaibo, across the Rafael Urdaneta Bridge from the city. Races are held on Wednesday starting at 5:30 pm.

Getting There & Away

Air La Chinita airport is about 12km southwest of the city center. There's no public transportation; you have to take a taxi, which will cost about US$8.

There are plenty of flights to the main cities in the country, including more than a dozen flights daily to Caracas serviced by most major airlines (US$68 to US$87). Air Venezuela and Avior fly direct to Mérida (US$55). Aeropostal and Air Venezuela service San Antonio del Táchira (US$58 to US$82). Aserca goes to Porlamar (US$92). There are also direct flights to Barquisimeto (US$58) and Las Piedras (US$55). Prices listed are one-way. For other domestic destinations you usually have to change planes in Caracas.

Bus The large and busy bus terminal is about 1km southwest of the old city center. Frequent local transportation links the terminal to the center and other districts.

Ordinary buses to Coro (US$7, four hours) run every half-hour; those to Barquisimeto (US$8, five hours) depart every hour. There are regular departures to Caracas (US$20 deluxe, 10½ hours). Four or five buses depart nightly for San Cristóbal (US$14 deluxe, eight hours).

There are half a dozen nightly buses to Mérida (US$14 deluxe, nine hours); they all go along the western side of Lago de Maracaibo and then via El Vigía. No direct buses run to Mérida via Valera and on the Trans-Andean mountain road through El Águila. You must go to Valera (US$6, four hours, buses every half-hour) and change there for

another one to Mérida (US$5, five hours, four buses a day).

To Colombia Two bus companies, Bus Ven and Expreso Brasilia, run air-conditioned buses to Cartagena (US$32, 10 hours) via Santa Marta (US$25, 6½ hours) and Barranquilla (US$28, eight hours). Both carriers have desks at Maracaibo's bus terminal, from where each company has one or two departures very early in the morning. Book your ticket a day or two in advance. The buses cross the border at Paraguachón (you actually change buses there) and continue through Maicao, the first Colombian town.

You can also go by por puesto to Maicao and change. Por puestos depart regularly from about 5 am to 3 pm (US$12, 2½ hours) and go as far as Maicao's bus terminal. From there, several Colombian bus companies operate buses to Santa Marta (US$11, four hours) and farther on; buses depart frequently until about 5 pm. Note that Maicao is widely and justifiably known as a lawless town and is far from safe – stay there as briefly as possible.

All passport formalities are completed in Paraguachón at the border. The Venezuelan immigration authorities there will charge you an exit tax *(impuesto de salida)* of US$15, to be paid in cash bolívares.

You can change bolívares into Colombian pesos at Maracaibo's terminal or in Paraguachón, but don't take them farther into Colombia. They are very difficult to change beyond Maicao.

Set your watch back one hour when crossing from Venezuela to Colombia. If you enter Venezuela this way from Colombia, expect a search of your luggage by Venezuelan officials.

AROUND MARACAIBO

Maracaibo is on the strait linking Lago de Maracaibo to the Caribbean Sea. The lake, at 12,800 sq km, is the largest on the continent. More than that, it is also the richest: Enormous deposits of oil discovered in the 1910s beneath the lake bed have made Venezuela a major oil exporter.

Although oil is the most obvious feature of the Maracaibo region, there's much more to see around the city. The region boasts a variety of attractions, some of which are detailed below.

Puente Rafael Urdaneta

Named after the greatest local hero, the Rafael Urdaneta Bridge spans the neck of Lago de Maracaibo just south of the city. It was built from 1959 to 1963 in order to provide a shortcut to the center of the country, and it was the first prestressed concrete bridge in the world. Measuring 8679m, it is the longest bridge in South America. A great achievement of local engineers, the bridge is the pride of maracuchos and appears in every local tourist brochure.

You'll cross the bridge if arriving in Maracaibo from anywhere in the east or southeast. There's a good view of the city from the bridge and vice versa.

Altagracia

This town faces Maracaibo from the opposite side of the strait. Altagracia has preserved some of its old architecture, particularly the charming, typical houses, painted in much the same style as those in Maracaibo.

The most interesting area is around Plaza Miranda, the square just one short block up from the lakefront. A stroll about the town, together with a pleasant boat trip from Maracaibo, justifies a half-day trip from the city.

Getting There & Away Boats from Maracaibo to Altagracia depart every two hours until about 6 pm from the wharf off Avenida Libertador. The trip takes 40 minutes and costs US$1.25. In Altagracia, the boats anchor at the pier one block below Plaza Miranda.

There are also por puestos that leave when full from next to either wharf. The ride (via the Rafael Urdaneta Bridge) takes 40 minutes and costs US$1.75.

Boats are the more pleasant means of transportation but sometimes break down, leaving por puestos as the only option.

Ciénaga de los Olivitos

Lying about 20km northeast of Altagracia, Ciénaga de los Olivitos (Marsh of the Little Olive Trees) is one of the major flamingo habitats and is the only place in Venezuela where they have built nests. These lovely birds live there year-round, though some fly temporarily to other regions, such as the Península de la Guajira and the Península de Paraguaná. The mangroves growing on the marshland are home to many other bird species as well; about 110 species have been recorded in the region. The area covering the marsh and its environs was decreed a wildlife refuge in 1986 and is currently administered by Profauna.

Getting There & Away The Ciénaga de los Olivitos is not easy to get to, as it is inaccessible by road. Ask the fishermen in Guarico (port of Altagracia) or (preferably) Sabaneta; they might take you across Bahía de Tablazo to the marsh. Alternatively, take a bus or por puesto from Altagracia to Quisiro, get off in the village of Ancón de Iturre (or get there by taxi) and talk to the local fishers. Before you set off to the marshes, contact the Profauna office in Maracaibo (☎ 61 49 59, 61 45 47) for more specific and detailed information.

Castillo de San Carlos de la Barra

This fort lies about 30km due north of Maracaibo, on the eastern tip of Isla de San Carlos. It was built in the second half of the 17th century to guard the lake entrance from pirates. Even though the mouth was largely protected by a sandbar, many marauders were eager to cross over and sack Maracaibo. The fort was in Spanish hands until the 1823 battle of Lago de Maracaibo, and after their defeat it passed over to the republicans.

In 1903 the fort was bombarded by a fleet of warships sent by Germany, Italy and Great Britain to blockade Venezuelan ports after the country failed to pay its foreign debts. During the dictatorship of Juan Vicente Gómez, the fort served as a jail for political prisoners, after which it was used as an arms depot. Finally decreed a national

Catatumbo Lightning

The 1937 tourist brochure *Venezuela Turística,* describing the Catatumbo Lightning as one of the country's tourist attractions, mentions that the natural phenomenon is found nowhere else on earth and that its cause is unknown. Both of these statements remain true today. The phenomenon, centered on the mouth of the Río Catatumbo at Lago de Maracaibo, consists of almost uninterrupted lightning. Observed from a distance, the thunder is unheard, which contributes to a very eerie sensation.

It's possible that Alonso de Ojeda and Amerigo Vespucci were the first Europeans to see the lightning (during their 1499 trip), but the oldest written historical record dates from a 1597 account by Lope de Vega. Later on, the lightning was watched and studied by various explorers and scientists, including Alexander von Humboldt and Agustín Codazzi, but none of them could explain it.

It seems that the luminosity and frequency of the lightning have been gradually diminishing over the past century, and particularly over recent decades. Today the lightning is more pronounced in the dry season, whereas it can stop for days in the wet season.

Various hypotheses have been put forth to explain the lightning, but so far none have been fully proven. One of the theories links the lightning with the presence of radioactive substances in the earth, but a thorough analysis of the soil's chemical composition is yet to be carried out.

Another theory that stands out is based on the topography of the region, characterized by the proximity of a vast lowland lake (Lago de Maracaibo) and a 5000m-high mountain (Sierra Nevada) – a dramatic configuration reputedly found nowhere else in the world. The clash of the cold winds descending from the cordillera and the hot, humid air evaporating from the lake is thought to produce the ionization of air particles, and thus to be responsible for the lightning. That the lightning is more pronounced in the dry season is explained by stronger sun radiation and consequently greater evaporation in that period, which in turn is likely to produce more powerful clashes.

monument, it was extensively restored in the late 1980s to become a tourist attraction.

Castillo de San Carlos is similar to the forts in Cumaná and those on Isla de Margarita. It's built on a four-pointed-star plan, with circular watchtowers at each corner and a square courtyard in the middle.

Getting There & Away The fort is accessible by passenger boats from the town of

San Rafael del Moján. San Rafael, about 40km north of Maracaibo, is serviced by a number of buses from the city's terminal. It's a fairly undistinguished town except for a huge, somewhat macabre sculptured head of Bolívar in the central plaza.

Laguna de Sinamaica

This lagoon is the most popular tourist sight around Maracaibo. It's noted for several hamlets with inhabitants who lived in palafitos on the lake's shore. Sinamaica is famous nationwide as the place where one can see roughly the same thing Alonso de Ojeda and Amerigo Vespucci saw in 1499, propelling them to name the entire region 'Venezuela' (see History, in the Facts about Venezuela chapter).

A boat will take you around the lagoon and the side *caños* (channels), passing scattered palafitos along the shores. However, don't expect too much. Some of the houses are still traditionally built of *estera,* a sort of mat made from a papyrus-like reed that grows in the shallows. If you ignore the TV antennas sticking out from the roof of almost every house, they probably don't look much different from their predecessors 500 years ago. Many houses, though, are now built from modern materials, including timber, brick and tin, which spoil the overall impression. Electric power lines over the lagoon don't add to the sense of authenticity either. A Parador Turístico (Tourist Stop) was built by Corpozulia in the middle of the lagoon and features a restaurant, craft shop and toilets. Every boat trip stops here.

Originally the lagoon was inhabited by the Paraujano (or Añú) Indians, but they are now extinct. Today, the local population, estimated at 2300, is almost exclusively mestizo.

Getting There & Away Laguna de Sinamaica makes for an easy day trip from Maracaibo. First you have to get to the town of Sinamaica, 60km north of Maracaibo and 19km past San Rafael. Take a bus to Guane or Los Filudos, whichever departs first, from the Maracaibo bus terminal. The trip to

Sinamaica takes up to two hours and costs US$1. Get off one block past the main square (just behind the police station). From there, por puestos do the 5km run on a paved road to Puerto Cuervito, which is situated on the edge of the lagoon (US$0.30, 10 minutes).

In Puerto Cuervito, a fleet of pleasure boats waits all day long to take tourists around the lagoon. A boat normally takes six passengers and costs about US$30 (for the whole boat). Bargaining is possible when there aren't many tourists around. The tour takes about an hour, longer if you feel like having lunch in the Parador Turístico (the boat will wait for you without any additional charge). There are two cheaper restaurants by the wharf in Puerto Cuervito.

Oil Towns

Although Maracaibo is considered Venezuela's oil capital, most oil drilling is undertaken along the northeastern shore of Lago de Maracaibo. Here is where genuine oil towns have sprung up, all the way from Cabimas to Bachaquero. **Cabimas**, with about 180,000 inhabitants, is the largest, followed by **Ciudad Ojeda**, with a population of 110,000. There's little to attract tourists in these towns, even though accommodations are available. What is interesting is the forest of old offshore oil derricks spread along the shore for some 50km or more. There are a number of viewpoints for these derricks, including the waterfronts of Tía Juana and Lagunillas. Although the Corpozulia tourist office says its OK to take photos, the local Guardia Nacional may have a different take, so be discreet.

Getting There & Away Half-hourly buses go from Maracaibo to Cabimas (US$1.50, 1½ hours), where you change for a por puesto to Lagunillas (US$1.75, 45 minutes). The road doesn't skirt the lakeside, and only occasionally will you catch distant views of the derricks. The lake views are further obstructed by the containing dike built to protect the area, which has sunk about 9m as a result of decades of oil exploitation. To get a closer look, walk right onto the dike.

Alternatively, ask a local taxi driver to take you to the best viewpoints.

Río Catatumbo

There are plenty of rivers emptying into Lago de Maracaibo, but the Río Catatumbo is exceptional – an almost uninterrupted lightning display occurs near its mouth. The phenomenon, referred to as 'Faro de Maracaibo' (Maracaibo Beacon) or 'Relámpago de Catatumbo' (Catatumbo Lightning), can be observed at night all over the region, weather permitting, from hundreds of kilometers away. It's visible, for example, from Maracaibo and San Cristóbal. Traveling by night on the Maracaibo–San Cristóbal or San Cristóbal–Valera roads, you'll get a glimpse of it. Obviously, the closer to the mouth of the Río Catatumbo you get, the more impressive the spectacle. Towns on the southern shores of Lago de Maracaibo (such as San Antonio, Bobures or Gibraltar) all provide good views, as do some of the towns up on the Andes slopes (including several viewpoints near La Azulita). See the boxed text for more information on the phenomenon.

The Andes

South America's spinal column, the Andes, runs the whole length of the continent, from Tierra del Fuego to the Caribbean Sea. In Venezuela, the Andes extend from the Táchira depression, near the Colombian border, northeast to Trujillo and Lara states. This part of the range is roughly 400km long and about 70km to 100km wide, and is Venezuela's highest outcrop.

Strictly speaking, the range continues farther to the northeast (past another depression east of Barquisimeto) to the Caribbean coast, then winds eastward. Although this coastal section is a structural continuation of the Andean cordillera, it's not commonly regarded as part of the Andes, but instead referred to as the 'Cordillera de la Costa.' Venezuela has another part of the Andes along its border with Colombia, west of Lago de Maracaibo. This range is called the Serranía de Perijá.

The state of Mérida is in the center of the Venezuelan Andes. The mountains here do not form a single ridge, but rather make up two roughly parallel chains separated by a verdant mountain valley. The southern chain culminates at the Sierra Nevada de Mérida, crowned by a series of snowcapped peaks. The country's highest summits are here, including Pico Bolívar (5007m), Pico Humboldt (4942m) and Pico Bonpland (4883m). This entire area was decreed as Parque Nacional Sierra Nevada in 1952, thus rendering it Venezuela's second national park. The northern chain, the Sierra La Culata, directly opposite the Sierra Nevada, reaches 4660m and is also a national park. In the deep valley between the two ranges sits the city of Mérida, the region's major urban center and the country's mountain capital. The Andes continue into the neighboring states of Táchira and Trujillo, and merge into single ridges, which gradually descend to the lowlands.

The mountains are dotted with small towns with inhabitants who continue the traditions of their predecessors, the roots of which go back to the Timote-Cuica Indians, the most advanced pre-Hispanic culture of present-day Venezuela. The land seems to be more actively cultivated here than elsewhere in the country, and the local campesinos appear to work harder than their lowland counterparts.

The Andes are popular hiking territory, offering a spectrum of habitats from lush cloud forest up to permanent snow. Sandwiched

Highlights

- Take a cable-car ride from Mérida up to Pico Espejo.
- Visit the remote village of Los Nevados.
- Go mountain trekking in the Sierra Nevada.
- Raft down the wild Andean rivers.
- Watch the mysterious Good Friday Passion play in Tostós.

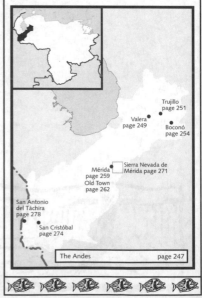

Trujillo page 251
Valera page 249
Boconó page 254
Sierra Nevada de Mérida page 271
Mérida page 259
Old Town page 262
San Antonio del Táchira page 278
San Cristóbal page 274
The Andes page 247

THE ANDES

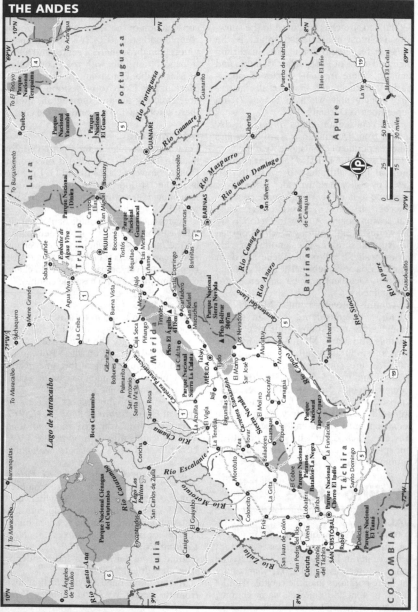

between the two is the *páramo,* a kind of open highland moor that begins at about 3300m and stretches up almost to the snowline. Its most characteristic plant is the *frailejón* (espeletia), found only in certain highland areas of Venezuela, Colombia and Ecuador. There are many species of espeletia in Venezuela, and they are all particularly spectacular when in bloom (from September to December).

The Venezuelan Andes undergo a dry season from December to April. May and June is a period of changeable weather, with a lot of sunshine but also frequent rain (or snow at high altitudes). It is usually followed by a short, relatively dry period from late June to late July (which some consider a second dry season) before a long, really wet season begins. August to October are the wettest months, during which hiking can be truly miserable. The amount of rain varies locally; Trujillo state is generally drier than Mérida and Táchira. The snowy period (June to October) may be dangerous for mountaineers.

Administratively, Trujillo, Mérida and Táchira are considered Andean states, though the mountains spill over into Barinas and Lara. Mérida state has the highest mountains and the best tourist infrastructure; consequently, it attracts the greatest number of visitors, both local and foreign. Trujillo remains undiscovered by tourism, despite its colonial gems and some splendid mountain scenery. Táchira also seems underestimated and glossed over by travelers, even though it boasts beautiful, unexplored mountains protected by four national parks.

Trujillo State

VALERA
☎ 071 (☎ 0271 from June 16, 2001)

Valera is the largest and most important urban center in Trujillo state; it's actually the state's only real city, with 140,000 inhabitants – far more populous than the capital, Trujillo. It lies at 40m and enjoys a warm climate, with an average annual temperature of 25°C.

Founded in 1820, Valera experienced an acceleration in growth propelled by the construction of the Trans-Andean highway, completed in the 1920s. It is now an important regional commercial center and a local transportation hub, with road connections to Maracaibo, Barquisimeto, Guanare and Mérida. It is likely to be a stopover if you are traveling around the region, though there's not much to see or do in the city.

Information
For tourist information, the Centro de Información Turística (☎ 542 86) is on Avenida Bolívar between Calles 10 and 11. The office is on the 1st floor, above a craft shop, and it is open 7:30 am to 1 pm and 2 to 5:30 pm weekdays, 7:30 am to 1 pm Saturday.

As for money, some of the banks that give advances on credit cards have been marked on the map. As elsewhere, you can change American Express traveler's checks at Corp Banca; however, no bank is likely to change cash, and there are no casas de cambio.

Places to Stay
Valera doesn't seem to have much to choose from as far as acceptable budget accommodations go. The very basic but very cheap *Hotel Central*, on Plaza Bolívar, was closed for refurbishing at the time of writing; it may improve upon reopening – check it out when you come.

You can probably expect better standards at *Hotel Aurora* (☎ 31 56 75, 31 59 67), Avenida Bolívar, which has air-conditioned doubles/triples with bathrooms and TV for US$18/24 and also a few singles with fan for US$13.

More respectable is *Hotel El Palacio* (☎ 529 23, 558 50), in the Centro Comercial Miami Center, on Calle 12, which costs US$33/42/48 single/double/triple and has a restaurant. Another of the few reasonable central options is the three-star *Hotel Camino Real* (☎ 537 95, 517 04), in a multicolored tower on Avenida Independencia, which has doubles for US$50.

If you don't mind staying farther away from the center, try *Hotel Country Valera* (☎ 31 13 62, 31 43 66), on Avenida Bolívar

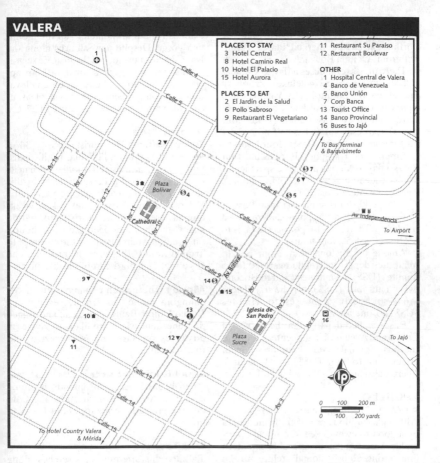

VALERA

PLACES TO STAY
3 Hotel Central
8 Hotel Camino Real
10 Hotel El Palacio
15 Hotel Aurora

PLACES TO EAT
2 El Jardín de la Salud
6 Pollo Sabroso
9 Restaurant El Vegetariano

11 Restaurant Su Paraíso
12 Restaurant Boulevar

OTHER
1 Hospital Central de Valera
4 Banco de Venezuela
5 Banco Unión
7 Corp Banca
13 Tourist Office
14 Banco Provincial
16 Buses to Jajó

3km southwest of the center. It's one of the best places in town, offering matrimoniales/triples for US$45/52, and it has its own restaurant as well.

Places to Eat

The city center is packed with eating outlets, though there's nothing really to send letters home about. For chicken, try *Pollo Sabroso*, on Avenida Bolívar. *Restaurant Boulevar*, also on Avenida Bolívar, serves local food, including arepas and cachapas.

Local budget vegetarian eateries include *Restaurant Su Paraíso*, on Calle 13 (closed Sunday), *Restaurant El Vegetariano*, on Calle 11 (closed weekends), and *El Jardín de la Salud*, on Avenida 11 (also closed weekends).

Getting There & Away

Air The airport is about 4km northeast of the city center. A taxi will cost about US$7; you can also take a La Cejita minibus from the corner of Avenida 6 and Calle 6. There are two flights a day to Caracas with LAI (US$65), one of which has a stopover in Barquisimeto (US$45). All prices listed are one-way.

THE ANDES

Bus The bus terminal is about 1.5km northeast of the center. To get there, take the northbound city bus marked 'Plata 3 Terminal' from Avenida Bolívar.

There are several buses a day to Caracas (US$11 ordinary, US$14 deluxe, 9½ hours), and all go via Barquisimeto, Valencia and Maracay. These apart, ordinary buses run to Barquisimeto every two hours (US$5, four hours). Expresos Valera has half-hourly departures to Maracaibo (US$6, four hours).

Empresa de Transporte Barinas has four buses a day to Mérida along the spectacular Trans-Andean highway (US$5, five hours). The road winds almost 3500m up to Paso El Águila, at 4007m (the highest road pass in Venezuela), before dropping 2400m down to Mérida. There are also por puesto taxis to Mérida (US$8.50, four hours).

Among the regional routes, por puesto minibuses depart to Trujillo every 10 to 15 minutes (US$1, 45 minutes), and to Boconó every half-hour (US$3, two hours). There are also hourly minibuses to Timotes (US$1.50, one hour).

Buses to Jajó depart from the corner of Calle 8 and Avenida 4 in the center (not from the bus terminal) every hour or so, from about 7 am to 5 pm (US$1.50, 1½ hours). There's also one daily direct bus to Tuñame.

TRUJILLO
☎ 072 (☎ 0272 from June 16, 2001)

Although Trujillo is just 35km from Valera by a good freeway, it seems a world apart. Unlike Valera, it has an agreeable climate, a fine setting, some colonial architecture, a small population (55,000) and the unhurried air of days gone by. It has also traditionally been (and remains) the state's capital.

Trujillo was the first town to be founded in the Andes (in 1557), but the continuous hostility of the local Indian group, the Cuicas, led to its being moved several times. Seven different locations were reputedly tried before the town, appropriately called the 'portable city,' was eventually permanently established in 1570 at its present site.

Trujillo's location in a long narrow valley, El Valle de los Cedros, determined the town's unusual and somewhat inconvenient layout. It's only a couple of blocks wide but extends for a few kilometers up the mountain gorge. Despite new suburbs along the Río Castán, at the foot of the historic sector, Trujillo remains a small town, in both appearance and atmosphere. Set on an elevation of around 800m, it enjoys a pleasant climate, with a mean temperature of 22°C.

Information
Tourist Offices The tourist office (☎ 36 14 55, 36 12 77) is in La Plazuela, Trujillo's distant suburb (once a small colonial town in its own right – see La Plazuela, later in this section), 3km north of Trujillo's center on the Valera freeway. It's open 8 am to 4 pm weekdays. There's also the tourist information stand (theoretically open the same hours) on Avenida Andrés Bello, at the entrance to Trujillo from Valera, near the bus terminal. It's about 1km northeast of Plaza Bolívar.

Money There aren't many options for changing money in Trujillo, except for Banco Unión, Banco Provincial and Banco de Venezuela, which are likely to give cash advances on Visa and MasterCard, but that's about it.

Email & Internet Access DMT Sistemas (☎ 36 40 52), in Edificio Almendrón, on the corner of Avenida Bolívar and Calle Candelaria, provides access for about US$3 an hour.

Old Town
Trujillo's historic quarter stretches along two parallel east-west streets, Avenidas Independencia and Bolívar. Bordered by these streets, at the eastern, lower end of the sector, is **Plaza Bolívar**, the town's historical heart and still the nucleus of the city's life today. The **Catedral**, completed in 1662, has a lovely whitewashed facade, but the refurbished interior has almost nothing left of its colonial fittings, except for the stone baptismal font.

There are still some graceful historic buildings around the plaza. The finest in the area is the large two-story mansion on the corner just north of the plaza. Built from

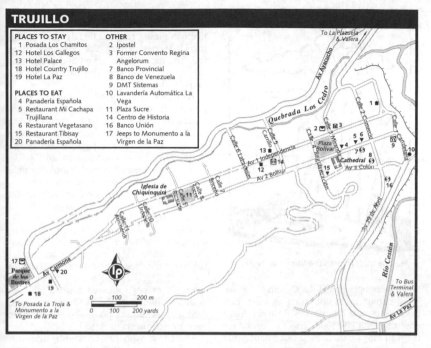

TRUJILLO

PLACES TO STAY
1. Posada Los Chamitos
12. Hotel Los Gallegos
13. Hotel Palace
18. Hotel Country Trujillo
19. Hotel La Paz

PLACES TO EAT
4. Panadería Española
5. Restaurant Mi Cachapa Trujillana
6. Restaurant Vegetasano
15. Restaurant Tibisay
20. Panadería Española

OTHER
2. Ipostel
3. Former Convento Regina Angelorum
7. Banco Provincial
8. Banco de Venezuela
9. DMT Sistemas
10. Lavandería Automática La Vega
11. Plaza Sucre
14. Centro de Historia
16. Banco Unión
17. Jeeps to Monumento a la Virgen de la Paz

1598 to 1617 as the Convento Regina Angelorum, it's now the public library. You'll find more surviving colonial houses west of the plaza, on Avenidas Independencia and Bolívar. Perhaps the best approach to sightseeing is to take either of the two streets uphill and return down by the other one. They merge 10 blocks farther up to become Avenida Carmona, but the best architecture is within a few blocks of the plaza.

The **Centro de Historia**, in a restored colonial mansion on Avenida Independencia, houses the town's history museum. Exhibits include old maps, armor, period furniture, pre-Columbian pottery and even a fully equipped kitchen with an old stove. It was in this house on June 15, 1813, that Bolívar signed his controversial Decreto de Guerra a Muerte (Decree of War to the Death), under which all captured royalists were to be summarily executed. The table on which the proclamation was signed and the bed in which Bolívar slept are part of the exhibition. The museum is open 9 am to 5 pm weekdays, 9 am to noon weekends.

Monumento a la Virgen de la Paz
This gigantic 47m-high monument, said to be the world's tallest statue of the Virgin Mary, is on the mountaintop overlooking Trujillo, 11km west of the town. Erected in 18 months and inaugurated in 1983, the massive, 1.2-million-kg concrete statue stands on the 1700m-high summit of Cerro Peña de la Virgen. The internal elevator and staircase provide access to five *miradores* (viewpoints). The highest mirador peeks out through the eyes of the Virgen, from which one can enjoy views over much of Trujillo state and beyond. On a clear day, the snow-capped peaks of the Sierra Nevada de Mérida and a part of Lago de Maracaibo are visible. The monument is open 9 am to 5 pm daily; the admission fee is US$1.25.

Jeeps to the monument leave from the upper end of Trujillo next to the Parque de

No one messes with the Virgen de la Paz.

los Ilustres, opposite Hotel Country Trujillo. They depart upon collecting at least four passengers and charge US$0.80 per head one-way for a 20-minute trip. On weekdays the wait may be quite long, but you can pay for four seats and have the jeep to yourself. It's best to start early, as later in the day the Virgin is often shrouded by clouds, even in the dry season. If you feel like going there on foot, it'll be a two- to three-hour walk uphill.

La Plazuela
This small colonial town, 3km north of Trujillo on the Valera *autopista* (freeway), has been partly rebuilt and partially restored to its former form. However, it's still not much more than one cobbled street, complete with a church and houses. In one of them is the tourist office.

Getting to La Plazuela is very easy – just get off the Valera-Trujillo por puesto there. Getting away may be a bit harder, as most por puestos come through full and won't stop.

Places to Stay
Probably the most pleasant budget place is *Posada Los Chamitos* (☎ 36 63 18), Calle Candelaria, two blocks downhill from Plaza Bolívar. It's a private house whose owners, a Chilean family, rent out three rooms, charging US$6 per person. The posada is often full. The place is unmarked and not immediately apparent from the street – see the map for the location.

Hotel Palace (☎ 36 69 36), Avenida Independencia, offers simple singles/matrimoniales/doubles/triples with bath and fan for US$12/14/16/18 and serves inexpensive meals. Nearby on the same street is the better *Hotel Los Gallegos* (☎ 36 31 93), which costs US$22/28 matrimonial/double with fan, US$25/30 with air-conditioning.

There are two reasonable options on Avenida Carmona at the upper end of town. First, the cheaper *Hotel La Paz* (☎ 36 48 64, 36 51 57) has suite-style doubles/triples/quads for US$28/32/35. Alternatively, a hundred meters up the road, the entirely refurbished *Hotel Country Trujillo* (☎ 36 35 76, 36 36 46) is the best place in town. It offers spacious air-conditioned doubles/triples for US$34/42, a restaurant, café and swimming pool. The pool can be used by nonguests for US$5.

For those who prefer countryside surroundings, there's the pleasant *Posada La Troja* (☎ 014-971 29 90), on the road to La Virgen de la Paz, a few kilometers out of Trujillo. It offers six rustic-style rooms, each different (about US$25 for up to four persons), as well as meals.

Places to Eat
The *Restaurant Tibisay*, just behind the cathedral, serves straightforward, cheap meals until about 8 pm (closed Saturday). It can be entered from either Calle Regularización or Avenida Colón. You can also try *Restaurant Mi Cachapa Trujillana*, Avenida Bolívar, which serves budget set lunches. Next door to that is the cheap, vegetarian *Restaurant Vegetasano*. Should you need somewhere more upmarket, try the restaurant of *Hotel Country Trujillo*, one of the best places to eat in town.

Panadería Española, at its two locations – Plaza Bolívar and Avenida Camona – has good bread, pastries, cakes and coffee.

Getting There & Away

Flight service to the area is provided by the airport in Valera, 30km from Trujillo.

The bus terminal is on Avenida La Paz, northeast of the town's center, beyond Río Castán. Urban minibuses link the terminal to the center. The terminal is rather quiet, and the only really frequent connection is with Valera (US$1, 45 minutes). There are a couple of night buses to Caracas (US$11 ordinary, US$14 deluxe, 9½ hours). Transportation to Boconó (US$3, two hours) thins out in the early afternoon. You may need to go to Valera, from where minibuses to Boconó depart regularly until about 5 pm.

BOCONÓ

☎ 072 (☎ 0272 from June 16, 2001)

Boconó is 50km southeast of Trujillo as the crow flies, but it's twice that distance by a spectacular, winding mountain road. The town sits at an altitude of about 1225m, and thus enjoys a pleasant temperature of around 20°C. The favorable climate and fertile soil of the region contributed to the development of agriculture. A variety of crops, including coffee, potatoes and chickpeas, are cultivated in the surrounding hills.

Boconó was founded as early as 1560. Its location is actually one of the previous foundation sites of Trujillo. Although the capital later moved, some of the inhabitants decided to stay and take their affairs into their own hands. Isolated for centuries from the outside world, Boconó grew painfully slowly and remained largely self-sufficient. It wasn't until the 1930s that the Trujillo-Boconó road was built, linking the town to both the state capital and areas to the north and west. The construction of the Guanare-Boconó road has recently provided access from the south and east.

Despite easy access by paved roads, this small town of 45,000 still maintains a sense of isolation, even though tourism has gradually increased. Agriculture apart, the town has developed into a regional craft center, specializing mostly in weaving, basketry and pottery. Boconó is also a jumping-off point for San Miguel, Tostós and Niquitao (see those sections, later in this chapter).

Information

The Oficina Municipal de Turismo, in the Alcaldía on Plaza Bolívar, may be able to provide some information, but the folks at Posada Machinipé (see Places to Stay, later) are probably more knowledgeable about the region.

As for money, it's better to come with local currency, unless you are traveling with a Visa or MasterCard, which can gain you an advance at the Banco Unión, Banco de Venezuela and Banco Provincial.

Things to See

The **Trapiche de los Clavo**, on Calle Jáuregui opposite the hospital, occupies a walled-in compound of a 19th-century sugarcane mill. It features some exhibits related to traditional sugar production, including the original mill. Other historic buildings on the grounds accommodate craft workshops and a restaurant, and an exhibition on coffee production is planned for the future. The place is pleasant enough to come and have a look around. Look for the textile workshop, where you can see artisans weaving their rags and blankets on their old rustic looms. The mill is open 9:30 am to 5 pm daily, but craft workshops may be closed on weekends.

The **Ateneo de Boconó**, on Calle Páez, is another place where you can see local weavers at work (weekdays only), in their textile workshop on the upper floor. It runs arts-and-crafts exhibitions from time to time.

The **Centro de Servicios Campesinos Tiscachic**, 400m off the road to Valera just past the bridge, has an exhibition of crafts – mostly woodcarving, pottery and basketry – fashioned by local artisans. The center also has a handicraft shop and hosts a lively food market on Saturday morning; on other days there are just a few food stalls. It's closed Sunday.

There are several home workshops in the town and its environs. One of the best known is the pottery workshop of the Briceño family, in the suburb of Primera Sabana on the eastern outskirts of Boconó, off the road to Guanare. The Briceños also

THE ANDES

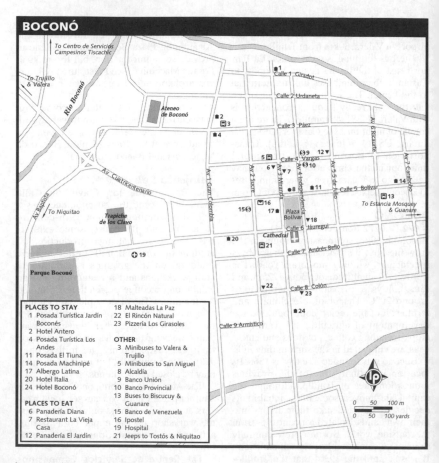

BOCONÓ

To Centro de Servicios
Campesinos Tiscachic

To Trujillo
& Valera

Río Boconó

Ateneo
de Boconó

Trapiche
de los Clavo

Parque Boconó

Av Cuatricentenario

Av Bautista

To Niquitao

Av 1 Gran Colombia

Av 2 Sucre

Av 3 Miranda

Av 4 Independencia

Av 5 de Julio

Av 6 Ricaurte

Av 7 Carache

Calle 1 Girardot
Calle 2 Urdaneta
Calle 3 Páez
Calle 4 Vargas
Calle 5 Bolívar
Calle 6 Jáuregui
Calle 7 Andrés Bello
Calle 8 Colón
Calle 9 Armístico

Plaza
Bolívar

Cathedral

To Estancia Mosquey
& Guanare

0   50   100 m
0   50   100 yards

PLACES TO STAY
1 Posada Turística Jardín
   Boconés
2 Hotel Antero
4 Posada Turística Los
   Andes
11 Posada El Tiuna
14 Posada Machinipé
17 Albergo Latina
20 Hotel Italia
24 Hotel Boconó

PLACES TO EAT
6 Panadería Diana
7 Restaurant La Vieja
   Casa
12 Panadería El Jardín

18 Malteadas La Paz
22 El Rincón Natural
23 Pizzería Los Girasoles

OTHER
3 Minibuses to Valera &
   Trujillo
5 Minibuses to San Miguel
8 Alcaldía
9 Banco Unión
10 Banco Provincial
13 Buses to Biscucuy &
   Guanare
15 Banco de Venezuela
16 Ipostel
19 Hospital
21 Jeeps to Tostós & Niquitao

have another workshop in the suburb of La
Vega, on the town's northern limits, off the
road to Valera.

Places to Stay

The new ***Posada Turística Jardín Boconés***
(☎ 52 01 71, Calle Girardot No 3-05) is a
charming, tranquil place established in a restored 100-year-old house with a spacious
leafy garden in the middle. It has five rooms
in all (two matrimoniales, two doubles and
one triple), all with private bath and each
priced at US$18.

The cozy ***Posada Machinipé*** (☎ 52 15 06,
Calle Bolívar 6-49) doesn't perhaps have
such natural beauty (or a garden), but is
otherwise a pleasant place with just three
rooms (with two, four and five beds). It costs
US$16 for two and US$8 for each additional person. The friendly owners are very
knowledgeable about the town and state,
and can provide excellent information. They
can also organize tours around the regional
attractions.

These two lovely posadas apart, Boconó
has quite a choice of budget hotels, including

Hotel Italia (☎ 52 25 65, Calle Jáuregui No 1-40), *Posada Turística Los Andes (☎ 56 15 42, Calle Páez No 1-08)*, *Hotel Antero (☎ 52 08 18, Avenida Gran Colombia No 2-47)*, *Albergo Latina (☎ 52 27 50, Avenida Miranda No 5-28)*, *Posada El Tiuna (☎ 52 27 78, Calle Bolívar No 4-39)* and *Hotel Boconó (Avenida Miranda No 8-45)*. Some of these places have changed their names to 'posada,' but don't be confused. They all are pretty undistinguished places that offer simple conditions and not much style; their major advantage over the two posadas mentioned earlier are lower rates: around US$10 to US$14 double. The basic El Tiuna is the cheapest, while the Antero is the most expensive of the lot.

Hotel Vega del Río (☎ 52 24 93, 52 29 92) and *Hotel Campestre La Colina (☎ 52 26 95, 52 19 60)*, both beyond the bridge in the northwestern part of Boconó, are appreciably better (and far more expensive) than the other hotels listed. Each has its own restaurant.

You can also stay in the pleasant *Estancia Mosquey (☎ 52 15 55, 56 18 86)*, 10km from Boconó on the road to Guanare, though it's rather inconvenient if you don't have your own transportation. The place costs about US$12 per person and has a restaurant and a pool.

Places to Eat

A number of budget places to eat are in the center, including the amazingly cheap and quite good *Pizzería Los Girasoles*. One of the most pleasant budget places for lunch is *Restaurant Mojos Chichas y Amasijos*, in the Trapiche de los Clavo, which serves a tasty *menú ejecutivo* (set lunch) for US$4. Cheap vegetarian fast food is available at *El Rincón Natural*.

More upmarket places to eat include *Restaurant La Vieja Casa* and the restaurants of *Hotel Vega del Río* and *Hotel Campestre La Colina*.

Malteadas La Paz, on Plaza Bolívar, serves good batidos, merengadas and malteadas. For breakfast, central bakeries include *Panadería Diana* and *Panadería El Jardín*.

Getting There & Away

The bus terminal is being built in the southern part of Boconó, but it may still be a while before it opens. So far, transportation companies have their own offices scattered throughout the central sector of the town (see the map for locations), from where their vehicles depart.

Minibuses to Valera (US$3, two hours) depart as soon as they're full (roughly every half-hour) until about 5 pm. From the same spot, there are minibuses to Trujillo (US$3, two hours), but they are not as regular and stop running earlier. If none are due to depart, take a minibus to Valera, get off in La Concepción and change buses.

Buses to Guanare depart until 3 pm (US$3, 3½ hours). If you miss the last one, take one of the half-hourly buses to Biscucuy, which operate until 5 pm (US$2, two hours). From there you may be able to catch a por puesto to Guanare (US$2.50, one hour).

Minibuses to San Miguel run every hour or so (US$0.75, 40 minutes).

Jeeps to Niquitao depart every half-hour or so until 5 to 6 pm on weekdays (US$1, 50 minutes). On weekends, they leave when full (every one to two hours). The road to Niquitao is paved all the way but is steep in parts and full of potholes, especially beyond Tostós. The Niquitao jeeps don't enter Tostós, but there are direct jeeps to Tostós (US$0.50, 20 minutes) departing from the same place in Boconó.

Also from the same place, there are jeeps to Las Mesitas, beyond Niquitao. In theory, three or four jeeps run per day, but only the first one, at about 11:30 am, and perhaps the second one, at 1 pm, are at all reliable.

SAN MIGUEL

A tiny town 27km north of Boconó, San Miguel is renowned for its colonial church. It's an austere, squat, whitewashed construction built around 1760. The structure's unusual features include roofed external corridors on both sides and a Latin-cross layout, a design rarely used in Venezuela. However, the highlight is inside: The church has one of the most beautiful folksy retables in the country.

The retable, dating from the church's construction, is a striking, colorful composition that is notable for its naive style. In the central niche, above the tabernacle, there used to be a statue of San Miguel, the patron saint of the church and the town, but it was stolen several years ago. Eight other niches – each one occupied by a winged archangel – are distributed symmetrically on two tiers, while the whole remaining surface of the retable is painted with decorative motifs in bright colors, mostly in red, green and yellow.

There are several statues of saints in the transept and on either side of the arch leading to the chancel. The statue of the blind Santa Lucía holding her eyes on a plate is particularly impressive. Also, side retables in the transept are worth a look.

The church is open daily except Wednesday from about 9:30 am to noon and 2 to 5 pm. Mass is at noon on Sunday.

About 1km outside San Miguel, on the only access road to the town, is the cemetery. Some of the curiously shaped tombstones have been painted with extremely bright colors.

The town's main event is the Romería de los Pastores y los Reyes Magos (Pilgrimage of the Shepherds and Magi), celebrated annually from January 4 to 7.

Places to Stay & Eat
The *Hostería San Miguel*, the state-owned hotel built during the fat years of the oil boom, is the only place to stay. It's pleasant and comfortable, and costs about US$20/28 double/quad with bath. Meals may be available by prior arrangement. The hostería is on the opposite side of the plaza from the church.

Getting There & Away
San Miguel lies 4km off the Boconó-Trujillo road. The narrow, paved side road to the town branches off 23km from Boconó.

The town has a public transportation link only with Boconó. Minibuses run between the two towns every hour or so (US$0.75,

40 minutes). In San Miguel they stop at the plaza in front of the church.

TOSTÓS
Diminutive Tostós, about 12km southwest of Boconó, is famous nationwide for its Easter celebrations, during which the Passion play is reenacted on Good Friday. On that day the town fills up, and the crowd's emotions reach fever pitch when Christ is crucified. The rest of the year, Tostós is a quiet town picturesquely stuck to a hillside, as it has been for 380 years.

The town can be easily reached by paved road from Boconó, from where it's serviced by regular por puesto jeeps (US$0.50, 20 minutes).

NIQUITAO
☎ 071 (☎ 0271 from June 16, 2001)
About 25km beyond Tostós is the larger town of Niquitao (population 5000). It was also a colonial settlement that was founded in 1625, and still has some of its historic architecture in place. The area around Plaza Bolívar, complete with the church, is particularly well preserved. As the town sits at an altitude of nearly 2000m, it has a typical mountain climate, with warm days but chilly nights. It's a good base for excursions (see Around Niquitao, later).

Places to Stay & Eat
The town has several accommodation options, of which the friendly *Posada Mama Chepy* (☎ 85 21 73), 400m south of Plaza Bolívar, is the cheapest. It has five simple rooms – two with bath, three without – but they all cost the same: US$12 for up to three persons. The family can prepare meals for you.

The pleasant *Posada Turística Guirigay* (☎ 85 21 49), on Avenida Bolívar one block south of the plaza, provides matrimonials/doubles/triples with bath for US$16/20/25 and also has its own restaurant. *Posada Don Jerez* (☎ 85 20 74), on Plaza Bolívar, offers and charges much the same as the Guirigay and also serves meals.

A recent addition, *Posada Turística Niquitao* (☎ 85 20 42), also on Plaza Bolívar, is stylish and elegant. Its rooms are perhaps a bit more comfortable than those of the Guirigay, but are twice as expensive. It too has its own restaurant.

Getting There & Away

Jeeps (taking up to 12 passengers) service the Boconó-Niquitao road every half-hour on weekdays and every one to two hours on weekends.

From Niquitao there's a 13km road (partly paved but in bad shape) to Las Mesitas. There are three or four jeeps servicing this route, all departing from Boconó (the most reliable is the jeep leaving Boconó at 11:30 am). Beyond Las Mesitas, a rough road leads to the town of Tuñame (transportation is scarce on this stretch), from where a better road continues downhill to Jajó. Tuñame has a couple of basic posadas and a bus link to Valera.

AROUND NIQUITAO

Niquitao is a convenient springboard for trips into the surrounding mountains, including Trujillo state's highest peak, **La Teta de Niquitao**, at 4006m. You can walk there all the way from Niquitao, but it will take two days roundtrip, so be prepared for camping. You can also go by jeep; the trip to the top will include a two- to three-hour jeep ride uphill via Las Mesitas to the Llano de la Teta, followed by an hour's walk to the summit.

Another possible mountaintop to climb in the area is **Pico Guirigay**, at about 3900m. It's also a long and hard hike, or an easy jeep trip plus an hour's walk to the top. Jeep excursions can be arranged through hotel managers in Niquitao, who will also suggest other interesting destinations in the region. Horse-riding trips are also possible.

You can make some shorter excursions around Niquitao, for which you need neither a jeep nor a guide. One such example is the **Viaducto Agrícola**, a spectacular old iron bridge over the lush Quebrada El Molino, 80m above its bed. You can go down to El Molino to take a refreshing bath. The bridge is on the Niquitao–Las Mesitas road, a half-hour walk from Niquitao.

In the same area, a bit farther up the road, is the site of the **Batalla de Niquitao**, which took place on July 2, 1813, and was one of the important battles of the War of Independence. The battlefield is a memorial site, boasting the busts of the battle heroes.

Another easy trip out of Niquitao is to **Las Pailas**, a set of scenic waterfalls in the Quebrada Tiguaní that lies a leisurely walk uphill from the town. You can bathe here too, though the water is pretty cold.

JAJÓ

☎ 071 (☎ 0271 from June 16, 2001)

Jajó, 48km south of Valera off the road to Mérida, is a tiny mountain town (population 4000) with a long history. It was founded in 1611 by Sancho Briceño Graterol in a remote place amid verdant mountains. Although paved roads now link the town with both Valera and Mérida, Jajó is still a tiny, sleepy place that has preserved much of its centuries-old urban fabric and atmosphere; it's one of the finest small colonial towns in Trujillo state. The town's prettiest part lies just north of Plaza Bolívar.

Places to Stay & Eat

Jajó has three budget hotels. The cheapest is the unmarked **La Pensión de Jajó**, on the southern side of Plaza Bolívar; you can recognize it by its balcony. Installed in an old house with a patio, it contains only a few rooms, all with one double and one single bed and a private bath with hot water. A room costs US$16, regardless of the number of people – up to three. Señora Amparo, who runs the place, can provide home-cooked meals if you wish, but let her know in advance.

On the western side of the plaza is **Hotel Turístico Jajó** (☎ 575 81), the only modern building on the square – it spoils the appearance of the plaza. It's OK but doesn't have the charm of the pensión; the cost is US$20/22/24 matrimonial/double/triple. The hotel has its own restaurant, which serves good trout.

The friendly **Posada Turística Marisabel** (☎ 569 99), on Calle Páez two blocks north of Plaza Bolívar, has clean (though dark) rooms that cost much the same as those in the Hotel Turístico. It also has its own restaurant.

Getting There & Away

The usual point of departure for Jajó is Valera. Hourly buses between Valera and Jajó (US$1.50, 1½ hours) operate until about 5 pm. They go not by the Valera-Mérida Trans-Andean highway through La Puerta, but rather along a shorter, eastern road. These buses depart from the corner of Calle 8 and Avenida 4, not from the Valera bus terminal.

If you want to get to Jajó from Mérida, you could take the morning bus to Valera, get off next to the gas station at the turnoff to Jajó and try to hitch the remaining 11km stretch to Jajó, though there are not many vehicles using this road.

Jajó is linked by an interesting but rough mountain road to Boconó (via Tuñame, Las Mesitas and Niquitao) that climbs nearly as high as 3800m. There's a bus to Tuñame (which has some places to stay and eat), but there's no regular transportation farther on to Las Mesitas. See the Niquitao section, earlier, for more information.

Mérida State

MÉRIDA

☎ 074 (☎ 0274 from Apr 21, 2001)

Mérida is arguably Venezuela's most popular destination among foreign back-packers. It has an unhurried and friendly atmosphere for a city of 250,000, plenty of tourist facilities, the famous *teleférico* (cable car) and beautiful mountains all around – the country's rooftop, the 5007m-high Pico Bolívar, is just 12km away. It's also the country's major center for outdoor activities.

Home to the large Universidad de los Andes (the second-oldest university in the country, founded in 1785 and now teaching about 35,000 students), the city has a pal-pable academic community, which gives it a cultured and bohemian air. Furthermore, Mérida is inexpensive and relatively safe by Venezuelan standards.

Although generally considered a cold city by Venezuelans (at 1625m, it's the highest state capital in the country), Mérida enjoys a pleasant, mild climate, with an average temperature of 19°C. The tourist season is at its peak here around Christmas, Carnaval and Easter, as well as from late July to early September.

History

La Ciudad de Santiago de los Caballeros de Mérida was founded in 1558 by Juan Rodrí-guez Suárez, who was from Pamplona, in Nueva Granada (now Colombia). Interest-ingly, most early towns in the region, includ-ing both San Cristóbal and Barinas, were founded by expeditions sent from Pamp-lona, an important political and religious center of the day, and they remained under Colombian jurisdiction for a long time afterward. It was not until 1777 that Mérida (as well as San Cristóbal) became part of Venezuela. The association with Colombia can still be perceived today and is notice-able in the people, culture and language.

Mérida was born illegally, since Rodrí-guez Suárez lacked the required Spanish approval to found a new city. Consequently, he was hunted down and taken to Bogotá, where he was placed on trial. Facing the death sentence, he miraculously escaped and fled to Trujillo, Venezuela, where he was granted political asylum – reputedly the first case of its kind in the New World.

The foundation controversy ended two years later, after Juan de Maldonado, again from Pamplona, was sent with all the paper-work in order, and Mérida was legally founded. However, the Rodríguez Suárez ad-venture has eventually come to be commonly recognized as marking the city's founding.

Separated by high mountains from both Colombia and the rest of Venezuela, Mérida grew very slowly during colonial times. The 1812 earthquake devastated most of the urban fabric and further hindered develop-ment. Two years later, the ruined town gave a warm welcome to Bolívar, who passed through leading his troops on to Caracas. In 1820, Mérida saw Bolívar again, this time on his march to Colombia.

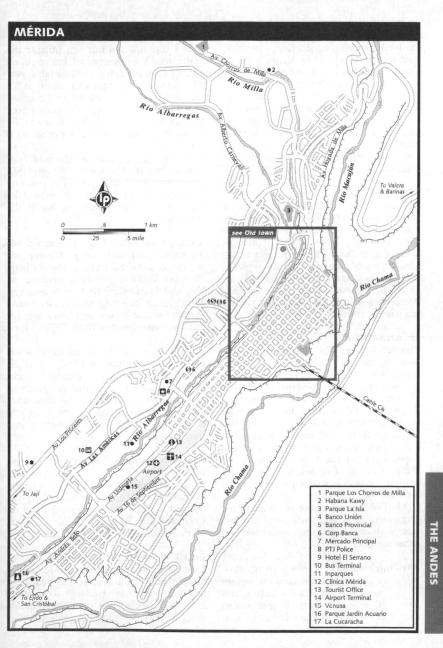

MÉRIDA

To Valera
& Barinas

see Old Town

To Jají

Airport

To Ejido &
San Cristóbal

1   Parque Los Chorros de Milla
2   Habana Kawy
3   Parque La Isla
4   Banco Unión
5   Banco Provincial
6   Corp Banca
7   Mercado Principal
8   PTJ Police
9   Hotel El Serrano
10 Bus Terminal
11 Inparques
12 Clínica Mérida
13 Tourist Office
14 Airport Terminal
15 Venusa
16 Parque Jardín Acuario
17 La Cucaracha

The isolation that had retarded Mérida's progress for centuries suddenly proved to be its ally. During the federation wars in the mid-19th century, when Venezuela was plunged into full-blown civil war, the city's isolation attracted refugees, and the population began to grow. It was not, however, until the 1920s that access roads were constructed and later paved, which smoothed the way for Mérida's subsequent development. Mérida's transition from a town into a city really took place only over the last few decades.

Orientation

Mérida sits on a flat *meseta,* an alluvial terrace that stretches for 12km between two parallel rivers; the edges of the terrace drop abruptly to the riverbanks. The historic quarter is at the northeastern end of the plateau, easily recognized by the typically Spanish chessboard street layout. Having filled the meseta as densely as possible, Mérida is now expanding beyond it, sprawling past the rivers.

Information

Tourist Offices The Corporación Merideña de Turismo (Cormetur) has its main office (☎ 63 59 18, 63 08 14 or toll-free 800 637 43) on Avenida Urdaneta, near the airport. The office is open 8 am to noon and 2 to 6 pm weekdays. Cormetur also operates several *módulos de información* throughout the city, including one at the airport (open during flight times), one at the bus terminal (open 8 am to 6 pm daily) and another at Parque Las Heroínas, close to the cable-car station (open 8 am to 3 pm Tuesday to Sunday).

Most of the major tour companies (see Organized Tours, later) will provide information about trekking, mountaineering and other activities.

Park Information The local Inparques administers two national parks in the region, Sierra Nevada and Sierra La Culata, and issues visitor permits for the former (so far, La Culata doesn't require permits). You need a permit if you are going to stay up in the mountains overnight.

The Inparques office lies outside the center, near the bus terminal, but you don't actually have to venture out that far, as permits are issued by Inparques outlets at the park entry points. If you go up the mountains by teleférico, you get your permit from the Inparques desk right next to the cable-car station (open whenever the cable car is operating).

The permit is issued on the spot (you have to show your passport) and costs US$1 per person per night. It should be returned after completing your hike – this is to make sure nobody is left wandering lost in the mountains.

Money Some of the banks that may possibly handle foreign-exchange transactions are marked on the Central Mérida map. They are likely to give cash advances on Visa and MasterCard, but that's about it. The Corp Banca, on Avenida Las Américas, outside the center (see the Mérida map for location), changes American Express traveler's checks.

The only official place to exchange cash is the Italcambio office (☎ 63 43 36) at the airport, which also changes traveler's checks of most major brands (bring the purchase receipt with you). There may be some other places to change cash by the time you come – tourist offices and tour companies should know of them.

Post & Communications CANTV and Ipostel are next door to each other on Calle 21. Ipostel has a poste restante facility. Letters sent here to you should be addressed as follows: your name, Lista de Correos, IPOSTEL, Calle 21 entre Av 4 y 5, Mérida, Estado Mérida, Venezuela.

Email & Internet Access For some reason, the cybercafé boom in Mérida has been phenomenal over recent years. By mid-2000, there were well over a dozen Internet facilities in town – more than in any other Venezuelan city, excepting perhaps

Caracas. And they were just about the cheapest in the country – US$1 to US$2 an hour – on average, five times cheaper than those in the capital. Central locations include the following:

Café Internet La Abadía
  (☎ 52 74 19) Avenida 3 No 17-45

Herald.Net
  Avenida 5 No 25-46

Info Net 2000
  (☎ 51 02 21) Calle 21 No 4-47

Inter-Planet
  (☎ 52 13 83) Calle 20 No 4-64

Zanzibar
  Avenida 4 No 19-37

There are also Internet facilities at Arassari Trek, Calle 24 No 8 301. Most of the listed places are open until 10 or 11 pm daily. There are no great price differences among them, but if you count every cent, start shopping around at Herald.Net, Info Net 2000 and Inter-Planet.

Laundry Many budget posadas offer laundry service; if not, they will direct you to a nearby *lavandería automática*. There are plenty of them across the central area, including the Lavandería Marbet, Calle 25 No 8-35; Lavandería Yibe, Avenida 6 No 19-25; and Lavandería Andina, Avenida 7 No 22-45. All offer full-service washing and drying for around US$3 per 5kg load.

Medical Services Mérida has an array of clinics and hospitals, including Clínica Mérida (☎ 63 06 52, 63 63 95), Avenida Urdaneta No 45-145, and Clínica Albarregas (☎ 44 81 01, 44 72 83), Calle Tovar No 1-26.

Teleférico
This is the world's highest and longest cable-car system and the highlight of any visit to Mérida. It was constructed in the late 1950s by a French company and runs 12.6km, from the bottom station of Barinitas (1577m), in Mérida, to the top of Pico Espejo (4765m), covering the 3188m climb in four stages (see the Sierra Nevada de Mérida map). The three intermediate sta-

tions are La Montaña (2436m), La Aguada (3452m) and Loma Redonda (4045m).

The cableway was in the past often out of order, closed totally or in some sections for extended periods of time. It was, fortunately, running the whole route up to Pico Espejo by late 2000, and let's hope it will stay this way.

The cableway normally operates from Wednesday to Sunday, though in the tourist season it may run every day. The first trip up is at 7:30 am and the last at noon (7 am and 2 pm, respectively, in peak season). The last trip down is at 1:30 pm (4 pm in peak season). The ascent to Pico Espejo takes about an hour if you go straight through. It's best to go up as early as possible, as clouds usually obscure views later on. There may be long lines during peak holiday periods. Don't forget to take warm clothes.

The roundtrip to Loma Redonda costs US$12, and you pay the same if you only go up and don't return by cable car. There are no cheaper fares for shorter trips – for example, to La Montaña or La Aguada. The last stage, from Loma Redonda to Pico Espejo, costs an additional US$8 roundtrip. No discount fares for students or senior citizens are offered. They may charge an additional US$3 to US$5 for large backpacks, depending on size and weight, at the attendants' discretion.

Apart from splendid views during the trip itself, the cableway provides easy access for high mountain hiking (see Around Mérida for details on hikes), saving you a day or two of puffing uphill. Bear in mind, however, that acclimatization problems can easily occur by quickly reaching high altitudes.

Old Town
The city center is quite pleasant for leisurely strolls, even though there's not much in the way of colonial architecture or outstanding tourist attractions. Plaza Bolívar is the city's heart, but it's not a colonial square. Work on the **Catedral** was begun in 1800, based on the plans of the 17th-century cathedral of Toledo in Spain, but it was not completed

THE ANDES

OLD TOWN

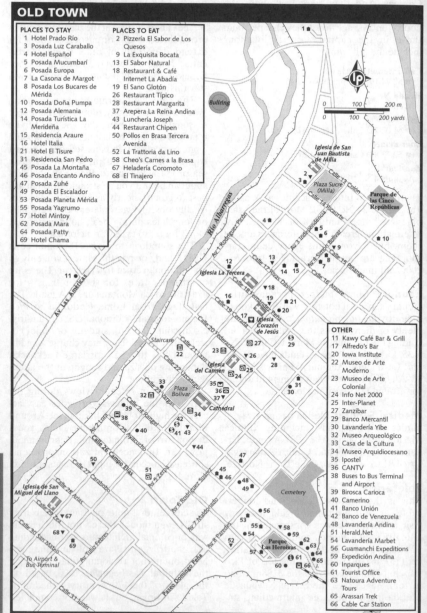

PLACES TO STAY
1 Hotel Prado Río
3 Posada Luz Caraballo
4 Hotel Español
5 Posada Mucumbarí
6 Posada Europa
7 La Casona de Margot
8 Posada Los Bucares de Mérida
10 Posada Doña Pumpa
12 Posada Alemania
14 Posada Turística La Merideña
15 Residencia Araure
16 Hotel Italia
21 Hotel El Tisure
31 Residencia San Pedro
45 Posada La Montaña
46 Posada Encanto Andino
47 Posada Zuhé
49 Posada El Escalador
53 Posada Planeta Mérida
55 Posada Yagrumo
57 Hotel Mintoy
62 Posada Mara
64 Posada Patty
69 Hotel Chama

PLACES TO EAT
2 Pizzería El Sabor de Los Quesos
9 La Exquisita Bocata
13 El Sabor Natural
18 Restaurant & Café Internet La Abadía
19 El Sano Glotón
26 Restaurant Típico
28 Restaurant Margarita
37 Arepera La Reina Andina
43 Lunchería Joseph
44 Restaurant Chipen
50 Pollos en Brasa Tercera Avenida
52 La Trattoria da Lino
58 Cheo's Carnes a la Brasa
67 Heladería Coromoto
68 El Tinajero

OTHER
11 Kawy Café Bar & Grill
17 Alfredo's Bar
20 Iowa Institute
22 Museo de Arte Moderno
23 Museo de Arte Colonial
24 Info Net 2000
25 Inter-Planet
27 Zanzibar
29 Banco Mercantil
30 Lavandería Yibe
32 Museo Arqueológico
33 Casa de la Cultura
34 Museo Arquidiocesano
35 Ipostel
36 CANTV
38 Buses to Bus Terminal and Airport
39 Birosca Carioca
40 Camerino
41 Banco Unión
42 Banco de Venezuela
48 Lavandería Andina
51 Herald.Net
54 Lavandería Marbet
56 Guamanchi Expeditions
59 Expedición Andina
60 Inparques
61 Tourist Office
63 Natoura Adventure Tours
65 Arassari Trek
66 Cable Car Station

THE ANDES

until 1958, and probably only then because things sped up to be in time for the 400th anniversary of the city's founding. Not surprisingly, the end result is very different from the initial design.

Next to the cathedral is the **Museo Arquidiocesano**, which features a collection of religious art; it's open 9 to 11:30 am Tuesday to Saturday. Note the bell cast in 909, thought by some to be the world's second-oldest surviving bell (the identity of the oldest is in dispute). Across the square, the **Casa de la Cultura** has temporary exhibitions of work by local artists and craftspeople. It's open 8 am to noon and 2 to 6 pm weekdays.

The Universidad de los Andes building, just off the plaza, houses the **Museo Arqueológico**, open 8 am to noon and 2 to 6 pm Tuesday to Friday, 1 to 6:30 pm weekends. A small but interesting collection, supported by extensive background information (in Spanish only), gives insight into the pre-Hispanic times of the region.

The large, modern Centro Cultural, one block north of the plaza, accommodates the **Museo de Arte Moderno**, open 9 am to noon and 2 to 6 pm Tuesday to Sunday. It stages changing exhibitions of modern art, so you never know what you'll find. The entrance is from Calle 21.

The **Museo de Arte Colonial**, two blocks northeast of the plaza, has a collection of mostly sacred art. It's open 8 am to noon and 2 to 6 pm Tuesday to Friday, 9 am to noon weekends.

Seven blocks northeast, at the end of Avenida 4, is the small **Parque de Las Cinco Repúblicas**, boasting the oldest monument to Bolívar, which dates from 1842.

Other Attractions

Some sights lie outside the city center. The scenic **Parque Los Chorros de Milla**, named after the waterfalls in the park, is on the northern outskirts of the city 4km from the center and is accessible by urban busetas. There's a small zoo in the park, which features some of the local fauna. It's open 8 am to 6 pm Tuesday to Sunday, and admission costs US$1.

In the southern part of the city, the new **Museo de Ciencia y Tecnología**, on Avenida Andrés Bello, combines the functions of a natural-history and a technology museum, featuring exhibitions on biodiversity, earthquakes, fauna and geology. It's open 8 am to noon and 2 to 6 pm Tuesday to Friday, 10 am to 6 pm weekends; admission is an overpriced US$5.

About 1.5km north along the same Avenida Andrés Bello, the **Parque Jardín Acuario** sports an aquarium with some fish typical of Venezuela and an exhibition devoted to the traditional culture of the region. The place was run down and unkempt when we were there, but it may improve one day. It's open 8 am to 6 pm Tuesday to Sunday.

Activities

While the city's cultural attractions listed above may not seem extremely fascinating, Mérida is easily Venezuela's major center for active tourism. The region provides excellent conditions for a range of activities as diverse as rock climbing, bird-watching and rafting, and local operators have been quick to make them easily accessible for visitors – see Organized Tours, later, for what's offered. Also see Around Mérida, later in this chapter, for more details about activities.

Language Courses

Mérida is an ideal place for travelers to study Spanish. First of all, it has a lot of attractions to offer visitors, so you won't be bored staying here while studying. Second, the Spanish spoken in the Andes is spoken more slowly than in other parts of the country, and many foreigners find it easier to understand. For this reason, it's a good place for practicing. Finally, Mérida is well prepared to teach you Spanish, and the prices of language courses tend to be lower here than just about anywhere else in the country.

The city has several language schools, plus plenty of students and tutors offering private lessons. They advertise through posadas, bars, tour companies etc. The major institutions offering Spanish courses include the following:

Instituto Latino Americano de Idiomas
(☎/fax 44 78 08, ildi@bolivar.funmrd.gov.ve) Centro Comercial Mamayeya, Piso 4, Oficina 26, Avenida Las Américas

Iowa Institute
(☎ 52 64 04, fax 44 90 64, iowainst@ing.ula.ve) Avenida 4 at Calle 18
Web site: www.ing.ula.ve/~iowainst

Venusa
(☎ 63 39 06, fax 63 35 25) Avenida Urdaneta No 49-49
Web site: www.flinet.com/~venusa

All these schools run courses of various lengths (from one week onward) at different levels. They are flexible at accommodating travelers' needs, and you usually don't have to wait long before the course starts.

Organized Tours

There are plenty of tour companies in Mérida, and prices are generally reasonable. Understandably, mountain trips feature most prominently on the operators' lists and include treks to the highest peaks, such as Pico Bolívar and Pico Humboldt; expect to pay about US$40 to US$50 per person per day, all-inclusive.

The village of Los Nevados is probably the most popular destination among those who don't attempt to climb the peaks. Most companies offer this trip, but you can easily do it on your own; all the tour companies listed here will give you details on how to do it and can arrange a jeep to Los Nevados without charging a commission. Refer to the Around Mérida section, later, for more about this trip.

The Sierra La Culata is a relatively easy and attractive destination and is available as a tour from most agents. It's usually a two- to three-day trip, costing around US$40 per person per day, all-inclusive.

A worthwhile excursion out of Mérida is a wildlife safari in Los Llanos, Venezuela's greatest repository of wildlife, particularly birds. There's a number of ecotourist camps in Los Llanos that offer tours in their ranches (known as *hatos*), but they are ex-

pensive (US$100 to US$150 per person per day). Mérida's companies (including those listed next) will organize a similarly fascinating excursion for around US$40 to US$50 a day. It's offered as a three- to five-day all-inclusive package.

The companies offer several options, such as mountain biking, paragliding, rafting and horseback riding. Some also handle rental of equipment, camping gear, bikes etc. As elsewhere in the country, Mérida's tour companies will normally accept cash payment for their services in US dollars. Most will accept traveler's checks, but not credit cards.

If you need just equipment, not a guide or a tour, check Expedición Andina (☎ 52 83 68), Calle 24 No 8-153. It's the only company that specializes in renting out camping, hiking and mountaineering stuff.

Tour Companies Following are some of the major, best-established and most reliable local tour companies:

Arassari Trek (formerly Bum Bum Tours)
(☎/fax 52 58 79, info@arassari.com) Calle 24 No 8-301. Run by Swiss polyglot Tom and his wife Raquel, the company has a wide range of tours, including mountain trekking, horseback riding and kayaking, as well as some of the most adventurous rafting and canyoning trips. Some of its Los Llanos tours are conducted by Alan Highton, one of the best bird and wildlife guides around. The company has a restaurant with fabulous views over the cableway and the mountains, as well as a cybercafé.
Web site: www.arassari.com

Guamanchi Expeditions
(☎/fax 52 20 80, info@guamanchi.com) Calle 24 No 8-39. One of Mérida's largest and longest-operating companies, it offers a good choice of well-prepared tours up to the mountain peaks and down to Los Llanos. It has bicycles for rent, bike tours and information about do-it-yourself bike trips, and it rents trekking equipment.
Web site: www.guamanchi.com

Natoura Adventure Tours
(☎/fax 52 42 16, 51 06 01, natoura@telcel.net.ve) Calle 24 No 8-237. Also boasting a long history and sound reputation, this company is particularly good for mountain trekking and climbing, though it runs a range of other tours as well, including bird-watching in the Mérida region and beyond. It offers Los Llanos tours with lodging

in beds (most other companies provide hammocks only). It also uses good-quality camping and mountaineering equipment on its tours, some of which can be rented.
Web site: www.natoura.com

All three companies have received excellent reports from travelers, and their prices are comparable. There are plenty of other tour companies in town (including several around Parque Las Heroínas) that may be as good and reliable and will cost much the same or even less. Shop around, talk to other travelers and check things thoroughly before you decide.

Special Events
The region is rich in festivals and festivities, many of which are confined to a particular small area or even a single town. The year begins with the Paradura del Niño, observed throughout the region during the whole of January. This traditional festival involves locals 'stealing' the infant Jesus from his crib, then searching for him and celebrating his 'finding.'

Reyes Magos (Epiphany), on January 6, is particularly solemn in the town of Santo Domingo. On February 2, the Vasallos de La Candelaria brings ritual dances to La Parroquia, Mucuchíes, Bailadores and La Venta.

The Feria del Sol is Mérida's Carnaval and the city's main annual party, replete with music, popular dance, sports events, major bullfights and a beauty pageant. It runs for nearly the whole week preceding Ash Wednesday.

Given the strong traditional character of the region, Semana Santa (Holy Week, leading up to Easter) is celebrated quite solemnly in many towns and villages, particularly so in La Parroquia, Lagunillas, Santo Domingo, Chiguará and La Azulita.

On May 15 there's the Fiesta de San Isidro Labrador. It's a sort of agrarian rite in honor of the patron saint of farmers, celebrated with processions featuring domestic animals and crops. It's most elaborate in Apartaderos, Mucuchíes, Tabay, Bailadores and La Azulita.

The Fiesta de Santiago Apóstol is held on July 25 in Lagunillas, Ejido and Jají. Los Negros de San Gerónimo is celebrated in Santo Domingo on September 30. The Fiesta de San Rafael takes place on October 24 in San Rafael.

The town of Mucurubá observes the Fiesta de la Inmaculada Concepción on December 8, with a spectacular display of some 20,000 candles, which are lit in the evening on the main plaza.

Christmas is essentially a family occasion that is celebrated at home. The Fiesta de San Benito springs to life on December 29 in Timotes, La Venta, Apartaderos and Mucuchíes. On this day the locals take to the streets in red-and-black costumes and sometimes black-colored faces, in honor of Venezuela's only black saint, and spend the day dancing to the rhythm of drums and parading from door to door.

The Despedida del Año Viejo (Farewell to the Old Year), at midnight on December 31, features the burning of life-size human puppets, often stuffed with fireworks, which have been prepared weeks before and placed in front of the houses.

Places to Stay – Budget
Mérida has heaps of budget places to stay, a good portion of which are *posadas*, or small, family-run guesthouses. There are around 50 posadas in the city – more than in all other major Venezuelan cities combined. Furthermore, despite the country's precarious economic climate and a seeming glut of accommodations in town, new posadas are popping up every month.

With such an assortment of options, enumerating all the guesthouses is nearly impossible. But don't worry: Most posadas are clean and friendly and a good value for money. Since many of the cheapest posadas are just ordinary private homes, with the family living in and renting some spare rooms, there are understandably only shared baths, but this is usually not a major problem because these places are very small. On the other hand, many posadas provide free access to the kitchen, and often can wash your clothes for a small fee.

The cheapest posada-style central places include ***Residencia San Pedro*** (☎ 52 27 35,

Calle 19 No 6-36), **Posada Patty** (Calle 24 No 8-265), the new **Posada Jama Chía** (☎ 52 57 67, Calle 24 No 8-223), **Posada Yagrumo** (☎ 52 95 39, Calle 24 No 8-78), **Posada Mundo Mérida** (☎ 52 26 44, Calle 24 No 8-16) and **Posada Mucumbarí** (☎ 52 60 15, Avenida 3 No 14-73). Any of these will cost US$5 to US$7 per person in doubles or triples with shared facilities. The Posadas Patty and Yagrumo are the cheapest but most basic of the lot, while the San Pedro is perhaps the best.

The German-run **Posada Alemania** (☎ 52 40 67), Avenida 2 at Calle 18, costs US$15/18 double/triple without bath and also has some more expensive rooms with private facilities. Additionally, it features a fine, leafy patio.

The cheapest posadas offering rooms with private bath (for about US$6 to US$8 per person) include **Posada Mara** (☎ 52 55 07, Calle 24 No 8-215) and **Residencia Araure** (☎ 52 51 03, Calle 16 No 3-34).

For a little more, you have a choice of pleasant, stylish posadas, all with private bath and hot water and often with TV. They include **Posada La Montaña** (☎ 52 59 77, Calle 24 No 6-47), **Posada Encanto Andino** (☎ 52 69 29, Calle 24 No 6-53), **Posada Luz Caraballo** (☎ 52 54 41, Avenida 2 No 13-80), **Posada Los Bucares de Mérida** (☎ 52 28 41, Avenida 4 No 15-05), **La Casona de Margot** (☎ 52 33 12, Avenida 4 No 15-17), **Posada Turística La Merideña** (☎ 52 57 38, Avenida 3 No 16-39) and **Posada Doña Pumpa** (☎ 52 72 86, Calle 14 No 5-11). In any of these, expect to pay US$20 to US$25 double or US$25 to US$30 triple.

Given the abundance of posadas, few backpackers bother to look for a hotel, even though there are quite a few budget hotels across the town. Few are anything special or have much character, but some may be useful. If price is your critical factor, try one of the cheapest: the 40-room **Hotel Italia** (☎ 52 57 37, Calle 19 No 2-55). It has small, basic singles/doubles without bath for US$6/8 and rooms with bath for US$10/12. The neat **Hotel Español** (☎ 52 92 35, Avenida 2 No 15-48) is one of the best budget hotels in town. It charges US$12/22/26/30

single/double/triple/quad with bath and cable TV.

Places to Stay – Mid-Range & Top End

Most travelers are perfectly satisfied with the standards offered by the budget posadas, but should you prefer a decent hotel, there's no problem finding one. Mérida has quite a few hotels in this price bracket, though most are mid-priced places without much luxury. There's nothing really very posh or expensive in town.

Central options include **Hotel Mintoy** (☎ 52 35 45, 52 03 40, Calle 25 No 8-130), just off Parque Las Heroínas, and **Hotel Chama** (☎ 52 48 51, 52 10 11), on Calle 29 near Avenida 4. Both have reasonable doubles with bath and cable TV for around US$40 to US$45, but otherwise they are not particularly memorable places.

A more stylish place in the center is **Hotel El Tisure** (☎ 52 60 61, 52 60 72, Avenida 4 No 17-47). Built in colonial style but offering modern facilities, it costs US$44/50 for an air-con double/triple. It's actually one of the very few hotels in Mérida that has air-conditioning – hardly anybody needs it here.

Hotel Prado Río (☎ 52 06 33, 52 05 81), Avenida Universidad, a bit farther from the center, certainly has character and style. Set in vast, walled-in grounds, it has a hotel building (US$35 for a spacious matrimonial room) and a colony of whitewashed cabañas arranged in the form of a Mediterranean town (US$50 for up to three persons), plus a restaurant, bar and a swimming pool.

One of the best options in town is the new **Hotel El Serrano** (☎ 66 74 47, 66 79 14), on Avenida Los Próceres 4km southwest of the center. It too has comfortable rooms (US$40/50 double/triple); you can also check in to an ample suite with two bathrooms and two TV sets (US$70 for up to four persons).

Places to Eat

If you are looking for unpretentious, budget dining, Mérida is for you. It's one of the cheapest places to eat in Venezuela, and the food is generally good. Plenty of restaurants serve set lunches for around US$2 to US$3.

Lunchería Joseph, just off Plaza Bolívar, is an example of a good central budget eatery; it's so popular that you may have to stand in line at the door during lunchtime. Other options for a US$2 set lunch include *Restaurant Típico (Calle 20 No 4-35)* and *Restaurant Margarita (Calle 19 No 5-14)*.

Outside the center, a good place for a budget local meal is the *Mercado Principal*, on Avenida Las Américas. It also has plenty of fruit and vegetable stalls, as well as an interesting crafts section.

Pollos en Brasa Tercera Avenida (Avenida 3 No 26-52) is one of the best budget outlets for chicken and is open late. The ordinary-looking *Arepera La Reina Andina (Avenida 5 No 21-46)* serves hearty arepas (two dozen different fillings to choose from) for around US$1 each. The popular *Pizzería El Sabor de Los Quesos*, Plaza Milla, does some of the cheapest pizzas, and they are not bad at all. Next door, the *Posada Luz Caraballo* has a good, inexpensive restaurant.

Cheap vegetarian set meals are served (at lunchtime only) in *El Sano Glotón (Avenida 4 No 17-84)*, *El Sabor Natural (Avenida 3 No 16-80)* and *El Tinajero (Calle 29 No 3-54)*. There are also two small vegetarian restaurants at both entrances to Alfredo's Bar, from Avenida 4 and Calle 19 (see Entertainment, later in this section).

Going a little bit up the price scale, *Restaurant Chipen (Avenida 5 No 23-67)* offers straightforward, tasty food, including churrasco and lomito. The well-appointed *La Trattoria da Lino (Pasaje Ayacucho No 25-38)* serves fine Italian fare at reasonable prices. *Cheo's Carnes a la Brasa (Calle 24 No 8-109, Parque Las Heroínas)* has juicy steaks. *La Exquisita Bocata (Avenida 4 No 14-99)* does delicious *bocatas* (a sort of sandwich with a meat filling).

One of the loveliest places to eat is the magical *Restaurant La Abadía (Avenida 3 No 17-45)*. Established in a beautifully reconstructed colonial mansion, the two-story *casona* (large house) has different dining spaces, each with its own ambience, plus a cybercafé.

You shouldn't miss *Heladería Coromoto (Avenida 3 No 28-75)*. Perhaps the most famous ice-cream parlor on the continent, it appears in *The Guinness Book of World Records*. The place offers about 750 flavors, though not all are available on an average day. Among the more unusual varieties are polar bear, shrimp, trout, chicken with spaghetti, and *el vegetariano*. You can even have the Lonely Planet flavor (which appears under its Spanish name, Planeta Solitario). The place is open 2 to 10 pm (closed Monday).

Entertainment

The noisy *Alfredo's Bar*, on the corner of Calle 19 and Avenida 4, is possibly the most popular watering hole in town, partly due to its incredibly cheap beer, reputedly the cheapest in Venezuela (about US$0.25 until 7 pm, US$0.40 after that). From the moment it opens its doors at 1 pm, it fills up gradually with guests, who in turn fill up gradually with beer and get ready to enter the dance floor by the evening, when the disco music reaches its zenithal volume. On weekend nights, it's so completely packed that it's impossible to get in, let alone sit or dance.

Birosca Carioca (Calle 24 No 2-04) is another popular central nightspot for fast dancing and drinking in a 'student' atmosphere, as is the nearby *Camerino (Avenida 3 No 24-55)*. Both discos are open nightly except Sundays, play the usual international disco fare, and attract mostly young clientele.

You can experience a completely different kind of entertainment at *La Abadía (Avenida 3 No 17-45)*, which has live music (to listen to, not to dance to) Friday to Sunday nights in a beautiful, atmospheric interior lit by candles rather than a stroboscope. The music can be jazz, Cuban song, Argentine *milonga* and the like.

Outside the town center, the invariably popular *La Cucaracha*, in the Centro Comercial Las Tapias on Avenida Urdaneta, is the oldest, largest and loudest discotheque. The music level is actually so high that it affects the body, not just the ears, and triggers off the alarms of cars parked outside. The 10-year-old place has a few different musical ambiences, with the main hall blasting with disco/techno music and the Latin-Caribbean rhythms played downstairs. Over 1000 guests can turn up and squeeze inside on a good weekend night.

Mega Tops, on Avenida Los Próceres, is the newest addition to Mérida's disco scene. It has more bells and whistles than La Cucaracha and draws in hordes of beautiful people to dance to a ragbag of everything from Beach Boys to Tito Puente.

The spacious *Habana Kawy*, Avenida Chorros de Milla, has live salsa and merengue Thursday to Saturday after 10 pm – a pleasant place to come and dance or just listen, if you like these rhythms.

Kawy Café Bar & Grill, Avenida Las Américas, also presents live music Thursday to Saturday, but it hosts various musical genres, including rock, salsa and jazz.

Getting There & Away

Air The airport is on Avenida Urdaneta, right inside the city, 2km southwest of Plaza Bolívar. Frequent urban busetas link the airport to the center. The runway is short, and the proximity of high mountains makes landing a difficult task, especially in bad weather. Consequently, particularly in the rainy season, flights can be diverted elsewhere, usually to El Vigía (accessible from Mérida by a new road via tunnels).

Avior, Lai and Santa Bárbara all fly daily to Caracas (US$58 to US$70). There are also flights to Maracaibo (US$55) and Barquisimeto (US$45), and to Porlamar via Maracay or Caracas (US$125). For other destinations, you usually have to change in Caracas. Prices listed are one-way.

Bus The bus terminal is on Avenida Las Américas, 3km southwest of the city center. It's linked with the center by frequent public transportation; alternatively, take a taxi (US$3). Half a dozen buses a day run to Caracas (US$17 ordinary, US$23 deluxe, 12 hours) and to Maracaibo (US$14 deluxe, eight hours). Busetas to San Cristóbal depart every 1½ hours from 5:30 am to 7 pm (US$7.50, five hours); you can also take a por puesto (US$11, four hours) – all

go via El Vigía and La Fría (not via the Trans-Andean route). A new road leading through a chain of tunnels between Mérida and El Vigía is now open, cutting down travel time and improving comfort.

Four buses a day run to Valera via the Trans-Andean highway (US$5, five hours), and five buses go to Barinas (US$4, four hours). Both roads are spectacular. Each route is also serviced by por puesto cars, which are about an hour faster but cost nearly twice as much as the bus. Por puestos also operate on many shorter, regional routes, including Apartaderos and Jají.

Getting Around

Bus & Taxi The city is well serviced by small buses and minibuses, and you can also move around by taxi. The latter may be particularly convenient for trips to and from the bus terminal and airport, when you're carrying all your bags with you. The taxi trip between the city center and the bus terminal or airport will cost about US$3 each way.

Línea Tele-Cars (☎ 63 95 89, 63 88 34) is a reliable taxi company with radio service. Apart from services within the city, the company organizes taxi trips around the region, including Lagunillas, Jají, El Águila and San Rafael.

Car Several car-rental companies have desks at the airport. Dávila (☎ 63 45 10) is possibly the most popular among travelers, but check others as well and compare.

AROUND MÉRIDA

The region that surrounds Mérida offers plenty of attractions, both natural and cultural. You could easily spend a month here and still only see a little of what the mountains have to offer. Many sights are accessible by road, so you can get around cheaply by public transportation. This is particularly the case with the towns and villages that dot the Trans-Andean highway and surrounding mountain slopes and valleys. Many of them have preserved their historic architecture and yesteryear's atmosphere.

Exploring the region is quite easy, as transportation and accommodations along the Trans-Andean highway are in good supply. Virtually every sizable village on the road has at least one posada, and there's a satisfactory number of roadside restaurants.

If you plan on hiking, you can get to many more attractions, mostly natural ones: mountain tops, verdant valleys, glacial lakes, waterfalls, hot springs and páramos among them. You don't necessarily need a tent, as some routes are one-day walks or have accommodation facilities on the way.

Jají & Around

About 38km west of Mérida, Jají is probably the best known of dozens of traditional mountain towns and villages in the region. It's easily accessible by por puestos from Mérida's bus terminal (US$1, 50 minutes). Jají was extensively reconstructed in the late 1960s to become a manicured, typical *pueblo andino* (Andean town), and it's pretty touristy. Its Plaza Bolívar has a choice of handicraft shops that enjoy particularly good trade on weekends, when most visitors come. There are two budget posadas on the plaza.

Eight kilometers before Jají, beside the road, is the Chorrera de Las González, a series of five waterfalls. You can stop here to bathe in the falls' ponds, or just to have a look. You can climb three of the waterfalls by taking side paths.

Instead of returning straight back to Mérida, you can walk 1.5km along the road (toward Mérida) to a junction, take a right turn and walk another 7km to La Mesa, a fine old town that's more authentic than Jají. Por puestos from La Mesa will take you to the larger town of Ejido, where you change for Mérida.

Mucuchíes & Around

Another authentic pueblo andino is Mucuchíes, about 48km northeast of Mérida. This 400-year-old town has a fine parish church on its Plaza Bolívar and a choice of accommodations, including the inexpensive *Hotel Los Andes*.

Several kilometers farther up the road is the village of San Rafael, noted for an amazing small stone chapel built by a local artist, Juan Félix Sánchez (1900–97), who is buried inside. This is his second chapel; the first, in similar style, was constructed two decades ago in the remote hamlet of El Tisure, a five- to seven-hour walk from San Rafael (there is no access road).

CIDA Astronomical Observatory

North of San Rafael, at an altitude of about 3600m, is the Centro de Investigaciones de Astronomía (CIDA), an astronomical observatory that includes a museum of astronomy. It's normally open to the public only on weekends, but in peak holiday seasons (Christmas, Carnaval, Easter) it's open daily. Information can be obtained by calling ☎ 71 27 80, 71 38 83; alternatively, check their Web site at www.cida.ve. The center is off the main road, and there is no public transportation on the access road that branches off the Mérida-Apartaderos road between Mucuchíes and San Rafael. Some Mérida companies may organize tours to the observatory.

Theme Parks

Two theme parks lie in the vicinity of Mérida. They have become favorite attractions for Venezuelan tourists, though they may look somewhat artificial and tacky to some foreign travelers. Put aside at least three hours to visit either park. Don't enter them if it's raining, because much of the action takes place outdoors. Both are open daily 8 am to 6 pm, but ticket desks close at 3 pm.

Los Aleros, on the road to Mucuchíes, shortly past Tabay, was opened in 1984. It's a re-creation of a typical Andean village from the 1930s, brought to life with period events, crafts and food, plus a few extra surprises. Por puestos from the corner of Calle 19 and Avenida 4 in Mérida will take you there. Admission is US$12.

The **Venezuela de Antier** opened in the early 1990s, following the success of Los Aleros. Here, the same entrepreneur, Romer Alexis Montilla, has created a sort of Venezuela-in-a-capsule by reproducing the country's landmarks, costumes and traditions. You'll find replicas of the Plaza Bolívar of Caracas, the Puente Urdaneta of Maracaibo and the oldest monument to

Bolívar (in Mérida). You'll see Amazonian Indians and Guajiro women in their traditional dresses, and General Juan Vicente Gómez will even show up in full uniform. The old *trapiche* (mill) serves sugarcane juice for guests, and cockfights may be held on weekends. There's also a collection of vintage cars. The park is 12km from Mérida on the Jají road; take a por puesto from Calle 26 between Avenidas 3 and 4. Admission is US$15.

Hiking & Mountaineering

Possibilities are almost unlimited. Some of the more popular destinations are detailed in this section, but there are plenty of other options. Except for the Pico Bolívar climb, the listed trips can be made without a guide, though it's more comfortable and safer to go on an organized tour. If you prefer to go on your own anyway, most of Mérida's tour operators, including Arassari, Guamanchi and Natoura, will provide information about these and other do-it-yourself tours. Don't ignore their comments about safety measures. Buy trekking maps at the Inparques office.

Bear in mind that weather can change frequently and rapidly even in the dry season. Rain (or snow, at upper reaches) can occur anytime, and visibility can drop dramatically within an hour, leaving you trapped high up in the mountains for quite a while. Be careful and hike properly equipped, with good rain gear and warm clothing, as well as some extra food and water. Particular care should be taken on remote trails, where you may not meet anyone for days. Also keep in mind the risk of altitude sickness (see Health, in the Facts for the Visitor chapter).

Sierra Nevada de Mérida One of the best ways to get a taste of what this range has to offer is to ride the spectacular teleférico from Mérida (see that section under Mérida, earlier). The mountain chain also offers several climbing opportunities, including Venezuela's two highest mountains.

Pico Bolívar This is possibly the most popular peak to climb, mostly because it's

Venezuela's highest point (5007m). Given the country's mania for Bolívar monuments, it probably shouldn't come as a surprise that a bust of the hero has been placed on the summit.

The climb requires a rope, and you shouldn't do it without a guide (particularly in the wet season) unless you have sound mountaineering experience. Several major tour companies in Mérida (including the three listed under Organized Tours in that section) organize trips to Pico Bolívar, usually offering a range of options, including combination trips to Pico Bolívar, Los Nevados and Pico Humboldt.

Pico Humboldt This is perhaps the second-most popular peak among climbers and high-mountain trekkers, and Venezuela's second-highest summit (4942m). There's not much here in the way of mountaineering, but the hike itself is marvelous.

The starting point for the trek is La Mucuy, accessible by road from Mérida. Take a carro to Tabay, from the corner of Calle 19 and Avenida 4. From Tabay's Plaza Bolívar, por puesto jeeps go to La Mucuy; Inparques has its post here.

A four- to six-hour walk will take you up to the small Laguna La Coromoto (3200m), where trekkers normally camp the first night. The next day, it's a four-hour walk to reach Laguna Verde (4000m), one of the largest lakes in the area. Some hikers stay here the second night, but if it's still not too late, you can walk for another hour to Laguna El Suero, a tiny lake at about 4200m, almost at the foot of the glacier. It gets freezing at night, so have plenty of warm clothes.

Pico Humboldt is a two- to four-hour ascent, depending on the weather. You reach the snowline at about 4800m. Farther up, crampons and an ice axe are recommended, and keep an eye out for crevasses. Again, this climb is best done with an experienced local guide, particularly in the rainy (snowy) season.

Back at Laguna El Suero, you can return the same way to La Mucuy or continue along the route known as La Travesía to

THE ANDES

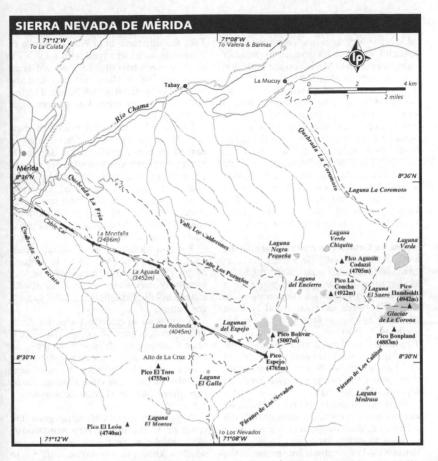

SIERRA NEVADA DE MÉRIDA

Pico Espejo (4765m). After an initial 500m ascent from the lake, the trail to Pico Espejo (four to six hours) goes for most of the way at roughly the same altitude, nearly 4700m. You can then climb Pico Bolívar before returning to Mérida by foot or teleférico. The whole loop will take four to seven days, or even longer, depending on how many peaks you climb and the weather conditions.

Some major tour operators in Mérida can provide full equipment and guides for these treks. If you just want equipment, it may be better to arrange rental at Expedición Andina, Calle 24 No 8-153.

Los Nevados If you are not up to scaling the peaks, you can try the easy and spectacular (and therefore very popular) trip to Los Nevados, a charming mountain pueblo set at an altitude of about 2700m (budget accommodations and food available). The trip is normally done as a two- to three-day loop and includes rides by jeep, mule and cable car.

One way of getting to Los Nevados is by jeep along a breathtaking mountain track hugging the cliffside (US$50 per jeep for up to five people, four to five hours). You stay the night in the village, from where you walk or ride on a mule to the Loma Redonda cable-car station. You can then return by cable car to Mérida, or walk downhill to the beautiful Valle Los Calderones for another night and return to Mérida on the third day.

It's perhaps more attractive to do the trip the other way around, as many travelers do. Go by cable car up to Pico Espejo, have a look around and go down (also by cable car) to Loma Redonda. Then walk to Los Nevados (four to five hours) for the night. From Los Nevados, you can walk back the same way (six hours) to Loma Redonda and return by cable car, or take a jeep to Mérida (63km). Some hikers continue walking for seven hours (24km) over to the village of El Morro (rooms and meals available), from where there are more jeeps to Mérida.

Sierra La Culata This national park, to the north of Mérida, also offers some amazing hiking territory and is particularly noted for its desertlike highland landscapes. Take a por puesto to La Culata (departing from Calle 19 between Avenidas 1 and 2), from where it's a three- to four-hour hike uphill northeast to a primitive shelter known as 'El Refugio,' at about 3700m. Continue the next day for about three hours to the top of Pico Pan de Azúcar (4660m). Return before 4 pm, when the last por puesto tends to depart back to Mérida.

Some guided tours don't return the same way but instead descend southeast through a deserted, moonscape-like terrain to a chain of mountain lakes and on down to Mucuchíes via the natural hot springs. Trails are faint on this route, and it's easy to get lost if you don't know the way; don't wander too far unless you're an experienced trekker.

Pico El Águila & Around This is another interesting area for hiking. Take a morning bus to Valera and get off at Venezuela's highest road pass (4007m), at the foot of Pico El Águila (4118m), about 60km from Mérida. Bolívar marched this way on one of his campaigns, hence the monument dedicated to the hero on the pass – it's the statue of a condor.

There's a roadside restaurant where you can have a hot chocolate before setting off. Take the side road up to Pico El Águila (a 20-minute walk), crowned with a CANTV mast, to reach beautiful páramo and great panoramic views. Here you may find the bearded helmetcrest, which lives at a higher altitude than any other known species of hummingbird.

Locals with mules often wait on the pass opposite the restaurant to take tourists to **Laguna Mucubají** (3540m), 5km due south, but it's perhaps better to walk there so as to get a closer look at the splendid páramo filled with *frailejones* (espeletia). The walk, downhill all the way, will bring you to the Barinas road and the lagoon, just off the road. It's one of the largest lakes in Parque Nacional Sierra Nevada.

You can walk from here (for one hour) up the reforested pine slope to **Laguna Negra**, a small, beautiful mountain lake with amazingly dark water. A 45-minute walk farther uphill is another fine lake, **Laguna Los Patos**.

If you want to camp, get a permit from Inparques at Laguna Mucubají. The office is open 8 am to 6 pm daily, and the staff can provide information on other sights in the area. There are two hotels by the road near the lake, including the good *Parador Turístico Sierra Nevada* (US$25 double with a fireplace).

A trail from Laguna Mucubají goes 7km south up to the top of **Pico Mucuñuque** (4672m), the highest peak in this range, which is known as the Serranía de Santo Domingo. The roundtrip will take you a good part of the day. It's a rather difficult hike, as the trail is not clear in the upper reaches and you have to ascend over 1100m from the lagoon. Ask for detailed instructions at the Inparques post.

Mountain Biking
Biking is becoming increasingly popular in the region. Several tour companies in Mérida organize bike trips and rent out bikes. Shop around, as bicycle quality and rental prices may differ substantially among tour companies.

One of the most popular bike routes is the loop around the remote mountain villages south of Mérida, known as 'Pueblos del Sur.' The loop normally includes the villages of San José, Mucutuy, Mucuchachí, Canaguá, Chacantá, El Molino, Capurí and Guaraque. It's a beautiful trip – provided you've got legs of iron.

Horseback Riding
Equestrian activities are organized by most operators, either as short leisurely rides based on a particular stud farm or as horse treks of several days on longer routes. Contact the companies for details, as their facilities and prices can vary considerably.

Paragliding
Another popular activity in the region is paragliding. Most area tour operators offer tandem flights with a skilled pilot, so no previous experience is necessary. The usual starting point for flights is Las González, an hour's jeep ride from Mérida, from where you fly for about 25 to 30 minutes, climbing over 850m in altitude from start to finish. The cost of the flight is much the same with all agencies (US$60); jeep transportation is included.

Some agencies offer paragliding courses that take five to eight days, and also cover theory (available in English) and practice (including solo flights); the cost is US$300 to US$350. The course allows you to fly solo, but you'll still have to rent a paraglider (US$50 a flight, US$200 a week, plus the cost of transportation).

One of the most experienced local gliding pilots and instructors is Raúl Penso, who runs tandem flights and conducts courses. He can be contacted through Arassari (see Tour Companies under Organized Tours in the Mérida section, earlier).

Rafting & Canyoning
River rafting was introduced in 1996 by Arassari, and other companies (including Natoura and Guamanchi; see Tour Companies under Organized Tours in the Mérida section, earlier) jumped on as well. It is done on some of the rivers at the southern foothills of the Andes, but new good sites have been found close to Mérida, allowing for attractive one-day tours, which are currently sold for about US$50 to US$60, all-inclusive. Rafting is a wet-season activity, normally from June to November, but climate anomalies over recent years make it difficult to determine the season.

The newest craze, also introduced by Arassari, is canyoning. Described by travelers as 'awesome, terrifying, beautiful, insane but amazing' or 'possibly the maddest thing you can do without getting killed,' canyoning is run as a full-day all-inclusive tour that costs much the same as a rafting tour. As we went to press, Arassari and Guamanchi were the only operators.

Fishing
Anglers may be interested in trout fishing. The most popular places to fish are Lagunas Mucubají and La Victoria, and, to a lesser extent, Lagunas Negra and Los Patos. The fishing season runs from mid March to the end of September. You need a permit from the Ministerio de Producción y Comercio (☎ 63 91 52, 63 52 58), Avenida Urdaneta, near the airport in Mérida. The permit costs US$15 and allows angling in the national park. Bring your own fishing equipment. You can buy some gear in Mérida, but don't count too much on renting the stuff from tour companies or anywhere else.

Táchira State

SAN CRISTÓBAL
☎ 076 (☎ 0276 from Aug 18, 2001)
The capital of Táchira state, San Cristóbal is today a thriving commercial center (population 340,000) fueled by the proximity of Colombia, just 40km away. Spread over a mountain slope at an altitude of about 800m, the city has an attractive location and agreeable climate, with an average temperature of 21°C. However, San Cristóbal has no extraordinary attractions; therefore, for most travelers it's just a place to pass through. It is a transit point on the Pan-American route between Venezuela and Colombia, and

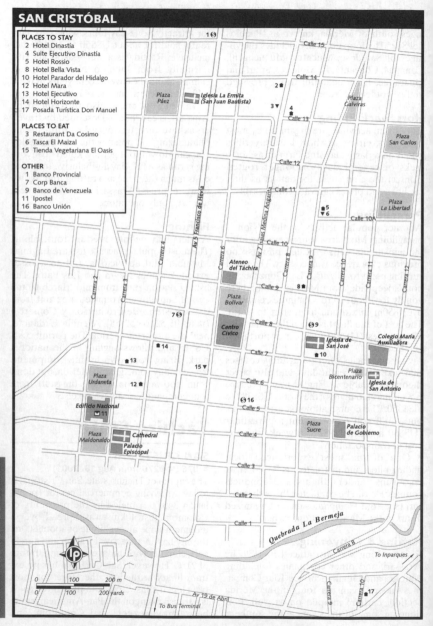

SAN CRISTÓBAL

PLACES TO STAY
2 Hotel Dinastía
4 Suite Ejecutivo Dinastía
5 Hotel Rossio
8 Hotel Bella Vista
10 Hotel Parador del Hidalgo
12 Hotel Mara
13 Hotel Ejecutivo
14 Hotel Horizonte
17 Posada Turística Don Manuel

PLACES TO EAT
3 Restaurant Da Cosimo
6 Tasca El Maizal
15 Tienda Vegetariana El Oasis

OTHER
1 Banco Provincial
7 Corp Banca
9 Banco de Venezuela
11 Ipostel
16 Banco Unión

you'll surely pass through if you come from or go to Cúcuta, in Colombia.

Founded in 1561 by Juan de Maldonado, the town grew slowly, and three centuries after its birth it was still not much more than an obscure settlement. This is why the city has almost no colonial architecture. For over 200 years, San Cristóbal was ruled from Nueva Granada (present-day Colombia). In 1777, with the rest of Táchira, it came under Venezuelan administration. Even then, though, because of the lack of roads to Caracas, the town was linked more to Colombia than to Venezuela. It wasn't until 1925 that the winding Trans-Andean road reached San Cristóbal from Mérida. And it was only in the 1950s that the Pan-American highway was completed, providing the city with a fast, lowland link to the center of the country.

Information
The Cotatur tourist office (☎ 55 96 55, 55 95 78) is on the corner of Avenidas España and Carabobo, about 2km northeast of the city center. It's open 8 am to noon and 2 to 5:30 pm weekdays. Cotatur has *módulos de información* at the airport terminals of Santo Domingo and San Antonio (open during flight times only) and in San Cristóbal's bus terminal (open 7 am to 6 pm daily).

The Bit Cyber Café (☎ 41 68 91), Calle 12 No 7-17, is one of the few central facilities offering Internet access. Most of the city's Internet cafés are in the Barrio Obrero, north of the center. They include Net-World Café, Calle 9 No 16-69; El Frontino Cyber Caffe, Calle 14 at Carrera 22; TNS Cyber C@fé, Carrera 21 between Calles 13 and 14; and Inter Conexion Cyber C@fe, Carrera 18 between Calles 9 and 10.

Things to See
San Cristóbal began its life around what is now Plaza Maldonado. The monumental **Catedral** wasn't completed until the early 20th century, after the previous church had been wrecked by an earthquake. It houses the venerated statue of San Sebastián, the city's patron saint. Next door to the cathedral is the fine **Palacio Episcopal**. On the northern side of the plaza is the massive **Edificio Nacional**, now home to courts of law.

Plaza Bolívar is not a colonial square either. The oldest building here is the **Ateneo del Táchira**, built in 1907 as the Sociedad Salón de Lectura. Do go inside to see what's on display in their art gallery.

There are some more historic buildings on and around Plaza Sucre, including the large **Palacio de Gobierno**. Also known as the Palacio de los Leones, because of the stone lions placed on the roof, the palace-like edifice was built in the 1910s as a government house.

The **Complejo Ferial**, 3km northeast of the center, is a large fairground and sports complex, complete with exhibition halls, a multisport stadium, a velodrome and Venezuela's second-largest bullring. About 1km north of the complex along Avenida Universidad is the **Museo del Táchira**, in an old hacienda. It features archaeology, history and arts-and-craft collections, and is open 9 am to noon and 2 to 5 pm Tuesday to Sunday.

Special Events
San Cristóbal's major annual bash is the Feria de San Sebastián, held in the second half of January. It includes agricultural and industrial fairs, bullfights, bicycle races and other sports events, a crafts fair, popular music, dances and parades, plus a lot of food and drink. Many events take place at the Complejo Ferial.

Places to Stay
If you're coming by bus and just need a budget shelter for the night, head for one of several basic hotels around the bus terminal. Alternatively, go to the city center (a 10-minute ride by local bus), where there are plenty of budget hotels (some double as love hotels). All places listed in this section have rooms with private bath and fan, unless specified otherwise.

The basic *Hotel Mara* (☎ 43 82 18, Carrera 4 No 5-29) is one of the cheapest central options, priced at US$10 matrimonial or double. The nearby *Hotel Ejecutivo* (☎ 44 62 98, Calle 6 No 3-25) is also on the basic side and costs US$10/13 matrimonial/double. *Hotel Horizonte* (☎ 43 00 11, 43 57 94), in the same area, is appreciably better and costs US$22/25/28 single/double/triple.

Five blocks toward the east lies *Hotel Parador del Hidalgo* (☎ 41 99 53, Calle 7 No 9-35). It's simple and lacks style but has clean rooms with private baths and hot water for US$12/14/16 matrimonial/double/triple. More prepossessing is the quiet *Hotel Rossio* (☎ 43 23 30, Carrera 9 No 10-98), which charges US$12/14 matrimonial/double.

For a bit more style and comfort, try the old-fashioned *Hotel Bella Vista* (☎ 43 78 66, 43 81 58), on the corner of Carrera 9 and Calle 9, which has spacious singles/doubles/triples for US$18/22/26.

One of the best places to stay in the center is *Hotel Dinastía* (☎ 42 11 10), Avenida 7 at Calle 14, which has neat air-conditioned singles/doubles/triples costing US$44/54/60. The hotel has an offspring, *Suite Ejecutivo Dinastía* (☎ 43 95 30), on Calle 13 near the corner of Avenida 7, which is newer and even more comfortable than its parent and costs exactly the same.

San Cristóbal has several posadas – a good budget alternative to hotels – worth considering, particularly so if you are in town for more than just one night. The cheapest and closest to the center is *Posada Turística Don Manuel* (☎ 47 80 82, Carrera 10 No 1-63), off Avenida 19 de Abril. It has just four rooms, costing US$18/20/28 single/double/triple with TV and fridge, and you can use the kitchen.

Other budget posadas include *Posada La Aragueña* (☎ 56 47 86, Avenida España No 0-90), in Urbanización Campo Alegre, Pueblo Nuevo, and *Posada La Fuente* (☎ 44 46 26, Avenida Principal de Pueblo Nuevo No 3-46), in Sector El Paraíso. Either will cost about US$25/30 double/triple. There's also the more expensive, friendly *Posada Los Pirineos* (☎ 55 65 28), Avenida Francisco Cárdenas, Quinta El Cerrito, Urbanización Pirineos. Its air-conditioned rooms cost US$50/60 matrimonial/triple.

The poshest place to stay in town is *Hotel El Tamá* (☎/fax 56 04 04, 56 06 41), Avenida 19 de Abril, Urbanización Los Pirineos. It

costs US$90 double and has a restaurant, bar, gym and swimming pool.

Places to Eat

There are many restaurants in the center, including numerous greasy spoons that serve set lunches for US$2 (eg, the *restaurant* in Hotel Parador del Hidalgo). More decent central eateries include *Restaurant Da Cosimo* (Avenida 7 No 13-51) and *Tasca El Maizal*, Carrera 9 at Calle 10A. Vegetarians can get budget lunches at *Tienda Vegetariana El Oasis* (Carrera 6 No 6-11).

Getting There & Away

Air San Cristóbal's airport is in Santo Domingo, about 35km southeast of the city, but there's not too much air traffic going through here. The airport in San Antonio del Táchira is far busier and just about the same distance from San Cristóbal.

Bus The bus terminal is about 2km south of the city center, linked by frequent city-bus services. There are about 10 buses daily to Caracas (US$24 deluxe, 13 hours); most depart in the late afternoon/early evening for an overnight trip via El Llano highway. Busetas to Barinas run every hour or so between about 5 am and 6 pm (US$7, five hours).

In theory, busetas to Mérida go every 1½ hours from 5:30 am to 7 pm (US$7.50, five hours); in practice, however, they depart as soon as all seats are taken. The 7 pm buseta is unreliable if fewer than 10 passengers show up. There are also por puesto cars to Mérida (US$11, four hours).

Por puesto minibuses to San Antonio del Táchira, on the Colombian border, run every 10 or 15 minutes (US$1.25, 1¼ hours); it's a spectacular road.

SAN PEDRO DEL RÍO
☎ 077 (☎ 0277 from Aug 18, 2001)

San Pedro del Río is an old town of 3000 inhabitants, about 40km north of San Cristóbal. It has been extensively restored and has some fine architecture. Colonial-looking, well cared for and clean, it has become a very popular weekend haunt among visitors from the region, mostly from San Cristóbal. On these days, food and craft stalls open and the town blossoms. During the rest of the week, by contrast, San Pedro is an oasis of peace and tranquility.

There are perhaps four calles and four carreras altogether, all cobblestoned and lined with single-story whitewashed houses. Calle Real is the town's central nerve, along which most craft shops and restaurants have nestled.

Places to Stay & Eat
The town's first and best-known place to stay is *Posada Turística La Vieja Escuela* (☎ 91 37 20, Calle Real No 3-61). Located in a fine vintage house that once was a school, the posada has spotless matrimoniales/ quads for US$16/24 and its own restaurant serving regional specialties.

Alternatively, you can stay in the less attractive *Posada Paseo La Chirirí* (☎ 91 01 57, Calle Los Morales No 1-27), which has matrimoniales/triples for US$16/22. Or try *Posada Valparaíso* (☎ 91 10 32), on the road to San Juan de Colón, about 3km out of San Pedro, which costs much the same and has its own restaurant.

There has been a proliferation of eating outlets in San Pedro over recent years, though most of them open only on weekends. The major restaurants include *La Casona de los Abuelos* and *Río de Las Casas*, on Calle Real; and *El Refugio de San Pedro*, on Plaza Bolívar.

Getting There & Away
San Pedro del Río lies just off the unfinished San Cristóbal–La Fría freeway. There are two large sections of the freeway still to be built, and traffic uses the old winding mountain roads on these parts.

From San Cristóbal, take the half-hourly Línea Colón bus to San Juan de Colón and ask the driver to let you off at the turnoff to San Pedro (US$1.50, 1¼ hour), about 10km before San Juan, from where it's a 10-minute walk to the town. To return from San Pedro to San Cristóbal, take the Expresos Ayacucho bus to San Juan de Colón (US$0.40, 20 minutes) and change for the

Línea Colón bus to San Cristóbal (US$1.50, 1½ hours). There may be one or two direct buses a day from San Pedro to San Cristóbal.

If you are coming from the north (eg, from Mérida or Maracaibo), get off at the turnoff to San Pedro, about 10km past San Juan de Colón (the driver will know where to let you off). To go to Mérida from San Pedro, go by the Expresos Ayacucho bus to San Juan de Colón, then change for one of the frequent buses to La Fría (US$1, 50 minutes); change there for a bus to El Vigía, and change again for a bus to Mérida.

SAN ANTONIO DEL TÁCHIRA
☎ 076 (☎ 0276 from Aug 18, 2001)
San Antonio is a Venezuelan border town of 55,000, sitting right on the busy San Cristóbal–Cúcuta route and living off trade with neighboring Colombia. You will pass through it if taking this way between the two countries. There's not much to see or do here except for passport formalities. Remember to set your watch back one hour when crossing from Venezuela to Colombia.

Information
Tourist Offices There's a tourist information desk at the airport, but it's open only during flight times. It's probably not worth a trip unless you're there anyway to take a flight. Any of several travel agencies on Avenida Venezuela (marked on the map) should solve your transportation problems.

Immigration The DIEX office is on Carrera 9 between Calles 6 and 7, and is theoretically open 6 am to 9 pm daily, though it may close earlier. You must get an exit or entry stamp in your passport here. There's a departure tax of US$15, which must be paid in bolívares and is required from all tourists who are leaving Venezuela overland.

Nationals of most countries don't need a visa for Colombia, but all travelers must get an entry stamp from DAS (Colombian immigration). The DAS office is just behind the bridge over the Río Táchira (the actual border) and has hours similar to DIEX's.

SAN ANTONIO DEL TÁCHIRA

COLOMBIA

Carrera 2

To Bus Terminal
& Airport

●1   To Cúcuta (Colombia)

Río Táchira

Carrera 3

🏠2

🏠3   📷7
●6 ●8   ●10

📷 4 5   9●

Carrera 4
●12
Av Venezuela (Carrera 4)
●13
●11

Cemetery

Carrera 5

🏠16
Carrera 6

14 🏠

Calle 1   Calle 2   Calle 3   Calle 4   Calle 5   Calle 6   Calle 7   Calle 8   Calle 9

Av Venezuela

Carrera 7

📷 15

Carrera 8

17 🏠

22 📷

To San Cristóbal

📷23
Carrera 9
●24

25 📷

18 🏠   19🔵 🔵20
Plaza
Bolívar   21 🏠

Carrera 10

📷   🔵
26   28
Cathedral   🔵29

27🏠

Carrera 11

Carrera 12

Quebrada La Dania

Plaza
Miranda

Carrera 13

Ⓛ🅿

0   100   200 m
0   100   200 yards

PLACES TO STAY
2   Hotel El Gran Neverí
3   Hotelito Frontera
14 Hotel Villa de San Antonio
16 Hotel Adriático
17 Hotel Terepaima
18 Hotel Frontera
21 Hotel Don Jorge
27 Hotel Colonial

OTHER
1   DAS Office (Colombian
    Immigration)
4   Expresos San Cristóbal
5   Viajes Turismo Internacional
6   Avensa Office
7   Infoplanet Cybercafé
8   Carven Viajes
9   Expresos Los Llanos
10 Viajes Turismo Uribante
11 Busetas to Bus Terminal &
    Airport
12 Expresos Mérida
13 Viajes Turismo Turvintel
15 CANTV
19 Banco de Venezuela
20 Corp Banca
22 Compunet Cybercafé
23 Por Puestos to Cúcuta
    (Colombia)
24 DIEX Office
25 Por Puestos to San Cristóbal
26 Ipostel
28 Banco Mercantil
29 Banco Unión

It's a short walk from San Antonio, but it's perhaps better not to walk over the bridge (especially after dark), as some cases of robbery have been reported: Someone 'accidentally' bumps into you, throwing you off balance, while your backpack is ripped off and thrown over the bridge, where accomplices lie in wait. Instead of walking, you may prefer to take a bus, which will let you off in front of DAS.

There's another DAS office in Cúcuta, in the suburb of San Rafael, Avenida 1 No 28-57, and also a DAS office at Cúcuta airport, but the latter deals only with air passengers.

Money There are more than half a dozen banks in San Antonio, none of which changes cash. Corp Banca will change your American Express traveler's checks, while Banco Unión, Banco de Venezuela and Banco Mercantil service MasterCard and Visa cardholders.

There are plenty of casas de cambio in the center, particularly on Avenida Venezuela and around the DIEX office. They all change US dollars, bolívares and pesos at rates similar to those in Cúcuta, across the border. None of the casas changes traveler's checks.

Email & Internet Access The town has several facilities, including Infoplanet Cybercafé (☎ 71 23 23), Calle 4 No 3-45, and Compunet Cybercafé, Calle 6 No 8-28.

Places to Stay & Eat
The cheapest, most basic options include *Hotel Villa de San Antonio* (☎ 71 10 23, Carrera 6 No 1-61) and *Hotel Frontera* (☎ 71 52 45, Calle 2 No 8-70). Either will cost US$7 double (US$10 with bath).

Hotel Colonial (☎ 71 26 79, Carrera 11 No 2-51) is a better budget bet and not much more expensive. It features clean matrimoniales/doubles/triples with fan and private bath for US$10/12/15 – ask for a room upstairs. The hotel has its own inexpensive restaurant.

Also a reasonable choice is *Hotelito Frontera* (☎ 71 62 38, Calle 3 No 3-51), which has larger rooms than the Colonial and costs much the same. It also has rooms with air-conditioning for US$12/14/18, which is as cheap as you can find in town.

Just half a block away, *Hotel El Gran Neverí* (☎ 71 57 02, Carrera 3 No 3-13) has good, spacious singles/doubles/triples/quads for US$14/16/22/26. *Hotel Terepaima* (☎ 71 17 63, Carrera 8 No 1-37) has slightly smaller rooms (US$20 double) but features a cheap restaurant.

The best accommodations in town are at *Hotel Don Jorge* (☎ 71 19 32, Calle 5 No 9-20) and *Hotel Adriático* (☎ 71 03 97, Calle 6 No 5-51). Either costs about US$24/34/40 for an air-con single/double/triple, and both have their own restaurants.

Getting There & Away
Air The airport is a couple of kilometers northeast of town on the road to Ureña. It can be reached by Ureña buses, which pass through from central San Antonio (catch them on Calle 6). Avensa, Aserca and Aeropostal have daily flights to Caracas (US$105 to US$127), and there are also flights to Maracaibo (US$58 to US$82). Local travel agencies will book and sell air tickets.

There are no direct flights to Colombia from San Antonio; go to Cúcuta, across the border, where flights leave to Medellín, Bogotá and other domestic destinations.

Bus San Antonio has a new bus terminal, halfway to the airport. Four bus companies – Expresos Mérida, Expresos Los Llanos, Expresos Alianza and Expresos San Cristóbal – operate buses to Caracas, with a total of seven buses daily. All depart between 4 and 7 pm and use El Llano route (US$26 deluxe, about 14 hours). Most bus companies maintain their offices in the town center, close to each other on Avenida Venezuela, where they sell tickets.

There are no direct buses to Mérida; go to San Cristóbal and change. Por puestos to San Cristóbal (US$1.25, 1¼ hours) leave frequently from Avenida Venezuela at Carrera 10.

To Colombia Buses and shared taxis run frequently to Cúcuta, in Colombia, 12km from San Antonio. Catch buses (US$0.40) on Calle 6 or Avenida Venezuela, and shared taxis (US$0.60) on Calle 6 near Carrera 9. Both will deposit you at the Cúcuta bus terminal, passing through the city center. You can pay in bolívares or pesos.

The Cúcuta terminal is dirty, busy and unsafe – one of the poorest in Colombia – so watch your belongings closely. You may be approached by well-dressed, English-speaking characters who will offer help in buying your bus ticket for you. Ignore them – they are con artists. Buy your ticket directly from the bus office.

There are frequent buses to Bucaramanga (US$10, six hours). Over two dozen air-conditioned buses run daily to Bogotá (US$25, 16 hours). If you plan on staying in Cúcuta, don't go all the way to the terminal, but get off in the center.

Los Llanos

Occupying the entire central part of Venezuela, roughly a third of the national territory, Los Llanos (The Plains) are pooltable-flat, low-lying savannas. They extend southwest well into Colombia, taking up just about as vast an area of that neighboring country as they do of Venezuela.

In administrative terms, the Venezuelan Llanos comprise the states of Barinas, Apure, Portuguesa, Cojedes and Guárico. Sometimes the southern parts of Anzoátegui and Monagas are also regarded as part of

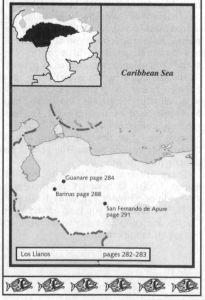

Caribbean Sea

Guanare page 284

Barinas page 288

San Fernando de Apure page 291

Los Llanos   pages 282-283

the Llanos (and called 'Llanos Orientales,' or 'Eastern Plains'). The Llanos are at their best down south, in Apure state, which is referred to as the 'Llano Bajo' (Lower Plain).

A result of the accumulation of sand, clay and mud deposited by rivers over millions of years, these eerie expanses lack distinguishing topographic features. They are mostly covered with grass, with ribbons of gallery forest along the rivers and scattered islands of woodland here and there. Rivers are numerous and, in the wet season, voluminous; the main ones are the Apure, Meta, Arauca and Capanaparo – all of which are left-bank tributaries of the Orinoco, which is itself the southeastern border of Los Llanos.

The climate of Los Llanos has a clearly defined pattern and is extreme in both wet and dry seasons. The former (referred to as *invierno*, or 'winter') lasts from May to November and is characterized by frequent and intense rains. The rivers overflow, turning much of the land into shallow lagoons. Humboldt, who was here in this season, compared Los Llanos to an ocean covered with seaweed. In December, the rains stop and rivers return to their normal courses, steadily getting narrower as the dry season (called *verano*, or 'summer') progresses. The sun beats down upon the parched soil, and winds blow the dust all around.

The Llanos are sparsely populated. Except for San Fernando de Apure, in the heart of the region, all the significant urban centers developed in the more hospitable environment at the northern outskirts of the plains. Roads are few, but the state, in an attempt to open up the plains, has built some access roads. San Fernando de Apure is accessible by paved roads from Maracay/Caracas, in the north, and Barinas/Guanare, in the northwest. The road from San Fernando southward to Puerto Páez, on the Colombian frontier, is in large part surfaced.

The inhabitants of the plains, the *llaneros*, are tough and resistant people used to a hard life. Consequently, Bolívar employed

The Music of Los Llanos

Música llanera, also known as *joropo,* has its origins in flamenco, although it has changed considerably over the centuries. It's a rhythmic form written in 6/8 time, usually sung and accompanied by the *arpa llanera* (a sort of local harp), a *cuatro* (small guitar) and *maracas* (gourd rattles). A modern joropo ensemble usually also includes the double bass as a part of its rhythmic section.

The harp came over from Spain during the colonial period, but it was not until the beginning of this century that it made its way into joropo music. By that time, it had evolved into quite a different instrument; it's smaller and less elaborate than its European parent. The cuatro has four nylon strings and accompanies the melody played by the harp. It too is of European origin and has gradually changed in the New World. Maracas are native American instruments. The harp is sometimes replaced by the *bandola,* another guitar derivative. It has a pearl-shaped body and four nylon strings, and is becoming popular in some areas after a long period during which it was in danger of disappearing.

Joropo has various forms, including *golpes* and *pasajes,* which can be further split into a variety of rhythms, such as *pajarillo, zumba que zumba* and *quirpa.* Generally speaking, pasajes are slower and gentler than golpes. The harp, normally associated with lyrical salon music, finds a different form of expression in joropo. Reflecting the hard life of the llaneros, the harp sounds clear and sharp, at times even wild.

Although joropo has conquered most of Venezuela and has become the national music, it's at its best and most original in Los Llanos. Every second inhabitant of the plains sings or plays one of the instruments, and every village has at least one joropo ensemble. Joropo is common in Venezuela and, to a lesser extent, Colombia, but is almost unknown beyond the borders of these two countries.

Feel the *llanero* groove.

the llaneros in his army to fight against the Spaniards, with great success. As the soil is not all that fertile, the people of the plains have dedicated themselves to raising cattle, and the region is Venezuela's major meat producer. It also produces dairy products and agricultural crops, and provides the country with river fish. Since the discovery of large oil reserves in Anzoátegui state and smaller ones in Barinas state, the Llanos have become increasingly important economically. Oil from both fields is pipelined north to the coast and from there is shipped overseas.

The llaneros have developed their own distinctive culture and folklore, which differ wildly from those elsewhere in Venezuela but have close affinities to those of the Colombian Llanos. One of the favorite pastimes is *coleo* or *toros coleados,* a sort of rodeo. Its aim is to bring down a bull by grabbing its tail while riding a galloping horse. Coleo is held at specially built tracks called *mangas de coleo.* Today, coleo can be seen in other parts of the country, usually accompanying local festivals, but in Los Llanos they are always more authentic and spontaneous.

★ Gravity Tours field camp

LOS LLANOS

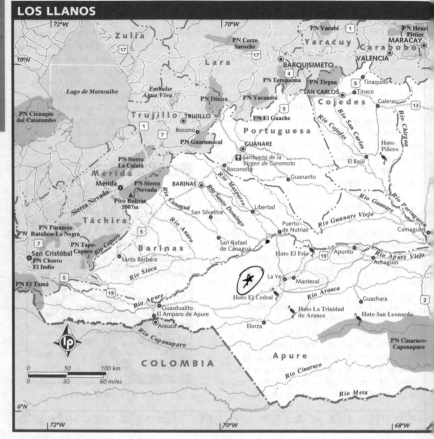

Another conspicuous trait of llanero culture is music – the *joropo* – which is an important part of local life, perhaps more so here than in other regions of the country. Joropo has successfully conquered the country to become Venezuela's national musical rhythm (see the boxed text).

Los Llanos is arguably Venezuela's least-visited region. Difficult access, an uninviting climate and a monotonous landscape are among the factors that deter tourists from coming here. Yet if you have the time and want something different from the usual tourist sights, the region is well worth ex-ploring for its fabulous wildlife, coleo, joropo and other aspects of the llanero lifestyle.

GUANARE

☎ 057 (☎ 0257 from Jun 16, 2001)

Set on the northwestern edge of Los Llanos, Guanare (population 130,000) is a 400-year-old city and the capital of Portuguesa state. Perhaps more remarkably, Guanare is Venezuela's spiritual capital, home of Nuestra Señora de Coromoto, the country's patron saint. Predictably, the city is Venezuela's major pilgrimage center, attracting some half million visitors each year.

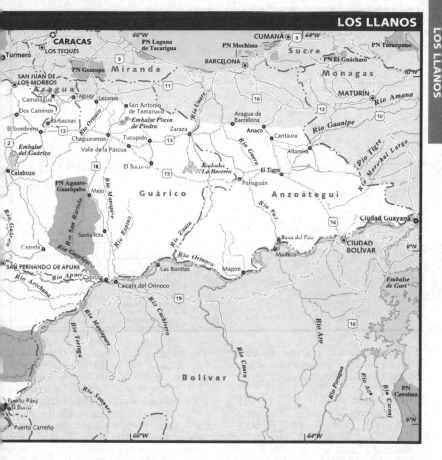

Founded in 1591 by Juan Fernández de León, La Ciudad del Espíritu Santo del Valle de San Juan del Guanaguanare is one of the few towns in Venezuela whose original Act of Foundation document has been preserved (it is kept in Seville, Spain). As with most early towns, Guanare's development was precarious and was hindered by Indians inhabiting the region. Things began to change on September 8, 1652, when the Virgen de Coromoto allegedly appeared miraculously before an Indian cacique on the Río Guanaguanare near the town (see the boxed text 'La Virgen de Coromoto,'

later in this section). As is generally the case with miracles of that kind, the place soon became a destination for pilgrims from the region and beyond.

A fair-sized church was built for the Virgin, and the town steadily developed around the cult. A serious earthquake in 1782 damaged many buildings, the church included, but the miraculous powers of the Virgin continued to draw the faithful in increasing numbers. By that time, the town's population had already reached 13,000. The canonization of the Virgin as the patron saint of Venezuela, in 1942, contributed to even larger

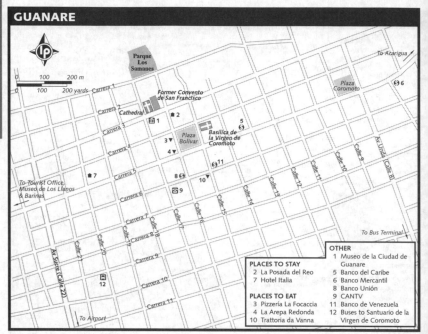

GUANARE

PLACES TO STAY
2 La Posada del Reo
7 Hotel Italia

PLACES TO EAT
3 Pizzería La Focaccia
4 La Arepa Redonda
10 Trattoria da Vanna

OTHER
1 Museo de la Ciudad de Guanare
5 Banco del Caribe
6 Banco Mercantil
8 Banco Unión
9 CANTV
11 Banco de Venezuela
12 Buses to Santuario de la Virgen de Coromoto

floods of pilgrims. Its religious status apart, Guanare has also developed into an important regional center for raising cattle.

Information

The Corpotur (Corporación Portugueseña de Turismo) tourist office (☎ 51 03 24) is in Pabellón de Exposiciones, Avenida IND, opposite the Instituto Nacional de Deporte, 1.5km southwest of the center. It's open 8 am to noon and 2 to 6 pm weekdays.

Some of the central banks useful for cash advances on Visa and/or MasterCard are marked on the map. Changing cash or traveler's checks may prove difficult in Guanare.

Basílica de la Virgen de Coromoto

This is by far the most important monument in the city, as well as the destination for every pilgrim. The church, on Plaza Bolívar, was constructed in 1710–42, but the 1782 earthquake almost completely destroyed it.

The image of the Virgin, which had been kept inside, was saved and temporarily guarded in the hospital chapel while the church was reconstructed in a different style; the work was completed in 1807.

Inside the church, your eyes will immediately be caught by a great, three-tier main retable, an excellent piece of colonial baroque art made by Pantaleón José Quiñones de Lara in 1739. It later took 16 months for Romualdo Antonio Vélez to gild it. In front of the retable stands the elaborate 3.4m-high *sagrario* (tabernacle), made entirely of silver in 1756. A painting on the dome over the high altar depicts the legend of the Virgen de Coromoto. The colorful stained-glass windows were commissioned in Munich, Germany.

The church's holiest possession, the Virgen's image, is far smaller and less conspicuous. It's at the head of the right-hand aisle, where a large statue of the Virgen de Coromoto is placed. Climb a few specially provided access stairs to the feet of the statue to have a look through the magnifying glass at the image. It's an oval painting measuring 22mm by 27mm, made on papyrus-like paper. Today its colors are almost totally washed out, and the picture is pretty faint and indistinct.

There's another sizable statue of the Virgin at the opposite end of the same aisle. Note the large number of commemorative plaques on the wall behind the statue.

Other Attractions

The mid-18th-century **Convento de San Francisco**, on the corner of Carrera 3 and Calle 17, no longer serves its original purpose. In 1825 it was turned into a school, the first institution of its kind in Venezuela. Today, the building accommodates the offices of the Universidad Nacional Experimental de Los Llanos. You can enter its spacious courtyard, which has retained much of its old style and charm. The cathedral church has a beautiful facade, but its interior lacks decoration; it's now used for university meetings and symposiums.

Directly opposite the church is the **Museo de la Ciudad de Guanare**. Housed in one of the few remaining colonial buildings, the museum presents a small collection related to the town's history. It's open 8 am to 5 pm Tuesday to Saturday.

Two blocks north from here is **Parque Los Samanes**, named after a species of the spreading trees that grow in the park. You'll find the first (rather impressive) specimen of the species in front of the entrance. Bolívar's troops reputedly camped here in 1813. The park is open 8 am to 5 pm daily except Monday.

There are several monuments dedicated to the Virgen de Coromoto in the town center, including the 1928 statue on Plaza Coromoto, seven blocks east of Plaza Bolívar along Carrera 5. On the same square you'll find a charming sculptured scene depicting the miraculous appearance of the Virgin to the Indian cacique and his family.

Outside the center, you can visit the **Museo de Los Llanos**, in the Complejo Ferial José Antonio Páez, half a kilometer beyond the tourist office. It has an archeological collection from the region and is open 8 am to 5 pm Tuesday to Friday, 10 am to 5 pm weekends.

Special Events

As might be expected, Guanare's annual celebrations revolve around the Virgen de Coromoto. Most pilgrims flock to the city in time for the Fiesta de la Virgen de Coromoto on September 8, the anniversary of the Virgin's appearance. There may also be crowds of believers on February 2, the anniversary of the day when the image of the Virgin was moved from the site of the apparition to the city.

Guanare is also noted for its Mascarada, a three-day-long colorful Carnaval celebration that culminates in a parade of *carrozas* (floats).

Places to Stay

There are two reasonable budget places right in the city center. One of these is *Hotel Italia* (☎ 53 12 13, 51 42 77), on Calle 20 off the corner of Carrera 5. Run by a friendly Italian, it offers air-conditioned singles/doubles/triples with private bath and TV for US$18/24/28. The other option is the marginally cheaper *La Posada del Reo* (☎ 51 57 57), on the corner of Calle 16 and Carrera 3. It too has air-conditioned rooms, which cost US$22/26 double/triple.

If this is still too much for you, try *Hotel El Llanero* (☎ 51 68 89), Avenida Juan Fernández de León (western continuation of Carrera 5), about 800m west of Avenida Sucre. It's basic but one of the cheapest in town – US$10/12/14 matrimonial/double/triple with fan, US$2 more if you want air-conditioning. Diagonally opposite is the better *Motel Arpe* (☎ 51 61 03), for US$18/25/30 with air-con and TV.

There are several reasonable options farther away from the center, including *Motel La Fontana* (☎ 51 35 42, 51 37 83), *Motel La Sultana* (☎ 53 17 23, 51 41 22) and the newest *Hotel Mirador* (☎ 53 45 20, 53 53 20), all three on Avenida Circunvalación. However, the title of most charming place in town goes to the 15-room *Posada del*

LOS LLANOS

La Virgen de Coromoto

The Virgen de Coromoto allegedly appeared on September 8, 1652, to the cacique of the Cospes Indians, some 20km south of Guanare. As legend has it, the Virgin not only appeared, but also talked to the Indian chief in his own language, trying to convince him to have holy water poured over his head so that he would be able to enter heaven. The Virgin also left the cacique an image of herself, radiating with rays of brilliant light.

Astonished and confused, the chief ignored the Virgin's advice and fled into the mountains. As soon as he entered the woods, however, he was bitten by a venomous snake. Only then, moments before his death, did he ask to be baptized, telling his tribe to do likewise.

On February 2, 1654, the Spanish brought the image to Guanare and placed it in a small sanctuary. News of the miracle spread throughout the region and beyond, and Guanare began to attract believers. As its fame spread far and wide, a good-sized church was commissioned to provide a more decent shelter for the image. The church was completed in 1742 after 30 years of work.

In 1942 the Virgen de Coromoto was declared the patron saint of Venezuela and solemnly crowned by Pope Pius XII in 1952, on the 300th anniversary of the miracle. A statue of the Virgin and an open-air chapel were erected at the site of the apparition, to be replaced by a huge church in the 1990s, which now looms like a gigantic beacon amid vast plains, showing pilgrims the way to the end of their journey.

Cabrestero (☎ 53 01 02), next door to the Museo de Los Llanos, which costs US40/45 double/triple with soundless air-con, fridge, cable TV and breakfast.

Places to Eat

The *Pizzería La Focaccia*, on Plaza Bolívar, has outside tables and is open until around 10 pm. It offers simple pizzas, spaghetti and some popular local dishes. Another place for pizzas and pastas is *Trattoria da Vanna*, on the corner of Carrera 6 and Calle 15, which also has some local food.

La Arepa Redonda, on Plaza Bolívar, does arepas and does them well. *Hotel Italia* runs its own restaurant, as does *Hotel Mirador* and most motels.

Getting There & Away

The bus terminal is on Avenida UNDA, 2km southeast of the city center, and is serviced regularly by local transportation. To get there from the center, take the eastbound buseta No 14 or 24 from Carrera 5.

Guanare sits on El Llano highway, so there is a fair bit of traffic heading southwest to San Cristóbal (US$11 deluxe, 6½ hours) and northeast to Caracas (US$9 ordinary, US$12 deluxe, seven hours). There are hourly buses to Barquisimeto (US$4, three hours) and several departures a day to Boconó (US$3, 3½ hours). Buses to Barinas run frequently until 6 pm (US$2, 1½ hours). If you are heading to Mérida, go to Barinas and change.

SANTUARIO DE LA VIRGEN DE COROMOTO

This is the place where the Virgen de Coromoto allegedly appeared in 1652. A cross was placed here after the event, and was later replaced with a chapel, but the site was isolated and rarely visited. Instead, the pilgrims flocked to Guanare's church, which for centuries has boasted the holy image and effectively acted as the Virgin's shrine.

But things have changed a bit. The construction of a huge church at the actual site of the apparition commenced in 1976 and was completed for the papal visit in February 1996, when 300,000 faithful attended the mass. It's planned that the image of the Virgin be brought here from Guanare and placed in the high altar.

The Templo Votivo – as the church is called – is monumental, strikingly modern and truly impressive. Designed by the Venezuelan architect Erasmo Calvani, the irregular concrete structure is laid out in the shape of a 4000-sq-meter heart. The high altar is believed to be at the exact location of the Indian cacique's hut where the Virgin appeared. The walls behind the church's altar are graced with marvelous stained-glass windows.

The church has two unequal bell towers (75m and 68m high). You can go up to a viewing platform (at 32m) between the towers, which is accessible by elevator for a small fee. A museum is planned in the basement of the church.

Getting There & Away

The Santuario is 25km south of Guanare – 10km by the main road toward Barinas plus 15km by the paved side road branching off to the south. Small buses, operated by Línea Los Cospes, depart regularly from the corner of Carrera 9 and Calle 20 in Guanare (US$0.60, 45 minutes) and will deposit you right at the church's entrance.

BARINAS

☎ 073 (☎ 0273 from Apr 21, 2001)

Barinas (population 225,000) was founded in 1577 by Spanish conquerors from Pamplona, in Nueva Granada, and it began to develop right from its birth. At the beginning of the 17th century, tobacco gave the town an economic base and overseas fame. Barinas was the only region in the colony allowed by the Crown to grow tobacco. Other crops, including sugarcane, bananas and cacao, were subsequently introduced to the region, as was raising cattle. By the end of the 18th century, Barinas was the second-largest town in Venezuela, after Caracas.

The War of Independence and the civil wars that plagued Venezuela during the 19th century seriously affected the development of both the town and the state, and many inhabitants fled, mostly to the Andes. During this period a lot of colonial architecture was lost, either destroyed during the struggles or abandoned.

Once the civil wars ended, a steady revival began. Agriculture and cattle raising were joined by a short-lived timber industry, which took advantage of the extensive rain forest in the western part of the state, rapidly and indiscriminately logging it until it was almost completely destroyed. Meanwhile, oil was discovered in the region 50km south of Barinas, and is now pipelined to the coast near Morón.

Today Barinas is both the capital of the state of the same name and the thriving center of a vast agricultural and ranching region. The climate is hot and damp, with an average temperature of 27°C and frequent rains from May through to November. There's not much to see or do in the city, and accordingly, few travelers bother to stop here.

Information

The Corbatur (Corporación Barinesa de Turismo) tourist office (☎ 270 91, 281 62) is on Avenida Marqués del Pumar, half a block back from Plaza Bolívar, and is open 8 am to noon and 2 to 6 pm weekdays. There are also three *módulos de información turística* (theoretically open daily): at the airport, at the bus terminal, and in the Parque Los Mangos, on Avenida Cuatricentenaria.

The locations of some major banks are indicated on the map.

LOS LLANOS

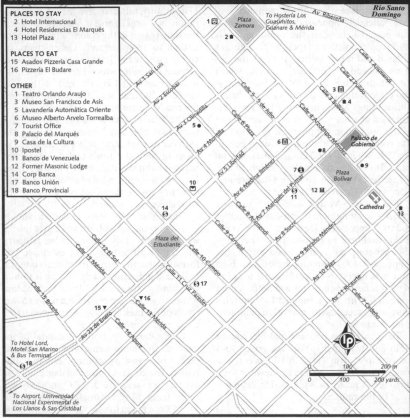

BARINAS

PLACES TO STAY
2 Hotel Internacional
4 Hotel Residencias El Marqués
13 Hotel Plaza

PLACES TO EAT
15 Asados Pizzería Casa Grande
16 Pizzería El Budare

OTHER
1 Teatro Orlando Araujo
3 Museo San Francisco de Asís
5 Lavandería Automática Oriente
6 Museo Alberto Arvelo Torrealba
7 Tourist Office
8 Palacio del Marqués
9 Casa de la Cultura
10 Ipostel
11 Banco de Venezuela
12 Former Masonic Lodge
14 Corp Banca
17 Banco Unión
18 Banco Provincial

Things to See

The unusual, two-block-long Plaza Bolívar still boasts some colonial buildings. The **Catedral** dates from the 1770s, except for the bell tower.

Opposite the cathedral, across the plaza, is the **Palacio del Marqués**, which occupies the entire side of the square. Commissioned by the Marqués de las Riberas de Boconó y Masparro as his private residence and constructed at the end of the 18th century, the palace reflected the owner's wealth and Barinas' prosperity at the time. It was partly

ruined during the Wars of Federation in the mid-19th century, but was restored in the 1940s. It now houses the municipal council and the police station.

A demonstration of Barinas' current fortunes is perhaps best encapsulated in the conspicuous **Palacio de Gobierno**, an eccentric edifice completed in 1999 and occupying half of the block off Plaza Bolívar. That President Hugo Chávez was born and raised in the state, and that his father is the current governor of Barinas, may be a pure coincidence.

On the northeastern side of the plaza is the **Casa de la Cultura**, built during the final decades of the 18th century as the town hall and jail. José Antonio Páez was imprisoned here but managed to escape, liberating 115 of his fellow prisoners in the process. The building was the town jail until 1966. Today it's a cultural center, holding art exhibitions and various other events. An auditorium hall for the local theater was being built at the back in late 2000.

The city has two small museums. The **Museo Alberto Arvelo Torrealba** (named after a local poet), on the corner of Calle 5 de Julio and Avenida Medina Jiménez, presents temporary exhibitions from time to time. The unsigned **Museo San Francisco de Asís**, Avenida Medina Jiménez, has a collection of colonial (mostly religious) objects. It normally stays locked – knock at the big blue gate in the middle of the block, and somebody may open it and let you in.

The **Jardín Botánico** and the small **Zoológico** are located on the campus of the Universidad Nacional Experimental de Los Llanos, 3km southwest of the center, on the road to San Cristóbal.

Places to Stay

If you are in Barinas for one or two nights only, it's probably best to look for a budget room around the bus terminal. There are half a dozen inexpensive hotels on the streets adjacent to the terminal. Among them, **Hotel Lord** (☎ 254 09) is one of the cheapest and a good value for money. It costs US$7/9/11 single/matrimonial/double with bath and fan. **Motel San Marino** (☎ 223 51) is also a reasonable choice, for US$10 double with private bath and fan (US$14 for air-conditioning).

In the city center, one of the cheapest places is the simple **Hotel Plaza** (☎ 249 18, Calle Arzobispo Méndez No 10-20), behind the cathedral. It has air-conditioned rooms with bath for US$14/16 double/triple and a basic restaurant. The **Hotel Residencias El Marqués** (☎ 265 76, Avenida Medina Jiménez No 2-88) is perhaps slightly better (and marginally more expensive).

The three-star **Hotel Internacional** (☎ 223 43, 233 03), on Calle Arzobispo Méndez facing Plaza Zamora, is the oldest hotel operating in town. It was built by Pérez Jiménez around 1950, when there was still no reliable road connection with Caracas. The hotel was certainly a better place 50 years ago than it is today, yet it's still probably worth the modest rates – US$25/30/35 for air-con matrimoniales/doubles/triples.

Other, better three-star options are outside the center and include **Hotel Bristol** (☎ 209 11, 208 40), **Hotel Turístico Varyná** (☎ 33 50 94, 33 39 84) and **Hotel Valle Hondo** (☎ 33 51 77, 33 58 77). They all are on Avenida 23 de Enero, southwest of the old center, near the airport. All three are comfortable and provide reasonable standards and facilities, and each has its own restaurant and bar. The Varyná is the cheapest of the lot at US$40/45 double/triple; the other two are almost twice as expensive.

Travelers with their own transportation may be interested in the comfortable country-style **Hostería Los Guasimitos** (☎ 46 15 46, 46 17 01), off the road to Guanare, about 5km northwest of the center.

Places to Eat

Several basic restaurants cluster in the bus terminal area. In the center, you'll find some fast food outlets around Plaza Bolívar. Additionally, **Hotel Plaza** has a restaurant serving cheap set meals.

Avenida Marqués del Pumar constitutes the main commercial street in the center, and some restaurants lie along it. There are more restaurants on Avenida 23 de Enero, including the popular **Asados Pizzería Casa Grande** and **Pizzería El Budare**.

Restaurant La Helice, near the Hostería Los Guasimitos, has some of the best *carne llanera* (the local version of *carne asada*) in town.

Getting There & Away

Air The airport is 1.5km southwest of Plaza Bolívar. Avior and LAI have several flights a day to Caracas (US$58 to US$67 one-way).

Bus The bus terminal is 2km west of Plaza Bolívar and is serviced by local buses. Barinas has regular bus services southwest to San Cristóbal (US$7 ordinary, US$9 deluxe, five hours), northeast to Caracas (US$11 ordinary, US$15 deluxe, 8½ hours) and all points in between, such as Guanare, Valencia and Maracay.

Transporte Barinas has five departures a day to Mérida (US$4, four hours). Several companies, including Expresos Los Llanos and Expresos Zamora, operate buses southeast into Los Llanos, with a total of up to 10 departures a day to San Fernando de Apure (US$10 ordinary, US$13 deluxe, eight hours). Buses to Guanare run every half-hour from 3 am until 6 pm (US$2, 1½ hours).

SAN FERNANDO DE APURE
☎ 047 (☎ 0247 from Apr 21, 2001)

The capital of Apure state, San Fernando de Apure is the largest city of the Llano Bajo; with a population of 90,000, it's actually the only city of any size for a couple of hundred miles around. Sitting on the southern bank of the Río Apure, in the very heart of Los Llanos, it is an important regional trading center for most of the Río Apure basin. Cattle raising and, to a lesser extent, farming are the two major activities in the region. Crops and livestock are funneled through San Fernando and trucked north to the central states of Aragua, Carabobo and Miranda, as well as the Distrito Federal.

The city of San Fernando was born as a missionary outpost at the end of the colonial era, and its development was for a long time hindered by its isolation. It wasn't until the road from Calabozo was extended south to the Río Apure that the town began to grow more swiftly. Today the city also has a paved road link with the western states of Barinas, Mérida and Táchira.

The city itself is not a tourist attraction and has little to keep you there. On the other hand, the vast region all around boasts some of the best of what Los Llanos has to offer, including several ecotourist ranches (see the Hatos section, later). San Fernando is the usual jumping-off point for trips to the hatos.

Information
The Coratur (Corporación Apureña de Turismo) tourist office is in a freestanding building in the middle of Paseo Libertador, about 700m south of the Monumento a Los Llaneros.

For information about the hatos, you can also try the Agencia de Viajes y Turismo Doña Bárbara (☎ 41 34 63, fax 41 22 35), Edificio Hotel La Torraca, Piso Bajo, Paseo Libertador. The company runs the Campamento Doña Bárbara in the Hato La Trinidad de Arauca (for which its staff can book and arrange transportation) and may provide information about other hatos in the region, including El Frío and El Cedral.

See the map for locations of potentially useful banks.

Things to See
Walk along Paseo Libertador, the city's main thoroughfare. At its northern end is a circular square with a large **fountain** adorned with six concrete caimans. Beside the fountain is the **Monumento a Pedro Camejo**, an equestrian statue of one of the bravest lancers to have fought under General José Antonio Páez in Bolívar's army. Camejo, who died in the battle of Carabobo, is commonly known as Negro Primero, as he was the first black person to distinguish himself in the War of Independence.

Just east of the fountain is the city's possibly most interesting architectural relic: **Palacio Barbarito**, built by Italian merchants at the turn of the 19th century. At that time the Río Apure used to pass just a few meters from the palace pier, and boats came directly from Europe up the Orinoco and Apure. Most of the trade was related to egret feathers and caiman leathers, and was initially very profitable. Later on, the business deteriorated, and the Italians sold the palace and left. It then passed through the hands of various owners who divided and subdivided it repeatedly, so much of the original internal design has been lost.

About 600m south along Paseo Libertador is the large **Monumento a Los Llaneros**, dedicated to the tough and brave people who made up the backbone of Bolívar's

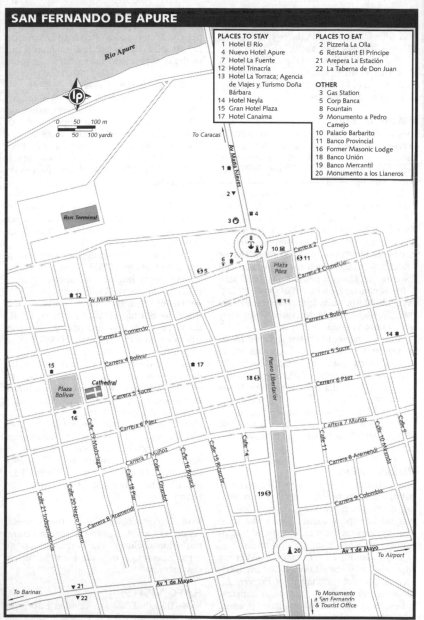

SAN FERNANDO DE APURE

PLACES TO STAY
1 Hotel El Río
4 Nuevo Hotel Apure
7 Hotel La Fuente
12 Hotel Trinacría
13 Hotel La Torraca; Agencia de Viajes y Turismo Doña Bárbara
14 Hotel Neyla
15 Gran Hotel Plaza
17 Hotel Canaima

PLACES TO EAT
2 Pizzería La Olla
6 Restaurant El Príncipe
21 Arepera La Estación
22 La Taberna de Don Juan

OTHER
3 Gas Station
5 Corp Banca
8 Fountain
9 Monumento a Pedro Camejo
10 Palacio Barbarito
11 Banco Provincial
16 Former Masonic Lodge
18 Banco Unión
19 Banco Mercantil
20 Monumento a los Llaneros

army. Another 600m down the paseo stands the **Monumento a San Fernando**, the largest and tallest monument in the city. The tourist office is 100m farther south.

The **Plaza Bolívar**, six blocks west of Paseo Libertador, boasts a modern cathedral and an old masonic lodge, and is pleasantly shaded with trees.

Places to Stay

One of the cheapest places in town is *Hotel Neyla* (☎ *41 14 87*), on Carrera Sucre four blocks east of Paseo Libertador. It's super basic but costs just US$6/8/10 single/double/triple with bath and fan.

If you need air-conditioning, reasonable budget options include *Hotel Trinacría* (☎ *235 78, 237 78*), Avenida Miranda, and *Hotel La Torraca* (☎ *227 77, 226 76*), Paseo Libertador. Both have acceptable matrimoniales/doubles/triples with bath and TV for US$22/24/26. For much the same, you can also stay at *Hotel Canaima* (☎ *41 37 03*), Calle Ricaurte; *Hotel El Río* (☎ *41 19 28*), Avenida María Nieves; or *Hotel La Fuente* (☎ *232 33*), Avenida Miranda – but they may be not as good.

More expensive but better is *Nuevo Hotel Apure* (☎ *41 44 83, 222 14*), Avenida María Nieves, which costs US$30/35 double/triple. If you decide to spend a little more, you can stay in the best place in town, *Gran Hotel Plaza* (☎ *215 04, 212 55*), on Plaza Bolívar. Here comfortable air-conditioned doubles/triples are priced at US$45/55. Choose one of the upper-floor rooms that look over the plaza.

Places to Eat

San Fernando has a satisfactory array of eating outlets across its central area, including many places on Paseo Libertador. As you might expect, carne llanera, the local beef, appears on the menus of many restaurants, as does fish from the local rivers.

Restaurant El Príncipe, Avenida Miranda, does tasty Middle Eastern food, including falafel and shawarma. *Pizzería La Olla*, Avenida María Nieves, has pizza, spaghetti and chicken. Diagonally opposite, the restaurant of *Nuevo Hotel Apure* cooks hearty food at reasonable prices. *Arepera La Estación*, Avenida 1 de Mayo, serves inexpensive arepas and is open until late. Across the street, *La Taberna de Don Juan* is one of the best places to eat and drink in town.

Getting There & Away

Air The airport is about 3km east of the city center; a taxi there shouldn't cost more than US$4. San Fernando is a stopover for Air Venezuela flights between Caracas and Puerto Ayacucho. There are three flights a week in each direction; the one-way airfare to Caracas is US$55; to Puerto Ayacucho, it's US$48.

Bus The bus terminal is on the northern outskirts of the city, near the river. You can either walk there (five minutes from Plaza Bolívar) or take a taxi (US$1).

There are about six departures a day directly to Caracas (US$10 ordinary, US$14 deluxe, eight hours), and about twice as many to Maracay (US$8 ordinary, US$12 deluxe, 6½ hours). Nine or 10 buses a day travel to Barinas (US$10 ordinary, US$13 deluxe, eight hours), and one of them continues on to San Cristóbal (US$20 deluxe, 13 hours).

Half a dozen buses a day (all in the morning) set off for an interesting ride south to Puerto Ayacucho (US$13 ordinary, seven hours) via Puerto Páez. The road is now paved almost all the way (except for about 30km), but the bridges on the Ríos Capanaparo and Cinaruco are incomplete, so the trip includes *chalana* (ferry) crossings across these two rivers and, obviously, across the Orinoco between Puerto Páez and El Burro. The route is traversable year-round.

Boat Despite its location on the large Río Apure (which was once the region's transportation lifeline), San Fernando has no regular passenger boat service, either up- or downstream.

HATO VISITS

Most of Los Llanos is divided into large ranches known as *hatos*. They are principally dedicated to cattle raising – as they have been for a century or more – but some of them have turned to ecotourism. The owners have built lodges equipped with reasonable facilities, which they call *campamentos,* and run excursions to show guests the local wildlife. Some hatos dealing with tourists have taken a serious approach to environmental issues, introducing the protection of wildlife within their ranches, installing research stations, contributing to ecological funds and the like.

A visit to an ecotourist hato is usually available only through an all-inclusive package, which has to be booked and paid for beforehand. Packages are normally three-day, two-night visits that include full board and one or two excursions each day.

Excursions are like safaris, in a jeep or boat. There's usually one trip in the morning and another in the afternoon – the best times to observe the wildlife and, coincidentally, to avoid the unbearable midday heat. More boat trips run in the rainy period, and more jeep rides run in the dry season. Whichever means of transportation is used, however, you are taken into wilderness areas where animals, mostly birds, are plentiful and easy to see. Among the mammals and reptiles, capybaras and caimans are particularly common. See the boxed text 'The Wildlife of Los Llanos' for more information about local fauna.

The wildlife is abundant in both rainy and dry seasons. The main difference is that in the dry season most animals flock to scarce sources of water, which makes them easy to watch. In the wet season, on the other hand, when most of the land is half-flooded, animals are virtually everywhere, but obviously not so concentrated.

The dry season is considered the peak season, and in most hatos this is reflected by higher tour prices. This is a good time to come, as you can expect good weather and more trip options to choose from, owing to greater land accessibility.

If you go in the dry season, take a hat, sunglasses and sunscreen. In the wet season, make sure to have wet-weather gear. Whenever you come, don't forget a flashlight,

good binoculars and plenty of film. Mosquito repellent is essential during the rainy season, but it is also highly advisable (even indispensable) in the dry period.

There are perhaps a dozen ecotourist hatos, but new ones spring up here and there. Some of the more established and perhaps most reputable hatos are detailed in the following sections, though they are not the cheapest ones. Their approximate locations are shown on the Los Llanos regional map, at the beginning of this chapter.

Most hatos offer pretty much the same services, and the fauna is similar across the region. For example, El Frío, El Cedral and La Trinidad are relatively close to each other, so you can expect similar wildlife habitats in each of them. You may consider factors such as price and facilities (eg, El Cedral has a tiny swimming pool and air-conditioning), but otherwise there is no great difference between the ranches.

Since many of the campamentos require advance booking and prepayment, plan ahead. Tours to some hatos have to be arranged in Caracas. Refer to the Organized Tours section in the Caracas chapter for relevant tour operators.

Tours in the ecotourist hatos are not that cheap. They cost somewhere between US$100 and US$150 per person per day, which adds up to some US$300 to US$450 for the whole tour. Some hatos are well off the beaten track, so you may need to pay extra for transportation to and from the campamento.

Cheaper wildlife safaris in Los Llanos are available from Mérida. Several of Mérida's tour companies have put together their own llano circuits and seem to do a good job. The companies don't use the ecotourist hatos' services; rather, they have their own campamentos or arrangements with local families and utilize their informal lodging and eating facilities. Conditions are usually rustic, and the whole trip is more casual, but you will see the same plethora of wildlife for roughly a third of the hato tour price. Travelers consistently recommend these tours. See the Mérida section, in the Andes chapter, for further information.

Gravity Tours $110 → 4d/3nights

Otherwise, you can explore Los Llanos on your own, particularly if you have your own transportation, ideally a 4WD. The Barinas–San Fernando road cuts through an interesting part of the plains and is serviced by regular transportation (up to 10 buses a day in either direction). The section of road between Bruzual and Apurito is perhaps the most spectacular as far as animal watching is concerned: Plenty of birds can be seen from the road itself. A choice of simple accommodations awaits in Bruzual and Mantecal, either of which can serve as jumping-off points for excursions around the area.

Hato El Frío

Occupying about 800 sq km, Hato El Frío lies on both sides of the Mantecal–San Fernando road and sports around 45,000 head of cattle. Its campamento is located 2km north of the road, 187km west of San Fernando (42km east of Mantecal). The campamento features a lodge with 10 double rooms (with the capacity for 20 guests), a pleasant dining room and a biological station where caimans, turtles and other endangered species are bred.

Boats and jeeps are available to take visitors for two four-hour excursions, in the morning and the afternoon. There's a choice of about 10 excursions in the *verano* (dry season) and five in *invierno* (wet season). It's estimated that about 13,000 *chigüires* (capybaras) and 25,000 *babas* (spectacled caimans) live in the hato.

So far, El Frío seems to be reasonably tolerant of individual travelers and will probably accept you if you turn up unexpectedly – as long as there are vacancies. The per-person price per day is about US$100 from April 1 to June 30, US$125 from July 1 to September 15, and US$145 from September 16 to March 31. El Frío has an office in Achaguas (☎/fax 047-812 23), 89km toward San Fernando, where you can book a tour. You can also call them on their cellular phone at ☎ 014-743 53 21. Various Caracas tour companies (including Orinoco Tours) organize tours to El Frío as well.

El Frío is easily accessible by public transportation; the San Fernando–Mantecal buses will drop you off at the main gate, a 20-minute walk to the campamento.

Hato El Cedral

About 70km southwest by paved road from El Frío, Hato El Cedral covers 560 sq km and has around 20,000 head of cattle. The campamento is 7km west off the road. It provides comfortable lodging in cabañas, which are equipped with air-conditioning and private hot-water baths, and there is also a tiny pool.

Half a dozen different excursions are offered, by boat or specially prepared minibus, but the trips seem to be shorter than those in El Frío. More than 250 bird species have been recorded on the ranch (much the same as in El Frío), as well as 14,000 capybaras, not to mention numerous representatives of other species.

El Cedral stringently requires advance booking in Caracas (see Organized Tours in the Caracas chapter for details). If you come without a booking, you are likely to be turned away. The price in the peak season (November 15 to April 15) is US$140 per person a day in a double room, and US$160 in a single room. In the off-season, it's about US$100 and US$120, respectively. This price doesn't include transportation to or from the hato; this can be arranged for an extra fee when you book your package. The roundtrip from San Fernando airport to El Cedral costs about US$30.

Hato La Trinidad de Arauca

Better known by the name of its campamento, Doña Bárbara, this hato is pretty close to El Cedral but is accessible only via a roundabout route through Elorza. In the dry season, the campamento can be reached by road, but in the wet season, the only access is by river (two hours from Elorza).

With 360 sq km, La Trinidad is smaller than the other hatos but has wildlife as rich and diverse as El Frío's and El Cedral's – except for capybaras, which are not so numerous here. Its campamento is pleasant and well organized and offers horse-riding excursions. Reservations should be made through the Doña Bárbara travel agency in San Fernando de Apure (see that section, earlier, for details). La Trinidad charges about US$125 per person a day.

The hato's campamento was named after Rómulo Gallegos' classic novel, for which the hato provided the setting and principal character. The grave of Francisca Vásquez de Carrillo (the real name of the hato's owner, on whom Doña Bárbara was based) is in the hato, as is a replica of her house, a modest, thatched adobe structure with some old objects inside. Today the campamento is run by the Estrada family.

Hato Piñero

The best-known ranch in the Llano Alto, Hato Piñero is in Cojedes state, close to the town of El Baúl. It's easily accessible by road from anywhere in the central states. If you are coming from Caracas, head first to Valencia. From that town, it's about 210km south.

The Wildlife of Los Llanos

Los Llanos is one of Venezuela's greatest repositories of wildlife, especially birds, which live here permanently or gather seasonally to breed and feed. About 350 bird species have been recorded in the region, which accounts for over a quarter of all the bird species found in Venezuela. Waterbirds and wading birds predominate, and the list includes ibis, herons, cormorants, egrets, jaçanas, gallinules and darters. The *corocoro*, or scarlet ibis (*Eudocimus ruber*), noted for its bright red plumage, is a spectacular sight when it appears in large colonies during the dry season. Three-quarters of the world's corocoro population live in Venezuela.

Among the more than 50 mammal species that inhabit the region is the *chigüire*, or capybara (*Hydrochoerus hydrochaeris*). This is the world's largest rodent, growing up to about 60kg. It has a face like a guinea and a bearlike coat, and it is equally at home on land and in the water, feeding mainly on aquatic plants. It's the most visible mammal in Los Llanos (apart from the ubiquitous zebu herds) and is often seen in families of two adults and several young, or in large groups.

Other local mammals include armadillos, peccaries, opossums, anteaters, tapirs, ocelots and the occasional jaguar. Two interesting aquatic mammals are the *tonina*, or freshwater dolphin (*Inia geoffrensis*), and the *manatí*, or manatee (*Trichechus manatus*), which inhabit the larger tributaries of the Orinoco. Both are endangered species, but numbers of the latter are dangerously low.

The capybara: Finally, someone's won the rat race.

Also threatened with extinction is the largest American crocodile, the *caimán del Orinoco* (*Crocodylus intermedius*). The population of these huge reptiles, which once lived in large numbers and measured up to 8m from head to tail, has been decimated by ranchers, who kill them for their skins. Far more numerous is the *baba*, or the spectacled caiman (*Caiman crocodylus*), the smallest of the family of local crocodiles, growing up to 3m in length.

Two large national parks, Cinaruco-Capanaparo (also known as 'Santos Luzardo') and Aguaro-Guariquito, protect important wildlife habitats of Los Llanos. A third, smaller park, Río Viejo, in the extreme western part of the region, is the most recent addition to Venezuela's natural-reserve system.

Given its location, Piñero has a somewhat different spectrum of wildlife from that of the hatos in the Llano Bajo. The topography of this 800-sq-km ranch is more diverse, and forests cover part of the hato. The wet season comes later (in late May or early June) and ends earlier (in September). Although capybaras and caimans are not so ubiquitous here, there are a variety of other animals, including ocelots, monkeys, anteaters, agoutis, foxes, tapirs and iguanas.

This is largely the effect of hunting and logging bans, which were introduced as early as the 1950s.

Tourist facilities accommodate about 25 guests, and packages should be booked in Caracas (see Organized Tours in that chapter for details). The package, including full board and excursions, will cost US$130 a day in the low season, which lasts from May to November, and US$150 from December to April.

The Northeast

Venezuela's northeast is a mosaic of diverse natural marvels, including white beaches, coral reefs, fresh mountains and verdant valleys, where fans of outdoor activities will find much to choose from. This is the region for sunbathing, snorkeling, diving, sailing, hiking and the like. The coast features some amazing stretches, including the marvelous Parque Nacional Mochida. The region also

boasts Venezuela's best cave, the Cueva del Guácharo.

Most of the cultural and historical attractions are close to the sea, for it was essentially the coast that the Spanish conquered and settled. However, even though the first colonists arrived here as early as 1498 and soon founded their towns, there's not much of the colonial legacy left, except for the partly preserved old quarters of Barcelona and Cumaná, and some old churches and forts scattered over the region.

Administratively, the northeast region is constituted by the states of Anzoátegui, Sucre and Monagas, plus the insular state of Nueva Esparta, which comprises the islands of Margarita, Coche and Cubagua.

Highlights

- Wander around picturesque Parque Nacional Mochima.

- Discover secluded beaches east of the Río Caribe.

- Explore the magnificent Cueva del Guácharo.

- Roam through Parque Nacional Península de Paria.

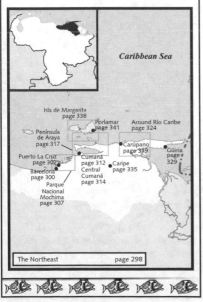

Caribbean Sea

Isla de Margarita page 338

Porlamar page 341

Around Río Caribe page 324

Península de Araya page 317

Carúpano page 339

Güiria page 329

Puerto La Cruz page 302

Cumaná page 312

Caripe page 335

Barcelona page 300

Central Cumaná page 314

Parque Nacional Mochima page 307

The Northeast .... page 298

Anzoátegui State

BARCELONA
☎ 0281

Barcelona was founded in 1671 by a group of Catalan colonists, who named it after their hometown in Spain. It was set on the Río Neverí, 5km from its outlet to the Caribbean. While the center is still there, the city now hosts a population of 290,000 and is gradually merging into a single urban sprawl with its dynamic young neighbor, Puerto La Cruz. Although Barcelona remains the capital of Anzoátegui state, it has already lost ground as a tourist and commercial center to Puerto La Cruz.

Central Barcelona is a pleasant enough place, with several leafy plazas and some colonial architecture. The historic quarter has been partly restored and whitewashed throughout, which gives it a pleasing appearance, even though the urban fabric is a mishmash of houses dating from different periods. The city doesn't seem to have rushed into modernity at the frenetic pace of Puerto La Cruz or other large Venezuelan cities, and the yesteryear feel is still noticeable within the old town.

THE NORTHEAST

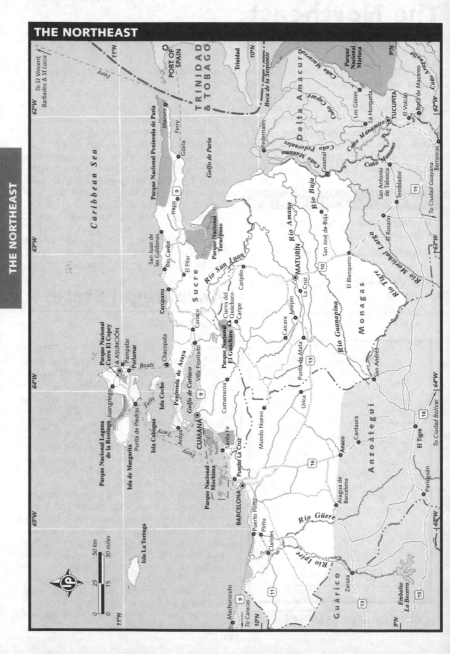

Information
Tourist Offices The official Corporación de
Turismo del Estado Anzoátegui (Coranztur) is the state's main tourist agency and
has its seat in Barcelona. The office (☎ 75 04
74) is on the ground floor of the building of
the Gobernación, on Avenida 5 de Julio, and
is open 8 am to noon and 2 to 5 pm weekdays. However, the staff is likely to direct
you to their tourist outlet in Puerto La Cruz
(see that section, later) rather than give information themselves. You may also try the
Dirección de Turismo (☎ 77 24 09), just off
Plaza Boyacá; it is open 8 am to noon and 2
to 5:30 pm weekdays.

Money Banco Unión, Banco de Venezuela
and Banco Mercantil will give cash advances on Visa and MasterCard, while Corp
Banca will change American Express traveler's checks. For changing cash, you'll need
to go to Barcelona's airport, which has two
casas de cambio: Italcambio (☎ 75 38 82)
and Oficambio (☎ 77 38 43). Alternatively,
you can use one of several casas de cambio
in Puerto La Cruz.

Things to See
The city's historic center, **Plaza Boyacá**,
boasts a statue of General José Antonio Anzoátegui, the Barcelona-born hero of the
War of Independence after whom the state
is named. On the western side of this tree-
shaded plaza stands the **Catedral**, built a
century after the town's founding. The most
venerated object in the church is the glass
reliquary in a chapel off the left aisle, where
the embalmed remains of the Italian martyr
San Celestino are kept. The richly gilded
main retable dates from 1744, but the
images of the saints were made in modern
times.

On the southern side of the plaza is the
Museo de Anzoátegui. Housed in the carefully restored, oldest surviving building in
town (1671), the museum features a variety
of objects related to Barcelona's history.
Note the collection of unusual religious
statues equipped with movable limbs; only
their faces, hands and feet have been properly finished. They were dressed in robes

and their pose adjusted to place them appropriately. The museum is open 9 am to
noon and 2 to 5 pm Tuesday to Friday, 9 am
to 3 pm Saturday, 9 am to 1 pm Sunday.
There may be a guide who can explain the
collection (in Spanish only).

An annex to the museum is housed in the
Ateneo de Barcelona (open 9 am to noon
and 2 to 5 pm weekdays), two blocks east.
On the 1st floor of this colonial-style building is a 44-piece collection of paintings
(most of which date from the 1940s and
1950s) by some of the prominent modern
Venezuelan artists. The collection belonged
to Miguel Otero Silva, a Barcelona-born
poet, novelist and journalist, who donated
the paintings to the state. The Ateneo also
presents temporary exhibitions on the
ground floor and conducts various cultural
activities. There's a small handicraft shop
attached, but a far larger selection of crafts
is offered by the Gunda Arte Popular craft
shop, on Carrera Bolívar.

Plaza Rolando is lined by more recent
buildings, including the **Iglesia del Carmen**
and the **Teatro Cajigal**, both dating from the
1890s. The latter is an enchanting, small
theater that seats 300 people, and is still
used for stage performances and concerts.
The security guards may let you in during
the day.

There are a few more plazas farther to
the northwest, including Plaza Miranda and
Plaza Bolívar, just one block from each
other. The western side of the latter is occupied by the **Casa Fuerte**, which was once a
Franciscan hospice but was destroyed by
the royalists in a heavy attack in 1817. Over
1500 people, both the defenders and the
civilians who took refuge here, lost their
lives in the massacre that followed the takeover. The surviving parts of the walls have
been left in ruins as a memorial.

The Palacio Legislativo, two blocks south
of Plaza Boyacá, houses the **Galería de Arte**,
which features temporary exhibitions. It's
open 9 am to 3 pm weekdays.

Places to Stay
Barcelona is not an accommodations paradise. It has nothing upmarket or trendy – for

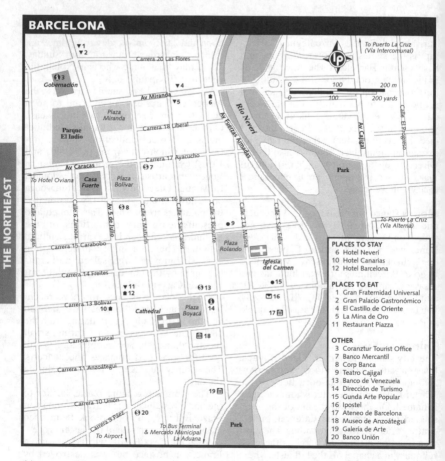

BARCELONA

PLACES TO STAY
6 Hotel Neverí
10 Hotel Canarias
12 Hotel Barcelona

PLACES TO EAT
1 Gran Fraternidad Universal
2 Gran Palacio Gastronómico
4 El Castillo de Oriente
5 La Mina de Oro
11 Restaurant Piazza

OTHER
3 Coranztur Tourist Office
7 Banco Mercantil
8 Corp Banca
9 Teatro Cajigal
13 Banco de Venezuela
14 Dirección de Turismo
15 Gunda Arte Popular
16 Ipostel
17 Ateneo de Barcelona
18 Museo de Anzoátegui
19 Galería de Arte
20 Banco Unión

this you need to go to Puerto La Cruz – and very little to offer as far as budget hotels go.

Hotel Canarias (☎ 77 10 34), Carrera Bolívar, is one of the cheapest acceptable places in town. It has rooms of different standards and prices, so have a look before booking in. Expect to pay about US$15/17 for a matrimonial/double with bath and fan, US$22/24 with air-conditioning.

The 70-room high-rise **Hotel Barcelona** (☎ 77 10 65, 77 10 66) enjoyed its best times long ago, but it's still perhaps worth US$24/30 for an air-conditioned double/triple with bath and TV. Probably better

cared for but noisy is **Hotel Neverí** (☎ 77 23 73, 77 64 02), Avenida Miranda, which costs US$25 for an air-conditioned double.

One of Barcelona's best central options is the **Hotel Oviana** (☎ 76 16 71, 76 41 47), Avenida Caracas, five blocks west of Plaza Bolívar. Rooms here will cost you US$35/45 double/triple.

Places to Eat

As with accommodations, dining out is better in Puerto La Cruz. However, Barcelona does have an array of eateries across the center, and the prices are reasonable.

A cheap and good place to eat is the **Mercado Municipal La Aduana**, right next to the bus terminal southeast of the city center. It has more than a dozen popular restaurants, which serve a variety of typical food from around 6 am to 2 pm daily (several may be closed Sunday).

In the center, Avenida 5 de Julio is the main culinary artery, lined with restaurants, luncherías, fuentes de soda and food vendors. The self-service **Gran Palacio Gastronómico**, near the Gobernación, offers a choice of fast food and snacks. Next door, **Gran Fraternidad Universal** serves cheap vegetarian meals at lunchtime weekdays. The 1st-floor **Restaurant Piazza**, next to the Hotel Barcelona, has pizzas and steaks at reasonable prices and is open until 11 pm – longer than most of the central restaurants.

There are also some places to eat on Avenida Miranda, including **El Castillo de Oriente**, which does parrillas, and **La Mina de Oro**, across the street, which serves chicken. **Hotel Oviana** runs its own restaurant, which offers pizzas and pastas.

Getting There & Away

Air The airport is 2km south of the city center and is accessible by urban transportation. Several carriers have flights to Caracas (US$65 to US$98). Avior flies to Puerto Ordaz (US$62). Aserca services Maracaibo, San Antonio del Táchira and Barquisimeto, all via Caracas. Several airlines, including Avior and Rutaca, fly direct to Porlamar, on Isla de Margarita (US$35). Prices listed are one-way.

Bus The bus terminal is about 1km southeast of the city center, next to the market. To get there, take a buseta going south along Avenida 5 de Julio, or walk 15 minutes.

The terminal handles mostly regional routes, including hourly buses to Píritu and Clarines. Few long-distance buses originate from here, but very occasionally buses from Puerto La Cruz call here on their way to Caracas (US$9 ordinary, five hours) and Ciudad Bolívar (US$8 ordinary, four hours). The terminal in Puerto La Cruz is far busier, so it's often better to go there instead of waiting in Barcelona for an infrequent and unreliable bus to come through.

To Puerto La Cruz, catch a city bus or buseta going north on Avenida 5 de Julio (US$0.25, 45 minutes). They use two routes, Vía Intercomunal and Vía Alterna. Either will set you down in the center of Puerto La Cruz. There are also por puesto minibuses (US$0.40), which depart from Avenida 5 de Julio 2½ blocks south of the Banco Unión; they are faster than the buses.

PUERTO LA CRUZ
☎ 0281

Puerto La Cruz is a youthful, dynamic and expanding city of 190,000. Until the 1930s it was no more than an obscure village, but it boomed after rich oil deposits were discovered in the region to the south. Port facilities have been built in Guanta and Guaraguao, just east of town; the latter serves as a main oil terminal, to ship oil piped from the wells overseas.

The city has become popular among Venezuelan holidaymakers and is very touristy. It's the major gateway to Isla de Margarita, Venezuela's number-one mass-tourist beach destination, and it's also a jumping-off point to the beautiful Parque Nacional Mochima, which stretches just north and east of the city. Taking advantage of its strategic position, Puerto La Cruz has grown into Venezuela's major water-sports center, with half a dozen marinas and yacht clubs, sailing and diving schools, yacht rental facilities, diving and fishing tours etc.

The city features a lively 10-block-long waterfront boulevard, Paseo Colón, packed with hotels, tour agencies, bars and restaurants. It comes to life in the late afternoon and evening, when plenty of craft stalls open and a gentle breeze sweeps away the heat of the day. This apart, however, the city has little to show tourists: a block or two back from the beach and it's just an ordinary place. Some travelers may be disappointed.

Information

Tourist Offices The Coranztur tourist office (☎ 68 81 70) is midway along Paseo Colón and is open daily 8 am to 9 pm.

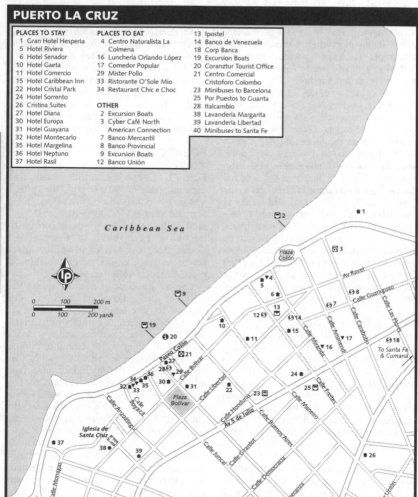

PUERTO LA CRUZ

PLACES TO STAY
1 Gran Hotel Hesperia
5 Hotel Riviera
6 Hotel Senador
10 Hotel Gaeta
11 Hotel Comercio
15 Hotel Caribbean Inn
22 Hotel Cristal Park
24 Hotel Sorrento
26 Cristina Suites
27 Hotel Diana
30 Hotel Europa
31 Hotel Guayana
32 Hotel Montecarlo
35 Hotel Margelina
36 Hotel Neptuno
37 Hotel Rasil

PLACES TO EAT
4 Centro Naturalista La
   Colmena
16 Lunchería Orlando López
17 Comedor Popular
29 Mister Pollo
33 Ristorante O'Sole Mio
34 Restaurant Chic e Choc

OTHER
2 Excursion Boats
3 Cyber Café North
   American Connection
7 Banco Mercantil
8 Banco Provincial
9 Excursion Boats
12 Banco Unión
13 Ipostel
14 Banco de Venezuela
18 Corp Banca
19 Excursion Boats
20 Coranztur Tourist Office
21 Centro Comercial
   Cristoforo Colombo
23 Minibuses to Barcelona
25 Por Puestos to Guanta
28 Italcambio
38 Lavandería Margarita
39 Lavandería Libertad
40 Minibuses to Santa Fe

Caribbean Sea

Money Most major banks are within a few blocks south of Plaza Colón (see the map for locations). There are several casas de cambio in the center that exchange cash and traveler's checks. Some of them are in the hotels on Paseo Colón, including the Oficambio in the Hotel Rasil, the Asecambio in the Hotel Gaeta, and Viajes Venezuela in the Hotel Riviera. Some casas may charge a commission, so shop around. Also check the Italcambio in the Centro Comercial Paseo del Mar, on Paseo Colón, which may give a bit better rates than the competitors and doesn't charge commission.

Email & Internet Access Two convenient Internet businesses are in the new Centro Comercial Cristoforo Colombo, on Paseo Colón: the Austrian Online Center (AOC; ☎ 68 60 10), Local 15, Planta Alta; and PC Mikros (☎ 68 54 42), Local 17, Planta Baja. You can also use the Cyber Café North American Connection (☎ 67 31 86), in the Centro Comercial Paseo Plaza, on Calle Carabobo. All three are open daily except Sunday and charge around US$5 an hour.

Laundry Central facilities include the Lavandería Margarita, on Calle Bolívar, and Lavandería Libertad, on Calle Libertad.

Complejo Turístico El Morro

This large and modern residential/tourist complex is being constructed on the waterfront, 4km west of the city center. It is one of the most ambitious urban projects ever to be carried out in the country.

Set on a coastal stretch of land, roughly in the form of a 1.5km by 2km rectangle, the complex is a model district, entirely designed and built from scratch. The area has already been crisscrossed by a maze of canals, on the banks of which a city of apartment blocks and houses is being built. Many of the inhabitants will have direct access to the waterfront with their own piers and slipways. The complex will boast commercial centers, hotels, parks, gardens and golf courses.

The project began in the 1970s, and some residential areas, the marina and a few of the planned chain of seaside hotels (including the Hotel Doral Beach and Hotel Maremares) have been completed. Also finished is the Centro Comercial Plaza Mayor, on the southern side of the complex, which has a multiscreen cinema. There's still a long way to go, but it's worth seeing if you are interested in urban planning or architecture. Night boat excursions around the canals are organized on weekends from the Centro Comercial Plaza Mayor.

To get to the complex from either Puerto La Cruz or Barcelona, take the Avenida Intercomunal bus and get off one block north of the Crucero de Lecherías, where five 20-story residential towers, known as the Conjunto Residencial Vistamar, loom. From there, por puestos go north, skirting the western, then northern side of the complex and take you to the marina.

Organized Tours

A score of travel agents have settled in the city, taking advantage of the tourist dollar. Many can be found on Paseo Colón: Some have their own offices, while others nestle in handicraft shops, hotel lobbies etc. They offer tours to anywhere in the country, from the Gran Sabana to the Andes, but it's cheaper to arrange one from the local center (Santa Elena de Uairén and Mérida, respectively). It may, however, be worth giving some thought to regional tours, principally around Parque Nacional Mochima. One-day tours are standard, but longer trips can be arranged with some operators. Tours usually include snorkeling (equipment provided), but may also feature fishing, scuba diving, water sports and the like. Note that boat trips are also organized from Santa Fe and Mochima, and they may be cheaper from there (see those sections, later).

Boat excursions to the nearby islands of Mochima have become popular with visitors (mostly Venezuelans) and depart regularly every morning from the three tourist piers, between the tourist office and Plaza Colón. They are either transportation-only trips or more complete tours that may include snorkeling, lunch and drinks.

One of the most popular trips includes Playa El Saco and Playa Puinare (both on

Isla Chimana Grande) and Playa El Faro (on Isla Chimana Segunda), all with food facilities. An additional attraction of Playa El Faro is iguanas. The tour costs US$7 to US$10 per person, transportation only.

Another popular tour goes to Islas Arapo and Arapito, and includes an hour's snorkeling in La Piscina between the two islands (equipment provided). The boats depart from Puerto La Cruz' waterfront from 9 to 10 am and return about 5 pm; tours cost around US$25 per person, including a lunch and soft drinks.

Some of the most popular insular beaches (including El Saco and El Faro) have boat services, so you don't need to take a tour and can choose to stay on one beach. Boats depart between about 8 am and noon from the city waterfront and return in the afternoon sometime between 2 and 5 pm. The roundtrip fare to El Faro or El Saco is US$4 to US$6 per person. There may also be some boats to Isla de Plata, but you can get there more cheaply from Guanta.

Lolo's Diving Center (☎ 67 39 63, 65 66 35), in the Marina Puerto La Cruz, and Explosub (☎ 65 36 11, ☎/fax 67 32 56), in the Gran Hotel Hesperia, are major local diving schools that organize diving courses and tours.

Places to Stay

Puerto La Cruz is an expensive place to stay by Venezuelan standards, and hotels fill up fast in the tourist season. It's difficult to find anything reasonable for below US$25 double. Many hotels have gathered on Paseo Colón and the adjoining streets, and this is the most lively and enjoyable area in which to stay. All the hotels listed below have rooms with private bath and air-conditioning, unless otherwise indicated.

Budget & Mid-Range Some of the cheapest options on Paseo Colón include *Hotel Montecarlo* (☎ 68 56 77), *Hotel Margelina* (☎ 68 75 45) and *Hotel Diana* (☎ 68 51 40). All three have rooms with air-conditioning, but are otherwise nothing special. Check a couple of them and inspect rooms before deciding. Expect a double to run about

US$25 in any of them, although the Montecarlo has some cheaper matrimoniales that cost US$20. The Diana has some doubles with fan for US$22. In the same area, *Hotel Neptuno* (☎ 65 32 61) is perhaps marginally better but costs US$32 for an air-conditioned double.

One block back from Paseo Colón, the eight-room *Hotel Guayana* (☎ 65 21 75), Plaza Bolívar, is one of the cheapest places in town, though its rooms are neither spotlessly clean nor very good. It has air-conditioned matrimoniales/doubles for US$20/24. There are more budget places in the back streets farther inland, but don't expect great bargains.

If you are prepared to spend a bit more, *Hotel Europa* (☎ 68 81 57), off Plaza Bolívar, may be an option. It's reasonably clean and well run, and costs US$35/40/45 for an air-conditioned matrimonial/double/triple. You may also try *Hotel Sorrento* (☎ 68 67 45, 68 85 50), Avenida 5 de Julio, which is less attractively located but offers cheaper prices – US$24/32/42 single/double/triple. For much the same, you can also stay in *Hotel Comercio* (☎ 65 14 29, 65 73 30), Calle Maneiro, though this is yet another unmemorable place.

Top End This section is for those who are ready to spend at least US$50 double per night. Puerto La Cruz has plenty of hotels in this price bracket, though most will cost much more than US$50.

Affordable options include *Hotel Gaeta* (☎ 65 04 11, fax 65 00 65), Paseo Colón, and *Hotel Senador* (☎ 67 35 22, fax 65 23 38), Calle Miranda. A double with a sea view in either will cost around US$55. The waterfront high-rise *Hotel Riviera* (☎ 67 21 11, fax 65 13 94) is probably a more attractive choice and costs much the same.

Without sea views but otherwise quite reasonable is *Hotel Cristal Park* (☎ 67 07 44, fax 65 31 05), Calle Buenos Aires, which also costs around US$55 double. Still more comfortable is the large, 11-story *Hotel Caribbean Inn* (☎ 67 42 92, fax 67 28 57), Calle Freites, which offers ample doubles/suites for about US$65/80. If you need a suite, you may also try **Cristina Suites** (☎ 67 47 12), Avenida Municipal, but it's several blocks back from the Paseo Colón. Its suites cost around US$90/100 for two/three persons.

The poshest hotels on the central waterfront are the four-star **Hotel Rasil** (☎ 67 24 22, fax 67 31 21) and the five-star **Gran Hotel Hesperia** (☎ 65 36 11, fax 65 31 17), both expensive. The Hesperia has a good swimming pool that fronts the beach and is open to nonresidents for US$8.

There are also some classy and costly options in the Complejo Turístico El Morro, including **Hotel Maremares** (☎ 81 10 11, fax 81 30 28) and **Hotel Doral Beach** (☎ 81 95 14, ☎/fax 81 72 10), both on Avenida Américo Vespucio. In the same area is the much cheaper **Hostería El Morro** (☎ 81 13 11, fax 81 42 26), which charges around US$50 double.

Places to Eat

The waterfront is essentially an upmarket area, but it also shelters some cheaper places, including half a dozen Middle Eastern eateries that have mushroomed over recent years and provide the usual repertoire of Arabian fast food, such as falafel and shawarma. Most of them also serve set lunches for less than US$5. Vegetarians can get budget set lunches (on weekdays only) at **Centro Naturalista La Colmena**, one of the very few vegetarian restaurants in town.

Some affordable Italian restaurants lie on Paseo Colón between Calles Boyacá and Juncal; the cheapest (and quite OK) is **Ristorante O'Sole Mio**. Next door is the good but expensive **Restaurant Chic e Choc**, which specializes in French cooking. In the same area is the top-floor restaurant of **Hotel Neptuno**, which is acceptable and relatively cheap. **Mister Pollo**, on Calle Sucre just off Paseo Colón, doesn't look very elegant but serves up tasty chicken at low prices.

For more budget eating, comb the streets back from the beach. **Comedor Popular**, Calle Arismendi, is one of the cheapest eateries in town, but it closes early in the afternoon. Better is **Lunchería Orlando López**, Calle Miranda, which offers a choice of set

meals from 11:30 am to 5 pm and also serves a hearty *desayuno criollo* (typical breakfast) in the morning from 7:30 am. Food is tasty, service efficient, portions generous and prices low (US$3 to US$4 for a meal) – all of which means that the place is consistently popular with the locals. There are more budget restaurants in the area, where a set lunch won't cost more than US$5.

The cream of the city's restaurants is along Paseo Colón. This area is alive well into the evening, when fresh breezes alleviate the day's heat and people gather in the numerous open-air establishments that overlook the beach.

Getting There & Away

Air The airport is in Barcelona (see that section, earlier).

Bus The busy bus terminal is conveniently situated in the middle of the city, just three blocks from Plaza Bolívar, though plans are in the works to build a new one outside the center. Frequent buses run west to Caracas (US$9 ordinary, US$12 deluxe, five hours) and east to Cumaná (US$3, 1½ hours); many of the latter continue east to Carúpano (US$7 deluxe, four hours) and some go as far as Güiria (US$11 deluxe, 6½ hours). If you go eastward (to Cumaná or farther on), grab a seat on the left side of the bus, as there are some spectacular views over the islands of Parque Nacional Mochima. Por puesto cars also run to Caracas (US$20, four hours) and Cumaná (US$5, 1¼ hours).

Buses to Ciudad Guayana run roughly every two hours (US$9 ordinary, US$12 deluxe, six hours), and all go via Ciudad Bolívar (US$7 ordinary, US$9 deluxe, four hours). There are also buses to Maturín (US$5 ordinary, US$7 deluxe, three hours), a few of which continue on to Tucupita (US$9 ordinary, US$12 deluxe, 6½ hours).

Por puesto jeeps to Los Altos depart regularly from the southern corner of the terminal (US$1.25, 40 minutes). Por puesto minibuses to Santa Fe park just outside the western corner of the terminal (US$2, 45 minutes). From the same place, private minibuses to Caripe depart at 1 pm (US$12, five hours).

To Barcelona, take a city bus from Avenida 5 de Julio. They go by either Avenida Intercomunal or Vía Alterna. Both will deposit you in Barcelona's center in 45 minutes to one hour, depending on the traffic. There are also por puesto minibuses to Barcelona, which are faster.

Boat Puerto La Cruz is the major departure point for Isla de Margarita. Conferry operates ferries to the island, with four departures a day (there may be fewer in the off season). The passenger fare is US$14/9 in 1st/2nd class and the trip takes 4½ hours. Conferry also operates the comfortable *Margarita Express,* which does the trip in two hours two times a day and costs US$35 per head. Additionally, another fast boat, *Gran Cacique Express,* shuttles twice a day in two hours and is cheaper (US$18). The Conferry terminal is accessible by por puestos from the center. Do this trip in the daytime – it's a spectacular journey between the islands of Parque Nacional Mochima.

CLARINES & PÍRITU
There are several colonial churches in small towns throughout the northern part of Anzoátegui state. Among them, those in Clarines and Píritu have been restored and are the most interesting. Both towns are on the Caracas-Barcelona highway.

Founded in 1694, **Clarines** is an old colonial town about 1km south of the highway. Its church, Iglesia de San Antonio, is at the upper end of the historic town. Built in the 1750s, the church is a massive, squat construction laid out on a Latin-cross floor plan, and is one of only a few examples of its kind in Venezuela. The austere facade is bordered by twin square towers. Perhaps the most unusual features of the structure are the two external arcades running between the towers and the transepts on both sides of the church.

The single-nave interior is topped with a wooden cupola and is refreshingly well balanced in both proportion and decoration. Over the high altar is a three-tier main retable from around 1760. It is placed against the wall, which still bears its original painting depicting a curtain. The church is open from approximately 9:30 to 11:30 am and 3 to 6 pm daily.

Sixteen kilometers east of Clarines, **Píritu** lies just north of the highway (but the access road branches off from the highway 2km before the town and rejoins it 2km beyond it). The town was founded in 1656, and about half a century later, the Iglesia de Nuestra Señora de la Concepción was built. Like the Iglesia San Antonio, it sort of resembles a fortress, though the structure's design is quite different: There's only one bell tower, no transept and no arcades.

This three-nave church has quite a number of remarkable colonial altarpieces. The main retable and the two side retables date from about 1745 and, like most of the others, are richly gilded. Note the painted decoration of the vault in the chancel.

Getting There & Away
As both towns are just off the Caracas-Barcelona highway, access is easy and transportation is frequent. Apart from the long-distance buses running between these two cities, there are regional hourly buses from Barcelona to both Píritu and Clarines.

PARQUE NACIONAL MOCHIMA
☎ 093 (☎ 0293 from Aug 18, 2001)
Roughly bisected by the border of Anzoátegui and Sucre states, the 950-sq-km Mochima national park covers the offshore belt of the Caribbean coast between Puerto La Cruz and Cumaná, complete with its 36 islands, a strip of the mountainous hinterland and its bays and beaches.

The main groups of islands include, from west to east, Islas Borrachas, Islas Chimanas and Islas Caracas. There are also a number of islands closer to the mainland, such as Isla de Plata and Isla de Monos. Most of the islands are barren, rocky in parts and quite spectacular, but some also have fine beaches. A few of the islands are surrounded by coral reefs and offer good snorkeling. The waters are warm and usually calm, abounding in marine life. The weather

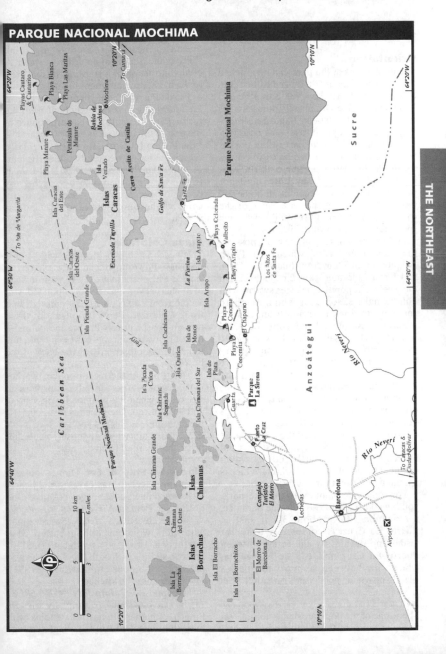

PARQUE NACIONAL MOCHIMA

THE NORTHEAST

is fine for most of the year, with moderate rainfall mainly between July and October.

Orientation

The insular part of the park can be reached only by boat. Trips are organized by boat operators from Puerto La Cruz, Santa Fe and Mochima (see the Organized Tours sections of those towns for details). Santa Fe is probably the cheapest place to go on a boat trip.

The mainland coastal part of the park is very easy to explore, as it's accessible from the Puerto La Cruz–Cumaná road. The road is serviced frequently by buses and por puestos, with lots of accommodations and food facilities along the way. Parts of the road skirt the seafront, so you'll have some spectacular glimpses of the islands.

A dozen beaches lie off the road, possibly the most popular of which are Playa Arapito, about 23km from Puerto La Cruz, and Playa Colorada, 4km farther east. On the weekends, popular beaches swarm with holidaymakers, some of whom seem to come just to drink beer and listen to loud music. On the other hand, some deserted beaches can be unsafe, particularly at night – use common sense. Camping on solitary beaches is not always safe either; there have been reports of robberies on both the islands and mainland beaches.

About 8km east of Playa Colorada is the ordinary town of Santa Fe, which has become a gringo haunt thanks to a beach and tourist facilities. Another 15km east along the Cumaná road, a side road branches off to the north and goes 4km downhill to the village of Mochima, which is a jumping-off point for nearby beaches.

For some panoramic views of the park, you can take a trip to Los Altos de Santa Fe, a mountain village about 30km east of Puerto La Cruz. A completely different visual approach is by the ferry between Puerto La Cruz and Isla de Margarita, which sails between some of the park's islands, providing good views on either side.

Isla de Plata

This is one of the popular islands among Venezuelan tourists, thanks to its beach and coral reefs, as well as its proximity to the mainland, which makes boat access frequent and cheap. There are food and drink stalls on the island but no drinking water. A bonus 'attraction' is a startling, surreal view of the nearby huge cement plant.

Isla de Plata is about 10km east of Puerto La Cruz and is accessible by boat from the pier at Pamatacualito, the eastern suburb of the port of Guanta (serviced by por puestos from Puerto La Cruz). Boats run regularly, especially during weekends, taking 10 minutes to get to the island (US$2.50 roundtrip). The island can also be reached by excursion boats directly from Puerto La Cruz, but these are more expensive and less regular.

Playa Colorada

This beach is neither long nor wide, but it does have fine orange sand and is pleasantly shaded with coconut groves. It has lost some of its charm ever since it was populated with a colony of cubic tin kiosks painted with Coca Cola and Pepsi propaganda; these now sit conspicuously among the palms. A line of rustic restaurants has been built, fortunately more discreetly, at the back of the beach.

This is one of the most popular beaches in the region, so try to avoid coming here on weekends, when it's swamped with visitors and left littered. The beach is just 200m off the road, and you'll get a good view of it (it's particularly attractive at sunset) while approaching by road from the east.

Places to Stay & Eat There's quite a choice of places to stay close to the beach, including some good budget posadas. One of these is *Posada Nirvana* (☎ 014-803 01 01), owned by Rita, a friendly Swiss woman who offers two rooms without bath (US$10 matrimonial), two rooms with bath (US$15) and two studios with bath (US$24). She also prepares fabulous breakfasts (US$4). Guests can use the kitchen.

Just opposite, *Quinta Jaly* (☎ 016-681 81 13), is run by Jacques, an equally friendly French Canadian. It has four rooms with bath that cost US$10/14/20 single/double/

triple. Here too guests have free access to the kitchen, and an optional breakfast is available for US$3.

Both places are on Calle Marchán, about 500m uphill from the main coastal road. If you don't feel like walking that far, check out the simple *Posada Edgar Lemus* (☎ 014-804 19 19), just off the road, and the two-room *Casa Carmita* (☎ 016-482 17 49), 150m up the hill. Either will cost around US$16 double.

Midway from the main road to the Nirvana and Jaly is the more upmarket *Hotel Tucusito* (☎ 016-681 63 65), which offers 12 spacious air-conditioned double rooms (US$50 each) and 16 large two-bedroom trailers (caravans) with kitchenette (US$50 for up to four people). It also has its own restaurant and a swimming pool.

Santa Fe

Going solely by its general appearance, Santa Fe is a drab fishing town where few travelers would bother to stop. However, the town has a beach, Playa Cochaima, that has become popular with foreign backpackers, who come here and stay for days. This is thanks to the grassroots initiative of some residents, inspired by an interesting journalist and writer, José Vivas, to make the place a small ecotourist resort.

The project has gone ahead with such enthusiasm and determination that there are now a dozen posadas along the kilometer-long beach, many of which are owned and managed by foreigners. The conditions are generally simple, but the prices are modest, and various facilities and activities, such as laundry, Spanish lessons, boat excursions, snorkeling and horse riding, are available. There's even a public phone right on the beach from where you can call around the world.

The place has become a lively traveler hangout. Some Venezuelans come here on weekends, but for the rest of the week it's essentially a gringo stronghold. The beach itself is nothing special, but it's regularly cleaned and the water is clear and sheltered.

If you're looking for a budget place to relax for some days, Santa Fe might be an option. You can spend mornings meditating in a hammock, days taking launches to nearby beaches and nights drinking fruity merengadas and cold beer. Bring insect repellent and sunscreen.

Organized Tours Tours and excursions by boat and/or car are organized by most posada and hotel managers. A standard full-day boat trip will normally feature La Piscina and the Islas Caracas, calling at two or three beaches and stopping for snorkeling (equipment provided). Tomás Fuentes (his *Gulliver* anchors next to Playa Santa Fe Resort) and Matthias, of Posada Café del Mar, offer some of the cheapest boat trips – about US$8 to US$10 a person, with a minimum of four people.

Places to Stay & Eat All but one of the places listed here are along the beach, just a stone's throw from each other. Each has rooms with fan and bath, unless otherwise specified.

Entering the beach, the first place you'll reach is *Posada Café del Mar* (☎ 21 00 09), run by a German, Matthias. It's one of the cheapest places, offering 14 rooms (about US$10 double) and a budget restaurant. If it's too busy or crowded, you can stay for a similar price in the four-room *Quinta La Jaiba* (☎ 21 00 27), the small white house just next to the Café del Mar. Next comes *La Sierra Inn* (☎ 21 00 42, 014-993 31 16), managed by José Vivas himself, who charges costs around US$18 double.

More budget places lie a bit farther down the beach, including the sizable *Hotel Cochaima* (☎ 21 00 71), which costs much the same as the Café del Mar and has a cheap restaurant. More pleasant and stylish is the eight-room *Bahía del Mar* (☎ 21 00 73), in the neighboring house, which is run by a friendly French Canadian, Lynn. Doubles without bath cost US$11 (US$18 with bath), and you can use the kitchen.

Another pleasant nearby place, *Hotel Las Palmeras* (☎ 014-773 61 52), 100m back from the beach, is managed by a helpful Frenchman, Michel. It has 10 comfortable double rooms for about US$20 each, plus the only air-conditioned room in the entire area (US$28).

The upper end of the local lodging ladder is represented by the distinctly upmarket *Playa Santa Fe Resort & Dive Center* (☎ 014-773 37 77, *santafe@telcel.net.ve*), owned and operated by a Californian, Jerry. The posada offers rooms of different standards and prices, ranging from US$25 to US$65 (the cheapest ones have shared baths) and offering an optional breakfast (US$10), plus a range of activities, including scuba diving, rafting, fishing and biking.

Getting There & Away Regular buses and por puestos from both Puerto La Cruz and Cumaná will deposit you on the highway at Santa Fe's main junction. Walk 1km through this unprepossessing town to the market on the seafront. Turn left and you'll soon get to the beach, which is lined with posadas and hotels.

Mochima

The small village of Mochima is clean and well cared for. It has no beach and is not a tourist destination per se, but it is a jumping-off point to half a dozen isolated mainland beaches that are inaccessible by road. The beaches are beautiful though shadeless, and are solitary except during some major holiday peaks. Only Playa Blanca and Las Maritas have established food facilities that are open daily, and they are the most visited beaches. Other beaches usually have food services only in high season.

Organized Tours Transportation to the beaches is provided from the wharf in the village's center, where boats anchor and *lancheros* (boatmen) sit on the shore and wait for tourists. They can take you to any beach, among them Playa Las Maritas (US$12), Playa Blanca (US$13), Playa Manare (US$16), and Playas Cautaro and Cautarito (US$16). The listed figures are roundtrip fares per boat (up to seven passengers), and you can be picked up whenever you want. The rates are posted at the wharf, but don't hesitate to bargain.

Some hotel managers can provide transportation to the beaches for their guests, which may work out to be cheaper than with lancheros. Some also organize trips around several islands, eventually leaving travelers for most of the day on a selected one. Longer tours, which can include cruises to Islas Caracas, La Piscina and Playa Colorada, plus snorkeling, are also available. Nené of the Posada Villa Vicenta (see Places to Stay & Eat, next) offers possibly the cheapest tours. His full-day trip will cost around US$15 per person.

Mochima has two scuba diving operators: Aquatics Diving Center (☎ 014-777 01 96, *diving@viptel.com*) and La Posada de Los Buzos (*faverola@cantv.net*). Both organize diving courses, dives and excursions, and handle snorkel rental; the latter also runs rafting trips on Río Neverí.

Places to Stay & Eat Mochima has an increasing choice of accommodation and food facilities. *Posada Villa Vicenta* (☎ 014-993 58 77), in the four-story building (the highest in town) one block back from the wharf, is probably the cheapest place – US$14 double or matrimonial with fan and bath. Some rooms on the upper floors have fine vistas over the bay.

The small *Posada Doña Cruz* (☎ 014-993 26 90), next to the wharf, has two double rooms with bath and fan (US$15) and four rooms with bath and air-conditioning (US$24). The nearby *Posada El Mochimero* (☎ 014-773 87 82) also has rooms with fan and air-conditioning. It provides a bit better standards than Doña Cruz for a marginally higher price.

Posada Gaby (☎ 014-773 11 04), at the far end of the village, is the largest and perhaps the best place to stay. It charges US$22 double with fan (US$28 with aircon). Locals also rent out rooms and houses if there is demand.

For somewhere to eat, you have four restaurants in the village: *El Mochimero*, *El Guayacán*, *Puerto Viejo* and *Brisas de Mochima*, of which El Mochimero is possibly the best. More restaurants open temporarily during holiday peaks.

Getting There & Away Jeeps departing from Cumaná will bring you to the village's center (US$1, 35 minutes), next to the wharf. There's no direct transportation from Puerto La Cruz.

Los Altos de Santa Fe

The mountain village of Los Altos is accessible by a winding paved road from the coast and is serviced regularly throughout the day by jeeps from Puerto La Cruz (US$1.25, 40 minutes). Sitting at an altitude of about 900m, it has a pleasant climate, about 5°C cooler than the coast. Los Altos is a typical one-street village, snaking up and down the rugged terrain for almost 5km without any pronounced center. It's surrounded by verdant highlands sprinkled with coffee and cacao haciendas, some of which can be visited.

Although Los Altos is only 4km back from the coast as the crow flies, it doesn't provide many panoramic views of the coast and the islands beyond. The best vistas are actually from the access road, as you approach the village. Once you enter it, which is roughly by the Bodega El Progreso (about 7km from the turnoff at the coastal highway), the road gradually descends inland, and there are no reasonable lookouts. Jeeps continue for about 5km to their terminus on the opposite end of the village, but it's probably not worth going that far.

Places to Stay & Eat Los Altos has just about one place to stay, *Posada El Paraíso*, 2km down the road from El Progreso. It offer 10 matrimoniales at US$18 and three doubles at US$22. Simple but agreeable, it does have its own restaurant. A few more places to eat are nearby, including the unusual *Petit Restaurant*, 700m inland from the posada, run by a Dutch-Moldavian couple that cook Indonesian-style food.

Long before you get to Los Altos, just 1.5km from the coastal highway, you'll pass by a curious restaurant-posada named *La Ventana de Real y Medio* (☎ 31 46 20, 014-809 05 52). The restaurant, arranged on a large terrace, serves comida criolla and also provides some of the best views over the islands of Parque Nacional Mochima. What's more, it's an amazing place in itself, decorated with folksy objects and other paraphernalia, which the owner, Victor Quintero, calls the 'Museo de la Tradición y del Humor.' Men shouldn't miss a visit to the toilet, which features mirrors installed at the urinals. The posada has three rustic suites for four, five and six guests, priced at US$40 for two people, plus US$8 for each additional person.

Sucre State

CUMANÁ

☎ 093 (☎ 0293 from Aug 18, 2001)

Founded by the Spaniards in 1521, Cumaná takes pride in being the oldest existing town on South America's mainland. There's not much colonial architecture left, however: Several earthquakes, including three serious ones in 1684, 1765 and 1929, reduced the town each time to little more than a pile of rubble, and its historic character largely disappeared in the subsequent reconstructions. Today the city is both the capital of Sucre state and an important port for sardine fishing and canning.

Cumaná (population 280,000) is noted more for its attractive environs than for the city itself. There are some beaches nearby, the closest being Playa San Luis, on the southwestern outskirts of the city. More beaches are in the Parque Nacional Mochima, a little farther down the coast. Cumaná is also one of the gateways to Isla de Margarita and is a convenient jumping-off point for the Península de Araya, the town of Santa Fe, the village of Mochima and the Cueva del Guácharo (see those sections for details).

Information

Tourist Offices The Dirección de Turismo (☎ 31 60 51) is on Calle Sucre, close to the Iglesia de Santa Inés. The office is open 8 am to noon and 2:30 to 5:30 pm weekdays. There's also a tourist stand at the airport.

Money Most major banks are on Calle Mariño and Avenida Bermúdez. Corp

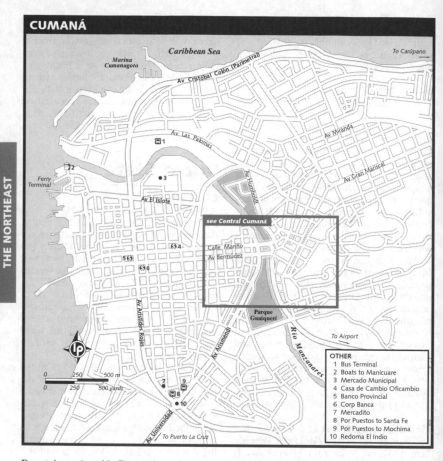

CUMANÁ

Caribbean Sea

To Carúpano

Marina
Cumanagoto

Av Cristóbal Colón (Perimetral)

Av Las Palmas

Av Miranda

Ferry
Terminal

Av El Islote

Av Humboldt

Av Gran Mariscal

see Central Cumaná

Calle Mariño

Av Bermúdez

Parque
Guaiquerí

Río Manzanares

To Airport

Av Aristides Rojas

Av Arismendi

To Puerto La Cruz

Av Universidad

OTHER
1 Bus Terminal
2 Boats to Manicuare
3 Mercado Municipal
4 Casa de Cambio Oficambio
5 Banco Provincial
6 Corp Banca
7 Mercadito
8 Por Puestos to Santa Fe
9 Por Puestos to Mochima
10 Redoma El Indio

Banca is on Avenida Bermúdez a few steps off Avenida Aristides Rojas. The only casa de cambio, Oficambio (☎ 33 16 26), on Calle Mariño 10 blocks west of Plaza Miranda, changes cash and traveler's checks. It's open 8:30 to 11 am and 2:30 to 5 pm weekdays, 8:30 to 11 am Saturday.

Central Cumaná

The streets around the **Iglesia de Santa Inés** have retained some of their appearance. The church itself dates from 1929 and has few objects from earlier times inside, apart from the 16th-century statues of El Nazareno (Christ with the Cross) and the patron saint Santa Inés, both in the chapels in the right-hand aisle. The **Catedral**, on Plaza Blanco, is also relatively young and has a hodgepodge of altarpieces in its largely timbered interior.

Perhaps the best-restored colonial structure in town is the **Castillo de San Antonio de la Eminencia**, overlooking the city from a hill just southeast of the center. Originally constructed in 1659 on a four-pointed-star plan, it suffered pirate attacks and earthquakes, but the coral-rock walls have survived and are in pretty good shape. The fort commands good views over the city and the bay. It's open from 8 am to noon and 3 to 6 pm on weekdays.

Next to the fort is the small **Museo de Arte Contemporáneo de Cumaná**, opened in 1998 in a modern building. It stages changing exhibits of modern art, which can be seen 9 am to noon and 3 to 6 pm Tuesday to Saturday. Some freestanding sculptures are scattered around the place.

The city has more museums, though all are pretty modest and of limited interest. The **Casa Natal de Andrés Eloy Blanco**, Plaza Bolívar, is the house where this poet, considered one of Venezuela's most extraordinary literary talents, was born in 1896. It's open 9 am to noon and 3 to 6 pm weekdays. Open the same hours is the **Casa Ramos Sucre**, on Calle Sucre. It is dedicated to another local poet, José Antonio Ramos Sucre, who was born here in 1890. Far less known than Blanco's, Ramos Sucre's poetry was well ahead of his time, and it was actually not before the 1960s that his verses began to attract the attention of scholars, critics, publishers and, finally, readers. Long before that, Ramos Sucre committed suicide at the age of 40.

Next door to the Casa Ramos Sucre, the **Museo de Arqueología e Historia del Estado Sucre** (also open the same hours) has a small archaeological collection. The **Museo Gran Mariscal de Ayacucho**, on Avenida Humboldt, is dedicated to the Cumaná-born hero of the War of Independence, General Antonio José de Sucre (1795–1830), best remembered for liberating Peru and Bolivia. It's open 9 am to noon and 3 to 6 pm Tuesday to Saturday.

Places to Stay

As the city has over 30 hotels, there's generally no problem finding somewhere to stay. Most budget places are conveniently located in the city center, within a few blocks of Plaza Bolívar. All the hotels listed here have rooms with a private bath and either fans or air-conditioning, as indicated; they can all be found on the Central Cumaná map.

There are several unremarkable cheapies on Calle Sucre, including *Hotel Vesubio* (☎ 31 40 77), *Hotel Cumaná* (☎ 31 05 45)

and *Hotel Italia* (☎ 66 36 78). They all are pretty simple but inexpensive – about US$10/12 matrimonial/double with bath and fan. The Italia also has some rooms with air-conditioning, which cost a bit more. Slightly better is *Hotel Astoria* (☎ 66 27 08), which charges US$12/15/18 for its air-conditioned singles/doubles/triples.

You can also try the small *Hospedaje Lucila* (☎ 31 18 08), Calle Bolívar, though there may be some passionate couples passing through for quick sex. Matrimoniales with fan/air-conditioning go for U3$10/14. Possibly even cheaper is the basic *Hotel La Gloria* (☎ 66 42 43), Calle Sucre.

There are also some inexpensive hotels across the river from Plaza Miranda, including *Hotel Regina* (☎ 32 25 81), *Hotel Turismo Gualyqueri* (☎ 31 08 21) and *Hotel Mariño* (☎ 32 07 51). Any of them will cost about US$22/24/28 for an air conditioned single/double/triple. None are memorable places. The Miranda is perhaps the best option – choose an east-facing room on the top floor for views over the city center, including its two churches and the fort.

Absolutely different from anything listed previously is the amazing *Posada San Francisco* (☎ 31 39 26, fax 33 39 17), Calle Sucre. Managed by an Italian, Roberto, this partly renovated, partly reconstructed old *casona* (large house) is easily one of the loveliest colonial mansions in town. It has eight ample rooms and a few apartments, all with private bath and fan and all arranged around two beautiful patios. Some restoration work is still going on, so prices are not that definite, but expect to pay up to US$30 double. (The rate is apparently open to negotiation.) In any case, it's an excellent value and is warmly recommended.

Another stylish and pleasant option, *Bubulina's Hostal* (☎/fax 31 40 25), around the corner from the tourist office, is also in a historic building, though the interior is a totally new construction. This posada-style place offers six comfortable matrimoniales and six doubles, all with air-conditioning, TV, bath and hot water, for US$32 each, breakfast included. The staff may organize budget tours in the region – ask about them.

THE NORTHEAST

THE NORTHEAST

CENTRAL CUMANÁ

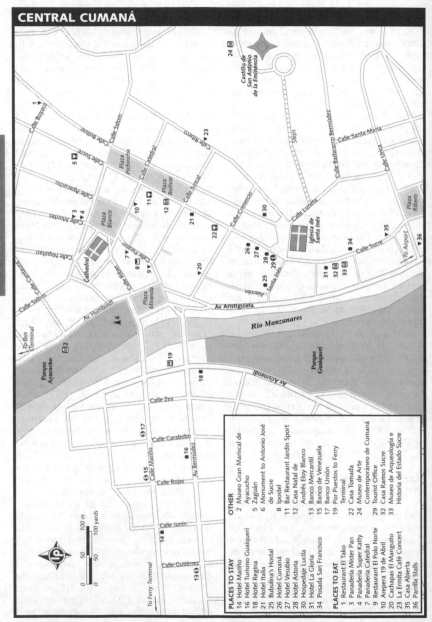

PLACES TO STAY
14 Hotel Mariño
16 Hotel Turismo Guaiqueri
18 Hotel Regina
21 Hotel Italia
25 Bubulina's Hostal
26 Hotel Cumaná
27 Hotel Vesubio
28 Hotel Astoria
30 Hospedaje Lucila
31 Hotel La Gloria
34 Posada San Francisco

PLACES TO EAT
1   Restaurant El Tako
3   Panadería Mister Pan
4   Panadería Super Katty
7   Panadería Catedral
9   Restaurant El Polo Norte
10 Arepera 19 de Abril
20 Cachapas El Manguito
23 La Ermita Café Concert
35 Casa Abierta
36 Parrilla Stalls

OTHER
2   Museo Gran Mariscal de
    Ayacucho
5   Zaguán
6   Monument to Antonio José
    de Sucre
8   Ipostel
11 Bar Restaurant Jardin Sport
12 Casa Natal de
    Andrés Eloy Blanco
13 Banco Mercantil
15 Banco de Venezuela
17 Banco Unión
19 Por Puestos to Ferry
    Terminal
22 Casa Tomada
24 Museo de Arte
    Contemporáneo de Cumaná
29 Tourist Office
32 Casa Ramos Sucre
33 Museo de Arqueología e
    Historia del Estado Sucre

Upmarket hotels are away from the center, mainly on Avenidas Perimetral and Universidad, both near the waterfront. The three poshest and most expensive places to stay in town – *Hotel Los Bordones* (☎ 51 31 11, fax 51 53 77), *Hotel Barceló Nueva Toledo* (☎ 51 95 95, fax 51 99 74) and *Hotel Cumanagoto Hesperia* (☎ 30 14 00, fax 52 18 77) – are all close to each other at the end of Avenida Universidad, near the beach but a long way from the center. The Cumanagoto provides some of the best luxuries, if you're up to paying US$300 double.

Places to Eat

The city center has few classy establishments, but budget eating is no problem. If you're yearning for arepas, you can choose from several central *areperas*, of which *Arepera 19 de Abril* is possibly the best. The simple *Cachapas El Manguito*, Calle Comercio, serves cachapas for just US$1.25 each. Some of the cheapest parrillas can be found at the *parrilla stalls* off Plaza Ribero, one long block south of Iglesia Santa Inés. Central panaderías include *Panadería Mister Pan* (which has some tables to sit and eat at), *Panadería Super Katty* and *Panadería Catedral*.

The restaurant in *Hotel Italia* serves unpretentious inexpensive meals, as does the *Restaurant El Polo Norte*. The ordinary-looking *Restaurant El Tako* has hearty budget set lunches (come just after noon, no later than 1 pm, because the food runs out quickly), including delicious *mondongo* (seasoned tripe with vegetables) on some days. For more pleasant surroundings, check *La Ermita Café Concert*, Calle Ribero, which has a good set menu for US$5 and a choice of dishes à la carte. Alternatively, head for *Bubulina's Restaurant*, in the hostel of the same name, which also serves tasty set lunches and other dishes, including paella.

Another charming place, *Casa Abierta*, Calle Sucre, is a restaurant/art gallery run by a French woman and accommodated in her private home, which you can visit (hence its 'Open House' moniker). Predictably, the cuisine is basically French; if you don't know what to choose, there's always the Plato de la Indecisión, which features a combination of various dishes.

Outside the center, some of the best budget food is available at the *Mercadito* (Small Market), Avenida Aristides Rojas, which has at least 15 typical restaurants. Fish and seafood are particularly good here. The *Mercado Municipal*, off Avenida El Islote, is also a good and cheap place to eat.

Entertainment

The informal open-air *Bar Restaurant Jardín Sport*, on Plaza Bolívar, serves inexpensive snacks, but it's essentially the cheap beer that draws people in. The place has long been popular with both locals and foreigners and is open late. The old jukebox has broken down, but now music videos are shown.

More bars have opened in recent years, including the rustic *Casa Tomada*, Calle Sucre, which has some of the cheapest beer in town. It features hot Afro-Caribbean rhythms at high volume, but if it's too loud for you, go upstairs and sit on a balcony, with a cold beer, a fresh breeze and the world going by at your feet.

Another recent addition, *Zaguán*, Calle Sucre, is a charming, cozy place serving beer, whiskey and a good choice of cocktails until late.

La Ermita Café Concert (see Places to Eat, earlier) may have live music or theater performances on weekends.

Getting There & Away

Air The airport is about 4km southeast of the city center. Avior, LAI and Air Venezuela service Cumaná, with seven direct flights daily to Caracas (US$66 to US$74) and six to Porlamar, on Isla de Margarita (US$33). Fares are one-way.

Bus The bus terminal is 1.5km northwest of the city center and is linked by frequent urban buses.

There is regular bus service to Caracas, operated by a number of companies (US$11 ordinary, US$15 deluxe, 6½ hours). All buses go through Puerto La Cruz (US$3, 1½ hours), and there are also frequent por puestos to Puerto La Cruz (US$5, 1¼ hours).

Half a dozen buses depart daily for Ciudad Bolívar (US$9 ordinary, US$12 deluxe, six hours) and continue on to Ciudad Guayana (US$11 ordinary, US$14 deluxe, 7½ hours). Five or six buses go daily to Güiria (US$8 deluxe, five hours). Buses to Carúpano run regularly throughout the day (US$3.50 ordinary, US$4.50 deluxe, 2½ hours), as do por puestos (US$6, two hours).

To Caripe, there are two departures daily, theoretically at 7:15 am and 12:30 pm (US$6, 3½ hours). More reliable, however, may be a private minibus, which is supposed to depart at 3 pm (US$7, three hours). They all pass the Cueva del Guácharo shortly before arriving at Caripe and can let you off at the cave's entrance.

Por puesto cars to Santa Fe (US$1.25, 45 minutes) depart from near the Mercadito, one block off the Redoma El Indio. Por puesto jeeps to Mochima (US$1, 35 minutes) depart from the same street.

Boat All ferries and boats to Isla de Margarita depart from the docks next to the mouth of the Río Manzanares and go to Punta de Piedras. There is no city bus service from the center to the ferry docks, but por puestos go there frequently from near the bridge (US$0.30).

Conferry runs two ferries a day (US$8, 3½ hours). The same route is serviced twice daily by the fast *Gran Cacique II* boat (US$15, two hours). Some departures may be suspended or canceled in the slow season.

From the same docks, Naviarca operates *La Palita* ferry to Araya on the Península de Araya (US$1, one hour), theoretically at 6 and 10 am and 3 pm on weekdays, and at 10 am on weekends, but their schedule is, as they say, 'flexible.' It's better to go by a small boat, popularly called a *tapadito*; they run from the same docks approximately every 20 to 30 minutes until about 4 or 5 pm (US$1, 20 minutes). They go to Manicuare (not Araya), from where por puestos travel the rest of the way on a paved road to Araya (US$0.30, 10 minutes). The area around the ferry docks in Cumaná is not famous for its safety, so use a por puesto instead of walking.

Cumaná has the good Marina Cumanagoto (☎ 31 14 23), which is tailor-made, well organized and reasonably cheap.

PENÍNSULA DE ARAYA
☎ 093 (☎ 0293 from Aug 18, 2001)
This 70km-long and 10km-wide peninsula stretches east-west along the mainland's coast, with its tip lying almost due north of Cumaná. Punta Arenas, on the peninsula's end, is just 5km from Cumaná as the crow flies, but it's some 180km by road. The peninsula is hilly, arid and infertile. Its eastern part is higher and more rugged, with the highest peak reaching 596m. The small population is scattered throughout a handful of coastal villages, mostly on the northern coast, along which the only peninsular road runs. Sandwiched between the peninsula and the mainland is the Golfo de Cariaco, a quiet, deep, intensely blue body of water.

Araya
The fort and the salinas – the peninsula's two major attractions – are both in the town of Araya, at the western end of the peninsula. Araya, the largest settlement on the peninsula, is easy to get to by boat or ferry from Cumaná. The town sits on the Bahía de Araya, with its pier in the middle. The fort is 750m to the south, while the salinas spread outward to the north.

Salinas de Araya Until the mid-1990s, the salt mining was managed by the state ENSAL company, which built installations on the seafront and operated the salinas. ENSAL organized free tours around the salt works, which could take up to three hours and were a great tourist attraction.

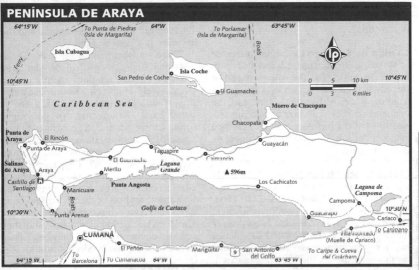

The tours included three areas to visit: the *salinas naturales* (called Unidad 1), *salinas artificiales* (Unidad 2) and the main complex of buildings, where the salt is sorted, packed and stored.

The salinas naturales, about 1km east of town, consist of an intriguingly pink salt lagoon, from which the salt is dragged to the shore by specially constructed boats and then put into piles for drying. The salinas artificiales, a couple of kilometers north of the town, are an array of rectangular pools that are filled in with salt water and left to dry out. Thanks to the intense strength of the sun, the water evaporates, leaving behind pure salt. The salt is then dragged out, the pool refilled, and the whole process begun again.

What is particularly amazing here is the unbelievable pink of the water. Since pools are in different stages of evaporation, there's an incredible variety of color tones, ranging from creamy pink to deep purple. The water coloration is due to the artemia, a microscopic saltwater shrimp. A *mirador* (lookout) has been built on the hill to the east of the salinas, and provides a good view over the whole chessboard of pools. It's on the road to Punta de Araya, 2km north of Araya.

In 1995, ENSAL was privatized and became SALARAYA. The new company doesn't seem to be particularly interested in conducting tours, but it can organize one for you. You need to send or fax them a letter, preferably a month in advance, stating the purpose of the visit, the names of those in your party, and the date of your intended visit. They also require that you have your own means of transportation (you can hire a pickup truck locally), in which they will take you on a short free tour around Unidades 1 and 2. Tours are conducted only on weekdays 8 to 10 am. Contact their Departamento de Relaciones Públicas (☎ 712 22, 711 91, 710 62, fax 711 82) for further information on seeing the salinas.

Even if you don't arrange a tour, the trip to Araya is still worth considering, if only to visit the fort and have a general look at the village. And you can still see a good bit of the salinas, including the mirador, from outside the installations and restricted areas. Start early in the morning and be prepared for baking heat. Adequate protection against the sun, such as good sunscreen, sunglasses and a hat, is essential. It's wise to carry a large bottle of water or other hydrating drink.

Castillo de Santiago Commonly referred to as the Castillo (Castle), this fort stands on the waterfront cliff at the southern end of the bay, a 10-minute walk along the beach from the wharf. Although it's damaged, the mighty coral-rock walls give a good impression of what the fort once looked like. You can wander freely around the place, as there's no gate.

Places to Stay & Eat There are five or six simple posadas in town, including the rustic *Posada Araya Wind* (☎ 014-774 54 85), near the fort, which is possibly the most stylish and pleasant of the lot. Next door is the larger *Posada Helen* (☎ 711 01), which has a variety of rooms with fan and air-conditioning, most with TV. Eating places in the same area include *Parador Turístico Eugenia* and *Restaurant Araya Mar*.

You'll find more posadas on the opposite side of the village, around Plaza Bolívar. These include *Posada Guacaraya* (☎ 710 75), Calle Bolívar, and *Posada Petrica* (☎ 713 35), Calle Brion.

In any of the listed posadas, expect to pay US$15 to US$18 double with fan. The Helen charges more for air-conditioned rooms.

Getting There & Away

There's a ferry service between Cumaná and Araya (US$1, one hour), but it's not very reliable. In theory, the ferry is scheduled to sail three times a day (once on weekends). It supposed to depart Araya at 7 am, noon and 4:30 pm on weekdays, 5 pm on weekends.

Boats are more frequent, faster and more reliable. They shuttle every 20 to 30 minutes until 4 or 5 pm between Manicuare and Cumaná (US$1, 20 minutes), and the remaining Araya-Manicuare leg is covered by frequent por puestos (US$0.30, 10 minutes).

Although there's a paved road between Araya and Cariaco (95km), there's not much traveling along it. There may be occasional por puestos from Araya to Cariaco, but you can't rely on them. You can try hitching, but the traffic is minimal and dies completely after 3 or 4 pm.

There's a boat service between Chacopata and Porlamar, on Isla de Margarita. Boats run from 8 am until about 4 pm, approximately every two hours. They may depart earlier than scheduled if full. On the other hand, if there are few passengers around, some scheduled departures may be canceled. Boats vary in size, capacity (from about 30 to 70 passengers) and quality – some look ready to sink at any moment. The trip takes between one and 1½ hours, depending on the particular crate, but the fare is the same with all of them – US$5. There's a por puesto service between Chacopata and Cariaco (US$2.50, 45 minutes), and there are also direct por puestos between Chacopata and Carúpano (US$6, 1½ hours).

CARÚPANO
☎ 094 (☎ 0294 from Aug 18, 2001)

Set on the coast 137km east of Cumaná, Carúpano (population 98,000) is the last city of any size on Venezuela's Caribbean coast. It has an airport where large jets can land, and it is linked by paved roads with Cumaná to the west and Maturín and Ciudad Guayana to the south. It's an active port for cacao that is cultivated in the region before being shipped overseas.

Despite its regular chessboard layout, suggesting colonial origins (indeed, it was founded in 1647), the town has no outstanding historic monuments. Of the minor sights, you might want to visit the two main churches, Iglesia de Santa Catalina and Iglesia de Santa Rosa de Lima; the modest Museo Histórico de Carúpano; and the unusually large Mercado Municipal. Carúpano is centered on Plaza Colón, while Plaza Bolívar is stranded far away in a southwestern suburb.

Information

Tourist Offices The Dirección de Turismo is in Edificio Rental Fundabermudez, Piso 1, Oficina 8, Avenida Independencia. It's open 8 am to noon and 2 to 5 pm weekdays.

CARÚPANO

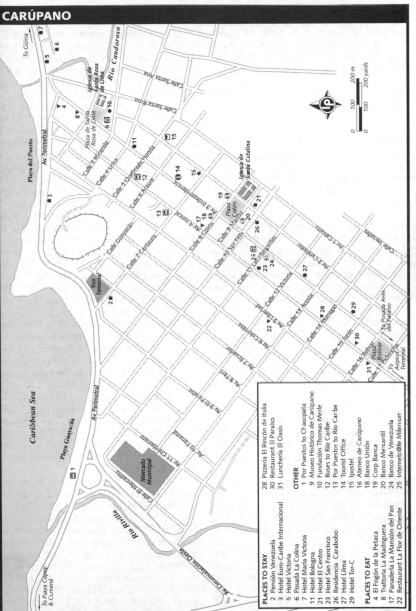

PLACES TO STAY
2 Pensión Venezuela
3 Hotel Euro-Caribe Internacional
5 Hotel Victoria
6 Posada La Colina
7 Hotel María Victoria
11 Hotel Bologna
21 Hotel El Centro
23 Hotel San Francisco
26 Residencia Carabobo
27 Hotel Lilma
29 Hotel Tor-C

PLACES TO EAT
4 El Fogón de la Petaca
8 Trattoria La Madriguera
17 Panadería La Mansión del Pan
22 Restaurant La Flor de Oriente

28 Pizzeria El Rincón de Italia
30 Restaurant El Paraíso
31 Lunchería El Oasis

OTHER
1 Por Puestos to Chacopata
9 Museo Histórico de Carúpano
10 Fundación Thomas Merle
12 Buses to Río Caribe
13 Por Puestos to Río Caribe
14 Tourist Office
15 Ipostel
16 Ateneo de Carúpano
18 Banco Unión
19 Corp Banca
20 Banco Mercantil
24 Banco de Venezuela
25 Internet@fe Milenium

Corpomedina (☎ 31 52 41, 31 39 17, 31 20 31), at the airport, will provide information and booking for their cabañas at Playa Medina and Playa Pui Puy. Fundación Thomas Merle (☎ 31 33 70, 31 38 47), in Plaza de Santa Rosa de Lima, and Posada La Colina (see Places to Stay, later) can give information about Hacienda Aguasana and Hato Río de Agua (see Orientation under Around Río Caribe, later).

Money Most major banks are located around Plaza Colón. Apart from the Corp Banca, which changes American Express traveler's checks, the other banks shown on the map are useful only for credit-card transactions.

Email & Internet Access Internetc@fe Milenium, in the Centro Comercial Olas del Caribe, Avenida Independencia No 136, is open Monday to Saturday and charges about US$5 per hour. The new Cyber Café Inversus.com, one block away on the same street, is cheaper and is open daily.

Special Events
Carúpano springs to life for the four days (Saturday to Tuesday) before Ash Wednesday, when Carnaval is held. There are dances, parades and a lot of music and rum, making it a good time to visit.

Places to Stay
For those coming by bus for just an overnight stay, the cheapest bet around the terminal is the very simple *Pensión Venezuela (Calle Cantaura No 49)*. It's reasonably clean and quiet, even though it has only shared bathrooms, and costs US$8/10 matrimonial/double with fan. In the center, the cheapest option is the basic *Residencia Carabobo*, Calle San Félix, which has doubles/triples with fan but no bath for US$10/15.

There are more undistinguished but cheap hotels across the central area. *Hotel Bologna (☎ 31 12 41, Avenida Independencia No 47)* has matrimoniales with bath and fan for US$12 (US$15 with air-con). *Hotel Tor-C (☎ 32 08 98, Avenida Independencia*

No 185) has air-conditioned doubles with bath for US$16. For a bit more you can stay in the similarly unmemorable *Hotel El Centro (☎ 31 36 73, Avenida Carabobo No 71)*. You can also try *Hotel María Victoria (☎ 31 11 70)*, on Avenida Perimetral, at the northeast end of the town, which offers air-conditioned doubles with bath for US$22.

For a little more comfort, check out *Hotel San Francisco (☎ 31 10 74, 31 32 84, Avenida Juncal No 87A)*, which provides air-conditioned doubles/triples with bath for around US$26/30. Alternatively, try the marginally better *Hotel Lilma (☎ 31 13 41, 31 13 61, Avenida Independencia No 161)*, for much the same price. Probably a wee bit better is *Hotel Victoria (☎ 31 39 10, 31 15 54)*, Avenida Perimetral, a 10-minute walk east of the bus terminal. It costs US$32/40 double/triple and has a small pool. None of the above places has much style or character.

If you need a more personal touch, the four-room *Posada Aves del Paraíso (☎ 31 04 06, 32 20 01, Avenida Independencia No 251)*, 1½ blocks up the road from Plaza Bolívar, is one of the loveliest places around. Arranged in a fine historic house with a flowering garden to one side, the posada is beautifully decorated with antiques and crafts, and has an atmospheric open-air bar (open also to nonguests) at the back. Rooms are simple but neat and comfortable, costing US$18/24 matrimonial/double without bath, US$30/36 with bath. All rooms have a fan and cable TV.

Corpomedina's more upmarket *Posada La Colina (☎ 32 05 27, 32 29 15)*, just behind the Hotel Victoria, is also an enjoyable place to stay, for US$50/60 double/triple, breakfast included.

The most luxurious place in town, the brand new *Hotel Euro-Caribe Internacional (☎ 31 39 11, fax 31 36 51)*, Avenida Perimetral, offers comfortable doubles/suites for US$55/80 and has its own restaurant.

There are some posadas outside Carúpano, including two good and pleasant places on Playa Copey, about 6km west of the city: *Posada Nena (☎ 31 76 24, 31 72 97)* and *Posada Casa Blanca (☎ 31 68 96)*. Either charges about US$25 double, and both have eating facilities.

The unusual Iglesia de San Antonio in Clarines

Asunción's colonial fort, Isla de Margarita

Earning *sal*aries in the Salinas de Araya

Chillin' at Playa El Agua, Isla de Margarita

The Iglesia San Nicolás in Porlamar

Checking out the catch of the day on Isla de Margarita

Away from the bustle on Isla de Margarita

Crystalline waters of Parque Nacional Mochima

Araya's Checkered History

The Spaniards first landed on the Península de Araya in 1499. After the unexpected discovery of fabulous pearl fisheries around the islands of Cubagua and Coche, Pedro Alonso Niño and Cristóbal de la Guerra sailed down to the western tip of the peninsula to find another, quite different treasure – extensive *salinas*, or salt pans. These salt beds were and still remain Venezuela's largest salt deposits.

At that time, salt was increasingly sought after in Europe as an indispensable means for preserving food, mainly fish. The Dutch, who by then already had a well-developed fishing industry but only a scarce supply of salt, were the first to realize the value of the Spanish discovery. They soon began to take advantage of it, extracting the salt from territory claimed by Spain. The Spaniards, on the other hand, who had some salt reserves at home, blindly concentrated on the pearl harvesting on Cubagua and Coche and largely ignored the deposits. It wasn't until the pearl beds were wiped out, around the mid-16th century, that the Spanish Crown eventually turned to the salt pans.

By that time, however, the salinas of Araya were being furtively exploited by the Dutch and English, and the Spanish couldn't do much about it. Various battles were fought by the Spaniards in an attempt to get control of their treasured possession, but the indiscriminate plundering of the salt continued. To prevent further attempts at theft, the Crown eventually set about constructing a fortress.

After careful selection of the location, work on the fort began in 1618 and took almost 50 years to be completed. Progress was interrupted by pirates and storms and was hindered by the heat, which was so extreme that most of the work had to be carried out at night. The fortress ended up being the most costly Spanish project to be realized in the New World up to that time; however, it was also the most powerful and magnificent. Equipped with 45 cannons and defended by a 250-man garrison, La Real Fortaleza de Santiago de León de Araya successfully repelled all attempts to take it.

A turning point in the fort's fortunes came in 1726 with a wild hurricane. The storm produced a tide that broke over the salt lagoon, flooding it and turning it into a gulf. Salt reserves could no longer be exploited, so the fort lost its role, and the Spanish decided to abandon the peninsula. Before leaving, however, they decided to blow up the fort, to prevent it from falling into foreign hands. Despite their using all the available gunpowder, the structure largely resisted efforts to pull it down. Damaged but not destroyed, the mighty bulwarks still proudly crown the waterfront cliff.

Meanwhile, as the years passed, the salinas slowly returned to their previous state, and mining was gradually reintroduced. Today they are Venezuela's largest salinas and provide a good part of the salt produced by the country – about half a million metric tons per year.

Places to Eat

There are plenty of eateries scattered throughout the city. The market is, as elsewhere, one of the cheapest options for unsophisticated local dishes, and Carúpano's **Mercado Municipal** is quite large. The **Panadería La Mansión del Pan**, on Avenida Juncal, is arguably the best central panadería, with good pasteles, cachitos and coffee.

Restaurant La Flor de Oriente, Avenida Libertad, serves hearty comida criolla at low prices. **Lunchería El Oasis**, on Plaza Bolívar, is a tiny Middle Eastern cubbyhole serving beautiful falafel, kafta, shawarma and the like. A few similar Arab eateries are nearby, including **Restaurant El Paraíso**, Avenida Juncal. In the same area, **Pizzería El Rincón de Italia** does some passable pizzas.

Trattoria La Madriguera (Avenida Independencia No 12) cooks delicious pastas at good prices. *El Fogón de la Petaca*, just around the corner on Avenida Perimetral, is also good, but more expensive. Of the hotel restaurants, those in *Hotel Lilma*, *Posada La Colina* and *Hotel Euro-Caribe Internacional* may be worth considering.

Getting There & Away

Air The airport is 1.5km west of the city center. There are two flights a day to Porlamar, on Isla de Margarita (US$33), and one to Caracas (US$64). Fares are one-way.

Bus The bus terminal is a short walk north of the center, on Avenida Perimetral. Buses to Caracas depart mostly in the morning and evening (US$14 ordinary, US$18 deluxe, 8½ hours), and they all run via Cumaná (US$3.50 ordinary, US$4.50 deluxe, 2½ hours) and Puerto La Cruz (US$6 ordinary, US$7 deluxe, 3½ hours). There are also frequent por puestos to Cumaná (US$6, two hours).

Half a dozen buses run to Güiria (US$4.50 deluxe, 2½ hours) coming through from Caracas/Puerto La Cruz; por puestos also go to Güiria regularly (US$6, two hours). Three or four buses go daily to Ciudad Guayana (US$9 ordinary, US$12 deluxe, seven hours).

For the Cueva del Guácharo, take the Caracas/Cumaná bus, get off by the gas station at Villa Frontado, also called Muelle de Cariaco (US$2.50, 1¼ hours), and catch one of the two buses coming through from Cumaná to Caripe (at about 8:30 am and 1:30 pm); it will drop you off at the cave (US$3.50, two hours). Alternatively, you can hitchhike, though the traffic is sporadic.

To Río Caribe, you can go either by por puesto (US$0.80, 30 minutes), departing from Avenida Juncal near the corner of Calle Cantaura, or by Ruta Popular bus (US$0.50, 45 minutes), which park two blocks down the road. You can catch these buses farther down the way, eg, on Avenida Perimetral.

For Isla de Margarita, the shortest and cheapest way is via Chacopata. Direct por

puestos to Chacopata depart from Avenida Perimetral near the market (US$6, 1½ hours), where you change for a boat to Porlamar (US$5, one to 1½ hours). See the Península de Araya section, earlier, for more about these boats.

RÍO CARIBE
☎ 094 (☎ 0294 from Aug 18, 2001)

Río Caribe is a seaside town 25km east of Carúpano. It's an old port that grew fat on cacao export, and the air of the former splendor is still palpable in the wide, tree-shaded Avenida Bermúdez with its once resplendent, now mostly decadent mansions.

Although Río Caribe has no beaches or great attractions, it nonetheless is a pleasant, peaceful town of 30,000, fairly popular with holidaymakers, and dotted with tourist facilities. It can be a useful springboard for beaches farther east, and perhaps a more attractive place to stay than Carúpano. If you happen to come here, visit the Centro Cívico Cultural, on Avenida Bermúdez, and the 18th-century church on Plaza Bolívar.

Information

Mareaje Tours (☎ 615 43) and Asociación de Turismo Paria (ATP), both on Avenida Bermúdez, can provide some information about the town and the region. Mareaje offers Internet access, as does Parian@ Café (see Places to Eat, later). Both facilities cost around US$5 per hour, but connections are unreliable.

Organized Tours

Mareaje Tours (see Information, earlier) organizes boat and car trips around the region, as do most of the posadas, including Pensión Papagayos, Villa Antillana, Posada Caribana and Posada de Arlet (see Places to Stay, later). Shop around, as routes, services and prices vary among the operators.

Places to Stay

The town has a rather developed range of accommodations, including several posadas. One of the cheapest is *Posada Don Chilo* (☎ 612 12, Calle Mariño No 27). It's basic and has only shared facilities, but it's quite acceptable and rather cheap – US$10/12 matrimonial/double.

The four-room **Pensión Papagayos** (☎ 618 68), Calle 14 de Febrero, costs US$7.50 per person. Rooms don't have private baths but are clean and pleasant, and you can use the kitchen and fridge.

Set in a restored 19th-century mansion, the friendly **Villa Antillana** (☎ 614 13), Calle Rivero, has just five rooms: three matrimoniales (US$20 each) and two double-level suites for four people (US$40). All rooms have been painstakingly reconstructed and decorated by the owner-architect and have a lot of personal style and charm, apart from their good modern amenities, such as comfortable mattresses, fans, private baths and hot water. An optional breakfast costs a couple of bucks.

The more upmarket **Posada Caribana** (☎ 612 42, Avenida Bermúdez No 25) is another lovely place, a typical Caribbean casona straight out of a picture postcard. It has 11 good-sized rooms (including three with air-conditioning) that line a spacious patio and cost US$45/55/65 double/triple/quad with breakfast. It also has its own restaurant.

Posada de Arlet (☎ 612 90), Calle 24 de Julio, is a cheaper and more modest option. Owned and managed by a polyglot Swiss woman, the place costs US$30 matrimonial with bath and fan.

Hotel Mar Caribe (☎ 614 94), near the waterfront, is the largest place to stay and must have once been the pride of the town. It's now a distant shade of its former self but still boasts 50 spacious air-conditioned rooms, a restaurant and a swimming pool, and it costs US$28/38/50 single/double/triple.

Places to Eat

The **Tasca Mi Cocina**, Calle Juncal near Plaza Sucre, is consistently popular among locals and visitors for good food at good prices. **Restaurant Doña Eva**, Calle Girardot near Plaza Miranda, is slightly cheaper and not bad either.

Parian@Café, Avenida Bermúdez, has become popular with foreign travelers. It serves food typical of the region, as well as plenty of drinks. **Abasto Independencia**, an ordinary-looking grocery store on Avenida Bermúdez, sells delicious pastelitos.

Getting There & Away

The best transportation link is with Carúpano; por puesto cars depart frequently from Plaza Bolívar (US$0.80, 30 minutes), and there are also buses marked 'Ruta Popular.'

Infrequent por puesto pickup trucks run to the villages of Medina (US$1), Pui Puy (US$1.50) and San Juan de las Galdonas (US$3). They don't get as far as the beaches of Medina and Pui Puy: You need to walk the rest of the way, but it's at most a pleasant half-hour walk in either case. Otherwise, you need to rent the vehicle, which will cost at least 10 times more than the por puesto fare. The trucks depart from the southeastern end of Río Caribe, opposite the gas station. The best chances for a short wait are in the morning. The traffic thins out gradually from the early afternoon onward.

AROUND RÍO CARIBE
☎ 094 (☎ 0294 from Aug 18, 2001)

The coast east of Río Caribe has some of the country's loveliest beaches. There are perhaps two dozen named beaches on the 50km coastal stretch between Río Caribe and San Juan de Unare, the last seaside village accessible by road. The best known (and arguably the nicest) are Playa Medina and Playa Pui Puy, but you're likely to find other amazing patches of sand.

The hinterland behind the beaches features a picturesque coastal mountain range that rolls down into the vast plains stretching to the south. The mountains and the plains shelter a variety of attractions, including a cacao hacienda, hot springs and a buffalo ranch. Farther to the south is the interesting but little-visited Parque Nacional Turuépano.

All in all, the compact region boasts a diversity of things to see and do to suit various tastes, making it a potential focus of tourism in the future. Unsurprisingly, places to stay and eat have been popping up over recent

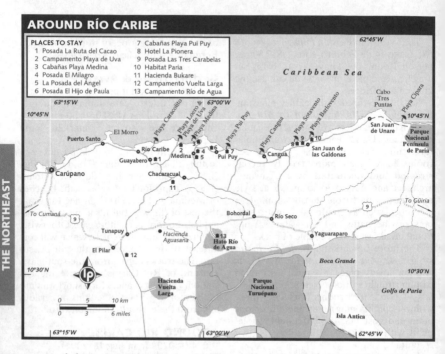

AROUND RÍO CARIBE

PLACES TO STAY
1 Posada La Ruta del Cacao
2 Campamento Playa de Uva
3 Cabañas Playa Medina
4 Posada El Milagro
5 La Posada del Ángel
6 Posada El Hijo de Paula
7 Cabañas Playa Pui Pui
8 Hotel La Pionera
9 Posada Las Tres Carabelas
10 Habitat Paria
11 Hacienda Bukare
12 Campamento Vuelta Larga
13 Campamento Río de Agua

years, and there are now at least a dozen posadas scattered across the mountains and beaches. Most are small and reasonably priced and also serve meals, so you can easily stay longer and on the cheap.

On the other hand, roads in the area are few, partly unpaved and in bad shape, and transportation services are infrequent (see the Río Caribe section, earlier, for details). This makes getting around a bit inconvenient and time-consuming, which paradoxically has some advantages: The region remains largely undeveloped and is not swamped with tourists. There are no classy high-rise beach hotels, and mass tourism is unknown.

Orientation

Many travelers come to the region for its beaches. Most are accessible by roads, though in many cases these access roads are unpaved.

The first beach east of Río Caribe, Playa Caracolito, is small and unattractive – probably not worth the 4km detour. A bit farther east, the side-by-side **Playa Loero** and **Playa de Uva** are better, as is the coast around them. They lie 6km from Río Caribe by the road to Bohordal (midway through this 6km stretch is the village of Guayabero, which has a posada), plus another 6km by a paved side road that branches off to the left and runs to the waterfront. There's a charming place to stay on Playa de Uva.

Back on the main road, 8km beyond the turnoff to Loero is the **Hacienda Bukare**, a working cacao plantation open to visitors; it has lodging and eating facilities and offers tours.

Proceeding east, a paved road branches off 4km beyond Bukare and goes 5km to the village of Medina (which has a posada). The road continues northward for 1km to a fork (where you'll find another posada). The left branch goes for 2km to the picture-postcard **Playa Medina** (with lovely ca-bañas), and you'll get a fantastic bird's-eye view of this tranquil, crescent-shaped beach from the road as it descends to the sea. The right branch leads 6km over a heavily pot-holed road to the village of Pui Puy (where there is another posada) and continues for 2km to the beautiful **Playa Pui Puy** (with cabañas).

Few travelers venture farther to the east, though beaches dot the coast as far as the eye can see. The most frequently visited place in the area is the seaside village of **San Juan de las Galdonas** (with several accom-modation options and tours), noted for its fine beaches. The main access to San Juan is by the recently improved, wholly paved 23km road that branches off the Río Caribe–Bohordal road 6.5km beyond the turnoff to Medina (this road is used by most vehicles to and from Río Caribe). Another access is by a potholed 22km road that branches off the Bohordal–Yaguaraparo road in the hamlet of Río Seco, 4km east of Bohordal (this route is serviced by infre-quent por puestos). Both roads wind up and down over the mountain range and are spectacular. If you have your own wheels, go by one and return by the other.

From San Juan de las Galdonas, a dirt road (serviced by sporadic transportation) goes for about 20km to the village of San Juan de Unare (where there are no reliable accommodations). An hour's walk east by a rough road will bring you to Playa Cipara (no accommodations), one of the longest beaches in the area. Just a few kilometers east of here, the Parque Nacional Península de Paria begins and stretches 100km along the coast, right to the eastern tip of the peninsula. See the separate section on the park, later in this chapter. The nearest village in the park, Santa Isabel, is accessible by a path from Playa Cipara.

There are more attractions farther inland, south of the Bohordal–El Pilar road (which is part of the Carúpano–Güiria highway, used by all the buses and por puestos running between these towns). Be-ginning from Bohordal and heading west for 10km, you'll find the entrance to **Hato Río de Agua**, a buffalo ranch that boasts its own accommodations and food facilities. Another 8km down the road, you'll reach the hot springs of **Hacienda Aguasana**.

Proceeding west for another 5km, you'll pass through the town of Tunapuy. About 2.5km farther west, a paved side road branches off to the south and goes for 1km to the campamento of **Hacienda Vuelta Larga** (which offers cabañas and tours). The road runs another 7km to the hacienda proper. East of here stretches the wild **Parque Nacional Turuépano**.

The following sections feature brief in-formation about the major attractions high-lighted above, in the same sequence, complete with their facilities and services.

You can explore the region on your own, using the local por puesto services and posadas, but should you need a more com-fortable form of sightseeing, there are plenty of tours offered. Tours are organized mostly by the managers of hotels and posadas in Río Caribe (see that section, earlier) and in the region.

Playa Loero & Playa de Uva

At the end of the 6km access road, Playa Loero is a pleasant if not particularly mem-orable beach. It has no facilities, but you can string your hammock under the roof of the churuata. Just to the east is the minuscule Playa de Uva and the idyllic *Campamento Playa de Uva*, right above the beach. The place consists of four charmingly rustic colonial-style houses, with 12 rooms alto-gether (some overlooking the beach), plus a palm-thatched restaurant. If you need a lovely place in lovely surroundings, in total isolation from the outside world, this might be the choice. It costs about US$60 per person for the bed and three meals. Infor-mation and booking is via Posada Caribana in Río Caribe (☎ 612 42).

If this is not exactly within your budget, try the simple but enjoyable *Posada La Ruta del Cacao (☎ 014-994 01 15)*, in the village of Guayabero, before the turnoff to the beach. Bed and breakfast will cost US$20 per person, and the manager organizes walking and horse-riding trips.

Hacienda Bukare

Near the small village of Chacaracual, 14km from Río Caribe, Hacienda Bukare (☎ 65 20 03, 014 226 82 01, fax 65 20 04, bukare@cantv.net) is an old cacao hacienda still in operation, albeit on a small scale. Hourlong tours around the grounds are conducted for US$3 per person. The historic main house, recently extended and refurbished, now offers four rooms for visitors (US$35/50/70 single/double/triple with breakfast) and a stylish cozy restaurant. You can also stay in the cheaper cabaña across the road (US$30 double without breakfast). The owner, Billy Esser, is an experienced and knowledgeable guide, and he organizes a variety of tours around the region. Billy also rents out bicycles for US$15 a day.

Playa Medina

With a reputation as the most beautiful beach in the region, if not on the entire Venezuelan coast, this golden 400m-long beach is marvelously set in a deep bay and shaded with a forest of coconut palms. Amid the palms is a collection of seven stylish cabañas and a restaurant, all operated by Corpomedina. Packages including accommodations and three meals cost about US$75 per person; they should be purchased in Carúpano's Corpomedina office (see Carúpano, earlier).

The beach can be visited and used by anybody, not just the guests of Corpomedina. Camping is not allowed, but food is available: Every day the señoras from the surrounding hamlets come and serve basic meals and snacks (such as fried fish and empanadas) for day trippers.

Some budget accommodation options lie not far from the beach. The four-room *Posada El Milagro* (☎ 014-782 11 27), 2km up the road from the beach, offers rustic rooms with bath and fan for US$14 per head. Meals are available on request.

One kilometer farther up the road, in the middle of the village of Medina, is the 19-room *La Posada del Ángel* (☎ 65 20 05, 65 20 06), priced at US$14 per person in rooms with bath and fan. It has its own budget restaurant.

Playa Pui Puy

Pui Puy cannot compete with Medina for a beauty title, but nonetheless it's one of the best beaches around. The 1300m-long beach is also finely shaded by coconut groves and has a colony of 16 cabañas and a restaurant operated by Corpomedina. Accommodations here are cheaper than on Playa Medina, priced at around US$60/100 per two/four persons with breakfast. The restaurant serves budget meals for guests and nonguests alike.

Camping on this beach is permitted for US$1.50 per tent, and you pay US$0.30 for using the bath. It may be possible to rent a hammock from the attendants for US$5 or so per night. If you come with your own hammock, you can sling it under the roof for a nominal fee or even free of charge. Mosquitoes and small biting flies appear in the mornings and evenings, particularly during the rainy season, so the usual protections (insect repellent, mosquito net for the hammock, long-sleeved shirts and so on) are recommended.

If you prefer to sleep in a bed, and are not up to the beach cabañas, try the basic *Posada El Hijo de Paula*, in the village of Pui Puy, 2km back from the beach, which costs approximately US$24 double with shared facilities.

San Juan de las Galdonas

Tiny San Juan is an old port of about 1500 inhabitants. Because of its isolation, it has remained an authentic little village, living its own lethargic life. These days, however, it sees an increasing number of visitors, due partly to the largely upgraded access road, and partly to a variety of lodging and eating facilities that have developed over recent years. The beaches around the village are fine and can keep you for a while, but if you feel like getting farther away, the local tour operators can take you just about anywhere in the region and beyond.

The cheapest place to stay, the Spanish-owned and -managed *Posada Las Tres Carabelas* (☎ 016-894 09 14), sits spectacularly on top of a cliff high above the beach, providing wide views over the sea. Run by a friendly couple, Mónica and Lalo, the posada offers 13 rooms with bath and fan for US$15/26/36 single/double/triple. If you prefer a package including breakfast and dinner, the cost rises to US$24/41/59. The couple runs the restaurant, which features some Spanish dishes.

Lalo takes travelers on budget hiking trips up the mountains of the Parque Nacional Península de Paria, while boat trips are organized by Botuto (☎ 014-779 83 98), who lives a few houses away.

The Mediterranean-style *Habitat Paria* (☎ 014-779 79 55) is off the far eastern end of the village, on the Playa Barlovento. It's an amazing place, offering 12 rooms with bath and fan at US$36/48 double/triple (or US$36 per person with breakfast and dinner), a restaurant, rooftop bar and tours, though the tours are more expensive than those with Lalo and Botuto.

The towering, five-level *Hotel La Pionera* (☎ 76 10 03, 016-694 01 13, fax 76 10 02) stands right on the beach, looming over it as the Potala Palace over Lhasa. It would probably fit better on Miami or Copacabana beaches rather than in this tiny, mostly single-story community. Otherwise, it's perfectly OK, offering more luxuries than anything else around the region. Owned and managed by a Frenchman, Richard Hassid, the 32-room hotel has its own restaurant, bar, Jacuzzi and fair-sized swimming pool. It costs US$45/55 double/triple, or US$40 per person including breakfast and dinner. Richard offers a thick package of tours within the region and beyond, though they are not that cheap.

Hato Río de Agua

This buffalo ranch, which occupies a 200-hectare chunk of marshland to the south of the El Pilar-Bohordal road, has 300 water buffalo and plenty of birds all over the place. The ranch's usual occupation has been the production of buffalo meat and cheese, but it has also turned to tourism. For this purpose, a campamento was built 2km off the road, which consists of six cabañas and a thatched restaurant. A package that includes accommodations and three meals, plus excursions within and outside the ranch (watching buffalo, bathing in hot springs, observing local wildlife by jeep and canoe) costs US$65/95/130 for one/two/three persons a day. Packages are booked and sold by the Fundación Thomas Merle in Carúpano (see that section, earlier, for contact details).

Day visits (without accommodations and meals) are also possible between 7 am and 6 pm daily; they cost US$3. The visit includes a brief look around the ranch, a short boat trip, a soft drink and a piece of buffalo cheese.

Hacienda Aguasana

This hacienda features *aguas termales*, or hot springs. There are 17 ponds of various sizes and with water of different temperatures scattered around the place and linked to each other by paths. Some ponds are natural, while others are shaped by human hand, and there are also a few ponds with hot mud instead of water. Visitors are welcome to bathe in any number of pools and for however long they wish.

The springs are open 8:30 am to 6 pm daily, and an hour of bathing costs US$3 (mud baths are more expensive). Other services, such as acupressure and massage with mud in coconut oil, are available. Bring your bathing suit and a towel. The hacienda is operated by the Fundación Thomas Merle in Carúpano (see that section, earlier), which may provide further information.

Hacienda Vuelta Larga

Operated by Klaus Müller, Hacienda Vuelta Larga (☎ 690 52, 690 74) is a 10-sq-km ecological ranch. It also has water buffalo, but the principal attraction here is birds: About 230 bird species have been recorded in the area. The hacienda has a campamento, about 7km north of the ranch, which provides lodging and eating facilities and is a point of departure for tours. A package, which costs US$80 per person a day, includes a bed and three meals plus two 3½-hour excursions daily, one usually within the ranch and the other outside. Birding trips, which are their specialty, are often conducted by Klaus' son, Daniel, who is an experienced bird-watcher.

Parque Nacional Turuépano

The 726-sq-km Turuépano national park is a wild world of marshlands crisscrossed by a maze of natural water channels and populated by a wealth of wildlife, principally birds and fish. The habitat is roughly similar to that of the Delta del Orinoco, characterized by high temperature and humidity, and a significant tide that gives rise to a peculiar type of vegetation. There have been no major studies on the park, so many of its features remain little known.

The park lacks tourist facilities and is rarely visited. Only recently have some of the regional tour operators begun to penetrate this mysterious place. Talk to Richard of Hotel La Pionera and Billy of Hacienda Bukare, who are possibly the most experienced in the subject.

IRAPA

☎ 094 (☎ 0294 from Aug 18, 2001)

Irapa (population 12,000) is an old port on the Golfo de Paria that flourished on cacao cultivated in the region and shipped overseas. Today it's a sleepy place that still bears traces of glory, namely some large houses influenced by the Trinidadian architectural style. The town lies about 2.5km south of the Carúpano-Güiria road, so it doesn't see much through traffic or many visitors. This gives it an air of isolation and tranquility in which not much seems to be going on.

Places to Stay & Eat

The cheapest of a few options is the friendly *Posada Chuchú Domínguez (☎ 978 10)*, Calle Carabobo, which costs US$8 for a simple room with bath (double or triple). More comfortable is *Posada Tierra de Gracia (☎ 978 63)*, Calle Bermúdez, one block back from the beach. It has air-conditioned matrimoniales and doubles for US$22 and a

pleasant open-air restaurant. Finally, you can stay in the central *Hotel Maryoli (☎ 973 15)*, Calle Anzoátegui, which provides air-conditioned matrimoniales/doubles/triples for US$18/22/26. It too has a restaurant, and you can also eat in the nearby *La Posada de Hilario*, Calle Monagas.

Getting There & Away

Por puestos depart from the town's center to Carúpano (US$6, 1½ hours) and Güiria (US$1.75, 40 minutes).

GÜIRIA

☎ 094 (☎ 0294 from Aug 18, 2001)

Güiria (population 27,000) is the easternmost point on Venezuela's coast reachable by road, 275km from Cumaná. It's the largest town on the Península de Paria and an important fishing port. It may also soon become an important oil center, since rich oil deposits were discovered in the region.

The town itself is a rather ordinary place with no significant tourist attractions. On the other hand, the neighboring region, particularly the rugged Parque Nacional Península de Paria, stretching along the peninsula's northern coast, is attractive.

Güiria is a major transit point on the Venezuela-Trinidad route. Although the ferry no longer operates, a passenger-boat service has taken its place.

Information

Acosta Asociados (☎ 82 00 58, 82 01 69, grupoacosta@cantv.net), Calle Bolívar, are representatives of Windward Lines, which operated the ferry to Trinidad and now conducts the *Sea Prowler* boat (see the Boat section, later).

Corp Banca changes American Express traveler's checks, while the other banks shown on the map can give advances on both Visa and MasterCard. Librería Las Novedades, Calle Bolívar, may change US dollars (at a low rate) or at least know where to change them.

Places to Stay & Eat

At the budget end, the most popular place to stay is *Hotel Plaza (☎ 82 00 22)*, on the

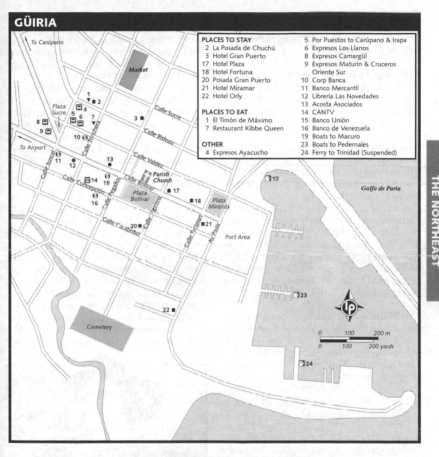

GÜIRIA

To Carúpano

Market

Plaza Sucre

To Airport

Parish Church

Plaza Bolívar

Plaza Miranda

Golfo de Paria

Port Area

Cemetery

PLACES TO STAY
2 La Posada de Chuchú
3 Hotel Gran Puerto
17 Hotel Plaza
18 Hotel Fortuna
20 Posada Gran Puerto
21 Hotel Miramar
22 Hotel Orly

PLACES TO EAT
1 El Timón de Máximo
7 Restaurant Kibbe Queen

OTHER
4 Expresos Ayacucho

5 Por Puestos to Carúpano & Irapa
6 Expresos Los Llanos
8 Expresos Camargüi
9 Expresos Maturín & Cruceros
   Oriente Sur
10 Corp Banca
11 Banco Mercantil
12 Librería Las Novedades
13 Acosta Asociados
14 CANTV
15 Banco Unión
16 Banco de Venezuela
19 Boats to Macuro
23 Boats to Pedernales
24 Ferry to Trinidad (Suspended)

0   100   200 m
0   100   200 yards

THE NORTHEAST

corner of Plaza Bolívar. It costs US$12 double with bath and fan (US$16 with air-conditioning) and has its own restaurant, which is one of the best inexpensive eateries in town. An extension to the hotel was being built in 2000, which may result in more comfort and higher rates.

For a similar price, you can stay in the primitive *Hotel Fortuna* (☎ 82 09 74), on Calle Bolívar 50m from the plaza, or in *Hotel Miramar* (☎ 82 07 32), Calle Turipi-ari, a little bit farther toward the port.

Posada Gran Puerto (☎ 810 85), Calle Vigirima, is a bit better and more expensive.

Its sibling, *Hotel Gran Puerto* (☎ 813 43), Calle Pegallos, provides slightly better standards in air-conditioned matrimoniales/doubles/triples for US$18/22/28. In much the same class is *Hotel Orly* (☎ 818 30), Avenida Paria, which is priced at US$24/30 matrimonial/double and has its own, reasonably priced restaurant.

A better value is *La Posada de Chuchú* (☎ 812 66), Calle Bideau, which costs about US$28 for an air-conditioned double or triple with bath and fridge. Its restaurant, *El Timón de Máximo*, is probably the best place to eat in town and is not too expensive.

You'll find more eating outlets around the central streets, including **Restaurant Kibbe Queen**, Calle Trinchera, serving inexpensive Middle Eastern food.

Getting There & Away

Air The airport is a 15-minute walk west of the town's center, but it hasn't been operating for years due to the snail's-pace construction of the control tower.

Bus There's no bus terminal. Several bus companies servicing Güiria have their offices close to each other around the triangular Plaza Sucre, where the Carúpano highway enters the town.

There are half a dozen buses a day to Caracas, departing early in the morning and late in the afternoon (US$22 deluxe, 12 hours). They all go via Cumaná (US$8, five hours) and Puerto La Cruz (US$11, 6½ hours). Por puestos run frequently to Carúpano (US$6, two hours) and less regularly to Irapa (US$1.75, 40 minutes).

Boat Windward Lines operated a ferry on the Güiria-Trinidad-St Vincent-Barbados-St Lucia route. The ferry still continues to shuttle between Trinidad and St Lucia, but the Güiria-Trinidad leg was suspended indefinitely in early 2000. The ferry used to come to Güiria from Port of Spain, Trinidad, every second Tuesday and depart back to Trinidad on Wednesday. On alternate weeks it went from Port of Spain to Pampatar, on Isla de Margarita, but this service has also been suspended. As of late 2000, Windward Lines planned to replace the suspended routes with the Puerto La Cruz–Isla de Margarita–Port of Spain weekly service operated by its new, larger ferry. Check with Acosta Asociados for news (see Information, earlier).

These days, the comfortable and air-conditioned *Sea Prowler* passenger boat runs between Güiria and Chaguaramas, near Port of Spain, Trinidad, which is supposed to arrive every Wednesday around noon and depart back to Chaguaramas at 2 pm. Fares are US$52 one-way, US$81 roundtrip.

Peñeros (open fishing boats) leave from the northern end of Güiria's port to Macuro every morning except Sunday; there's no fixed schedule, but they normally leave around 11 am. They charge US$3.50, and the trip takes 1½ to two hours.

Irregular fishing and cargo boats (a few per week) go to Pedernales, at the northernmost mouth of the Delta del Orinoco. The trip takes four to five hours and the fare is largely negotiable; you probably should not pay more than US$10 per person. From Pedernales, boats go south to Tucupita.

MACURO
☎ 094 (☎ 0294 from Aug 18, 2001)

Macuro is a remote fishing village (population 2000) near the eastern tip of the Península de Paria that has claim to more fame than its size suggests. It was reputedly somewhere here that Columbus landed in August 1498, though no records state the exact landing site. What is known is that this was the only place on South America's mainland where Columbus came ashore.

Although Macuro is a poor place, it has lots of character. While the village itself is not particularly inspiring, being in such a

Columbus: 'If I say it's India, it's India.'

historically significant place may be. If you decide to come, visit the little history museum and consider a hike to Uquire (see Walking Trails, in the following section). The friendly *Posada Beatriz* (☎ 816 99), Calle Mariño, provides budget shelter, and there are one or two other places to stay.

Macuro is accessible only by water. Boats from Güiria depart daily except Sunday, somewhere between 10 am and noon (US$3.50, 1½ to two hours). Boats depart Macuro for Güiria early in the morning, between 5 and 6 am.

So far, there are no access roads, but plans to link the village to Güiria over land are in the works. A part of this road, from Güiria to Río Salado, already exists and is being gradually extended eastward.

PARQUE NACIONAL PENÍNSULA DE PARIA

This 375-sq-km park stretches for 100km along the northern coast of the peninsula, right up to its eastern tip. It encompasses a coastal mountain range, which looms up almost right from the sea and reaches its maximum elevation point at Cerro Humo (1257m). The coast is graced with many coves, in which tiny fishing villages have nestled. Going from west to east, they include Santa Isabel, Mejillones, Uquire and Don Pedro.

The mountain is largely covered with forest, and the higher you go, the wetter it is. The upper reaches of the outcrop (roughly above 800m) form a typical cloud-forest habitat, with characteristic epiphytes, lianas, ferns and the like. This part is largely unexplored and intact, and there has been no comprehensive inventory of the wildlife compiled, though it's certainly rich and diverse.

On the other hand, the range's southern foothills, along the park's border areas, are increasingly affected by local farmers who clear the forest and claim the land for agriculture. An additional, new danger threatening the peninsula is the discovery of offshore oil, the exploitation of which may alter this remote bucolic corner of Venezuela completely.

Orientation

The park has no tourist facilities and is rarely visited by travelers. Access is not straightforward, despite the proximity of human settlements. The villages on the northern coast are best (or only) accessed by boat, the closest points of departure being Macuro and San Juan de Unare. However, boat trips are irregular and expensive. Access from the south is from the Carúpano-Güiria highway, but there are few gateways here leading into the park.

A few trails cross the park north to south, and these are the best way to get deeper into the wilderness. Ideally, you should be accompanied by a local guide, because the trails are not always easy to follow.

Walking Trails

One of the trails goes between the villages of Manacal and Santa Isabel, in the western end of the park. The rough road to Manacal branches off the Carúpano-Güiria highway 20km east of Yaguaraparo and winds uphill to the village at 750m. There are few vehicles along this road, so you may need to walk (three hours). There are no hotels in Manacal, but some sort of informal accommodations, eg, in the school, can usually be arranged. It's still easier if you have a hammock, as you'll be allowed to sling it under the roof in some homes.

The trail from Manacal winds to the hamlet of Roma and then uphill to the crest, at almost 1000m. It then goes down to Santa Isabel, on the coast. Guides can be found in Manacal, and the hike will take five to seven hours. The trail goes close to the park's highest peak, Cerro Humo; you can walk to the top from the crest along a side path.

Stuck to the hillside high above the bay and dotted with rocky islets, Santa Isabel is a charming old fishing village of 25 families. It shelters the rustic *Posada de Cucha*, which offers beds and meals (US$8 each) and a marvelous view over the rugged coast from its balcony. There's no electricity in the hamlet, but Cucha has a small generator.

There's no way out by road from the village, but a path goes westward to Boca del Río Cumaná (two to four hours), then continues along the shore to Playa Cipara (one hour) and onward by a dirt road to San Juan de Unare (one hour). The first part of the trail, from Santa Isabel to Río Cumaná, can be faint and confusing, so a guide is recommended (available in Santa Isabel). Otherwise, negotiate for a boat to San Juan de Unare, from where you can continue overland or directly to San Juan de las Galdonas. Alternatively, walk back the same way you came.

A variation of the previous route is the Las Melenas–Santa Isabel trail. The road to Las Melenas branches off 8km east of the turnoff to Manacal (5km west of the turnoff to Irapa) and goes to the village of Río Grande Arriba (4km). It then continues uphill as a jeep trail to Las Melenas (8km), where you're likely to find a guide. The trail that goes from here to Santa Isabel joins the trail from Manacal in Roma, forming one path farther on.

On the opposite, eastern end of the park is a path from Macuro to Uquire on the northern coast (a five- to six-hour walk). Guides for this hike can be found in Macuro. Uquire has a good beach, and you may be able to arrange a room or hammock for the night (or take your own hammock). You can either walk back or hunt for a boat to return you to Macuro around the peninsula's tip, but it's expensive.

If you don't plan on walking much, you can hire a boat in Macuro to take you to Uquire and other nearby places, such as Don Pedro and San Francisco, and then bring you back. The roundtrip fare won't be much more than the one-way trip. Tours along the coast are organized from San Juan de las Galdonas (see the Around Río Caribe section, earlier).

Monagas State

MATURÍN
☎ 091 (☎ 0291 from May 19, 2001)

Founded in 1760 as a Capuchin mission, Maturín has grown into a hub of the agro-industrial development of the eastern Llanos. Large deposits of oil found and ex-

ploited in the region have augmented the city's status. Maturín is also a busy regional transportation hub, connecting routes from the northeastern coast to the Delta del Orinoco and the Gran Sabana.

The town is the capital of Monagas state and is a modern industrial city of wide avenues, thrilling commerce and 320,000 people, but it has little to offer tourists. However, you are likely to pass through if traveling around the region, and may need to change buses here. Occasionally travelers end up staying the night in the city.

Information
Tourist Offices The Diturmo (Dirección de Turismo del Estado Monagas) tourist office (☎ 43 07 98) is in Hacienda Sarrapial, Elevado de Boquerón, a long way north from downtown on the Caripito road. To get there, take the Ruta 4 carrito from the center. The office is open 8 am to noon and 3 to 6 pm Monday to Thursday, 8 am to 3 pm Friday.

Money Most major banks have at least one branch in the center, mostly on Avenida Bolívar or just off it. Corp Banca is on the traffic circle on Avenida Bolívar at Calle 8.

Italcambio (☎ 60 15 70) is in Centro Comercial Petroriente, Nivel PB, Local No 23, Avenida Alirio Ugarte Pelayo.

Email & Internet Access Postnet (☎ 43 32 49), at Carrera 8A No 38, is right in the heart of the city, one block west of Plaza Ayacucho.

Organized Tours
One of the major operators offering tours along the Río Morichal Largo (see the following section) is El Centro del Mundo (☎/fax 41 35 01), Centro Comercial Fiorca, Planta Baja, Local 13, Avenida Libertador. All-inclusive full-day tours include round-trip transportation from Maturín, a boat trip and lunch, and they cost US$90/80 per person for four/six people. Discounts are available for larger parties. The company also runs tours in the Río Buja area, where it has its own campamento. A two-day tour

will cost about US$150 per person, with a minimum of four people.

The Boca de Tigre Tours (☎ 52 65 71), in the lobby of the Hotel Morichal Largo, also have their campamento in the Río Buja area; their two-day tours may be slightly cheaper.

Places to Stay

The budget hotel inside the bus terminal building has been closed. Now you'll probably need to go to the center for a cheap bed, even if you are in town just for the night.

A range of budget hotels around the central Plaza Ayacucho is easily accessible from the bus terminal by frequent city buses; you can also take a taxi (US$3). One of the cheapest here is *Hotel La Trinidad* (☎ 42 93 56, Carrera 8A No 37). It has matrimoniales with bath and fan for US$13 and matrimoniales/doubles/triples with bath and air-conditioning for US$16/24/28. The hotel is well managed and well kept, and it has two branch outlets just around the corner: at Calle 18 No 6 (☎ 41 06 26) and Calle 18 No 13 (☎ 42 24 76). Both are very similar to the original.

Hotel Europa (☎ 42 82 92), on Plaza Ayacucho, is marginally cheaper (US$12 matrimonial with fan, US$15 with air-conditioning), but it's basic. Next door is the slightly better *Hotel Ayacucho Plaza* (☎ 41 30 80), which costs US$18/20/24 for an aircon matrimonial/double/triple. Alternatively, try *Hotel París* (☎ 41 40 28, Avenida Bolívar No 133), priced at US$24/28/34, but avoid front rooms, which can be noisy from the heavy traffic. For much the same price, you can stay in the quieter *Hotel Iruña* (☎ 42 94 86, Carrera 7 No 64), two blocks east of Plaza Bolívar.

Hotel Colonial (☎ 42 11 75, fax 42 53 16, Avenida Bolívar No 58) is a more upmarket central option. It costs US$55/60 double/triple and has a choice of suites for marginally more. Should you need a decent option that's close to the buses, the high-rise *Hotel Monagas Internacional* (☎ 51 88 11, fax 51 87 27), on Avenida Libertador right next to the bus terminal, comes in handy and charges US$50/60 double/triple. One of the

largest and poshest places in the area is *Hotel Morichal Largo* (☎ 51 61 22, 51 54 22, fax 51 55 44), 3km out of town on the road to La Cruz (US$120/140).

Getting There & Away

Air The airport is 2km east of the city center; eastbound buses Nos 1 and 5 from Avenida Bolívar will let you off near the terminal. Aeropostal and Aserca operate flights to Caracas (US$72 to US$97 one-way), while Rutaca, LAI and Avior fly to Porlamar (US$42 one-way). Rutaca has three flights a week to Port of Spain, Trinidad (US$90 one-way, US$120 for a 30-day roundtrip).

Bus The bus terminal is on Avenida Libertador near Avenida Orinoco. It's about 2km southwest of the city center, and the two are linked by frequent urban transportation.

Several buses a day run to Caracas, mostly in the evening (US$14 ordinary, US$17 deluxe, 8½ hours). There are buses to Ciudad Guayana (US$5, 3½ hours), Tucupita (US$6, four hours) and Caripe (US$3, three hours); all these regional routes are also serviced by por puestos for nearly double the bus fare.

For the Cueva del Guácharo, take the Caripe bus or por puesto, get off at the turnoff to Cariaco at the village of El Guácharo (9km before Caripe) and walk or hitch to the cave (2.5km).

RÍO MORICHAL LARGO

The lower course of the Río Morichal Largo, southeast of Maturín near the Delta del Orinoco, has beautiful lush vegetation (including the *moriche* palm, after which it was named), rich wildlife and Warao Indian settlements. These features prompted the development of a tourist infrastructure, which includes a pleasure-boat service on a stretch of the river. The embarkation point is on the highway to Ciudad Guayana, about 90km southeast of Maturín, where excursion boats await to take tourists down the river.

The boat trips give a taste of the wildlife and the Indian communities typical of the

Delta del Orinoco without penetrating far into the delta proper. They are popular as an easier, shorter and cheaper alternative to the delta tours out of Tucupita. A number of tour companies in Maturín (see that section, earlier) and elsewhere offer tours along the river. You can also go on your own to the embarkation point and negotiate a trip directly with the boat operators, but be prepared for long waits (or pay for the empty seats) on weekdays.

The village of San José de Buja, 85km southeast of Maturín, is another springboard for a delta-like experience down along the Río Buja and is used by various tour companies.

CARIPE

☎ 092 (☎ 0292 from May 19, 2001)

Set in a verdant mountain valley midway between Maturín and the Caribbean coast, Caripe (population 12,000) is an easygoing town renowned for its agreeable climate, attractive environs, coffee and orange plantations, and proximity to Cueva del Guácharo, Venezuela's most magnificent cave.

The town is clean and appears quite prosperous, with fine villas and well-kept gardens. The place is touristy, and on weekends it's full of people escaping the steamy lowlands. It's also very full for Caripe's elaborate Easter celebrations. Caripe itself is little more than two parallel streets, on and around which most activities and services are centered.

Information

Local tour operators (see Organized Tours, later) may provide some information about the town and the region.

Banco Unión and Banco de Venezuela give advances on Visa and MasterCard. Corp Banca changes American Express traveler's checks.

For Internet access, head to Cyber Café Belén (☎ 519 37, 513 25), on Avenida Enrique Chaumer opposite Hotel Samán.

Things to See & Do

Save for a beautiful colonial high altar in the modern parish church, there's nothing really to see in town, but the rugged surroundings are amazing and pleasant for walks. The number-one attraction in the region is certainly the Cueva del Guácharo, 12km from the town (see that section, later).

El Mirador (1100m), to the north of the town, commands sweeping views over the Valle del Caripe. It's an hour's walk from town; you can also get there by road. Among the other sights are two beautiful waterfalls: the 30m-high **Salto La Payla**, near the Cueva del Guácharo, and the 80m-high **Salto El Chorrerón**, an hour's walk from the village of Sabana de Piedra. Farther away are the **Puertas de Miraflores**, a spectacular river canyon; and the **Mata de Mango**, which features 22 caves, including the impressive Cueva Grande and Cueva Clara.

Organized Tours

Oscar Gregori, manager of Hotel Samán (☎ 511 83, oscargh@cantv.net.ve), organizes some of the cheapest tours around the region, including Salto El Chorrerón (half-day trip, US$10 per person), Puertas de Miraflores (full day, US$30) and Mata de Mango (three days, about US$100). He also rents out bicycles (US$6 per day).

Enzo Cammareri of Bohemia Café (☎ 014-772 19 96, bohemiacafe@hotmail .com) has a similar program of tours for slightly more.

Alexander Rodríguez of Trekking Travelers Tours (☎ 014-790 12 31), Calle Guzmán Blanco, also offers various hiking and caving trips, though these may be a bit more expensive than those of the other operators.

Places to Stay & Eat

Caripe has become popular with tourists, and there's a score of places to stay and eat in and around the town. Hotel prices tend to rise on weekends.

La Posada, opposite the church, is essentially a restaurant, but it has some acceptable simple rooms at the back, which makes it perhaps the cheapest place to stay in town (US$8 double without bath). The restaurant itself is also cheap and OK, as is *Trattoria Da Antonio*, Calle Cabello, which serves some basic Italian fare. However, the best

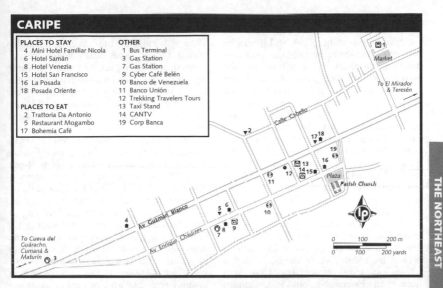

CARIPE

PLACES TO STAY	OTHER
4 Mini Hotel Familiar Nicola	1 Bus Terminal
6 Hotel Samán	3 Gas Station
8 Hotel Venezia	7 Gas Station
15 Hotel San Francisco	9 Cyber Café Belén
16 La Posada	10 Banco de Venezuela
18 Posada Oriente	11 Banco Unión
	12 Trekking Travelers Tours
PLACES TO EAT	13 Taxi Stand
2 Trattoria Da Antonio	14 CANTV
5 Restaurant Mogambo	19 Corp Banca
17 Bohemia Café	

pasta in town is in the charming *Bohemia Café*, which also has the best espresso.

Across the street from La Posada, *Hotel San Francisco* (☎ 510 18) has rooms with bath for US$12/13/14 single/double/triple. *Posada Oriente* (☎ 519 71), Avenida Guzmán Blanco, cost much the same. A little bit better is *Hotel Venezia* (☎ 510 35), with its rooms for US$13/15/18 single/double/triple. It has its own restaurant. You can also try *Restaurant Mogambo*, right across the road.

Hotel Samán (☎ 511 83, 519 50) has reasonable rooms costing US$14/24/30 single/double/triple, its own restaurant and laundry service. The manager offers special rates for backpackers – be sure to ask for one. Guests can use the hotel's Internet facility.

You can also try *Mini Hotel Familiar Nicola* (☎ 514 89), which is a family house renting a few rooms for about US$16/20 double/triple.

There are more places to stay and eat around the town, particularly along the road between Caripe and the village of El Guácharo. Some of them have cabañas, which may work out cheaply if you are in a large party.

Getting There & Away

The bus terminal is at the northeastern end of the town, behind the market. There's an evening bus that goes directly to Caracas via Cumanacoa (US$14, nine hours) or via Maturín (US$18, 11 hours). Buses to Maturín depart approximately every 1½ hours until about 5:30 pm (US$3, three hours), and there are also por puestos (US$4.50, two hours).

Two buses daily run to Cumaná, at 6 am and noon (US$6, 3½ hours); the more reliable private minibus goes at 6 am (US$7, three hours). They all pass the Cueva del Guácharo on the way. A roundtrip by taxi from Caripe to the Guácharo cave (including waiting as you visit the cave) shouldn't cost more than about US$16. Some tour operators and hotel managers may organize trips to the cave – ask around.

CUEVA DEL GUÁCHARO

The Guácharo cave, 12km from Caripe on the road toward the coast, is Venezuela's longest, largest and arguably most magnificent cave. It had been known to the local Chaima Indians long before Columbus crossed the Atlantic and was later explored by Europeans. The eminent scientist Alexander von Humboldt penetrated 472m into the cave in September 1799, and it was he who first classified its unusual namesake inhabitant, the *guácharo,* or oilbird (see the boxed text). In February 1835, Agustín Codazzi explored 1200m into the cave, much the same depth as tourists go today.

Even apart from the guácharo, the cave has an impressive variety of wildlife, such as fish, crabs, crickets, mice, rats, spiders, ants, centipedes and bats. It also shelters some amazing natural formations, including a maze of stalactites and stalagmites. Some speleologists consider this one of the most complete cave ecosystems found anywhere in the world.

The cave was declared Venezuela's first natural monument, Monumento Natural Cueva del Guácharo, in 1949. In order to protect the habitat where the birds feed, a 627-sq-km area around the cave was decreed the Parque Nacional El Guácharo in 1975.

All visits to the cave are by guided tours in groups of up to 10 people; tours depart from the reception building and take about 1½ hours. A 1200m portion of the total 10.2km length of the cave is normally visited, though occasionally water rises in August and/or September and can limit sightseeing to half a kilometer. Bags have to be left in the building by the ticket office, but cameras with flash are permitted in the cave beyond the area where the guácharos live.

The reception building has a small museum and cafeteria. These have the same opening hours as the cave, 8 am to 4 pm daily. The admission fee for foreigners is now a hefty US$10 (US$4 for Venezuelans) and there are no student discounts.

You can camp next to the building at the entrance to the cave, but only after closing time; it costs US$5 per tent and the bathroom is open 24 hours. If you camp here, be sure to watch the hundreds of birds pouring out of the cave mouth at around 6:30 pm and returning at about 4 am. You can also take a short trip to the waterfall of Salto La Payla, a 25-minute walk from the cave.

The Guácharo

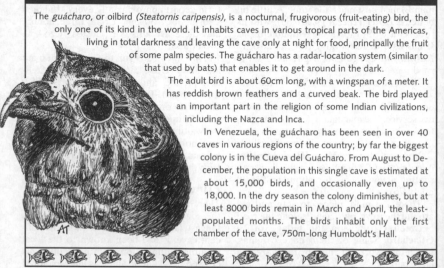

The *guácharo,* or oilbird *(Steatornis caripensis),* is a nocturnal, frugivorous (fruit-eating) bird, the only one of its kind in the world. It inhabits caves in various tropical parts of the Americas, living in total darkness and leaving the cave only at night for food, principally the fruit of some palm species. The guácharo has a radar-location system (similar to that used by bats) that enables it to get around in the dark.

The adult bird is about 60cm long, with a wingspan of a meter. It has reddish brown feathers and a curved beak. The bird played an important part in the religion of some Indian civilizations, including the Nazca and Inca.

In Venezuela, the guácharo has been seen in over 40 caves in various regions of the country; by far the biggest colony is in the Cueva del Guácharo. From August to December, the population in this single cave is estimated at about 15,000 birds, and occasionally even up to 18,000. In the dry season the colony diminishes, but at least 8000 birds remain in March and April, the least-populated months. The birds inhabit only the first chamber of the cave, 750m-long Humboldt's Hall.

Getting There & Away

The possible jumping-off points for the cave include Cumaná, Carúpano, Caripe and Maturín. See those sections, earlier, for transportation details.

Isla de Margarita

With an area of 1071 sq km, Isla de Margarita is Venezuela's largest island, 69km from east to west and 35km from north to south. It lies some 40km off the mainland, due north of Cumaná, and is composed of what were once two neighboring islands, now linked by a narrow, crescent-shaped sandbank, La Restinga.

Margarita's eastern section is the larger and more fertile area and contains 95% of the island's total population of 340,000. The thriving city of Porlamar and all the major towns are here, connected by a reasonably well developed array of roads. The western part, known as the Península de Macanao, is arid and sparsely populated, with 17,000 or so people living in a dozen villages located mostly along the coast. Both sections of the island are mountainous, their highest peaks approaching 1000m.

Generally speaking, people are drawn to the island for two reasons. The first is the beaches that skirt its coast. Thanks to them, Margarita has become the prime destination for Venezuelan holidaymakers seeking white sand and sunbathing with decent facilities at hand. The islands are also popular with international visitors, most brought here on charter flights. The tourism infrastructure is well developed, and Margarita has a collection of posh hotels comparable only to that in Caracas.

The island's other magnet is shopping. Margarita is a duty-free zone, so the prices of consumer goods are supposed to be lower than on the mainland, though in many cases there is no significant difference. Despite that, local shops are packed with bargain seekers.

However, Margarita is much more than just beaches and shopping, even though it's possible that few Venezuelans would think about coming here for any other reason. The island's geography makes for a colorful spectrum of habitats, including mangrove swamps, cloud forest and semidesert. No fewer than five nature reserves, among them two national parks, have been established on Margarita.

The island is also interesting culturally, featuring some important historic monuments that include two fine Spanish forts and just about the oldest church in the country. The island is sprinkled with small old towns, some of which have preserved much of their traditional culture and are vivid centers of craftwork. Finally, since Margarita has become a touristy place, it has a wide range of facilities, plenty of comfortable hotels, fine restaurants, experienced tour operators, good road infrastructure and reasonable transportation, all of which makes travel easy.

The island's climate is typical of the Caribbean: The average temperature ranges between 25°C and 28°C, and the heat of the day is agreeably mitigated in the evening by breezes. The rainy period lasts from November to January, with rain falling mostly during the night. Peak seasons for Venezuelan tourists include Christmas, Easter and the August holiday period. May, June and October are the quietest months.

Administratively, Isla de Margarita and the two small islands of Cubagua and Coche make up the state of Nueva Esparta. Although Porlamar is by far the largest urban center on the island, the small, sleepy town of La Asunción is the state capital.

Getting There & Away

Air Margarita's airport is in the southern part of the island, 20km southwest of Porlamar, and can be reached by por puestos (US$2). A taxi on this route will cost about US$10. The airport is identified in all the flight schedules as 'Porlamar.'

The island is a busy and lucrative market, so all the major national airlines fly here and fight for passengers. There are about 20 flights a day to Caracas with various carriers, including Aeropostal, Aserca and Laser. The normal one-way fare is US$74, but

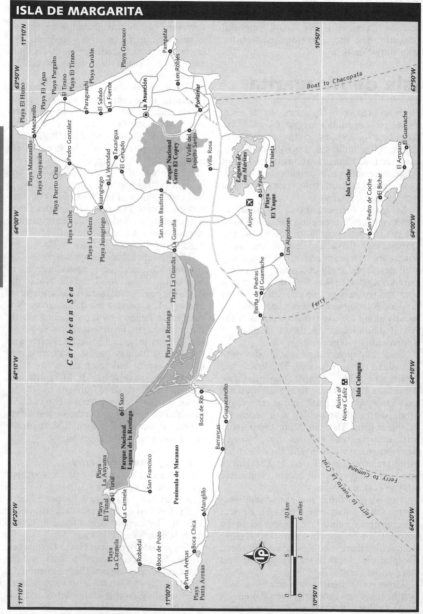

THE NORTHEAST

ISLA DE MARGARITA

Caribbean Sea

Playa El Humo
Playa El Agua
Playa Parguito
Playa El Tirano
Playa Cardón
Playa Guacuco
Pampatar
Los Robles
Porlamar

Boat to Chacopata

Macanao
Playa Guayacán
Playa Manzanillo
Manzanillo
Pedro González
Playa Puerto Cruz
Playa La Galera
Playa Caribe
Playa Juangriego
Juangriego

Paraguachi
El Tirano
El Salado
La Fuente
Paraguachí
La Asunción
La Vecindad
Tacarigua
El Cercado
San Juan Bautista
La Guardia
La Guardia

Parque Nacional
Cerro El Copey
El Valle del
Espíritu Santo
Villa Rosa

Laguna de
las Marites
El Yaque
Playa
El Yaque
La Isleta

Airport

Los Algodones
Punta de Piedras
El Guamache

Isla Coche
El Bichar
San Pedro de Coche
El Amparo
El Guamache

Ferry

Playa La Restinga

Playa La Guardia

El Saco
Boca de Río
Guayacancito
Barrancas

Ruins of
Nueva Cádiz
Isla Cubagua

Parque Nacional
Laguna de la Restinga

Playa
La Auyama
El Tunal
La Carmela

San Francisco

Península de Macanao

Mangillo
Boca Chica

Playa
El Tunal
Playa
La Carmela
Robledal
Boca de Pozo

Punta Areñas
Punta Arenas

Playa
Punta Arenas

Ferry to Puerto La Cruz

Ferry to Cumaná

10 km
6 miles

0   5
0   3

discounted fares, sometimes as cheap as US$46, are available. There are scheduled direct flights to Barcelona (US$35), Carúpano (US$33), Cumaná (US$33), Maturín (US$42) and Puerto Ordaz (US$73), and indirect flights to just about anywhere else in the country. Aereotuy and Aeroejecutivos fly to Los Roques (US$90). Aeropostal flies twice weekly to Port of Spain, Trinidad (US$120).

Boat Isla de Margarita has links with the mainland via Puerto La Cruz and Cumaná (both from Punta de Piedras, 29km west of Porlamar) and Chacopata (from Porlamar).

The Puerto La Cruz route is operated by the Conferry car/passenger ferries, with four departures a day (up to six in holiday peaks). Passengers fares are US$14/9 in 1st/2nd class. Cars go for US$26, jeeps for US$28 and motorcycles for US$7. The trip takes about 4½ hours. Conferry also operates its modern *Margarita Express* on this route, which takes up to 500 passengers and 150 cars and runs at up to 36 knots. It sails twice a day and takes just two hours, costing US$35 per passenger, US$38 per car and US$48 per jeep. Additionally, the route is operated by the passenger-only *Gran Cacique Express* hydrofoil, with two departures a day (US$18, two hours).

The Cumaná route is serviced by Conferry, with two departures a day. Fares are US$8 per passenger, US$16 per car, US$18 per jeep and US$5 per motorcycle, and the trip takes 3½ hours. The route is also operated by *Gran Cacique II*, which shuttles two times a day (US$15, two hours).

In the off season, there may be fewer departures than listed. Tickets for the Conferry ferries can be bought at the office in Porlamar (☎ 61 92 35, 61 67 80) or at the ferry terminal in Punta de Piedras (☎ 983 40, 984 40). Tickets for Gran Cacique are available in the Porlamar office (☎ 64 17 62, 64 29 45) and in Punta de Piedras (☎ 983 39, 984 39). Frequent small buses (US$0.80) run between Punta de Piedras and Porlamar; taxis charge US$10.

The Chacopata route is operated by small passenger-only boats from the breakwater near the old lighthouse in central Porlamar (US$6, one to 1½ hours). The boats depart every two hours or so. There's frequent onward por puesto transportation from Chacopata to Cariaco (US$2.50, 45 minutes). See the Península de Araya section, earlier in this chapter, for further details.

There's also a ferry service between Punta de Piedras and Isla de Coche, operated once a day by Conferry (US$1.25, one hour).

International The ferry service between Pampatar and Trinidad, operated by Windward Lines, was suspended in 2000. The ferry arrived at Pampatar from Trinidad every other Wednesday morning and departed back to Trinidad on the afternoon of the same day. It then continued to St Vincent, Barbados and St Lucia. The ferry may be back on Margarita by the time you read this. See the Güiria section, earlier in this chapter, for further details.

Getting Around

Porlamar is the island's transportation hub, from where frequent small buses (locally called *micros* or *busetas)* service towns and beaches around the main, eastern part of the island. Public transportation on the Península de Macanao is poor.

Renting a car may be worthwhile, especially if there are others in your party to share the cost. There are at least a dozen car rental companies in the oval building opposite the airport's international terminal, and most have another office in Porlamar. Rental rates are lower than those on the mainland: You can get a small car for about US$40 per day. Scooters and bicycles can be hired at several places in Porlamar.

If you prefer a more comfortable form of sightseeing, plenty of travel agencies/tour operators will happily show you around the island and beyond. Most companies are in Porlamar, but there are also some in Juangriego and elsewhere. They offer general-interest tours around the island, as well as more specific trips (eg, Parque Nacional Laguna de La Restinga) and activity tours (horse riding, fishing, snorkeling, scuba

THE NORTHEAST

diving). The Archipiélago Los Fraíles, northeast of Margarita, has become a popular destination for snorkeling (see the Juangriego section, later).

PORLAMAR
☎ 095 (☎ 0295 from Mar 24, 2001)

With a population of 210,000, Porlamar is the largest center on the island and is likely to be your first stop when coming from the mainland. It's a bustling city replete with shopping centers, hotels and restaurants. Tree-shaded Plaza Bolívar is Porlamar's historic center, but the city is expanding eastward, with new suburbs and tourist facilities being built all the way along the coast up to as far as Pampatar. Porlamar offers little sightseeing other than wandering around trendy shops packed with imported goods.

Information
Tourist Offices The government-run Corporación de Turismo (☎ 62 23 22, 62 30 98) is based at the Centro Artesanal Gilberto Menchini, Avenida Jóvito Villalba, Los Robles, midway between Porlamar and Pampatar. The office is open 9 am to noon and 2 to 5 pm weekdays.

The private corporation Cámara de Turismo (☎ 63 56 44), on Avenida Santiago Mariño in Porlamar, is open 8 am to noon and 2 to 5:30 pm weekdays.

The Fondo de Promoción Turística Pro Margarita (☎ 61 01 68, 61 22 91) is in Edificio Universidad Santa María, Avenida 4 de Mayo, midway between central Porlamar and Los Robles.

Pick up a copy of *Margarita La Guía,* a useful quarterly guide published in Spanish, English and German. Also get hold of *Mira!,* an English-language monthly paper that features practical details and background information about the island and beyond. Both are published irregularly, with shorter or longer breaks, but when they do appear they are distributed free through some travel agencies, upmarket hotels and other tourist establishments.

Money Banks that handle some foreign-currency transactions are marked on the

map. There are also casas de cambio, mostly in the new center around Avenida Santiago Mariño, including Casa de Cambio For You (☎ 61 44 42) and Cambios Cussco (☎ 61 33 79). Italcambio (☎ 65 93 92) is in Ciudad Comercial Jumbo, Nivel Ciudad. They all change cash and traveler's checks, and some don't charge a commission on checks. There are also a few casas de cambio in the airport terminal. Some stores will exchange cash dollars and/or will accept them for payment. Credit cards are widely accepted in shops, upmarket hotels and restaurants.

Email & Internet Access Porlamar has a number of Internet facilities. Most are open until 8 to 10 pm Monday to Saturday and often Sunday afternoon, and will cost US$4 to US$5 an hour. Central locations include:

Cabinas Telefónicas Privadas (CTP)
    (☎ 63 80 63) Calle Malavé
Cyber Café Jumbo
    Ciudad Comercial Jumbo, Nivel Fiesta
Cyber Room Internet & Art
    (☎ 64 47 07) Calle Fermín
Mega-Tech
    (☎ 64 33 94) Calle Tubores

Outside the center, you may want to use FL Video (☎ 64 25 81), Avenida 4 de Mayo near the Pro Margarita tourist office, which is one of the cheapest and is open till 11 pm, longer than most others.

Laundry There are several places for laundry, including Lavandería Edikö's and Lavandería Wash Quick, both in the new center, and Lavandería La Burbuja, at two locations in the old quarter.

Medical Services The Hospital Central Dr Luis Ortega (☎ 61 11 01) is on Avenida 4 de Mayo in Porlamar's center. Other major medical facilities include Clínica La Fe (☎ 62 44 55), Avenida Jóvito Villalba in Los Robles, and Centro Médico Nueva Esparta (☎ 42 00 11), in La Asunción.

Things to See
One of the few real tourist sights is the **Museo de Arte Contemporáneo Francisco**

PORLAMAR

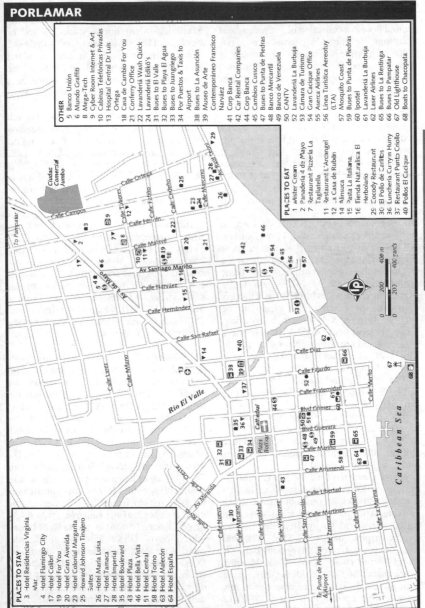

PLACES TO STAY
3 Hotel Residencias Virginia
    Mar
4 Hotel Flamingo City
17 Hotel Colibrí
19 Hotel For You
20 Hotel Gran Avenida
23 Hotel Colonial Margarita
25 Howard Johnson Tinajero
    Suites
26 Hotel María Luisa
27 Hotel Tamaca
28 Hotel Imperial
35 Hotel Plaza
43 Hotel Boulevard
46 Hotel Bella Vista
51 Hotel Central
58 Hotel Torino
63 Hotel Malecón
64 Hotel España

PLACES TO EAT
1 Mister Cream
2 Panadería 4 de Mayo
7 Restaurant Pizzeria La
    Tagliatella
11 Restaurant L'Arcangel
12 La Casa de Rubén
14 Pasta La Italiana
15 Alinsuca
16 Tienda Naturalista El
    Herbolario
29 Cocody Restaurant
30 El Pollo de Carlitos
36 Luncheria Curryn Hurry
37 Restaurant Punto Criollo
40 Pollos El Cacique

OTHER
5 Banco Unión
6 Mundo Graffiti
8 Mega-Tech
9 Cyber Room Internet & Art
10 Cabinas Telefónicas Privadas
13 Hospital Central Dr Luis
    Ortega
18 Casa de Cambio For You
21 Conferry Office
22 Lavandería Wash Quick
24 Lavandería Ediko's
31 Buses to El Valle
32 Buses to Playa El Agua
33 Buses to Juangriego
34 Por Puestos & Taxis to
    Airport
38 Buses to La Asunción
39 Museo de Arte
    Contemporáneo Francisco
    Narváez
41 Corp Banca
42 Car Rental Companies
44 Corp Banca
45 Cambios Cussco
47 Buses to Punta de Piedras
48 Banco Mercantil
49 Banco de Venezuela
50 CANTV
52 Lavandería La Burbuja
53 Cámara de Turismo
54 Gran Cacique Office
55 Aserca Airlines
56 Línea Turística Aereotuy
    (LTA)
57 Mosquito Coast
59 Buses to Punta de Piedras
60 Ipostel
61 Lavandería La Burbuja
62 Laser Airlines
65 Buses to La Restinga
66 Buses to Pampatar
67 Old Lighthouse
68 Boats to Chacopata

Narváez, in a large, modern building on the corner of Calles Igualdad and Díaz. On the ground floor is a collection of sculptures and paintings by this Margarita-born artist (1905–82), while the salons on the upper floor are used for temporary exhibitions. The museum is open 8:30 am to 3:30 pm Tuesday to Friday, 10 am to 4 pm weekends.

Places to Stay

Porlamar has loads of hotels for every budget. As a general rule, prices and standards rise from west to east. Accordingly, if you're after a budget shelter, the best choice is in the area of Plaza Bolívar, but if fancy lodging is what you need, look around Avenida Santiago Mariño and farther east.

Budget A score of budget hotels lies within the few blocks southwest of Plaza Bolívar. All the hotels listed in this section have private facilities, unless indicated otherwise.

One of the cheapest options is the basic *Hotel España* (☎ 61 24 79), on Calle Mariño near the waterfront. It has a variety of rooms, some better than others, so be sure to inspect a few before deciding. Expect to pay about US$11/13 double/triple with bath and fan, a dollar less without bath. The hotel has its own restaurant, which is as basic and cheap as the hotel itself.

The nearby *Hotel Malecón* (☎ 64 25 79), Calle La Marina, charges US$12 for simple but acceptable doubles with fan (US$15 with air-conditioning). Choose a room overlooking the sea. *Hotel Plaza* (☎ 63 03 95), on Calle Velázquez a block west of Plaza Bolívar, offers similar standards and costs much the same as the Malecón.

Hotel Central (☎ 61 47 57) is another budget option with air-conditioning. It's conveniently located on Boulevard Gómez and has a large balcony from which to watch the world go by. It offers air-con doubles/triples/quads for US$16/20/26 and has a budget restaurant. Marginally better is *Hotel Torino* (☎ 61 71 86), Calle Mariño, which costs US$20/22/25 double/triple/quad with air conditioning and also has a few small cheap rooms with fan (US$10/12 single/matrimonial).

Budget accommodations in Porlamar's new center, around Avenida Santiago Mariño, do exist, but they are few and far between. They're not as cheap as their old-town counterparts, but it may be worth spending a few extra dollars for nicer surroundings; finer restaurants; more bars, cybercafés and discos; and reputedly better security, particularly at night.

Hotel Tamaca (☎ 61 16 02), on Avenida Raúl Leoni at Calle Campos, is the most popular gringo haunt in the area – and deservedly so. Clean rooms cost US$13/17/22 single/double/triple with fan, US$16/20/24 with air-conditioning, and the hotel has its own, reasonably priced restaurant and a bar with a good atmosphere.

In case Tamaca is full, you'll find the undistinguished but acceptable *Hotel Colonial Margarita* (☎ 63 98 23) on Calle Fermín, just a two-minute walk away, which has a choice of rooms with fan and air-conditioning and costs much the same as the Tamaca. Or walk a few blocks up the same street to *Hotel Residencias Virginia Mar* (☎ 61 23 73), which also offers rooms with both fan and air-conditioning for prices similar to the Colonial's.

Mid-Range Several hotels in this price bracket lie in the historic center, but not many of them are a good value. *Hotel Boulevard* (☎ 61 05 22, 61 07 32), Calle Marcano, has doubles/triples for US$32/36 and is one of the establishments you might consider.

There are also some affordable hotels farther east, around Avenida Santiago Mariño. One of the cheaper options in the area is the small *Hotel Gran Avenida* (☎ 61 74 57), Calle Cedeño, but it's nothing particularly special. It has air-conditioned doubles/triples for US$32/40. Better and even cheaper is *Hotel Imperial* (☎ 61 64 20, 61 48 23, fax 61 50 56), Avenida Raúl Leoni, which costs US$30/35/40 double/triple/quad. Ask for a room in one of the upper floors with a view over the sea. Alternatively, try *Hotel Flamingo City* (☎ 64 55 64, 64 45 57), strategically placed on Avenida 4 de Mayo at Avenida Santiago Mariño. All its rooms have one double and one single bed and quiet air-conditioning, and cost US$30/35/40 single/double/triple.

Top End Porlamar has plenty of hotels in this category. Virtually all of them are in the eastern part of the city, from Avenida Santiago Mariño eastward up to Pampatar.

There are some reasonable upmarket hotels on the trendy Avenida Santiago Mariño itself, including the good and pleasant *Hotel Colibrí* (☎ 61 63 46, 61 56 45, fax 63 94 98), priced at US$42/56/70 single/double/triple with breakfast. It has a small pool on the roof. One block up the street is *Hotel For You* (☎ 63 86 35, 63 97 93, fax 61 87 08), formerly Stauffer Hotel, which offers and costs roughly the same as the Colibrí.

The three-star *Hotel María Luisa* (☎/fax 61 05 64, 63 79 40), Avenida Raúl Leoni, is a good value at US$45/55/60 single/double/triple. The large high-rise four-star *Hotel Bella Vista* (☎ 61 72 22, fax 61 25 57) is one of the poshest options in the area. It offers most facilities you'd wish for, including a swimming pool, five restaurants and a nightclub, for about US$100 double with breakfast.

Perhaps not as swanky but nonetheless comfortable is *Howard Johnson Tinajero Suites* (☎ 63 83 80, fax 63 91 63), Calle Campos. Each of its 66 suites is equipped with a kitchenette, fridge, microwave and coffeemaker, plus all the pots and pans. They cost US$60/75/90 for two/three/four persons with breakfast (about US$25 more per suite in the high season, July 15 to September 15 and December 15 to January 15).

The five-star establishments, including *Hotel Marina Bay* (☎ 62 52 11, fax 62 41 10) and *Margarita Hilton* (☎ 62 33 33, fax 62 08 10), are farther east.

Places to Eat

There's a wide choice of budget eateries across the city, mostly in the old town but also in the newer districts to the east. *Pasta La Italiana*, Calle Cedeño, offers some of the cheapest pasta in town until about 8 pm (closed Sunday). Two blocks west, *Alinsuca* is another low-budget pasta outfit that also has pizzas; you can carry out or eat in (open noon to 4 pm Monday to Saturday).

The rustic *El Pollo de Carlitos* does chicken and does it very well. Half a chicken with *hallaca* (chopped meat in maize dough, steamed in banana leaves) and salad costs US$3 – an excellent value. The place is open daily until 1 am. *Pollos El Cacique*, Calle Igualdad, is another good chicken affair, but is a bit more expensive. Two blocks west along the same street, *Restaurant Punto Criollo* is deservedly popular with locals and visitors for its solid Venezuelan food and reasonable prices.

Vegetarians will find budget meals and snacks at *Tienda Naturalista El Herbolario*, Calle Cedeño, which is one of the very few vegetarian eateries in town (closed Sunday). The minute *Lunchería Curry n Hurry*, Calle Gómez, also has some cheap vegetarian dishes on its small menu.

Most of the finer restaurants are in the eastern sector of the city, east of Avenida Santiago Mariño. The cozy *Restaurant Pizzería La Tagliatella* has beautiful Italian food, and you'll easily find several other Italian restaurants within a few blocks around. In the same area, the appropriately craft-decorated *La Casa de Rubén*, Calle Campos, cooks typical local food at reasonable prices.

Restaurant L'Arcangel, Calle Malavé, offers mouthwatering French fare, prepared by an experienced French chef, Jean Claude. Alternatively, check *Cocody Restaurant*, Avenida Raúl Leoni, which also serves fine French food. Just one block away is *Hotel Tamaca*, with its charming open-air garden restaurant serving tasty food at good prices.

The smart new *Mister Cream* café, Avenida 4 de Mayo, opens at 7:30 am and serves good breakfasts, pasteles and sandwiches, as well as some of the best ice cream in town. Some good panaderías lie on Avenida 4 de Mayo, including the invariably popular *Panadería 4 de Mayo*, on the corner of Calle Fermín.

Entertainment

Discotheques appear and disappear frequently, so you may find a picture quite different from the one painted here. One of the few discos that had kept going for years with invariable popularity is the waterfront *Mosquito Coast*, near the Hotel Bella Vista, but it too underwent some rough patches recently.

Among the most popular discos at the time of writing were *Dady's Latino*, in the Centro Comercial Jumbo, and *Señor Frog's*, in the Centro Comercial Costa Azul, on Avenida Bolívar. Also worth checking is *Woody's Pub*, Avenida 4 de Mayo, 150m beyond Dady's. It's an enjoyable wood-decked pub with a bar in the middle and a dance floor around.

Shopping

Oh yes, ask Venezuelans and they'll all agree that Porlamar is a fantastic place for shopping. Some foreign visitors may be a little bit disappointed, however, as there are actually no great bargains, unless paying just a few dollars less for your blue jeans than on the mainland is enough to keep you happy. And, as always, keep in mind that a cheap price often means mediocre quality.

The old center has some of the cheapest shops. Many of these nestle in two central pedestrian malls, Boulevard Guevara and Boulevard Gómez, south of Plaza Bolívar, and trade mostly in clothing, footwear, electrical goods, watches etc.

The most elegant and expensive shopping areas are on and around Avenidas Santiago Mariño and 4 de Mayo. Here you'll find jewelry, imported spirits, fashionable clothing, audio and video equipment, computers etc. For clothes, check Mundo Graffiti, on the corner of Avenidas Santiago Mariño and 4 de Mayo, which is one of the cheaper retailers around. And, of course, don't miss combing the huge, sparkling six-level Ciudad Comercial Jumbo, on Avenida 4 de Mayo at Calle Campos.

In the afternoon, craft and souvenir stalls mushroom along Avenida Santiago Mariño, selling their wares until 9 or 10 pm.

Getting There & Away

There's frequent transportation to most of the island, including Pampatar, La Asunción and Juangriego, operated by small buses. They leave from different points in the city center; the departure points for some of the main tourist destinations are indicated on the map.

PAMPATAR

☎ 095 (☎ 0295 from Mar 24, 2001)

Pampatar (population 15,000) is 10km northeast of Porlamar, but the two urban centers are gradually merging into a single conurbation. Founded in the 1530s, Pampatar was one of the earliest settlements on Margarita, and within 50 years it grew into the largest shipping center in what is now Venezuela. It still shelters some colonial buildings and a nostalgic hint of bygone days, but it's increasingly circled by new constructions.

Things to See

Pampatar's fort, the **Castillo de San Carlos Borromeo**, was built from 1662 to 1684 on the site of the previous stronghold (which was destroyed by pirates). It's the best-preserved and -restored construction of its type on the island. A classic example of Spanish military architecture, it's similar to other forts built around the colony. In the rooms surrounding the central courtyard is a small exhibition of period weapons, paintings and coats of arms. The fort is right in the center of town, on the waterfront, and can be visited 9 am to noon and 2 to 5 pm daily except Monday.

Opposite the fort is the **parish church**, a sober whitewashed construction dating from the mid-18th century. Go inside to see the crucifix, Cristo del Buen Viaje, over the high altar. Legend has it that the ship that carried the crucifix from Spain to Santo Domingo called en route at Pampatar, but despite repeated efforts it couldn't depart until the Christ image had been unloaded. It has remained in Pampatar since and is much venerated by local fisherfolk.

A hundred meters east of the church is a neoclassical building from 1864, formerly the **Casa de la Aduana**. It's now home to Fondene, the state's development foundation, which holds temporary exhibitions on the ground floor.

The beach, which extends for a kilometer east of the fort, has some old-world charm, with rustic boats anchored in the bay and on the shore, and fishers repairing nets on the beach. The large community of pelicans adds color to this picture-postcard scene. The beach is more suitable for watching fishing activities than for sunbathing or swimming, owing to water pollution. The cape at the far eastern end of the bay is topped by another fort, the ruined **Fortín de la Caranta**, which provides better views than the castillo.

Language Courses

Pampatar's Centro de Lingüística Aplicada (CELA; ☎/fax 62 81 98), Calle Coromoto, Quinta Cela, Urbanización Playa El Ángel, offers several intensive Spanish language courses of different levels, with optional accommodations and meals in family homes. The school complements the courses with excursions and cultural activities. Check their Web site, www.cela-ve.com, for details.

Places to Stay & Eat

Few travelers stay in Pampatar, but there is a choice of places for those who do. Many of them are the so-called *apart-hoteles,* offering studio apartments that include a fully equipped kitchenette.

Some of the cheapest places are on Calle Almirante Brion, one block back from the beach. The simplest here is **Hotel Apache** (☎ 62 40 30), which has doubles with bath and fan for US$18. The nearby *Aparthotel Don Juan* (☎ 62 36 09) has doubles for US$18 and suites for up to four people for US$25; all have air-conditioning, private bath, fridge and gas stove. Across the street, *Posada La Bufonera* (☎ 62 84 18, 62 99 77) is the most attractive of the lot, but also the most expensive: Its fully equipped, cozy suites cost US$35/40 for two/three people.

More places to stay are on Calle El Cristo, a five-minute walk eastward, including *Los Chalets de la Caranta* (☎ 62 12 14). A bit farther east is the three-star *Hotel Flamingo Beach* (☎ 62 45 94), which costs US$35 per person with breakfast.

When you're hungry, head for the uninterrupted line of palm-thatched shack restaurants on the beach, each with its very powerful sound system and good supply of cold beer. Other than beer, fried fish is the principal fare.

Getting There & Away

Buses between Porlamar and Pampatar make the trip every five to 10 minutes (US$0.25, 20 minutes).

EL VALLE DEL ESPÍRITU SANTO
☎ 095 (☎ 0295 from Mar 24, 2001)
Commonly called just 'El Valle,' this is Margarita's spiritual capital, home to the miraculous Virgen del Valle and a population of 10,000. It's actually the major religious sanctuary for all of eastern Venezuela, drawing pilgrims from the region and beyond year-round – particularly on September 8, the Virgin's day. Perhaps equally remarkably, El Valle is the first Marian religious sanctuary in the Americas. According to local history, the image of the Virgin was brought here around 1510.

Things to See

The characteristic pink-and-white mock-Gothic **Basílica de Nuestra Señora del Valle**, on the central plaza, was built in form 1894 to 1906 and is the current home to the Virgin. Her statue is in the niche high above the high altar. You can buy a plaster copy of the Virgin in any size from religious stalls next to the church, which are particularly numerous and active on Sundays and major holy days.

The **Museo Diocesano**, right behind the church, features objects related to the Virgin, as well as votive offerings presented by the faithful. It's open 9 am to noon and 2 to 5 pm Tuesday to Saturday, 9 am to 1 pm Sunday.

The **Casa Museo Santiago Mariño**, diagonally opposite the church, is the house where this hero of the War of Independence, often referred to as 'El Libertador de Oriente' was born in 1788. The sizable country mansion has been painstakingly reconstructed and fitted with vintage furniture, portraits of the independence leaders and period memorabilia, and it is open to the public 9 am to 5 pm weekdays, 9 am to 2 pm weekends. The building is meticulously kept, as are the gardens around.

Getting There & Away
Buses between Porlamar and El Valle shuttle frequently (US$0.25, 15 minutes).

LA ASUNCIÓN
☎ 095 (☎ 0295 from Mar 24, 2001)

La Asunción (population 18,000), set in a fertile valley in the island interior, is the capital of Nueva Esparta state, even though it's far smaller than Porlamar. It's distinguished for its tranquility and verdant environs. There's little duty-free commerce here, and hotels and restaurants are scarce.

Things to See
Built in the second half of the 16th century, the **Catedral** on the tree-shaded Plaza Bolívar is one of the oldest surviving colonial churches in the country, possibly the second after Coro's cathedral. It has an unusual bell tower at the back corner, a delicate Renaissance portal on the facade and two more doorways on the side walls.

On the northern side of the plaza is the **Museo Nueva Cádiz**, named after the first Spanish town in South America, which was established around 1500 (but officially founded in 1519) on Isla Cubagua, south of Margarita. An earthquake in 1541 completely destroyed the town. It wasn't until an excavation in 1950 that the town's foundations were uncovered, along with some architectural details and various period objects. The museum displays a small collection of exhibits related to the region's history. It's open 9 am to 4 pm daily, except Monday.

On the western side of the plaza is the modern **Casa de la Cultura**, which stages changing exhibitions.

Just outside town, a 10-minute walk southward up the hill, is the **Castillo de Santa Rosa**, one of seven forts built on the island to protect it from pirate attacks. It provides a good view over the town and the valley, and has some old armor on display. The opening hours are the same as the museum's.

Places to Stay & Eat
The **Hotel de la Asunción** (☎ 42 06 66), Calle Unión, two blocks east of Plaza Bolívar, is one of the very few places to stay in town. It costs US$16/22 for a simple airconditioned matrimonial/double with bath, and has its own restaurant.

Getting There & Away
Buses from Porlamar will let you off on the tree-shaded Plaza Bolívar of La Asunción (US$0.40, 20 minutes). After having a look around, you can return to Porlamar or continue on to Juangriego (US$0.40, 20 minutes) – frequent transportation runs to both these destinations. If you opt for the latter, you can stop in Santa Ana to see its church, which is similar to the La Asunción cathedral but is two centuries younger. In the nearby village of El Cercado, typical Venezuelan pottery is made.

JUANGRIEGO
☎ 095 (☎ 0295 from Mar 24, 2001)

Set on the edge of a fine bay in the northern part of Margarita, Juangriego is a relaxing backwater of 18,000 people. It has become popular with tourists, even though there's really not much to see or do here except for watching the marvelous sunsets.

The town is swiftly spreading inland from the waterfront, but the place to hang around is the beach along the bay, with rustic fishing boats, visiting yachts and pelicans. Far away on the horizon, the peaks of Macanao are visible, and are spectacular when the sun sets behind them.

The **Fortín de la Galera**, the fort crowning the hill just north of town, is today nothing more than stone walls with a terrace and a refreshment stand on the top. At sunset it is packed with tourists who come for the view, though you can have almost as good a vista right from the beach.

The town is a convenient springboard for **Los Frailes**, a small archipelago of coral islands northeast of Margarita. The tours organized by two Norwegian guys, Bent and Bjørn, are the best deal you can find around – call them at ☎ 014-995 42 61 or ask for them at Hotel Nuevo Juangriego or

Hotel Patrick's (see Places to Stay & Eat, next). The full-day trip includes snorkeling (equipment provided) and lengthy stops on three different beaches, plus barbecue and drinks; it costs US$45.

Places to Stay & Eat

Juangriego is now increasingly catering to tourism and already has a dozen hotels and even more restaurants. In the middle of the beach is the simple Dutch-operated *Hotel Nuevo Juangriego* (☎ 53 24 09). Doubles with bath and fan on the waterfront side go for US$25, while those without sea views are US$18. If you choose a room facing the bay, you'll enjoy a postcard view of the sunset from your window.

About 200m north along the beach, the Portuguese-owned four-room *Posada Los Tucanes* (☎ 53 17 16), Calle El Fuerte, doesn't provide sea views, but otherwise is a pleasant, friendly and cheap place that costs US$12 to US$20 (depending on the room) for an air-conditioned matrimonial with bath and cable TV. Next door, the French-run *Hotel Patrick's* (☎ 53 62 18) offers nine good rooms, which each cost US$18 double with bath and fan (US$25 if you want air-conditioning).

All the hotels listed above have their own restaurants (Patrick's, predictably, offers French fare), and there are more places to eat. Particularly pleasant are several beach restaurants, including *El Búho*, *El Fortín*, *El Viejo Muelle*, and *La Mamma*. They all are romantic places for a meal or just a beer, and all provide perfect settings for the sunset view.

Just back from the beach, in the Centro Comercial Juangriego, on Calle La Marina, are two uninspiring but cheap hotels: *Hotel La Coral* (☎ 53 24 63) and *Hotel Gran Sol* (☎ 53 32 16), both priced at US$15/18 double/triple. Several other accommodation and food options are set farther back from the beach.

Getting There & Away

Frequent buses run between Porlamar and Juangriego (US$0.80, 40 minutes); all pass via La Asunción.

In order to draw tourists into Juangriego, the local government put into operation free transportation between the ferry docks in Punta de Piedras and Juangriego. A small white bus marked 'Asociación Civil Plan Desarrollo Pro Juangriego,' waits for incoming Conferry ferries and whisks visitors at no charge directly to Juangriego.

PARQUE NACIONAL LAGUNA DE LA RESTINGA

Laguna de la Restinga is one of two national parks on the island (the other is Cerro El Copey, near La Asunción). The park covers the lagoon and a mangrove area at its western end. This is a habitat for a variety of birds, including pelicans, cormorants and scarlet ibis.

Buses from Porlamar go regularly to La Restinga (US$1) and will deposit you at the entrance to the embarkation pier. From there, five-seat motorboats will take you on a half-/full-hour trip (US$12/18 per boat) along the *caños* (channels) that cut through the mangroves. The boats can also take you to a fine shell beach, where you can grab fresh fried fish in one of the open-air restaurants before returning (US$15 roundtrip per boat). In the low season, be prepared for long waits, or pay for the empty seats.

BEACHES

Isla de Margarita has 167km of coastline endowed with some 50 beaches big enough to bear proper names, not to mention smaller bits of sandy coast. Many beaches have been developed with a range of services, such as restaurants, bars, and deck chairs and sunshades for rent. Though the island is no longer a virgin paradise, you can still find a relatively deserted strip of sand.

On the whole, Margarita's beaches have little shade, and some are virtually barren. The beaches on the northern and eastern coasts are better than those skirting the southern shore of the island. You can camp on the beaches, but use common sense and be cautious. Don't leave your tent unattended. Swimmers should be aware of the dangerous undertows on some beaches, including Playa El Agua and Playa Puerto Cruz.

Playa El Agua

This wonderful 3km-long stretch of white sand is the most heavily promoted and developed beach on the island. Effectively, it has become Margarita's trendiest beach, full of Venezuela's beautiful and arty people, their chocolate bodies contrasting finely with lobster-colored gringos. It may be a sardine-can experience in the short holiday peaks, but at other times it's quite OK, especially if you walk to the northern, less developed part of the beach.

The beach is shaded with coconut groves and densely dotted with palm-leaf-thatched restaurants and bars offering a good selection of food, cocktails and frequent live music. Various beach and water sports services are available, including flights along the coast in ultralight planes (US$30/50 for a 15-/30-minute flight).

Behind the beach is a collection of hotels and holiday homes, though not many would really fall into the budget price bracket. *Hostería El Agua* (*☎/fax 49 12 97*), on the Manzanillo road 350m back from the beach, is one of the cheapest places around. Run by a friendly French couple, the hotel has 15 air-conditioned rooms for US$20/25/30 single/double/triple April 1 to July 15 and US$30/35/40 during the rest of the year, and offers a variety of services, including tours and bicycle and motorcycle rental.

The beach has regular bus transportation from Porlamar (US$0.80, 45 minutes), so you can easily come here for the day if you can't afford to stay overnight.

Other Beaches

Other popular destinations include **Playa Guacuco** and **Playa Manzanillo**. Perhaps Margarita's finest beach is **Playa Puerto Cruz**, which has arguably the widest, whitest stretch of sand and still isn't overdeveloped. **Playa Parguito**, next to Playa El Agua, has strong waves good for surfing, while **Playa El Yaque**, south of the airport, has tranquil waters and steady winds, perfect for windsurfing. It has already gained some international reputation and has become a hangout for the windsurfing community from Venezuela and beyond. If you want to escape from people, head for **Macanao**, which is the wildest part of the island – so are some of its beaches.

Guayana

Guayana encompasses the whole of Venezuela's southeast – everything that lies to the south of the Río Orinoco, including its delta. Geographically, it's composed of several wildly diverse regions, including the

Guiana Highlands, which are dotted with massive table mountains known as *tepuis;* the basins of the upper Orinoco and the Amazon, which are carpeted with thick rain forest; and the swampy Delta del Orinoco, with its extensive mangroves. In administrative terms, Guayana comprises the states of Bolívar, Amazonas and Delta Amacuro.

Although it covers approximately half of the country's area, Guayana is home to only 1.4 million people, a mere 6% of the nation's population. More than two-thirds of that population is concentrated in the region's only two important cities, Ciudad Bolívar and Ciudad Guayana, while the rest are scattered over a vast area without any significant urban centers.

Guayana is home to the majority of Venezuela's Indian groups. Although the most numerous group, the Guajiro, lives in Zulia state, all the other main communities, including the Warao, Pemón, Yanomami and Piaroa, inhabit Guayana. They constitute about 10% of the total population of the region.

Rich in natural resources, Guayana shelters considerable deposits of iron ore and bauxite (from which aluminum is made), and two particular treasures: gold and diamonds. Almost all of these riches are in Bolívar state. The Lower Orinoco comprises Guayana's most industrialized area; Ciudad Guayana has become Venezuela's major center of heavy industry.

From a traveler's point of view, Guayana is one of Venezuela's most amazing regions, renowned for its mysterious tepuis, spectacular waterfalls, wild jungles and sweeping savannas. The region boasts seven national parks (covering about 20% of Guayana), including Venezuela's three largest nature reserves (Parima-Tapirapecó, Canaima and Serranía La Neblina).

Most parts of the region are barely explored, and large areas have hardly ever been penetrated. As roads are few and far between, most transportation is by jeep,

GUAYANA

GUAYANA

boat or light plane. Exploring the region on your own is not easy or cheap, except in more developed areas. Organized tourism has developed considerably over the past decade, cutting farther and farther into the wilderness. However, traveling in this area is not inexpensive at all.

Delta del Orinoco

Covering an area of about 25,000 sq km, the Orinoco's delta is the second largest on the continent, after the Amazon Delta. In its lower course, the river reaches a width of 20km and splits into about 40 major *caños* (channels), which carry the waters down into the Atlantic. Their *bocas* (mouths) are distributed along 360km of coast. The southernmost channel, Río Grande, is the main one and is used by oceangoing vessels sailing upriver to Ciudad Guayana.

The delta formed over millennia by accumulated sediments that were brought down by the river. As the process continues, the delta is slowly extending out into the ocean. In the course of the last century alone, about 900 sq km of new land appeared. The delta area consists of a maze of islands separated by *caños*. A good part of the channel banks are lined by mangroves. The land is largely covered by mixed forest that includes a variety of palms, of which the *moriche* is the most typical of the region. The tree has traditionally provided the staple food of the delta's inhabitants, the Warao Indians, as well as material for their dwellings, crafts, tools and household implements.

The climate of the delta is hot and humid, with an average annual temperature of around 26°C that changes little throughout the year. However, temperature variation between day and night can be considerable. Annual rainfall is relatively high, exceeding 2000mm in many areas, and, in general, the closer you get to the coast the more it rains. The driest period is from January to March; the remaining part of the year is wet or very wet.

This rainfall pattern doesn't exactly correspond with the water level of the Orinoco,

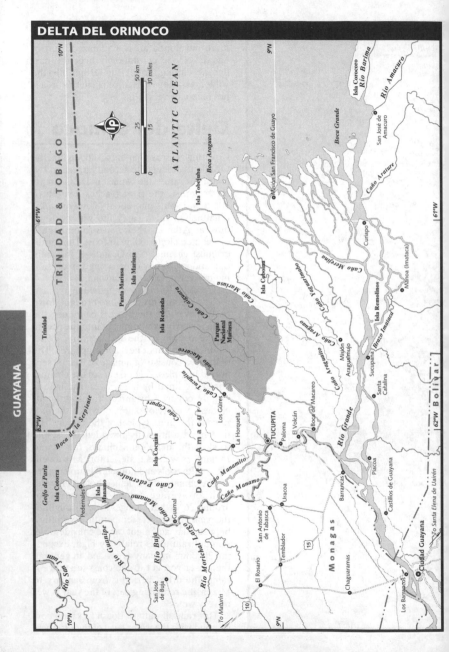

DELTA DEL ORINOCO

The cathedral in downtown Ciudad Bolívar

Elegance in road crossing, Ciudad Bolívar

The irrestible lure of the falls, Parque Nacional Canaima

The tippy-top of Roraima

Heading to Roirama

The Quebrado de Jaspe, La Gran Sabana

Salto Angel's unparalleled drop

Golden falls in Parque Nacional Canaima

The Warao

The Delta del Orinoco is inhabited by the Warao (or Guarao) Indians, the second-largest indigenous group in Venezuela (after the Guajiro), numbering about 24,000. They dwell along the *caños* (channels), constructing their *palafitos* (houses on stilts) on riverbanks, and live mostly off fishing. Water is pivotal in their lives, as indicated by the tribe's name *(wa* in the local language means 'canoe,' *arao* means 'people').

Many of the Waraos still use their native language (classified as 'independent' – in other words, not belonging to any of the major linguistic families); only half the indigenous population speaks Spanish. Two-thirds of the Waraos live in the eastern part of the delta, between the Caño Mariusa and the Río Grande, and are distributed across about 250 tiny communities.

The Waraos are very skillful craftspeople. They are renowned for their basketry and woodcarvings, especially *curiaras* (dugouts) and animal figures carved from balsa wood. Their *chinchorros* (hammocks), made from the fiber of the *moriche palm*, are also widely known

which essentially depends on the climate in the upper reaches of the river and its major tributaries. The water level is usually at its lowest in March and highest from August to September; in that time, parts of the delta become marshy or flooded.

Curiously enough, the state that encompasses the delta is not named after the Orinoco, but after the Río Amacuro, a small river that runs along a part of the Guyana border and empties into Boca Grande, the Orinoco's main mouth. Tucupita is the state capital and its largest town.

Tucupita is the major point of departure for organized tours to the delta and the place to arrange a tour. However, the nondescript town of Barrancas (not to be confused with Los Barrancos, opposite San Félix) is the delta's busiest port, from which nontourist boats run through to most delta destinations, particularly toward the Lower Delta, to the east.

The delta has long been one of Venezuela's wildest and best-preserved regions. But this is now being changed, following the discovery and subsequent exploitation of large oil reserves in the area of Pedernales. Another dangerous addition to the delta's traditional life is drug smuggling. The delta is increasingly used for the trafficking of cocaine from Colombia via the Río Orinoco and out into the Caribbean through the maze of delta waterways. It may have an ir-

reversible impact on the local population and the safety of the region. So far, however, there have been no reports of incidents involving tourists. However, travelers should avoid any contact with the drug trade.

TUCUPITA
☎ 087 (☎ 0287 from Jun 16, 2001)

The capital of Delta Amaruco state is a hot river town of 60,000. It sits on the banks of Caño Manamo, the westernmost channel of the delta, which flows northward for 110km before emptying into the Golfo de Paria near the town of Pedernales. Caño Manamo has been blocked by a dike built 22km south of Tucupita. The dike was erected in the 1960s as part of a flood-control program that aimed to secure land in the northern delta for farming and stock raising. The road that runs along the top of the dike is Tucupita's only overland link with the rest of the country.

Tucupita evolved in the 1920s as one of a chain of Capuchin missions founded in the delta to convert the indigenous peoples. This opened up the region for both governmental activities and criollo colonists. The missions established social programs that focused on providing Indians with education and health services. Other missions scattered throughout the region include Araguaimujo, Nabasanuka and San Francisco de Guayo.

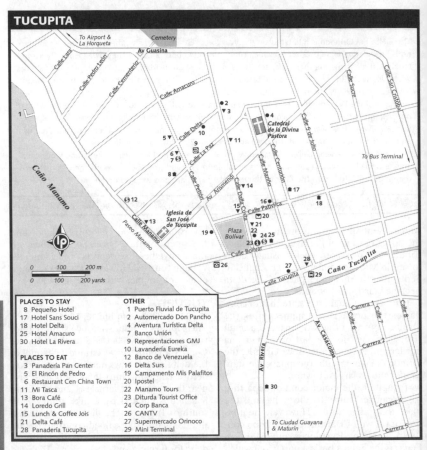

TUCUPITA

PLACES TO STAY
8   Pequeño Hotel
17 Hotel Sans Souci
18 Hotel Delta
25 Hotel Amacuro
30 Hotel La Rivera

PLACES TO EAT
3   Panadería Pan Center
5   El Rincón de Pedro
6   Restaurant Cen China Town
11 Mi Tasca
13 Bora Café
14 Loredo Grill
15 Lunch & Coffee Jois
21 Delta Café
28 Panadería Tucupita

OTHER
1   Puerto Fluvial de Tucupita
2   Automercado Don Pancho
4   Aventura Turística Delta
7   Banco Unión
9   Representaciones GMJ
10 Lavandería Eureka
12 Banco de Venezuela
16 Delta Surs
19 Campamento Mis Palafitos
20 Ipostel
22 Manamo Tours
23 Diturda Tourist Office
24 Corp Banca
26 CANTV
27 Supermercado Orinoco
29 Mini Terminal

Tucupita is essentially a base for exploring the delta rather than an attraction in itself. Although you may find it pleasant enough to stroll around the central streets or along Paseo Manamo, the riverbank esplanade, there are no special sights in town.

Information
Tourist Offices The Diturda (Dirección de Turismo del Estado Delta Amacuro) municipal tourist office (☎ 21 68 52) is in the Edificio San Juan, Piso 2, Oficina 18, Calle Bolívar, just off Plaza Bolívar. It's open 8 am to noon and 3 to 6 pm weekdays.

Money Banco de Venezuela and Banco Unión will give cash advances on Visa and MasterCard. The latter bank may also change traveler's checks and cash, but it's likely to charge a commission. American Express checks can also be cashed at Corp Banca. Most of the tour agencies will accept cash payments, often also traveler's checks, but not credit cards.

Email & Internet Access Representaciones GMJ (☎ 21 01 63, 21 67 96), Calle La Paz, provides Internet access for about US$6 an hour.

Things to See

The **Iglesia de San José de Tucupita**, the Capuchin mission church built in 1930, is the oldest building in town. It served as a parish church until the monumental **Catedral de la Divina Pastora** was completed in 1982, after nearly three decades of construction.

Organized Tours

The picture of tour companies in Tucupita is changing rapidly, with new agencies appearing on the market and others going out of business. At the time of writing, there were half a dozen tour operators in town, all focusing on trips into the delta. The tourist office keeps track of the current situation and has a list of registered companies. It may be useful to consult the staff before you strike a deal with an unregistered operator, as you won't be able to get your money back if the company doesn't provide the services to which it has committed itself.

Another useful resource is Manamo Tours (☎ 21 01 79), on Plaza Bolívar, managed by Antonio. The agency doesn't organize tours but does sell tours of selected local operators, so you'll get some information about the major players and their prices, and you can arrange a tour if you so choose. The agency also sells plane tickets.

Tours are usually all-inclusive two- to four-day trips (there are hardly any one-day tours), and the going rate is about US$60 to US$120 per person a day, depending principally on the number of people in the group. Most agencies say they can provide a guide who speaks English and sometimes other languages, such as German, Italian or French, though it's better to check this by meeting the guide personally before you commit yourself.

Most agents offer tours to the northern part of the delta, toward Pedernales. Of these, Aventura Turística Delta (☎ 21 08 35, a_t_d_1973@hotmail.com), Calle Centurión, is perhaps the most popular with travelers, but unfortunately, their prices have gone up considerably over recent years. Alternatively, check Tucupita Expeditions (☎ 21 08 01, 21 19 53, ducexpdelta@cantv.net), Calle Las Acacias, nine blocks east of Plaza Bolívar. The newest competitor, Campa-

mento Mis Palafitos, used to operate from Hotel Saxxi (see Places to Stay, later), but it now has a new office on Plaza Bolívar. The 32-cabin campamento is 1½ hours by boat from Tucupita and serves as a base for tours around the area.

Delta Surs (☎ 21 26 66, 21 05 53), on Calle Mariño at Calle Pativilca, is the only local operator offering tours to the far eastern area of the delta, which is arguably more interesting due to its more diverse wildlife and more numerous Indian population. Delta Surs also has a campamento in San Francisco de Guayo.

Despite tourist office efforts to eliminate pirate guide services, independent guides will descend like vultures as soon as you arrive in town. Their tours may be cheaper, though you never actually know what you'll get for your money; Lonely Planet has received very mixed (even totally contradictory) comments about their services.

If you decide on one of these guides, clarify all the details of the trip (duration, places to be visited, food and lodging etc) and have a look at the boat before you commit yourself. Make sure the boat has two engines (required by law) and preferably a roof, and that mosquito nets are provided for hammocks. After you and your guide agree on a price, you should pay only the money necessary for predeparture expenses (gasoline and food). Insist on paying the remaining part only upon your return.

Places to Stay

Accommodations are limited in Tucupita. There are only four or five hotels in the town center, and two or three more are outside the central area. All the hotels listed have rooms with private baths.

The cheapest, *Pequeño Hotel* (☎ 21 05 23), Calle La Paz, has basic doubles with fan for US$9 (US$12 with noisy air-con). They lock the door at 10:30 pm, so don't be late. *Hotel Delta* (☎ 21 24 67), Calle Pativilca, offers similarly basic rooms for US$10 matrimonial with fan, US$16/18 matrimonial/double with air-conditioning.

The *Hotel Amacuro* (☎ 21 04 04), on Calle Bolívar, is better and features quieter air-conditioning. Its matrimoniales/doubles cost US$17/19. The best central option is the neat **Hotel Sans Souci** (☎ *21 01 32)*, Calle Centurión, at US$12/14/20 matrimonial/double/triple with fan (US$16/21/24 with aircon); it has its own restaurant.

Hotel La Rivera (☎ *21 05 55)*, a short walk south from the center, is not significantly better than Sans Souci but is more expensive: US$22/27/30 single/double/triple. If you need somewhere appreciably better, try **Hotel Saxxi** (☎ *21 21 12)*, in Paloma, 6km south of Tucupita on the main road, perhaps the best place to stay in the area. It costs US$36/44/56 for an air-conditioned matrimonial/double/triple and has a swimming pool, restaurant and bar. Check if they have discos on Friday and Saturday nights, which are probably not the best days to sleep there unless you plan to join the dancing party.

Places to Eat

There's a range of simple places to eat in town, of which *Mi Tasca*, Calle Dalla Costa, is popular with travelers for its hearty food at low prices. *El Rincón de Pedro*, Calle Petión, has good budget chicken, among other dishes, while the nearby *Restaurant Cen China Town* does some reasonable Chinese cooking. *Tasca Sans Souci*, in the hotel of the same name, is good and inexpensive; you can also try *Loredo Grill*, which is a bit more expensive.

For breakfast, there are a few central panaderías, including *Panadería Pan Center* and *Panadería Tucupita*. *Lunch & Coffee Jois* and *Delta Café*, both on Plaza Bolívar, serve coffee and snacks. A bit more expensive is the pleasant *Bora Café*, Calle Manamo. Should you require food provisions for a trip, try *Automercado Don Pancho* or *Supermercado Orinoco*.

Getting There & Away

Air The airport is 3km north of town; the San Rafael carrito goes there from the town center. Avior has flights to Porlamar (US$59) and Caracas (US$96), both with a connection in Carúpano (US$34). Prices are one-way.

Bus Tucupita has a new bus terminal that handles all intercity buses and por puestos. It's about a kilometer southeast of the center; a taxi between the center and the terminal will cost about US$1.25. The Mini Terminal, on Calle Tucupita in the center, handles local and suburban bus traffic.

Four buses nightly make the run to Caracas (US$20 deluxe, 11 hours), with either Expresos Camargüi, Expresos del Mar or Expresos Los Llanos; they all go via Maturín. Expresos La Guayanesa has two buses daily to Ciudad Guayana (US$5, 3½ hours), but por puestos service this route regularly (US$7, two hours). The trip includes a ferry ride across the Orinoco from Los Barrancos to San Félix (no extra charge).

Several buses a day go to Maturín (US$6, four hours); you can also go by a more frequent and faster por puesto (US$9, three hours).

Boat Passenger boats are supposed to depart daily from Puerto Fluvial de Tucupita to Pedernales (US$18, four to five hours). No boat services operate from Tucupita to the eastern part of the delta. There may be some boats from El Volcán, the port near the dike, 22km south of Tucupita. However, most boats to the eastern delta (Curiapo, Misión San Francisco de Guayo, Misión Araguaimujo, San José de Amacuro etc) depart from Barrancas.

Lower Orinoco

The Lower Orinoco is the industrial heart of Guayana. This is the most densely populated part of the region, and is the only one with a road network to speak of. Here are Guayana's only two cities, Ciudad Bolívar and Ciudad Guayana, both of which sit on the right bank of the Orinoco, in Bolívar state (Venezuela's largest state, occupying over a quarter of the country's territory).

While Ciudad Bolívar is an important historic city with character and charm, Ciudad Guayana is not much more than a vast urban sprawl dotted with industrial installations. Either of the two cities makes a

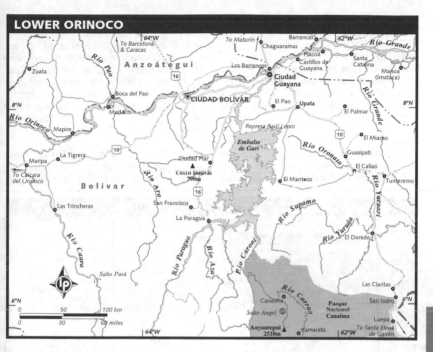

LOWER ORINOCO

convenient starting point for exploring Bolívar state, especially its most attractive southeastern part, which includes Salto Angel (Angel Falls), La Gran Sabana and Roraima (a large table mountain). The state is bisected by an excellent and spectacular highway that runs from Ciudad Guayana south all the way to Santa Elena de Uairén, on the Brazilian border.

CIUDAD BOLÍVAR
☎ 085 (☎ 0285 from Jun 16, 2001)

Ciudad Bolívar is a hot city set on the southern bank of the Orinoco, about 420km upstream from the Atlantic. Founded in 1764 on a rocky elevation at the river's narrowest point, the town was appropriately named Angostura (literally, 'narrows') and grew slowly as a sleepy river port hundreds of miles away from any important population centers. Then, suddenly and unexpectedly, Angostura became the spot where much of the country's (and the continent's) history was forged.

It was here that Bolívar came in 1817 – soon after the town had been liberated from Spanish control – and set up the base for the military operations that led to the final stage of the War of Independence. The town was made the provisional capital of the yet-to-be-liberated country. It was in Angostura that the British Legionnaires joined Bolívar before they all set off for the battle of Boyacá, which secured the independence of Colombia. The Angostura Congress convened here in 1819 and gave birth to Gran Colombia, a unified republic comprising Venezuela, Colombia and Ecuador. In honor of Bolívar, the town was renamed 'Ciudad Bolívar' in 1846.

Today, Ciudad Bolívar is the capital of Bolívar state and a city of 290,000 with quite a number of tourist attractions. Its center has retained the flavor of an old river town and still conserves some of the architecture dating from its 50-year-long colonial era. It's a popular stop for travelers, partly for the city itself, and partly as a jumping-off point for Salto Angel.

Information

Tourist Offices The Dirección de Turismo del Estado Bolívar (☎ 216 13, 223 62, fax 245 25) is in Quinta Yeita, Avenida Bolívar No 59, four blocks north of the airport, and is open 8 am to noon and 2 to 5:30 pm weekdays.

Money The Banco Unión, Banco Mercantil and Banco de Venezuela give advances on Visa and Mastercard. The Banco Mercantil branch on Paseo Orinoco may also change US cash at good rates. The Corp Banca, on the corner of Avenidas Aeropuerto and Andrés Bello, near the airport, will change American Express traveler's checks. Across the road, in Hotel Laja Real, is the only authorized money-exchange office in town, Casa de Cambio Febres Parra (☎ 284 53, 226 02), which changes cash and checks but charges a commission on transactions.

Email & Internet Access Posada Amor Patrio and Hotel Caracas provide Internet facilities (see Places to Stay, later).

CIUDAD BOLÍVAR

see Paseo Orinoco & Colonial Quarter

Piedra del Medio

Río Orinoco

Paseo Orinoco

Calle Bolívar

Jardín Botánico del Orinoco

GUAYANA

PLACES TO STAY
11 Laja City Hotel
13 Hotel Valentina
18 Hotel Laja Real
20 Hotel Da Gino

PLACES TO EAT
7 Restaurant El Rincón Criollo
12 Ristorante Mezza Luna
14 La Traviata Café
15 Parrillas Alfonso

OTHER
1 Banco Mercantil
2 Mercado La Carioca
3 Fortín El Zamuro
4 Museo Casa San Isidro
5 Ipostel
6 Lavandería Gladys Martínez
8 Tourist Office
9 Museo de Arte Moderno Jesús Soto
10 Supermercado El Diamante
16 Bus Terminal
17 Jimmie Angel's Airplane
19 Corp Banca
21 Museo Geológico y Minero

Av Cumaná
Av 5 de Julio
Av Táchira
Av Gaspari
Av San Félix
Paseo Heres
Av Moreno Mendoza
Paseo Meneses
Av Cruz Verde
Calle Caracas
Calle 19 de Abril
Av Guasipati
Av Bolívar
Av Briceño Iragorry
Av Germania
Av Andrés Bello
Calle José Méndez
Av Maracay
Av Ceder
Av P Reverend
Av Upata
Av La Paragua
Av Aeropuerto
Airport Terminal
Airport
Av Independencia
Av Sucre
Av Pichincha
Av República
Av 17 de Diciembre
Río San Rafael

To Barcelona
To Ciudad Guayana
To Ciudad Piar

0   200   400 m
0   200   400 yards

Laundry In the center is Lavandería Woo Lee & Co, Calle Zea. Outside this area, you can use Lavandería Gladys Martínez, Avenida 19 de Abril.

Paseo Orinoco

This lively waterfront boulevard is lined with arcaded houses, some of which date back to Bolívar's days. Midway along the Paseo is the **Mirador Angostura**, a rocky headland that juts out into the river at its narrowest point. If you happen to be here in August, when the water is at its highest, you may have the river just below your feet. This is also the time to watch fishermen with their *atarrayas* (fishing nets) trying to catch the delicious *sapoara* (or *zapoara*), which appear only during this short period. In March, by contrast, the water level may be more than 15m lower.

The lookout commands good views up and down the Orinoco. Five kilometers upriver you'll see a suspension bridge, **Puente de Angostura**, which was constructed in five years and opened in 1967. It's the only bridge across the Orinoco along the river's entire 2150km length. It's 1678m long, and its central, highest section is 45m above the river (in the low-water season). Walkers are not allowed on the bridge – you must have a vehicle in order to make the crossing.

Close to the lookout is a restored 18th-century prison building that functioned as a jail until 1952. It now shelters the **Museo Etnográfico del Orinoco**, which features the crafts of Indian communities from Venezuela's south. It also has a large aquarium with fish species typical of the Orinoco, including the sapoara.

Two blocks west along the paseo is the **Museo de Ciudad Bolívar**, in a spacious colonial residence known as the Casa del Correo del Orinoco. It was here that the republic's first newspaper was printed, from June 1818 until 1821, and you can see the original press on which it was published, along with other objects related to the town's history and a collection of modern paintings and sculptures. The museum is open 9 am to noon and 2 to 5 pm weekdays.

Colonial Quarter

The historic heart of the city is on a hillside to the south of the river and is centered on the finely restored and tranquil **Plaza Bolívar**. Apart from the usual monument to Bolívar in the middle, there are five allegorical statues on the square that personify the five countries Bolívar liberated. To the east looms the massive **Catedral**, begun right after the town's founding and completed 80 years later.

Half of the plaza's western side is taken up by the **Casa del Congreso de Angostura**, built in the 1770s. In 1819 it housed lengthy debates of the Angostura Congress. You can have a look around the interior.

On the northern side of the square is the **Casa Piar**, where General Manuel Piar was kept prisoner in October 1817 before being placed before the wall of the cathedral and executed by a firing squad. Piar liberated the city from Spanish control but rejected Bolívar's authority and was sentenced to death in a controversial and much criticized trial.

Other historic buildings around the plaza include the **Casa Parroquial** and the **Gobernación**. Just one block south is the **Alcaldía de Heres**, a pair of fine old buildings on both sides of Calle Igualdad that are linked by an intriguing aerial walkway.

Don't miss visiting **Parque El Zanjón**, a most unusual city park, replete with massive boulders (called *lajas*). The fine old-style **Casa de Tejas**, picturesquely set on one of the boulders, houses a small art exhibition.

On the southern edge of the colonial sector is the pleasantly shaded **Plaza Miranda**. A sizable building on its eastern side was constructed in 1870 as a hospital, but it never served that purpose. In 1892 it was turned into barracks and served the army until 1954, only to become a police station afterward. Eventually, after extensive refurbishing, it reopened in 1992 as the **Centro de las Artes**, which now stages temporary exhibitions (open 9 am to noon and 3 to 5:30 pm Tuesday to Friday, 10 am to 4 pm weekends). Ask to be let up to the mirador on the roof (closed to the general public), which provides a good view of **Fortín El Zamuro**,

GUAYANA

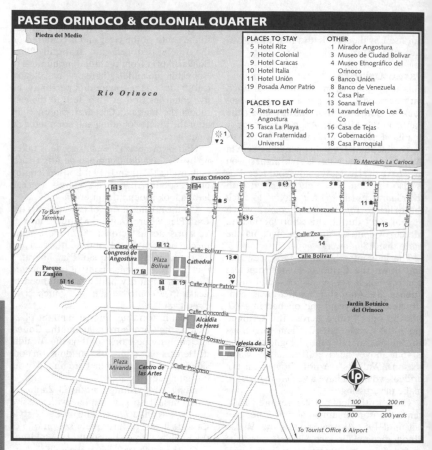

PASEO ORINOCO & COLONIAL QUARTER

PLACES TO STAY
5   Hotel Ritz
7   Hotel Colonial
9   Hotel Caracas
10   Hotel Italia
11   Hotel Unión
19   Posada Amor Patrio

PLACES TO EAT
2   Restaurant Mirador Angostura
15   Tasca La Playa
20   Gran Fraternidad Universal

OTHER
1   Mirador Angostura
3   Museo de Ciudad Bolívar
4   Museo Etnográfico del Orinoco
6   Banco Unión
8   Banco de Venezuela
12   Casa Piar
13   Soana Travel
14   Lavandería Woo Lee & Co
16   Casa de Tejas
17   Gobernación
18   Casa Parroquial

crowning the top of the highest hill in the city, half a kilometer to the south. The fort is open to visitors from 9 am to noon and 2:30 to 5:30 pm Tuesday to Saturday, from 9 am to noon Sunday (the entrance is from Paseo Heres), and it provides fine views over the old town.

Other Attractions

Beyond the fort, on Avenida Táchira, is the **Museo Casa San Isidro**, in a beautiful colonial mansion of the coffee hacienda that once stretched as far as the airport. Bolívar stayed here for 29 days, during which he re-

putedly composed his vehement speech for the Angostura Congress. The house's interior is maintained in the style of Bolívar's era and has the same opening hours as the fort.

Proceed 1km south on Avenida Táchira and take the perpendicular Avenida Briceño Iragorry to the left, which will lead you to the **Museo de Arte Moderno Jesús Soto**. The museum has a good collection of works by this renowned kinetic artist (who was born in Ciudad Bolívar in 1923), as well as works by other national and international modern artists. The museum is open 9:30 am to 5:30 pm Tuesday to Friday, 10 am to 5 pm weekends.

In front of the airport terminal, a 10-minute walk from the museum, stands the legendary **airplane of Jimmie Angel** (see the Salto Angel section, later, for more about him). This is the original plane, which was removed from the top of Auyantepui in 1970 and restored in Maracay.

In the southwestern suburb of the city is the **Museo Geológico y Minero**, which introduces Guayana's mines, mining techniques, machinery etc.

Organized Tours

Ciudad Bolívar abounds with tour operators, though some have received mixed comments from travelers. Talk to others who have just returned from a tour before strik ing a deal. Never buy tours offered by individuals on the street or in the bus terminal. If they approach you and take you to their agency office, check the agency's credentials before buying a tour. Be wary of small agencies that have just opened makeshift stalls in a lobby of a cheap hotel or a cubbyhole in a backstreet – some of these may be rogues that intend to disappear with your money. The agencies listed below are all reputable.

Most major tour operators are either around Paseo Orinoco or at the airport. In the former area, check the offers of two companies nestled in riverfront hotels: Neckar Tour (☎ 244 02), in the Hotel Colonial, and Expediciones Dearuna (☎ 285 12), in the Hotel Caracas. In the airport terminal, Turi Express (☎ 297 64) has received the best comments, followed perhaps by Gekko Tours (☎ 232 23). Here you'll also find the desk of Tiuna Tours (☎ 286 97, 265 00), Canaima's major boat-tour operator; and Sapito Tours (☎ 014-854 82 34), an offspring of Bernal Tours, another Canaima-based tour company.

Probably none of the tour operators and airlines listed here will accept payment by credit card; even if they do, they'll charge about 10% more if you pay with one. The usual form of payment is cash (US dollars or bolívares), and some agents also accept traveler's checks. The prices listed are only ballpark figures; they may vary among the companies and largely depend on the number of people in the group, your bargaining skills and other circumstances (season, number of boats in repair etc).

Tours to Salto Angel Ciudad Bolívar is the main gateway to Salto Angel, and tours to the falls are the staple of most city tour operators. The most common tour offered is a day trip that includes a roundtrip flight to Canaima, a flight over Salto Angel, lunch in Canaima and a short boat excursion to other nearby falls (usually Salto El Sapo). Tours depart from Ciudad Bolívar between 7 and 8 am and return between 4 and 5 pm, costing about US$160 to US$180 per person. Some agents may offer Kavac as an alternative to Canaima, in which case the tour will include, apart from the Salto Angel flyover, an excursion to the Cueva de Kavac; this tour costs around US$180 to US$200.

A Canaima-Kavac two-day tour that combines all the attractions of the two one-day trips is available from some agencies for about US$230 to US$260. Three-day tours are also offered, particularly in the rainy season, when they will include a boat trip to the foot of Salto Angel (but no flight over the falls) for roughly US$230 to US$260. There are also likely to be some longer tours offered, usually including other regional sights along with Salto Angel.

Most agents will be able to tailor tours to suit your particular requirements. For example, if you don't want to come back to Ciudad Bolívar but would rather continue to Santa Elena de Uairén, the tour operators will replace the Canaima-Ciudad Bolívar return portion with the Canaima–Santa Elena ticket, charging you about US$25 extra for the difference in airfares.

The tour companies use the services of small regional airlines, all of which are based at the airport. There are half a dozen of them, including Rutaca, Convallés, Ciaca, Transmandú and Aerobol. Free luggage allowance is 10kg. Tour operators sell plane tickets for flights with these carriers.

The airlines can fly you to Canaima (US$50 each way) and can also include a flight over Salto Angel for about US$30 extra. In other words, they can put together a no-frills tour to Salto Angel (without lunch or side trips) for around US$130, which is probably the minimum you have to pay for the pleasure of seeing the falls.

The usual scenario of these tours is as follows. You depart in the morning, heading toward Canaima. If the pilot expects the sky over Salto Angel to be clear, he flies first to the waterfall and then puts you down at Canaima, picking you up later in the afternoon after he has completed his scheduled flights for that day. If the pilot suspects bad weather, he flies you straight to Canaima and tries the falls in the afternoon, after he's finished his rounds. See the Salto Angel section for more information. The prices of tours to Salto Angel don't include the US$12 entrance fee to the national park, which is collected by Inparques upon your landing at Canaima.

Other Tours All the tour companies offer a range of other tours, of which trips to La Gran Sabana are possibly the most popular among travelers – even though they can be organized more cheaply from Santa Elena de Uairén. These tours are normally offered by agents as four-day jeep trips for about US$200 per person, all-inclusive.

Another tour appearing on the menu of various operators is Río Caura, which is normally scheduled as a five-day trip, costing US$300 to US$360 per person. A minimum of four people is usually necessary for these tours. Soana Travel (☎ 220 30, soanatravel@gmx.de), Calle Bolívar, is one of the major operators doing this tour. As of early 2001, Soana Travel was considering moving its offices to Posada Amor Patrio (see Places to Stay, later).

Roraima is another destination and costs roughly US$300 to US$350 per person for a six- to seven-day tour. It's cheaper to do this trip on your own, contracting a guide in Paraitepui (see the Roraima section, later).

Special Events

The city's major annual bash is the Feria del Orinoco, held in late August to correspond with the massive appearance of the sapoara in the river. The celebrations include – you guessed it – a sapoara fishing competition, tons of sapoara on the local menus, aquatic sports, an agriculture fair, and a range of cultural and other popular events. The Fiesta de Nuestra Señora de las Nieves, the patron saint of the city, is held on August 5.

Places to Stay

Budget The small *Posada Amor Patrio* (*☎ 288 19*), on Plaza Bolívar behind the cathedral, is the loveliest budget place. Set in a historic house, the posada has just four rooms, all with fan and shared facilities (it may have two more by the time you read this), for US$10/15/20 single/matrimonial/triple. In the evening, travelers gather in the front common room, which is decorated with antiques and old photos and reverberates with old Cuban rhythms – the favorite music of the German manager, Fidi. The posada also offers the use of kitchen as well as Internet facilities for guests.

The Posada Amor Patrio is the only place to stay in the colonial quarter around Plaza Bolívar. More budget hotels lie on or just off Paseo Orinoco (a pleasant area to stay), but nothing really compares with the posada. *Hotel Caracas* (*☎ 260 54, Paseo Orinoco No 82*) has long been a popular travelers' haunt, but it had some room security problems, which, hopefully, are over. It is quite simple but cheap (US$10/12/14 matrimonial/double/triple with bath and fan) and has a lovely large terrace overlooking the paseo, where you can sit with a bottle of beer, watch the world go by and enjoy the evening breeze. The hotel has Internet facilities and a tour agency.

Hotel Italia (*☎ 278 10, Paseo Orinoco No 131*) has been another popular backpacker shelter over the years. It doesn't offer much luxury either, and it now has problems with cleanliness and security. Once a lively travelers' hangout, the now-overpriced restaurant, much like the hotel, is increasingly run down. Rooms costs US$9/10/13 single/double/triple with fan, US$14/15/17 with air-conditioning.

Hotel Unión (☎ *233 74, Calle Urica No 11)* is clean if styleless and has rooms with fan or air-conditioning for slightly more than those in the Italia. The Brazilian-run *Hotel Ritz* (☎ *238 86, Calle Libertad No 3)* offers air-conditioned doubles/triples with bath for US$12/14, and doubles with fan but no bath cost US$9.

The best place to stay on Paseo Orinoco is the old-style *Hotel Colonial* (☎ *244 02, 201 01)*, where spacious air-conditioned singles/doubles/triples cost US$22/26/30. Grab a room in front, overlooking the river. The hotel has some smaller and less attractive rooms for US$12/15 double/triple.

Mid-Range & Top End Most of the mid-range and top-end hotels are away from the river. Some are near the airport, which may be convenient if you plan on catching a morning flight to Canaima. *Hotel Da Gino* (☎ *203 13, 283 67)* is just a two-minute walk from the airport terminal and charges US$28/30 for good-sized air-conditioned doubles/triples.

The nearby *Hotel Laja Real* (☎ *279 11, 279 44)* is one of the best hotels in town, and it's not absurdly expensive at US$35/44 single/double. Although its rooms are not as large as those of Da Gino, they're neat and have quiet air-conditioning. The hotel has a swimming pool, which is accessible to non-guests for US$6, and a casa de cambio.

There's a cheaper outlet of the same Laja business, *Laja City Hotel* (☎ *299 19, 299 20)*, Avenida Bolívar, which is priced at US$24/28/30 matrimonial/double/triple. Midway between the two, on Avenida Maracay, is the small and quiet *Hotel Valentina* (☎ *221 45 272 53)*, which costs much the same as Laja City and has its own restaurant.

Places to Eat

Good, inexpensive local food is served at the *Mercado La Carioca* (popularly called 'La Sapoara'), a well-organized market at the eastern end of Paseo Orinoco. It has a row of restaurants lining the riverfront and is a clean and pleasant place to eat. The market is open from about 6 am until midafternoon.

In the central waterfront area, *Restaurant Mirador Angostura* is one of cheapest places around and is popular with locals. *Gran Fraternidad Universal*, Calle Amor Patrio, has cheap vegetarian meals at lunchtime on weekdays only. Get there just after noon, as they run out of food quickly. *Tasca La Playa*, Calle Urica, has good food and good prices.

Farther away from the river, *Restaurant El Rincón Criollo*, Avenida Andrés Bello, offers hearty comida criolla. *La Traviata Café*, next to the Hotel Valentina, has beautiful salads, sandwiches and Tex-Mex food at reasonable prices. *Parrillas Alfonso*, across the street, has rich parrillas. A bit more upmarket, *Ristorante Mezza Luna*, Avenida Bolívar in the same area, does good Italian food.

Should you need provisions for an off-the-beaten-track trip (eg, Roraima), try *Supermercado El Diamante*, Avenida Germania, which is one of the better-stocked supermarkets in town.

Shopping

Ciudad Bolívar is an important center of the gold trade. It may be worth checking local jewelers if you plan on buying gold and are not going to El Callao (which is arguably the cheapest place in the country to buy gold – see that section, later in this chapter). Many of the gold shops nestle in two passageways off Paseo Orinoco – Pasaje Bolívar and Pasaje Trivigno-Guayana – both of which are near the Hotel Colonial.

Getting There & Away

Air The airport is 2km southeast of the central riverfront and is linked to the city center by frequent busetas. Busetas marked 'Ruta 1' going eastbound along Paseo Orinoco will take you there.

Ciudad Bolívar has few links with the country's other major cities (nearby Ciudad Guayana is a much more important air transportation hub). Lai provides link with Caracas (US$88 one-way), and through it connections with the rest of the country. Ciudad Bolívar is the major jumping-off point for Canaima, which is serviced by light planes of half a dozen small carriers (see Organized Tours, earlier).

Bus The bus terminal is at the junction of Avenidas República and Sucre, about 2km south of the center. To get there, take the westbound buseta (marked 'Terminal') from Paseo Orinoco. Busetas heading to farther southern suburbs will also drop you at the terminal.

Buses to Caracas run regularly throughout the day, though most depart in the evening for an overnight trip (US$15 ordinary, US$19 deluxe, nine hours). There are a dozen departures a day to Puerto Ayacucho (US$12 ordinary, US$15 deluxe, 10 to 11 hours); the road is now fully paved (though it still hasn't been marked on some of the local maps). Buses to Puerto La Cruz depart every hour or two (US$7 ordinary, US$9 deluxe, four hours).

Turgar, Línea Orinoco, Expresos San Cristóbal, Expresos Los Llanos and Expresos Caribe service the route to Santa Elena de Uairén, with a total of nine departures daily (US$12 ordinary, US$15 deluxe, 10 to 11 hours). To Ciudad Guayana, buses depart every 15 to 30 minutes (US$2, 1½ hours).

Six buses a day depart for Ciudad Piar (US$2.50, two hours), three of which continue up to La Paragua (US$4.50, four hours). There are also por puestos to both Ciudad Piar (US$5, 1½ hours) and La Paragua (US$8, 3½ hours).

Boat Boats go regularly across the Orinoco to the town of Soledad, but there is no regular passenger boat service farther up or down the river.

RÍO CAURA

The Río Caura is a right-bank tributary of the Orinoco, about 200km southwest of Ciudad Bolívar. A singularly beautiful and picturesque river, it's graced with islands, beaches and huge granite boulders. It's cut by rapids and falls, of which Salto Pará are among Venezuela's most spectacular waterfalls. For a good part of its course, the Caura

flows through the wildlife-rich rain forest. The riverbanks are inhabited by indigenous communities, of which the Yekuana is the major group. They are renowned for particularly fine basketry.

All in all, the Caura offers a variety of natural and cultural experiences few other rivers can match. Furthermore, it is one of Venezuela's least-polluted rivers. Gold mining hasn't yet affected the river, though prospectors have been combing the region for a while. Boat trips on the Caura can be run year-round, unlike excursions on some other rivers, which are only possible during the rainy season. The Caura is also what as known as a 'black river' (see the boxed text 'River Coloration' in the Ciudad Guyana section, later), so mosquitoes are scarce.

Unsurprisingly, Caura has become a popular tourist destination, and an increasing number of tour companies include a boat trip on this river in their program. Doing the trip on your own is neither easy nor cheap, as you need to rent a boat anyway, which may be almost as expensive as a tour.

Organized Tours
Various travel operators in Caracas (including Cacao Expediciones), Ciudad Bolívar (Soana Travel, among others) and other cities offer Caura tours. It's most often a five-day package that costs US$60 to US$90 a day, all-inclusive (accommodations are in hammocks). Tour operators in Ciudad Bolívar are likely to be the cheapest.

The usual starting point for tours is Ciudad Bolívar, from where tourists are driven west for 205km along the Puerto Ayacucho road, then along a small side road branching off to the south and running for about 50km to Las Trincheras. In the area, there are several campamentos, where tours stay the first (and last) night. The next day, boats take tourists 130km upriver (a five- to six-hour ride) to a sandbank known as El Playón, where another night is spent. The following day, a two-hour walk uphill takes visitors to the amazing Salto Pará, consisting of five 50m-high falls.

CIUDAD GUAYANA

☎ 086 (☎ 0286 from Jun 16, 2001)

Set on the southern bank of the Orinoco at its confluence with the Río Caroní, Ciudad Guayana is quite an unusual city. It was officially founded in 1961 to serve as an industrial center for the region, and included in its metropolitan boundaries two distinct urban components – the colonial town of San Félix, on the eastern side of the Caroní, and the newborn Puerto Ordaz, on the opposite bank.

At the time of the city's founding, the total population of the area was about 40,000. Forty years later, the two parts have merged and become a 20km-long urban sprawl populated by about 620,000 people. Indeed, Ciudad Guayana is Venezuela's fastest-growing city, and it may remain so for a while until the population reaches the government and city planners' target of one million.

Three bridges have been built across the Río Caroní to unify the two sections of the city, which apparently still can't come to terms with the 'Ciudad Guayana' moniker. The inhabitants persistently refer to their hometown as either 'San Félix' or 'Puerto Ordaz,' depending on which part they are talking about. Similarly, businesses label their addresses with the respective component, without bothering to include the united name. And don't look for 'Ciudad Guayana' in air and bus schedules, because there's no such destination. The airport and bus terminal appear under the name of the sector where they are located.

San Félix was founded sometime in the 16th century, but don't let this date confuse you – there's nothing colonial about the town, apart perhaps from its original chessboard layout. The town center is today a busy, dirty commercial sector, parts of which resemble a street bazaar, with rather nondescript architecture. It's essentially a workers' suburb and can be unsafe.

Puerto Ordaz is quite a different story: It's modern and well planned, and has a good infrastructure of roads, supermarkets, and services. The center is quite clean and pleasant, and it's here that the cream of restaurants and trendy shops is located. It's basically the executive zone, as you can easily tell from the people, their cars and the general atmosphere. Yet there's something eerie about the place; it lacks the feel of older cities that have evolved in a natural way over centuries.

The city garnered its moniker from Diego de Ordaz, the Spanish explorer who, in 1531–32, first sailed up the Orinoco as far as Raudales de Atures, near what is now Puerto Ayacucho. He was searching for gold, as it was thought that the Orinoco was one of the gateways to the mythical land of El Dorado. However, it wasn't until the mid-19th century that gold was found in the region around El Callao, which constitutes today the main area for gold mining. It's estimated that the total gold reserves of Guayana are about 8000 metric tons.

Puerto Ordaz is the seat of the CVG, or Corporación Venezolana de Guayana. This is the regional governmental body founded in 1960 to manage and integrate the industrial development of the region with ecological protection and conservation.

Save for three scenic parks, there's not much to see or do in the city. For most travelers it's a transit point between Caracas/Ciudad Bolívar and Gran Sabana/Brazil, rather than a destination in its own right. On the other hand, as with any city of that size, Ciudad Guayana has well-established tourist facilities, so you can eat and sleep well, change money easily, arrange a tour or buy any provisions you need for further travel.

Information

Tourist Offices The main seat of the Almacaroní municipal tourist office (☎ 440 77) is in central San Félix, at the intersection of Calle 1 and Carrera 1, on the riverfront. It's open 8 am to noon and 2 to 5:30 pm weekdays. They also operate tourist information desks at the airport terminal and at Puerto Ordaz' bus terminal.

Embassies & Consulates The Brazilian consulate (☎ 23 52 43) is in the Edificio

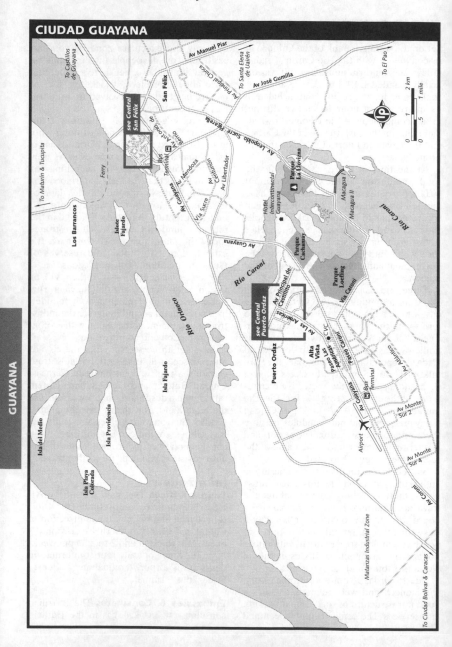

CIUDAD GUAYANA

Amazonas, Avenida Las Américas, Puerto Ordaz. The only other consulate on the way to Brazil is in Santa Elena de Uairén, on the border.

Money Some of the potentially useful central banks are marked on the Puerto Ordaz and San Félix maps. For changing cash, try the Italcambio (☎ 51 72 66) at the airport terminal.

Email & Internet Access Internet access is reasonably cheap in Ciudad Guayana, about US$3 to US$4 an hour. Most facilities are in Puerto Ordaz. All the cybercafés listed in this section are open until 9 or 10 pm daily, unless otherwise indicated.

X-Net Café (☎ 23 39 16), in the Centro Comercial La Gaviota, Local 8, Calle Los Llanos, is one of the most central facilities (closed Sunday). Also close to the center is the Navigator in line (☎ 23 18 82), in the Torre Loreto 2, Nivel 3, Local 19, Avenida Las Américas.

There are various Internet facilities in Alta Vista, including two in the Centro Ciudad Comercial Alta Vista (commonly called Macro Centro): Net Celular (☎ 62 30 27) and CANTV.Net (☎ 61 58 88), both on Piso 1.

Parque Cachamay
This scenic riverside park is just 1km south of Puerto Ordaz' center. The showpiece here is the view of the Río Caroní, which turns into a series of rapids and eventually into a spectacular 200m-wide line of waterfalls. The park is open 7 am to 5 pm Tuesday to Sunday; there's a small admission fee.

Parque Loefling
The 245-hectare Loefling city park adjoins Cachamay park from the southwest and is open the same hours. It has a small zoo featuring native fauna, with some animals in cages and others (including tapirs, capybaras and capuchin monkeys) wandering freely. The park was named after a Swedish botanist, Peter Loefling (1729–56), who came to Venezuela in 1754 and studied plants in the eastern part of the colony.

Parque La Llovizna
La Llovizna park has been established on a group of islands in the Río Caroní, about 5km upstream from where it spills into the Orinoco. The 30-odd islands are separated by many narrow water channels and interconnected by 36 footbridges. The highlight is the 20m-high Salto La Llovizna, and the *llovizna* (drizzle) it produces provided the name of the waterfall and park. Several vantage points provide dramatic views over the falls from various angles, and the walking trails around the park give access to other attractions, including small lakes, exuberant vegetation and even a beach. The park is open 8 am to 5 pm Tuesday to Sunday.

Avenida Leopoldo Sucre Figarella, which crosses over the Caroní next to the Macagua hydroelectric scheme, provides access to the park, but no urban buses service this route. A taxi from either Puerto Ordaz or San Félix shouldn't cost more than US$6. To return to the city, hunt down a lift around the visitor parking lot. Plans are in the works to open a walking trail to the park over the dikes from Parque Loefling – ask about them.

Other Attractions
If you decide to visit San Félix, walk to the Orinoco bank, just off Plaza Bolívar, and watch the river, which at this point is 7km downstream from its confluence with the Caroní. As you'll notice, the river has two distinct colors: The waters closer to your bank (originating from the Caroní) are conspicuously darker than the farther-out waters of the Orinoco proper. The phenomenon is also visible from the San Félix–Los Barrancos ferry.

Organized Tours
There are two-dozen tour operators in town – virtually all in Puerto Ordaz – and competition is fierce, but don't expect prices to be cheaper than elsewhere.

The staple offer of most operators is the three- to five-day tour around the Gran Sabana, which will cost around US$60 to US$90 per person a day. It may be cheaper to arrange this tour with some of Ciudad

GUAYANA

River Coloration

An notable aspect of rivers is their color, which can range from light grayish or yellowish (*ríos blancos*, or 'white rivers'), to dark coffee or even ink (*ríos negros*, or 'black rivers'). The coloration is a complex response to the chemical components of the rock and soil of the riverbed and shores, the flora along the banks, the climate, the season, and many other factors. Generally speaking, dark color is the result of a low level of organic decomposition, which can be caused by either of two factors. First, poor nutrient levels may prevail in the soils (this is the case in the Amazon rain forest). Alternatively, acid formation, caused by a lack of calcium, may slow the decaying process (this is common in areas where igneous rock is prevalent). Interestingly enough, black rivers are almost free of mosquitoes and other insects, and caimans are virtually unknown there. In contrast, all these creatures abound in white rivers.

Among the Orinoco tributaries, the Ríos Caroní, Atabapo and Sipapo are examples of dark rivers, while most of the rivers of Los Llanos (eg, Río Apure or Río Arauca) have a light coloration. Understandably, the color of the Orinoco itself largely depends on the colors of its affluents. Broadly speaking, the lower its course, the lighter the color. Río Negro, as its name suggests, is a black river.

The best place to see the color difference of any two rivers is, naturally, at their confluence. The waters of the tributary don't usually mix with the main river immediately, but rather gradually, over a longer or shorter distance downstream from the confluence, initially forming two parallel flows of different colors. This phenomenon is clearly visible at the confluence of the Ríos Caroní and Orinoco.

Bolívar's tour companies, but the cheapest option is to go by bus to Santa Elena and buy the tour there (see the Santa Elena de Uairén section, later in this chapter, for details).

Another standard package offered by agents is Salto Angel; these tours, too, are probably cheaper to organize from Ciudad Bolívar (likewise with Río Caura tours; see the Ciudad Bolívar section, earlier). Some operators offer trips to the Delta del Orinoco, but you may want to check the Tucupita-based companies before deciding.

Among the shorter regional tours, some companies offer half-day trips to the Castillos de Guayana and day trips to Represa de Guri and Cerro Bolívar (all these places are detailed in separate sections later in this chapter).

The local tour operators worth checking include Kuravaina Tours (☎ 62 08 17, 014-862 36 23), Bagheera Tours (☎ 52 94 81, 52 87 67) and the smaller Ivarkarima Expedi-

ciones (☎ 014-386 49 13). Tobé Lodge (☎ 52 18 42) and Sacoroco Tours (☎ 61 55 26) specialize in Delta del Orinoco tours, but they are not cheap.

CVG organizes tours to its industrial establishments in the city, including the steel mill and aluminum plant. It will also have updated information about visiting Represa de Guri and Cerro Bolívar. The CVG headquarters (☎ 22 61 55) are in Edificio CVG, Calle Cuchiveros, Alta Vista Norte, Puerto Ordaz.

Places to Stay

Both Puerto Ordaz and San Félix have a range of hotels, but it's probably better to stay in Puerto Ordaz for the convenience, nicer surroundings and security. All hotels listed have a private bath, unless indicated otherwise, as well as either fan or air-conditioning. Only the top-end hotels have hot water, but it's hardly necessary in this steamy climate.

Puerto Ordaz Some of the cheapest hotels are around Avenida Principal de Castillito, though they are very basic and rent rooms by the hour. If this is OK with you, try *Hotel Montecarlo*, which costs US$9 matrimonial, US$10 with bath and US$12 with bath and air-conditioning.

Hotel Roma (☎ 22 37 80), next door, is also basic and costs slightly more than the Montecarlo. There are more cheapies in the back streets to the north, but try to avoid venturing there at night. It's more pleasant to stay farther to the west and south of Avenida Principal de Castillito. The cheapest places in this area include *Hotel Rayoli* (☎ 23 72 70), *Hotel Saint Georges* (☎ 22 00 79), *Hotel Habana Cuba* (☎ 22 19 01) and *Hotel La Guayana* (☎ 23 48 66). None of them is a memorable place, and they are not good values for the prices they ask: US$24 to US$28 for an air-conditioned double (a triple will cost about US$3 more).

The posada-like *Residencias Tore* (☎ 23 17 80, 23 13 89, fax 23 17 43), on Calle San Cristóbal at Carrera Los Andes, provides a hell of a difference in style and atmosphere from the hotels listed previously. Set in a quiet, leafy backstreet (yet a manageable walking distance from the center), it's an enjoyable, family-run 25-room guesthouse. Simple but comfortable air-conditioned doubles are US$40 with breakfast, and guests can have other meals in the hotel's own open-air restaurant. Not surprisingly, the hotel is popular with tour operators and individual guests, and is often fully booked. A 13-room extension opened diagonally across the street in 2000. Named *Residencias Tore 2* (☎ 23 06 79, 22 04 92), it offers better standards and larger rooms for marginally more.

Another recommended family-run place, *Residencias Ambato 19* (☎ 23 20 72, Carrera Ambato No 19), has seven comfortable rooms, all with one double bed, air-conditioning and private bath, each priced at US$38.

Puerto Ordaz has a number of upmarket hotels, including the affordable, very central *Hotel Tepuy* (☎ 22 01 11, 22 01 20), Carrera

Upata, which costs US$42/48/60 for an air-conditioned single/double/triple and is possibly the cheapest hotel with hot water.

Hotel Embajador (☎ 22 55 11, 22 57 65), on the corner of Avenida Principal de Castillito and Calle Urbana, is another central place to stay, for US$54/60 single/double. Alternatively, check the huge, 316-room *Hotel Rasil* (☎ 22 02 30, 23 33 48), which has rooms of different standards ranging between US$60 and US$100 double. The smaller and cheaper *Hotel Dos Ríos* (☎ 22 06 79, 22 91 88), Calle México, has recently been refurbished and is a reasonable value for US$50/55/60 single/double/triple.

Hotel Intercontinental Guayana (☎ 20 11 11, fax 23 19 14), on the bank of the Caroní, is the best hotel in Puerto Ordaz.

San Félix There are about a dozen hotels in the town center, all of which are budget establishments. Most are basic and double as sex hotels. The few more tolerable places include *Hotel Águila* (☎ 442 91), Calle 4; *Hotel Excelsior* (☎ 413 75), Calle 3; *Hotel Miranda* (☎ 420 68), Plaza Miranda; and *Hotel Yoli* (☎ 433 41), Carrera 3. Any of them will cost about US$24/28 double/triple, and none is anything special.

Places to Eat

With a wide selection of restaurants in both San Félix and Puerto Ordaz, you can eat quite well. Most of the upmarket establishments are in Puerto Ordaz, which is a much more pleasant area for dining, while San Félix abounds in rather ordinary eateries. On Sunday many restaurants close, especially in Puerto Ordaz.

In Puerto Ordaz, the budget end of the gastronomic scene is represented by the *Boulevar de la Comida Guayanesa*, Calle Guasipati, a line of food kiosks that serve low-priced typical local fare until about 3 or 4 pm. Later in the afternoon and in the evening, you can eat cheaply at the street stalls along Calle Los Llanos. There are several chicken outlets there, where half a chicken with yucca and salad goes for less than US$4 and makes a filling meal.

GUAYANA

CENTRAL PUERTO ORDAZ

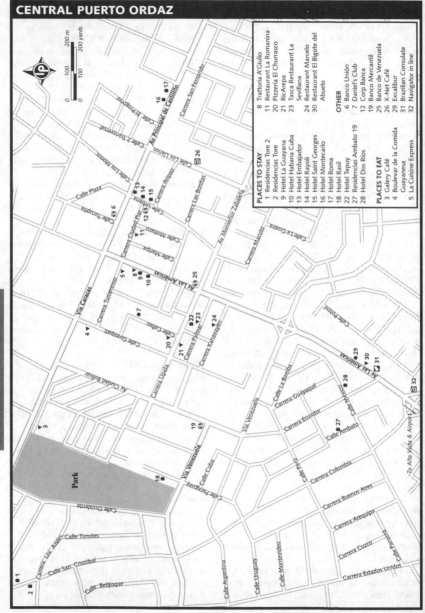

PLACES TO STAY
1   Residencias Tore 2
2   Residencias Tore
9   Hotel La Guayana
10 Hotel Habana Cuba
13 Hotel Embajador
14 Hotel Rayoli
15 Hotel Saint Georges
16 Hotel Montecarlo
17 Hotel Roma
18 Hotel Rasil
22 Hotel Tepuy
27 Residencias Ambato 19
28 Hotel Dos Ríos

PLACES TO EAT
3   Galery Café
4   Boulevar de la Comida
    Guayanesa
5   La Cuisine Express
8   Trattoria A'Giulio
11 Restaurant La Romanina
20 Pizzeria El Churrasco
21 RicArepa
23 Tasca Restaurant La
    Sevillana
24 Restaurant Marcelo
30 Restaurant El Bigote del
    Abuelo

OTHER
6   Banco Unión
7   Daniel's Club
12 Corp Banca
19 Banco Mercantil
25 Banco de Venezuela
26 X-Net Café
29 Excalibur
31 Brazilian Consulate
32 Navigator in line

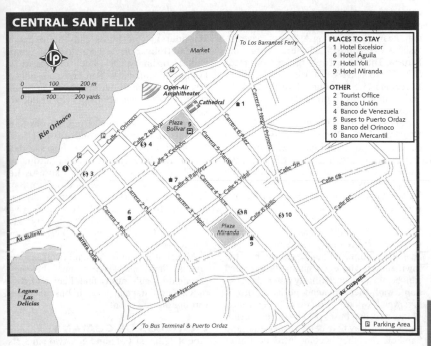

CENTRAL SAN FÉLIX

Río Orinoco

To Los Barrancos Ferry

Market

Open-Air Amphitheater

Cathedral

Plaza Bolívar

Calle 1 Orinoco

Calle 2 Bolívar

Calle 3 Credeiho

Carrera 7 Negro Primero

Carrera 6 Páez

Carrera 5 Merino

Calle 4 Ramírez

Carrera 4 Sucre

Calle 5 Vidal

Calle 5 Bello

Carrera 3 Infia

Carrera 2 Pil

Carrera 1 Siyo

Carrera Orta

Av Bolívar

Plaza Miranda

Calle Alvarado

Calle 5JA

Calle 68

Calle 6C

Av Guayana

Laguna Las Delicias

To Bus Terminal & Puerto Ordaz

PLACES TO STAY
1 Hotel Excelsior
6 Hotel Águila
7 Hotel Yoli
9 Hotel Miranda

OTHER
2 Tourist Office
3 Banco Unión
4 Banco de Venezuela
5 Buses to Puerto Ordaz
8 Banco del Orinoco
10 Banco Mercantil

0   100   200 m
0   100   200 yards

Parking Area

Other inexpensive places in the area include **RicArepa**, Calle Upata, which has arepas and other typical local food, **Trattoria A'Giulio**, adjoining the Hotel La Guayana, which does some Italian fare, and **Pizzería El Churrasco**, Calle Callao.

More upmarket dining in the central area is provided, among other places, by **Restaurant La Romanina** (both Italian food and steaks), **Tasca Restaurant La Sevillana** (Spanish cuisine, including seafood) and **Restaurant Marcelo** (mostly Italian food). Farther south, on Avenida Las Américas, is the good **Restaurant El Bigote del Abuelo**.

Galery Café is a beautiful arty café that has quickly become a trendy place. It features live music most days, as well as lovely salads, sandwiches and fondue, and it is open late. Next door, the new **Restaurant Pancho Villa** serves Mexican specialties in its appropriately decorated, charming interior.

More cafés lie in Puerto Ordaz' center, including the enjoyable **La Cuisine Express**,

Carrera Tumeremo. You'll find many more cafés in Alta Vista – the Centro Ciudad Comercial Alta Vista (Macro Centro) alone has half a dozen of them.

Entertainment

For nighttime dancing, try **X Tremo's** or **Cannibal Club**, two popular discos in Macro Centro that draw in essentially young clientele. Slightly more mature folks flock to **Excalibur**, on Avenida las Américas. If playing pool and drinking are all you're after, check **Daniel's Club**, on Calle Callao in the center.

Getting There & Away

Air The airport is at the western end of Puerto Ordaz, on the road to Ciudad Bolívar. Buses marked 'Sidor Directo' from Alta Vista will leave you at the terminal's entrance. Note that the airport appears in all schedules as 'Puerto Ordaz,' not 'Ciudad Guayana.'

GUAYANA

Puerto Ordaz is the busiest air hub in eastern Venezuela and is serviced by most major carriers, including Avensa/Servivensa, Aserca, Aeropostal, Laser, Avior and Rutaca. There are direct flights to Caracas (US$52 to US$88), Porlamar (US$73), Barcelona (US$62) and Maturín (US$57), and connections to other destinations. The prices are one-way.

Servivensa has daily flights on DC-3s to Canaima (US$122) and on to Santa Elena de Uairén (an additional US$107; if you don't stop in Canaima, it's US$122 for the whole Puerto Ordaz–Santa Elena route). The planes fly at low altitudes, thus providing spectacular views over the Gran Sabana and its tepuis.

Bus Ciudad Guayana has two bus terminals. The main one is in San Félix, on Avenida Gumilla, about 1.5km south of the town center. The environs of the terminal can be unsafe, particularly after dark, so don't walk there. Instead, go by carrito or taxi, which will drop you off at the entrance. Plenty of urban buses pass by the bus terminal on their way between Puerto Ordaz and San Félix, but they become infrequent after 8 pm and stop running around 9 pm. If you arrive later, you'll probably need a taxi to move around, which will cost US$6 to central Puerto Ordaz.

The other terminal is in Puerto Ordaz, on Avenida Guayana, about 1km east of the airport. It's smaller, cleaner, quieter and safer, and handles far fewer buses than the San Félix terminal. It's essentially a transit point rather than a destination, but not all buses pass through here.

There are regular departures from San Félix's terminal to Caracas (US$17 ordinary, US$21 deluxe, 10½ hours); most of these buses call en route at Puerto Ordaz' terminal. There are also buses direct to Maracay (US$19 deluxe, 10 hours) and Valencia (US$21 deluxe, 11 hours) that don't pass through Caracas. They are convenient for all those who wish to go straight to Venezuela's northwest or the Andes, avoiding spending time and money on connections in the capital.

Buses to Ciudad Bolívar depart from both terminals every half-hour or so (US$2, 1½ hours). Nine buses daily arrive from Ciudad Bolívar on their way to Santa Elena (US$11 ordinary, US$14 deluxe, nine to 10 hours); they all call at San Félix, but only a few do so in Puerto Ordaz. No direct buses run to Ciudad Piar from San Félix or Puerto Ordaz.

Expresos Maturín has buses from San Félix to Maturín every hour or two (US$5, 3½ hours) and also several buses a day farther north to Carúpano (US$9 ordinary, US$12 deluxe, seven hours). Expresos La Guayanesa has two buses a day from San Félix to Tucupita (US$5, 3½ hours), but por puestos go there regularly (US$7, two hours). All these trips involve a ferry ride across the Orinoco from San Félix to Los Barrancos.

Most buses going to Ciudad Guayana are labeled 'San Félix,' since it's here that they terminate. You'll rarely find 'Puerto Ordaz' or 'Ciudad Guayana' listed in bus schedules throughout the country.

CASTILLOS DE GUAYANA

About 38km east of San Félix, two old forts sit on the hilly right bank of the Orinoco, overlooking the river. They were built to protect Santo Tomás, the first Spanish settlement founded on the riverbank in 1595.

The older fort, the **Castillo de San Francisco** (named after the monastery of San Francisco de Asís that had previously stood on the site) dates from the 1670s. As pirate raids continued unabated, a second fort, the **Castillo de San Diego de Alcalá**, went up in 1747 on a nearby, higher hill. However, this didn't provide adequate protection either. The settlement was eventually moved upriver in 1762 and refounded two years later as Santo Tomás de la Guayana de Angostura (present-day Ciudad Bolívar), while the forts were abandoned. At the end of the 19th century, the forts were remodeled and used to control river traffic, which they did until 1943. In the 1970s, they were restored to their original condition and became tourist attractions. The higher fort commands fine views over the Orinoco and beyond. The forts are open to visitors from Tuesday to Sunday.

Getting There & Away

The forts are accessible by road from San Félix. Por puestos take you there from the place known as 'El Mirador,' at the eastern end of San Félix, which can be reached by city buses. The ride to the forts costs US$1.75 and takes 1¼ hours.

Alternatively, take a tour. Several travel agencies operate half-day tours to the Castillos for around US$25 per person.

REPRESA DE GURI

Due south of Ciudad Guayana is a large artificial lake, Embalse de Guri. This is the reservoir of the second-largest hydroelectric project in the world (Itaipú on the border of Brazil and Paraguay is the largest).

The Represa Raúl Leoni – as it is officially named, though commonly referred to as the Represa de Guri (Guri Dam) – was built in the lower course of the Río Caroní, about 100km upstream from its inlet into the Orinoco. The work was carried out in stages from 1963 to 1986. Eight million cubic meters of concrete were used to build a gigantic 1304m-long dam that is 162m high at its highest point. Covering an area of about 4250 sq km, the reservoir created by the dam is Venezuela's largest lake after Lago de Maracaibo. It now abounds in fish, mainly *pavón* (peacock bass) and its equally ferocious cousin, the *payara*. The lake has grown in popularity as a good sport-fishing destination.

With an electric potential of 10 million kilowatts, the complex satisfies over half of the country's electricity demand. The Guri Dam not only provides power for the giant industrial plants of the region, but also supplies electricity to central Venezuela, Caracas included. The dam and some of the installations can be visited.

Organized Tours

EDELCA (Electrificación del Caroní), the state company that operates the dam, runs free daily tours at 9 and 10:30 am and 2 and 3:30 pm. From the visitors center, you are taken by bus for a one-hour trip around the complex. Although you don't see much of the installations, you get a feeling for how enormous the project is.

The tour will include a stopover at a lookout, from where you get a good general view of the dam and of a large kinetic sculpture by Alejandro Otero. You are then shown one of the units of the powerhouse, embellished with a geometrical decoration by Carlos Cruz Díez. Finally you go to the Plaza del Sol y la Luna, noted for a huge sundial showing months, hours and minutes.

Tours to the Represa de Guri (usually combined with a visit to Cerro Bolívar) are available from a few travel agents in Ciudad Guayana. Expect to pay US$60 to US$80 for this tour.

Getting There & Away

This is a bit complicated, as there's no public transportation to the dam. The entrance to the complex is at the northwestern end of the Embalse de Guri, about 80km by road from Puerto Ordaz. You first go along the Ciudad Guayana–Ciudad Piar highway, then along the Guri side road, which branches off and goes to the *alcabala* (checkpost) at the entrance to the Guri complex. No public buses go along this road, so taking a taxi or hitching are the only options.

EDELCA vehicles run regularly from Puerto Ordaz to the dam, so it may be worth checking the office. Otherwise, take the bus going along the old road (not the autopista) between Ciudad Guayana and Ciudad Bolívar, and get off at km 70. From here, hitchhike the remaining distance. At the alcabala, you will be given a permit; the visitors center is 5km farther inside the compound, so you will again have to rely on someone's vehicle.

CERRO BOLÍVAR

Jutting 600m out of the surrounding plains some 100km south of Ciudad Bolívar, Cerro Bolívar is a huge, oval, iron-ore mountain, 11km long and 3km wide. The mountain has intrigued explorers since the early days of the Spanish conquest. Around the mid-18th century, Capuchin missionaries set up the first forges here, but it actually was not until 1947 that US geologists confirmed the unusually high grade of the ore (up to 60% pure iron in some parts), which paved the way for large-scale exploitation. Since then, the ore has been systematically stripped from the mountain by humans and machines, and now Cerro Bolívar is terraced all around. After being mined, the ore is loaded onto railcars and transported to the steel mill in Ciudad Guayana.

About 10km east of Cerro Bolívar is **Ciudad Piar**, a town founded in the 1950s to provide an operational and administrative center for the state-run Ferrominera Orinoco mining company as well as accommodations for the workers. Today, it's a town of 23,000 inhabitants. Ferrominera organizes tours at 9 am and 2 pm weekdays. The Ferrominera administration building, where the tours begin, is at the western end of the town, at the entrance to the mine's restricted area.

Getting There & Away

Ciudad Piar is accessible by bus from Ciudad Bolívar (US$2.50, two hours); there are no buses from Ciudad Guayana.

If you fly from Ciudad Bolívar to Canaima, you are likely to get a bird's-eye view of Cerro Bolívar, as planes normally pass directly over it.

EL CALLAO
☎ 088 (☎ 0288 from Jun 16, 2001)

El Callao is an old gold town that is set on the Río Yuruarí, about 180km southeast of Ciudad Guayana, in what has been Venezuela's richest gold region. The gold-rich basin spreads from El Callao southward for 200km, right up to the edge of La Gran Sabana, and is dotted with hundreds of gold mines.

The gold rush hit the region in 1849, when prospectors found exceptionally rich lodes in the Río Yuruarí. Fortune seekers from all corners of Venezuela, as well as Trinidad, British Guiana and beyond, were quick to rush in and take part in what was one of the world's greatest gold rushes in

modern history. El Callao, the early product of that rush, developed dramatically.

Today El Callao is a quiet and tidy town of 12,000, the gold-shopping mecca of the region. It boasts a quite spectacular number of gold jewelers – possibly as many as 25 on Plaza Bolívar alone – and many more down side streets. The jewelry is not renowned for any particular artistic quality, but it's arguably the cheapest in the country.

Gold jewelry is produced locally in numerous small workshops, using rudimentary manual techniques. Some workshops can be visited; just walk around the central streets and look for 'Taller de Oro' signs.

The town's other distinctive feature is its Trinidad-influenced Carnaval, accompanied with calypso, steel bands and floats – a palpable mark of the substantial Antillan migration during the gold rush.

There are several gold mines around the town, of which the Mina Colombia, operated by the Minerven state company, is the largest. It's the deepest gold mine in Venezuela, with galleries spread over seven levels, from 130m to 479m below the ground surface. It produces about three tons of gold per year. The mine is 3km from El Callao and is serviced by por puestos and taxis.

Mina Colombia is occasionally open to tourists from 8 am to noon weekdays. The visits are by a 1½-hour free tour, organized by request at least one or two days in advance. Participants need to be in good health, between 18 and 60 years of age. Contact the mine's Departamento de Relaciones Públicas (☎ 612 16, fax 612 15) for further details.

Places to Stay

Several budget hotels lie within a few blocks northwest of Plaza Bolívar, including *Hotel Italia (☎ 617 70)* and *Hotel Ritz (☎ 619 33),* diagonally opposite each other on Calle Ricaurte. Both are basic but acceptable and cost about US$10 matrimonial with bath and fan. The Italia also has some rooms with air-conditioning, as well as a cheap restaurant.

If you need more comfort, try *Hotel El Arte Dorado (☎ 615 35, 616 37),* Calle

Roscio, 300m south of Plaza Bolívar, which has reasonable air-con singles/doubles/triples/quads with bath for US$20/24/28/32. In late 2000, *Hotel New Millennium* was just about to open on Plaza Bolívar, and it's likely to be the best place in town. Its owner may organize tours around the mines in the region.

Getting There & Away
El Callao sits a kilometer off the main highway. Some of the long-distance buses enter the town and stop near the bridge. There's regular service to San Félix by bus (US$6, three hours) and por puesto (US$8, 2½ hours). A few buses a day pass through on their way to Santa Elena (US$9 ordinary, US$11 deluxe, six to seven hours).

EL DORADO
☎ 088 (☎ 0288 from Jun 16, 2001)
Appropriately named 'El Dorado' (Golden One), this is another gold town, on the Cuyuní River, 108km south of El Callao. It grew fat on the 19th-century gold rush, and a number of mines still operate in the area. In the 1950s, a maximum-security prison was built across the river from the town; it remains in use today. The famous French convict Papillon stayed here for a while. The jail can no longer be visited, since a couple of tourists under military guidance were taken hostage by prisoners in 1992.

Unlike the orderly and tranquil El Callao, El Dorado (population 5000) looks chaotic and retains much of the gold-rush atmosphere. It appears a tough town, with filthy streets and a busy triangular square, around which much of the town's life is concentrated.

It's possible to visit some of the rudimentary gold mines in the El Dorado area. Jeeps and pickup trucks park in the square and go to the mines on demand, usually with miners early in the morning. Talk to the drivers, some of whom will be eager to take you for a trip around the mines.

Places to Stay
There are three budget hotels on the triangular square: *Hotel Edgar*, *Hotel El Dorado* and *Hotel San Antonio*. All have

rooms with private baths and fans, and cost US$16/20 single/double. Some more basic hotels lie on the street going from the square to the river.

Getting There & Away
El Dorado is 6km off the Ciudad Guayana–Santa Elena highway. The turnoff (marked 'km 0') is a point of reference from which road distances are measured and signed for every kilometer all the way south to the Brazilian border.

Santa Elena buses don't normally call at El Dorado, but buses to Ciudad Guayana run every two to three hours from the triangular square (US$8, five hours). There are also por puestos to Tumeremo, from where there are more buses to Ciudad Guayana.

Salto Angel & Around

Commonly known to the English-speaking world as 'Angel Falls,' this is the world's highest waterfall. Its total height is 979m, recorded by a National Geographic Society expedition in 1949. It also has the world's greatest uninterrupted drop – 807m, which is 16 times the height of Niagara Falls. The waterfall has clearly become Venezuela's number-one promotional landmark, and you will find photos of it in just about every tourist brochure.

Salto Angel spills from the heart-shaped Auyantepui ('Mountain of the God of Evil' in the Pemón language), one of the largest tepuis, with a flat top of about 700 sq km. The waterfall is in the central portion of the tepui and drops into what is known as Cañón del Diablo (Devil's Canyon).

The waterfall is not named, as one might expect, after a divine creature, but after an American bush pilot, Jimmie Angel (1899–1956), who landed on the boggy top of Auyantepui in 1937 in a four-seater airplane, in search of gold. The plane stuck in the marshy surface, preventing Angel from taking off again. He, his wife and two companions trekked through the rough virgin

GUAYANA

SALTO ANGEL & AROUND

terrain to the edge of the plateau, then descended over a kilometer of almost vertical cliff to return to civilization after an 11-day odyssey.

Orientation

Salto Angel is in a distant wilderness without any road access. The village of Canaima, about 50km northwest of Salto Angel, is the major gateway to the falls. Canaima doesn't have any overland link to the rest of the country either (except for a couple of adventurous, seasonal trails), but it does have an airport. The small Indian settlement of

Kavac, at the southeastern foot of Auyantepui, is another jumping-off point for the falls, but it's far less popular than Canaima and is used mostly by organized tours. It's also isolated, but it has its own airstrip.

A visit to Salto Angel is usually undertaken in two stages, with Canaima as the stepping-stone. Most tourists fly into Canaima, from where they take a light plane or boat to the falls. No walking trails go all the way from Canaima (or Kavac) to the falls.

There are a number of other attractions in the Canaima area, mostly waterfalls, of which the most popular is Salto El Sapo.

In Kavac's area, the most frequently visited sight is the Cueva de Kavac.

Salto Angel, Auyantepui, Canaima and the surrounding area lie within the boundaries of Parque Nacional Canaima, which is Venezuela's second-largest national park and covers 30,000 sq km. The park stretches eastward and southward almost to the international border and encompasses most of La Gran Sabana (see that section, later in this chapter). All visitors coming to Canaima pay the US$12 national-park entrance fee, which is collected upon arrival at the airport.

Planning

When to Go The dry season in the region normally lasts from January to May; rains tend to begin in late May or early June and continue until November. They gradually ease in December and stop by January. Recent climatic anomalies throughout the world were also felt in the Salto Angel region; since 1996 the rainy season has continued well into February, and even in the dry season, rains have occurred more frequently than before.

Understandably, the season determines the volume of Salto Angel (and other waterfalls). At times in the dry season, it can be pretty faint – just a thin ribbon of water fading into mist halfway down its drop. In the rainy months, on the other hand, it's often voluminous and spectacular.

The waterfall is at its most impressive after heavy rains, which occur frequently in August and September. Unfortunately, this is precisely the period when it is hardest to see, as it is often covered by clouds. In general, the waterfall shows up more often in the morning than in the afternoon, but there are no hard and fast rules here. Morning hours are the best for taking photos of the waterfall, as it faces east and is in direct sunlight until around noon.

The rainy season is certainly a better time to admire Salto Angel and other waterfalls, although, of course, it's more risky. One of the other advantages of coming in the wet period is that you can take a boat tour to Salto Angel, which is only organized when the water level of local rivers is sufficiently high (roughly from June to January). However, due to the recent climatic changes, there has been sufficient water for the tours to be run for most of the year. Over the past five years, tours continued for at least 10 months each year, with February to April being the only uncertain period.

What Kind of Trip Numerous tour operators in virtually every corner of the country offer trips to Salto Angel – this is, after all, Venezuela's top tourist attraction – so there's never a problem whatsoever getting there. If there's any trouble, it may be money, as none of these trips is cheap: You need at least US$130 or so for a glimpse of the falls.

The cheapest way to get to Salto Angel is to take a no-frills day trip with one of the small airlines from Ciudad Bolívar (see Organized Tours in the Ciudad Bolívar section, earlier). However, you may end up not seeing the waterfall, especially in the rainy season. The airlines offering these trips are essentially commercial passenger carriers that fly people (mainly miners and their families) between the scattered towns and villages of the region on a more or less regular schedule. Flying around Salto Angel is only part of their activity, and not necessarily the major one. The pilots will fly you there, but according to their schedule (ie, on the way to Canaima or another regional destination in the morning or on the way back to Ciudad Bolívar in the afternoon). If the waterfall happens to be visible, you are lucky; if not, you've paid for nothing.

The second-cheapest option (costing about US$160 to US$180) is a day tour organized by Ciudad Bolívar's tour operators; these tours add some other local attractions to Salto Angel, plus a lunch. The tour companies use the same local airlines but charter the whole flight, so they are less dependent on the carriers' schedules.

Some travelers prefer to fly to Canaima on their own and arrange the flight over Salto Angel (or the boat trip to the falls, or both) from there with local operators. This can be more expensive than a package from

GUAYANA

Ciudad Bolívar and will involve shopping around in Canaima, yet it gives you more flexibility, especially if you plan on staying in Canaima for a while. To keep costs down, camping equipment would be a good idea, as well as some food brought in from Ciudad Bolívar.

If money is not a problem, Hoturvensa's packages may appear to provide a comfortable and easy solution (see Organized Tours under Canaima, later), but be warned that they are a terrible value.

What to Bring Bring waterproof gear, a swimsuit and plenty of film. Efficient insect repellent is essential – insects abound on the savanna, though not so much in the jungle. A long-sleeved shirt will further protect you from insects and occasional chills at night. A hat or other head protection from sun and rain is also a wise idea; a flashlight may be useful as well. If you plan on boat excursions, make sure to have a plastic sheet or bag to protect your gear. A tent or hammock (preferably with a mosquito net) will save you from having to spend money at Canaima's hotels, while food brought from outside will save you money on restaurants.

CANAIMA
☎ 086 (☎ 0286 from Jun 16, 2001)
Canaima (population 1200) is a mixed tourist-Indian village that serves as a springboard for Salto Angel. It first appeared on travelers maps in the 1960s, after a large holiday camp named Campamento Canaima and an airport capable of receiving commercial jets were built here. Today it blends an Indian settlement of some 150 Pemón families with a tourist resort.

Without a doubt, Canaima's location is spectacular. It sits on a peaceful, wide stretch of the Río Carrao known as Laguna de Canaima, just below the point where the river turns into a line of magnificent falls, Saltos Hacha. The rose-colored lagoon is bordered by a pink beach. The falls, too, have conspicuously colored water, ranging from yellowish to brownish tones that are vaguely reminiscent of beer or brandy. The coloring of these (as well as of other rivers and falls in the region) is caused by *tanino* (tannin), a solid compound found in some local trees and plants, especially in the Bonnetia tree.

Campamento Canaima is right on the bank of the romantic lagoon. The airport is a five-minute walk to the west, while the Indian village stretches to the south of the camp.

Information
Tourist Offices There's no specific tourist information office here, but tour operators are knowledgeable about the region and are usually helpful.

Money There are no banks in Canaima. Tienda Quincallería Canaima (a souvenir and grocery store), near the airport, changes US cash and traveler's checks at possibly the best rate in town; however, it's obviously lower than in the cities, so it's best to come with a sufficient amount of bolívares. Some other establishments, including Campamento Canaima, change cash and sometimes traveler's checks, but the rate may be still lower. Most of Canaima's tour operators accept payment in US cash but refuse payment by credit cards, or charge 10% more if you pay with plastic.

Things to See & Do
Most regional attractions are inaccessible on your own, so you'll have to use the services of tour operators (see Organized Tours, next). What you can do are short walks in the environs of Canaima, such as a hike to the top of the hill east of the village. It's a steep, 20-minute ascent (ask for directions) rewarded with great views. You can also stroll around the dusty streets of the village. There's an interesting thatched Pemón church at the southern end of Canaima.

Like most visitors, you'll probably spend some time in Campamento Canaima, enjoying the beach and views of the falls. The lagoon looks wonderfully calm, but the waterfalls cause treacherous undercurrents. Some people have drowned trying to swim from the camp to the opposite island. Be careful and find out where it's safe to swim before you go into deep water. Also, the beach may have some *niguas* (chigoes or chiggers), small sand fleas that tend to burrow into skin.

Organized Tours

Canaima is a hive of tour-business activity, with half a dozen tour operators and their planes, boats and jeeps. They offer tours to Salto Angel, other nearby falls, Indian villages and whatever other interesting sights they have discovered in the area.

Tour Operators Hoteles y Turismo Avensa (Hoturvensa), a travel offspring of Avensa/Servivensa airlines, runs Campamento Canaima. The agency offers packages that include accommodations and full board in its camp, Servivensa's flight over Salto Angel (weather permitting), a short boat trip on Laguna de Canaima and a complimentary drink on arrival. Two kinds of packages are available: a two-day, one-night stay for US$295/485/600 for one/two/three

persons, and a three-day, two-night stay for US$570/675/875.

The packages don't include the flight into and out of Canaima, so keep US$200 in reserve. Also keep in mind that if you don't see the falls because of bad weather, Hoturvensa won't give you any money back; it's just your bad luck. The packages can be bought from any Avensa office in Venezuela and from most travel agencies. This is the most expensive way to visit Canaima and Salto Angel, and it is a really bad value. Hoturvensa doesn't offer any tours other than these two packages.

There are several real tour operators in Canaima, including Canaima Tours, Tiuna Tours, Bernal Tours and Kamaracoto Tours. Canaima Tours (☎ 62 55 60, 61 69 81) is Hoturvensa's agent and has its office in Campamento Canaima. It's the most expensive operator, essentially catering to guests of Campamento Canaima, to complement Hoturvensa's limited tour offer. The remaining companies are cheaper, and their advertised prices can be negotiated to some extent.

Harried travelers endure yet another stressful day in Parque Nacional Canaima.

GUAYANA

JANE SWEENEY

They all wait for incoming flights at the airport – this is the right place and time to shop around for a tour.

Tiuna Tours (☎ 62 42 55) has grown into the major local operator and does a good job. The company provides local services for most packaged groups that are organized by Ciudad Bolívar's tour agencies and flown into Canaima, and also services individual travelers who arrive at Canaima independently. It has a large campamento in Canaima that provides lodging and meals for the participants of its tours and, if there are vacancies, for anybody else. The tours are conducted by bilingual guides. Tiuna has its offices in Ciudad Bolívar and Caracas – see those sections for details.

Bernal Tours (☎ 62 04 43) is now run by Tomás Bernal's sons, after Tomás tragically died in 1998. Their campamento is on the island in Laguna de Canaima, opposite Campamento Canaima. Tour participants stay and eat in the rustic house and sleep in hammocks. Facilities are quite simple, but there is a certain charm about the place, plus a fine pink beach in front of Saltos Hacha. If you can't find Tomás' sons at the airport, inquire at the Tienda Quincallería Canaima. Bernal Tours has recently opened its outlet (named Sapito Tours) at the airport in Ciudad Bolívar, where it sells its Canaima trips.

Kamaracoto Tours have roughly similar tours and comparable prices to the Tiuna and Bernal, and they too have their own campamento, near the church in Canaima, with accommodations in hammocks only.

As the major attraction, Salto Angel is the focus of the tour companies. As there are no trails to the waterfall, you have to take a tour, either by plane or boat.

Salto Angel by Plane Flights to the waterfall are serviced by light (usually five-seat) planes of various small airlines that come to Canaima, mostly from Ciudad Bolívar. The pilots fly two or three times back and forth over the face of the falls, circle the top of the tepui and then return. The roundtrip out of Canaima takes about 40 minutes and costs roughly US$40. These trips can be arranged directly with the pilots at the airport or with local tour operators.

Servivensa flies the guests of Campamento Canaima to Salto Angel in its 22-seater DC-3s. These planes – which hark back to the World War II era – have been remodeled by enlarging the windows to provide better views. Nonguests can use Servivensa's services, if there are vacancies, for US$50 per person. Canaima Tours handles information and bookings.

Salto Angel by Boat This is a memorable experience – arguably even more fascinating than the flight – that allows you to see the waterfall from a different perspective, and, more importantly, to enjoy it at a more leisurely pace.

Motorized canoes depart from Ucaima, above Saltos Hacha, and go up the Ríos Carrao and Churún to Isla Ratoncito, at the foot of Salto Angel. From there, an hour's walk will take you uphill to Mirador Laime, the outcrop right in front of the falls.

All Canaima-based tour companies (except Hoturvensa) offer all-inclusive boat trips to the falls. A minimum of five to six persons is usually required (boats have a capacity of 10 to 12 passengers), but some operators may be satisfied with just four, particularly in the slow season.

The shortest and cheapest is a full-day roundtrip, which requires an early start at around 5 am and gives you about 30 minutes to an hour face to face with Salto Angel. The package usually includes a trip to Salto El Sapo, and the whole tour costs US$120 to US$140. The more relaxing three-day, two-night tours (all-inclusive) are offered for US$150 to US$180, and they also include Salto El Sapo. Each company has its own campamento upriver, where travelers stay the two nights (in hammocks). Most operators have camps in the area of Isla Orquídea; only Bernal Tours has a camp at Isla Ratoncito.

The boats operate in the rainy season, but as mentioned earlier, they have been running for most of the year over several past years. For example, in 2000 there was a break of only a few weeks in March, plus some dry days in the neighboring months. However, you should bear in mind that the waterfall may be barely a trickle in the dry season, even though it's accessible by boat. The view of the falls may be a little bit different from what you've seen on postcards. Be prepared for a disappointment if traveling in the middle of the dry period, although the boat trip is a great fun and the scenery is spectacular all the way, particularly in the Cañón del Diablo.

Other Tours The most popular short trip is to Salto El Sapo. It's usually included in the Salto Angel boat package but can be an excursion in its own right (US$20 per person, two to three hours). It's a 10-minute boat trip from Canaima plus a short walk. You can't get to the falls on foot from Canaima (it's on the other side of the Río Carrao), so you'll have to take a tour (unless you're staying at the Bernal camp on the island).

Salto El Sapo is beautiful, and unusual in that you can walk under it. Be prepared to get drenched by the waterfall in the rainy season – take a swimsuit. A few minutes' walk from El Sapo is Salto El Sapito, another attractive waterfall that is normally included in the same excursion.

Salto Yuri is another nearby destination. It's a half-day jeep and boat trip and is offered by most local operators (US$30 to US$40 per person).

Places to Stay & Eat

Canaima's main lodging/eating venue is *Campamento Canaima (☎ 61 17 91, fax 61 30 71)*, operated by Hoturvensa. The camp consists of about 35 palm-thatched cabañas (109 rooms in all, with bath and hot water), its own restaurant, bar and *fuente de soda* (snack bar). The cabañas, which are scattered along the lagoon bank, are built in traditional style, and the elevated churuata-style restaurant offers an excellent view over the lagoon and falls.

Accommodations are available only as part of a package (see Tour Operators, earlier), but the camp's restaurant, bar and fuente de soda are open to all. The restaurant does not provide à la carte dishes; it serves only expensive set meals (breakfast US$14, lunch US$21, dinner US$21), which don't seem to be a good value. The meals do not include soft drinks and fruit juices, which you can buy separately, and the food can be monotonous.

Some potential travelers to Canaima may be put off by the apparent monopoly of the camp, but don't worry, as there are cheaper options for both accommodations and food. There are now more than half a dozen other campamentos and posadas in Canaima, some of which also serve meals. Some camps service organized tours but usually have vacancies that they rent out to individual tourists. At most places, expect to pay US$6 to US$10 for a hammock and US$12 to US$25 for a bed. Some campamentos will let you string up your own hammock under their roof (and use their facilities) for US$3 to US$5.

The eight-room *Posada Kaikusé (☎ 014-884 90 31)*, in the northern end of the village, is possibly the cheapest place to stay, for about US$12 per bed in doubles, triples or quads with bath. Just next to it is the similarly simple *Posada Kusarí*, which charges US$16 per bed – inquire at Tienda Quincallería Canaima for vacancies and current rates.

In the southern portion of the village, *Posada Wey Tepuy (☎ 014-884 09 93)*, opposite the school, is one of the cheapest places, for US$16 per bed in a double or triple with bath. In the same area, the *Campamento Churún Vená*, opposite the soccer field, is another option, for US$8/18 hammock/bed. The nearby *Restaurant Imawary* (popularly known as 'Simón') is reasonably cheap by Canaima standards – US$12 for lunch or dinner – and has some still cheaper offerings such as spaghetti (US$6) and sandwiches (US$3).

Tiuna and Kamaracoto possess campamentos and may have some vacant hammocks or beds – ask their agents at the airport upon arrival. The Tiuna camp also serves meals, for much the same as Restaurant Imawary.

If you have your own tent, you can camp free in Canaima, but get a permit from the

GUAYANA

Inparques officer at the airport. The usual place to camp is on the beach next to the helpful Guardia Nacional post, just off Campamento Canaima. You may be able to arrange with the Guardia to leave your stuff at the post while you are away.

A few shops in Canaima sell basic supplies, such as bread, pasta, canned fish and biscuits, but prices are rather high. If you plan on self-catering, it's best to bring some essential supplies with you.

Getting There & Away

Servivensa no longer has jet flights from Caracas and Porlamar to Canaima. It now flies daily on its veteran DC-3s all the way from Caracas via Puerto Ordaz to Canaima, and continues on to Santa Elena de Uairén. As DC-3s are not permitted at Maiquetía, Servivensa uses the Aeropuerto Caracas, an obscure airport near Charallave, about 50km from Caracas, without any reliable public transportation except for taxis.

If you buy either of Hoturvensa's packages, Servivensa will sell you a discount ticket to Canaima, which is US$108 from Caracas, US$57 from Puerto Ordaz and US$57 from Santa Elena. Otherwise, it will charge its inflated regular fares of US$183, US$122 and US$107, respectively. The airline may not want to sell tickets in advance, hoping to fill flights with package-tour passengers. Even if you succeed in buying a ticket, there may still be difficulties at the airport. The figures are one-way fares and are the same in both directions – ie, you need another US$183 to return to Caracas. There are no discounts on roundtrip fares: They are just two one-ways. Whichever route you're traveling, make sure to book your onward ticket in high season, otherwise you may have to wait for several days for a seat to become available.

Several small regional carriers fly between Ciudad Bolívar and Canaima on a semiregular or charter basis (US$50). See Organized Tours in the Ciudad Bolívar section, earlier, for details. Rutaca has daily flights between Canaima and Santa Elena for US$75 each way.

Flights to Kavac are difficult to arrange in Canaima, unless there are four or five of you, in which case you can just charter a small plane. It's easier to buy just a seat to Kavac from Ciudad Bolívar, as there are more planes flying from there.

KAMARATA

Kamarata is an old Pemón village on the Río Acanán, at the southeastern foot of Auyantepui. Some decades ago, it was discovered as a possible alternative jumping-off point for Salto Angel, and since then it has been slowly attracting adventurous travelers. There are a few simple places to stay and eat in town, and you can even camp next to the Capuchin mission.

In order to attract tourists, the locals built the village of Kavac (see the next section), which has since taken over most of Kamarata's tourist traffic. It's a hot two-hour walk from Kamarata, or a short drive on a dirt road.

KAVAC

Kavac is the tourist outlet of Kamarata. It consists of 20-odd churuatas built in traditional style, making it a fine if slightly artificial example of a typical Pemón settlement. Neat, quiet and almost devoid of people, it is situated on the plain savanna close to Auyantepui.

The vast majority of tourists coming to Kavac are package groups put together by tour companies from outside, mostly from Ciudad Bolívar. Individual travelers are rare guests here. They should be aware of a potential risk of being overcharged for tours, accommodations and food by the local operators, as has happened in the past.

Organized Tours

Kavac plays host to three small tour/hotel operators – Asociación Civil Kamarata Kavac, Makunaima Tours and Excursiones Pemón – that organize tours in the region.

The area's major attraction is the Cueva de Kavac, which despite its name is not a cave but a deep gorge with a waterfall plunging into it. There's a natural pool at the foot of the waterfall; you reach it by swimming upstream in the canyon, so bring your swimsuit with you. You actually don't need a guide to get to the falls; it's a pretty straightforward half-hour walk from Kavac. If in doubt, discreetly follow any of the tour groups.

Boat trips to Salto Angel are organized in the rainy season only. The boats go from Kamarata down the Ríos Acanán and Carrao, then up the Río Churún to Isla Ratoncito. Following a walk to the Mirador Laime, the boats then sail down the Ríos Churún and Carrao to Canaima, where the tours conclude. It's normally a four-day tour that costs US$200 to US$300 per person, with a minimum of about six persons.

Kavac is one of the starting points for a trip (or, rather, an expedition) to the top of Auyantepui. Guides for this long and adventurous hike can be contracted through local tour agencies in Kavac or Kamarata. The trail leads from Kavac via Santa Marta to Guayaraca, from where it approaches the foot of the tepui before snaking uphill, following roughly the same route Jimmie Angel used for his descent in 1937. In three days (from Kavac), you'll reach a place called El Libertador, so named after Bolívar's bust was placed here. You need another week or so to get to the point from where Salto Angel plunges. Count on roughly US$25 a day per guide for the group, plus another US$25 per porter.

Places to Stay
The *Hotel Kavaikoden* is the only place in Kavac that has beds, but it was being refurbished when we were there and may still be when you read this. There are more places offering accommodations in hammocks (US$8 to US$12 per head), and these are fairly easy to come by.

Getting There & Away
Kavac has an airstrip where light planes land several times a week from Ciudad Bolívar and Santa Elena de Uairén (about US$75 to or from either). Flights to or from Canaima are mostly on a charter basis.

La Gran Sabana

The Gran Sabana, a rolling grassy highland in Venezuela's far southeastern corner, is vast, wild, beautiful, empty and silent. In geographical terms, it's the upland region lying in the basin of the upper Río Caroní at an elevation of over 800m. Its area is estimated at some 35,000 sq km, and much of it lies within the limits of the Parque Nacional Canaima. Correctly speaking, La Gran Sabana doesn't include either the Valle de Kamarata or the Sabanas of Urimán and Canaima.

The only town in the region is Santa Elena de Uairén, close to the Brazilian frontier. The remaining part of the sparse population – mostly Pemón Indians, the land's indigenous inhabitants – live in scattered villages and hamlets. It's estimated that there are about 15,000 Indians living in some 270 settlements.

The most striking natural feature dominating the skyline of the Gran Sabana are gigantic flat-topped mountains called tepuis (see the boxed text 'Tepuis & Simas'). The best known of all the tepuis is Roraima, which was the first to be climbed and is increasingly popular among travelers, although the trip to the top and back takes at least five days.

Many other sights in La Gran Sabana are easier to visit, and some of them are conveniently located on the main road. Particularly amazing are the many waterfalls.

Orientation
Up to not long ago, the Gran Sabana was virtually inaccessible. It wasn't until 1973 that a road between El Dorado and Santa Elena was completed, and not until 1990 that the last stretch of this road was paved. Today it's one of the best highways in the country, and one of the most spectacular. The entire length of the road is signposted with kilometer marks, telling you how far you are from El Dorado. The El Dorado fork is km 0 and Santa Elena is km 316. These are a great help and are often included in

LA GRAN SABANA

tourist publications to help you determine
the location of the sights.

Traveling southward from El Dorado,
you'll find the fine ***Campamento La Montañita*** at km 70 just by the road, which has
several inexpensive cabañas, a restaurant
and a campsite.

At km 85 you reach **Las Claritas**, a particularly dirty and busy ramshackle town, and
3km farther south is **San Isidro** (often
simply called 'Km 88'), another unsavory
collection of tin-and-rubbish shacks. Both
settlements have grown as gold-mining
supply centers for what is today one of Ve-

nezuela's major gold-rush areas. These localities rekindle memories of the old American gold outposts you have seen in the
movies, with prospectors much in evidence
and noisy bars crammed with tipsy miners.
Neither of the two seems to be the safest
spot on earth, but for those who wish to
hang around for a while anyway, both towns
offer a choice of accommodations; ***Campamento Turístico Anaconda***, in Las Claritas,
is one of the best options around.

Proceeding south, at km 95 the road
begins to wind up the so-called **La Escalera**
(Stairway). This portion of road, snaking

through lush rain forest and ascending about 800m over 40km, is reputed to be one of the best bird-watching roads on the continent.

At km 99 you pass a huge sandstone boulder, **Piedra de la Virgen**, which marks the entrance to Parque Nacional Canaima. At km 120 is a 40m-high waterfall called **Salto El Danto**. It's not visible from the road but is very close to it.

The road continues to wind uphill to km 135, where the rain forest suddenly ends and you enter a vast, flat grassland. This is the beginning of La Gran Sabana, which stretches south for nearly 200km. You are now at an altitude of about 1200m, which is clearly evidenced by more moderate temperatures, particularly during cloudy days, and by chilly nights.

At km 141 is the Inparques office, and 2km farther on you'll pass by a military outpost at Luepa. At km 147 a side road branches to the west and runs for 70km to the village of **Kavanayén**. Midway down this road, a dust trail departs south to the Indian hamlet of Iboribó, from where you will be able to walk to the marvelous **Salto Aponguao**.

The main road continues south to **Rápidos de Kamoirán**, at km 172, where there's a hotel, restaurant and gas station, and small rapids behind the complex. At km 195 is **Salto Kawí**, a small but lovely cascade spilling onto red jasper rock, and at km 202 you'll find the frequently visited **Salto Kamá**.

The **Quebrada Pacheco**, noted for yet another waterfall, is at km 237, and **Balneario Soruapé**, a kilometer off the road at km 244, is a popular place to bathe in natural pools. Just 3km farther south you'll find the amazing **Salto Yuruaní** before reaching the village of **San Francisco de Yuruaní** at km 250. Here a side road runs east to the Indian village of Paraitepui, from where a fascinating hike will take you to the even more fascinating top of **Roraima**.

The main road proceeds south to the impressive **Quebrada de Jaspe**, at km 273, one of the most popular attractions in the region. Five kilometers down the highway, a rough jeep trail branches off to the east and

runs for 3km to two picturesque waterfalls, **Salto Agua Fría** and **Salto Puerta del Cielo**.

At km 316, you will finally reach **Santa Elena de Uairén**, the region's only town to speak of. The highway heads south to the Brazilian border, at km 331, and continues to Boa Vista, 223km beyond the borderline.

There's an unpaved road heading west from Santa Elena to the mining settlement of **Icabarú**, 115km away. Tours around this part of La Gran Sabana are normally available from Santa Elena, but they were not organized in 2000 because of the disastrous state of the road. However, more adventurous travelers may want to go on their own to the friendly village of **El Paují**, at km 73, which offers a reasonable choice of simple places to stay and eat, and use it as a base for exploring the area. Nearby attractions include **Salto Catedral**, **Pozo Esmeralda**, **Salto El Paují** and **El Abismo**.

Some of the major attractions mentioned in this section are detailed separately later.

Getting Around

Getting around the Gran Sabana is not all that easy, as public transportation operates only along the highway and is infrequent (nine buses a day in each direction, with half running at night). Given time, you can visit the sights on the main road using a combination of hitching and buses. Heading toward Kavanayén, however, may prove difficult, as there are no buses on this road and traffic is sporadic. A comfortable solution is a tour from Santa Elena (see that section, later, for details).

Whichever way you choose to explore the region, bring plenty of good insect repellent. The Gran Sabana is infested by a kind of gnat known as *jején,* commonly (and justifiably) called *la plaga* (plague). They are ubiquitous and voracious, especially so in the morning and late afternoon, and their bites itch for days.

SALTO APONGUAO

Salto Aponguao, also known by its Indian name of Chinak-Merú (merú means 'waterfall' in the Pemón language), is one of the most impressive and photogenic waterfalls

GUAYANA

Tepuis & Simas

Tepuis are flat-topped, cliff-edged mountains typical of southern Venezuela. There are over a hundred such plateaus dotting the vast region from the Colombian border in the west up into Guyana and Brazil in the east. However, they are most concentrated in the Gran Sabana.

Tepui (also spelled 'tepuy') is the Pemón Indian word for 'mountain,' and it has been adopted as the term to identify this specific type of table mountain. Interestingly, the term 'tepui' is used only in the Pemón linguistic area – ie, in the Gran Sabana and its environs. Elsewhere, the table mountains are called either *cerros* or *montes*.

Geologically, these sandstone mesas are the remnants of a thick layer of Precambrian sediments (some two billion years old) that gradually eroded, leaving behind only the most resistant rock 'islands.' Effectively isolated over millions of years from each other and from the eroded lower level, the tops of tepuis saw the independent evolution of flora and fauna. Developing in such a specific environment, many species have preserved features of their remote ancestors, and outside of their tepuis they can be seen only in fossilized remains.

Every tepui has a characteristic plant life, different from any of its neighbors. Scientific explorations show that roughly half of some 2000 plant species found on top of the tepuis are endemic – that is, they grow only there. This is about the highest percentage of endemic flora found anywhere in the world. Yet only a handful of tepuis have been researched, and many remain virtually untouched by humans.

Another geological curiosity of southern Venezuela is the huge round holes in the ground known as *simas*. They have vertical walls and flat bottoms – you might say they are a mirror image of tepuis. Like their aboveground reflections, simas are formed by erosion of softer rock. These unique phenomena were explored for the first time in 1974. Only a few of them so far have been found, the largest of which is about 350m in diameter and 350m deep. They all are in Parque Nacional Jaua Sarisariñama, some 400km west of La Gran Sabana. The region is accessible only by air.

in the Gran Sabana, though it's not all that easy to get to on your own. The waterfall is off the highway, 30km along an unpaved road toward Kavanayén, plus another 10km south to the Indian hamlet of Iboribó (no public transportation on these roads). Villagers offer rustic lodging in hammocks under a roof and serve simple meals.

Locals will take you in a *curiara* (dugout canoe) to the opposite side of the Río Aponguao and provide a mandatory guide for a trip to the falls (though the path is so clear that no guide is necessary). It's a half-hour walk to the falls. The fee for the roundtrip boat ride and the guide is about US$5 per person.

The waterfall is about 105m high, and even in the driest season it's pretty spectacular. In the wet season it can be a wall of water nearly 100m wide. There's a well-marked path leading downhill to the foot of the falls, where you can bathe in natural pools and take excellent pictures; sunlight strikes the falls from midmorning until very early afternoon.

KAVANAYÉN

Kavanayén is a small Indian village lost in the middle of the Gran Sabana, about 70km west of the highway, and accessible by a rough road. It developed around the Capuchin mission established here half a century ago. The missionaries erected a massive stone building for themselves and apparently assumed that the Indians wanted to live in a similar type of dwelling: Almost all houses in the village are heavy stone constructions, a striking contrast to the thatched adobe churuatas you'll see elsewhere in the region.

Kavanayén enjoys a spectacular location. Set on the top of a small mesa, the village is surrounded by tepuis, and one can see at least half a dozen of these mountains, including the unique cone-shaped Wei Tepui (Mountain of the Sun).

A rough jeep trail leads from Kavanayén to the Karuai-Merú, a fine waterfall at the base of Ptari Tepui, 20km away. The road is so bad that the trip may take up to 1½ hours. If you walk, it's five hours each way. The scenery is fabulous.

There's an adventurous trail from Karuai to Kamarata that takes at least a week to complete. One of the most competent guides for this trip is Carlos Enrique Calcaños – ask for him in Kavanayén. Ruta Salvaje Tours, in Santa Elena de Uairén (see that section, later), also organizes trips on this route.

Places to Stay & Eat

The mission provides basic dormitory-type accommodations for around US$7 per hard bed. There are two informal restaurants in the village (recognized by the names of their owners as *Señora Guadalupe* and *Señora Rosa*), which serve unsophisticated but cheap and filling meals.

There are also accommodations (US$25 per person with breakfast and dinner) in Chivatón, 17km before Kavanayén. The place is frequently used by tours as an overnight stop, but it's not convenient for individual travelers without any transportation of their own.

Getting There & Away

The road leading to Kavanayén is almost traffic-free, so it may take a long time to hitchhike. A quicker option is a tour, but not all tours go as far as Kavanayén. The last stretch of the road to Kavanayén is in very poor shape, especially in the wet season, and the road may sometimes be passable only by jeep.

SALTO KAMÁ

Salto Kamá, or Kamá-Merú, is a lovely, 50m-high waterfall 200m west of km 202. Do not miss walking down the right (north)

bank to its base (for a small fee). The locals can take you on a boat trip (US$2) around the waterfall's pool and behind its water curtain; be prepared to get completely wet. Photographers should note that sunlight strikes the falls from midmorning to midafternoon.

Places to Stay & Eat

There are two basic campamentos next to the falls (about US$25 per triple), each with its own simple restaurant. You can also pitch your tent in the camps for a small fee.

Rápidos de Kamoirán, at km 172, has a restaurant and a hotel (US$18 per bed in a double); it's one of the usual overnight stops for tours around the Gran Sabana.

Getting There & Away

If you're traveling on your own, just stay on the road and flag down anything heading in your direction. Keep an eye out for parked cars belonging to tourists visiting the falls; they may give you a ride when they leave.

QUEBRADA PACHECO

Also known as Arapán-Merú, this is a handsome multistep cascade just 100m to the east of the road, at km 237. It's much nicer up close than you'd imagine from the road. Keep in mind that the best light for photos is in the afternoon.

Basic tourist facilities include hammock lodgings in a churuata (US$7 per person) and, sometimes, meals during holiday peaks.

SALTO YURUANÍ

Ten kilometers south of Quebrada Pacheco, at km 247, you pass over a bridge across the Río Yuruaní. From the bridge you'll see the waterfall, about a kilometer to the east, with the Yuruaní tepui in the background. The way to the falls is along both the southern and northern banks of the river. It's a wonderful waterfall, about 6m high and 60m wide, with an amazing water coloration reminiscent of beer. The best sunlight strikes the falls in the afternoon. You can walk behind the curtain of water, but only during low-water periods, and you shouldn't do it without a guide. There's a place for

GUAYANA

camping next to the falls, but bring a lot of insect repellent, as this waterfall is notorious for jejenes.

RORAIMA

Roraima, on the tripartite border of Venezuela, Guyana and Brazil, is one of the largest and highest tepuis: Its plateau is at about 2700m, and the highest peak is at 2810m. The first of the tepuis on which a climb was recorded (in 1884), it has been much explored by botanists. Interestingly, although Roraima is a classic example of a tepui and lies within the Pemón linguistic area, it is not called a 'tepui' but a *monte* (mountain) – nobody knows why.

Roraima is the easiest table mountain to ascend, and is increasingly popular among travelers. More than 80% of people that trek to the top are foreigners. The climb doesn't require any particular skills and can be done by anyone reasonably fit and healthy. The route does not require elements of technical climbing or ropes, ladders etc.

However, it's not an easy or short walk. To make the trip, you need camping equipment, food and a minimum of five days. Be prepared for a hard trek and some discomfort, including plenty of rain and jejenes. Still, you'll be rewarded by some of the most unusual and memorable experiences you will have in Venezuela. The hike is fascinating, and the top of the mesa is nothing short of a dream.

Orientation

Roraima lies approximately 40km off the El Dorado–Santa Elena highway, just east of San Francisco de Yuruaní, which is the usual starting point for the trip. From here, you walk or go by jeep to the Indian village of Paraitepui, where you hire a (compulsory) local guide and continue by path for two days to the top of Roraima. Give yourself at least two days on the top to be able to visit some of the major attractions and to enjoy the beauty and atmosphere of this unique place. You then return along the same way down to San Francisco.

Planning

When to Go The dry season in the region is from December to April, but the tops of the tepuis receive rain off the Atlantic all year round. The weather up there changes in a matter of minutes, with bright sunshine or heavy rain possible at any time.

What Kind of Trip You have basically two options: Bring and carry all your camping gear and food and only hire a local guide; or to purchase a tour and not worry about anything. There's obviously a big difference in price between the former and the latter, but take some time to calculate all the costs precisely. Given that few travelers come to Venezuela with full high-mountain camping equipment, you'll probably need to rent all of it locally, which will substantially add to your do-it-yourself tour. You also must buy all your food (and rent pots and pans to cook it). Finally, if you don't want to walk from San Francisco to Paraitepui and back, you'll need to rent a jeep, which will again add to the expense of your tour. If you sum it all up, the difference in cost between going solo and taking a tour may not be so drastic.

If you consider a tour option, check the tour operators in Santa Elena (see that section, later), who are possibly the best and cheapest you can get. Visit them even if you just need some camping gear, as they rent the stuff out.

What to Bring A good tent, preferably with a flysheet (an outer canvas layer), is a must. It gets bitterly cold at night on the top, so bring a good sleeping bag and warm clothes too. You also need reliable rain gear, sturdy shoes, a cooking stove and the usual hiking equipment. Bring enough food to share with your guide and to last one or two days more than planned: You may not be able to resist the temptation of staying longer on the top, or you may be stuck at Río Kukenán, unable to cross. A rope may be useful for crossing the river.

There's no plaga atop Roraima, but you'll have plenty of these nasty biting gnats on the way, so take an effective insect repellent. Don't forget a good supply of film. A macro lens is a great help in photographing the unique small plants. Make sure to bring along plastic bags to take *all* your garbage back down to civilization. However, also be sure not to remove anything that belongs to the mountain – plants, rocks, crystals etc. Searches are often conducted on returning travelers, and crystals are subject to heavy on-the-spot fines. Furthermore, locals believe that these crystals bring bad luck.

San Francisco de Yuruaní

This small village, 66km north of Santa Elena de Uairén by the highway, is the starting point for the trip. There are two small tour operators, Roraima Tours and Arapena Tours, but it's better to buy a tour in Santa Elena. Even if you don't want to go on a tour, you still need a guide; you can arrange one in San Francisco. Guides charge US$25 a day per group of up to about six people. Porters, should you need one, charge another US$25 per day and can carry up to about 15kg. Both guides and porters can also be hired in the village of Paraitepui, your next stop on the way to Roraima.

Accommodation options in San Francisco include the roadside *Hospedaje Minina*, 100m north of the bus stop (US$8 per person) and an *unmarked house* next to Roraima Tours (US$10 per person). The few basic places to eat include *Restaurant Roraima*, at the central junction. The restaurant also provides accommodations in hammocks (US$4).

Paraitepui

Paraitepui is about 25km east of San Francisco. To get there, rent a jeep from the tour operators in San Francisco (US$50 for up to about eight passengers) or walk. The road to Paraitepui branches off the highway 1km south of San Francisco. It's a hot, steady seven-hour walk, uphill most of the way, to Paraitepui (back to San Francisco, it's six hours).

The road is not difficult to follow, except for one point (about a five-hour walk from San Francisco) where it divides. The road going straight ahead leads to the hamlet of Chirimatá, while the Paraitepui road proper (which you should follow) branches off sharply to the right. Don't worry too much if you miss this turnoff, as there's a path from Chirimatá to Paraitepui.

You may be lucky enough to hitch a jeep ride on this road, but traffic is sporadic and drivers will probably charge you for the lift (a more reasonable fare than jeep rental in San Francisco).

Paraitepui is a nondescript Indian village of about 250 people whose identity has been largely shattered by tourists and their money. Upon arrival, you will invariably be greeted by one of the village headmen, who will show you the list of guides (apparently every adult male in the village is a guide) and inform you about prices. They are much the same as in San Francisco. Although you don't really need a guide to follow the trail up to the tepui, the village headmen won't let you pass through without one.

There are no hotels in the village, but you can camp on the square near the school and have hot meals at the small local restaurant. A few shops in the village sell basic food (canned fish, biscuits, packet soups) at inflated prices.

Climbing Roraima

Once you have arranged your guide, you can set off for Roraima. The trip to the top takes two days (total walking time is about 12 hours uphill and 10 hours down). There are several good places to camp (with water) on the way. The most popular campsites are on the Río Tek (four hours from Paraitepui), the Río Kukenán (30 minutes farther on) and the so-called *campamento base* (base camp) at the foot of Roraima (three hours uphill from Río Kukenán). The steep and tough four-hour ascent from the base camp to the top is the most difficult but also the most spectacular part of the hike.

The volume of the Río Kukenán depends on the highly changeable and unpredictable rainfall on the Kukenán and Roraima tepuis, and the river level can change substantially in an hour or less. After rains, the river can be impassable, and you may need to wait for several hours or even a day until the level drops. As a rough rule, the water level is lower in the evening than in the morning. Don't camp right on the shore, unless you don't mind taking an unexpected bath.

Once you reach the top, you walk for some 15 minutes to the place known as El Hotel, one of the few good campsites. It's actually a patch of sand large enough for about four small tents, partly protected by an overhanging rock. There are already half a dozen other 'hotels' in the area.

The scenery that surrounds you is a dreamscape, evocative of a science-fiction movie: impressive blackened rock of every imaginable shape, gorges, creeks, pink beaches, and gardens filled with unique flowering plants. Frequent and constantly changing mist and fog add to the mysterious air.

It's here that a guide finally becomes handy, as it's very easy to get lost on the vast plateau. Your guide will take you to some attractions, including El Foso, a curious round pool in a deep rocky hole. It's about a three-hour walk north from El Hotel. On the way, you'll pass the amazingly lush Valle Arabopo. Beyond the pool is the Valle de los Cristales and the Laberinto, both well worth a trip. Another fascinating area is the southwestern part of Roraima, where attractions include La Ventana (Window), El Abismo (Abyss) and La Piscina (Swimming Pool). Plan on staying at least two days on the top, though it's better to allow longer.

Getting There & Away
San Francisco de Yuruaní is on the Ciudad Guayana–Santa Elena highway, and nine buses a day run in each direction. Buy all food at either starting point; don't count on shopping in San Francisco, let alone in Paraitepui.

QUEBRADA DE JASPE
Between San Francisco and Santa Elena, at km 273, is yet another Gran Sabana waterfall. This one is small and faint, but what is truly amazing is the intense orange-red color of the pure jasper rock over which the creek flows. The Quebrada is 200m to the east of the highway, hidden in a stretch of woodland.

SANTA ELENA DE UAIRÉN
☎ 088 (☎ 0289 from Jun 16, 2001)
Founded in 1924, Santa Elena began to grow when diamonds were discovered in the 1930s in the Icabarú region, 115km to the west. However, isolated from the center of the country by a lack of roads, it remained a small village. The second development push came with the opening of the highway from El Dorado.

Today, Santa Elena is a pleasant, easy-going border town with an agreeable if damp climate and a Brazilian air thanks to the significant number of residents from across the border.

The Carnaval here has a distinctly Brazilian feel, with samba rhythms and a parade of *carrozas* (floats). Small as it is, Santa Elena is the main town of the Gran Sabana and the largest before you reach Tumeremo, 385km to the north.

Information
Tourist Offices Tour agencies (see Organized Tours, later) are good sources of information about the region.

Immigration Both Venezuelan and Brazilian passport formalities are now done at the border itself, locally known as La Línea, 15km south of Santa Elena.

Embassies & Consulates The Brazilian consulate is at the northeastern end of town and is open 8 am to noon weekdays. It normally takes one day to issue a visa. It may be a good idea to get your visa beforehand, because if this consulate fails to give you a visa for whatever reason, you'll have a long way to go to get one (the next-nearest Brazilian consulate is in Ciudad Guayana). A yellow-fever vaccination certificate is likely to be required by the officials before they issue you a visa, and it will probably be checked again on the border.

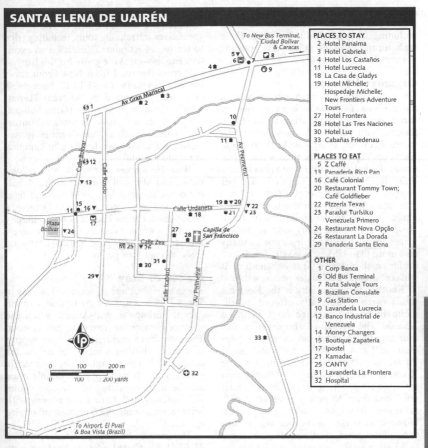

SANTA ELENA DE UAIRÉN

To New Bus Terminal, Ciudad Bolívar & Caracas

Av Gran Mariscal

Calle Bolívar

Calle Roscio

Plaza Bolívar

Calle Urdaneta

Calle Zea

Capilla de San Francisco

Calle Icabarú

Av Perimetral

Av Perimetral

To Airport, El Puaí & Boa Vista (Brazil)

0   100   200 m
0   100   200 yards

PLACES TO STAY
2 Hotel Panaima
3 Hotel Gabriela
4 Hotel Los Castaños
11 Hotel Lucrecia
18 La Casa de Gladys
19 Hotel Michelle;
    Hospedaje Michelle;
    New Frontiers Adventure
    Tours
27 Hotel Frontera
28 Hotel Las Tres Naciones
30 Hotel Luz
33 Cabañas Friedenau

PLACES TO EAT
5 Z Caffé
13 Panadería Rico Pan
16 Café Colonial
20 Restaurant Tommy Town;
    Café Goldfieber
22 Pizzería Texas
23 Parador Turístico
    Venezuela Primero
24 Restaurant Nova Opção
26 Restaurant La Dorada
29 Panadería Santa Elena

OTHER
1 Corp Banca
6 Old Bus Terminal
7 Ruta Salvaje Tours
8 Brazilian Consulate
9 Gas Station
10 Lavandería Lucrecia
12 Banco Industrial de
    Venezuela
14 Money Changers
15 Boutique Zapatería
17 Ipostel
21 Kamadac
25 CANTV
31 Lavandería La Frontera
32 Hospital

GUAYANA

Money Banco Industrial de Venezuela gives cash advances on Visa (but so far not on MasterCard). US cash can be easily exchanged with the money changers who hang around the corner of Calles Bolívar and Urdaneta, popularly known as Cuatro Esquinas. They are there every day except Sunday afternoon and usually give quite good rates. By the time you come, they may already have their own money-exchange offices somewhere around the area.

If you are heading north into Venezuela, keep in mind that the nearest place you can easily change money is likely to be Ciudad Guayana, 600km away, so change enough in Santa Elena to last you until you get there. If you're heading south for Brazil, get rid of all your bolívares in Santa Elena and buy Brazilian currency (from the money changers).

Email & Internet Access There are Internet facilities in the CANTV office on Calle Zea, and in La Casa de Gladys (see Places to Stay, later).

Laundry Some hotels, including La Casa de Gladys, provide laundry service for their guests. If your hotel doesn't have this facility, use one of several launderettes in town, including Lavandería La Frontera, Calle Icabarú, and Lavandería Lucrecia, Avenida Perimetral.

Organized Tours

There are perhaps a dozen tour agencies in Santa Elena. Their staple is a one-, two- or three-day jeep tour around La Gran Sabana, with visits to the most interesting sights. They can bring you back to Santa Elena or drop you on the road at the northernmost point of the tour if you plan to continue north. Count on roughly US$25 per day per person for a group of four or more. This price includes transportation and a guide, but no accommodations or food. However, tours normally stop in budget places, where beds and meals don't usually cost more than US$5 to US$10 each. If you prefer an all-inclusive Gran Sabana tour, it will cost around US$50 per person a day.

Another local specialty is the Roraima tour, which is normally offered as all-inclusive six-day package for US$200 to US$300. The operators who organize this tour usually also rent out camping equipment and can provide transportation to Paraitepui, the starting point for the Roraima trek, for around US$80 per jeep for up to six people (plus another US$80 if you want them to pick you up on a prearranged date and take you back). However, it works out cheaper to go by bus to San Francisco and either rent a jeep there (US$50) or walk.

Managed by knowledgeable Iván Artal, Ruta Salvaje Tours (☎ 95 11 34, rutasalvaje@ cantv.net), is one of the best all-around companies in Santa Elena, strategically situated in a churuata-style pavilion at the town's entrance. The agency offers a wide choice of tours, including Gran Sabana sightseeing, the Roraima trek and rafting trips. It also rents out camping gear and bicycles (US$10 a day) and can provide tourist information about the region.

Another recommended company, New Frontiers Adventure Tours (☎ 95 15 83, 95 14 43, info@newfrontiersadventures.com) is run by two experienced guides, Mario Rojas and Kendall Donald Mitchell. The agency specializes in trekking tours, including trips to the top of Roraima (Kendall is an excellent English-speaking guide for this trip).

Across the road from New Frontiers is the new Kamadac (☎ 95 13 12, kamadac@ cantv.net), operated by Andreas Hauer, which offers popular tours (Gran Sabana, Roraima) as well as some more adventurous projects (such as nine-day trips to Auyantepui and Acopan Tepui), plus camping equipment rental.

Raúl Helicopter's (☎ 95 11 59), on Avenida Gran Mariscal 1km east of the Brazilian consulate, provides air services in light planes and helicopters. This is not exactly a proposition for backpackers, but if money is not a problem it can take you anywhere – for example, the top of Roraima (around US$1300 per four persons).

Places to Stay

There's no shortage of accommodations in Santa Elena, and it's easy to find a room, except perhaps in mid-August, when the town celebrates the feast of its patron saint. The town has a problematical water supply, so check whether your hotel has water tanks. Few hotels in Santa Elena have single rooms; you'll have to pay the double price and be accommodated in a double room. All hotels listed here have rooms with private bathrooms and fan unless otherwise specified.

The friendly *La Casa de Gladys* (☎ 95 11 71, 95 15 30), Calle Urdaneta, has long been a popular travelers' lodge. Neat singles/doubles/triples are US$7/12/15, or you can stay in a dorm for US$4. Guests can use the kitchen and fridge for no extra fee. Gladys provides laundry facilities for guests only, and offers Internet access for everybody, but hotel guests get discounts. She also rents out tents, sleeping bags etc for Roraima.

Another good place is the new *Hotel Michelle* (☎ 95 14 15), Calle Urdaneta, which offers 10 ample rooms, all with private bath, for US$6 per person. At the back of the building is the simpler *Hospedaje Michelle*, which costs US$5 per person in rooms with shared baths. Guests have free access to the kitchen, and the management provides laundry services.

Other cheap places (costing much the same as La Casa de Gladys) include the pleasant *Hotel Los Castaños* (☎ 95 14 50) and the basic *Hotel Luz* (☎ 95 15 05). For a little more (say, US$14 to US$16 double), you have several options, including *Hotel Gabriela* (☎ 95 13 79), *Hotel Las Tres Naciones* (☎ 95 15 86) and *Hotel Panaima* (☎ 95 14 74).

The *Hotel Frontera* (☎ 95 10 95), Calle Icabarú, has long passed its best days, but still has its spacious charming patio around which the rooms are arranged, and it costs just US$16/18 double/triple. Another pleasant place with a lovely patio, *Hotel Lucrecia* (☎ 95 11 30) provides good standards with air-conditioning for US$24/28 double/triple.

If you are in a larger party, you may be interested in *Cabañas Friedenau* (☎ 95 13 53), which offers cabañas with kitchenette and fridge for five to nine people at US$12 per bed.

In the northern Akurima suburb, *Posada Villa Fairmont* (☎ 95 10 22) is one of the best places in town, at US$30/38/44 for a large air-con single/double/triple; it also has its own restaurant.

The best place to stay is probably the new 58-room *Hotel Gran Sabana* (☎ 95 18 10, fax 95 18 13), on the road to Brazil 3km from the town's center. Its ample air-con rooms cost US$55/65/80 single/double/triple. The hotel has a swimming pool and a snack bar.

Places to Eat

Plenty of inexpensive eateries cluster all around the central streets. *Café Colonial*, Avenida Urdaneta, does rich breakfasts, salads, soups and set lunches. *Restaurant La Dorada* is the place for cheap chicken. For pizza, choose between the *Z Caffé*, in the Centro Dextino, and *Pizzería Texas*, on Avenida Perimetral. *Restaurant Tommy Town*, Avenida Urdaneta, has authentic and tasty Chinese food. Next door, the *Café Goldfieber* serves filling breakfasts and mouthwatering Hungarian-style goulash.

The self-service *Restaurant Nova Opção*, Plaza Bolívar, sells food (chicken, beef, potatoes, rice etc) by weight, so you can choose what you want and how much you want. A bit more expensive is *Parador Turístico Venezuela Primero*, Avenida Perimetral. Still a bit more expensive but good is the pleasant *Restaurant El Churuaney de Akurima*, in the Posada Villa Fairmont.

For breakfast, there are several central panaderías, including *Panadería Santa Elena*, which opens early, and *Panadería Rico Pan*, which has tables outside at which to sit and watch the unhurried world go by.

Getting There & Away

Air The airport is 7km southwest of town, off the road to the border. There's no public transportation; a taxi will cost around US$4. Tour operators are often waiting for incoming flights and will usually give you a free lift to town, hoping you might be interested in their offers.

Prices given in this section are one-way. Servivensa has weekly flights to Puerto Ordaz (US$122), with a stopover in Canaima (US$107). If you've bought Hoturvensa's package in Campamento Canaima, you are entitled to a discount ticket to Canaima for US$57. These flights are serviced by the 60-year-old DC-3s, which aren't the safest planes in the world.

Rutaca travels daily to Ciudad Bolívar (US$75), also via Canaima (US$75). These flights are also on light planes, which fly at only about 1000m, close to the tepuis.

Bus The new bus terminal is on the Ciudad Guayana highway, about 2km east of the town center. It was almost completed by early 1997, but then construction was virtually abandoned. It was still not open in late 2000. It may or may not be open by the time you read this. Meanwhile, buses flock around the primitive facilities of the existing terminal, near the corner of Avenidas Gran Mariscal and Perimetral.

Nine buses run daily to Ciudad Bolívar (US$12 ordinary, US$15 deluxe, 10 to 11 hours), all passing through Ciudad Guayana (US$11 ordinary, US$14 deluxe, nine to 10 hours). A jeep to El Paují departs around 6 am (US$10, three hours).

There are two buses a day to Boa Vista, Brazil (US$10, three to four hours). The road is now paved all the way. The bus calls at the Venezuelan and Brazilian immigration posts on the border, which is open from 7am to 10pm, for passport formalities.

Amazonas

Venezuela's southernmost state, Amazonas, covers an area of 175,000 sq km, or approximately one-fifth of the national territory, yet it has at most 1% of the country's population. Despite its name, most of the region lies in the Orinoco drainage basin, while the Amazon basin takes up only the southwestern portion of the state. The two basins are linked by the unusual Brazo Casiquiare, a natural channel that sends a portion of the Río Orinoco's waters to the Río Negro and down to the Amazon.

The region is predominantly a thick tropical forest crisscrossed by a maze of rivers and sparsely populated by a mosaic of indigenous communities. The current Indian population is estimated at 40,000, half of what it was in 1925. The three main groups –

A Yanomami Indian in ceremonial garb

Piaroa, Yanomami and Guajibo – make up about three-quarters of the indigenous population, while the remaining quarter is composed of the Yekuana (Maquiritare), Curripaco, Guarekena, Piapoco and a number of smaller communities. Approximately 20 Indian languages are used in the region.

In contrast to the central Amazon basin in Brazil, Venezuelan Amazonas is quite diverse topographically, its most noticeable feature being the tepuis. Though not as numerous or as classical as in La Gran Sabana, they do give the green carpet a distinctive and spectacular appearance.

The best known of the Amazonas tepuis is Cerro Autana, about 80km south of Puerto Ayacucho. It is the sacred mountain of the Piaroa Indians, who consider it the birthplace of the universe. The tepui is reminiscent of a gigantic tree trunk, looming about 700m above the surrounding plains. There's a unique cave about 200m below its top that cuts right through the tepui.

At the far southern end of the region, along the border with Brazil, is the Serranía de la Neblina (the Misty Mountain Range); it is hardly ever explored and is virtually unknown. At 3014m, it's the tallest mountain on the continent east of the Andean chain. The canyon running through its middle is considered one of the world's deepest. It's also thought that La Neblina has some of the richest endemic plant life anywhere in the world.

Puerto Ayacucho, situated at the northwestern tip of Amazonas, is the only town of significance and is the main gateway and supply center for the entire state. It's also the chief transportation hub, from where a couple of small regional airlines fly in light planes to the major settlements of the region.

As there are no roads, transportation is by river or air. There's no regular passenger service on virtually any stretch of any river, which makes independent travel difficult, if not impossible. Tour operators in Puerto Ayacucho have swiftly filled the gap and can take you just about everywhere – at a price, of course.

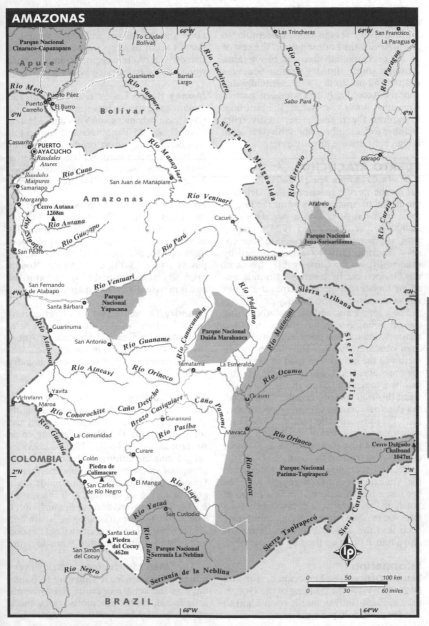

The climate is not uniform throughout the region. At the northern edge, there's a distinctive dry season from December to April. April is the hottest month. The rest of the year is marked by frequent heavy rains. Heading south, the dry season becomes shorter and not so dry, and eventually disappears. Accordingly, the southern part of Amazonas is wet year-round. The best time to explore the region is reputedly from October to December, when the river level is high but rains are already easing.

PUERTO AYACUCHO
☎ 048 (☎ 0248 from Apr 21, 2001)
Set on the middle reaches of the Orinoco, the capital of Amazonas is by far the largest town in the region, with a population of 75,000. It was founded in 1924, together with another port, Samariapo, 63km upriver. The two ports have been linked by road to bypass the unnavigable stretch of the Orinoco cut by a series of rapids, enabling timber to be shipped from the upper Amazonas down to the country's center.

For a long time, and particularly during the oil boom, Amazonas was a forgotten territory, and the two ports were little more than obscure villages. The link between them was the only paved road in the whole region; connection to the rest of the country was by a rough trail. Only in the late 1980s, when this trail was improved and surfaced, did Puerto Ayacucho start to grow dramatically. Paradoxically, the port, which was responsible for the town's birth and initial growth, has lost its importance, as most cargo is now trucked by road.

Puerto Ayacucho is the main gateway to the Venezuelan Amazon region and has become a tourist center. There's a range of hotels and restaurants, and travel agents can take you up the Orinoco and its tributaries, deep into the jungle. Puerto Ayacucho is also a transit point on the way to Colombia.

Information
Tourist Offices The Dirección de Turismo (☎ 21 00 33) is in the building of the Gobernación, Plaza Bolívar, and is open 8 am to noon and 2 to 5:30 pm weekdays.

Immigration The DIEX office is on Avenida Aguerrevere and is open 8 am to noon and 2 to 5 pm weekdays, though it doesn't seem to keep to these hours very strictly. Get your passport stamped here when leaving or entering Venezuela.

Money Banco Unión changes cash and American Express traveler's checks and gives cash advances on Visa and Master-Card. Banco de Venezuela and Banco Caroní don't change cash or checks, but they do service credit-card holders. Some tour agencies may change your dollars or at least accept them as payment for their services.

Email & Internet Access Biblionet, on the upper floor of the Biblioteca Pública (☎ 21 47 02), Avenida Río Negro, provides access 8 to 11:30 am and 2 to 5:30 pm weekdays (US$5 per hour). Cibercafé Compuserv (☎ 21 43 72), Calle Evelio Roa, is open similar hours and also on Saturday, and is marginally more expensive.

Laundry There are two launderettes next to each other on Avenida Aguerrevere: Lavandería Parima and Lavandería Aquario. If you're staying in the nearby Residencia Internacional, you can use its laundry facility.

Things to See
Puerto Ayacucho is hot, but it's pleasantly shaded by luxuriant mango trees and has some attractions. The **Museo Etnológico de Amazonas**, Avenida Río Negro, provides insight into the culture of the main Indian groups of the region, including the Piaroa, Guajibo, Yekuana and Yanomami. It has a good selection of exhibits with interesting background information (in Spanish only). The museum is open 8:30 to 11:30 am and 2:30 to 6 pm Tuesday to Friday, 9 am to noon and 3:30 to 7 pm Saturday, 9 am to 1 pm Sunday.

The **Mercado Indígena**, held every morning (busiest from Thursday to Saturday) on the square opposite the museum, sells Indian crafts. For more crafts, check out the nearby handicraft shop, Artesanías

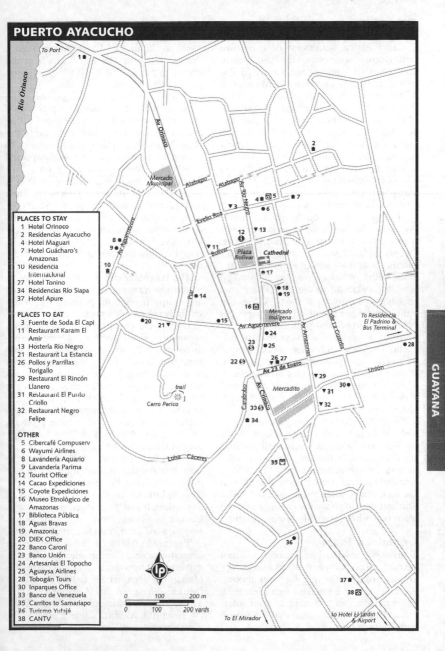

PUERTO AYACUCHO

Río Orinoco

To Port

Mercado Municipal

Av Orinoco

Atabapo

Atabapo

Av Río Negro

Evelio Roa

Av Aguerrevere

Bolívar

Plaza Bolívar

Cathedral

Piar

Av Aguerrevere

Av Amazonas

Calle La Guardia

Mercado Indígena

To Residencia El Padrino & Bus Terminal

Unión

Av 23 de Enero

Carabobo

Av Orinoco

Mercadito

trail
Cerro Perico

Luisa Cáceres

To Hotel El Jardín & Airport

To El Mirador

0   100   200 m
0   100   200 yards

GUAYANA

PLACES TO STAY
1 Hotel Orinoco
2 Residencias Ayacucho
4 Hotel Maguari
7 Hotel Guácharo's Amazonas
10 Residencia Internacional
27 Hotel Tonino
34 Residencias Río Siapa
37 Hotel Apure

PLACES TO EAT
3 Fuente de Soda El Capi
11 Restaurant Karam El Amir
13 Hostería Río Negro
21 Restaurant La Estancia
26 Pollos y Parrillas Torigallo
29 Restaurant El Rincón Llanero
31 Restaurant El Punto Criollo
32 Restaurant Negro Felipe

OTHER
5 Cibercafé Compuserv
6 Wayumi Airlines
8 Lavandería Aquario
9 Lavandería Parima
12 Tourist Office
14 Cacao Expediciones
15 Coyote Expediciones
16 Museo Etnológico de Amazonas
17 Biblioteca Pública
18 Aguas Bravas
19 Amazonia
20 DIEX Office
22 Banco Caroní
23 Banco Unión
24 Artesanías El Topocho
25 Aguaysa Airlines
28 Tobogán Tours
30 Inparques Office
33 Banco de Venezuela
35 Carritos to Samariapo
36 Turismo Yutajé
38 CANTV

El Topocho. Also visit the **Catedral** on Plaza Bolívar to see its colorful interior.

Cerro Perico, southwest of the town center, provides views over the Río Orinoco and the town. Another hill, Cerro El Zamuro, commonly known as **El Mirador**, is 1.5km south of the center and overlooks the Raudales Atures, the spectacular rapids that block river navigation (the other rapids, the Raudales Maipures, are near Samariapo). Both are more impressive in the rainy season, when the water level is high. The difference between the water level in the dry and rainy periods can surpass 15m. The two viewpoints are a bit isolated and solitary, so be careful and don't walk alone.

A couple of attractions lie around Puerto Ayacucho. **Parque Tobogán de la Selva** is a picnic area developed around a large, steeply inclined smooth rock with water running over it – a sort of natural slide. It's 30km south of town along the Samariapo road, then 6km off to the east. There's no transportation directly to the park: You can either take a por puesto to Samariapo, get off at the turnoff and walk the remaining distance, or negotiate a taxi in Puerto Ayacucho. The rock is a favorite weekend spot among the townspeople, who, unfortunately, leave it littered (watch out for broken glass). There's a less well known natural waterslide, called Tobogancito, a short walk farther upriver.

Cerro Pintado is a large rock with pre-Columbian petroglyphs carved high above the ground in a virtually inaccessible place. It's 17km south of the town and a few kilometers off the main road, to the left. A roundtrip taxi ride from Puerto Ayacucho to the rock can be arranged for about US$15. The best time to go see the carvings is in the afternoon, when the glyphs are in sunlight.

Organized Tours

Tourism business has flourished over the past decade, and probably as many as a dozen operators are now hunting for your money. Agents offer some standard tours, but most can arrange a tour according to your interests and time. Be sure to carry your passport and tarjeta de ingreso on all trips.

Among the popular shorter tours are a three-day trip up the Sipapo and Autana rivers to the foot of Cerro Autana, and a three-day trip up the Río Cuao. You can expect to pay US$50 to US$70 per person per day, all-inclusive.

If you're looking for a longer and more adventurous journey, consider the so-called Ruta Humboldt, following the route of the great explorer. The route goes along the Ríos Orinoco, Casiquiare and Guainía up to Maroa. From there the boat is transported overland to Yavita, and you then return down the Atabapo and Orinoco to Puerto Ayacucho. This trip takes eight to 12 days and will cost around US$80 to US$120 per person a day. Tour operators don't usually do the whole loop, but rather only its most attractive fragments, including Casiquiare, skipping over the less interesting parts by plane.

The far southeastern part of Amazonas, where the Yanomami live, is a restricted area requiring special permits, which are virtually impossible to get.

One of the cheapest and most popular companies with travelers is Coyote Expediciones (☎ 21 45 83, coyotexpedition@cantv.net). It's one of the few operators that focus on servicing individual backpackers who come to town, rather than groups put together by associated agencies in Caracas or other big cities and sent to Puerto Ayacucho as packages. Coyote's main products are three-day Autana and Cuao tours, but they also have longer trips.

Cacao Expediciones (☎ 21 39 64), Calle Piar, has roughly similar tour offers and prices as Coyote, but because it's younger there is little information on the quality of its services. If you buy a three-day tour with Coyote or Cacao, try to negotiate bonus side trips to Cerro Pintado and/or Tobogán.

Turismo Yutajé (☎ 21 06 64) is one of the longest-established companies, but it's more expensive. It runs three-day tours to the Río Manapiare area, where it has its campamento, and seven-day Casiquiare tours. Yutajé also has fishing trips. Tobogán Tours (☎ 21 48 65), Avenida 23 de Enero, is the oldest operator in Puerto Ayacucho. It now mostly caters to organized groups, only occasionally servicing individual travelers. Amazonia (☎ 21 49 26), Avenida Río Negro, is yet another upmarket operator that also mostly deals with incoming package tours.

Aguas Bravas (☎ 21 05 41, 21 44 58) offers rafting over the Atures rapids. It runs two trips a day (about three hours long) for US$35 each. The owners, Claudia and Jorge, are knowledgeable about the region and may provide information about other options for exploring the rain forest, including the Refugio Yagrumo-Cataniapo.

If there's a serious discrepancy between what an agency promises and what it actually provides, complain to the tourist office and insist on receiving part of your money back.

Places to Stay

The town has two dozen hotels, some of which have become popular with foreign travelers. All those listed have private baths and a fan or air-conditioning.

The most popular choice with backpackers has long been the simple but pleasant **Residencia Internacional** (☎ 21 02 42), Avenida Aguerrevere. It has matrimoniales/doubles/triples with fan for US$12/16/24, and it now also offers rooms with air-conditioning for US$20/24/30. The hotel also offers laundry service and may have a bar-restaurant by the time you come. The more central **Hotel Maguarí** (☎ 21 31 89), Calle Evelio Roa, is probably less popular with travelers but is OK and costs much the same as the Residencia Internacional.

If you're looking for the cheapest place in town, head for **Residencias Ayacucho** (☎ 21 07 79), which costs just US$8 double; however, it's very basic and has barrels of water instead of showers. A better budget option, if also on the basic side, is **Residencia El Padrino** (☎ 21 05 65), off Avenida 23 de Enero 700m east of Tobogán Tours. It has just a few rooms, which cost US$9 double.

Hotel Tonino (☎ 21 14 64), Avenida 23 de Enero, offers five neat matrimoniales/

The Río Orinoco provides splashy thrills near Puerto Ayacucho.

GUAYANA

KRZYSZTOF DYDYŃSKI

doubles or triples with bath and (slightly noisy) air-conditioning for US$18/22/24. The nearby *Residencias Río Siapa (☎ 21 01 38)* is another reasonable central place, at US$20/24/28. There's no sign at the entrance, so keep your eyes open when walking down the street.

Other inexpensive hotels lie farther away from the center, including *Hotel Orinoco (☎ 21 02 85),* on the northern fringes of town, and *Hotel El Jardín (☎ 21 46 47),* at the southern end. Both have air-conditioned rooms priced about US$20/24/28 matrimonial/double/triple. About 250m before El Jardín is the more comfortable *Hotel Apure (☎ 21 05 16),* which costs US$24/34/42.

The central *Hotel Guácharo's Amazonas (☎ 21 03 28),* previously called Gran Hotel Amazonas, was perhaps the best hotel in town when built, but gradually began falling into ruin. Recently partly refurbished, it again boasts a great covered patio and remains the only city hotel with a swimming pool. Rooms cost US$30/35/40 for a double/triple/suite.

Places to Eat

There's quite a selection of eating outlets in town, but many are closed on Sunday. *Fuente de Soda El Capi*, Calle Evelio Roa, has savory food, including salads, at reasonable prices. For tasty chicken and parrillas, try the cheap *Pollos y Parrillas Torigallo*, on Avenida 23 de Enero. Hearty falafel, shawarma and other Middle Eastern specialties are served at *Restaurant Karam El Amir*, Avenida Orinoco. Some of the better pizzas in town are found at *Pizzería El Padrino*, in the hotel of the same name.

One of the favorite budget places to eat among locals is the *Mercadito* (Little Market), which boasts half a dozen rudimentary eateries, including *Restaurant El Rincón Llanero*, *Restaurant El Punto Criollo* and *Restaurant Negro Felipe*. The *Mercado Municipal*, Avenida Orinoco, also has some simple budget restaurants, though these are perhaps less frequented by the locals.

Among some more expensive places, you may want to check *Restaurant La Estancia*, Avenida Aguerrevere, or *Hostería Río Negro*, Avenida Río Negro.

Getting There & Away

Air The airport is 6km southeast of the town center; taxis cost US$4. Air Venezuela has one direct flight daily to Caracas (US$60) and three flights a week via San Fernando de Apure (US$48).

Two small local carriers, Aguaysa and Wayumi, operate flights within Amazonas. There are daily flights (except Sunday) to San Fernando de Atabapo (US$60) and San Juan de Manapiare (US$60), two weekly flights to La Esmeralda (US$80), and one flight a week (usually on Friday) to San Carlos de Río Negro (US$80). Other, smaller localities are serviced irregularly on a charter basis.

Bus The bus terminal is 6km east of the center, on the outskirts of town. To get there, take the city bus from Avenida 23 de Enero or a taxi (US$2). Buses to Ciudad Bolívar depart every few hours throughout the day and more often in the evening (US$12 ordinary, US$15 deluxe, 10 to 11 hours). There are half a dozen departures a day to San Fernando de Apure (US$13 ordinary, seven hours), from where you catch buses to Caracas, Maracay, Valencia, Barinas and San Cristóbal. There are also direct buses from Puerto Ayacucho to Caracas, Maracay and Valencia, but they go via a longer route through Caicara del Orinoco.

Por puestos to El Burro run from the terminal (US$4, 1½ hours). Carritos to Samariapo depart from Avenida Orinoco, one block south of the Banco de Venezuela (US$2.50, 1½ hours).

Boat There is no passenger boat service down the Río Orinoco, and cargo boats are infrequent.

To Colombia Puerto Carreño, the nearest Colombian town, is at the confluence of the Ríos Meta and Orinoco and is accessible from Puerto Ayacucho in two ways. Remember to get an exit stamp in your passport at DIEX before setting off.

The first way leads via Casuarito, a Colombian hamlet right across the Orinoco from Puerto Ayacucho. A boat between Puerto Ayacucho's port (at the northeastern end of town) and Casuarito shuttles regularly throughout the day (US$1.50). From Casuarito, there's the *voladora* (high-speed boat) once a day to Puerto Carreño (US$9, one hour); check the time of departure when you arrive in Puerto Ayacucho. In the dry season (December to April), there may also be some jeeps from Casuarito to Puerto Carreño.

The other way goes via Puerto Páez, a Venezuelan village about 95km north of Puerto Ayacucho. Get there by a San Fernando bus (US$3, two hours); the trip includes a ferry crossing of the Orinoco from El Burro to Puerto Páez. The bus will drop you off in the center of the village. Go to the wharf and take a boat across the Río Meta to Puerto Carreño (US$1.50); they run regularly between 6 am and 6 pm.

Puerto Carreño is a long, one-street town with an airport, half a dozen hotels and a number of places to eat. Go to the DAS office (Colombian immigration), one block west of the main square, for an entry stamp in your passport. A number of shops will change bolívares to pesos.

There are two flights per week to Bogotá (US$110). Buses go only in the dry season, approximately from mid-December to mid-March. They depart once a week for the two-day journey by rough road to Villavicencio (US$60), which is four hours by bus from Bogotá. The region is unsafe, however, because of the presence of guerrillas.

To Brazil Take a flight from Puerto Ayacucho to San Carlos de Río Negro, from where irregular boats will take you to San Simón de Cocuy, on the border. Take a bus to São Gabriel (Brazil) and search there for cargo boats down the Río Negro to Manaus.

Language

Every visitor to Venezuela should attempt to learn some Spanish, the basic elements of which are easily acquired (perhaps more so for speakers of English and Romance languages). A monthlong language course taken before departure can go a long way toward facilitating communication and comfort on the road. Language courses are also available in Venezuela; Mérida and Caracas have the most options, but Isla de Margarita has some facilities too (see those sections for more information). Even if classes are impractical, you should make the effort to learn a few basic phrases and pleasantries. Do not hesitate to practice your new skills – in general, Latin Americans meet attempts to communicate in the vernacular, howsoever halting, with enthusiasm and appreciation.

Latin American Spanish

The Spanish of the Americas comes in a bewildering array of varieties. Depending on the areas in which you travel, consonants may be glossed over, vowels squashed into each other, and syllables and even words dropped entirely. Slang and regional vocabulary, much of it derived from indigenous languages, can add even further to your bewilderment.

Throughout Latin America, the Spanish language is referred to as *castellano* more often than *español*. Unlike in Spain, the plural of the familiar *tú* form is *ustedes* rather than *vosotros*; the latter term will sound quaint and archaic in the Americas. In addition, the letters 'c' and 'z' are never lisped in Latin America; attempts to do so could well provoke amusement or even contempt.

Spanish in Venezuela

Venezuelan Spanish is not the clearest or easiest to understand. Venezuelans (except those from the Andes) speak more rapidly than most other South Americans and tend to drop some endings, especially plurals.

The use of the forms *tú* (informal 'you') and *usted* (formal 'you') is very flexible in Venezuela. Both are used, but with regional variations. Either is OK, though it's best to answer using the same form in which you are addressed. Always use the *usted* form when talking to the police and the Guardia Nacional.

Greetings in Venezuela are more elaborate than in Spain. The short Spanish *hola* has given way to a number of expressions, which are exchanged at the beginning of a conversation. Listen to how the locals greet you and learn some of these expressions in order to keep to the local style.

Although Venezuelans don't seem to be devoutly religious, the expressions *si Dios quiere* (God willing) and *gracias a Dios* (thanks to God) are used frequently in conversation.

Phrasebooks & Dictionaries

Lonely Planet's *Latin American Spanish phrasebook,* by Anna Cody, is a worthwhile addition to your backpack. Another exceptionally useful resource is the *University of Chicago Spanish-English, English-Spanish Dictionary* – its small size, light weight and thorough entries make it ideal for travel. It also makes a great gift for any newfound friends upon your departure.

Pronunciation

The pronunciation of written Spanish is, in theory, consistently phonetic. Once you are aware of the basic rules, they should cause little difficulty. Speak slowly to avoid getting tongue-tied until you become confident of your ability. Of course, the best way to familiarize yourself with the pronunciation of the area you're traveling in is to chat with locals, keeping an ear out for any regional variations.

Traditionally, there were three Spanish letters that did not exist in English: 'ch,' 'll' and 'ñ.' These followed 'c,' 'l,' and 'n' respectively in the alphabet, and had their own corresponding sections in the dictionary. However, in the mid-1990s, Spain's Academia Real de la Lengua Española abolished 'ch' and 'll' as separate letters; hence, newer Spanish dictionaries list them in their English alphabetical order. The practice varies from region to region, so look for a 'ch' section in the phone book if you can't find 'Chávez' under 'c.'

Vowels Spanish vowels are generally consistent and have close English equivalents:

a is like the 'a' in 'father'
e is somewhere between the 'e' in 'met' and the 'ey' in 'hey'
i is like the 'ee' in 'feet'
o is like the 'o' in 'note'
u is like the 'oo' in 'boot'; it is silent after 'q' and in the pairings 'gue' and 'gui,' unless it's carrying a dieresis ('ü,' as in *güero*)

Consonants Spanish consonants generally sound like their English equivalents. The following are the major differences in the pronunciation of consonants.

b resembles the English 'b,' but is a softer sound produced by holding the lips nearly together. When beginning a word or when preceded by 'm' or 'n,' it's pronounced like the 'b' in 'book' *(bomba, embajada)*. The Spanish 'v' is pronounced almost identically; for clarification, Spanish speakers refer to 'b' as 'b larga' and to 'v' as 'b corta.'
c is like the 's' in 'see' before 'e' and 'i'; otherwise, it's like the English 'k.'
d is produced with the tongue up against the front teeth, almost like the 'th' in 'feather'; after 'l' and 'n,' it's pronounced like the English 'd' in 'dog.'
g before 'e' and 'i' acts as a more guttural English 'h'; otherwise, it sounds like the 'g' in 'go.'
h is invariably silent; if your name begins with this letter, listen carefully when immigration officials summon you to pick up your passport.
j acts as a more guttural English 'h.'
ll acts as a Spanish 'y,' although it is never a vowel; see Semiconsonant, below.

ñ is like the 'ny' in 'canyon.'
r is produced with the tongue touching the palate and flapping down, almost like the 'tt' of 'butter.' At the beginning of a word or following 'l,' 'n' or 's,' it is rolled strongly.
rr is a very strongly rolled Spanish 'r.'
t resembles the English 't,' but without the puff of air.
v is pronounced like the Spanish 'b.'
x is generally pronounced like the 'x' in 'taxi' except for a few words in which it acts as the Spanish 'j' (as in 'México').
z is like the 's' in 'sun.'

Semiconsonant The Spanish **y** is a semiconsonant; it's pronounced as the Spanish 'i' when it stands alone or appears at the end of a word. Normally, 'y' is pronounced like the 'y' in 'yesterday'; however, in some regions it may be pronounced as the 's' in 'pleasure' or even the 'j' in 'jacket.' Hence, *yo me llamo* can sound like 'joe meh jahm-oh.'

Diphthongs Diphthongs are combinations of two vowels that form a single syllable. In Spanish, the formation of a diphthong depends on combinations of the two 'weak' vowels, 'i' and 'u,' or one weak and one of the three 'strong' vowels, 'a,' 'e' and 'o.' Two strong vowels form separate syllables.

An example of two weak vowels forming a diphthong is the word *viuda* (widow; pronounced **vyu**-tha). The initial syllable of 'Guatemala' is a combination of weak and strong vowels. In contrast, the verb *caer* (to fall) has two syllables (pronounced ca-**er**). Other examples include the following:

ai as in 'hide'
au as in 'how'
ei as in 'hay'
ia as in 'yard'
ie as in 'yes'
oi as in 'boy'
ua as in 'wash'
ue as in 'well' (unless preceded by 'q' or 'g')

Stress Stress is extremely important, as it can change the meaning of words. In general, words ending in vowels or the letters 'n' or 's' have stress on the next-to-last syllable, while those with other endings have stress on the last syllable. Thus *vaca* (cow) and *caballos* (horses) are both stressed on their penultimate syllables, while *catedral* (cathedral) is stressed on its last syllable.

To indicate departures from these general rules, Spanish employs the acute accent, which can occur anywhere in a word. If there is an accented syllable, stress is always on that syllable. Thus *sótano* (basement), 'América' and 'Panamá' have the first, second and third syllable stressed, respectively. When words are written in capital letters, the accent is often omitted, but the stress still falls where the accent would be.

Basic Grammar

Although even colloquial Spanish comprises a multitude of tenses and moods, learning enough grammar to enable basic conversation is not particularly difficult. In general, Spanish word order in sentences resembles that of English.

Nouns & Pronouns Nouns in Spanish are masculine or feminine. In general, nouns ending in 'o,' 'e' or 'ma' are masculine, while those ending in 'a,' 'ión' or 'dad' are feminine. Of course, there are scores of exceptions to this rule: both *día* (day) and *mapa* (map) are masculine, while *mano* (hand) is feminine. To pluralize a noun, add 's' if it ends in an unaccented vowel – eg, *libro* (book) becomes *libros* – and 'es' if it ends in a consonant or accented vowel – eg, *rey* (king) becomes *reyes*. Fortunately for speakers of English, there is no declension of nouns as in Latin.

The personal pronouns are *yo* (I), *tú* or *vos* (you, informal), *usted* (you, formal; abbreviated Ud), *el/ella* (he/she), *nosotros/nosotras* (we), *ustedes* (you, plural; abbreviated Uds) and *ellos/ellas* (they). Note that to use the feminine plurals *nosotras* and *ellas,* the group referred to must be entirely composed of females; the presence of even one male calls for the masculine pronoun. In common speech, the personal pronoun may

be omitted when it is the subject of a sentence if the subject's identity is made clear by the verb ending: *estoy aquí* rather than *yo estoy aquí* (both mean 'I am here').

The possessive pronouns are *mi* (my), *tu* (your, informal), *nuestro* (our) and *su* (his/her/their/your, formal; singular and plural). As in English, possessive pronouns precede the noun they modify; however, they must agree in number and gender with that noun – not with the possessor. Thus we get *nuestro hombre* (our man), *nuestra mujer* (our woman), *nuestros novios* (our boyfriends) and *nuestras novias* (our girlfriends). *Mi, tu* and *su* do not change with gender, but add an 's' for plural nouns: *mis libros* means 'my books.'

The demonstrative pronouns are *este* (this) and *ese* (that). Gender and number also affect demonstrative pronouns:

este libro	this book
estos cuadernos	these notebooks
esta carta	this letter
estas tijeras	these scissors
ese chico	that boy
esos muchachos	those guys
esa chica	that girl
esas muchachas	those gals

Articles, Adjectives & Adverbs The definite articles ('the' in English) are *el, la, los* and *las*. These four forms correspond to the four possible combinations of gender and number. Similarly, the indefinite articles ('a,' 'an' and 'some') are *un, una, unos* and *unas*. In Spanish, the definite article is used more extensively than in English, while the indefinite article is utilized less. As in English, the articles precede the nouns they modify, eg, *el papel* (the paper), *unas frutas* (some fruits).

In contrast, adjectives in Spanish usually follow the noun they modify. Adjectives ending in 'o' agree with the noun in gender and number (thus *alto* means 'tall,' while *mujeres altas* means 'tall women'); those ending in other letters merely agree in number. To form a comparative, add *más* (more) or *menos* (less) before the adjective. For superlatives, add the *más* or *menos* as well as *lo, la, los* or *las* (depending on gender and number). For example, *pequeño* is 'small,' *más pequeño* 'smaller' and *lo más pequeño* 'the smallest.'

Adverbs can often be formed from adjectives by adding the suffix *-mente*. If the adjective ends in an 'o,' convert it to an 'a' before affixing the ending. Thus *actual* (current) becomes *actualmente* (currently) and *rápido* (rapid) becomes *rápidamente* (rapidly).

Verbs Spanish has three main categories of verbs: those ending in 'ar,' such as *hablar* (to speak); those ending in 'er,' such as *comer* (to eat); and those ending in 'ir,' such as *reir* (to laugh). Verbs are conjugated by retaining the verb's stem and altering the ending depending on subject, tense and mood. While most verbs follow a complicated yet predictable pattern of conjugation, there are scores of 'irregular' verbs, often the most commonly used, that must be memorized. For a more detailed explanation of verb conjugation, refer to Lonely Planet's *Latin American Spanish phrasebook*.

Greetings & Civilities
In public behavior, Latin Americans are often cordial yet polite and expect others to reciprocate. Never, for example, address a stranger without extending a greeting such as *buenos días* or *buenas tardes*. The usage of the informal second-person singular *tú* and *vos* differs from country to country; when in doubt, use the more formal *usted*. You must *always* use *usted* when addressing the police or persons with considerable power.

Hello	*Hola*
Good morning/Good day	*Buenos días*
Good afternoon	*Buenas tardes*
Good evening/Good night	*Buenas noches*

(The above three are often shortened to *Buenos* or *Buenas*.)

Goodbye	*Adiós* or *Hasta luego*
Please	*Por favor*
Thank you	*Gracias*
I'm sorry	*Lo siento*

My name is …	*Me llamo …*
Excuse me	*Discúlpeme* or *Perdón*
What is your name?	
¿Cómo se llama usted?	
A pleasure (to meet you)	
Mucho gusto	
You're welcome/It's a pleasure	
De nada/Con mucho gusto	
Excuse me (when passing someone)	
Permiso	

Useful Words & Phrases

yes	*sí*
no	*no*
and	*y*
to/at	*a*
for	*por, para*
of/from	*de/desde*
in/on	*en*
with	*con*
without	*sin*
before	*antes*
after	*después de*
soon	*pronto*
already	*ya*
now	*ahora*
right away	*ahorita, en seguida*
here	*aquí*
there	*allí* or *allá*
I understand.	*Entiendo.*
I don't understand.	*No entiendo.*

I don't speak much Spanish.
  No hablo mucho castellano.
I would like …
  Me gustaría … or *Quisiera …*

Is/are there …?	*¿Hay …?*
Where?	*¿Dónde?*
Where is/are …?	*¿Dónde está/están …?*
When?	*¿Cuándo?*
What?	*¿Qué?*
Which (ones)?	*¿Cuál(es)?*
Who?	*¿Quién?*
Why?	*¿Por qué?*
How?	*¿Cómo?*
How much?	*¿Cuánto?*
How many?	*¿Cuántos?*

(use *¿Cómo?* to ask someone to repeat something)

Emergencies

Help!	*¡Socorro!* or *¡Auxilio!*
Help me!	*¡Ayúdenme!*
Thief!	*¡Ladrón!*
Fire!	*¡Fuego!*
police	*policía*
doctor	*doctor*
hospital	*hospital*
I've been robbed.	*Me han robado.*
They took my ...	*Se me llevaron ...*
money	*el dinero*
passport	*el pasaporte*
bag	*la bolsa*
Leave me alone!	*¡Déjeme!*
Go away!	*¡Váyase!*

Getting Around

plane	*avión*
train	*tren*
bus	*bus*
small bus	*por puesto, colectivo, micro, buseta, carrito*
ship	*barco, buque*
boat	*bongo, lancha, bote*
car	*auto, carro*
taxi	*taxi*
truck	*camión*
pickup	*camioneta*
bicycle	*bicicleta*
motorcycle	*motocicleta*
hitchhike	*hacer dedo, pedir una cola*
airport	*aeropuerto*
train station	*estación de ferrocarril*
bus terminal	*terminal de pasajeros*

I would like a ticket to ...
Quiero un boleto/pasaje a ...
What's the fare to ...?
¿Cuánto cuesta el pasaje a ...?
When does the next plane/train/bus leave for ...?
¿Cuándo sale el próximo avión/tren/bus para ...?
Are there student discounts?
¿Hay descuentos estudiantiles?/¿Hay rebajas para estudiantes?

first/last/next *primero/último/próximo*
first/second class *primera/segunda clase*
one-way/roundtrip *ida/ida y vuelta*

left luggage *guardería de equipaje*
tourist office *oficina de turismo*

Traffic Signs Keep in mind that traffic signs will invariably be in Spanish and may not be accompanied by internationally recognized symbols. Pay especially close attention to signs reading *Peligro* (Danger), *Cede el Paso* (Yield, or Give Way; especially prevalent on one-lane bridges), and *Hundimiento* (Dip; often a euphemistic term for 'axle-breaking sinkhole'). Disregarding these warnings could result in disaster.

Adelante	Ahead
Alto	Stop
Cede el Paso	Yield/Give Way
Curva Peligrosa	Dangerous Curve
Derrumbes en la Vía	Landslides or Rock falls (in the Road)
Despacio	Slow
Desvío	Detour
Hundimiento	Dip
Mantenga Su Derecha	Keep to the Right
No Adelantar/No Rebase	No Passing
No Estacionar	No Parking
No Hay Paso	No Entrance
Peligro	Danger
Trabajos en la Vía	Construction/ Roadwork
Tránsito Entrando	Entering Traffic

Accommodations

hotel	*hotel, pensión, residencia*
single room	*habitación sencilla*
double room	*habitación doble*
What does it cost?	*¿Cuánto cuesta?*

Can you give me a deal?
¿Me puede hacer precio?/¿Me puede hacer promoción?/¿Me puede rebajar?

per night	*por noche*
full board	*pensión completa*
shared bath	*baño compartido*
private bath	*baño privado*
too expensive	*demasiado caro*

cheaper	*más económico/barato*
May I see it?	*¿Puedo verlo?*
I don't like it.	*No me gusta.*
the bill	*la cuenta*

Toilets

The most common word for 'toilet' is *baño*, but *servicios sanitarios* or just *servicios* (services) is a frequent alternative. Men's toilets will usually be signaled by *hombres*, *caballeros* or *varones*. Women's toilets will say *señoras* or *damas*.

Eating & Drinking

Only some basic terms are given here. Please see the Food & Drink Glossary, later, for more vocabulary.

I (don't) eat/drink …	*(No) como/tomo …*
I'm a vegetarian.	*Soy vegetariano/a.*
water	*agua*
purified water	*agua purificada*
bread	*pan*
meat	*carne*
cheese	*queso*
eggs	*huevos*
milk	*leche*
vegetables	*vegetales* or *legumbres*
fish	*pescado*
coffee	*café*
tea	*té*
beer	*cerveza*
alcohol	*alcohol*

Post & Communications

post office	*correo*
letter	*carta*
parcel	*paquete*
postcard	*postal*
airmail	*correo aéreo*
registered mail	*correo certificado*
stamps	*estampillas*
phone call	*llamada (telefónica)*
collect call	*llamada a cobro revertido*
public telephone	*teléfono público*
local call	*llamada local*
long-distance call	*llamada de larga distancia*
person to person	*persona a persona*
email	*correo electrónico*

Geographical Expressions

The expressions below are among the most common you will encounter in Spanish-language maps and guides.

avenida	avenue
bahía	bay
calle	street
camino	road
campo, finca, fundo, hacienda	farm
carretera, camino, ruta	highway
cascada, salto	waterfall
cerro	hill
cerro	mount
cordillera	mountain range
estancia, granja, rancho	ranch
estero	marsh, estuary
lago	lake
montaña	mountain
parque nacional	national park
paso	pass
puente	bridge
río	river
seno	sound
valle	valley

Countries

The list below includes only countries whose names are spelled differently in English and Spanish.

I am from *Soy de…*
Where are you from?
  ¿De dónde viene usted?
Where do you live?
  ¿Dónde vive usted?

Canada	*Canadá*
Denmark	*Dinamarca*
England	*Inglaterra*
France	*Francia*
Germany	*Alemania*
Great Britain	*Gran Bretaña*
Ireland	*Irlanda*
Italy	*Italia*
Japan	*Japón*
Netherlands	*Holanda*
New Zealand	*Nueva Zelandia*
Scotland	*Escocia*
Spain	*España*

Sweden	*Suecia*
Switzerland	*Suiza*
United States	*Estados Unidos*
Wales	*Gales*

Numbers

1	*uno*
2	*dos*
3	*tres*
4	*cuatro*
5	*cinco*
6	*seis*
7	*siete*
8	*ocho*
9	*nueve*
10	*diez*
11	*once*
12	*doce*
13	*trece*
14	*catorce*
15	*quince*
16	*dieciséis*
17	*diecisiete*
18	*dieciocho*
19	*diecinueve*
20	*veinte*
21	*veintiuno*
22	*veintidós*
23	*veintitrés*
24	*veinticuatro*
30	*treinta*
31	*treinta y uno*
32	*treinta y dos*
33	*treinta y tres*
40	*cuarenta*
50	*cincuenta*
60	*sesenta*
70	*setenta*
80	*ochenta*
90	*noventa*
100	*cien*
101	*ciento uno*
102	*ciento dos*
110	*ciento diez*
200	*doscientos*
300	*trescientos*
400	*cuatrocientos*
500	*quinientos*
600	*seiscientos*
700	*setecientos*
800	*ochocientos*
900	*novecientos*
1000	*mil*
1100	*mil cien*
1200	*mil doscientos*
2000	*dos mil*
10,000	*diez mil*
50,000	*cincuenta mil*
100,000	*cien mil*
1,000,000	*un millón*
2,000,000	*dos millones*
1,000,000,000	*un billón*

Ordinal Numbers

As with other adjectives, ordinals must agree in gender and number with the noun they modify. Ordinal numbers are often abbreviated using a numeral and a superscript 'o' or 'a' (depending on gender) in street names, addresses, and so forth: Calle 1a, 2o piso (1st Street, 2nd floor).

1st	*primero/a*
2nd	*segundo/a*
3rd	*tercero/a*
4th	*cuarto/a*
5th	*quinto/a*
6th	*sexto/a*
7th	*séptimo/a*
8th	*octavo/a*
9th	*noveno/a*
10th	*décimo/a*
11th	*undécimo/a*
12th	*duodécimo/a*
20th	*vigésimo/a*

Days of the Week

Monday	*lunes*
Tuesday	*martes*
Wednesday	*miércoles*
Thursday	*jueves*
Friday	*viernes*
Saturday	*sábado*
Sunday	*domingo*

Time

The time is expressed by saying *la* or *las* followed by the hour number and how far it is past or until the hour. Thus, eight o'clock is *las ocho*, while 8:30 is *las ocho y treinta* (eight and thirty) or *las ocho y media* (eight and a half). However, 7:45 is *las ocho menos quince* (eight minus fifteen) or *las ocho menos cuarto* (eight minus one quarter).

Times are modified by morning *(de la mañana)* or afternoon *(de la tarde)* instead of am or pm. Use of the 24-hour clock, or military time, is also common, especially with transportation schedules.

What time is it?	*¿Qué hora es?*
It's one o'clock.	*Es la una.*
At three o'clock…	*A las tres…*
It's two/three/etc o'clock.	*Son las dos/tres/etc.*

Glossary

abasto – grocery store

acure – hare-sized rodent, species of agouti

AD – Acción Democrática, or Democratic Action Party; populist party created in 1941 by Rómulo Betancourt. It is one of the two major traditional parties.

adeco – member or follower of the Acción Democrática party

adobe – sun-dried brick made of mud and straw, used in traditional rural constructions

alcabala – road checkpost operated by the Guardia Nacional

alcaraván – stone curlew, a large shorebird

andino/a – inhabitant of the Andes

araguaney – *Tabebuia chrysantha,* or trumpet tree; a large tree with yellow flowers (Venezuela's national tree)

atarraya – kind of traditional circular fishing net used on the coast and rivers

ateneo – cultural center

autopista – freeway

azulejos – ornamental handmade tiles brought to South America from Spain and Portugal in colonial times

baba – spectacled caiman, the smallest of this family of crocodiles

balneario – sea-, lake- or riverside bathing place with facilities

bandola – four-string guitar-type instrument used by some *joropo* bands instead of the harp

Baré – also *Balé*; an Indian group living in southern Amazonas

barrio – shantytown built of *ranchos* by the poor around the big city centers. Particularly numerous and extensive in Caracas, they are found throughout South America, though they are named differently in different countries: *tugurios* in Colombia, *favelas* in Brazil, *villas miserias* in Argentina, *cantegriles* in Uruguay, *barriadas* in Peru and *callampas* in Chile.

bodega – warehouse; also used to mean 'grocery,' especially in small localities and rural areas

bolo – informal term for the bolívar (Venezuela's currency); see also *real*

bonche – party (informal)

bongo – large dugout canoe; traditionally hand-hewn, today usually equipped with outboard motor

bora – aquatic plant with mauve or white flowers and leaves that resemble small balloons; favorite treat of the capybara

broma – literally 'joke'; a problem, or an object or entity that need not be precisely named (informal)

bucare – *Erythrina poeppigiana,* a large tree with red flowers that often provides shade to coffee or cacao plantations. Its branches house orchids and bromeliads.

buhonero – street vendor

buseta – small bus

cabaña – cabin, found mostly on the coast and in the mountains

cachicamo – armadillo

caimán – caiman, or American crocodile; similar to alligators but with a more heavily armored belly

caminata – trek

campamento – countryside lodging facility, usually in cabins, with its own food services and often a tour program

campesino/a – rural dweller, usually of modest economic means; peasant

canoa – a dugout canoe

CANTV – the national telecommunications company

caño – natural water channel

carabobeño/a – inhabitant of Carabobo state, particularly Valencia

Caracazo – violent Caracas riots of February 27–29, 1989, in which more than 300 people died

caraqueño/a – person born and/or residing in Caracas

cardón – columnar type of cactus typical of the Península de Paraguaná

casa – house; used for anything from a rustic hut to a rambling colonial mansion

casa de cambio – money-exchange office

cascabel – rattlesnake

caserío – hamlet

casona – large, usually historic mansion; stately home

catire – person of light complexion

caudillo – South American dictator, normally a military man who assumes power by force and is noted for autocratic rule. Caudillos governed Venezuela from 1830 to 1958.

Causa R – Causa Radical, a left-wing political party founded by unionists in opposition to the traditional parties

cédula – identity document of Venezuelan citizens and residents

ceiba – common tree of the tropics. It can reach a huge size.

chalana – river ferry for people and vehicles

chaguaramo – popular term for royal palm

chamo/a – boy/girl, young person, friend, pal (informal)

chapaletas – fins, flippers (rubber paddle-like devices used for swimming, snorkeling and the like)

chévere – good, fine (informal)

chigüire – capybara, the world's largest rodent

chimó – tobacco tar used by people in the Amazon, the Andes and other regions; a 'nicotine candy.' A ball of chimó is placed under the tongue or between the gum and check until it dissolves.

chinchorro – hammock woven of cotton threads or palm fiber like a fishing net; typical of many Indian groups, including the Warao and Guajiro

chiripa – crawling insect; also used to describe a small, newly born political party (informal)

churuata – traditional palm-thatched circular Indian hut

cinemateca – art cinema that focuses on screening films of a high artistic quality

cogollos – top ranks of the political parties

cola – literally 'tail'; also used in the sense of 'ride,' as in *dar una cola* (to give a ride) and *pedir una cola* (to ask for a ride) – useful expressions when hitchhiking

coleo – form of rodeo practiced in Los Llanos, also known as *toros coleados*. The aim is to overthrow a bull by grabbing its tail from a galloping horse.

colibrí – hummingbird

cónchale – informal tag word, used on its own or added to the beginning of a sentence to emphasize emotional involvement

conuco – small cultivated plot, usually obtained by slashing-and-burning

Copei – Partido Social Cristiano, or Social Christian Party; founded by Rafael Caldera in 1946 in opposition to the leftist AD party. Initially conservative and Catholic-oriented, since the 1970s it has gradually moved leftward to become the essentially populist party. Until the 1993 election, Copei and AD almost monopolized the popular vote.

copeyano – member of Copei

corrida – bullfight

criollo/a – Creole, a person of European (especially Spanish) ancestry but born in the Americas

cuadra – city block

cuatro – sort of small four-stringed guitar, used in *joropo* music

cuñado – literally 'brother-in-law'; pal, friend (informal)

curiara – small dugout canoe

danta – tapir; large hoofed mammal of tropical and subtropical forests. The danta is a distant relative of the horse.

denuncia – official report/statement to the police

DIEX or **DEX** – Dirección Nacional de Identificación y Extranjería, the Venezuelan immigration authority

embalse – reservoir formed by a dam built for hydroelectric or water-supply purposes

E'ñepá – see *Panare*

esquina – street corner

estacionamiento (vigilado) – (guarded) parking lot

farmacia – pharmacy

flamenco – flamingo

flor de mayo – species of orchid that is Venezuela's national flower

flux – suit

fortín – small fort

fósforos – matches

frailejón – espeletia; a species of plant typical of the *páramo*

franela – literally 'flannel'; commonly refers to a T-shirt

fuerte – fort

fundo – country estate

furruco – musical instrument consisting of a drum and a wooden pole piercing the drumhead; used in some kinds of popular music including the *gaita*. The sound is produced via striking the drumhead by moving the pole up and down.

gaita – popular music played in Zulia state

gallera – cockfight ring

garimpeiro – illegal gold miner

garza – heron

gavilán – sparrow hawk

gringo/a – any white foreigner; sometimes, not always, derogatory

guacamaya – macaw

guácharo – oilbird, a species of nocturnal bird living in caves

Guajibo – or *Guahibo* (*Hiwi* in the native language); an Indian group living in parts of Los Llanos and Amazonas along the frontier with Colombia

Guajiro – Venezuela's most numerous Indian group, living in Zulia state (Venezuela) and Península de la Guajira (Colombia); often referred to by their native name of *Wayú*

guardaequipaje – left-luggage office; checkroom

guardaparque – national-park ranger

Guardia Nacional – military police responsible for security

guarupa – jacaranda; a tall tropical tree with lavender-blue blossoms

hacienda – country estate

hato – large cattle ranch, typical of Los Llanos

Hiwi – see *Guajibo*

hospedaje – cheap hotel

invierno – literally 'winter'; refers to the rainy season

Ipostel – state company operating a network of post offices

IVA – *impuesto de valor agregado*, a value-added sales tax (VAT)

jején – species of small biting fly that infests La Gran Sabana and, to a lesser extent, some other regions

jíbaro – drug dealer (informal)

joropo – typical music of Los Llanos, today widespread throughout the country; considered Venezuelan national rhythm

lapa – species of agouti, a rabbit-sized rodent whose brown skin is dotted with white spots

libre – taxi

liqui liqui – men's traditional costume, typical of most of the Caribbean; a white or beige suit comprising trousers and a blouse with a collar, usually accompanied by white hat and shoes

llanero/a – inhabitant of Los Llanos

(Los) Llanos – literally 'plains'; Venezuela's vast central region

loro – parrot

malecón – waterfront promenade

manatí – manatee; a cetaceous herbivore living in calm rivers. Manatees can reach up to 5m in length.

manga de coleo – place where *coleos* are held

mapanare – venomous snake common in Venezuela

Maquiritare – see *Yekuana*

maracas – gourd rattles; an indispensable accompanying instrument of *joropo*

maracucho/a – person from Maracaibo; often extended to mean anyone from the Zulia state

margariteño/a – person from the Isla de Margarita

MAS – Movimiento al Socialismo; leftist political party created by former guerrilla leaders after the insurgent forces were dismantled in the early 1970s

matrimonial – hotel room with a double bed intended for married couples

médanos – sand dunes near Coro

merengue – musical rhythm originating from the Dominican Republic, today widespread throughout the Caribbean

merú – Pemón Indian word for 'waterfall'

mestizo/a – person of mixed European-Indian blood

micro – in some regions, a term for a minibus or van used as local transportation

mirador – lookout, viewpoint

monedero – originally, a term referring to public telephone operated by coins, but now extended to any public phone

moriche – palm common in Los Llanos and the Delta del Orinoco, used by Indians for construction, food, household items, handicrafts etc

morocho/a – person of dark complexion; usually a mix of black and white ancestry

morrocoy – tortoise typical of some regions, including Los Llanos and Guayana

mosquitero – mosquito net

muelle – pier, wharf

mulato/a – mulatto; a person of mixed European African ancestry

musiú – old-fashioned term for 'foreigner,' derived from the French *monsieur* and used by elderly locals in some rural areas

MVR – Movimiento Quinta República; populist leftist party formed by Hugo Chávez as a platform for his presidential campaign

Navidad – Christmas

nevado – snowcapped peak

orquídea – orchid

oso hormiguero – anteater

palafito – house built on stilts over the water; a typical Warao dwelling in the Delta del Orinoco. Also found in Zulia state, especially in Laguna de Sinamaica

palos – literally 'sticks'; drinks (informal)

pana – pal (informal)

Panare – indigenous group living in Bolívar and Amazon states; also known by their native name of *E'ñepá*

paño – small towel, the one you'll get in cheap hotels

parada – bus stop

páramo – open highlands above about 3300m; typical of Venezuela, Colombia and Ecuador

parapente – paraglider

pardo/a – mulatto; person of mixed European and African descent

paují – a black bird that inhabits cloud forest in the north and west of Venezuela

Pemón – Indian group inhabiting La Gran Sabana and neighboring areas

peñero – open fishing boat made from wood

pereza – sloth

Piaroa – originally called *Wóthuha;* an Indian group living in Amazonas state

plaza de toros – bullfight ring

por puesto – cross between a bus and taxi that plies fixed routes and departs when full; a popular means of transportation

posada – small, family-run guesthouse

primo – literally 'cousin'; pal, brother (informal)

propina – tip

Pumé – see *Yaruro*

puri-puri – small biting flies, similar to *jejenes*

quinta – house with a garden. Quintas originally took up a fifth of a city block hence the name.

ranchería – Indian hamlet

rancho or **ranchito** – ramshackle dwelling built of waste materials

raudales – rapids

real – informal term for the bolívar (Venezuela's currency)

redoma – traffic circle, roundabout

refugio – rustic shelter in a remote area, mostly in the mountains

residencia – cheap hotel or, more often, apartment building.

rústico – jeep

salinas – seaside salt pans or shallow lagoons used for extraction of salt

salsa – literally 'sauce'; a type of Caribbean dance music of Cuban origin. It evolved and matured in New York, from where it has conquered the entire Caribbean basin and surrounding countries.

Semana Santa – Holy Week, the week before Easter Sunday

shabono – large circular house typical of the Yanomami

SIDA – AIDS

sifrino/a – yuppie (informal)

sima – sinkhole; depression in the ground, usually of a circular shape and often of a large depth, characteristic for its vertical walls

soroche – altitude sickness

tapara – cuplike vessel made from a hollowed-out pumpkin cut in half; traditionally used in some rural areas for drinking, washing etc

tarjetero – public telephone operated by phone cards

teleférico – cable car

telenovela – TV soap opera

tepui – also spelled *tepuy*; a flat-topped sandstone mountain with vertical flanks. The term is derived from the Pemón Indian word for 'mountain.'

terminal de pasajeros – bus terminal

tigre – jaguar

tonina – freshwater dolphin

toros coleados – see *coleo*

trapiche – traditional sugarcane mill

turpial – small black, red and yellow bird; Venezuela's national bird

urbanización – suburb

vallenato – typical Colombian music, now widespread throughout Venezuela

vaquero – cowboy of Los Llanos

vená – the Pemón Indian word for 'high waterfall'

verano – literally 'summer'; used in the sense of 'dry season'

Warao – Indian group living in the Delta del Orinoco

Wayú – see *Guajiro*

viaje expreso – literally 'express trip'; refers to paying for the whole trip in a car, jeep, boat etc, as in a taxi

Wóthuha – see *Piaroa*

yagrumo – wtree with large palmate silver-colored leaves

Yanomami – indigenous group living in the Venezuelan and Brazilian Amazon

Yaruro – known in their native language as *Pumé*; an Indian group living in Apure state (Venezuela) and Arauca and Casanare states (Colombia)

Yekuana – also referred to as *Maquiritare*; an Indian group inhabiting parts of Amazonas and Bolívar states

yoppo – hallucinogenic powder inhaled through the nostrils using a long pipe; traditionally used by Yanomami shamans

zambo/a – person of mixed Indian-African ancestry

zamuro – vulture

Food & Drink Glossary

aceite – oil
aceituna – olive
agua – water
aguacate – avocado
aguardiente – sugarcane spirit flavored with anise; typical of Colombia, similar to *miche*
ají – red hot chili pepper
ajo – garlic
ajoporro – leek
alcaparra – caper
aliño – combination of spices
almeja – clam
almendra – almond
almuerzo – lunch
arepa – small maize pancake, which in itself is plain and comes as an accompaniment to some dishes. More popularly, it's served as a snack in its own right, stuffed with a variety of fillings including cheese, beef, ham, octopus, shrimp, sausage, eggs, salad, avocado and just about anything you might think of. In the Andean region, there's also the quite different *arepa de trigo,* which is made from wheat.
arepera – eating place that serves arepas. It can be just a self-service arepa snack bar, or a restaurant with table service that, apart from arepas, offers other typical dishes, such as *mondongo, hervido, pabellón* etc.
arroz – rice
arvejas – green peas
atún – tuna
auyama – pumpkin
avellana – hazelnut
azúcar – sugar

bagre – catfish
batata – sweet potato
batido – fresh fruit juice (pure or watered down)
bebida – drink, beverage
berenjena – eggplant
bienmesabe – sponge cake with coconut flavor
brócoli – broccoli

cachapa – round juicy pancake made of fresh corn, usually served with cheese and/ or ham
cachito – a sort of croissant filled with chopped ham and served hot
calabacín – zucchini, courgette
calabaza – squash
calamar – squid
calentado – typical drink of the Andean highlands made from *miche* and milk, sweetened with *papelón,* seasoned with herbs and served hot
camarón – small shrimp
cambur – banana
canela – cinnamon
cangrejo – crab
canilla – small baguette
carabina – Mérida version of *hallaca*
caracol – snail
caraota – black bean
carite – kingfish
carne – meat
carne de cochino – pork
carne de res – beef
carne guisada – stewed beef
carne mechada – shredded beef
carne molida – minced (ground) meat
casabe – very large, dry flat bread made from *yuca amarga* (bitter yucca, grated, pressed and dried) that has traditionally been an important part of the diet of the Indian communities
cazón – baby shark
cebolla – onion
cebollín – scallion, spring onion
céleri – celery
cereza – cherry
cerveza – beer
champiñón – mushroom
charcutería – pork butcher's shop selling hams, sausages, salamis etc
chayote – chayote, christophine; a light green pear-shaped fruit
chicha – thick, filling nonalcoholic drink made from corn or rice. It also has an alcoholic variety.

chicharrones – pork cracklings
chimbombo – okra
chivo – goat
chorizo – seasoned sausage
chuleta – chop, rib steak
churro – fried pastry stick sprinkled with sugar; often sold on the street
ciruela – plum
cocada – blended drink made from coconut milk
cochino – pork
coco – coconut
coctel – cocktail
cocuy – a kind of liqueur that is made from sugarcane
codorniz – quail
coliflor – cauliflower
contorno – accompaniment to the main dish
cordero – lamb
corocoro – grunt (fish)
corvina – bluefish
costilla – rib
cotufa – popcorn
crema agria – sour cream

dátil - date
desayuno – breakfast
dorado – mahimahi, dolphinfish (not the mammalian dolphin)
dulce – small cake
durazno – apricot

empanada – crescent-shaped, deep-fried cornmeal turnover stuffed with ground beef (*empanada de carne*), chicken (*empanada de pollo*) or cheese (*empanada de queso*). A ubiquitous snack found throughout the continent, with numerous local varieties.
ensalada – salad
espárrago – asparagus
espinaca – spinach

falda – flank
frambuesa – raspberry
fresa – strawberry
frijoles – red beans
fruta – fruit
frutería – fruit shop or place that serves fruit salads, fruit juices, *merengadas* etc
fuente de soda – budget eating place serving snacks and drinks

galleta – biscuit, cracker
gallina – hen
garbanzo – chickpea
grasa – fat
guacuco – clam
guanábana – soursop
guarapita – drink made from a sugarcane spirit and fruit juice
guasacaca – piquant sauce made of peppers, onions and seasoning; the red-colored varieties are hotter than the green ones. The sauce is served with chicken, *parrillas,* empanadas etc, and you'll often find it on restaurant tables.
guayaba – guava
guayoyo – weak black coffee
guisante – pea

haba – broad bean/large lima bean, common in the Andes
hallaca – chopped pork, beef and/or chicken with vegetables and olives, all folded in a maize dough, wrapped in banana leaves and steamed; particularly popular during Christmas
helado – ice cream
hervido – a hearty soup made of beef (*hervido de res*) or chicken (*hervido de gallina*) with potatoes, carrots and a variety of local root vegetables
hielo – ice
hígado – liver
higo – fig
hongo – mushroom, fungus
huevo – egg
huevos fritos – fried eggs
huevos revueltos – scrambled eggs

jamón – ham
jamón serrano – cured ham that is sliced paper-thin
jengibre – ginger
jojoto – kernel corn, fresh corn
jugo – juice
jurel – a type of fish, which is similar to saurel or scad

langosta – lobster
langostino – large shrimp, large prawn
lebranche – black mullet
leche – milk

leche de burra – thick alcoholic beverage made of *miche,* egg and milk; common in the Andes

leche descremada – skim milk

lechón – pig stuffed with its own meat, as well as rice and dried peas, then baked

lechosa – papaya, pawpaw

lechuga – lettuce

lenguado – sole, flounder

lenteja – lentil

lima – lime

limón – lemon

limonada – lemonade

lisa – silver mullet, gray mullet

lomito – tenderloin

lunchería – cheap restaurant serving staple food and snacks

maíz – corn, maize

maíz pelado – shucked corn

mamón – grape-sized fruit, with green skin and reddish edible flesh that you suck until you get to the core

mandarina – mandarin, tangerine

maní – peanuts

mantecado – vanilla or dairy ice cream

mantequilla – butter

manzana – apple

margarina – margarine

mariscos – shellfish, seafood

masa – dough

mayonesa – mayonnaise

mejillones – mussels

melocotón – peach

melón – honeydew, rock melon

merengada – fruit milk shake

merey – cashew

mero – grouper or sea bass

miche – anise-flavored spirit made from sugarcane, similar to the Colombian *aguardiente,* and so called in some areas

milanesa – thin steak

mondongo – seasoned tripe cooked in bouillon with maize, potatoes, carrots and other vegetables

mora – blackberry

mostaza – mustard

muchacho – roast beef served in sauce

nabo – turnip

naranja – orange

nata – thick sweet cream

natilla – sour-milk butter

níspero – fruit of the medlar tree

nuez – nut, walnut

ñame – a type of yam, edible tuber

ocumo – root vegetable with dark skin and white meat; basic food for many Indian groups

ostra – oyster

pabellón criollo – main course consisting of shredded beef, rice, black beans, cheese and *tajada.* It's Venezuela's national dish.

paella – Spanish dish of rice, pork, chicken and seafood

pámpano – pompano (fish)

pan – bread

panqueca – pancake, crêpe

papa – potato

papas fritas – french fries

papelón – crude brown sugar; sold in solid blocks in cubes or pyramids

parchita – passion fruit

pargo – red snapper

parrilla – also called *parrillada;* a mixed grill of different kinds of meat, usually including steak, pork, chops, chicken and a variety of sausages. Originally an Argentine specialty but now widespread in Venezuela.

parrillada – see *parrilla*

pasapalos – hors d'oeuvres, small snacks, finger food

pastel – pastry

pasticho – lasagna

paticas – pig's feet

patilla – watermelon

pato – duck

pavo – turkey

pavón – peacock bass; a tasty freshwater fish common in Los Llanos

payara – type of peacock bass common in the Río Orinoco and its tributaries

pechuga – breast (poultry)

pepino – cucumber

pepitona – ark-shell clam

pera – pear

perejil – parsley

pernil – leg of pork

perro caliente – hot dog

pescado – fish that has been caught to eat
pez – live fish
pimentón – sweet green pepper (capsicum)
pimienta – pepper
piña – pineapple
plátano – plantain (green banana)
pollo – chicken
pulpo – octopus
punta trasera – rump roast

quesillo – caramel custard
queso – cheese

rábano – radish
raspao – shaved ice with flavored sugar syrup; sold only in the street
refresco – soft drink
refresquería – place serving soft drinks and snacks
reina pepiada – chicken with avocado, a tasty stuffing for *arepas*
remolacha – beet
repollo – cabbage
riñon – kidney
róbalo – snook, bass
ron – rum
rosbif – roast beef
rueda – fish steak

sal – salt
salchicha – sausage
salmón – salmon
salsa – sauce
salsa de tomate – tomato sauce, ketchup
sancocho – vegetable stew with fish, beef or chicken
sangría – red wine diluted with soda water, mixed with chunks of fruit
sardina – sardine
sierra – king mackerel, sawfish
solomo – sirloin
sopa – soup

tajada – fried ripe plantain
tamarindo – tamarind

tapas – typical Spanish hors d'oeuvres, a staple offering of the *tascas*. The most common include empanadas, *tortillas, jamón serrano, calamares, camarones, chorizos a la plancha* (grilled sausage) and *pimientos fritos* (fried peppers). Some of the dishes are served cold, others hot, and some of the latter variety may constitute the core of a main course.
tasca – Spanish-style bar-restaurant, ubiquitous in Venezuela, which serves Spanish *tapas* and other dishes, plus a variety of drinks
té – tea
tequeño – white cheese strips wrapped in pastry and deep fried
teta – iced fruit juice in a plastic wrap, consumed by sucking
tizana – a variety of chopped fruit in fruit juice; usually includes pieces of papaya, banana, watermelon, cantaloupe, pineapple and orange
tocineta – bacon
tomate – tomato
toronja – grapefruit
torta – cake
tortilla – omelet
tostón – fried plantain
trago – alcoholic drink
trigo – wheat
trucha – trout

uva – grape
uva pasa – raisin

vieira – scallop
vinagre – vinegar
vino blanco – white wine
vino espumoso – sparkling wine
vino rosado – rosé or blush wine
vino tinto – red wine

yuca – yucca (edible root)

zanahoria – carrot

Acknowledgments

THANKS

We'd like to thank the following travelers, who read the previous edition of this book and wrote to us about their experiences in Venezuela (apologies if we misspelled your name):

Lynn Achee, Holly Ackerman, Sherry Ackerman, Theo van Aerts, Wolf Albermann, Beth & Skip Albertson, Carmen Alfonso, Lucy de Alio, Tanya Ammann, Marzio Andrea Pistilli, Harold Armitage, Dan Arrowood, Guy Atherton, Nicolas Atwood, Ted Bachrach, Francoise Balconi, Brad Ballard, R A Balmanoukian, CJ Bayman, Carsten Dehme, Federico Belline, Tony Bennee, Kim Bennett, Robert J Bennett, Marty Berke, A Bernard, Petra Biderman, Fabio Biserna, R Bisset, Erica Blatchford, Roland Bogers, Sue Bokowski, Stephane Borella, Kris Borring, Martijn van den Bosch, Roy & Audrey Bradford, Christopher Branahan, Nick Branch, Kerstin Brandes, Carl Bray, Richard J Bray, Capt MJ Bristow, Mag Bruno Korinek, Nina Bryggemann, Wim Buesink, Neil Burditt, CD Burgess, Nicki Burston, Veronica Byrne, Elisabetta Cammarota, Fabio Cannavale, Georg Capart, Pernille Carlson, Geerg Caspary, Sabas Castillo, Rowan Castle, Stephen Chan, Morag Chase, Kelly Chisholm, Thomas Christen, Dale R Christiansen, Eva Christiansen, C Christopher Gaunt, Liam Clancy, Claudia Cleff, Paolo Cocchiglia, Juan Claudio Coello Pantojo, Rachel Cook, David & Diana Copp, Aaron Corcoran, Erika Cordes, James Cornish, Elizabeth MG Court, Bruce Cowley, John Crandon, Martin Crone, Peter D, Wojciech Dabrowski, Kerstin Daemen, Christopher & Victoria Darke, Justa Denning, Pieter Dings, Jens Dube, Vanessa Eden Evans, David Edwards, Ron Edwardson, Anna Elfors, Sarah Ellis, Hans en Marjan van den Enag, P Enea, Manon Ensing, Cristina Esther Pulido, Chris P Evans, Sabine Exner, Igor Fabjan, Donatella Fachin, Mike Farrell, Tracy Ferrell, Alex Fontanini, Richard Fowkes, Jill Frazer, Frank Ftl, S Garrett, Jeannie Gellatly, David Gerez, Michael Gerth, Sherry Gibson, William Gibson, Gregory Gilbert, Werner Ginzky, Peter Goeltenboth, Tulio Gomez, Shannon Gorman, John Gravley, Stephanie Greene, Danny Grobben, Michael Grundke, Katja Grunow, Daniel Guerrero C, Eileen Hallstrom, Jessica Hanlaoui, Paula Hanna, Joan Hannum, Donna & Dan Hardy, John C Harley, Colin Harvey, Ineke van Hassel, Steve Hauser, Roland Helmi, Deborah Herbint, Jacob Henriksen, Silvia Hincapie, Heidi Hirsh, Anita Hoback, Beth Hocking, Carla Holden, John Holman, Susanne Hrinkov, Serge Huguet, Diana Humple, David L Huntzinger, Jan Hutta, Andrew Inchley, Stephanie Inglesfield, Judy Isikow, Greg Jones, Peter Jones, D Josephson, Sabine Joyce, Admir Jukanovic, Leonard Kahansky, D Kakimoto, Georg Karl, Nils Karmann, Kryss Katsiavriades, Chris Kelley, Mrs R & Dr Key, M Kilpatrick, Andy King, Katie Kipper, Rachel Kirsch, Marc Kish, Robert Koepcke, Jaap Koerce, Michael Koest, Nadja Kos, Margaret Kostaszuk, Ken Kramer, P Lack, Coby Laird, Lewis Laura, Ino Laurensse, Robert Layne, Jonathan Legg, Dominique Leon, Guy Leonard, Wim Leuppens, Nadine Lewin, Laura Lewis, Verhofstadt Lieven, John P Linstroth, Cor Lionel, Stephen Lloyd, Lutz & Beate Logemann, Denise Perreault & David Low, Dieter Lubitz, Hermann Luyken, Hugh MacDonald, Ruth Magden, Arlette Marcer, Chris Marks, Alyssa M Martin, Philip B Martin, Bob Masters, Laurence Mathelin, Akira Maya, Ronan McCabe, Kathleen McGurk, Bill McKnight, Randy Mead, Manfred Melchinger, Tony Mendoza, Johan van der Merwe, Christian Messerschmidt, Gabriele Mills, Simon Moore, Jacob E Moss, Asia Motyl, Mohan Mukhoty, Juan Nagel, John T Nasci, Tino Naumann, Peter Necas, Angie & Yannick Neron, Christph Neunzig, Victoria Neves Pedro, Grant Nielsen, Gitte Norgaard, Loma Norgrove, Frederique Numerol, Mike O'Connor, N Okwudili, Conny Olde Olthof, Anders Olsson, Sian Oram, Simon Orr, Robert H Packard, Natalie Paganelli, Markus Pallor, Beryl Park, Rhonda Payget, Sacha Pearson, G Percontino, Cheryl Petreman, M Philippe Queriaux, Cameron Phillips, Paseal Pin, Helen & Anthony Pink, Michael Post, Inga Poy, Philip Preston, Alex Price, Martyn Pronk, Franca Pugnaghi, Kevin Ransom, Prasada Rao, Sandra Reauu, Sarah Reid, Teus Renes, Kristen Reynolds, David Rheault, Thomas Ribisel, Mary Richards, Alexander Robinson, Don Rogers, Peter Roose, Daniel Ross, Steffen Rossel, Tom Roth, Nareg

Roubinian, Ollie Royer, Diarmuid Russell, Stephen Ryan Chan, Scott Savoie, Sue Savoy, Paul Schaffrath, Andreas Scharew, Ron Scharis, Gabriele Schindl, Marc Schipperheyn, Katja Schwoerke, Matt Scott, Steve Seamark, Davide Selva, Yiftah Shalev, Eran Shayshon, Ron Shell, Andrew Sherwin, Martin Shippen, Gayle Short, Andy Shorwin, Jochen Siepmann, Christian Silkenath, Tom Simpson, Luke Skinner, Caroline Smith, Peter Smith, TJ Snow, EG Stack III, David Stephnes, Morten Stige, Thomas Stodulka, David Strachan, Francesca Symmons, Danko Taborosi, Beth Taylor, M Taylor, Carolina Tenias, Isabel B Terry, Jonas Teubner, Elke Thape, Stèphane Tiberghien,

Steve Tietsworth, M Tilman, Anne Tobin, GB Toppelwell, Alistair Towers, Samuel Trickey, Roland Ulrich, Richard Vader, L Valles, Michel Van Velde, Pascal Vervacke, Thomas Villette, Antonio Vizamora, Helene Vroegh, Mike Wagner, Jonathan Waldie, Peter Walker, Hans Warmerdam, Paul Webb, Jonathan Weber, Jorn Weigle, Ina Wenig, Maaike van Westen, Michael Wheelahon, Richard Wherry, RA Wilmore, Ian Wilson, Tristram Winfield, Thomas Winter, Alan H Witz, Anja Wohlgemuth, Meike Wolf, Christopher Woods, Jonathan Woolrich, Alexander Wuerfel, Dirk Wutherich, Jackie Wynn, Andrew Yale, Vamosi Zoltan

LONELY PLANET

You already know that Lonely Planet produces more than this one guidebook, but you might not be aware of the other products we have on this region. Here is a selection of titles which you may want to check out as well:

South America on a Shoestring
ISBN 1864502835
US$29.99 • UK£17.99

Read this First: Central & South America
ISBN 1864500670
US$14.99 • UK£8.99

Latin American Spanish phrasebook
ISBN 30864425589
US$6.95• UK£4.50

Brazil
ISBN 1864501464
US$24.99 • UK£14.99

Panama
ISBN 1864503076
US$16.99 • UK£10.99

Healthy Travel: Central & South America
ISBN 1864500530
US$5.95 • UK£3.99

Available wherever books are sold.

Guides by Region

Lonely Planet is known worldwide for publishing practical, reliable and no-nonsense travel information in our guides and on our Web site. The Lonely Planet list covers just about every accessible part of the world. Currently there are 16 series: Travel guides, Shoestring guides, Condensed guides, Watching Wildlife guides, Pisces Diving & Snorkeling guides, City Maps, Road Atlases, Out to Eat, World Food, Journeys travel literature and Pictorials.

AFRICA Africa on a shoestring • Cairo • Cairo City Map • Cape Town • Cape Town City Map • East Africa • Egypt • Egyptian Arabic phrasebook • Ethiopia, Eritrea & Djibouti • Ethiopian Amharic phrasebook • The Gambia & Senegal • Healthy Travel Africa • Kenya • Malawi • Morocco • Moroccan Arabic phrasebook • Mozambique • Read This First: Africa • South Africa, Lesotho & Swaziland • Southern Africa • Southern Africa Road Atlas • Swahili phrasebook • Tanzania, Zanzibar & Pemba • Trekking in East Africa • Tunisia • Watching Wildlife East Africa • Watching Wildlife Southern Africa • West Africa • World Food Morocco • Zimbabwe, Botswana & Namibia
Travel Literature: Mali Blues: Traveling to an African Beat • The Rainbird: A Central African Journey • Songs to an African Sunset: A Zimbabwean Story

AUSTRALIA & THE PACIFIC Auckland • Australia • Australian phrasebook • Australia Road Atlas • Cycling Australia • Cycling New Zealand • Fiji • Fijian phrasebook • Healthy Travel Australia, NZ and the Pacific • Islands of Australia's Great Barrier Reef • Melbourne • Melbourne City Map • Micronesia • New Caledonia • New South Wales • New Zealand • Northern Territory • Outback Australia • Out to Eat – Melbourne • Out to Eat – Sydney • Papua New Guinea • Pidgin phrasebook • Queensland • Rarotonga & the Cook Islands • Samoa • Solomon Islands • South Australia • South Pacific • South Pacific phrasebook • Sydney • Sydney City Map • Sydney Condensed • Tahiti & French Polynesia • Tasmania • Tonga • Tramping in New Zealand • Vanuatu • Victoria • Walking in Australia • Watching Wildlife Australia • Western Australia
Travel Literature: Islands in the Clouds: Travel in the Highlands of New Guinea • Kiwi Tracks: A New Zealand Journey • Sean & David's Long Drive

CENTRAL AMERICA & THE CARIBBEAN Bahamas, Turks & Caicos • Baja California • Belize, Guatemala & Yucatán • Bermuda • Central America on a shoestring • Costa Rica • Costa Rica Spanish phrasebook • Cuba • Dominican Republic & Haiti • Eastern Caribbean • Guatemala • Havana • Healthy Travel Central & South America • Jamaica • Mexico • Mexico City • Panama • Puerto Rico • Read This First: Central & South America • World Food Mexico • Yucatán
Travel Literature: Green Dreams: Travels in Central America

EUROPE Amsterdam • Amsterdam City Map • Amsterdam Condensed • Andalucía • Austria • Baltic States phrasebook • Barcelona • Barcelona City Map • Belgium & Luxembourg • Berlin • Berlin City Map • Britain • British phrasebook • Brussels, Bruges & Antwerp • Brussels City Map • Budapest • Budapest City Map • Canary Islands • Central Europe • Central Europe phrasebook • Copenhagen • Corfu & the Ionians • Corsica • Crete • Crete Condensed • Croatia • Cycling Britain • Cycling France • Cyprus • Czech & Slovak Republics • Denmark • Dublin • Dublin City Map • Eastern Europe • Eastern Europe phrasebook • Edinburgh • England • Estonia, Latvia & Lithuania • Europe on a shoestring • Europe phrasebook • Finland • Florence • France • Frankfurt Condensed • French phrasebook • Georgia, Armenia & Azerbaijan • Germany • German phrasebook • Greece • Greek Islands • Greek phrasebook • Hungary • Iceland, Greenland & the Faroe Islands • Ireland • Italian phrasebook • Italy • Krakow • Lisbon • The Loire • London • London City Map • London Condensed • Madrid • Malta • Mediterranean Europe • Mediterranean Europe phrasebook • Moscow • Munich • Netherlands • Normandy • Norway • Out to Eat – London • Out to Eat – Paris • Paris • Paris City Map • Paris Condensed • Poland • Polish phrasebook • Portugal • Portuguese phrasebook • Prague • Prague City Map • Provence & the Côte d'Azur • Read This First: Europe • Rhodes & the Dodecanese • Romania & Moldova • Rome • Rome City Map • Russia, Ukraine & Belarus • Russian phrasebook • Scandinavian & Baltic Europe • Scandinavian phrasebook • Scotland • Sicily • Slovenia • South-West France • Spain • Spanish phrasebook • St Petersburg • St Petersburg City Map • Sweden • Switzerland • Tuscany • Ukrainian phrasebook • Venice • Vienna • Walking in Britain • Walking in France • Walking in Ireland • Walking in Italy • Walking in Spain • Walking in Switzerland • Western Europe • World Food France • World Food Ireland • World Food Italy • World Food Spain
Travel Literature: After Yugoslavia • Love and War in the Apennines • The Olive Grove: Travels in Greece • On the Shores of the Mediterranean • Round Ireland in Low Gear • A Small Place in Italy

LONELY PLANET

Mail Order

Lonely Planet products are distributed worldwide. They are also available by mail order from Lonely Planet, so if you have difficulty finding a title please write to us. North and South American residents should write to 150 Linden St, Oakland, CA 94607, USA; European and African residents should write to 10a Spring Place, London NW5 38H, UK; and residents of other countries to Locked Bag 1, Footscray, Victoria 3011, Australia.

INDIAN SUBCONTINENT & THE INDIAN OCEAN Bangladesh • Bengali phrasebook • Bhutan • Delhi • Goa • Healthy Travel Asia & India • Hindi & Urdu phrasebook • India • Indian Himalaya • Karakoram Highway • Kerala • Madagascar • Maldives • Mauritius, Réunion & Seychelles • Mumbai (Bombay) • Nepal • Nepali phrasebook • Pakistan • Rajasthan • Read This First: Asia & India • South India • Sri Lanka • Sri Lanka phrasebook • Tibet • Tibetan phrasebook • Trekking in the Indian Himalaya • Trekking in the Karakoram & Hindukush • Trekking in the Nepal Himalaya
Travel Literature: The Age of Kali: Indian Travels and Encounters • Hello Goodnight: A Life of Goa • In Rajasthan • Maverick in Madagascar • A Season in Heaven: True Tales from the Road to Kathmandu • Shopping for Buddhas • A Short Walk in the Hindu Kush • Slowly Down the Ganges

MIDDLE EAST & CENTRAL ASIA Bahrain, Kuwait & Qatar • Central Asia • Central Asia phrasebook • Dubai • Farsi (Persian) phrasebook • Hebrew phrasebook • Iran • Israel & the Palestinian Territories • Istanbul • Istanbul City Map • Istanbul to Cairo • Istanbul to Kathmandu • Jerusalem • Jerusalem City Map • Jordan • Lebanon • Middle East • Oman & the United Arab Emirates • Syria • Turkey • Turkish phrasebook • World Food Turkey • Yemen
Travel Literature: Black on Black: Iran Revisited • The Gates of Damascus • Kingdom of the Film Stars: Journey into Jordan

NORTH AMERICA Alaska • Boston • Boston City Map • Boston Condensed • British Columbia • California & Nevada • California Condensed • Canada • Chicago • Chicago City Map • Florida • Great Lakes • Hawaii • Hiking in Alaska • Hiking in the USA • Las Vegas • Los Angeles • Los Angeles City Map • Louisiana & the Deep South • Miami • Miami City Map • Montréal • New England • New Orleans • New York City • New York City City Map • New York City Condensed • New York, New Jersey & Pennsylvania • Oahu • Out to Eat – San Francisco • Pacific Northwest • Rocky Mountains • San Francisco • San Francisco City Map • Seattle • Southwest • Texas • Toronto • USA • USA phrasebook • Vancouver • Virginia & the Capital Region • Washington, DC • Washington, DC City Map • World Food New Orleans
Travel Literature: Caught Inside: A Surfer's Year on the California Coast • Drive Thru America

NORTH-EAST ASIA Beijing • Beijing City Map • Cantonese phrasebook • China • Hiking in Japan • Hong Kong • Hong Kong City Map • Hong Kong Condensed • Hong Kong, Macau & Guangzhou • Japan • Japanese phrasebook • Korea • Korean phrasebook • Kyoto • Mandarin phrasebook • Mongolia • Mongolian phrasebook • Seoul • Shanghai • South-West China • Taiwan • Tokyo • World Food Hong Kong
Travel Literature: In Xanadu: A Quest • Lost Japan

SOUTH AMERICA Argentina, Uruguay & Paraguay • Bolivia • Brazil • Brazilian phrasebook • Buenos Aires • Chile & Easter Island • Colombia • Ecuador & the Galápagos Islands • Healthy Travel Central & South America • Latin American Spanish phrasebook • Peru • Quechua phrasebook • Read This First: Central & South America • Rio de Janeiro • Rio de Janeiro City Map • Santiago de Chile • South America on a shoestring • Trekking in the Patagonian Andes • Venezuela
Travel Literature: Full Circle: A South American Journey

SOUTH-EAST ASIA Bali & Lombok • Bangkok • Bangkok City Map • Burmese phrasebook • Cambodia • Hanoi • Healthy Travel Asia & India • Hill Tribes phrasebook • Ho Chi Minh City • Indonesia • Indonesian phrasebook • Indonesia's Eastern Islands • Java • Lao phrasebook • Laos • Malay phrasebook • Malaysia, Singapore & Brunei • Myanmar (Burma) • Philippines • Pilipino (Tagalog) phrasebook • Read This First: Asia & India • Singapore • Singapore City Map • South-East Asia on a shoestring • South-East Asia phrasebook • Thailand • Thailand's Islands & Beaches • Thailand, Vietnam, Laos & Cambodia Road Atlas • Thai phrasebook • Vietnam • Vietnamese phrasebook • World Food Thailand • World Food Vietnam

ALSO AVAILABLE: Antarctica • The Arctic • The Blue Man: Tales of Travel, Love and Coffee • Brief Encounters: Stories of Love, Sex & Travel • Chasing Rickshaws • The Last Grain Race • Lonely Planet...On the Edge: Adventurous Escapades from Around the World • Lonely Planet Unpacked • Not the Only Planet: Science Fiction Travel Stories • Sacred India • Travel Photography: A Guide to Taking Better Pictures • Travel with Children

Index

Text

Bold indicates maps.

Boxed Text

MAP LEGEND

ROUTES

City   Regional

............Freeway
.......Primary Road
.......Primary Dirt
........Secondary Road
........Tertiary Road
........Tertiary Dirt

............Pedestrian Mall
............Steps
............Tunnel
............Trail
............Walking Tour
............Path

TRANSPORTATION

............Train
............Metro
............Bus Route
............Ferry

HYDROGRAPHY

............River; Creek
............Canal
............Lake
............Spring; Rapids
............Waterfalls
............Dry; Salt Lake

ROUTE SHIELDS

[1] Venezuela National Highway
[BR 364] Brazil National Highway

BOUNDARIES

............International
............Provincial
............County
............Disputed

AREAS

............Beach
............Building
............Campus
............Cemetery
............Forest; Reserve
............Garden; Zoo
............Golf Course
............Park
............Plaza
............Reservation
............Sports Field
............Swamp; Mangrove

POPULATION SYMBOLS

✪ **NATIONAL CAPITAL** ...National Capital
◎ **Provincial Capital** .....Provincial Capital
❶ **Large City** ....Large City
❶ **Medium City** ....Medium City
● **Small City** ....Small City
● **Town; Village** ....Town; Village

MAP SYMBOLS

■ ....Place to Stay
▼ ....Place to Eat
● ....Point of Interest

✈ ....Airfield	✝ ....Church	⊞ ....Museum	⚡ ....Skiing - Downhill
✈ ....Airport	⊞ ....Cinema	⚞ ....Observatory	⊞ ....Stately Home
⊞ ....Archeological Site; Ruin	⊡ ....Embassy; Consulate	⚑ ....Park	⚑ ....Surfing
⊛ ....Bank	⊱ ....Footbridge	⊡ ....Parking Area	⚙ ....Synagogue
⬟ ....Baseball Diamond	⊛ ....Garden	)(............Pass	⊡ ....Tao Temple
⚐ ....Beach	◉ ....Gas Station	⚘ ....Picnic Area	⊟ ....Taxi
⚲ ....Bike Trail	✚ ....Hospital	⬟ ....Police Station	☎ ....Telephone
⚐ ....Bird Sanctuary	❶ ....Information	⬛ ....Pool	⊟ ....Theater
⚑ ....Buddhist Temple	⊡ ....Internet Café	⬛ ....Post Office	♿ ....Toilet - Public
⊟ ....Bus Station; Terminal	⚔ ....Lighthouse	⬛ ....Pub; Bar	⬛ ....Tomb
⊟ ....Cable Car; Chairlift	☀ ....Lookout	⟁ ....RV Park	⚐ ....Trailhead
⛺ ....Campground	⊠ ....Mine	⬛ ....Shelter	⊟ ....Tram Stop
⊞ ....Castle	⊠ ....Mission	⚓ ....Shipwreck	⊟ ....Transportation
⊞ ....Cathedral	⚑ ....Monument	⚓ ....Shopping Mall	▲ ....Volcano
⌂ ....Cave	▲ ....Mountain	⚐ ....Skiing - Cross Country	⊞ ....Winery

Note: not all symbols displayed above appear in this book

LONELY PLANET OFFICES

Australia
Locked Bag 1, Footscray, Victoria 3011
☎ 03 8379 8000 fax 03 8379 8111
email talk2us@lonelyplanet.com.au

USA
150 Linden Street, Oakland, California 94607
☎ 510 893 8555, TOLL FREE 800 275 8555
fax 510 893 8572
email info@lonelyplanet.com

UK
10a Spring Place, London NW5 3BH
☎ 020 7428 4800 fax 020 7428 4828
email go@lonelyplanet.co.uk

France
1 rue du Dahomey, 75011 Paris
☎ 01 55 25 33 00 fax 01 55 25 33 01
www.lonelyplanet.fr

World Wide Web: www.lonelyplanet.com *or* AOL keyword: lp
Lonely Planet Images: lpi@lonelyplanet.com.au